BRIEF EDITION Volume I: To 1877

America

PAST AND PRESENT

BRIEF EDITION Volume I: To 1877

PAST AND PRESENT

Robert A. Divine
University of Texas

T. H. Breen
Northwestern University

George M. Fredrickson
Stanford University

R. Hal Williams
Southern Methodist University

and

Randy Roberts
Sam Houston State University

Scott, Foresman and Company

Glenview, Illinois
London, England

123456-VHJ-908988878685

Library of Congress Cataloging in Publication Data
Main entry under title:
America, past and present.
    Includes bibliographies and indexes.
    Contents: v. 1. To 1877—v. 2. From 1865.
    1. United States—History.   I. Divine, Robert A.
E178.1.A4894   1986b   973   85-22250
ISBN 0-673-18138-3 (pbk. : v. 1)
ISBN 0-673-18139-1 (pbk. : v. 2)

About the Authors

Robert A. Divine

Robert A. Divine, the George W. Littlefield Professor in American History at the University of Texas at Austin, received his Ph.D. degree from Yale University in 1954. A specialist in American diplomatic history, he has taught at the University of Texas since 1954, where he has been honored by the Student Association for teaching excellence. His extensive published work includes *The Illusion of Neutrality, Second Chance: The Triumph of Internationalism in America During World War II* (1968) and *Blowing on the Wind* (1978). His most recent book is *Eisenhower and the Cold War* (1981). In 1962–1963, he was a fellow at the Center for Advanced Study in the Behavioral Sciences and in 1968 he gave the Albert Shaw Lectures in Diplomatic History at Johns Hopkins University.

T. H. Breen

T. H. Breen received his Ph.D. from Yale University in 1968. Since 1975 he has been a Professor of History and American Culture at Northwestern University. Breen's major books include *The Character of the Good Ruler: A Study of Puritan Political Ideas in New England* (1974), *Puritans and Adventurers: Change and Persistence in Early America* (1980), with S. Innes of the University of Virginia, *"Myne Owne Ground": Race and Freedom on Virginia's Eastern Shore* (1980), and *Tobacco Culture: The Great Tidewater Plant-*ers on the Eve of Revolution (1985). In addition to receiving an award for outstanding teaching at Northwestern, Breen has been the recipient of research grants from the American Council of Learned Societies, the Guggenheim Foundation, the Institute for Advanced Study (Princeton), and the National Humanities Center. He is currently preparing a volume for the Oxford University Press *History of the United States in Early America.*

George M. Fredrickson

George M. Fredrickson is Edgar E. Robinson Professor of United States History at Stanford University. He is the author or editor of several books, including *The Inner Civil War* (1965), *The Black Image in the White Mind* (1971), and *A Nation Divided* (1975). His latest work, *White Supremacy: A Comparative Study in American and South African History* (1981) won both the Ralph Waldo Emerson Award from Phi Beta Kappa and the Merle Curti Award from the Organization of American Historians. He received both the A.B. and Ph.D. degrees from Harvard and has been the recipient of a Guggenheim Fellowship, two National Endowment for the Humanities Senior Fellowships, and a Fellowship from the Center for Advanced Studies in the Behavioral Sciences. He has also served as Fulbright lecturer in American History at Moscow University and as a Mellon visiting professor at Rice University.

R. Hal Williams

R. Hal Williams has been Dean of Dedman College at Southern Methodist University since 1980. He received his A.B. degree from Princeton University (1963) and his Ph.D. degree from Yale University (1968). His books include *The Democratic Party and California Politics, 1880–1896* (1973) and *Years of Decision: American Politics in the 1890s* (1978). He taught at Yale University from 1968 to 1975 and came to SMU in 1975 as Chair of the Department of History. He has received outstanding teaching awards at both Yale and SMU. Williams has received grants from the American Philosophical Society and the National Endowment for the Humanities, and he serves on the Texas Committee for the Humanities.

Randy Roberts

Randy Roberts has taught history at Sam Houston State University since 1980. He received his Ph.D. from Louisiana State University in 1978. A specialist in cultural history and the history of sport, he has published widely in those fields. His books include *Jack Dempsey: The Manassa Mauler* (1979) and *Papa Jack: Jack Johnson and the Era of White Hopes* (1983). He is on the editorial board of the *Journal of Sport History* and *Arete: The Journal of Sport Literature*, and he is co-editor of the Illinois University Press series Studies in Sports and Society. He has received several grants from the National Endowment for the Humanities. He is currently finishing a book on sport and American society from 1945 to the present for the Johns Hopkins University Press and preparing a biography of Ernest Hemingway.

America

PAST AND PRESENT

Preface to Brief Edition

This Brief Edition of *America: Past & Present*, prepared by Professor Randy Roberts with the collaboration of the four authors of the full-length edition published in 1984, is intended to serve the needs of instructors in one-semester courses and those who supplement the main assigned text with a wide variety of other readings. Enriched by the use of primary sources, monographs and scholarly articles, and fiction, a foundation text helps the student grasp the sweep and complexity of the American past.

The full-length edition won acclaim for its skillful integration of political, diplomatic, economic, social, and cultural history, its clarity of organization, and its stylistic grace. The goal of this abridgment is to produce a condensation true to the original in all its dimensions—a miniaturized replica or *bonsai*, as it were—retaining the style and tone, and the interpretations, with their nuances and subtleties intact. To achieve that goal, factual coverage and thematic advancement have been closely monitored; we have gone over the text line by line and the intent of every paragraph has been retained. This version contains about two thirds of the narrative of the longer book, one half of the highly praised maps, charts and graphs, and a commensurate proportion of the outstanding illustration program.

What is new in this edition? Added material includes a new map series entitled *Growth of the United States* at the front of the book, a number of new and improved thematic, military, and current international maps, and a 1984 electoral map; *a final section in the last chapter* covering the years 1984 and 1985; new bibliographies for every chapter; *an augmented Choosing the President chart in the Appendix* with additional categories for presidential popular and electoral vote tabulations.

A full complement of ancillary support items accompany the Brief Edition: a one-volume study guide *(Studying America Past & Present)*; an *Instructor's Resource Manual*; and a *Test Item File*. A packet of forty four-color *Map Transparencies* from the full-length text is available for classroom use, and a new 72-page book (in full color) comprising thirty-two *Special Feature Essays* on topics of high interest and instructional value, will be made available to students.

Many thanks to the following academic reviewers, whose critiques and suggestions were extremely valuable in preparing the final version of the Brief Edition:

F. Ross Peterson, Utah State University
George Rable, Anderson College, Anderson, Indiana
Salme Harju Steinberg, Northeastern Illinois University
Kenneth Weatherbie, Del Mar College, Corpus Christi, Texas

This project was a collective effort in which the staff of my publisher, Scott, Foresman, played an integral part. I am grateful to Bruce Borland, editorial vice president, and Barbara

Muller, history editor, for their help, to Charlotte Iglarsh, developmental editor, with whom I worked most closely in preparation of the text, and to the editorial and production people on the team. I am also indebted to Christine Silvestri.

A special note of appreciation to my friend and colleague, Professor Terry Bilhartz for his careful reading and critique of this work, and to Suzy Rankin for her support.

R. R.

Preface to Full Length Edition

America: Past and Present is a history of the United States that tells the unfolding story of national development from the days of the earliest inhabitants to the present. We emphasize *telling the story* because we strongly believe in the value of historical narrative to provide a vivid sense of the past. Weaving the various strands of the American experience, we have sought in each chapter to blend the excitement and drama of that experience with insights into the underlying social, economic, and cultural forces that brought about change.

In a clear chronological organization, we have used significant incidents and episodes to reflect the dilemmas, the choices, and the decisions made by the people as well as by their leaders. After the colonial period, most of the chapters deal in short time periods, usually about a decade, that permit us to view major political and public events as points of reference and orientation around which social themes are integrated. This approach gives unity and direction to the text.

As the title suggests, our book is a blend of the traditional and the new. The strong narrative emphasis and chronological organization are traditional; the incorporation of the many fresh insights that historians have gained from the social sciences in the past two decades is new. In recounting the story of the American past we see a nation in flux. The early Africans and Europeans developed complex agrarian folkways that departed greatly from their experiences in the Old World—an evolution that established new cultural identities and finally led the settlers to accept the idea of political independence. People who had been subjects of the British Crown created a system of government that challenged later Americans to work out the full implications of social and economic equality. As we move to the growing sectional rift between North and South, the focus shifts to divergent modes of labor utilization and disparate social values that culminated in civil war. The westward movement and the accompanying industrial revolution severely tested the values of an agrarian society, while leading to an incredibly productive economic system. In the early twentieth century, progressive reformers sought to infuse the industrial order with social justice, and the First World War demonstrated the extent of American power in the world. The resiliency of the maturing American nation was tested by the Great Depression and World War II but despite setbacks, the United States overcame these challenges. The Cold War ushered in an era of crises, foreign and domestic, that revealed both the strengths and weaknesses of modern America.

The impact of change on human lives adds a vital dimension to historical understanding. We need to comprehend how the Revolution affected the lives of ordinary citizens; what it was like for both blacks and whites to live in a plantation society; how men and women fared in the shift from an agrarian to an industrial economy; and what impact technology, in the form of the automobile and the computer, has had on patterns of life in the twentieth century.

Our primary goal has been to write a clear,

relevant, and balanced history of the United States. Our commitment is not to any particular ideology or point of view; rather, we hope to challenge our readers to rediscover the fascination of the American past and reach their own conclusions. At the same time, we have not tried to avoid controversial issues and have sought to offer reasoned judgments on such morally charged subjects as the nature of slavery and the advent of nuclear weapons. We believe that what happened in the entire nation, not just New England and the Northeast, deserves retelling, and thus we have given special emphasis to developments in the South and West.

The structure and features of the book are intended to stimulate student interest and reinforce learning. Chapters begin with a **vignette** or incident that relates to the chapter themes stated in the introductory section, which also serves as an overview of the topics covered. Each chapter has a **chronology, recommended readings,** and **bibliography.** In addition, the very extensive **map program,** the many **charts and graphs,** and the **illustrations** throughout are directly related to the narrative. They serve to advance and expand the themes, provide elaboration and contrast, tell more of the story,

and generally add another dimension of learning. A six-page **map series** at the front of the text highlights the sweep of American history. The **Appendix** contains the vital documents, a ten-column chart on choosing the president and other political information, the cabinet members in every administration, and the Supreme Court justices.

Although this book is a joint effort, each author took primary responsibility for writing one section. T. H. Breen contributed the first eight chapters from the Native American period to the second decade of the nineteenth century; George M. Fredrickson wrote chapters 9 through 16, carrying the narrative through the Reconstruction era. R. Hal Williams is responsible for chapters 17 through 24, focusing on the industrial transformation and urbanization, and the events culminating in World War I; and Robert A. Divine wrote chapters 25 through 32, bringing the story through the Depression, World War II, and the Cold War to the present. Each contributor reviewed and revised the work of his colleagues and helped shape the material into its final form.

This book owes much to the conscientious historians who reviewed chapters and sections, and offered valuable suggestions that led to many important improvements in the text. We are grateful to the following:

Frank W. Abbott
University of Houston

Kenneth G. Alfers
Mountain View College
Dallas

Thomas Archdeacon
University of Wisconsin-Madison

Kenneth R. Bain
Pan American University
Edinburg, Texas

Lois W. Banner
Hamilton College
Clinton, New York

Thomas Camfield
Sam Houston State University
Huntsville, Texas

Clayborne Carson
Stanford University

Jerald Combs
San Francisco State University

John Cooper
University of Wisconsin-Madison

Nancy F. Cott
Yale University

Eric Foner
Columbia University

Stephen Foster
Northern Illinois University

Sondra Herman
DeAnza Community College
Cupertino, California

John R. Howe
University of Minnesota

Nathan I. Huggins
Harvard University

John Kelley
Shawnee State Community College
Portsmouth, Ohio

Richard S. Kirkendall
Iowa State University

Harbert F. Margulies
University of Hawaii

Myron Marty
National Endowment for the Humanities
Washington, D.C.

John M. Murrin
Princeton University

John K. Nelson
University of North Carolina at Chapel Hill

Nora Ramirez
San Antonio Community College

Ronald Walters
Johns Hopkins University

Frank Wetta
Galveston Community College

We are also indebted to many people at Scott, Foresman.

Finally, each author received aid and encouragement from many colleagues, friends, and family members over the four years to research, reflection, drafting, and revising that went into this book.

THE AUTHORS

CONTENTS

xvii
Contents

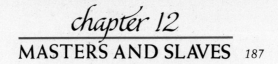

Maps

Front Pages

Political and Physical Map of the United States
The Growth of the United States
1783 / 1803 / 1819 / 1853 / American Empire, 1900 /
United States and Its Possessions
Major Armed Interventions of the United States

Charts and Graphs

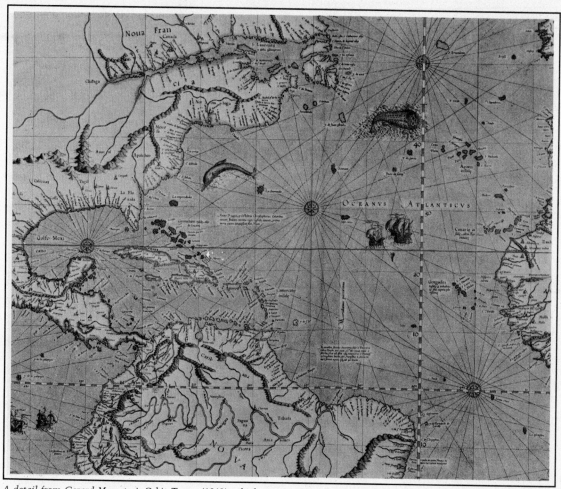

A detail from Gerard Mercator's Orbis Terrae *(1569), which expressed the sum total of geographic knowledge of its day.*

Map Series

Political and Physical Map of the United States
The Growth of the United States
1783 / 1803 / 1819 / 1853 / American Empire, 1900 /
United States and Its Possessions
Major Armed Interventions of the United States

CANADA

Lake of the Woods.

Lake Superior

Duluth

MINNESOTA

St. Paul

Minneapolis

WISCONSIN

Green Bay

Madison

Milwaukee

IOWA

Cedar Rapids

Des Moines

Davenport

MICHIGAN

Lake Michigan

Lake Huron

Grand Rapids

Lansing

Detroit

Rockford

Chicago

Gary

Ft. Wayne

Toledo

Cleveland

Akron

Lake Erie

Peoria

Illinois River

CENTRAL

INDIANA

OHIO

Columbus

ILLINOIS

Springfield

Indianapolis

Cincinnati

PLAINS

Ohio River

Missouri River

Kansas City

St. Louis

Jefferson City

MISSOURI

OZARK PLATEAU

Topeka

Louisville

Frankfort

Lexington

KENTUCKY

Nashville

Knoxville

TENNESSEE

Tennessee River

ARKANSAS

Fort Smith

Little Rock

Memphis

Pine Bluff

Mississippi River

MISSISSIPPI

Birmingham

ALABAMA

Montgomery

Jackson

Meridian

Alabama River

Shreveport

LOUISIANA

Baton Rouge

New Orleans

Biloxi

Mobile

COASTAL PLAIN

Mississippi Delta

Gulf of Mexico

PENNSYLVANIA

ADIRONDACK MTS

Lake Ontario

Rochester

Buffalo

NEW YORK

Albany

Susquehanna River

Harrisburg

Pittsburgh

Wheeling

ALLEGHENY MTS

WEST VIRGINIA

WASHINGTON D.C.

Huntington

Charleston

VIRGINIA

James River

Richmond

Newport News

APPALACHIAN MTS

BLUE RIDGE MTS

Mt. Mitchell
6,684 ft.
(2,030 m)

Greensboro

Raleigh

PIEDMONT

NORTH CAROLINA

Charlotte

Greenville

SOUTH CAROLINA

Columbia

COASTAL PLAIN

Cape Fear

Atlanta

GEORGIA

Columbus

ATLANTIC

Savannah

Charleston

Jacksonville

Tallahassee

FLORIDA PENINSULA

FLORIDA

Tampa

St. Petersburg

Lake Okeechobee

Cape Canaveral

Miami

Florida Keys

Straits of Florida

CUBA

MAINE

Augusta

Burlington

Montpelier

Lewiston

Portland

VT.

N.H.

Concord

Manchester

MASS.

Boston

Worcester

Cape Cod

CONN.

Hartford

Providence

R.I.

Bridgeport

Jersey City

New York City

Newark

LONG ISLAND

Trenton

NEW JERSEY

Philadelphia

Wilmington

DELAWARE

Baltimore

Dover

Annapolis

MARYLAND

DELMARVA PENINSULA

Chesapeake Bay

Norfolk

Cape Hatteras

ATLANTIC OCEAN

Hudson River

St. Lawrence River

Bay of Fundy

40°N

35° North Latitude

70° West Longitude

20°N

Tropic of Cancer

	International boundaries
	State boundaries
⊛	National capital
★	State capitals
•	Other cities
▲	Mountain peaks

ATLANTIC OCEAN

PUERTO RICO
(U.S.)

San Juan

0   100 Miles

0   100 Kilometers

0   100   200 Miles

0   100   200   Kilometers

95°W   90°W   85°W   80°W   75°W   70°W   65°W   50°N

The Growth of the United States

1783

The Treaty of Paris gave the Americans a western boundary at the Mississippi River. The value of the Mississippi was enhanced when Spain, in 1795, agreed to permit free navigation to the port of New Orleans.

Because some original land grants extended from "sea to sea," certain states laid claim to the newly acquired lands beyond the Appalachians. States without such claims demanded that the land be held in common. It was not until the early 1800s that this problem was settled.

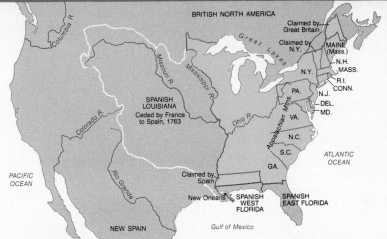

1819

Following the War of 1812, the United States and Great Britain established the 49th Parallel as their boundary. In 1818 they agreed to a joint occupation of the disputed Oregon Country.

The United States had annexed parts of Spanish West Florida in 1810 and 1812. Spain, fearing the possible occupation of East Florida and New Spain, sold East Florida for $5 million and established a firm boundary in place of the vague natural boundary of Louisiana.

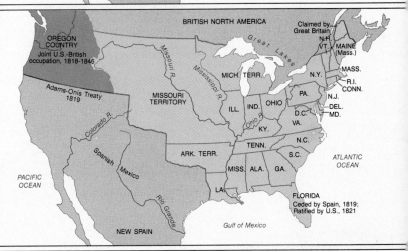

American Empire, 1900

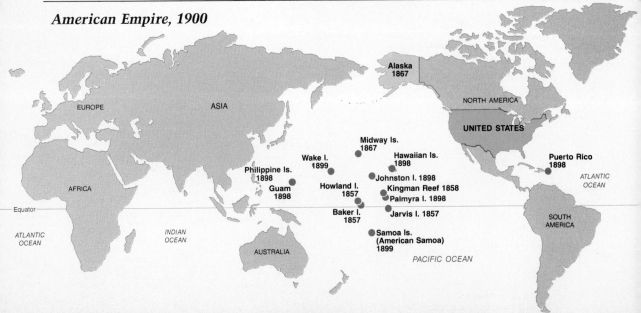

1803

The purchase of Louisiana nearly doubled the size of the United States. France had ceded Louisiana to Spain in 1763, but in 1801 Spain gave the territory back to France. While still in New Orleans, Spanish officials closed the port to American shipping. President Jefferson offered to buy the port, but the French made a counterproposal— to sell all of Louisiana for $15 million. At the time of the purchase, the extent of Louisiana was not known.

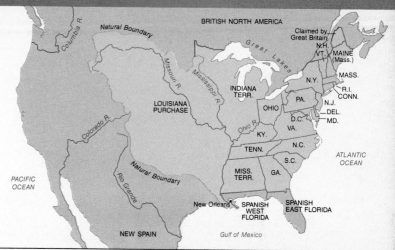

1853

By 1853 the continental boundary of the United States was established. The Maine and Minnesota boundary disputes were settled in 1842. The Treaty of Guadalupe Hidalgo (1848) which followed the Mexican War, ceded to the U.S. all Mexican holdings north of the Rio Grande and Gila River; the treaty, however, left some boundary questions open. In 1853 the Gadsden Purchase not only settled the question, but also provided the U.S. with a possible southern railroad route.

Present-day Possessions of the United States

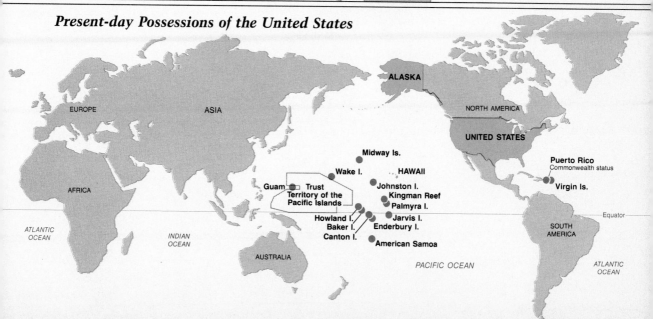

Major United States' Armed Interventions (excluding declared wars)

NORTH AMERICA

UNITED STATES

EUROPE

Iceland 1941
Greenland 1941
U.S. troops land

Tunis
Algiers
MOROCCO
Tripoli
**Wars Against
the Barbary States
1801–1815**

**Dominican Republic
1916–1924**
U.S. occupation
1965
U.S. troops land

Vera Cruz 1914
Seized by U.S. Navy

**Haiti
1915–1934**
U.S. occupation

Grenada 1983
U.S. troops land

**Nicaragua
1912–1925, 1927–1933**
Marines enforce
U.S. position

ATLANTIC
OCEAN

AFRICA

Equator

SOUTH
AMERICA

PACIFIC
OCEAN

Map shows present-day boundaries

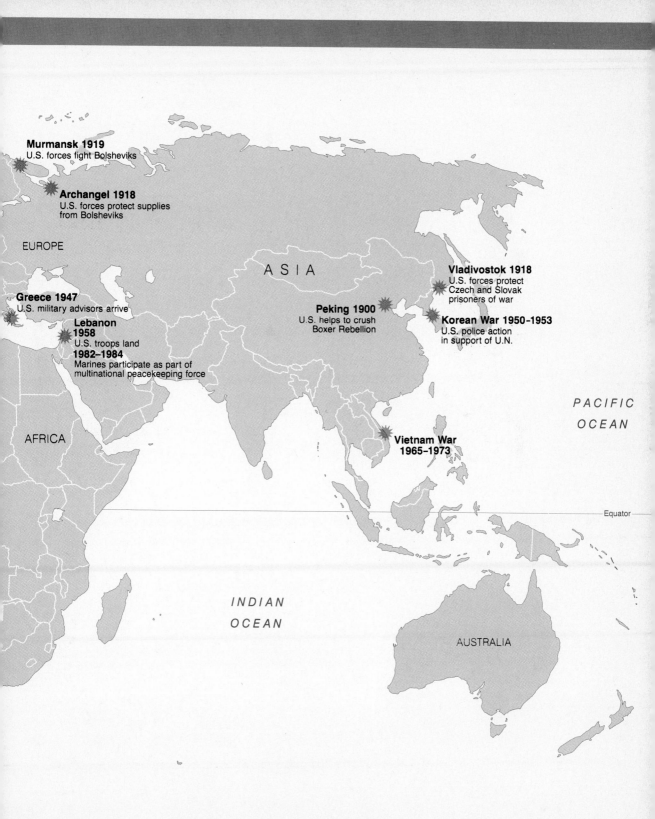

Murmansk 1919
U.S. forces fight Bolsheviks

Archangel 1918
U.S. forces protect supplies
from Bolsheviks

EUROPE

ASIA

Vladivostok 1918
U.S. forces protect
Czech and Slovak
prisoners of war

Greece 1947
U.S. military advisors arrive

Peking 1900
U.S. helps to crush
Boxer Rebellion

Korean War 1950–1953
U.S. police action
in support of U.N.

**Lebanon
1958**
U.S. troops land
1982–1984
Marines participate as part of
multinational peacekeeping force

AFRICA

**Vietnam War
1965–1973**

PACIFIC
OCEAN

Equator

INDIAN
OCEAN

AUSTRALIA

chapter 1

PATTERNS OF DISCOVERY

One day in 1926 while riding along a dry creek bed near Folsom, New Mexico, George McJunkin, a black cowboy, noticed some unusual bones protruding from the mud. Probing these remains with his knife, he uncovered several flint points as well that somewhat resembled Apache arrowheads. Archaeologists later concluded that McJunkin had stumbled across an ancient bison skeleton and the tips from the spears of the hunters who had killed the beast 10,000 years ago. This discovery of the "Folsom Man" demonstrated that Native American civilizations were far older than had been assumed. Later discoveries revealed that Stone Age hunters first migrated to North America from Siberia some 30,000 years ago.

Native Americans had inhabited the continent for millennia when European explorers crossed the Atlantic Ocean in the fifteenth century and proclaimed the discovery of a New World. But, as historian J. H. Parry observed, "Columbus did not discover a new world; he established contact between two worlds, both already old."

The dream of vast treasure first lured Europeans to the New World, but there was no typical pattern of settlement once they arrived. The experiences of the immigrants varied widely, as they attempted to transfer familiar institutions to America. They wanted to reproduce the particular societies that they had left behind.

Often the success of these ventures depended on factors over which the colonists had little control. The support of the mother countries and the availability of investment capital, for example, profoundly affected the character of colonial settlements. The land itself played an important role, for not all areas were equally fertile or rich in mineral deposits. Given the differences in game and timber alone, it is not surprising that English, French, and Spanish colonies developed in substantially different ways.

Native American Cultures

When the peopling of America began some 30,000 years ago, the Earth's climate was considerably colder than it is today. Much of the world's moisture was transformed into ice. The oceans dropped several hundred feet below their current level, creating a land bridge between Asia and America. The first people to cross this land bridge were small bands of Siberian hunters in pursuit of giant mammals, woolly mammoths, and mastodons. The migration of these nomadic groups took place over thousands of years. By 8000 B.C. men and women had ventured to the tip of South America.

Survival in the harsh environment forced the separate groups to look inward. Native Americans did not think of themselves as representatives of a single people or race. Over the centuries relatively isolated tribal groups developed their own cultures, patterns of kinship, and spoken languages. By the time that

Europeans first arrived, Native Americans who had settled north of Mexico had evolved between 300 and 350 separate languages. The concept of an homogeneous Native American culture was invented in a much later period by persons largely ignorant of the complexity of the history of these early people.

The introduction of agriculture revolutionized the life of Native Americans. As early as 2000 B.C. some groups in the Southwest began farming, and over the centuries their knowledge spread north and east. The impact of agriculture upon Native American societies was immense. Freed from the insecurity of an existence based solely upon hunting and gathering, Native Americans settled in permanent villages. An increased food supply led to a population boom, freeing some people for artistic endeavors. The Agricultural Revolution further divided North American tribes; groups in Mexico and the Southwest relied heavily on domesticated plants while those who had no agriculture or who learned of it late continued to depend mainly on hunting and gathering.

An interesting division of labor between the sexes is depicted in this sixteenth-century engraving by Jacques Le Moyne of American Indians sowing beans and maize. The men prepare the ground with hoes made of fishbones attached to wooden handles; one woman digs holes with a dowel while the other two drop in the seeds. Le Moyne visited Florida between 1564 and 1565.

Development of Civilizations

The most advanced Native American cultures appeared in Mexico and Central America. The Maya and Toltec peoples built vast cities, organized sophisticated government bureaucracies, and developed an accurate calendar and a complex form of writing. When the Spanish conquerors first saw the impressive cities of the New World, they compared them to Venice, one of Italy's most stunning artistic and engineering achievements. One explorer even proclaimed one Mexican city "the most beautiful . . . in the world."

Over the centuries, Native American civilizations rose and fell. By the time Columbus set sail in 1492, the Aztec, an aggressive, militant people, dominated the Valley of Mexico. They ruled by the sword and carried out human sacrifice on a scale previously unknown in Mexico.

The people who inhabited the present-day territories of the United States and Canada were less technologically advanced than their Mexican neighbors. Although tribes in the Southwest and the Mississippi valley practiced intensive agriculture, eastern tribes mixed farming with hunting and gathering. Small bands among the Algonquian tribes on the Atlantic coast, for example, formed villages and cultivated corn in the warm summer months. But with the hardships of winter, the bands dispersed, and each family lived off the land as best it could. The dangers were great; survival could never be taken for granted.

Despite common linguistic roots, the members of the different Algonquian groups, such as the Narragansett and the Powhatan, communicated only with greatest difficulty. The distinct dialects that developed in the isolated environments were as different from one another as modern Romanian is from Portuguese.

Native American cultures were never static. Tribal migration was common, and distances traveled were sometimes considerable. The Ojibway tribe of the famed Iroquois League, for example, seems to have originated in the Saint Lawrence valley. Whether driven west by their enemies or by the search for better hunting grounds, the Ojibway were well established in the Lake Superior region by the time European explorers met them (see map of Indian tribes, p. 4).

European Contact

The arrival of Europeans on this continent radically altered the lives of the native inhabitants. Whether English or Spanish, the colonizers regarded their own cultures as superior to those of the Native Americans, and they quickly tried to introduce their concept of civilization to those they considered savages. The attempt was a universal failure.

Some Native Americans—or Indians, as they came to be called by the Europeans—paid lip service to Christianity, but neither Catholic nor Protestant dogma deeply affected their inner convictions. Indian concepts of sin and the afterlife differed markedly from Christian theology. The white settlers' educational system proved no more successful in winning converts to European culture. Stuffy classrooms held little attraction for young Indian scholars. And, as Benjamin Franklin was told by tribal leaders in 1753, college education did not teach Indian students "the true methods of killing deer, catching Beaver or surprising an enemy."

The Native Americans clung tightly to their own ways, showing little enthusiasm for European clothes, diet, or houses. And when an Indian married a white—unions which the English found less desirable than did the French or Spanish—the European partner usually elected to live among the Indians. Even slavery failed to achieve cultural conversion. Enslaved Indians either ran away or died; they did not become Europeans.

Indians did, however, covet the products of European technology. Arrows tipped with metal rather than flint were obviously superior. Hunting became more efficient, and with the introduction of firearms, Indian warfare became more deadly. The tribes located closest to the white settlements obtained firearms more quickly than did those that lived farther west. This put the interior tribes at a great dis-

3

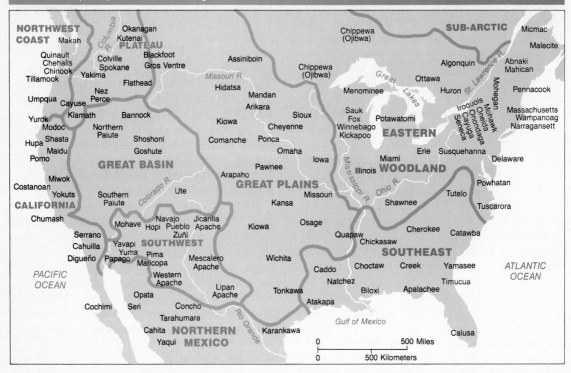

The First Americans:
Location of Major Indian Groups and Culture Areas in the 1600s

NORTHWEST COAST Makah
Quinault
Chehalis
Chinook
Tillamook
Umpqua Cayuse
Yurok
Modoc
Hupa Shasta
Maidu
Pomo
Costanoan Miwok
CALIFORNIA Yokuts
Chumash
Serrano
Cahuilla
Digueño

PLATEAU Okanagan
Kutenai
Colville Blackfoot
Spokane Gros Ventre
Yakima
Nez Flathead
Perce
Klamath Bannock
Northern
Paiute Shoshoni
Goshute
GREAT BASIN
Southern
Paiute Ute
Mohave Navajo Jicarilla
Hopi Pueblo Apache
Zuñi
Yavapi **SOUTHWEST**
Yuma Pima
Papago Maricopa
Western Mescalero
Apache Apache
Opata Lipan
Cochimi Seri Concho Apache
Tarahumara
Cahita **NORTHERN**
Yaqui **MEXICO**

Assiniboin
Missouri R.
Hidatsa
Mandan
Arikara
Kiowa Sioux
Cheyenne
Comanche Ponca
Omaha
Pawnee Iowa
Arapaho
GREAT PLAINS Missouri
Kansas
Osage
Kiowa
Quapaw
Wichita
Caddo
Tonkawa Natchez
Atakapa
Karankawa
Rio Grande

Chippewa
(Ojibwa)
Chippewa
(Ojibwa)
Menominee
Sauk
Fox Potawatomi
Winnebago
Kickapoo **EASTERN**
Miami
Illinois **WOODLAND**
Shawnee
Chickasaw
Choctaw Creek
Biloxi Apalachee
SOUTHEAST
Yamasee
Timucua

SUB-ARCTIC Micmac
Malecite
Algonquin Abnaki
Ottawa Mahican
Huron Pennacook
Iroquois Mohawk Massachusetts
Oneida Wampanoag
Onondaga Narragansett
Cayuga
Seneca
Mohegan
Erie Susquehanna
Delaware
Powhatan
Tutelo
Tuscarora
Cherokee Catawba

Calusa

ATLANTIC OCEAN

PACIFIC OCEAN

Gulf of Mexico

| 0 | | 500 Miles |
| 0 | | 500 Kilometers |

---

advantage, and it is not surprising that the tribes trading directly with the whites dominated other Native Americans armed only with bows and arrows.

Effects of Disease

Disease ultimately destroyed the cultural integrity of many North American tribes. European explorers exposed Native Americans to germs against which they possessed no natural immunities—smallpox, measles, and typhus. Settlers who possessed no knowledge of germ theory speculated that God had providentially cleared the wilderness of heathens.

Modern historians believe that some tribes suffered a 90 to 95 percent population loss within the first century of European contact. The death of so many Indians deprived the conquerors, especially the Spanish, of indigenous workers needed to operate new mines

and plantations. This loss may have caused colonists throughout the New World to seek a substitute labor force in Africa.

The Indian survivors of the terrible epidemics often suffered profound psychological consequences. Some questioned their own religious beliefs and practices. One Canadian tribe, the Micmac, seems to have reacted to the demographic disaster by slaughtering the wild animals that they had once held as sacred. They reasoned that the game had betrayed them. The animals had lost their magic, and in their anger and confusion, the Micmac retaliated by killing as many animals as they could. This wholesale slaughter of an important element of their economy only added to the Indians' suffering.

Some tribes, the Iroquois, for example, withstood the threat of disease better than did others. On the whole this disaster reinforced racial stereotypes in the minds of Europeans already predisposed to view Indians as inferior and uncivilized. European colonists may have described Native Americans in derogatory terms because they were seeing sick and dispirited men and women whose lives had been shattered.

European Background of Exploration

In ancient times the West possessed a mythical appeal to people living along the shores of the Mediterranean Sea. Classical writers speculated about the fate of the legendary Atlantis, a great civilization that had mysteriously sunk beneath the ocean waves. In the fifth century A.D. an intrepid Irish monk, Saint Brendan, reported finding enchanted islands far out in the Atlantic where he also met a talking whale. Such stories aroused curiosity but proved difficult to verify.

About 1000 A.D., Scandinavian seafarers known as Norsemen or Vikings actually established settlements in the New World. In the year 984 a band of Vikings led by Eric the Red sailed west from Iceland to a large island in the North Atlantic, which Eric inappropriately named Greenland in an effort to attract colonists to this icebound region. A few years later Eric's son, Leif, pushed even farther west to northern Newfoundland. Poor communications, hostile Indians, and political upheavals at home, however, made maintenance of these distant outposts impossible. The Viking adventurers were not widely known; when Columbus set out on his great voyage in 1492, he seemed to have been unaware of these earlier exploits.

Rise of Nation-States

The Viking achievement went unnoticed partly because other Europeans were not prepared to sponsor trans-Atlantic exploration and settlement. Medieval kingdoms were loosely organized, and for several centuries fierce provincial loyalties, widespread ignorance of classical learning, and dreadful plagues such as the Black Death discouraged people from thinking about the world beyond their immediate villages.

In the fifteenth century these conditions began to change. The expansion of commerce, a more imaginative outlook, fostered by the Renaissance, and a general population growth after 1450 contributed to the exploration impulse. Land became more expensive, and landowners prospered. Demands from wealthy landlords for such luxury goods as spices and jewels, obtainable only in distant ports, introduced powerful new incentives for exploration and trade.

This period also witnessed the victory of the "new monarchs" over feudal nobles; political authority was centralized. The changes came slowly, and in many areas violently, but wherever they occurred, the results altered traditional political relationships between the nobility and the crown, between the citizen and the state. The new rulers recruited national armies and paid for them with national taxes. These rulers could be despotic, but they usually restored a measure of peace to communities tired of chronic feudal war.

The story was the same throughout most of western Europe. Henry VII in England, Louis XI

■ *Population increase, high land prices, and a demand for luxury goods contributed to the exploration impulse.*

in France, and Ferdinand of Aragon and Isabella of Castile in Spain forged strong nations from weak kingdoms. If these political changes had not occurred, the major European countries could not possibly have generated the financial and military resources necessary for worldwide exploration. Indeed, the formation of aggressive nation-states prepared the way for the later wars of empire.

Technology and Knowledge

During this period naval innovators revolutionized ship design and technology. Before the fifteenth century the ships that plied the Mediterranean were clumsy and slow. But by the time Columbus sailed from Spain, they were faster, more maneuverable, and less expensive to operate. Most important of all was a new type of rigging developed by the Arabs, the lateen sail, which allowed large ships to sail into the wind, permitting trans-Atlantic travel and difficult maneuvers along the rocky, uncharted coasts of North America. By the end of the fifteenth century, seafarers set sail with a new sense of confidence.

The final prerequisite to exploration was knowledge. The rediscovery of classical texts and maps in the humanistic renaissance of the fifteenth century helped stimulate fresh investigation of the globe. And, because of the invention of the printing press, this new knowledge could spread across Europe. The printing press opened the European mind to exciting possibilities that had only been dimly perceived when the Vikings sailed the North Atlantic.

Spain and the New World

In the early fifteenth century, Spain was politically divided, its people were poor, and its harbors were second-rate. There was little to indicate that this land would take the lead in conquering the New World. But in the early sixteenth century Spain came alive. The union of Ferdinand and Isabella sparked a drive for political consolidation which, because of the monarchs' militant Catholicism, took on the characteristics of a religious crusade. The new monarchs waged a victorious war against the Moslem states in southern Spain, which ended in 1492 when Granada, the last Moslem stronghold, fell. Out of this volatile political and social environment came the *conquistadores*, men eager for personal glory and material gain, uncompromising in matters of religion, and unswerving in their loyalty to the Crown. These were the men who first carried European culture to the New World.

Admiral of the Ocean Sea

If it had not been for Christopher Columbus (Cristoforo Colombo), Spain might never have gained an American empire. Born in Genoa, Italy, in 1451 of humble parentage, Columbus devoured classical learning and became obsessed with the idea of sailing west across the Atlantic Ocean to reach Cathay, as China was then known. In 1484 he presented his plan to the king of Portugal, who was also interested in a route to Cathay. But the Portuguese were more interested in the route that went around the tip of Africa. After a polite audience, Columbus was refused support.

Undaunted by rejection, Columbus petitioned Isabella and Ferdinand for financial backing. They were initially no more interested in his grand design than the Portuguese had been. But fear of Portugal's growing power as well as Columbus' confident talk of wealth and empire led the new monarchs to reassess his scheme. Finally the two sovereigns provided the supremely self-assured navigator with three ships, the *Niña*, *Pinta*, and *Santa Maria*. The indomitable admiral set sail for Cathay in August 1492, the year of Spain's unification.

Educated Europeans in the fifteenth century knew without question that the earth was round. The question was size, not shape. Columbus estimated the distance to the mainland of Asia to be about 3000 nautical miles, a

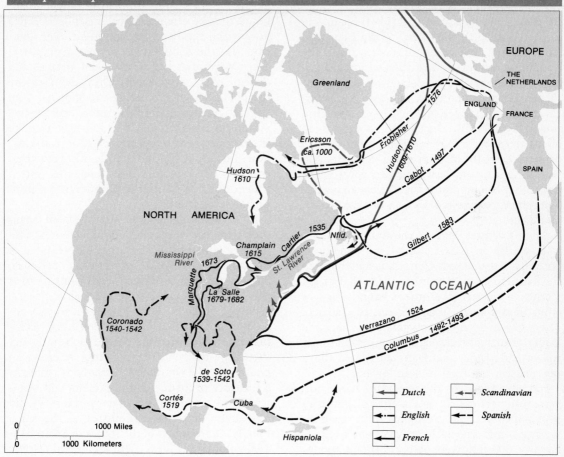

EUROPE

THE NETHERLANDS

Greenland

1576

ENGLAND

FRANCE

Frobisher

Ericsson
ca. 1000

Hudson
1609-1610

Cabot 1497

SPAIN

Hudson
1610

NORTH AMERICA

Cartier 1535

Nfld.

Champlain
1615

Gilbert 1583

Mississippi
River 1673

Marquette

St. Lawrence River

ATLANTIC OCEAN

La Salle
1679-1682

Coronado
1540-1542

Verrazano 1524

Columbus 1492-1493

de Soto
1539-1542

Cortés
1519

Cuba

← Dutch	←·· Scandinavian
←·−· English	←−− Spanish
←— French	

Hispaniola

0 1000 Miles

0 1000 Kilometers

voyage that his small ships would have had no difficulty in completing. The actual distance is 10,600 nautical miles, however, and had the New World not been in his way, his crew would have run out of food and water long before they reached China.

After stopping in the Canary Islands for ship repairs and supplies, Columbus crossed the Atlantic in thirty-three days, landing on an island in the Bahamas. He searched for the fabled cities of Asia, never considering that he had stumbled upon a large land mass completely unknown in Europe. Since his mathematical calculations had been correct, he assumed he would soon encounter the Chinese.

Instead he met friendly, though startled, Native Americans, whom he called Indians.

Three more times Columbus returned to the New World—in search of fabled Asian riches. He died in 1506, a frustrated, impoverished dreamer, unaware that he had reached a previously unknown continent. The final blow came in December 1500 when an ambitious falsifier, Amerigo Vespucci, published a sensational travel account that convinced German mapmakers that he had beaten Columbus to the New World. Before the deception was discovered, "America" gained general acceptance throughout Europe as the name for the newly discovered continent.

7

The Rise of the Conquistadores

By the Treaty of Tordesillas (1494) Spain and Portugal divided the New World. Portugal gained Brazil, and Spain laid claim to all the remaining territories. Spain's good fortune unleashed a horde of conquistadores on the Caribbean. They came not as colonists but as fortune hunters seeking instant wealth, preferably gold, and they were not squeamish about the means they used to obtain it. The primary casualty of their greed were the Native Americans. In less than two decades the tribes that had inhabited the Caribbean islands had been exterminated, victims of exploitation and disease.

After a quarter century the rumors of fabulous wealth in Mexico lured the conquistadores from the islands Columbus had found to the mainland. On November 18, 1518, Hernán Cortés, a minor government functionary in Cuba, and a small army set sail for Mexico. There Cortés soon demonstrated that he was a leader of extraordinary ability, a person of intellect and vision who managed to rise above the goals of his avaricious followers.

His adversary was the legendary Aztec emperor Montezuma. It was a duel of powerful personalities. After burning his ships to cut off his army from a possible retreat, Cortés led his band of 600 followers across difficult mountain trails toward the Valley of Mexico. The sound of gunfire and the sight of armor-clad horses, both unknown to Native Americans, frightened the Indians. Added to these technological advantages was an important psychological factor. At first Montezuma thought that the Spaniards were gods, representatives of the fearful plumed serpent, Quetzalcoatl. By the time the Aztec ruler realized his error, it was too late to save his empire.

The Spanish Colonial System

Cortés' victory in Mexico, coupled with other Spanish conquests, notably in Peru, transformed the mother country into the wealthiest nation in Europe. But the Spanish crown soon faced new difficulties. The conquistadores had to be brought under royal authority. Adventurers like Cortés were stubbornly independent, quick to take offense, and thousands of miles away from the seat of government. One solution was the *encomienda* system. Conquistadores were rewarded with Indian villages and control over native labor. They also had the responsibility of protecting the Indians, who suffered terribly under this cruelly exploitative system of labor tribute. The system did make the colonizers very dependent upon the king, however, for it was he who legitimized their title. As one historian has noted, the system transformed "a frontier of plunder into a frontier of settlement."

Bureaucrats dispatched directly from Spain soon replaced the aging conquistadores. Unlike the governing system that later existed in England's mainland American colonies, Spain's rulers maintained tight control over their American possessions through their government officials. After 1535 a viceroy, a nobleman appointed to oversee the king's colonial interests, ruled the people of New Spain. Working independently of the viceroy, an *audiencia*, the supreme judicial body, brought a measure of justice to the Indians and Spaniards and made certain that the viceroys did not slight their responsibilities to the king. Finally, the Council of the Indies in Spain handled colonial business. Although cumbersome and slow, somehow this rigidly controlled system worked.

The Spanish also brought Catholicism to the New World. The Dominicans and Franciscans, the two largest religious orders, established Indian missions throughout New Spain, and some barefoot friars protected the Native Americans from the worst forms of exploitation. One courageous Dominican, Fra Bartolomé de Las Casas, even published an eloquent defense of Indian rights, *Historia de las Indias*, that among other things questioned the European conquest of the New World. The book led to reforms designed to bring greater "love and moderation" to Spanish-Indian relations.

About 750,000 people migrated to the New World from Spain. Most of the colonists were impoverished, single males in their late twen-

■ *The Dominicans and Franciscans established Indian missions throughout New Spain to convert the Native Americans. Some friars protected the Native Americans from the worst forms of Spanish exploitation.*

ties in search of economic opportunities. They generally came from the poorest agricultural regions of southern Spain. Since few Spanish women migrated, especially in the sixteenth century, the men often married Indians and, later, blacks, unions which produced "mestizos" and "mulattos." The frequency of interracial marriage created a society of more fluid racial categories than there were in the English colonies, where the sex ratio of the settlers was more balanced and the racially mixed population comparatively small.

The Spanish Borderlands

The lure of gold drew Spanish conquistadores to the unexplored lands to the north of Mexico. Between 1539 and 1541, Hernando de Soto trekked across the Southeast from Florida to the Mississippi River looking for gold and glory, and at about the same time, Francisco Vasquez de Coronado set out from New Spain in search of the fabled "Seven Cities of Cibola." Neither conquistador found what he was searching for. In the seventeenth century

when Juan de Oñate established outposts in the Southwest, the Spanish came in open conflict with Native Americans in that region. In 1680 the Indians drove the whites completely out of the territory. Thereafter the decision was made to maintain only a token presence in present-day Texas and New Mexico in order to discourage French encroachment upon Spanish lands. For the same reason, the Spanish colony of St. Augustine was established in Florida in 1565. Little interest was shown by Spanish authorities in California, a land of poor Indians and even poorer natural resources. Had it not been for the work of a handful of priests, Spain would have had little claim to California.

Even so, Spain claimed far more of the New World than it could possibly manage. After the era of the conquistadores, Spain's rulers regarded the American colonies primarily as a source of precious metal, and between 1500 and 1650 an estimated 200 tons of gold and 16,000 tons of silver were shipped back to the Spanish treasury in Madrid. The resulting inflation hurt the common people in Spain and prevented the growth of Spanish industry. Poor leadership and debilitating wars hastened the Spanish decline. As one insightful observer declared in 1603, "the New World conquered by you has conquered you in its turn." Nonetheless, Spain's great cultural contribution to the American people is still very much alive today.

French Exploration and Settlement

French interest in the New World developed more slowly. In 1534 Jacques Cartier first sailed to the New World in search of a northwest passage to China. At first he was de-pressed by the rocky, barren coast of New-foundland. He grumbled, "I am rather inclined to believe that this is the land God gave to Cain." But the discovery of a large, promising waterway raised Cartier's spirits. He reconnoi-tered the Gulf of the Saint Lawrence, traveling up the river as far as Montreal, but he did not discover a northwest passage, gold, or other precious metals. After several voyages to Can-ada, Cartier became discouraged by the harsh winters and meager findings; he returned home for good in 1542. Not until seventy-five years later did the brilliant navigator Samuel de Champlain rediscover this region for France. He founded Quebec in 1608.

In Canada the French developed an economy based primarily on the fur trade, a commerce

In the dead of winter the streams of New France were frozen solid. The French voyageurs built sledges, placed their canoes and their supplies on them, and proceeded down the frozen course into the heart of the continent.

that required close cooperation with the Native Americans. They also explored the heart of the continent. In 1673 Père Jacques Marquette journeyed down the Mississippi River, and nine years later Sieur de La Salle traveled all the way to the Gulf of Mexico. In the early eighteenth century, the French established small settlements in Louisiana, the most important being New Orleans.

Although the French controlled the region along the Mississippi and its tributaries, their dream of a vast American empire suffered from several serious flaws. From the first, the king remained largely indifferent to colonial affairs. An even greater problem was the nature of the land and climate. Few rural peasants or urban artisans wished to venture to the inhospitable northern country, and throughout the colonial period, New France was underpopulated. By the first quarter of the eighteenth century, the English settlements had outstripped their French neighbors in population as well as in volume of trade.

Background of English Exploration

The first English visit to North America remains something of a mystery. Fishermen working out of the western English ports may have landed in Nova Scotia and Newfoundland as early as the 1480s. John Cabot (Giovanni Caboto), a Venetian sea captain, completed the first recorded trans-Atlantic voyage by an English vessel in 1497. Henry VII had rejected Columbus' Enterprise for the Indies, but the first Tudor monarch apparently experienced a change of heart after hearing of Spain's success.

Like other explorers of the time, Cabot believed that he could find a northwest passage to Asia. He doggedly searched the northern waters for a likely opening, but a direct route to Cathay eluded him. Cabot died during a second attempt in 1498. Although Sebastian Cabot continued his father's explorations in the Hudson Bay region in 1508–1509, English interest in the New World waned. For the next three quarters of a century, the English people were preoccupied with more pressing domestic and religious concerns. The Cabot voyages did, however, establish an English claim to American territory.

The English Reformation

The reign of Henry VII was plagued by domestic troubles. England possessed no standing army, a small, weak navy, and many strong and independent local magnates. During the sixteenth century, however, the next Tudor king, Henry VIII and his daughter Elizabeth I developed a strong central government and transformed England into a Protestant nation. These changes propelled England into a central role in European affairs and were crucial to the creation of England's North American empire.

The Protestantism that eventually stimulated colonization was definitely not of English origin. In 1517 a relatively obscure German monk, Martin Luther, publicly challenged certain tenets and practices of Roman Catholicism, and within a few years the religious unity of Europe was forever shattered. Luther's message was straightforward. God spoke through the Bible, Luther maintained, not through the pope or priests. Pilgrimages, fasts, alms, indulgences, none of these traditional acts could assure salvation. Luther's ideas spread rapidly across northern Germany and Scandinavia.

Other Protestant reformers soon spoke out against Catholicism. The most important of these was John Calvin, a lawyer turned theologian, who lived in the Swiss city of Geneva. Calvin stressed God's omnipotence over human affairs. The Lord, he maintained, chose some persons for "election," the gift of salvation, while condemning others to eternal damnation. Human beings were powerless to alter this decision by their individual actions.

Common sense suggests that such a bleak doctrine might lead to fatalism or hedonism. After all, why not enjoy worldly pleasures if they have no effect on God's judgment? But common sense would be wrong. Indeed, Cal-

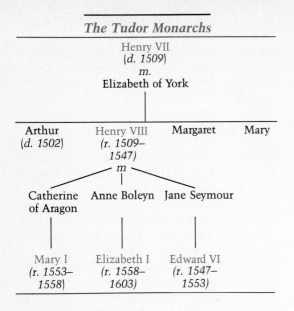

The Tudor Monarchs

Henry VII
(d. 1509)
m.
Elizabeth of York

| Arthur (d. 1502) | Henry VIII (r. 1509–1547) | Margaret | Mary |

m

| Catherine of Aragon | Anne Boleyn | Jane Seymour |

| Mary I (r. 1553–1558) | Elizabeth I (r. 1558–1603) | Edward VI (r. 1547–1553) |

vinists were constantly busy searching for signs that they had received God's gift of grace. The uncertainty of their eternal state proved a powerful psychological spur, for as long as people did not know whether they were scheduled for heaven or hell, they worked diligently to demonstrate that they possessed at least the seeds of grace. This doctrine of "predestination" became the distinguishing mark of Calvin's followers throughout northern Europe. In the seventeenth century, they were known in France as Huguenots, and in England and America as Puritans.

Popular anticlericalism was the basis for the Reformation in England. The English people had long resented paying monies to Catholic churchmen. Early in the sixteenth century, opposition to the clergy grew increasingly vocal. Cardinal Thomas Wolsey, the most powerful prelate in England, flaunted his immense wealth and became a symbol of spiritual corruption. Parish priests were ridiculed for their ignorance and greed. Anticlericalism did not run as deep in England as in Germany, but by the late 1520s the Roman Catholic clergy had strained the allegiance of the great mass of the population. Ordinary men and women throughout the kingdom were ready to leave the institutional church.

The catalyst for Reformation in England was Henry VIII's desire to end his marriage to Catherine of Aragon, daughter of the king of Spain. Their union in 1509 had produced a daughter, Mary, but no son. The need for a male heir obsessed Henry. He and his counselors assumed that a female ruler could not maintain domestic peace and that England would fall once again into civil war. Henry petitioned Pope Clement VII for a divorce. Unwilling to tolerate the public humiliation of Catherine, Spain forced the pope to procrastinate. In 1527 time ran out. Henry fell in love with Anne Boleyn, who later bore him a daughter, Elizabeth. The king divorced Catherine without papal consent.

The final break with Rome came swiftly. Between 1529 and 1536, the king, acting through Parliament, severed all ties with the pope, seized church lands, and dissolved many of the monasteries. In March 1534 the Act of Supremacy boldly named Henry VIII "supreme head of the Church of England." Land formerly owned by the Catholic church passed quickly into private hands, and property holders acquired a vested interest in Protestantism. In 1539 William Tyndale and Miles Coverdale issued an English edition of the Bible, which made it possible for the common people to read the scriptures in their own language. The separation was complete.

When Henry died in 1547, his young son Edward VI came to the throne. But he was a sickly child. Militant Protestants took advantage of the political uncertainty to introduce Calvinism into England. In breaking with the papacy, Henry had shown little enthusiasm for theological change; most Catholic ceremonies remained. But opponents now insisted that the Church of England remove every trace of its Catholic origins. Edward died in 1553, and these ambitious efforts came to a sudden halt. Henry's eldest daughter, Mary I, next ascended the throne. Fiercely loyal to the Catholic faith, she vowed to return England to the pope. Hundreds of Protestants were executed, others

■ Foxe's Book of Martyrs *provided powerful propaganda for the ever growing Protestant religion in England.*

scurried off to Geneva and Frankfurt where they absorbed radical Calvinist doctrines. When Mary died in 1558 and was succeeded by Elizabeth I, these "Marian exiles" returned, more eager than ever to purify the Tudor church of Catholicism. Mary had inadvertently advanced the cause of Calvinism by creating so many Protestant martyrs. The Marian exiles controlled the Elizabethan church, which remained fundamentally Calvinist until the end of the sixteenth century.

Elizabeth Settles the Question

Elizabeth I was a woman of extraordinary talent. She governed England from 1558 to 1603, an intellectually exciting period during which some of her subjects took the first halting steps toward colonizing the New World.

Elizabeth's most urgent duty was to end the religious turmoil that had divided the country for a generation. Following Henry VIII's break with Rome, each new Tudor sovereign had introduced a different theology—Catholicism, Anglo-Catholicism, Calvinism, something in

between—until, in the words of one confused Englishman, people's consciences were *"tost up and Down (even like Tenis-bals)."* Elizabeth had no desire to restore Catholicism. After all, the pope openly referred to her as a woman of illegitimate birth. Nor did she want to recreate the church exactly as it had been in the final years of her father's reign. Rather, Elizabeth established a unique church, near-Catholic in ceremony, but Protestant in doctrine. The examples of Edward and Mary had demonstrated that neither radical change nor widespread persecution gained a monarch lasting popularity.

Elizabeth still faced serious religious challenges. Catholicism and Protestantism were warring faiths; each was an ideology, a body of deeply held beliefs that influenced the way that average men and women across the continent interpreted the experiences of everyday life. The confrontation between Protestantism and Catholicism affected Elizabeth's entire reign. Militant Calvinists urged her to drop all Catholic rituals, and fervent Catholics wanted her to return to the Roman church. Pope Pius excommunicated her in 1570. Spain, the most intensely Catholic state in Europe, vowed to restore England to the "true" faith, and Catholic terrorists constantly plotted to overthrow the Tudor monarchy.

Religion, War, and Nationalism

English Protestantism and English nationalism slowly merged. A loyal English subject in the late sixteenth century loved the queen, supported the Church of England, and hated Catholics, especially those who happened to live in Spain. Elizabeth's subjects adored the Virgin Queen, and they applauded when her famed "Sea Dogs"—dashing figures such as Sir Francis Drake and Sir John Hawkins—seized Spanish treasure ships in American waters. The English sailors' raids were little more than piracy, but they passed for grand victories. With each engagement, each threat, each plot, English nationalism took deeper root. By the 1570s, the English people were driven by powerful ideological forces similar to those that had moved the subjects of Isabella and Ferdinand almost a century earlier.

In the mid-1580s, Philip II of Spain constructed a mighty fleet carrying thousands of Spain's finest infantry. This Armada was built to cross the English Channel and destroy the Protestant queen. When one of Philip's lieutenants viewed the Armada at Lisbon in May 1588, he described it as "La felicissima armada," the invincible fleet. The king believed that with the support of England's oppressed Catholics, Spanish troops would sweep Elizabeth from power.

It was a grand scheme; it was an even grander failure. In 1588 a smaller, more maneuverable English navy dispersed the Armada and revealed Spain's vulnerability. Philip's hopes for a Catholic England lay wrecked along the rocky shores of Scotland and Ireland. Elizabeth's subjects remained loyal throughout the crisis. Inspired by success in the Channel, bolder personalities dreamed of acquiring riches and planting colonies across the North Atlantic. Spain's American monopoly had been broken.

Irish Rehearsal for American Colonization

England's first colony was Ireland. On that island enterprising Englishmen first learned to subdue a foreign population and seize its lands. Ireland's one million inhabitants were scattered mainly along the coast, and there were few villages. To the English, the Irish seemed wild and barbaric. They were also fiercely independent. The English dominated a small region around Dublin, but much of Ireland remained in the hands of Gaelic-speaking Catholics who presumably lived beyond the reach of civilization.

During the 1560s and 1570s the English decided that money could be made in Ireland, despite the hostility of the Irish. English colonists moved in and forced the Irish either into

tenancy or off the land altogether. Semi-military colonies were planted in Ulster and Munster.

Colonization produced severe cultural strains. The English settlers, however humble their own origins, felt superior to the Irish. After all, the English had championed the Protestant religion, constructed a complex market economy, and created a powerful nation-state. To the English, the Irish appeared lazy, lawless, superstitious, and oftimes stupid. Even educated representatives of the two cultures found communication almost impossible. English colonists, for example, criticized Ireland's pastoral farming methods. It seemed perversely wasteful for the Irish to be forever moving about because this practice retarded the development of towns. Sir John Davies, a leading English colonist, declared that if the Irish were left to themselves, they would "never . . . build houses, make townships or villages or manure or improve the land *as it ought to be*." Such wastefulness became the standard English justification for seizing more land. No matter what the Irish did, they could never be sufficiently English to please their new masters.

English ethnocentrism was relatively benign so long as the Irish accepted subservient roles. But they rebelled frequently, and English condescension turned quickly to violence. Resistance smacked of disrespect, and for the good of the Irish and the safety of the English, it had to be crushed. Sir Humphrey Gilbert was especially brutal. A talented man who wrote treatises on geography, Gilbert explored the coast of North America and entertained Queen Elizabeth with witty conversation. But as military governor in Ireland, he tolerated no opposition.

In 1569, when the Irish rose up in Munster, he executed everyone he could catch, "mane, woman and childe." He cut off the heads of many enemy soldiers killed in battle, and in the words of one contemporary, Gilbert laid his macabre trophies "on the ground by each side of the way leading into his tent, so that none should come into his tent for any cause but commonly he must pass through a lane of heads." Instead of bringing peace and security, such behavior generated a hatred so deep that Ireland remains divided to this day.

The Irish experiments served as models for later English colonies in the New World, shaping the English view of America and its people. English adventurers in the New World compared Native Americans with the "wild" Irish. This ethnocentrism was a central element in the transfer of English culture to America. The English, like the Spanish and the French, did not perceive America in objective terms. They had already constructed an image of America, and the people and objects that greeted them on the other side of the Atlantic were forced into Old World categories, some of them Irish.

England Turns to America

By the 1570s, England was ready to challenge Spain and reap the profits of Asia and America. Only dimly aware of Cabot's voyages and with very limited colonization experience in Ireland, the English adventurers made almost every mistake that one could possibly imagine between 1575 and 1600. They did, however, acquire valuable information about winds and currents, supplies and finance, which laid the foundation for later, more successful ventures.

Gilbert's Adventure and the Roanoke Tragedy

The pioneer of English colonization in the New World was the same Sir Humphrey Gilbert who had experimented with colonization in Ireland. Gilbert originally set out to discover the northwest passage to Cathay. He published an entire book on the subject, showing exactly where the passages might be found. He tantalized readers and potential investors with stories of the fabulous riches awaiting those who first seized control of the short route to Asia. Gilbert also envisioned vast New World estates, much like those he had created in Ireland.

Gilbert's enterprise got off to a bizarre start. In 1576, he sent Martin Frobisher, a courageous sea captain, to find the passage. Frobisher missed it, but he returned with tons of American "gold" from desolate Hall's Island. The sparkling dirt turned out upon closer analysis to be worthless chunks of iron pyrite (fool's gold).

In 1578 Gilbert tried a different approach. He persuaded Elizabeth to grant him a charter for "remote heathen and barbarous landes." After one abortive attempt and against the advice of the queen, Gilbert sailed to Newfoundland in 1583 and claimed the territory as his very own.

■ *The wife and daughter of an Algonquin chief, drawn by John White. The child is holding an English doll.*

On the return voyage his ship was lost without a trace. The tough old adventurer was last sighted sitting on the open deck during a storm reading from the works of Sir Thomas More.

Sir Walter Raleigh shared Gilbert's dreams. The men were half-brothers, and after Gilbert's death, Raleigh announced his own intention of establishing a colony in America. In 1585 the optimistic Raleigh dispatched two captains to the coast of the present-day North Carolina to claim land granted to him by Eliza-

beth. The men returned with glowing reports about the fertility of the soil. Diplomatically, Raleigh renamed this marvelous region Virginia, in honor of his patron, the Virgin Queen.

Raleigh's enterprise seemed ill-fated from the start. Though encouraged by Elizabeth, he received no financial backing from the crown, and despite careful planning, everything went wrong. In 1585 Sir Richard Grenville transported a group of men to Roanoke Island, but the colonists did not arrive in Virginia until nearly autumn. The settlement was also poorly located, and even experienced navigators found it dangerous to reach. Finally, Grenville alienated the local Indians when he senselessly destroyed an entire Indian village in retaliation for the theft of a silver cup.

Grenville hurried back to England in the autumn of 1585, leaving the colonists to fend for themselves. They performed quite well. But when an expected shipment of supplies failed to arrive on time, the colonists grew discontented. In the spring of 1586 Sir Francis Drake unexpectedly landed at Roanoke, and the colonists impulsively decided to return home with him. They were apparently relieved to escape an island that contained neither gold nor silver. Their irresponsible behavior nearly destroyed the entire experiment.

In 1587 Raleigh launched a second colony. The new settlement was more representative, containing men, women, and even children. The settlers feasted upon Roanoke's fish and game and bountiful harvests of corn and pumpkin. Yet within weeks after arriving, the leader of the settlement, John White, returned to England at the colonists' urging to obtain additional food and clothing and to recruit new immigrants.

Once again, Raleigh's luck turned sour. War with Spain pressed every available ship into military service. When rescuers eventually reached the island in 1590, they found the village deserted. The fate of the "lost" colonists remains a mystery. The best guess is that they paid for Grenville's attack upon the Indians with their lives.

The Roanoke debacle discouraged others from emulating Raleigh. He had squandered a fortune and had nothing to show for it. During the 1590s smart investors put their money into privateering or other less exhausting ventures. Had it not been for Richard Hakluyt, who publicized the explorers' accounts of the New World, the dream of American colonization by the English might have ended.

Keeping the Dream of America Alive

Hakluyt, a supremely industrious man, never saw America. Nevertheless, his vision of the New World powerfully shaped public opinion. He interviewed captains and sailors and carefully collected their travel stories in a massive book entitled *The Principall Navigations, Voyages, and Discoveries of the English Nation* (1589). Although each tale appeared to be a straightforward narrative, Hakluyt edited each piece to drive home the book's central point: England needed American colonies. English settlers, he argued, would provide the mother country with critical natural resources, and in the process they would grow rich themselves.

As a salesman for the New World, Hakluyt was as misleading as he was successful. He led many ordinary men and women who traveled to America to expect nothing less than a paradise on earth. As the history of Jamestown was soon to demonstrate, the harsh realities of America bore little relation to those golden dreams.

Recommended Reading

The events surrounding the exploration of the New World have been the subject of a rich historical literature. A particularly well-written account of the background of European expansion is J. H. Parry, *The Age of Reconnaissance* (1963). A book of narrower focus is Samuel E. Morison, *The European Discovery of America: The Southern Voyages, 1492–1616* (1971). The transformation of early modern Europe, especially economic shifts, is discussed in Ralph Davis' brilliant synthesis, *The Rise of Atlantic Economies* (1973). Alfred Crosby provides insights into the unintended results of exploration in *Columbian Exchange: Biological and Cultural Consequences of 1492* (1972). Spain's rise to a world power can be traced in J. H. Elliott, *Imperial Spain, 1469–1716* (1963), and J. H. Parry, *The Spanish Seaborne Empire* (1966). Charles Gibson provides an excellent introduction to the history of New Spain in *Spain in America* (1966). Two books by W. J. Eccles, *Canada Under Louis XIV, 1663–1701* (1964) and *The Canadian Frontier, 1534–1760* (1969), provide considerable insight into the development of New France.

There are many fine studies of sixteenth-century England, but one might start with G. R. Elton, *England Under the Tudors* (1974), and J. E. Neale, *Queen Elizabeth I* (1934). A. G. Dickens examines England's religious transformation in *The English Reformation* (1964). One should also look at Patrick Collinson, *The Religion of Protestants: The Church in English Society, 1559–1625* (1982). The two best studies of Ireland in this period are Nicholas P. Canny, *The Elizabethan Conquest of Ireland* (1976), and David B. Quinn, *The Elizabethans and the Irish* (1966).

Two sensitive books on Native American cultures are Bruce Trigger, *The Children of Aataentsic: A History of the Huron People to 1660* (1976), and Cornelius Jaenen, *Friend and Foe: Aspects of French-Amerindian Cultural Contact in the Sixteenth and Seventeenth Centuries* (1976). Sherburne F. Cook and Woodrow Borah provide a comprehensive analysis of the demographic crisis in *The Aboriginal Population of Central Mexico on the Eve of the Spanish Conquest* (1963). See Calvin Martin, *Keepers of the Game: Indian-Animal Relationships and the Fur Trade* (1978) on the Indians' responses to white culture. Also of interest are Shepard Krech, ed., *Indians, Animals, and the Fur Trade: A Critique of Keepers of the Game* (1918), and James Axtell, *The European and the Indian* (1981).

chapter 2

THE SPECTRUM
OF
SETTLEMENT

English monarchs, often without the slightest knowledge of local geography, awarded large tracts of land in North America to merchant adventurers or court favorites. The results were boundary conflicts and disputes that often lasted a hundred years or more. In 1665, for example, Connecticut, Massachusetts Bay, Plymouth, and Rhode Island threatened war with each other over an area of land around Narragansett Bay. Each colony claimed the land, and each colony possessed documents signed by the king of England supporting its claim. Royal commissioners prevented a war, but almost a century passed before the boundary dispute finally was resolved. This dispute revealed how English colonization transformed maps of North America into a crazy quilt of territorial claims and counterclaims.

Such a haphazard method of granting land also suggests the diverse origins of England's American colonies. English colonization did not spring from a desire to build a centralized empire, like that of Spain or France. Instead,

the Crown awarded colonial charters to a wide variety of merchants, religious idealists, and aristocratic adventurers who established separate and profoundly different colonies. In this atmosphere a variety of religious practices, political institutions, and economic arrangements thrived.

Motives for Migration

Changes in the mother country occurring throughout the period of settlement help explain the diversity of English colonization. Far-reaching economic, political, and religious transformation affected seventeenth-century England. Many people left the villages where they were born in search of fresh opportunities. Thousands traveled to London, by 1600 a city of several hundred thousand inhabitants. Others set out for more exotic destinations. A large number of English settlers migrated to

Ireland; lucrative employment and religious freedom attracted others to Holland. The most adventurous individuals, however, went to the New World—to Caribbean islands such as Barbados or to the mainland colonies.

Various reasons drew the colonists across the Atlantic. The quest for a purer form of worship motivated many, while the dream of owning land attracted others. And a few came to escape bad marriages, jail terms, and poverty. But whatever their reasons for crossing the ocean, English men and women who emigrated to America in the seventeenth century left a mother country wracked by recurrent, often violent, political and religious controversies. During the 1620s the Stuart monarchs—James I (1603–1625) and his son Charles I (1625–1649)—fought constantly with the elected members of Parliament. In 1640 the conflict escalated into a bloody civil war between the king and supporters of Parliament. Finally, in 1649 the victorious parliamentarians beheaded Charles, and for almost a decade Oliver Cromwell, a brilliant general and religious reformer, governed England.

The unrest did not end with the death of Charles I. After Cromwell's death the Stuarts were restored to the throne (1660). But through the reigns of Charles II (1660–1685) and James II (1685–1688) the political turmoil continued. When the authoritarian James openly favored his fellow Catholics, the nation rose up in the "Glorious Revolution" (1688), sent him into permanent exile, and placed his staunchly Protestant daughter and son-in-law (William and Mary) upon the throne.

Political turmoil, religious persecution, and economic insecurity determined the flow of emigration. Men and women thought more seriously about living in the New World at such times. Ever changing conditions in England help to explain the diversity of American settlement.

Regardless of when they came, the colonists carried with them a bundle of ideas, beliefs, and assumptions that shaped the way they viewed their new environment. The New World tested and sometimes transformed their

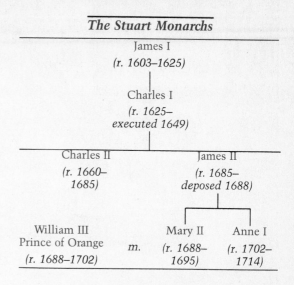

The Stuart Monarchs

James I
(r. 1603–1625)

Charles I
(r. 1625–executed 1649)

Charles II
(r. 1660–1685)

James II
(r. 1685–deposed 1688)

William III Prince of Orange
(r. 1688–1702)   m.   Mary II
(r. 1688–1695)

Anne I
(r. 1702–1714)

values, but never destroyed them. The different subcultures that emerged in America were determined largely by the interaction between these values and such physical elements as climate, crops, and soil. The Chesapeake, the New England Colonies, the Middle Colonies, and the Carolinas formed distinct regional identities that persisted long after the first settlers had passed from the scene.

The Chesapeake

The Roanoke debacle (see Chapter 1) raised questions about America's promise, but with the aid of visionaries like Richard Hakluyt the dream persisted. Writers insisted that there were profits to be made in the New World. In addition, goods from America would supply England with items that it would otherwise be forced to purchase from European rivals—Holland, France, and Spain. The thought of making money, helping England, and annoying Catholic Spain was a powerful incentive. Shortly after James I ascended to the throne, the settlers were given an opportunity to test their theories in the Chesapeake colonies of Virginia and Maryland.

■ *Surrounded by water on three sides, the marshy peninsula on the James River seemed an easy-to-defend location for the Jamestown fort.*

Tragic Adventure at Jamestown

Money had been an early obstacle to colonization. The "joint-stock company" removed the barrier. A business organization in which scores of people could invest without fear of bankruptcy, it proved very successful. A person could purchase a share of stock at a stated price, and at the end of several years, could anticipate recovering the initial investment plus a portion of whatever profits the company had made. Within a very short time, some of these enterprises were able to amass large amounts of capital, enough certainly to finance a new colony. Virginia was the first such venture.

On April 10, 1606, James I issued a charter authorizing the London Company under the dynamic leadership of Sir Thomas Smith (no relation to Captain John Smith) to establish plantations in Virginia. Although the boundaries mentioned in the charter were vague, the London Company promptly renamed itself the Virginia Company and set out to find the treasure that Hakluyt had promised. In December 1606, the *Susan Constant*, the *Godspeed*, and the *Discovery*, with 104 men and boys aboard, sailed for America. The land the voyagers found was lush and well-watered with "faire meaddowes and goodly tall trees."

They soon found something else—death and dissension. The low-lying ground on which they set up their base was thirty miles up the James River on a marshy peninsula they named Jamestown. It proved to be a disease-ridden death trap; even the drinking water was contaminated with salt. However, a peninsula was easier to defend and they feared a surprise attack more than sickness.

Almost instantly the colonists began quarreling. Tales of beaches strewn with rubies and diamonds had lured them to Virginia. Once there, instead of cooperating for the common good—guarding the palisade or farming—each individual pursued personal interests. Meanwhile, disease, hostile Indians, and then starvation ravaged the hapless settlers.

Had it not been for Captain John Smith, Virginia might have gone the way of Roanoke. Smith told tales of fighting the Turks and being saved from certain death by various beautiful women, claims that modern historians have largely verified. In Virginia, Smith brought order out of anarchy. He traded with the Indians for food, mapped the Chesapeake Bay, and was even rescued from execution by a precocious Indian princess, Pocahontas. After seizing control of the ruling council in 1608, he instituted a tough military discipline, forcing the lazy to work and breathing life back into the dying colony.

Leaders of the Virginia Company in London soon recognized the need to reform the entire enterprise. A new charter in 1609 granted the company the right to make all commercial and political decisions affecting the colonists. Moreover, in an effort to obtain scarce capital, the original partners opened the "joint stock" to the general public. The company sponsored a spirited publicity campaign; pamphlets and sermons extolled the colony's potential and exhorted patriotic English citizens to invest in the enterprise.

This burst of energy came to nothing. Bad luck and poor planning plagued the Virginia Company. A ship carrying settlers and supplies went aground in the Caribbean; the governor, Lord De La Warr postponed his departure for America; and Captain Smith suffered a debilitating accident and had to return to England.

As a result, between 1609 and 1611 the remaining settlers lacked capable leadership. Food supplies grew short. The terrible winter of 1609–1610—termed the "starving time"—drove a few desperate colonists to cannibalism. Smith reported that one crazed settler killed, salted, and ate parts of his wife before the murder was discovered. Many people lost their will to live.

Governor De La Warr finally arrived in June 1610. He and the deputy governors who succeeded him ruled by martial law. Men and women marched to work by the beat of the drum. These extreme measures saved the colony but Virginia did not flourish. Nothing produced in the colony came close to covering the company's expenditures. In 1616, the year profits were to be distributed to shareholders, the company hovered near bankruptcy, with only a vast expanse of unsurveyed land three thousand miles from London to show for all its efforts.

A "Stinking Weed" Saves the Colony

The solution to Virginia's problems grew in the vacant lots of Jamestown. Only Indians cultivated tobacco—for religious purposes—until John Rolfe realized that this local weed might be a valuable export crop. Rolfe, who married Pocahontas, developed a milder tobacco leaf that greatly appealed to European smokers.

Virginians suddenly possessed a means to make money. Tobacco was easy to grow, and settlers who had avoided work now threw themselves into its production with singleminded diligence. James I initially considered smoking immoral and unhealthy; he changed his mind as the duties he collected on tobacco imports mounted.

The Virginia Company in 1618 launched one last effort to transform Virginia into a profitable enterprise, promising a series of reforms—relaxation of martial law and establishment of a representative assembly were among these. Sir Edwin Sandys (pronounced Sands), a gifted

■ *Pocahontas took the name Rebecka when she converted to Christianity. This portrait was painted during a visit to London in 1616.*

entrepreneur, led the faction of stockholders who pumped life into the faltering organization, encouraging private investors to develop their own estates in Virginia. Sandys even introduced a new method for distributing land. Colonists who paid their own way to Virginia were guaranteed a "headright," a fifty-acre lot for which they paid only a small annual rent. Additional headrights were granted to the adventurers for each servant that they brought to the colony. This procedure enabled planters to build up huge estates with dependent labor, a land system that persisted long after the Company's collapse.

Sandys had only just begun. He also urged the settlers to diversify their economy. He envisioned colonists busily producing iron and tar, silk and glass, sugar and cotton, as well as tobacco. To finance such a huge project, Sandys relied upon a lottery. The final element in the grand scheme was people. Sandys sent

Life and Death in Virginia

Between 1619 and 1622 colonists arrived in Virginia in record numbers. Most of the 3570 individuals who emmigrated to the colony during those years were single males in their teens or early twenties. Most of them came as indentured servants. In exchange for transportation across the Atlantic, they agreed to serve a master for a stated number of years. The younger the servant, the longer he or she was expected to serve. In return, the master promised to give the laborers proper care and, at the conclusion of their contracts, to provide them with tools and clothes according to "the custom of the country."

Since the Virginia masters needed strong servants able to do heavy field work, young males were preferred. Thus the sex ratio in Virginia was dramatically skewed. In the early decades, men outnumbered women by as much as six to one. Even if a man lived to the end of his indenture, he could not realistically expect to start a family of his own. Moreover, servants were often treated harshly. They were sold, traded, even gambled away in a hand of cards. It does not require much imagination to see that a society that tolerated such an exploitative labor system might later embrace slavery.

Most Virginians did not live long enough to worry about marrying and starting a family. Between 1618 and 1622 perhaps three out of every four persons in Virginia died. Contagious diseases killed the most. Salt poisoning also took a toll. And on Good Friday, March 22, 1622, the local Indians slew 347 settlers in a well-coordinated surprise attack. Those who survived must have lived with a sense of impermanence and a desire to escape Virginia with a little money before they too met an early death.

On both sides of the Atlantic people wondered who should be blamed for the debacle. The burden of responsibility lay with the Virginia Company, whose planning and funding were woefully inadequate. Neither food nor shelter awaited the settlers when they arrived in Virginia. Weakened by the long sea voyage, the malnourished colonists quickly succumbed to contagious diseases.

Officials in Virginia also shared the guilt. Their greed caused them to overlook both the common good and the public defenses. Jamestown took on the characteristics of a "boom town." Unrestrained self-advancement was the dominant feature of this highly individualistic, competitive society.

In 1624 the king took charge, dissolving the bankrupt enterprise and finally transforming Virginia into a royal colony. The Crown appointed a governor and a council, but made no provision for the continuation of Virginia's representative assembly. Even without the king's authorization, however, the House of Burgesses gathered annually, and in 1639 Charles belatedly recognized its existence.

He had no choice. The colonists who served on the council or in the assembly were strong-willed ambitious men. Having survived privation, disease, and Indian attacks, they were singlemindedly out to get rich and had no intention of surrendering their control over local affairs. Governors who opposed the council did so at considerable personal risk. Nor was Charles, encountering his own problems at home, much disposed to intervene. In 1634 the assembly divided the colony into eight counties, each of which was governed by a justice of the peace. The "county court"—as these officers were called—remained the center of Virginia's social, political, and commercial life long after the American Revolution.

The changes in government had little impact upon the character of daily life in Virginia. The isolated tobacco plantations that dotted Virginia's many navigable rivers were the focus of the settlers' lives. This dispersed pattern of settlement retarded the development of institutions such as schools and churches. And for more than a century Jamestown was the only place that could reasonably be called a town.

Maryland: A Refuge for Catholics

Maryland's roots lay not in a wild scramble for wealth, but in a nobleman's desire to create a sanctuary for England's persecuted Catholics. The driving force behind the settlement of Maryland was Sir George Calvert, later Lord Baltimore. Well-educated, charming, ambitious, and from an excellent family, he became a favorite of James I. Although he kept his religious beliefs private, he showed great interest in the progress of Virginia and New England. By the late 1620s it was clear that he longed to establish a colony of his own.

On June 30, 1632, Charles I granted George Calvert's son, Cecilius, a charter for a colony to be located on the Chesapeake Bay north of Virginia. George died while the negotiations were in progress, but his vision shaped the character of the new settlement, named "Mariland, in honor of the Queene." For his part, Charles wanted to halt the southward spread of Dutch influence from New Netherland and regarded Baltimore's project as a cheap and convenient way to do so.

The charter itself is an odd document, part medieval and part modern. Lord Baltimore held absolute authority over the colonists. He was as powerful in his colony as a lord on a feudal estate. As proprietor, Baltimore owned the land outright, but he subdivided it into manors where landed aristocrats could establish their own courts of law. The more land a person owned, the more privileges that person enjoyed in the government.

Embedded in this feudal scheme was a concept that broke boldly with the past. Unlike the European leaders of his day, Baltimore championed religious freedom for all people who accepted the divinity of Christ. Even though Maryland's early settlers—Catholic as well as Protestants—occasionally persecuted each other, Baltimore's commitment to toleration never flagged.

In 1634 the first of Maryland's immigrants landed at St. Mary's, near the mouth of the Potomac River. Maryland attracted both Catholics and Protestants, and for a brief period, the two groups seemed capable of living in peace. Unlike the Virginia settlers, these early colonists were not threatened by starvation, and they maintained friendly relations with the local Indians.

Lord Baltimore's feudal system never took root in Chesapeake soil. People simply refused to play the social roles that he had assigned. Most importantly, the elected assembly, which first met in 1635, insisted upon exercising traditional parliamentary privileges that eventually undermined Baltimore's authority. With each passing year, the proprietor's absolute control over the men and women of Maryland progressively weakened.

Despite Baltimore's efforts to establish liberty of conscience, Maryland's gravest problems grew out of the colonists' religious intolerance. Aggressive Jesuits frightened Protestants, who in turn tried to unseat the proprietor on the grounds that he and his chief advisors were Catholic. In fact, Baltimore's experiment led to chronic instability during the first thirty years after settlement. Violence, not toleration, resulted from his efforts to put freedom of conscience into practice.

In this troubled sanctuary, planters cultivated tobacco on dispersed riverfront plantations. No towns developed. The tobacco culture permeated every aspect of society. A steady stream of indentured servants supplied the plantations with dependent laborers, until they were replaced at the end of the seventeenth century by slaves. Both Maryland and Virginia were peopled by settlers principally concerned with their individual interests.

The Colonies of New England

Legend surrounds the Pilgrims. These brave refugees crossed the cold Atlantic in search of religious liberty, signed a democratic compact aboard the *Mayflower*, landed at Plymouth Rock, and gave us our Thanksgiving Day. As with most mythic accounts, this one contains only a core of truth.

The Pilgrims were not crusaders who set out to change the world. They were humble English farmers from Scrooby Manor. They believed that the Church of England retained too many traces of its Catholic origin, that its very rituals compromised God's true believers. And so, in the early years of the reign of James I, the Scrooby congregation formally left the state church. Like others who followed this logic, they were called "Separatists." Since English statute required citizens to attend established Church of England service, the Scrooby Separatists moved to Holland in 1608–1609 rather than compromise their souls.

The Netherlands provided the Separatists with a good home—too good. They feared that their distinct identity was threatened, that their children were becoming Dutch. By 1617 a portion of the Scrooby congregation vowed to sail to America. A group of English investors who were only marginally interested in Separatism underwrote their trip. In 1620 they sailed for Virginia aboard the *Mayflower.*

Hardship soon shattered the voyagers' optimism. Because of an error in navigation, the Pilgrims landed not in Virginia, but in New England, where their land patent from the Virginia Company had no validity. Without a patent, the colonists possessed no authorization to form a civil government, a serious matter since some sailors who were not Pilgrims threatened mutiny. To preserve the struggling community from anarchy, forty-one men agreed on November 11 to "covenant and combine our selves together into a civill body politick."

Unfortunately, the Mayflower Compact, as this voluntary agreement was called, could not ward off disease and hunger. During the first months in Plymouth, death claimed approximately half of the 102 people who had initially set out from England. Moreover, debts contracted in the mother country severely burdened the new colony. Through strength of will and self-sacrifice, their elected leader, William Bradford, persuaded frightened men and women that they could survive in America.

The Pilgrims never became very prosperous. But they did build a humble farm community and practice their Separatist beliefs. Although they experimented with commercial fishing and the fur trade, most families relied upon mixed husbandry, grain and livestock. Not a populous colony, in 1691 Plymouth was absorbed into its thriving, larger neighbor, Massachusetts Bay.

The Power of Puritanism

During the seventeenth century Puritan zeal transformed the face of England and America. The popular image of a Puritan—a carping critic who condemned liquor and sex, who dressed in drab clothes, and minded the neighbors' business—is based on a fundamental misunderstanding of the actual nature of Puritanism. Puritans were radical reformers committed to far-reaching institutional change, not Victorian prudes. Not only did they found several American colonies, but they sparked the English civil war and the bold new thinking about popular representation that accompanied it.

The Puritan movement came out of the Protestant Reformation. It accepted the notion that an omnipotent God predestined some people to salvation and damned others throughout eternity (see Chapter 1). Puritans constantly monitored themselves for signs of grace, hints that God had in fact placed them among his "elect." And their attempt to live as if they *were* saved—that is, according to the Scriptures—became the driving engine for reform on this earth.

They saw their duty clearly: to eradicate unscriptural elements and practices from the Church of England; to campaign vigorously against the sins of sexual license and drunkenness; and to inveigh against alliances with Papist (Catholic) states. Puritans were more combative than the Pilgrims had been. They wanted to purify the English Church from within, and before the 1630s at least, Separatism held little appeal for them.

From the Puritan perspective, the early Stuarts, James I and Charles I, seemed unconcerned about the spiritual state of the nation. The monarchs, Puritans believed, courted Catholic alliances and showed no interest in purifying the Church of England. As long as Parliament met, Puritan voters in the various boroughs and counties throughout the nation elected men sympathetic to their point of view. These outspoken representatives criticized royal policies. And because of their defiance, Charles decided in 1629 to rule England without Parliament. Four years later he named as Archbishop of Canterbury the Puritans' most conspicuous clerical opponent, William Laud. The last doors of reform slammed shut; the corruption remained.

John Winthrop, the future governor of Massachusetts Bay, was caught up in these events. A man of modest wealth and education, he believed God would punish England, although he was confident that the Lord would provide shelter somewhere for his Puritan flock. Other

■ *John Winthrop was a friendly and outgoing person by nature, but he deliberately trained himself from boyhood to show reserve and sobriety.*

Puritans, some of them wealthier and better connected than Winthrop, reached similar conclusions about England's future. They turned their attention to the possibility of establishing a colony in America. On March 4, 1629, their Massachusetts Bay Company obtained a charter directly from the king.

The king may have believed that Massachusetts Bay would be simply another commercial venture, but Winthrop and his associates knew better. In the Cambridge Agreement (August 1629) they pledged to emigrate, knowing that their charter allowed the company to hold meetings wherever the stockholders desired, *even in America*. And if they were in America, the king could not easily interfere in their affairs.

"A City on a Hill"

The Winthrop fleet departed England in March 1630. By the end of the year, almost 2000 people had arrived in Massachusetts Bay, and before the "Great Migration" concluded in the early 1640s, almost 20,000 men and women would arrive in the new Puritan colony.

Unlike the early immigrants to Virginia and Maryland, they moved to Massachusetts Bay as nuclear families: fathers, mothers, and their dependent children. This guaranteed a more balanced sex ratio than in the Chesapeake colonies. Finally, and perhaps more significantly, these colonists survived. Indeed, their life expectancy compares favorably to that of modern Americans. This remarkable phenomenon alleviated the emotional shock of long-distance migration.

Their common sense of purpose provided another source of strength and stability. God, they insisted, had formed a special covenant with them. On his part, the Lord expected them to live according to scripture, to reform the church, in other words, to create a "city on a hill" that would stand as a beacon of righteousness for the rest of the Christian world. If everyone fulfilled their bargain, the colonists could expect peace and prosperity. They fully expected to transform a religious vision into a social reality.

They arrived in Massachusetts Bay without a precise plan for their church, other than that they refused to separate formally from the Church of England. Reform, not separation, was their mission. Gradually, they came to accept a form of church government known as Congregationalism. Under this system, each congregation was independent of outside interference. The people (the "saints") *were* the church. They pledged as a body to uphold God's law. In Congregational churches, full members—men and women who testified that they were among the Lord's "elect"—selected a minister, punished errant members, and determined matters of theology. This loose structure held together for more than a century.

In creating a civil government, the Bay Colony faced a particularly difficult challenge. Their charter allowed the investors in a joint-stock company to set up a business organization. When the settlers arrived in America, however, company leaders—men like Winthrop—moved quickly to transform the commercial structure into a colonial government. In 1631 they expanded the franchise to include all adult males who had become members of a Congregational church. During the 1630s, at least 40 percent of the adult male population could vote in elections—a percentage far above the standards in England. These "freemen" elected their own governor, magistrates, local representatives, and even military officers.

Two popular misconceptions about the government should be dispelled. It was neither a democracy nor a theocracy. Magistrates ruled in the name of the electorate but believed their responsibilities as rulers were to God. And second, the Congregational ministers possessed no formal political authority. They could not even hold civil office.

Unlike in Virginia, the town, rather than the county, became the center of public life in the Bay colony. Groups of men and women voluntarily covenanted together to live by certain rules. They constructed their communities around a meetinghouse where church services and town meetings were held. Each townsman received land sufficient to build a house and to support a family. The house lots were clustered around the meetinghouse; the fields were located on the village perimeter. Land was free, but villagers were obliged to contribute to the minister's salary, to pay local and colony taxes, and to serve in the town militia.

The settlers of Massachusetts Bay managed to live in peace. When differences arose, as they often did, the courts settled matters. People believed in a rule of law, as was illustrated in 1648 when the colonial legislature drew up the *Laws and Liberties*, the first alphabetized code of law printed in English. This code clearly stated the colonists' rights and responsibilities as citizens of the commonwealth. It engendered public trust in government and discouraged magistrates from the arbitrary exercise of authority.

The most serious challenges to Puritan orthodoxy in Massachusetts Bay came from two remarkable individuals. The first, Roger Williams, arrived in 1631. He was well liked and immediately attracted a body of loyal followers. But he preached extreme separatism. Moreover, he questioned the validity of the colony's charter since the king had not first purchased the land from the Indians. Williams also insisted that the civil rulers of Massachusetts had no business punishing settlers for their religious beliefs. The magistrates believed that Williams threatened the social and religious foundation of the colony, and in 1636 they banished him. Williams then bought a tract of land from the Narragansett Indians and founded the Providence settlement in Rhode Island.

The magistrates of the Bay Colony believed that Anne Hutchinson posed an even graver threat to the peace of the commonwealth. Intelligent and outspoken, she questioned the authority and theology of some of the most respected ministers of the colony. As justification for her own views, known as Antinomianism, she cited divine inspiration, rather than the Bible or the clergy. In other words, Hutchinson's teachings could not be tested by Scripture, a position that Puritan leaders regarded as dangerously subjective. Without clear, external standards, one person's truth was as valid as that of anyone else, and from Winthrop's perspective, Hutchinson's teachings invited civil and religious anarchy.

When she described some of the leading ministers as unconverted men, the General Court intervened. Hutchinson was cross-examined for two days in 1637, but she knew Scripture too well to be easily tripped up. Then she made a slip that led to her undoing. She stated that what she knew of God came "by an immediate revelation." She had heard a voice. This "heretical" declaration challenged the authority of the Bay rulers and they were relieved to exile Hutchinson and her followers to Rhode Island.

Breaking Away

Massachusetts Bay spawned four new colonies, three of which survived to the American Revolution. New Hampshire became a separate colony in 1677, although its population grew slowly, and for much of the colonial period it remained economically dependent upon Massachusetts.

Far more people were drawn to the fertile lands of the Connecticut River valley. Populated by settlers from the Bay Colony under the ministry of Thomas Hooker, the valley took on the religious and cultural characteristics of Massachusetts. In 1639 representatives from the Connecticut towns drafted the Fundamental Orders, a blueprint for civil government; and in 1622 Charles II awarded the colony a charter of its own. That same year Connecticut absorbed the New Haven colony, a struggling Puritan settlement on Long Island Sound.

Rhode Island experienced a wholly different history. From the beginning, it was populated by exiles and "troublemakers." One Dutch visitor uncharitably characterized it as "the receptacle of all sorts of riff-raff people." However, the colony's broad toleration attracted many men and women who held unorthodox religious beliefs.

Toleration, however, did not mean cooperation. Villagers fought over land and schemed with outside speculators to divide the tiny colony into even smaller pieces. Even a royal charter obtained in 1663 did not calm the political turmoil. For most of the seventeenth century, colonywide government existed in name only. But despite all the bickering, Rhode Island's population grew, and the colony's commerce flourished.

Diversity in the Middle Colonies

New York, New Jersey, Pennsylvania, and Delaware were founded for quite different reasons. William Penn, for example, envisioned a Quaker sanctuary; the Duke of York worried chiefly about his own income. Despite the founders' intentions, however, some common characteristics emerged. Each colony developed a strikingly heterogeneous population, men and women of different ethnic and religious backgrounds. This cultural diversity became a major influence upon the economic, political, and ecclesiastical institutions of the Middle Colonies, and foreshadowed later American society.

English Conquer a Dutch Colony

By the early decades of the seventeenth century, the Dutch had established themselves as Europe's most aggressive traders. Holland's merchant fleet was second to none, trading in

Asia, Africa, and America. While searching for the elusive Northwest Passage in 1609, Henry Hudson, an English explorer employed by a Dutch company, sailed up the river that bears his name and claimed the area for Holland. Hudson's sponsors, the Dutch West Indies Company, established two permanent settlements, Fort Orange (Albany) and New Amsterdam (New York City) in the colony of New Netherland.

The first Dutch settlers in New Netherland were not actually colonists. Rather they were salaried employees of the Company, who were expected to spend most of their time gathering animal fur pelts. They received no land for their efforts. Needless to say, this arrangement attracted relatively few Dutch immigrants.

Although the colony's population was small, only 270 in 1628, it contained an extraordinary ethnic mix. By the 1640s Finns, Germans, and Swedes lived there, along with a sizable community of free blacks. Another contribution to the hodgepodge of languages was added by New England Puritans who moved to New Netherland to stake out farms on Long Island.

The Company sent a succession of directors-general to oversee and govern. Without exception, these men were temperamentally unsuited to govern an American colony. They were autocratic, corrupt, and above all, inept. The Long Island Puritans complained bitterly about the absence of any sort of representative government, and none of the colonists felt much loyalty to the trading company.

In August 1664 the Dutch lost their tenuous hold on New Netherland. The English Crown, eager to score an easy victory over a commercial rival, dispatched a fleet of warships to New Amsterdam (renamed New York City). No real fighting was needed. Although the last director-general, Peter Stuyvesant (1647–1664), urged resistance, the settlers decided otherwise. They accepted the Articles of Capitulation, a generous agreement that allowed Dutch nationals to remain in the province and to retain their property.

Charles II had already granted his brother, James, the Duke of York, a charter for the newly captured territory and much else be-

■ *Fort New Amsterdam, 1626. First settled by Dutch West Indies Company employees, the colony of New Netherlands attracted few immigrants.*

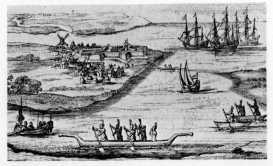

sides. He became absolute proprietor of Maine, Nantucket, Martha's Vineyard, and land extending from the Connecticut River to Delaware Bay. The duke was no more receptive to the idea of a representative government than the Dutch trading company had been; but to appease the complaining colonists, the governor, Colonel Richard Nicolls, drew up a legal code known as the Duke's Laws. It guaranteed religious toleration and created local governments.

There was no provision, however, for an elected assembly. Nor was there much harmony in the colony. The Dutch, for example, continued to speak their own language, worship in their own churches (Dutch Reformed Calvinists), and eye their English neighbors with suspicion. In fact, the colony seemed little different from what it had been under the Dutch West India Company, a loose collection of independent communities ruled by an ineffectual central government.

Divisions in New Jersey

Only three months after receiving a charter for New York, the duke made a terrible blunder—something this stubborn, humorless man was quite prone to do. He awarded the land lying between the Hudson and Delaware rivers to two courtiers, John, Lord Berkeley, and Sir George Carteret. This colony was named New Jersey in honor of Carteret's birthplace, the Isle of Jersey in the English Channel.

The duke's impulsive act bred confusion. Before learning of James' decision, the governor of New York allowed migrants from New England to take up farms west of the Hudson River, promising them an opportunity to establish an elected assembly and liberty of conscience in exchange for the payment of a small annual quitrent to the duke. Berkeley and Carteret recruited colonists on similar terms. The new proprietors assumed, of course, that they would receive the rent money.

The result was chaos. Legally, only James could set up a colonial government or authorize an assembly. But knowledge of the law failed to quiet the controversy, and through it

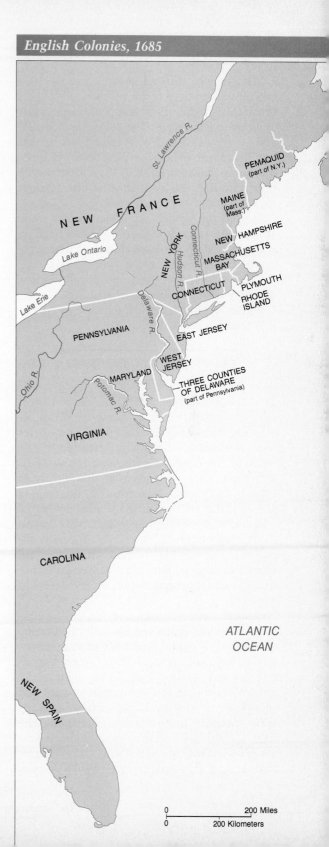

English Colonies, 1685

all, the duke showed not the slightest interest in the peace and welfare of the people of New Jersey.

Matters were further complicated in 1674 when Berkeley tired of the venture and sold his proprietary rights to a group of surprisingly quarrelsome Quakers. The colony was legally divided into East and West Jersey, but neither half prospered. When the West Jersey proprietors went bankrupt in 1702, the Crown mercifully reunited the two Jerseys into a single royal colony.

In 1700 the population of New Jersey stood at approximately 14,000. Its residents lived on scattered, often isolated farms; villages of more than a few hundred people were rare. And, as in New York, the ethnic and religious diversity of the settlers was striking. Yet the colonists of New Jersey somehow managed to live together peaceably.

The Quaker Colony: Penn's "Holy Experiment"

Quakers founded Pennsylvania. This radical religious group gained its name from the derogatory term that English civil authorities used to describe those who "tremble at the word of the Lord." George Fox (1624–1691) was the tireless spokesman of the Society of Friends, as Quakers were formally known. He preached that every man and woman possessed a powerful, consoling "inner light." This was a wonderfully liberating message, especially for persons of lower class origin. Gone was the stigma of original sin; discarded was the notion of eternal predestination. Everyone could be saved.

Quakers practiced humility. They wore simple clothes and employed old-fashioned terms of address that set them apart from their neighbors. They were also pacifists. According to Fox, all persons were equal in the sight of the Lord, a belief that annoyed people of rank and achievement. Moreover, they refused to keep their thoughts to themselves, spreading the light throughout England, Ireland, and America. Harassment, imprisonment, and even execution failed to curtail their activities. In fact,

such measures proved counterproductive, for persecution only inspired the Quakers to redouble their efforts.

William Penn lived according to the Inner Light, a commitment that led eventually to the founding of Pennsylvania. He was a complex man: an athletic person interested in intellectual pursuits; a visionary capable of making pragmatic decisions; and an aristocrat whose religious beliefs involved him with the lower classes. Penn's religious commitment irritated his father, who hoped William would become a favorite at the Stuart Court. Instead Penn was expelled from Oxford University for holding unorthodox religious views, moved to the forefront of the Quaker movement, and even spent two years in an English jail for his beliefs.

Precisely when Penn's thoughts turned to America is not known. In any case, Penn negotiated in 1681 one of the more impressive land deals in the history of American real estate. Charles II awarded Penn a charter making him the sole proprietor of a vast area called Pennsylvania (literally, Penn's woods), a name that embarrassed the modest Quaker. The next year, Penn purchased from the Duke of York the so-called Three Lower Counties that eventually became Delaware. This astute move guaranteed that Pennsylvania would have open access to the Atlantic and determined even before Philadelphia had been established that it would become a great commercial center.

Penn lost no time in launching his "holy experiment." His plan blended traditional notions about the privileges of a landed aristocracy with quite daring concepts of personal liberty. Penn guaranteed that the settlers would enjoy among other things liberty of conscience, freedom from persecution, no taxation without representation, and due process of law. He believed that both the rich and poor had to have a voice in political affairs; neither should be able to overrule the legitimate interests of the other class. In his Frame of Government (1682), he envisioned a governor appointed by the proprietor, a Provisional Council responsible for initiating legislation,

and an Assembly that could accept or reject the bills presented to it. Penn apparently thought that the Council would be filled by the colony's richest landholders and that the Assembly would be peopled by the smaller landowners. It was a fanciful, clumsy structure, and in America the entire edifice crumbled under its own weight.

Penn promoted his colony aggressively throughout England, Ireland, and Germany. The response was overwhelming. People poured into Philadelphia and the surrounding area. Most of the early settlers were Irish, Welsh, and English Quakers. But men and women from other lands soon joined the Quaker surge toward Penn's woods. One newcomer called the vessel that brought him to Philadelphia a "Noah's Ark" of nationalities and religions.

Penn himself emigrated to America in 1682. His stay, however, was unexpectedly short and unhappy. The Council and Assembly fought over the right to initiate legislation. Wealthy Quaker merchants dominated the Council, and rural settlers unconcerned about the "holy experiment" controlled the Assembly. Many colonists refused to pay quitrents, and the Baltimore family claimed that much of Pennsylvania actually lay in Maryland. In 1684, to defend his charter against Baltimore's attack, Penn returned to London.

Penn did not see his colony again until 1699. By that time, the settlement had changed considerably. Although it had prospered, a contentious quality pervaded its politics. Even the Quakers briefly split into hostile factions. As the seventeenth century closed, few colonists still shared the founder's desire to create a godly, paternalistic society.

In 1701 legal challenges in England again forced Penn to depart for the mother country. Just before he sailed, Penn signed the Charter of Liberties, a new framework of government that established a unicameral or one-house legislature (the only one in colonial America) and gave the representatives the right to initiate legislation. The charter also provided for the political separation of the Three Lower Counties (Delaware) from Pennsylvania, something people living in this area had demanded for years. This hastily drafted document served as Pennsylvania's constitution until the American Revolution.

His experience in America must have depressed Penn, now both old and sick. In England Penn was imprisoned for debts incurred by dishonest colonial agents, and in 1718 Pennsylvania's founder died a broken man.

Carolina Proprietors and the Barbadian Connection

In some ways Carolina society looked very much like the one that had developed in Virginia and Maryland. In both areas white planters forced unfree laborers to produce staple crops for a world market. But such superficial similarities masked substantial regional differences. In fact, "The South"—certainly the fabled solid South of the early nineteenth century—did not exist during the colonial period. The Carolinas, joined at a much later date by Georgia (in Chapter 4), stood apart from their Chesapeake neighbors.

Carolina owed its establishment to the Restoration of the Stuarts to the English throne. Court favorites who had followed the Stuarts into exile during the civil war demanded tangible rewards for their loyalty. New York and New Jersey were obvious plums. So too was Carolina. On March 24, 1663, the king granted Sir John Colleton and seven other courtiers a charter to the vast territory between Virginia and Florida and running west as far as the "South Seas."

Like so many Englishmen before them, the eight proprietors thought of America in terms of instant wealth. Their plan involved luring settlers from established American colonies by means of an attractive land policy and such other incentives as a representative assembly, liberty of conscience, and a liberal headright system. In exchange for their privileges, they demanded only a small annual quitrent.

After dividing their grant into three distinct jurisdictions, Albemarle, Cape Fear, and Port Royal, the proprietors waited for the money to roll in; to their dismay, no one seemed particularly interested in moving to the Carolina frontier. Plans for the settlement of Cape Fear and Port Royal fell through, and the majority of the surviving proprietors gave up on Carolina.

Anthony Ashley Cooper, later earl of Shaftesbury, was an exception. In 1669 he persuaded the remaining proprietors to invest their own capital in the colony. He then dispatched over 300 English colonists to Carolina. After a rough voyage that saw one ship destroyed by Atlantic gales, the settlers arrived at the Ashley River. Later the colony's administrative center, Charles Town (it did not become Charleston until 1783), was established at the junction of the Ashley and Cooper rivers.

Ashley also wanted to bring order to the new society. With assistance from John Locke, the famous English philosopher (1632–1704), Ashley devised the Fundamental Constitutions of Carolina. His goal was to create a landed aristocracy that governed the colony through the Council of Nobles, a body designed to administer justice, oversee civil affairs, and initiate legislation. A parliament in which smaller landowners had a voice could accept or reject bills drafted by the Council. The very poor were excluded from political activity altogether. Ashley's plans for a "balance of government" between aristocracy and democracy, however, never conformed to the realities of Carolina society, and his Council of Nobles remained a paper dream.

Before 1680 almost half the men and women who settled in the Port Royal area came from Barbados. This small Caribbean island, which produced an annual fortune in sugar, depended upon slave labor. By the third quarter of the seventeenth century, Barbados had become over-populated, and Barbadians looked to Carolina for relief. These migrants, many of whom were quite rich, traveled to Carolina both as individuals and family groups. Some brought slave gangs with them. The Barbadians carved out plantations on the tributaries of the Cooper River and established themselves used to maintain ocean vessels). It was not until the 1690s that the planters came to appreciate fully the value of rice, but once they had done so, it quickly became the colony's main staple.

Proprietary Carolina was in a constant political uproar. Barbadian settlers resisted the proprietors' policies, and the proprietors appointed a series of utterly incompetent governors. By the end of the century, the lower houses of assembly had assumed the right to initiate legislation. In 1719 the colonists overthrew the last proprietary government, and in 1729 the king created separate royal governments in North and South Carolina.

Seventeenth-Century Legacy

The seventeenth-century English colonies had little in common beyond their allegiance to the king. A contemporary visitor could find along the Atlantic coast a spectrum of settlements, one that ranged from the almost feudal hierarchy of Carolina to the visionary paternalism of Pennsylvania to the Puritan commonwealth of Massachusetts Bay. The diversity of English colonization needs to be emphasized precisely because it is so easy to overlook. Even though the colonists eventually banded together and fought for independence and established a federal government, persistent differences separated New Englanders from Virginians, Pennsylvanians from Carolinians.

immediately as the colony's most powerful political faction. The society they created was closer to the slave-based plantation society they left than to any of the other English colonies.

Much of the planters' time was taken up with the search for a profitable crop. They experimented with a number of plants—tobacco, cotton, silk, and grapes. The most successful items in the early years turned out to be beef, cattle, furs, and naval stores (especially tar,

Recommended Reading

The most detailed investigation of the founding of the early American colonies remains Charles M. Andrews, *The Colonial Period of American History*, 4 vols. (1934–1938). A full discussion of the historiography of colonial America is Jack P. Green and J. R. Pole, eds., *Colonial British America* (1984).

To understand the English background of colonization, see Carl Bridenbaugh, *Vexed and Troubled Englishmen, 1590–1642* (1968). T. H. Breen, *Puritans and Adventurers: Change and Persistence in*

Early America (1980), explores the problem of cultural transfer. Also helpful is David Grayson Allen, *In English Ways: The Movement of Societies and the Transferal of English Local Law and Custom* (1981).

The best analysis of the early settlement of Virginia is Edmund S. Morgan, *American Slavery, American Freedom* (1975). An exciting account of the founding of Jamestown is John Smith, *Travels and Works*, edited by Edward Arber (2 vols., 1910). On Roanoke, see D. B. Quinn, ed., *The Roanoke Voyages, 1584–1590* (1967). For a masterful analysis of current research see Thad W. Tate and David L. Ammerman, eds., *The Chesapeake in the Seventeenth Century* (1979). New insights are offered in Gloria L. Main, *Tobacco Colony, Life in Early Maryland, 1650–1720* (1982).

Studies of early New England are Kenneth A. Lockridge, *A New England Town: The First Hundred Years* (1970), and E. S. Morgan, *Puritan Dilemma: The Story of John Winthrop* (1958). On Puritan ideas, see Perry Miller, *New England Mind: From Colony to Province* (1953), and *Errand into the Wilderness* (1956).

The best account of New York and the transition from Dutch to English rule is Michael Kammen, *Colonial New York* (1975). The best single book on the political history of early Pennsylvania is Gary B. Nash, *Quakers and Politics: Pennsylvania, 1681–1726* (1968). To understand the Quaker movement, read Frederick B. Tolles, *Quakers and the Atlantic Culture* (1960). William Penn's life and political thought are the subject of Mary M. Dunn, *William Penn, Politics and Conscience* (1967). A comprehensive general description of the early Carolina settlements can be found in Wesley F. Craven, *The Southern Colonies in the Seventeenth Century, 1607–1689* (1949).

chapter 3

COLONISTS IN AN EMPIRE: REGIONAL PATTERNS

During the 1640s, Governor John Winthrop of the Massachusetts Bay Colony recorded in his diary the story of a master who could not afford to pay his servant's wages. To meet this obligation, the master sold a pair of oxen, but that transaction barely covered the cost of keeping the servant. In desperation, the master asked the employee, a man of a lower social status, "How shall I do . . . when all my cattle are gone?" The servant replied, "You shall then serve me, so you may have your cattle again." In the margin of his diary next to this account, Winthrop scribbled, "insolent."

The servant's actions violated the governor's concept of social order. From Winthrop's perspective, the idea of improving one's social status was unthinkable. Since God had assigned every person a place, it seemed blasphemous for any man or woman to attempt to alter the Lord's plan. Conditions in the New World, however, eroded this conception of the structure of society. Some individuals rose, others fell, and the American social order seemed oblivious to any divine plan. Instead, it was the product of several critical elements: shortage of labor, abundance of land, unusual demographic patterns, and commercial ties with European markets.

These factors varied from place to place. In the Chesapeake, for example, the staple economy based on tobacco created an almost insatiable demand for the controlled labor of slaves and servants. In Massachusetts Bay, the extraordinary longevity of the early settlers generated a level of social and political stability that Virginians and Marylanders did not attain until the end of the seventeenth century. In short, regional differences appeared during the earliest decades of settlement as European and African ideas and assumptions were recast to meet the demands of the particular colonial environments.

Stable Societies: The New England Colonies in the Seventeenth Century

The family was central to the development of social stability in early New England. This observation may seem commonplace, but the modern reader must remember that in the seventeenth century many activities now performed by the state were the responsibility of the family. It was within the family unit that men and women earned a livelihood, educated their children, maintained religious traditions, and nursed each other in sickness. New En-

■ *This painting depicts Anne Pollard at age 100. Her life span exemplifies the striking longevity of New England settlers.*

glanders expected social institutions—church and state, in particular—to complement and support rather than to take over family functions. Any understanding of patterns of stability in colonial New England, therefore, must begin with the character of the family.

Immigrant Families and Social Order

Early New Englanders believed that God ordained the family for human benefit. It was essential to the maintenance of social order, since outside the family, men and women succumbed to carnal temptation. Such people had no one to sustain them, no one to remind them of Scripture. And just as Scripture taught obedience to the Lord, the godly seventeenth-century family was patriarchal in structure.

This familial experience exercised a powerful influence upon early New England life. Mature adults who migrated to America within nuclear families, preserved local English customs more fully than did the youths who traveled to other parts of the continent as single men and women. Not only did traveling with one's family help to reduce the shock of migration, it ensured that the ratio between men and women would be fairly well balanced. In addition, persons who had not already married in England could expect to form nuclear families of their own.

The great migration of the 1630s and 1640s brought approximately 20,000 persons to New England. The English Civil War reduced this flood to a trickle, but by the end of the century, the population of New England had reached almost 150,000, an amazing increase considering the small number of original immigrants. Historians have long searched for the reason. Men and women in New England married no earlier than they did in England; for a first marriage men's average age was in the mid-twenties; women, the early twenties. Nor, for that matter, were Puritan families unusually large by the standards of the period.

The reason turned out to be longevity. Put simply, people who, under normal conditions, would have died in contemporary Europe survived in New England. Indeed, the life expectancy of seventeenth-century settlers was not very different from our own. Males who survived infancy could expect to see their seventieth birthday. The figures for women were only slightly lower. No one is sure why they lived longer, but pure drinking water, a cool climate that retarded the spread of fatal contagious disease, and a dispersed population promoted general good health.

Longer life altered family relations. New England may have been one of the first societies in recorded history in which a person could reasonably anticipate knowing his or her grandchildren. The traditions of particular families and communities, therefore, remained alive, literally, in the memories of the colony's oldest citizens.

Family Life Cycle

The life cycle of the family in New England began with marriage. Young men and women generally selected their own partners, usually a neighbor. Prospective brides were expected to possess a dowry worth approximately one half what the bridegroom brought to the union. The overwhelming majority of the region's population married, for in New England, the single life was not only physically difficult, but also morally suspect.

The household was primarily a place of work—very demanding work. It has been estimated that a family of five needed seventy-five acres of cleared land just to feed itself. But a family also needed a surplus crop to pay for items that could not be manufactured at home—metal tools, for example. The belief that early American farmers were self-sufficient is a popular misconception.

During the seventeenth century, men and women generally lived in the communities of their parents and grandparents. Towns, in fact, were collections of families, not individuals. Over time, these families intermarried, so that the community became an elaborate kinship network. In many towns the original founders dominated local politics and economic affairs for several generations. Not surprisingly, new-

To seek the Word of God, young people had to learn to read. The New England Primer, shown here, taught the alphabet and the Lord's Prayer.

comers who were not absorbed into the family system tended to move away from the village with greater frequency than did the sons and daughters of the established lineage groups.

Congregational churches were also built upon a family foundation. During the earliest years of settlement, the churches accepted persons who could demonstrate that they were among God's "elect." But when sons and daughters of the "elect" failed to experience saving grace, a synod in 1662 adopted the so-called Half-Way Covenant. The compromise allowed the grandchildren of persons in full communion to be baptized even though *their* parents could not demonstrate conversion. Obsession with family meant that by the end of the century, Congregational churches often failed to meet the religious needs of New Englanders who were not members of the select families.

Colonists regarded education as primarily a family responsibility. The ability to read was considered essential for learning the principles of Christianity. For this reason, the Massachusetts legislature ordered towns containing at least fifty families to open an elementary school supported by local taxes. Larger towns supported more advanced grammar schools, which taught a basic Latin curriculum. After 1638, young men could attend Harvard College, the first institution of higher learning founded in England's mainland colonies.

This family-based education system worked. A majority of the region's adult males could read and write, an accomplishment not achieved in the Chesapeake colonies for another century. The literacy rate for women was somewhat lower, but by the standards of the period, it was still impressive.

Women's Work and Women's Rights

The status of women in colonial New England was complex. Although subordinate to men by law and custom, their productive labor was essential to the survival of most households. They cooked, washed, made clothes, milked cows, gardened, and raised poultry. Sometimes, by selling surplus fowl, wives achieved some economic independence. Women also joined churches in greater numbers than did men, and it is possible that their involvement in these institutions encouraged them to express their ideas.

In political and legal matters, society sharply curtailed the rights of colonial women. According to common law practice, a wife exercised no control over property. And since a divorce was extremely difficult to obtain, a woman married to a cruel or irresponsible spouse had little recourse but to run away or accept the unhappy situation.

Yet most women were neither prosperous entrepreneurs nor abject slaves. Like men, they generally accepted the roles that they thought God had ordained. Although Puritan couples worried that the affection they felt for a husband or a wife might turn their thoughts away from God's perfect love, this was a danger they were willing to risk.

Rank and Status

During the seventeenth century the New England colonies attracted neither noblemen nor paupers, an incomplete social structure by contemporary European standards. The lack of very rich, titled persons was particularly troublesome. According to the prevailing hierarchical view of the structure of society, well-placed individuals were *natural rulers*, people intended by God to exercise political authority over the rank and file. Migration forced the colonists, however, to choose their rulers from men of more modest status, ignoring the "ordinariness of their persons."

The colonists gradually sorted themselves out into distinct social groupings. To become part of the ruling elite it helped to possess at least modest wealth and education; it was also expected that leaders would belong to a Congregational church and defend religious orthodoxy. The Winthrops, Dudleys, and Pynchons fulfilled these expectations, and in public affairs they assumed dominant roles. They took their responsibility quite seriously and certainly did not look kindly upon anyone who spoke of their "ordinariness."

The problem was that while most New Englanders accepted a hierarchical view of society, they disagreed over their assigned places. Both Massachusetts Bay and Connecticut passed sumptuary laws—statutes that limited the wearing of fine apparel to the wealthy and prominent—designed to curb the pretentions of lower status individuals. By the end of the century, the character of the ruling class in New England had changed, and personal piety figured less importantly in social ranking than did family background and large estate.

Most northern colonists were yeomen (independent farmers), few of whom became rich and even fewer of whom fell hopelessly into debt. Possession of land gave agrarian families a sense of independence from external authority, but during the seventeenth century, this independence was balanced by an equally strong feeling of local identity. Not until the late eighteenth century, when a large number of New Englanders left their familial villages in search of new land, did many northern yeomen place personal material ambition above traditional community bonds.

It was not unusual for northern colonists to work as servants among their neighbors at some point in their lives. New Englanders recruited few servants from the Old World. Their forms of agriculture, which mixed cereal with dairy farming, made employment of large gangs of dependent workers uneconomical.

New England servants more resembled apprentices than anything else, and servitude was more a vocational training program than an exploitive system. This was vastly different from the institutions that developed in the southern colonies.

Roots of Southern Plantation Societies

An entirely different regional society developed in England's Chesapeake colonies. Although the two areas were founded at roughly the same time by Protestant Englishmen, the two regions were worlds apart in terms of environmental conditions, labor systems, and agrarian economies. The most important reason for the distinctiveness of these early southern plantation societies, however, turned out to be the Chesapeake's death rate, a frighteningly high mortality that tore at the very fabric of family life.

Family Life in a Perilous Environment

Unlike New England settlers, the men and women who migrated to the Chesapeake region did not move in family units. Nor were most entirely free when they arrived. Between 70 and 80 percent of the white colonists who went to Virginia and Maryland during the seventeenth century owed four or five years' labor in exchange for the cost of passage to America. Most of these indentured servants were men, and although more women made the voyage after 1640, the sexual ratio in the Chesapeake was never as balanced as it had been in early Massachusetts.

Most immigrants to the Chesapeake region died soon after arriving. Malaria and other diseases took a frightful toll, and drinking water contaminated with salt killed many colonists living in low-lying areas. Life expectancy for Chesapeake males was about forty-three, some ten to twenty years less than for men born in New England! For women, life expectancy was even shorter. A full 25 percent of all children died in infancy: Another 25 percent did not see their twentieth birthday. The survivors were often weak or ill, unable to perform hard physical labor.

These demographic conditions retarded normal population increase. Young women who might have become wives and mothers could not do so until they had completed their terms of servitude. They thus lost several reproductive years, and in a society in which so many children died in infancy, late marriages greatly restricted family size. Moreover, the unbalanced sex ratio meant that many men could not find wives. Without a constant flow of immigrants, the population of Virginia and Maryland would have actually declined.

High mortality compressed the family cycle into a few short years. Marriages were extremely fragile, and one partner usually died within seven years. Not only did children not meet grandparents, they often did not even know their own parents. Widows and widowers quickly remarried, and children frequently grew up with persons to whom they had no blood relation. People had to adjust to the impermanence of family life and to cope with a high degree of personal insecurity.

The unbalanced sex ratio in the Chesapeake may have provided women with the means to improve their social status. Because of the uneven sex ratio, women could be confident of finding husbands, regardless of their abilities, attractiveness, or moral character. Despite liberation from some traditional restraints, however, women as servants were still vulnerable to sexual exploitation by their masters. Moreover, childbearing was extremely dangerous; women in the Chesapeake usually died twenty years earlier than their New England counterparts.

Rank and Status in Plantation Society

Tobacco cultivation formed the basis of the Chesapeake economy. Although anyone with a few acres of cleared land could grow leaves for export, cultivation of the Chesapeake staple did not produce a society of individuals roughly similar in wealth and status. To the contrary, it generated inequality. The amassing of a large fortune involved the control of a large labor force. More workers in the fields meant larger harvests, and, of course, larger profits. Since free persons showed no interest in toiling away in another man's fields of tobacco, not even for wages, wealthy planters relied upon laborers who were not free as well as on slaves. The social structure that developed in the seventeenth-century Chesapeake reflected a wild, often unscrupulous scramble to bring men and women of three races—black, white, and Indian—into various degrees of dependence.

Great planters dominated Chesapeake society. The group was small, and during the early decades of the seventeenth century, constantly changing. Not until the 1650s did the family names of those who would become famous eighteenth-century gentry appear on the records. These ambitious men arrived in America with capital. They invested immediately in laborers, and one way or another, they obtained huge tracts of the best tobacco-growing land. Although not aristocrats, but rather the younger sons of English merchants and artisans, they soon acquired political and social power. Over time, these gentry families—such as the Burwells, Byrds, Carters, and Masons—intermarried so frequently that they created a vast network of cousins. During the eighteenth century it was not uncommon to find a half dozen men with the same surname sitting simultaneously in the Virginia House of Burgesses.

Freemen formed the largest class in this society. Most came as indentured servants, unlike New England's yeomen farmers, and by sheer good fortune, managed to stay alive to the end of their contracts. When their period of indenture was over, many freemen lived on the edge of poverty. After 1660, opportunities for upward mobility decreased dramatically.

Below the freemen came indentured servants. Membership in this group was not demeaning; after all, servitude was a temporary status. But servitude in the Chesapeake colonies was not the benign institution it was in New England. Great planters purchased servants to grow tobacco, and they were not overly concerned with the well-being of these laborers. The unhappy servants regarded their servitude as a form of "slavery," while the planters worried that discontented servants and impoverished freemen would rebel at the slightest provocation. Later events would justify these fears.

The character of social mobility changed during the seventeenth century. Before the 1680s, movement into the planter elite by newcomers who possessed capital was relatively easy. After the 1680s, however, life expectancy rates improved in the Chesapeake colonies and the sons of great planters replaced their fathers in powerful government positions. New arrivals, even those with funds to invest, found it increasingly difficult to move into a ruling class tightly knit by blood and marriage.

Opportunities for advancement also decreased for the region's freeman. As the gentry consolidated its hold on political and economic institutions, ordinary people discovered that it was much harder to rise in Chesapeake society. Men and women with more ambitious dreams headed for Pennsylvania, North Carolina, and western Virginia.

Social institutions that figured importantly in the New Englanders' daily lives were either weak or nonexistent in the Chesapeake, partly due to the high infant mortality rates. There was little incentive to build elementary schools, for example, since only half the children would reach adulthood. The development of higher education languished, too, and the great planters sent their sons to English or Scottish schools through much of the colonial period.

Tobacco also inhibited the growth of towns in this region. Owners of isolated plantations along the river banks traded directly with English merchants and had little need for local markets. People met sporadically at scattered churches, courthouses, and taverns. Seventeenth-century Virginia could not boast of even one printing press.

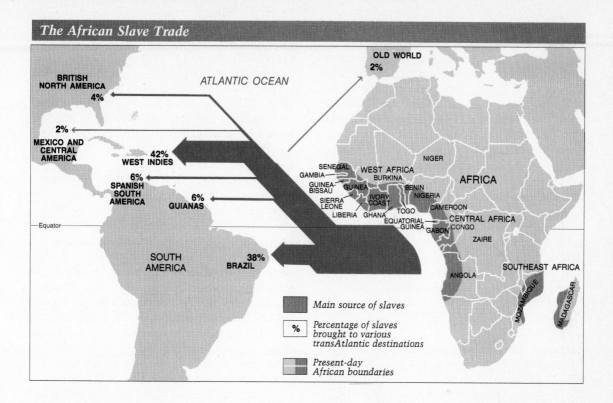

OLD WORLD 2%

ATLANTIC OCEAN

BRITISH NORTH AMERICA 4%

2%
MEXICO AND CENTRAL AMERICA

42% WEST INDIES

6% SPANISH SOUTH AMERICA

6% GUIANAS

Equator

SOUTH AMERICA

38% BRAZIL

SENEGAL
GAMBIA
GUINEA-BISSAU
SIERRA LEONE
LIBERIA

WEST AFRICA
BURKINA
GUINEA
IVORY COAST
GHANA
TOGO
BENIN
NIGERIA
CAMEROON
EQUATORIAL GUINEA
GABON
CONGO

NIGER

AFRICA

CENTRAL AFRICA

ZAIRE

ANGOLA

SOUTHEAST AFRICA

MOZAMBIQUE

MADAGASCAR

Main source of slaves

% *Percentage of slaves brought to various transAtlantic destinations*

Present-day African boundaries

The Black Experience in English America

Many people who landed in the colonies had no desire to come to the New World; they were brought from Africa as slaves to cultivate rice, sugar, and tobacco. As the Native Americans were exterminated and the supply of white indentured servants dried up, white planters demanded ever more African laborers.

Roots of Slavery

Between the sixteenth and nineteenth centuries, slave traders carried 8 to 11 million blacks from Africa to the New World, mainly to Brazil and the Caribbean. Only a small part of this commerce involved British North America. Young black males predominated in the human cargo; the planters preferred this group for the hard physical labor of the plantations. In many early slave communities, black men outnumbered women by a ratio of two to one.

English colonists did not hesitate to enslave black people; the decision to import African slaves to the British colonies was based primarily upon economic considerations. But English masters never justified the practice purely in terms of planter profits. They associated blacks in Africa with heathen religion, barbarous behavior, sexual promiscuity, in fact, with evil itself. From such a perspective, the enslavement of African men and women seemed unobjectionable. Planters avowed that loss of freedom was a small price for the civilizing benefits of conversion to Christianity.

Africans first landed in Virginia in 1619. For the next fifty years, their status remained unclear. English settlers classified some black laborers as slaves for life, others as indentured servants. A few blacks purchased their freedom. Several seventeenth-century Africans even became successful Virginia planters.

One reason that Virginia lawmakers tolerated such confusion was that the black population remained very small. Planters wanted more African slaves, but during this period, slave traders sold their cargoes on Barbados or the other sugar islands of the West Indies, where they fetched a higher price than Virginians could afford. In fact, before 1680 most blacks who reached England's colonies on the North American mainland came from Barbados or through New Netherland rather than directly from Africa.

By the end of the seventeenth century, the status of Virginia's black people was no longer in doubt. They were slaves for life, as were their children after them. Slavery was unequivocally based on skin color alone. This transformation reflected an increase in the supply of Africans to British North America. After 1672 the Royal African Company undertook to meet the colonial planters' rising demands for black laborers, and during the eighteenth century many American merchants entered the lucrative trade.

The expanding black population apparently frightened white colonists, and lawmakers drew up ever stricter slave codes. The white planter could deal with his black property as he alone saw fit, and one extraordinary Virginia statute excused a master who killed a slave on the grounds that no rational person would purposely "destroy his own estate." Furthermore, children born to a slave woman became slaves regardless of the father's race. Nor did conversion to Christianity free blacks from bondage. Unlike the Spanish colonies where persons of lighter color enjoyed greater privileges in society, in the English colonies racial mixing was not tolerated, and mulattos received the same treatment as did pure Africans.

Afro-American Cultures

The slave experience varied substantially from colony to colony. The size and density of the slave population determined in large measure how successfully blacks could maintain a separate cultural identity. On isolated rice plantations in South Carolina, where during the eighteenth century 60 percent of the population was black, Afro-Americans developed creole languages that blended English with words from African tongues. Slaves on these large plantations were also able to establish elaborate and enduring kinship networks that may have helped reduce the more dehumanizing aspects of bondage.

Blacks made up a smaller percentage of the population in New England and the Middle Colonies (less than 10 percent) and even in Virginia (40 percent). Most slaves in the northern

■ *In 1660 only about 1500 blacks lived in Virginia. Colonial demands for slave laborers pushed that number beyond 12,000 by the turn of the century.*

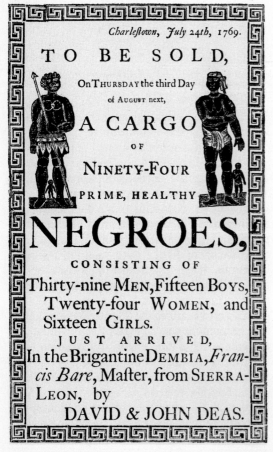

■ *On larger plantations, some African identity and customs survived.*
These slaves are performing a West African religious dance in a rare
moment of leisure.

colonies worked as domestics and lived in their masters' homes. Close contact with whites made it more difficult to preserve and reaffirm an African heritage and identity.

In eighteenth-century Virginia, native-born blacks had learned to cope with whites on a daily basis. They looked with disdain upon slaves who had just arrived from Africa. Blacks as well as whites pressed these "outlandish" newcomers to accept elements of English culture, especially to speak the English language.

Despite their wrenching experiences, black slaves did establish cultural traditions that involved an imaginative reshaping of African and European customs into something that was neither African nor European; it was Afro-American. For example, slaves embraced Christianity, but transformed it into an expres-

sion of religious feeling in which an African element remained vibrant.

During the early decades of the eighteenth century, blacks living in England's mainland colonies began to reproduce themselves successfully; that is, live births exceeded deaths. This demographic shift did not take place in the Caribbean or South American colonies until a much later date. Historians believe that North American blacks enjoyed a healthier climate and better diet than did other New World slaves.

But longer lives did not make them any less slaves. Nor did it prevent slave protests, including organized revolt. The most serious slave rebellion of the colonial period was the Stono Uprising, which took place in September 1739. One hundred and fifty South Carolina blacks rose up and murdered several whites. They marched toward Florida and the promise of freedom, but the local militia overtook and crushed the rebellious slaves. Such rebellions were rare; in fact, the level of interracial violence in colonial North America was quite low. But the fear of slave rebellions was pervasive, prompting whites to take drastic defensive measures.

Blueprint for Empire

Until the middle of the seventeenth century, English political leaders largely ignored the American colonists. After the Restoration of Charles II in 1660, however, intervention replaced indifference. The Crown, Parliament, and the mercantile interests decided that the colonies should be brought more tightly under the control of the mother country. Regulatory policies that evolved during this period formed a framework for empire that survived with only minor adjustment until 1765.

Fitting the Colonies into a Mercantilist System

The famous eighteenth-century Scottish economist, Adam Smith, coined the term *mercantilism* to describe the system on which England based its commercial regulations. As administered by the policymakers of the late seventeenth century, however, the system was not nearly as well thought out or organized as Smith suggested. Rather, it represented a series of individual responses to the needs of several powerful interest groups.

Each group looked to colonial commerce to solve a different problem. Charles wanted money to pay his enormous debts. English merchants were eager to exclude Dutch rivals from lucrative American markets, but without government assistance they could not compete successfully with the Dutch Merchant Marine. Parliament wanted to strengthen England's navy, and the expansion of the domestic shipbuilding industry was a fine starting place.

And almost everyone agreed with the mercantilistic view that the mother country should establish a more favorable balance of trade, that is, increase exports, decrease imports, and grow richer at the expense of other European states. Together, these ideas provided a blueprint for England's first empire.

Navigation Acts Transform Colonial Trade

In 1660 Parliament passed a Navigation Act, the most important piece of imperial legislation drafted before the American Revolution. It stated (1) that no ship could trade in the colonies unless it had been constructed in either England or America and carried a crew that was at least 75 percent English, and (2) that certain enumerated goods of great value that were not produced in England—tobacco, sugar, cotton, indigo, dye, wool, ginger—could be transported from the colonies *only* to an English or another colonial port. Early in the next century, Parliament added rice, molasses, wood resins, tars, and turpentines to the enumerated list.

The Act of 1660 was masterfully conceived. It encouraged the development of domestic shipbuilding, prohibited European rivals from obtaining enumerated goods anywhere except in England, and provided the Crown with added revenue. Parliament supplemented this act in 1663 with a second Navigation Act, known as the Staple Act, that closed off nearly all direct trade between European nations and the American colonies. With a few noted exceptions, nothing could be imported into America unless it had first been transshipped through the mother country.

During the 1660s Virginians showed little enthusiasm for the new imperial system. Not only did the collection of customs on tobacco greatly reduce profits, but with the exclusion of the Dutch as the middlemen in American commerce, tobacco planters had to sell their crops to English merchants at artificially low prices. Virginia's loss (£100,000 in import duties collected for the Crown by 1670) was Charles II's gain. New England merchants ignored or cleverly circumvented the commercial restrictions. These crafty traders picked up cargoes of enumerated goods such as sugar or tobacco, sailed to another colonial port (thereby technically fulfilling the letter of the law), and then made directly for Holland or France. Along the way they paid no customs.

To plug this loophole, Parliament passed another Navigation Act in 1673. This statute established a *plantation duty*, to be collected at the various colonial ports. New Englanders could no longer escape paying customs. And in 1675, as part of this new imperial firmness, the Privy Council formed a powerful subcommittee, the Lords of Trade, whose members monitored colonial affairs.

Despite these legal reforms, serious obstacles impeded the execution of imperial policy. The customs service did not have enough effective agents in American ports to enforce the Navigation Acts fully, and imperial officials of various independent agencies often worked at cross-purposes.

Parliament passed the last major piece of imperial legislation in 1696. First, the statute ordered all colonial governors to swear oaths promising to uphold the Navigation Acts. Second, Parliament established a regular, greatly expanded American customs service. Collectors had broad powers to search vessels and ferret out smugglers. Third, the act called for the creation of American vice-admiralty courts. Established to settle disputes that occurred at sea, vice-admiralty courts required neither juries nor oral cross-examination. In time, the expansion of the admiralty court system became a major colonial grievance.

Parliament thus compelled the colonists to accept, belatedly, the Navigation Acts. By 1700 American goods transshipped through the mother country accounted for a quarter of *all* English exports, an indication that the colonists found it profitable to obey the commercial regulations. In fact, during the eighteenth century, smuggling from Europe to America dried up almost completely.

Finally, in 1696 the Crown replaced the now moribund Lords of Trade with a body usually referred to as the Board of Trade. Unlike the Lords of Trade, the members of this body were not Privy Councillors; half the members were politicians, the rest were civil servants, presumably well informed about American affairs. The Crown and Parliament usually listened to the Board of Trade's recommendations. Eventually the Board became a refuge for political hacks, but in the first decades of the eighteenth century it aggressively addressed imperial problems.

Colonial Gentry in Revolt, 1676–1691

The Navigation Acts created an illusion of unity; these imperial statutes superimposed a system of commercial regulations on all the colonies. But within each society men and women struggled to bring order out of disorder, to establish stable ruling elites, to defuse ethnic and racial tensions, and to cope with population pressures that imperial planners only dimly understood. During the final decades of the seventeenth century, these efforts sometimes sparked revolt between factions of the local gentry, usually the "outs" versus the "ins," for political power.

Bacon's Rebellion Sweeps Virginia

Virginia was the first colony to experience this political unrest. After 1660, the Virginia economy steadily declined. Returns from tobacco had not been good for some time, and the Navigation Acts reduced profits even further. Into this unhappy environment came thousands of ambitious indentured servants.

It was not a land where ambitions could easily be satisfied. Servants complained about the lack of food and clothing. Those who managed to win their freedom found little opportunity to better their lives. In 1670 Virginia's governor, Sir William Berkeley, and the House of Burgesses disenfranchised all landless freemen, persons they regarded as troublemakers, but the threat of social violence remained.

Nathaniel Bacon arrived in Virginia in 1674.

He came from a respectable English family and brought enough money to America to set himself up immediately as a substantial planter. Berkeley even appointed Bacon to the Virginia Council. But when Bacon attempted to obtain a license to trade furs with the local Indians, he was rebuffed. This commerce was Berkeley's monopoly, and Virginia's ruling elite had not yet accepted Bacon as a full member.

In 1675, Indian attacks on outlying plantations thrust Bacon suddenly into the center of Virginia politics. Virginians expected the governor to send an army to retaliate. Instead, Berkeley called for the construction of a line of defensive forts. Settlers suspected that the governor was simply trying to protect his own fur interests and was rewarding his friends with contracts to build useless forts.

In response, Bacon boldly offered to lead a volunteer army against the Indians at no cost to the hard-pressed Virginia taxpayers. All he demanded was an official commission from Berkeley giving him military command. The governor steadfastly refused. Berkeley believed that Bacon was a fanatic on the subject of Indians who would make matters worse along the frontier.

What followed would have been comic had not so many people died. Bacon thundered against the governor's treachery; Berkeley labeled Bacon a traitor. Bacon led several campaigns against the Indians, failing to kill any enemies, but managing to massacre some friendly Indians. Bacon also burned Jamestown to the ground, forcing Berkeley to flee to the colony's eastern shore. Charles II sent troops to aid the governor, but by the time they arrived, Berkeley had gained full control of the colony's government. In October 1676, Bacon died after a brief illness, and his band of rebels dispersed within a few months.

Order was soon restored, and in 1677 the Crown recalled the embittered Berkeley. The governors who followed were unusually greedy, and the local gentry formed a united front against them. Bacon's Rebellion had been a revolt without an ideology or a reform program; it soon faded from popular memory.

The Glorious Revolution in the Bay Colony

During John Winthrop's lifetime, the settlers of Massachusetts developed an inflated sense of their independence from the mother country. After the Restoration in 1660, however, the Crown put an end to that illusion. Royal officials demanded full compliance with the Navigation Acts, which were constant reminders of New England's colonial status. The growth of commerce attracted new merchants who were there to make money and were restive under the Puritan strictures. These developments divided Bay leaders. A few Puritan ministers and magistrates regarded compromise with England as treason, a breaking of the Lord's covenant. Other spokesmen recognized the changing political realities within the empire and urged a more moderate course.

In 1675, the Indians dealt the New Englanders a terrible setback. Metacomet, a Wampanoag chief whom the whites called King Philip, declared war against the colonists; he was joined by the powerful Narragansetts. In little more than a year of fighting, the Indians destroyed scores of frontier villages, killed hundreds of colonists, and disrupted the entire regional economy. "In proportion to population, King Philip's War inflicted greater casualties upon the people than any other war in our history," writes historian Douglas Leach.

Another shock followed. In 1684, the Court of Chancery, sitting in London and acting under a petition from King James II, annulled the charter of the Massachusetts Bay Company. The decision forced the most stubborn Puritans to recognize that they were part of an empire run by people who did not share their particular religious vision.

In the place of representative governments, James II created the Dominion of New England. In various stages from 1686 to 1689, it incorporated Massachusetts, Connecticut, Rhode Island, Plymouth, New York, New Jersey, and New Hampshire under a single appointed royal governor. For this demanding position, James selected Sir Edmund Andros

■ *Metacomet, called King Philip by the whites, waged a war against the Massachusetts colonists that left at least a thousand New Englanders dead.*

(pronounced Andrews), a military veteran of tyrannical temperament. He quickly abolished elective assemblies and town meetings, and enforced the Navigation Acts so rigorously that he brought about a commercial depression. His high-handed methods alienated almost all the colonists.

Early in 1689 the news of the Glorious Revolution (see the chart on p. 19) reached Boston. The English people had deposed James II, an absolutist monarch who openly espoused Catholicism. His daughter Mary and her husband William of Orange ascended the throne as joint monarchs in James' place. William and Mary had accepted a Bill of Rights that stipulated the constitutional rights of the English subject. Almost immediately the Bay colonists over-

threw the hated Andros regime and jailed the governor. No one came to Andros' defense.

However united they were, the Bay colonists could not take the newly crowned monarch's support for granted. But thanks largely to the tireless efforts of Increase Mather, a Congregational minister and father of Cotton Mather, who pleaded the colonists' case in London, King William abandoned the Dominion of New England and in 1691 conferred a new royal charter upon Massachusetts. This document provided for a Crown-appointed governor and a franchise based on property ownership rather than church membership. On the local level, town government remained much as it had been in Winthrop's time.

Troubles with Witches

During these politically troubled times, hysterical men and women living in Salem Village, a small, struggling farming community, created panic in Massachusetts Bay. In late 1691, during a very cold winter, several adolescent girls began to behave in strange ways. They cried for no apparent reason; they twitched on the ground. The girls attributed their suffering to the work of witches. The arrest of several alleged witches did not relieve the girls' "fits," and other arrests followed. At least one person confessed, providing a frightening description of the devil as "a thing all over hairy, all the face hairy, and a long nose." By the end of the summer, a specially convened court had hanged nineteen people; another was pressed to death. Many more suspects awaited trial.

Then suddenly, the storm was over. Led by Increase Mather, a group of prominent Congregational ministers urged leniency and restraint. Especially troubling to the clergymen was the court's decision to accept "spectral evidence," that is, reports of dreams and visions in which the accused appeared as the devil's agent. The colonial government accepted the ministers' advice and convened a new court, which promptly acquitted, pardoned, or released the remaining suspects.

No one knows exactly what sparked the terror in Salem Village. The community had a history of discord, and during the 1680s the people split into angry factions over the choice of a minister. Jealousy and bitterness apparently festered to the point that adolescent girls who normally would have been disciplined were allowed to incite judicial murder. As often happens in incidents like this one, the accusers later came to their senses and apologized for the cruel suffering that they had inflicted.

The Glorious Revolution in New York and Maryland

When news of the Glorious Revolution reached New York City in May 1969, Jacob Leisler, a German immigrant with mercantile ties to the older Dutch elite, raised a group of militiamen and seized a local fort in the name of William and Mary. For a short time he controlled the city. But English newcomers and powerful Anglo-Dutch families who had recently risen to prominence opposed the older Dutch group to which he was allied, and Leisler never was able to construct a secure political base.

In 1691 a new royal governor, Henry Sloughter, reached New York and ordered Leisler to surrender his authority. Leisler hesitated; he may have feared the vengeance of rival factions. The pause cost Leisler his life. He was declared a rebel, promptly tried, and executed in grisly fashion. Four years later, Parliament officially pardoned him, but the decision came a bit late. The bitter political factionalism of which this unfortunate episode was a part plagued New York throughout the next century.

Tensions in Maryland between Protestants and Catholics ran high during the last third of the seventeenth century. When news of James' overthrow reached Maryland early in 1689, pent-up anti-proprietary and anti-Catholic sentiment exploded. John Coode, a member of the Assembly and an outspoken Protestant, formed a group called the Protestant Associa-

tion, which forced the governor appointed by Lord Baltimore to resign.

The Protestant Association petitioned the newly crowned Protestant monarchs to transform Maryland into a royal colony, alleging many wrongs suffered at the hands of the Catholic-dominated upper house. William complied, sending a royal governor in 1691. The new Assembly then proclaimed the Church of England as the established religion and excluded Catholics from public office. Baltimore lost control of the colony's government. A quarter century later, however, the fourth Lord Baltimore, who had been raised a member of the Church of England, regained full proprietorship from the Crown. Maryland remained in the hands of the Calvert family until 1776.

Colonists in an Empire: Regional Patterns

Common Experiences, Separate Cultures

In the years since Winthrop had sailed to the New World, colonial Americans had become more, not less, English. They had been drawn into an imperial system—Carolinians, Virginians, New Englanders, all regulated now by the same commercial statutes. They had not, however, developed a sense of unity as Americans. Profound sectional differences remained, indeed had grown stronger, so that during the eighteenth century, the colonists felt increasingly torn between the culture of the mother country and the culture of their own region.

Recommended Reading

The best account of seventeenth-century New Englanders' views on the family remains Edmund S. Morgan, *The Puritan Family* (1966). Morgan has also produced a masterful analysis of a southern colony; his *American Slavery, American Freedom: The Ordeal of Colonial Virginia* (1975) examines the impact of an extraordinarily high death rate upon an evolving triracial plantation society. Anyone interested in the history of slavery should start with David B. Davis, *The Problem of Slavery in Western Culture* (1966), and Winthrop D. Jordan, *White over Black: American Attitudes Toward the Negro, 1550–1812* (1968). A complete discussion of the drafting of the Navigation Acts and England's efforts to enforce them can be found in C. M. Andrews, *The Colonial Period of American History*, vol. 4 (1938). David S. Lovejoy provides a comprehensive survey of the various late seventeenth-century rebellions in *The Glorious Revolution in America* (1972).

Stephen Foster, *Their Solitary Way* (1971), is a highly readable analysis of the ways in which Puritans perceived their society. Two books that examine the relationship between the life cycle and social structure are John Demos, *A Little Commonwealth* (1970), and Philip J. Greven, *Four Generations* (1969). The role of women in this society is the subject of Lyle Koehler, *A Search for Power: "The Weaker Sex" in Seventeenth-Century New England* (1980), and Laurel T. Ulrich, *Good Wives: Image and Reality in the Lives of Women in Northern New England, 1650–1750* (1982).

The development of colonial society in the South is explored in T. W. Tate and D. L. Ammerman, eds., *The Chesapeake in the Seventeenth Century* (1979). In *Colonists in Bondage* (1947), A. E. Smith discusses indentured servitude, but see also David W. Galenson, *White Servitude in Colonial America: An Economic Analysis* (1981). T. H. Breen speculates on the cultural values of early Virginians in *Puritans and Adventurers* (1980).

The black experience in colonial America has been the topic of several recent interdisciplinary studies: Philip D. Curtin, *The Atlantic Slave Trade: A Census* (1969); Peter Wood, *Black Majority* (1974); G. W. Mullin, *Flight and Rebellion* (1972); and T. H. Breen and Stephen Innes, *"Myne Owne Ground," Race and Freedom on Virginia's Eastern Shore* (1980).

The best study of King Philip's War is by Douglas Leach, *Flintlock and Tomahawk* (1958). Of the many studies of Salem Village witchcraft, the most imaginative are Paul Boyer and Stephen Nissenbaum, *Salem Possessed* (1974), and John Demos, *Entertaining Satan: Witchcraft and the Culture of Early New England* (1982).

chapter 4

EXPANDING HORIZONS: EIGHTEENTH-CENTURY AMERICA

In the 1970s a group of archaeologists excavated an area in northwest Massachusetts where more than 200 years earlier the royal governor of the Bay colony had ordered construction of a line of forts. Artifacts taken from the site provide insights into eighteenth-century American culture. The provincial militiamen wore clothes made from textiles manufactured in Great Britain, drank rum from imported glasses, sipped tea from delicate Staffordshire ceramicware, smoked pipes produced in London, and killed Indians and Frenchmen with guns produced in the mother country.

Life in the colonies had changed from the days of Captain John Smith and John Winthrop. After 1690, men and women were gradually drawn into the larger Anglo-American world. Colonists whose parents or grandparents had tamed a "howling wilderness" relied increasingly upon imported goods, read London journals, traveled to the mother country,

fought Britain's enemies, and sought favors from royal officials. Colonial women modeled themselves on the ideal of the English "genteel lady." A love–hate relationship with England began.

Tensions arose and there were many contradictions. It was not unusual for colonists who adopted the latest London fashions to condemn the corrupting influence of British life. Colonists eagerly read sophisticated English journals, yet extolled the virtues of simplicity and provincial society. Benjamin Franklin, one of the most cosmopolitan colonial figures of the age, championed American liberties. And William Byrd, a Virginia planter who spent most of his adult life in Great Britain chasing celebrities, insisted that America had purer air than England. Trapped between cultures, the colonists were neither Englishmen nor Americans. In time, however, they would have to choose between the two worlds.

People and Trade in an Expanding Empire

During the eighteenth century, the American population doubled approximately every twenty-five years. Not only was the total population increasing at a very rapid rate, it was also becoming more dispersed and heterogeneous. Each year witnessed the arrival of thousands of non-English Europeans, most of whom were soon scattered along the colonial frontier.

Population Explosion

The estimated white population of Britain's mainland colonies rose from about 250,000 in 1700 to 2,150,000 in 1770, an annual growth rate of 3 percent. Few societies in recorded history have expanded so rapidly. Natural reproduction was responsible for most of the growth. The population of the late colonial period was strikingly young; approximately one half of the population at any given time was under the age of sixteen.

Immigration further swelled the colonial population. The largest group of newcomers consisted of Scotch-Irish. During the seventeenth century, English rulers sent thousands of Scottish Presbyterians as colonists to Catholic Ireland in an attempt to pacify that wartorn country. The plan failed, and after a short time, many of the Scotch-Irish elected to immigrate to America where they hoped to find the freedom and prosperity that they had been denied in Ireland. By the time of the American Revolution, perhaps 250,000 Scotch-Irish had migrated to America.

Most Scotch-Irish immigrants landed initially in Philadelphia, but they soon headed for the fertile land on Pennsylvania's western frontier. They were welcomed, for the colony's proprietors believed that the Scotch-Irish would serve as a buffer between the Indians and the older, coastal communities. The Penn family soon had second thoughts, however.

The Scotch-Irish settled wherever they found unoccupied land, regardless of who owned it, and challenged established authority.

A second large body of non-English settlers, more than 100,000 people, came from the Upper Rhine Valley, in the German Palatinate. Some of these people belonged to small, pietist Protestant sects, and they came to America in search of religious toleration. Most Germans, however, sought the peace and good land of the colonies. By 1766 persons of German stock—mistakenly called Dutch—accounted for more than one third of Pennsylvania's total population. Even their detractors admitted that the Germans were the best farmers in the colony.

Ethnic differences in Pennsylvania bred disputes. The Scotch-Irish and the Germans preferred to live with people of their own background, and they sometimes fought to keep members of the other nationalities out of their neighborhood. Further complicating the problem, the English were suspicious of both groups. Indeed, many Pennsylvanians shared

Estimated Population, 1720–1760

		New England Colonies	Middle Colonies	Southern Colonies
1720	White	166,937	92,259	138,110
	Black	3,956	10,825	54,098
1730	White	211,233	135,298	191,893
	Black	6,118	11,683	73,220
1740	White	281,163	204,093	270,283
	Black	8,541	16,452	125,031
1750	White	349,029	275,723	309,588
	Black	10,982	20,736	204,702
1760	White	436,917	398,855	432,047
	Black	12,717	29,049	284,040

New England Colonies *New Hampshire, Massachusetts, Rhode Island, and Connecticut*

Middle Colonies *New York, New Jersey, Pennsylvania, and Delaware*

Southern Colonies *Maryland, Virginia, North Carolina, South Carolina, and (after 1740) Georgia*

Source: Adapted from R. C. Simmons, *The American Colonies: From Settlement to Independence* (1976).

Benjamin Franklin's opinion that the Germans posed a threat to the primacy of the English language and government in that colony.

Prejudice and hostility may have persuaded the Germans and the Scotch-Irish to head for western Pennsylvania, the Shenandoah Valley of Virginia, and the backcountry of the Carolinas. The Germans usually remained wherever they found unclaimed fertile land. The Scotch-Irish tended to move two or three times and acquired a reputation as a rootless people.

Culture of the Cities

Considering the rate of population growth, few eighteenth-century Americans lived in cities. Boston, Newport, Philadelphia, New York, and Charleston—the five largest cities—contained only about 5 percent of the colonial population. In 1775 none had more than 40,000 persons. The explanation for the dearth of city dwellers can be found in the highly specialized nature of colonial commerce. Port towns served as intermediary trade and shipping centers where bulk cargoes were broken up for inland distribution; they did not support large-scale manufacturing. Also, men who worked for wages in the colonies usually became farmers, rather than urban laborers.

Yet American cities profoundly affected colonial culture, for it was in the cities that the English influence was most pronounced. Wealthy merchants and lawyers tried to emulate the culture of the mother country. They went to the theater, listened to concerts, and dressed in the high fashion of London society.

The architectural splendor was especially noticeable. Homes of enduring beauty, modeled on English country houses, were constructed during the reign of Britain's early Hanoverian kings. Since all these kings were named George, the term "Georgian" was applied to this style of architecture.

Their owners filled these houses with fine furniture. Each city patronized certain skilled craftsmen, but the artisans of Philadelphia were known for producing magnificent copies of the works of Thomas Chippendale, Great Britain's most famous furniture designer. These developments gave American cities an elegance that they had not possessed in the previous century.

For some American artists colonial society did not fulfill their needs. They could not find the training they required, and America seemed devoid of the kind of subject matter that inspired the great European masters. John Singleton Copley, perhaps colonial America's finest and most highly regarded painter, always wondered whether the English would respect his work. Sir Joshua Reynolds, the preeminent English painter of the age, admired Copley's *The Boy with the Squirrel* and urged the artist to pursue his career in England. In 1774 Copley moved to London.

Economic Expansion

The colonial economy kept pace with the stunning growth in population. *Per capita* income never fell behind the population explosion. An abundance of land and the extensive

Estimated Population of Colonial Cities, 1720–1770
showing decennial percentage increases

	Boston	%	Newport	%	New York	%	Philadelphia	%	Charleston	%
1720	12,000	—	3,800	—	7,000	—	10,000	—	3,500	—
1730	13,000	8	4,640	22	8,622	23	11,500	15	4,500	29
1740	15,601	20	5,840	26	10,451	21	12,654	10	6,269	39
1750	—	—	6,670	14	14,225	36	18,202	44	7,134	14
1760	15,631	—	7,500	12	18,000	27	23,750	30	8,000	12
1770	15,877	2	9,833	31	22,667	26	34,583	46	10,667	33

Source: R. C. Simmons, *The American Colonies: From Settlement to Independence* (1976).

Expanding Horizons: 18th-Century America

This eighteenth-century Philadelphia parlor shows how carefully wealthy urban Americans copied the culture of the mother country.

on the English markets. The emerging Industrial Revolution in Great Britain was beginning to create a new generation of consumers who possessed enough income to purchase American goods, especially sugar and tobacco. This rising demand was the major market force shaping the colonial economy.

Roughly one fourth of all American exports went to the West Indies. Colonial ships carrying food sailed for the Caribbean and returned *immediately* to the Middle Colonies or New England with cargoes of molasses, sugar, and rum. "Triangular trade" including the west coast of Africa was insignificant. In addition, the West Indies played a vital role in preserving American credit. Without this source of income, colonists would not have been able to pay for the manufactured items that they purchased in the mother country. The cost of goods imported from Great Britain normally exceeded the revenues collected on American exports to the mother country. To cover this small but recurrent deficit, colonial merchants relied upon profits made in the West Indies.

After mid-century, however, the balance of trade turned dramatically against the colonists. Americans began buying more English goods than their parents and grandparents had done. Between 1740 and 1770 English exports to the American colonies increased by an astounding 360 percent.

In part, this shift reflected the increased production of British industries. Because of technological advances in manufacturing, Great Britain was able to produce certain goods more efficiently and more cheaply than the colonists could. Americans started to buy as never before; Staffordshire china and imported cloth replaced crude earthenware and rough homespun. In this manner, British industrialization undercut American handicraft and folk art.

To help Americans purchase manufactured goods, British merchants offered generous credit. For many people, the temptation to acquire English finery blinded them to hard economic realities. Colonists deferred settlement by agreeing to pay interest on their debts, and by 1760 total indebtedness had reached £2 million. Colonial governments could delay the

growth of agriculture accounted for this economic success. Each year more Americans produced more tobacco, wheat, and rice—just to cite the major export crops—and by this means, they maintained a high level of individual prosperity without developing an industrial base.

One half of American goods produced for export went to Great Britain. The Navigation Acts (see Chapter 3) were still in effect and "enumerated" items such as tobacco and furs had to be landed first at a British port. Over the years, specific Acts brought white pine trees, molasses, hats, and iron under imperial control as England regulated colonial trade to her advantage.

The statutes might have created tensions between the colonists and the mother country had they been rigorously enforced. Crown officials, however, generally ignored the new laws. But even without the Navigation Acts, a majority of colonial exports would have been sold balance-of-payment crisis for a time by issuing paper money, but the problem was not resolved.

The eighteenth century brought a substantial increase in intercoastal trade. Southern planters sent tobacco and rice to New England and the Middle Colonies where these staples were exchanged for meat and wheat as well as for goods imported from Great Britain. By 1760 approximately 30 percent of the colonists' total tonnage capacity was involved in this extensive "coastwise" commerce. In addition, American colonists carried on a substantial amount of commerce over the rough, backcountry highway known as the "Great Wagon Road," which stretched 735 miles along the Blue Ridge Mountains from Pennsylvania to South Carolina. The long, gracefully designed Conestoga wagon was vital to this overland trade.

These shifting patterns of trade had an immense effect on the development of an American culture. First, the flood of British imports eroded local and regional identities. Deep sectional differences remained, of course, but Americans from New Hampshire to Georgia were increasingly drawn into a sophisticated economic network centered in London.

Second, the expanding coastwise and overland trade brought colonists of different backgrounds into more frequent contact, exchanging ideas and experience as well as tobacco and wheat. New journals and newspapers appeared. Americans were kept abreast of the latest news in the colonies as well as in London. Americans were expanding their horizons, and slowly, sometimes painfully, a distinct culture was emerging.

Religious Revival in an Age of Reason

Two great forces—one intellectual, the other religious—transformed the character of eighteenth-century American life. Although both movements originated in Europe, they were redefined in a New World context and soon re-

flected the peculiarities of the colonial experience. The *Enlightenment* changed the way that educated, urbane colonists looked at their world; the *Great Awakening* brought a rebirth to thousands of men and women scattered along the Atlantic coast. Both movements made Americans aware of other persons, often complete strangers, who shared their beliefs. These voluntary networks undercut traditional community ties and helped the colonists forge new cultural identities.

American Enlightenment

European historians often refer to the eighteenth century as an Age of Reason. During this period a body of new ideas, called the Enlightenment, altered the way that educated Europeans thought about God, nature, and society. Enlightenment philosophers replaced the concept of original sin with a much more optimistic view of human nature. A benevolent God, they argued, having set the universe in motion, gave human beings the power of reason to enable them to comprehend the orderly workings of His creation. Everything, even human society, operated according to these mechanical laws. It was the duty of men and women, therefore, to make certain that institutions such as church and state conformed to self-evident natural laws. Through the use of reason, they asserted, human suffering could be eliminated and perfection could be achieved.

The American Enlightenment was a rather tame affair compared to its European counterpart. Colonists welcomed the advent of experimental science but stoutly defended the tenets of traditional Christianity. Americans emphasized the search for useful knowledge, ideas, and inventions. What mattered was practical experimentation, and the Enlightenment spawned scores of earnest scientific tinkerers, people who dutifully recorded changes in temperature, the appearance of strange plants or animals, and the details of astronomic phenomena.

The greatest of all these American experimenters was Benjamin Franklin (1706–1790).

54

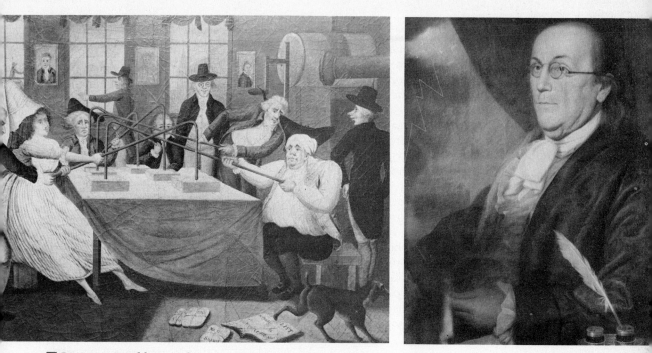

■ *Benjamin Franklin's (right) experiments with electricity became world famous and motivated others to study this strange force. The people at left are rubbing rods together to produce static electricity.*

As a young man working in his brother's Boston printshop, he discovered a copy of a new British journal, the *Spectator*. It was like a breath of fresh air to a boy growing up in Puritan New England. In August 1721 he and his brother founded the *New-England Courant*, a weekly newspaper that satirized Boston's political and religious leaders in the manner of the contemporary British press. Proper Bostonians were not prepared for such a critical journal, and in 1723 Franklin left Massachusetts in search of a less hostile intellectual environment.

He settled in Philadelphia. There he devoted himself to the pursuit of useful knowledge. Franklin never denied the existence of God. Rather, he pushed the Lord aside, making room for the free exercise of reason. A naturally curious man, he was constantly experimenting and broadening his understanding of science, always with some practical end in mind. The lightning rod and a marvelously ef-

ficient stove are only two of Franklin's important contributions to material progress through human ingenuity.

Franklin energetically promoted the spread of Enlightenment ideas. In Philadelphia he formed "a club for mutual Improvement, which we call'd the Junto" and a library association to discuss literature, philosophy, and science. The members of these groups communicated with Americans living in other colonies, providing them not only with the latest information from Europe, but also with models for their own clubs and associations. Such efforts broadened the intellectual horizons of many colonists, especially city dwellers.

Great Awakening

The Great Awakening had a far greater impact on the lives of the common people than did the Enlightenment. This unprecedented evangelical outpouring caused men and women to rethink basic assumptions about society, church, and state. In our own time we have witnessed the forces of religious revival in different regions throughout the world. It is no exaggeration to claim that a similar revolution took place in mid-eighteenth-century America.

Only with hindsight does the Great Awakening seem a unified religious movement. Revivals occurred in different places at different times. The first signs of a spiritual awakening appeared in New England during the late 1730s. The intensity of the event varied from region to region. Revivals were most important in Massachusetts, Connecticut, Rhode Island, Pennsylvania, New Jersey, and in the 1750s and 1760s in Virginia. No single religious denomination or sect monopolized the Awakening; mainly Congregationalist churches were affected in New England, but elsewhere revivals involved Presbyterians, Methodists, and Baptists.

The evangelism of the Great Awakening infused a new sense of vitality into religions that had lost their fervor. People in New England complained that Congregational ministers seemed obsessed with dull, scholastic matters; their sermons no longer touched the heart. And in the southern colonies, there were simply not enough ordained ministers to tend to the religious needs of the population.

The Great Awakening began unexpectedly in Northampton, a small farm community in western Massachusetts, sparked by the preaching of Jonathan Edwards, the local Congregationalist minister. With fervent zeal, Edwards reminded his flock that their fate had been determined for all eternity by an omnipotent God. He thought his fellow ministers had grown soft and were preaching easy salvation. Edwards disabused his congregation of that false comfort. With calm self-assurance he described in vivid detail the torments of the damned, those whom God had not elected to receive divine grace.

Why this uncompromising Calvinist message set off religious revivals during the late 1730s is not known. Whatever the explanation

for the sudden popular response to Edwards' preaching, young people began flocking to church. They experienced a searing conversion, a sense of "new birth" and utter dependence upon God. The excitement spread, and evangelical ministers concluded that God must be preparing Americans, His chosen people, for the millennium.

The best-known figure of the Great Awakening was George Whitefield, a young inspiring preacher from England who toured the colonies from Georgia to New Hampshire. He was an extraordinary public speaker who cast a spell over the throngs who came to see and hear him.

Whitefield's audience came from all groups of American society, rich and poor, young and old, rural and urban. While Whitefield described himself as a Calvinist, he welcomed all Protestants, and he spoke from any pulpit that was available. "Don't tell me you are a Baptist, an Independent, a Presbyterian, a dissenter," he thundered, "tell me you are a Christian, that is all I want."

Other, American-born, itinerant preachers followed Whitefield's example. The most famous was Gilbert Tennent, a Presbyterian of Scotch-Irish background who had been educated in the Middle Colonies. He, and other revivalists of like mind, traveled from town to town, colony to colony challenging local clergymen who seemed hostile to evangelical religion. Many ministers remained suspicious of the itinerants and their methods. Some complaints may have amounted to little more than jealousy. Others raised serious questions: How could the revivalists be certain that God had sparked the Great Awakening? And how could the revivalists be certain that the "dangers of enthusiasm" would not lead them astray? During the 1740s and 1750s, many congregations split between defenders of the new emotional preaching, the "New Lights," and those who regarded the entire movement as dangerous nonsense, the "Old Lights."

While Tennent did not condone the excesses of the Great Awakening, his attacks on formal learning invited the crude anti-intellectualism of such deranged revivalists as James Davenport. Davenport preached under the light of smoky torches; he danced and stripped, shrieked and laughed. He also urged people to burn books written by those who had not experienced the "new light."

To concentrate upon occasional anti-intellectual outbursts is to obscure the positive ways in which this vast revival changed American society. First, the New Lights founded several important centers of higher education. They wanted to train young men who would carry on the good works of Edwards, Whitefield, and Tennent. Princeton (1747), Dartmouth (1769), Brown (1764), and Rutgers (1766) were all colleges founded by revivalist leaders.

Second, the Great Awakening encouraged men and women who had been taught to remain silent before traditional figures of authority to take an active role in their own salvation. They could no longer rely upon ministers or institutions. The individual alone stood before God. This emphasis upon personal religious choices shattered the old harmony that existed among Protestant sects and in its place introduced a noisy, often bitterly fought competition.

With religious contention, however, came an awareness of a larger community, a union of fellow believers that extended beyond the boundaries of town and colony. In fact, evangelical religion was one of several forces at work during the mid-eighteenth century that brought scattered colonists into contact with one another for the first time. In this sense, the Great Awakening was a "national" event long before a nation actually existed.

People who had been touched by the Great Awakening saw America as "an instrument of Providence." With God's help, social and political progress was achievable, and from this perspective, of course, the New Lights did not sound much different than the mildly rationalist American spokesmen of the Enlightenment. Both groups prepared the way for the development of a revolutionary mentality in colonial America.

Anglo-American Politics: Theory and Practice

The balanced constitution of Great Britain was an object of nearly universal admiration during the eighteenth century. According to its defenders, it protected life, liberty, and property better than did any other contemporary government. The constitution incorporated three distinct parts: the monarch, the House of Lords, and the House of Commons. Thus, in theory the government represented the socioeconomic interests of the king, nobility, and common people. Acting alone, each body would run to excess, even tyranny, but operating within a mixed system, they automatically checked each other's ambitions for the common good.

The Reality of British Politics

The reality of daily political life, however, bore little relation to theory. The three elements of the constitution did not, in fact, represent distinct socioeconomic groups. Men elected to the House of Commons often came from the same social background as did those who served in the House of Lords. All represented the interests of Britain's landed elite. Moreover, there was no attempt to maintain strict constitutional separation. The king exerted considerable influence, for example, in the House of Commons.

The claim that the members of the House of Commons represented all the people of England also seemed farfetched. In 1715 only about 20 percent of British adult males had the right to vote, and there was no standard size for electorate districts. Some representatives to Parliament were chosen by several thousand voters; some, by only a handful of electors.

Before 1760 few people in England spoke out against these constitutional abuses. The main exception was a group of radical publicists whom historians have labeled the "Commonwealthmen." These writers decried the corrup-

The Election by William Hogarth illustrates just one aspect of electoral corruption in England—voters were openly willing to sell their votes to either (or both) sides in an election. The practice was by no means remarkable.

tion of political life, warning that the nation that compromised its civic virtue deserved to lose its liberty and property. The most famous Commonwealthmen were John Trenchard and Thomas Gordon, who penned a series of essays entitled *Cato's Letters* between 1720 and 1723. They warned the nation to be vigilant against tyranny by England's rulers.

But however shrilly these writers protested, however many newspaper articles they published, the Commonwealthmen won little support for their political reforms. Englishmen were not willing to tamper with a system of government that had so recently survived a civil war and a Glorious Revolution. Americans, however, took Trenchard and Gordon to heart.

American Political Culture in the Mid-Eighteenth Century

The colonists assumed—perhaps naively—that their own governments were modeled upon the balanced constitution of Great Britain. They argued that within their political systems, the governor corresponded to the king, the governor's council to the House of

Lords, and the colonial assemblies to the House of Commons. As the colonists discovered, however, English theories about the mixed constitution were no more relevant in America than they were in the mother country.

By mid-century royal governors appointed by the Crown ruled a majority of the mainland colonies. Many of the appointees were career army officers who through luck, charm, or family connection had gained the ear of someone close to the king. These patronage posts did not generate income sufficient to interest the most powerful or talented personalities of the period, but they did draw middle-level bureaucrats who were ambitious, desperate, or both.

Before departing for the New World, royal governors received an elaborate set of instructions drafted by the Board of Trade. The document dealt with almost every aspect of colonial life, political, economic, and religious, and no one knew for certain that these orders even possessed the force of law.

About the governors' powers, however, there was no doubt; they were enormous. In fact, royal governors could do certain things in

America that a king could not do in eighteenth-century Britain. Among these were the right to veto legislation and dismiss judges. The governors also served as commanders in chief in each province.

Royal governors were advised by a council, usually a body of about twelve wealthy colonists selected by the Board of Trade in London upon the recommendation of the governor. By the eighteenth century, however, the council had lost most of its power. This body was certainly no House of Lords.

Nor were the colonial assemblies much like the House of Commons. A far greater proportion of men could vote in America than in Great Britain. In most colonies adult white males who owned a small amount of land could vote in county-wide elections. Although participation in government was not high, and most colonists were content to let gentry represent them in the assemblies, the potential for throwing the rascals out was always present.

Rise of the Colonial Assemblies

Members of the assemblies were convinced that they had a special obligation to preserve colonial liberties. Any attack upon the legislature was perceived as an assault upon the rights of Americans. So aggressive were these bodies in seizing privileges, determining procedures, and controlling money bills that some historians have described the political development of eighteenth-century America as "the rise of the assemblies."

This political system seemed designed to generate hostility. There was simply no reason for the colonial legislature to cooperate with appointed royal governors. A few governors managed briefly to create in America a political culture of patronage akin to what they knew in England. But usually such efforts clashed with the colonists' perceptions of politics. They *really* believed in the purity of the balanced constitution, and attempts to revert to a patronage system were met by their loud protests in language that seemed to be directly lifted from the pages of *Cato's Letters.*

The major source of shared political information was the weekly journal, a new and vigorous institution in American life. In New York and Massachusetts especially, weekly newspapers urged readers to preserve civic virtue, and to exercise extreme vigilance against the spread of privileged power. Through such journals, a pattern of political rhetoric that in Britain had gained only marginal respectability, became after 1765 America's normal form of political discourse.

The rise of the assemblies shaped American culture in other, subtler, ways. Over the course of the century, the language of the law became increasingly anglicized. Varying local legal practices that had been widespread during the seventeenth century became standardized. Indeed, by 1750 there was little difference between the colonial legal system and that of the mother country. Not surprisingly, many men who served in colonial assemblies were either lawyers or persons who had received legal training. When Americans from different regions met they discovered that they shared a commitment to the preservation of the English common law.

But if eighteenth-century political developments drew the colonists closer to the mother country, they also brought Americans a greater awareness of each other. As their horizons widened, they learned that they operated within the same general imperial system and that they shared similar problems. Like the revivalists and merchants—people who crossed old boundaries—colonial legislators laid the foundation for a broader cultural identity.

Century of Imperial War

The scope and character of warfare in the colonies changed radically during the eighteenth century. Local conflicts with the Indians, such as King Philip's War (1675–1676) in New England, gave way to hostilities that originated on the other side of the Atlantic, in rivalries between Great Britain and France over geopolitical considerations and commercial ambitions. The external threat to security forced people in different colonies to devise unprecedented measures of military and political cooperation.

By 1750 the French had established a chain of settlements southward through the heart of the continent from Quebec to New Orleans. But few French troops were stationed in the New World. The Crown left the defense of Canada and the Mississippi valley to the companies engaged in the fur trade. This seemed an impossible task for the French outposts strung out along the St. Lawrence River, the Great Lakes, and the Mississippi banks.

On paper, at least, the British settlements enjoyed military superiority. Nonetheless, for most of the first half of the eighteenth century, their advantage proved more apparent than real. While the British settlements possessed a larger and more prosperous population than the French—1,200,000 to 75,000—they were divided into separate governments that sometimes seemed more suspicious of each other than of the French. When war came, French officers and Indian allies exploited these jealousies with considerable skill. Moreover, the small population of New France was concentrated along the St. Lawrence, and it could easily mass the forces needed to defend Montreal and Quebec.

King William's and Queen Anne's Wars

Colonial involvement in imperial war began in 1689, when England's new king, William III, declared war on France's Louis XIV. Europeans called this struggle the War of the League of Augsburg, but to the Americans, it was simply King William's War. Canadians raided the northern frontiers of New York and New England, and although they made no territorial gains, they caused considerable suffering among the civilian population of Massachusetts and New York.

The war ended with the Treaty of Ryswick (1697), but the colonists were drawn almost immediately into a new conflict, Queen Anne's War, a dynastic conflict known in Europe as the War of Spanish Succession (1702–1713). Colonists in South Carolina as well as New England battled against the French and Indians. The bloody combat along the American frontier was formally terminated in 1713 when Great Britain and France signed the Treaty of Utrecht. European concerns were paramount in the peace negotiations. Although two decades of fighting had taken a fearful toll in North America, neither France nor the English colonists had much to show for their sacrifice.

When George I, the first Hanoverian king of Great Britain, replaced Queen Anne in 1714, parliamentary leaders determined to preserve peace. But on the American frontier hostilities continued. At stake was the entire West, including the Mississippi valley. English colonists believed that the French planned to "encircle" them, to confine them to a narrow strip

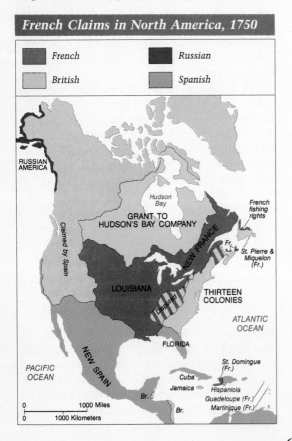

French Claims in North America, 1750

French Russian
British Spanish

RUSSIAN AMERICA

Hudson Bay

GRANT TO HUDSON'S BAY COMPANY

Claimed by Spain

NEW FRANCE

French fishing rights

Fr.
St. Pierre & Miquelon (Fr.)

LOUISIANA

THIRTEEN COLONIES

Disputed

ATLANTIC OCEAN

FLORIDA

PACIFIC OCEAN

NEW SPAIN

St. Domingue (Fr.)

Cuba
Jamaica   Hispaniola
Br.   Guadeloupe (Fr.)
    Martinique (Fr.)
Br.

0   1000 Miles
0   1000 Kilometers

■ *Founded by the French in 1699, New Biloxi was part of a chain of settlements established in an attempt to maintain control of the Louisiana Territory.*

of land along the Atlantic coast. As evidence they pointed to the French forts that had been constructed through the heart of America. On their part, the French suspected that their rivals intended to seize all of North America. They noted that land speculators and Indian traders were pushing aggressively into territory claimed by France. And so the two sides lined up their Indian allies and made ready for war.

Founding of Georgia

In these wars for empire, Spain often acted as France's ally against Great Britain. Spanish bases in Florida could be used to harass English settlements in the South. In part, this imperial struggle led to the foundation of the last of the mainland colonies, Georgia.

The colony owed its existence primarily to James Oglethorpe, a British general and member of Parliament who believed that he could thwart Spanish designs on the area south of Charleston while at the same time providing a fresh start for London's debtors. Although Oglethorpe envisioned Georgia as an asylum

as well as a garrison, the military aspects of his proposal were especially appealing to the leaders of the British government. In 1732 the king granted Oglethorpe and a board of trustees a charter for a new colony. The trustees living in the mother country were given complete control over Georgia politics, a condition the settlers soon found intolerable.

At first the colony did not fare very well. Few English debtors showed any desire to move there, and the trustees provided little incentive for emigration. No settler could amass more than 500 acres of land. Moreover, land could be passed only to an eldest son, and if a planter died without a son, the holding reverted to Oglethorpe and the trustees. Slavery and rum were prohibited.

The settlers wanted more—slaves, a voice in local government, unrestricted land ownership. Oglethorpe met their demands with angry rebuffs. Eventually, however, Oglethorpe lost interest in his colonial experiment, and the trustees were then forced to compromise their principles. In 1738 they eliminated all restrictions on the amount of land a person could own; they allowed women to inherit land. Slaves came next, then rum. In 1751 the trustees gave up on what had become a hard-drinking, slave-holding plantation society and returned Georgia to the king. That same year, the king authorized an assembly. But even with these social and political changes, Georgia attracted very few new settlers.

King George's War and Its Aftermath

In 1743 the Americans were dragged once again into the imperial conflict. During King George's War (1743–1748), known in Europe as the War of Austrian Succession, the colonists scored a magnificent victory over the French. In June 1745, an army of New England troops under the command of William Pepperrell captured Louisbourg, a gigantic fortress on Cape Breton Island guarding the approaches to the Gulf of St. Lawrence and Quebec. The Americans, however, were in for a shock. When the war ended with the signing of the Treaty of Aix-la-Chapelle in 1748, the British government handed Louisbourg back to the French in exchange for concessions elsewhere! New Englanders saw this as an insult, one they did not soon forget.

By the conclusion of King George's War, the goals of the conflict had clearly changed. Americans no longer aimed simply at protecting their territory from attack. They now wanted to gain complete control over the West, a region obviously rich in economic opportunity. Vast tracts of land and lucrative trade with the Indians awaited ambitious colonists.

The French were not prepared to surrender an inch. But time was running against them. Not only were the English colonies growing more populous, they also possessed a seemingly inexhaustible supply of manufactured goods to trade with the Indians. The French decided in the early 1750s, therefore, to seize the Ohio valley before their rivals could do so. They established forts throughout the region, the most formidable being Fort Duquesne, located at the strategic fork in the Ohio River near the modern city of Pittsburgh.

Although France and England had not officially declared war, British officials advised the governor of Virginia to "repell force by force." The Virginians, who had their eyes on the Ohio valley, needed no encouragement. In 1754 several militia companies under the command of a promising young officer, George Washington, constructed Fort Necessity not far from Fort Duquesne. The plan failed. French and Indian troops overran the badly exposed outpost (July 3, 1754). Among other things, this humiliating setback revealed that a single colony could not defeat the French.

Albany Congress and Braddock's Defeat

Benjamin Franklin, for one, understood the need for intercolonial cooperation. When British officials invited representatives from the northern colonies to Albany (June 1754) to discuss relations with the Iroquois, Franklin used the occasion to present a bold blueprint for colonial union. His so-called Albany Plan envisioned the formation of a Grand Council, made up of elected delegates from the various colonies, to oversee matters of common defense, western expansion, and Indian affairs. Most daring of all, he wanted to give the council the power of taxation.

■ *The first political cartoon to appear in an American newspaper. Drawn by Benjamin Franklin in 1754, it portrays his belief in colonial union.*

First reaction to the Albany Plan was enthusiastic, but neither the separate colonial assemblies nor Parliament finally approved the plan. The assemblies were jealous of their fiscal authority, and the English thought the scheme undermined the Crown's power in the colony.

Even though there was still no formal declaration of war, the British resolved to destroy Fort Duquesne, and to that end, in 1755 they dispatched units of the regular army to the Ohio valley under the command of Major General Edward Braddock. A poor leader who inspired no respect, on July 9 Braddock led his force of redcoats and colonists into one of the worst defeats in British military history. The French and Indians opened fire as Braddock's army was wading across the Monongahela River, about eight miles from Fort Duquesne. Enraged, Braddock ordered a senseless counterattack. In the end, nearly 70 percent of Braddock's troops were either killed or wounded, and Braddock himself was dead. The French remained in firm control of the Ohio valley.

French and Indian War

Britain's imperial war effort had hit rock bottom. No one in England or America seemed to possess the leadership necessary to drive the French from the Mississippi valley. Still, on May 18, 1756, Great Britain declared war on France, a conflict called the French and Indian War in America and the Seven Years' War in Europe.

William Pitt, the most powerful minister in the cabinet of George II, finally provided Great Britain with what it needed most, a forceful leader. Arrogant and conceited, Pitt nevertheless offered a bold, new imperial policy. Rather than fight great battles in Europe where France had the advantage, Pitt decided that the critical theater of the war would be in North America, where Britain and France were struggling for control of colonial markets and raw materials. His goal was clear; he was determined to expel the French from the continent, however great the cost.

To effect this ambitious scheme, Pitt took

personal command of the army and navy. He mapped strategy; he promoted young promising officers over the heads of their superiors. He convinced Parliament to pour millions of pounds into his imperial efforts, thus creating an enormous national debt that would soon haunt both Britain and its colonies.

To direct the grand campaign, Pitt selected two relatively obscure colonels, Jeffrey Amherst and James Wolfe. It was a masterful choice, one that soon proved sound. Forces under their direction captured Louisbourg on July 26, 1758, a victory that cut the Canadians' main supply line with France. Time was now on the side of the British. Two poor harvests, in 1756 and 1757, and a population too small to meet the military demands of the accelerated conflict, led to a desperate situation for the French empire in North America. Frontier

The British soundly defeated the French at Quebec in 1759 with superior strategy and force of arms in a battle that proved to be the climax of the French and Indian War. However, it cost the British the life of their brilliant commander, General James Wolfe.

forts began to fall; Fort Duquesne was abandoned in 1758. French and Indian troops retreated to Quebec and Montreal, surrendering key outposts at Ticonderoga, Crown Point, and Niagara as they withdrew.

The climax to a century of war came dramatically in September 1759. Wolfe, now a major general, assaulted Quebec, held by the brilliant French commander, the Marquis de Montcalm. It was a remarkable campaign, which saw Wolfe's men scale a cliff under the cover of darkness and launch a successful surprise attack at dawn on September 13, 1759. Both Wolfe and Montcalm were mortally wounded. When an aide informed Wolfe that the French had been routed, he sighed, "Now, God be praised, I will die in peace." One year later, Amherst accepted the final surrender of the French army at Montreal.

The Peace of Paris signed on February 10, 1763, almost fulfilled Pitt's grandiose dreams. Great Britain took possession of an empire that stretched around the globe. After a century-long struggle, the French had been driven from the mainland of North America, retaining only their sugar islands in the Caribbean. The treaty gave Britain title to Canada, Florida, and all the land east of the Mississippi River. The colonists were overjoyed. It was a time of good feelings and imperial pride.

The Seven Years' War made a deep impression upon American society. The military struggle had forced the colonists to cooperate on an unprecedented scale. It also drew them into closer contact with the mother country. They became aware of being part of a great empire, but in the very process of waging war, they acquired a more intimate sense of an America that lay beyond the plantation and the village. Moreover, the war trained a corps of American officers, people like George Washington, who learned from firsthand experience that the British were not invincible.

Forging an Identity

In 1754 John Dickinson, a young American, visited Great Britain on the eve of a parliamentary election. He looked forward to seeing and hearing the great English political leaders. What he saw, however, was the most corrupt sort of political activity. Vice had become vir-

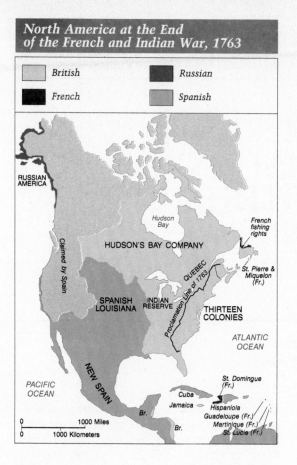

North America at the End of the French and Indian War, 1763

British
French
Russian
Spanish

RUSSIAN AMERICA

Hudson Bay

HUDSON'S BAY COMPANY

French fishing rights

Claimed by Spain

QUEBEC

St. Pierre & Miquelon (Fr.)

Proclamation Line of 1763

SPANISH LOUISIANA

INDIAN RESERVE

THIRTEEN COLONIES

ATLANTIC OCEAN

PACIFIC OCEAN

NEW SPAIN

St. Domingue (Fr.)

Cuba
Jamaica

Br.

Hispaniola
Guadeloupe (Fr.)
Martinique (Fr.)
St. Lucie (Fr.)

Br.

0   1000 Miles
0   1000 Kilometers

tuous in the sordid world of English society and politics. He left England disillusioned, but prouder than ever to be an American.

Dickinson's intellectual odyssey was not unusual. After 1760, other provincials, persons who had been attracted to Great Britain by the chance to advance their careers, denounced the luxury and corruption that seemed to have swept the mother country. Perhaps they resented being treated as cultural inferiors; perhaps they reflected the spirit of the Great Awakening. Whatever their personal motives, many colonial leaders had become convinced

that Britain's rulers threatened what one Marylander called "the reign of American freedom."

Recommended Reading

A well-written introduction to the topic of Anglo-American relations in the late colonial period is Richard Hofstadter, *America at 1750: A Social Portrait* (1971). For the wars of empire, see Howard H. Peckham, *The Colonial Wars, 1689–1762* (1964). The state of eighteenth-century religion is examined in Sydney E. Ahlstrom's encyclopedic *Religious History of the American People* (1972). A useful discussion of the revivals can be found in Edwin S. Gaustad, *Great Awakening in New England* (1957). Anyone curious about intellectual history should read Henry F. May, *The Enlightenment in America* (1976). The most imaginative analysis of eighteenth-century colonial politics is Bernard Bailyn, *The Origins of American Politics* (1968).

The growth of the American population in this period is traced in Carl Bridenbaugh, *Myths and Realities, Societies in the Colonial South* (1952); James T. Lemon, *The Best Poor Man's Country* (1972); and Gary B. Nash, *The Urban Crucible* (1979). The economic development of colonial America and England is discussed in Gary M. Walton and James F. Shepherd, *The Economic Rise of Early America* (1979).

The most engaging account of the imperial wars is Francis Parkman's nineteenth-century work, *France and England in North America*. More recent studies include Douglas E. Leach, *Arms for Empire: A Military History of the British Colonies in North America, 1607–1763* (1973).

Verner W. Crane, *Benjamin Franklin and a Rising People* (1952) is a good biography of the scientist/statesman. Several excellent editions of his *Autobiography* are available.

Eighteenth-century English politics is the subject of J. H. Plumb, *Sir Robert Walpole*, 2 vols. (1956–1960); Leonard W. Labaree, *Royal Government in America* (1930); Robert E. Brown, *Middle-Class Democracy and the Revolution in Massachusetts, 1691–1780* (1955); and J. R. Pole, *Political Representation* (1966).

chapter 5

THE AMERICAN REVOLUTION: FROM PROTEST TO INDEPENDENCE, 1763-1783

During the Revolutionary War, a captured British officer spent some time at the plantation of Colonel Thomas Mann Randolph, a leader of Virginia's gentry. The Englishman described with a note of disgust the arrival of three farmers who were members of the local militia—the way the militiamen drew chairs up to the fire, pulled off their muddy boots, and began spitting. Randolph explained that such behavior demonstrated "the spirit of independency" in America. Indeed, every American who "bore arms" during the Revolution considered himself as good as his neighbors.

This chance encounter illuminates the character of the American Revolution. The initial stimulus for rebellion came from the gentry—from the rich and wellborn. They voiced their unhappiness in public statements and in speeches before elected assemblies. However, soon they lost control as the revolutionary movement generated a momentum of its own. As relations with the mother country deteriorated, the traditional leaders of colonial society were forced to invite the common folk to join the protest—as rioters, as petitioners, and finally as soldiers. What had begun as a squabble among the gentry had been transformed into a mass movement, and as Randolph learned, once the common people had become involved in shaping the nation's destiny, they could never again be excluded.

The incident at Randolph's plantation reveals a second, often overlooked, aspect of the American Revolution. It involved a massive military commitment. If mud-covered Virginia militiamen had not been willing to stand up to seasoned British troops, to face the terror of the bayonet charge, independence would have remained a dream of intellectuals. Proportionate to the population, a greater percentage of Americans died in military service during the Revolution than in any war in American history, with the exception of the Civil War. Liberty to them was more than an abstraction studied by political theorists like Thomas Jefferson and John Adams, and those Americans who risked death and survived the ordeal saw new meaning in the concept of equality as well.

Imperial Crisis: Failure of Imagination

No one consciously set out in 1763 to achieve independence. The bonds of loyalty that had cemented the British empire dissolved slowly. At several points British rulers and American colonists could have compromised. Their failure to do so was the result of thousands of separate decisions, errors, and misunderstandings. The Revolution was, in fact, a complex series of events, full of unexpected turns, extraordinary creativity, and great personal sacrifice.

Ultimate responsibility for preserving the empire fell to George III, whose reign began in 1760. He was only twenty-two years old; had led a sheltered, loveless life; and was poorly educated. He displayed little understanding of the larger implications of government policy, and many people who knew him considered him dull-witted. Unfortunately, the king could not be ignored, and during a difficult period that demanded imagination, generosity, and wisdom, George muddled along as best he could.

Unlike the preceding Georges, George III decided to play an aggressive role in government. He selected as his chief minister the Earl of Bute, a Scot whose only qualification for office appeared to be his friendship with the young king and the young king's mother. The Whigs, a political faction that dominated Parliament, believed that George was attempting to turn back the clock, to reestablish a monarchy free from traditional constitutional restraints. George did not, in fact, harbor such arbitrary ambitions, but his actions threw customary political practices into doubt.

In 1763 Bute left office. What followed was a seven-year period of confusion, during which ministers came and went, often for no other reason than George's personal distaste. Because of this chronic instability, subministers, the minor bureaucrats who directed routine colonial affairs, did not know what was expected of them. In the absence of a long-range policy, the ministers showed more concern for

Despite his insecurity over an inadequate education, George III was determined to take over an active role in reigning over Parliament and the colonies.

their own future than for coping with the problems of empire-building.

The king does not bear the sole blame for England's loss of empire in the American colonies. The members of Parliament, the men who actually drafted the statutes that drove a wedge between the colonists and the mother country, failed to respond creatively to the challenge of events. They clung doggedly to the principle of parliamentary sovereignty, and when Americans questioned whether that legislative body in London should govern colonial affairs, parliamentary spokesmen provided no constructive basis for compromise. They refused to see a middle ground between the supreme authority of Parliament and total American independence.

Parliament's attitude was in part a product of ignorance. Few men active in English government had visited America. For those who attempted to follow colonial affairs, accurate information proved extremely difficult to obtain. One could not expect to receive an answer from America to a specific question in less than three months. As a result of the lag in communication between England and America, rumors sometimes passed for true accounts, and misunderstanding influenced the formulation of colonial policy.

American Perspective on Internal Politics

At the conclusion of the French and Indian War, it seemed inconceivable that the colonists would challenge the supremacy of Parliament. But the crisis in imperial relations that soon developed impelled the Americans first to define and then to defend principles that were rooted deeply in the colonial political culture.

For more than a century, the colonists' ideas about their role within the British empire had remained a vague, untested bundle of assumptions about personal liberties, property rights, and representative institutions. But by 1763 certain fundamental American beliefs had become clear. They accepted the authority of representative local assemblies to tax their constituents. But to declare that the House of Commons in London enjoyed the same right made no sense to them. Moreover, the colonists rejected the distinction that British officials sometimes made between taxes imposed directly on a person's estate and taxes on trade that could be passed on to consumers. Americans firmly believed that a tax was a tax by whatever name and that Parliament had no right to collect taxes on the American side of the Atlantic, especially since no Americans sat in Parliament.

Political thought in the colonies contained a strong moral component, one that British rulers and American Loyalists (people who sided with the king during the Revolution) never fully understood. The origins of this perspective on civil government are difficult to pinpoint but, certainly, the moral fervor of the Great Awakening and the reformist writings of the "Commonwealthmen" played a part (see Chapter 4). Whatever the intellectual sources may have been, colonists viewed *power* as extremely dangerous, unless it was countered by *virtue*.

Insistence upon civic virtue—sacrifice of self-interest to the public good—became the dominant theme of revolutionary political writing. American pamphleteers shared the outlook of those who regarded bad government not as human error, but as sin. They saw a host of external threats and plots—arbitrary taxation, standing armies, bishops sent over by the Church of England—all designed to crush American liberty. Popular writers seldom took a dispassionate, legalistic approach in their analysis of Anglo-American relations. They described events in conspiratorial terms, using language charged with emotion.

Colonial newspapers spread these ideas through a large, dispersed population. A majority of adult white males—a great majority in the northern colonies—were literate, and the number of journals in the country increased dramatically during the revolutionary period. The newspaper united the colonies, informing each colony about the political activities in the others, and provided the rhetoric that successfully roused ordinary folk to take up arms against Britain.

Eroding the Bonds of Empire: Challenge and Resistance

Following the Seven Years' War, more than 7000 British troops, members of the regular army, remained in North America. Their alleged purpose was to provide a buffer between Indians and frontiersmen and to preserve order in the newly conquered territories of Florida and Quebec. But not one person in the British government actually made the decision to

British Legislation and Colonial Reaction

Legislation	Date	Provisions	Colonial Reaction
Sugar Act	April 5, 1764	Imposition of duties on sugar, coffee, tea, wine, other imports; expanded jurisdiction of vice-admiralty courts	Several assemblies protest taxation for revenue
Stamp Act	March 22, 1765; repealed March 18, 1766	Printed documents (deeds, newspapers, marriage licenses, etc.) issued only on special stamped paper purchased from stamp distributors	Riots in cities; collectors forced to resign; Stamp Act Congress (October 1765)
Quartering Act	May 1765	Colonists must supply British troops with housing and other items (candles, salt, rum, etc.)	Protest in assemblies; New York Assembly punished for failure to comply (1767)
Declaratory Act	March 18, 1766	Parliament declares its sovereignty over the colonies "in all cases whatsoever"	Ignored in celebration over repeal of the Stamp Act
Townshend Revenue Acts	June 26, 29, July 2, 1767; all repealed except duty on tea, March 1770	New duties on glass, lead, paper, paints, tea; customs collections tightened in America	Nonimportation of British goods; assemblies protest; newspapers attack British policy
Tea Act	May 10, 1773	Parliament gives East India Company right to sell tea directly to Americans; some duties on tea reduced	Protests against favoritism shown to monopolistic company; tea destroyed in Boston (December 16, 1773)
Coercive Acts (Intolerable Acts)	March–June 1774	Closes port of Boston; restructures Massachusetts government; restricts town meetings; troops quartered in Boston; British officials accused of crimes sent to England or Canada for trial	Boycott of British goods; First Continental Congress convenes (September 1774)
Prohibitory Act	December 22, 1775	Declares British intention to coerce Americans into submission; embargo on American goods; American ships seized	Drives Continental Congress closer to decision for independence

keep an army in the colonies. The army was not recalled simply because of bureaucratic confusion and inertia.

The war had saddled Britain with a national debt so huge that over one half of the annual budget went to interest payments. A peacetime army, so far from the mother country, fueled the budgetary crisis. The growing financial burden weighed heavily on restive English taxpayers and sent government leaders scurrying in search of new sources of revenue.

For their part, colonists doubted the value of this very expensive army. First, British troops did not maintain peace effectively. This was demonstrated in 1763 when Ottawa Chief Pontiac, who had been allied with the French and hated the British, organized a general uprising along the western frontier. His warriors easily slipped by the redcoats and slew several thousand settlers. Second, the colonists resented the Proclamation of 1763 which attempted unsuccessfully to restrain Americans from moving into Indian lands west of the Appalachian Mountains, and they identified the hated policy with the British troops who guarded the frontier.

The task of reducing England's debt fell to George Grenville, the somewhat unimaginative chancellor of the exchequer who replaced Bute in 1763 as the king's first minister. He decided that the colonists would have to contribute to the maintenance of the army. The first bill he steered through Parliament was the Revenue Act of 1763, known as the Sugar Act.

This legislation represented a major break with the Navigation Acts that had governed the flow of colonial commerce for almost a century (see Chapter 3). The earlier acts were designed to force Americans to trade with the mother country; their primary purpose was not to raise money. The Sugar Act, on the other hand, was specifically designed to generate revenue. It imposed new import duties on sugar, coffee, wines, and other imports, instituted tougher customs collection methods, and expanded the jurisdiction of the vice-admiralty courts. The act also included provisions aimed at curbing colonial smuggling of molasses and bribery of customs officials.

American reaction came swiftly. James Otis, a fiery orator from Massachusetts, exclaimed that the legislation deprived Americans of "the rights of assessing their own taxes." Petitions of protest involved no violence, but to Grenville and persons of his temperament, even petitions smacked of ingratitude. After all, they reasoned, had not the mother country saved the Americans from the French? But Grenville's perspective overlooked the contribution of colonial staples such as rice and tobacco to the prosperity of the mother country. Moreover, American markets helped sustain British industry (see Chapter 4). The colonists saw no justification for Grenville's aggressive new policy now that the military emergency had passed.

The Stamp Act: A Political Crisis

Even before the Sugar Act had gone into effect, Grenville put the final touches on a second revenue measure, the Stamp Act. Although a few members of Parliament warned that the Americans would bitterly resent the act, the majority of the House of Commons supported the legislation. Specifically, the Stamp Act required printed documents—such as legal contracts, newspapers, and marriage licenses—to bear revenue stamps purchased from royal stamp distributors. The act was to go into effect November 1, 1765.

Word of the Stamp Act reached America by May, and the colonial reaction against it was swift. In Virginia's House of Burgesses, eloquent young Patrick Henry introduced five resolutions protesting the act. He timed his move carefully. It was late in the session; many of the more conservative burgesses had already departed for their plantations. Even then, Henry's resolves declaring that Virginians had the right to tax themselves as they alone saw fit passed by narrow margins.

The Virginia Resolves might have remained a local matter had it not been for the colonial press. Newspapers throughout America printed Henry's resolutions. The newspaper accounts, however, were not always accurate. Some accounts said that all five of Henry's resolutions had passed, when, in fact, the fifth resolution, which announced that Britain's actions were "illegal, unconstitutional, and unjust," had been stricken from the legislative records. Several newspapers even printed two resolutions that Henry had not dared to introduce. The result of this misunderstanding, of course, was that the Virginians appeared to have taken an extremely radical position on the issue of the supremacy of Parliament, one that other Americans now trumpeted before their own assemblies.

Not to be outdone by Virginia, the Massachusetts assembly in June proposed a general meeting to protest Grenville's policy. Nine colonies sent representatives to the Stamp Act Congress that convened in New York City in October 1765. The delegates drafted petitions to the king and Parliament which restated the colonists' belief "that no taxes should be imposed on them, but with their own consent, given personally, or by their representatives." There was no mention of independence or disloyalty to the Crown.

Resistance to the Stamp Act soon moved from assembly petitions to mass protests in the streets. In Boston, the Sons of Liberty burned the local stamp distributor in effigy. The violent outbursts of these mobs frightened colonial leaders; yet the evidence suggests that they encouraged the lower classes to intimidate royal officials. After 1765, it was impossible for either royal governors or patriot leaders to take the common folk for granted.

By November 1, 1765, stamp distributors in almost every American port had publicly resigned, and without distributors, the hated revenue stamps could not be sold. The Sons of Liberty convinced colonial merchants to boycott British goods. Grenville had fallen from power. His replacement as first lord of the treasury, Lord Rockingham, envisioned a prosperous empire founded upon an expanding commerce, with local government under the gentle guidance of Parliament. Grenville, now simply a member of Parliament, urged a tough policy toward America, but important men, such as William Pitt, defended the colonists' position. Finally, Rockingham called for the repeal of the Stamp Act. On February 22, 1766, the House of Commons complied.

Repeal failed to restore imperial harmony. Lest its retreat on the Stamp Act be interpreted as weakness, the House of Commons passed the Declaratory Act (March 1766), a shrill defense of parliamentary supremacy over the Americans "in all cases whatsoever." The colonists' insistence upon no taxation without representation failed to impress British rulers. Clearly, if America thought it won the Stamp Act battle, Parliament was announcing that it fully expected to win the war.

In America, too, attitudes hardened. Respect for imperial officeholders as well as Parliament had diminished. Suddenly, royal governors, customs collectors, and military personnel appeared alien, as if their interests were not those of the people over whom they exercised authority. Indeed, it is testimony to the Americans' lingering loyalty to the British Crown and constitution that rebellion did not occur in 1765.

Townshend's Boast: Tea and Sovereignty

Rockingham's ministry soon gave way to a government headed once again by William Pitt, now the Earl of Chatham. The aging Pitt suffered horribly from gout, and during his long absences from London, Charles Townshend, his chancellor of the exchequer, made important political decisions. Townshend's mouth often outran his mind, and in January 1767 he pleased the House of Commons by announcing that he knew a way to obtain revenue from the Americans.

His plan turned out to be a grab bag of duties on American imports of paper, glass, paint, and tea, collectively known as the Townshend Revenue Acts (May 1767). To collect these duties he created an American Board of Customs Commissioners, a body based in Boston and supported by reorganized vice-admiralty courts in port cities.

Americans were no more willing to pay Townshend's duties than they had been to buy Grenville's stamps. In major ports, the Sons of

Liberty organized boycotts of British goods. Imported finery came to symbolize England's political corruption. Americans prided themselves on wearing homespun clothes, a badge of simplicity and virtue. Women were ardent supporters of the boycott, holding public spinning bees to produce more homespun.

On February 11, 1768, the Massachusetts House of Representatives drafted a circular letter, which it then sent to other colonial assemblies. The letter requested suggestions on how best to thwart the Townshend Acts. Although the letter was mild, Lord Hillsborough, England's secretary for American Affairs, took offense. He called the letter a "seditious paper" and ordered the Massachusetts representatives to rescind it; the legislators refused.

Suddenly, the circular letter became a *cause célèbre*. When the royal governor of Massachusetts dissolved the House of Representatives, the other colonies demonstrated their support of the Bay Colony by taking up the circular letter in their assemblies. Hillsborough promptly dissolved more colonial legislatures. Parliament's challenge had brought about the very results it most wanted to avoid: a basis for intercolonial communication and a growing sense among the colonists of the righteousness of their position.

The Boston "Massacre"

In October 1768 British rulers made another critical mistake. The issue was the army. In part to intimidate colonial troublemakers, the ministry stationed 4000 regular troops around Boston. The armed strangers camped on Boston Commons, sometimes shouting obscenities at citizens passing the site. To make relations worse, the redcoats—soldiers who were ill-treated and underpaid—competed in their spare time for jobs with local dockworkers and artisans.

When citizens questioned why the army had been sent to a peaceful city, pamphleteers claimed that the soldiers in Boston were simply another phase of a conspiracy originally conceived by the Earl of Bute to oppress Americans, to take away their liberties, and to col-

Outrage over the Boston Massacre was fanned by the propaganda of this etching by Paul Revere, which showed British redcoats firing on unarmed civilians.

lect illegal revenues. Grenville, Hillsborough, Townshend, were all, supposedly, part of the plot. To Americans raised on the political theories of the Commonwealthmen, the pattern of tyranny seemed obvious.

Colonists had no difficulty interpreting the violence that erupted in Boston on March 5, 1770. In the gathering dusk of that afternoon, young boys and street toughs used rocks and snowballs to bombard a small isolated patrol outside the offices of the hated customs commissioners in King Street. The details of this incident are obscure, but it appears that as the mob grew and became more threatening, the troops panicked and fired, leaving five Americans dead.

Pamphleteers promptly labeled the incident a "massacre." The victims were seen as martyrs. To the propagandists, what actually happened mattered little. Their job was to inflame emotions; they performed their work well.

Confronted with such an intense reaction and with the possibility of massive armed resistance, Crown officials wisely moved the army to an island in Boston Harbor.

At this critical moment, the king's new first minister restored a measure of tranquility. Lord North, congenial, well-meaning, but not very talented, became the first minister in 1770, and for the next twelve years—indeed, throughout most of the American crisis—he managed to retain his office. His secret formula seems to have been an ability to get along with George III and to build an effective majority in Parliament.

One of North's first recommendations to Parliament was the repeal of the ill-conceived Townshend duties. Not only had the duties enraged Americans, they hurt British manufacturers by encouraging Americans to develop their own industries. Parliament responded by dropping all the duties with the notable exception of tea. But Parliament still maintained that it held total supremacy over the colonies. For a time, Americans drew back from the precipice of confrontation, frightened by the events of the past two years.

An Interlude of Order, 1770–1773

For a brief moment, American colonists and British officials put aside their recent animosities. Merchants returned to familiar patterns of trade, and American indebtedness grew. Even in Massachusetts, the people decided that they could accept their new royal governor, an American, Thomas Hutchinson.

But appearances were deceiving. The bonds of imperial loyalty remained fragile, and even as Lord North attempted to win the colonists' trust, Crown officials in America created new strains. Customs commissioners abused their powers of search and seizure and in the process lined their own pockets. Any failure to abide by the Navigation Acts, no matter how minor, could bring confiscation of ship and cargo.

The commissioners were not only corrupt, they were also foolish. They harassed the wealthy and powerful as well as the common folk. The commissioners' actions drove members of the colonial ruling class, men like John Hancock of Boston, into opposition to the king's government. Eventually, the commissioners' greed brought the colonists closer together.

Samuel Adams (1722–1803) refused to accept the notion that the repeal of the Townshend duties had secured American liberty. During the early 1770s, while colonial leaders turned to other matters, Adams kept the cause alive with a drumfire of publicity. He never allowed the people of Boston to forget the many real and alleged wrongs perpetrated by the Crown. Adams was a genuine revolutionary, seemingly obsessed with the need to preserve civic virtue and moral values in the conduct of public affairs. With each new attempt by Parliament to assert its supremacy over the colonists, more and more Bostonians listened to what Adams had to say. By 1772 Adams had broad support for the formation of a committee of correspondence to communicate grievances to villagers throughout Massachusetts. People in other colonies soon copied his idea and established intercolonial committees as well. It was a brilliant stroke; Adams developed a structure of political cooperation completely independent of royal government.

The Boston Tea Party Provokes Punishment

In May 1773 Parliament resumed its old tricks. It passed the Tea Act, a strange piece of legislation that Parliament thought the colonists would welcome. The statute was designed to save the floundering East India Company, not to raise revenue. It allowed the company to ship tea directly to America, thereby eliminating the colonial middlemen and permitting Americans to purchase tea at bargain rates. The plan, however, was flawed. First, since the Townshend duty on tea remained in effect, this new act seemed like a devious way to win popular support for Parliament's right to tax the colonists without representation. Second, the act threatened to undercut tea smugglers and powerful mercantile groups in Boston.

Americans soon registered their protest. Boston took the most dramatic stand. Although colonists in Philadelphia and New York City turned back tea ships before they could unload, in Boston Governor Hutchinson would not permit the vessels to return to England. Local patriots would not let them unload. So the ships sat in Boston Harbor crammed with tea until the night of December 16, 1773. That night a group of men in Indian dress boarded the ships and pitched 340 chests of tea worth £10,000 into the water.

When news of the Tea Party reached London in January 1774, the North ministry was stunned. The people of Boston had treated parliamentary supremacy with utter contempt, and British rulers saw no humor whatsoever in the destruction of private property by subjects of the Crown dressed in costume. To quell such rebelliousness, Parliament passed a series of laws called the Coercive Acts. (In America they were referred to as the Intolerable Acts.) This legislation (1) closed the port of Boston until the city fully compensated the East India Company for the lost tea; (2) restructured the Massachusetts government by transforming the upper house from an elective to an appointed body and restricting the number of legal town meetings to one a year; (3) allowed the royal governor to transfer British officials arrested for offenses committed in the line of duty to England or Canada, where there was little likelihood they would be convicted; and (4) authorized the army to quarter troops wherever they were needed, even if this required the compulsory requisition of uninhabited private buildings. George III enthusiastically supported this tough policy; he appointed General Thomas Gage to serve as the colony's new royal governor.

This sweeping series of laws confirmed the colonists' worst fears. The vindictiveness of the Acts strengthened the influence of men like Samuel Adams and undermined the influence of colonial moderates. In Parliament, a saddened Edmund Burke, one of America's few remaining friends, warned his countrymen that the Acts could lead to war.

In the midst of this constitutional crisis, Parliament announced plans to establish a new civil government for the Canadian province of Quebec (Quebec Act, June 22, 1774), which extended the province's boundaries all the way south to the Ohio River and west to the Mississippi. The act made no provision for an elective assembly, but it granted French-speaking Roman Catholics religious and political rights and a large voice in local affairs. These measures were seen by Americans as a denial of *their* rights to settle and trade in this fast-developing region.

Americans everywhere rallied to Massachusetts' defense. Few persons advocated independence, but they could not remain passive while Boston was destroyed. They sent food and money and, during the autumn of 1774, reflected more deeply than ever on what it meant to be a colonist in the British Empire. And the more they reflected, the more they objected to the idea of the sovereignty of Parliament.

Decision for Independence

Samuel Adams had prepared Americans for this moment. Something had to be done. But what? The committees of correspondence endorsed a call for a continental congress, a gathering of fifty-five elected delegates from twelve colonies (Georgia sent none but agreed to support the action taken). This momentous gathering convened in Philadelphia on September 5, 1774, and included such respected leaders as John and Samuel Adams, Patrick Henry, Richard Henry Lee, and George Washington.

But the delegates were strangers to one another. They knew little about the customs and values, the geography and economy of Britain's other provinces. Differences of opinion soon surfaced. Delegates from the Middle Colonies wanted to proceed with caution, but before they knew what had happened, Samuel Adams maneuvered these moderates into a position far more radical than they found comfortable. Boston's master politician engineered congres-

The American Revolution: From Protest to Independence

■ The Battle of Lexington (1830). *The militia of Lexington gathered on the village green in response to Paul Revere's midnight alarm. No one knows who fired the first shot that led to the death of eight Americans.*

sional commendation of the Suffolk Resolves, a bold statement drawn up in Suffolk County, Massachusetts, that encouraged Americans to resist the Coercive Acts forcibly.

The tone of the meeting was set. The more radical delegates carried the day. They agreed to form an "Association" to halt all commerce with the mother country until Parliament repealed the Intolerable Acts. They also agreed to meet in the coming year. Meanwhile, in London, George III told his confidants, "blows must decide whether [New England governments] are to be subject to this country or independent."

"Shots Heard Around the World"

Before Congress reconvened, "blows" fell at Lexington and Concord, two small farm villages in eastern Massachusetts. On the evening of April 18, 1775, General Gage dispatched troops from Boston to seize rebel supplies. Paul Revere, a renowned silversmith and active patriot, warned the colonists that the redcoats were coming. The militia of Lexington, a collection of ill-trained farmers, decided to stand on the village green the following morning, April 19, as the British soldiers passed on the road to Concord. No one planned to fight, but in a moment of confusion someone (probably a colonist) fired; the redcoats discharged a volley, and eight Americans lay dead.

Word of the incident spread rapidly. "Minutemen," special companies of Massachusetts militia prepared to respond instantly to military emergencies, went into action. The redcoats found nothing of significance in Concord, and turned back to Boston. The long march back became a rout; the minutemen swarmed all over the redcoats. On June 17 colonial militiamen again held their own against seasoned troops at the Battle of Bunker Hill (actually Breed's Hill). The British finally captured the hill, but after this costly "victory" in which he lost 10 percent of his troops, Gage took the American militiamen more seriously.

The Second Continental Congress Directs the War Effort

Members of the Second Continental Congress gathered in Philadelphia in May 1775. They faced an awesome responsibility. British government in the mainland colonies had almost ceased to function; Americans were fighting redcoats; and the country desperately needed strong central leadership. Congress provided that leadership. The delegates formed a Continental army, appointed George Washington its commander, purchased military supplies, and, to pay for them, issued paper money. But they refused to take the final step—independence.

Indecision drove John Adams nearly mad with frustration. He and other like-minded delegates ranted against their timid colleagues. Haste, however, would have been a terrible mistake, for many Americans were not convinced that independence was either necessary or desirable. If Congress had moved too quickly, it might have faced charges of extremism and thereby lost mass support for its cause.

The British government appeared intent upon transforming colonial moderates into angry rebels. In December 1775 Parliament passed the Prohibitory Act, declaring war on American commerce. The British navy blockaded colonial ports and seized American ships on the high seas. Lord North also hired German mercenaries to put down the rebellion. And in America, royal governors like Lord Dunmore further undermined the possibility of reconciliation by urging Virginia's slaves to take up arms against their masters.

Thomas Paine (1737–1809) pushed the colonists even closer to independence. In January 1776, Paine, a recent arrival from England, published a pamphlet entitled *Common Sense*. In this powerful democratic manifesto, Paine urged the colonists to resist "tyranny and false systems of government." The essay became an instant best-seller. More than 120,000 copies were sold in the first three months after publication. *Common Sense* systematically stripped kingship of historical and theological justification. Contrary to traditional English belief, Paine said, monarchs could and did commit many wrongs. George III was simply a "royal brute," who by his arbitrary behavior had surrendered his claim to the colonists' obedience.

Paine's greatest contribution to the revolutionary cause was persuading common folk to sever their ties with Great Britain. "Europe, and not England," he exclaimed, "is the parent country of America. This new world hath been the asylum for the persecuted lovers of civil and religious liberty from *every part* of Europe." The time had come for the colonists to form an independent republic. "We have it in our power," Paine wrote in one of his most

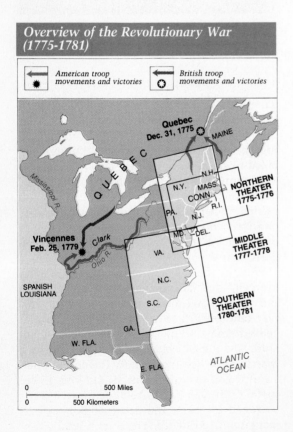

Overview of the Revolutionary War (1775-1781)

American troop movements and victories

British troop movements and victories

Quebec Dec. 31, 1775

MAINE

QUEBEC

N.H.
N.Y. MASS.
CONN.
PA. R.I.
N.J.

NORTHERN THEATER 1775-1776

MD. DEL.

MIDDLE THEATER 1777-1778

Vincennes Feb. 25, 1779

Clark

Ohio R.

VA.

Mississippi R.

N.C.

SPANISH LOUISIANA

S.C.

SOUTHERN THEATER 1780-1781

GA.

W. FLA.

E. FLA.

ATLANTIC OCEAN

0   500 Miles

0   500 Kilometers

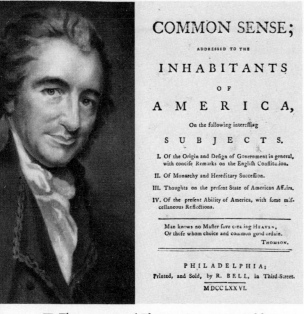

COMMON SENSE;

ADDRESSED TO THE

INHABITANTS

OF

AMERICA,

On the following interesting

SUBJECTS.

I. Of the Origin and Design of Government in general,
with concise Remarks on the English Constitution.

II. Of Monarchy and Hereditary Succession.

III. Thoughts on the present State of American Affairs.

IV. Of the present Ability of America, with some mis-
cellaneous Reflections.

Man knows no Master save creating Heaven,
Or those whom choice and common good ordain.
THOMSON.

PHILADELPHIA;

Printed, and Sold, by R. BELL, in Third-Street.

MDCCLXXVI.

The message of Thomas Paine's pamphlet, Common Sense (title page shown), was easy to follow. His stark phrases calling for "The Free and Independent States of America" reverberated in people's hearts and minds.

moving statements, "to begin the world over again . . . the birthday of a new world is at hand."

On July 2, 1776, after a long and tedious debate, Congress finally voted for independence. The motion passed; twelve states *for*, none *against*. Thomas Jefferson, a young Virginia lawyer and planter who enjoyed a reputation as a graceful writer, drafted a formal declaration that was accepted two days later with only minor alterations. Much of the Declaration of Independence consisted of a list of specific grievances against George III and his government. But the document's enduring fame rests upon statements of principle that are tested anew in each generation of Americans; that "all men are created equal," that they are endowed with certain rights, among which are "life, liberty, and the pursuit of happiness," and that governments are formed to protect these rights.

War for Independence

Only fools and visionaries were optimistic about America's prospects of winning independence in 1776. The Americans had taken on a formidable military power whose population was perhaps four times greater than their own. Britain also possessed a strong industrial base, a well-trained regular army supplemented by thousands of hired German troops (Hessians), and a navy that dominated the world's oceans. Many British officers had battlefield experience. They already knew what the Americans would slowly learn, that waging war requires great discipline, money, and sacrifice.

The British government entered the conflict fully confident that it could beat the Americans. Lord North and his colleagues regarded the war as a police action. They anticipated that a mere show of armed force would intimidate the upstart colonists. Humble the rebels in Boston, they reasoned, and Americans will abandon independence like rats fleeing a burning ship.

As later events demonstrated, of course, Britain had become involved in an impossible military situation, somewhat analogous to that in which the United States found itself in Vietnam. Three separate elements neutralized advantages held by the larger power over its adversary. First, the British had to transport men and supplies across the Atlantic, a logistic challenge of unprecedented complexity. Second, America was too vast to be conquered by conventional military methods. Redcoats might gain control over the major port cities, but as long as the Continental army remained intact, the rebellion continued. And third, British strategists never appreciated the depth of the Americans' commitment to a political ideology. Unlike the military forces in traditional eighteenth-century European wars, Americans fought for liberty, not for money or because the military was their vocation.

During the earliest months of rebellion, American soldiers—especially those of New England—suffered no lack of confidence. Indeed, they interpreted their engagements at Concord and Bunker Hill as evidence that brave, yeoman farmers could lick British regulars on any battlefield. George Washington spent the first years of the war disabusing the colonists of this foolishness. As he had learned during the French and Indian War, military success depended upon careful planning, endless drill, and tough discipline.

Washington insisted upon organizing a regular, well-trained field army. He rejected the idea of waging a guerrilla war. He recognized that the Continental army served not only as a fighting force but also as a symbol of the republican cause. Its very existence would sustain American hopes, and so long as the army survived, American agents could plausibly solicit foreign aid. This thinking shaped Washington's cautious wartime strategy; he studiously avoided any "general actions" in which the Continental army might be destroyed.

If the commander in chief was correct about the army, however, he failed to comprehend the importance of local militia. These scattered, almost amateur, military units seldom altered the outcome of a battle, but they did maintain control over large areas of the country not directly affected by the British army. Throughout the war, they compelled men and women who would rather have remained neutral to support actively the American effort. Without their local political coercion, Washington's task would have been considerably more difficult.

Early Disasters: "Times That Try Men's Souls"

After the embarrassing losses in Massachusetts, the king appointed General Sir William Howe to replace the ill-fated Gage. British rulers now understood that a simple police action would not be sufficient to crush the American rebellion. Howe promptly evacuated Boston—an untenable strategic position—and on July 3, 1776, his forces stormed Staten Island in New York harbor. From this central position, he hoped to cut off New Englanders from the rest of America.

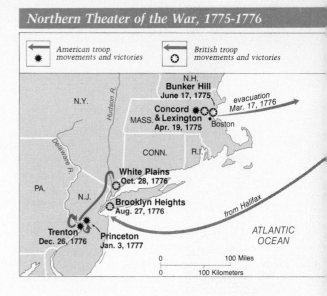

Northern Theater of the War, 1775-1776

American troop movements and victories

British troop movements and victories

N.Y.

Hudson R.

Delaware R.

N.H.

Bunker Hill June 17, 1775

Concord & Lexington Apr. 19, 1775

MASS. Boston

evacuation Mar. 17, 1776

CONN.

R.I.

White Plains Oct. 28, 1776

PA.

N.J.

Brooklyn Heights Aug. 27, 1776

from Halifax

ATLANTIC OCEAN

Trenton Dec. 26, 1776

Princeton Jan. 3, 1777

0   100 Miles

0   100 Kilometers

When Washington learned that the British were digging in at New York, he transferred many of his inexperienced soldiers to Long Island where they suffered a serious defeat (August 26, 1776). Howe drove the Continental army across the Hudson River into New Jersey, but he failed to annihilate Washington's entire army. Nevertheless, the Americans were on the run, and in the fall of 1776, contemporaries predicted that the rebels would soon capitulate.

His swift victories in New York and New Jersey persuaded General Howe that few Americans enthusiastically supported independence. He issued a general pardon, therefore, to anyone who would swear allegiance to George III. More than 3000 Americans responded to Howe's peaceful overtures. However, the pardon plan eventually failed partly because Howe's soldiers and officers regarded loyal Americans as inferior provincials, an attitude that did little to promote good relations, and partly because the rebel militia often retaliated against Americans who had deserted the patriots' cause.

In December 1776, Washington's bedraggled army retreated across the Delaware River into Pennsylvania. American prospects appeared bleaker than at any other time during the war.

"These are the times that try men's souls," Tom Paine wrote in a pamphlet entitled *American Crisis.* "The summer soldier and the sunshine patriot will, in this crisis, shrink from the service of their country, but he that stands it *now* deserves . . . love and thanks of man and woman." Before winter, Washington determined to attempt one last desperate stroke.

Howe played into Washington's hands. The British army was strung out across New Jersey. On the night of December 25, Continental soldiers slipped over the ice-filled Delaware River and at Trenton took 900 sleeping Hessian mercenaries by complete surprise. Cheered by success, Washington returned a second time to Trenton, but on this occasion a large British force under Lord Cornwallis trapped the Americans. Washington secretly, by night, marched his little army around Cornwallis' left flank. On January 3, 1777, the Americans surprised a British garrison at Princeton. Having regained their confidence, Washington's forces then went into winter quarters. The British, fearful of losing any more outposts, consolidated their troops, thus leaving much of the state in the hands of the patriot militia.

Victory in a Year of Defeat

In 1777 England's chief military strategist, Lord George Germain, still perceived the war in conventional European terms. He believed that England could achieve a complete victory by crushing Washington's army in a major battle. Unfortunately, the Continental forces proved extremely elusive, and while one British army vainly tried to corner Washington in Pennsylvania, another was forced to surrender in the forests of upstate New York.

In the summer of 1777 General John Burgoyne marched south from Canada determined to clear the Hudson Valley of rebel resistance. He intended to join Howe's army, which was to come up to Albany, thereby cutting New England off from the other states. Burgoyne moved slowly, weighed down by a German band, thirty carts filled with the general's liquor and belongings, and 2000 dependents and

camp followers. The campaign was a disaster. American military units cut the enemy force apart in the deep woods north of Albany, and overwhelmed Burgoyne's German mercenaries at Bennington. After it became clear that Howe could provide no relief, the haughty Burgoyne was forced to surrender 5800 men to the American General Horatio Gates at Saratoga (October 17).

General Howe could provide no support to Burgoyne because about the time Burgoyne left Canada, Howe quite unexpectedly decided to move his main army from New York City to Philadelphia, trying to devise a way to destroy Washington's forces. The British troops sailed to the head of the Chesapeake Bay and then marched north to Philadelphia. Washington's troops obstructed the enemy's progress, but they could not stop the British from entering the city on September 26, 1777.

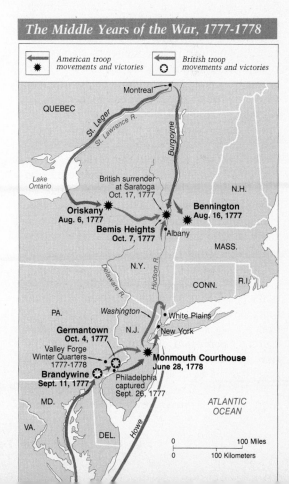

The Middle Years of the War, 1777-1778

American troop movements and victories

British troop movements and victories

Montreal

QUEBEC

St. Leger

St. Lawrence R.

Burgoyne

Lake Ontario

British surrender at Saratoga Oct. 17, 1777

N.H.

Oriskany Aug. 6, 1777

Bennington Aug. 16, 1777

Bemis Heights Oct. 7, 1777

Albany

MASS.

Delaware R.

N.Y.

Hudson R.

CONN.

R.I.

PA.

Washington

White Plains

Germantown Oct. 4, 1777

N.J.

New York

Valley Forge Winter Quarters 1777-1778

Monmouth Courthouse June 28, 1778

Brandywine Sept. 11, 1777

Philadelphia captured Sept. 26, 1777

Howe

MD.

ATLANTIC OCEAN

VA.

DEL.

0   100 Miles

0   100 Kilometers

Lest these defeats discourage Congress and the American people, Washington attempted one last battle before the onset of winter. In a curious engagement at Germantown (October 4), beset by bad luck and confusion, the Americans launched a major counterattack on a fog-covered battlefield, but just at the moment when success seemed assured, the Americans broke off the fight. A discouraged Continental army dug in for the winter at Valley Forge, twenty miles outside of Philadelphia, where camp diseases took 2500 American lives.

The French Alliance

Even before the Americans declared their independence, agents of the government of Louis XVI began to explore ways to aid the colonists, not so much because the French monarchy favored the republican cause, but because it hoped to avenge its defeat in the Seven Years' War and lessen the power of Britain. During the early months of the Revolution the French covertly sent tons of essential military supplies to the Americans, but refused to recognize American independence or sign an outright military alliance with the rebels. The international stakes were too great for the king to openly back a cause that had little chance of success.

The American victory at Saratoga convinced the French that the rebels had formidable forces and were serious in their resolve. Meanwhile, in Paris, American representative Benjamin Franklin hinted that Congress might accept a recently tendered British peace overture. Hence, if the French wanted the war to continue, if they really wanted to strike at their old rival, then they had to formally recognize the independence of the United States.

The stratagem paid off handsomely. On February 6, 1778, the French presented American representatives with two separate treaties. The first, called the Treaty of Amity and Commerce, established commercial relations between France and the United States. It tacitly accepted the existence of a new, independent republic. The Treaty of Alliance was even more generous. In the event that France and

Chronology

1763	Peace of Paris ends the Seven Years' War
1764	Parliament passes Sugar Act to collect American revenue
1765	Stamp Act receives support of House of Commons (March)
	Stamp Act Congress meets in New York City (October)
1766	Stamp Act repealed the same day that Declaratory Act becomes law (March 18)
1767	Townshend Revenue Acts stir American anger (June–July)
1768	Massachusetts assembly refuses to rescind circular letter (February)
1770	Parliament repeals all Townshend duties except one on tea (March)
	British troops "massacre" Boston civilians (March)
1772	Samuel Adams forms committee of correspondence
1773	Lord North's government passes Tea Act (May)
	Bostonians hold Tea Party (December)
1774	Parliament punishes Boston with Coercive Acts (March–June)
	First Continental Congress convenes (September)
1775	Patriots take stand at Lexington and Concord (April)
	Second Continental Congress gathers (May)
	Americans hold their own at Bunker Hill (June)
1776	Congress votes for independence; Declaration of Independence is signed
	British defeat Washington at Long Island (August)
	Americans score victory at Trenton (December)
1777	General Burgoyne surrenders at Saratoga (October)
1778	French treaties recognize independence of the United States (February)
1780	British take Charleston (May)
1781	Washington forces Cornwallis to surrender at Yorktown (October)
1783	Peace treaty signed (September)
	British evacuate New York City (November)

England went to war (they did so on June 14), the French agreed to reject any peace initiative until Britain recognized American independence. The Americans pledged that they would not sign a separate peace with Britain without first informing their new ally. Amazingly, France made no claim to Canada or any territory east of the Mississippi River.

French intervention instantly transformed British military strategy. What had been a colonial rebellion suddenly became a world conflict, a continuation of the great wars for empire of the late seventeenth century (see Chapter 4). Scarce military resources, especially newer fighting ships, had to be diverted from the American theater to guard the English Channel. England realized that the French navy posed a serious challenge to the overextended British fleet.

The Final Campaign

British General Henry Clinton replaced Howe, who resigned after the battle of Saratoga. As a subordinate officer, Clinton was imaginative, but as commander of British forces in America, his resolute self-confidence suddenly dissolved. Perhaps he feared failure? Whatever the explanation for his vacillation, Clinton's record in America was little better than Howe's or Gage's.

Military strategists calculated that Britain's last chance of winning the war lay in the southern colonies, a region largely untouched in the early years of fighting. They believed that with proper support and encouragement the Loyalists in Georgia and South Carolina would take up arms for the Crown. The southern strategy devised by Germain and Clinton in 1779 turned the war into a bitter guerrilla conflict, and during the last months of battle, British officers worried that their search for an easy victory had inadvertently opened a Pandora's box of uncontrollable partisan furies.

The southern campaign opened in the spring of 1780. Savannah had already fallen, and Clinton reckoned that if the British could take Charleston, they would be able to control the entire South. Clinton and his second in command, General Cornwallis, gradually encircled the city, and on May 12, the six thousand-man American army in Charleston surrendered.

The defeat took Congress by surprise, and without making proper preparations, it dispatched a second army to South Carolina under Horatio Gates, the hero of Saratoga. He, too, failed. At Camden, Cornwallis outmaneuvered the raw American recruits (August 16). Poor Gates galloped from the scene and did not stop until he reached Hillsboro, North Carolina, two hundred miles away.

Even at this early stage of the southern campaign, the savagery of partisan warfare had become evident. Loyalist raiders plundered or occasionally killed neighbors against whom they harbored ancient grudges. Men who supported independence or who had merely fallen victim to the Loyalist guerrillas bided their time. On October 7 at King's Mountain, North Carolina, they struck back against a force of

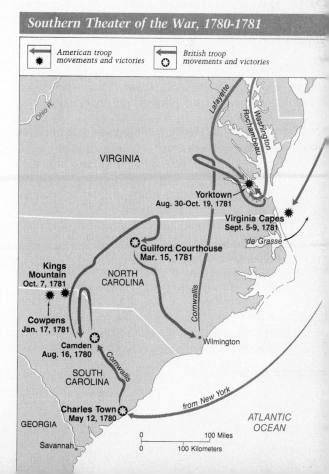

Southern Theater of the War, 1780-1781

■ *With the aid of the French fleet by sea and well-trained French troops on land, Washington and his lieutenants forced Cornwallis to surrender at Yorktown, thus ending the Revolutionary War.*

Loyalists and British regulars who had strayed too far from base. This was the most vicious fighting of the Revolution; the Americans gave no quarter.

Cornwallis, badly confused and poorly supported, proceeded to squander his strength senselessly chasing American forces across the Carolinas in the winter and early spring of 1781. When he did engage a freshly formed army under the command of Nathanael Greene, the most capable general on Washington's staff, Cornwallis was outmaneuvered and outfought at Cowpens and Guilford Courthouse. His army's strength sapped, Cornwallis pushed north into Virginia, planning apparently to establish a base of operations on the coast.

He selected Yorktown, a sleepy tobacco market town located on a peninsula bounded by the York and James rivers. Washington watched these maneuvers closely. The canny Virginia planter knew this territory intimately, and he sensed that Cornwallis had made a serious blunder. When Washington learned that the French fleet could gain temporary dominance in the Chesapeake Bay, he rushed south from New Jersey. With him marched thousands of well-trained French troops commanded by the Comte de Rochambeau; they were joined along the way by a sizable contingent of forces under the Marquis de Lafayette. All the pieces fell into place. The French admiral, Comte de Grasse, cut Cornwallis off from the sea, while Washington and his lieutenants encircled the British on the land. On October 19, 1781, Cornwallis surrendered his entire army of 6000 men. The Continental army had completed its mission; the task of securing independence now rested in the hands of American diplomats.

The Losers: The American Loyalists

The war lasted longer than anyone had predicted in 1776. While the nation won its independence, many Americans paid a terrible price. Indeed, a large number of men and women decided that however much they had loved colonial society, they could not accept the new government.

No one knows for certain how many Americans supported the Crown during the Revolution. But more than 100,000 men and women permanently left America. Although a number of these exiles had served as British officeholders, they came from all ranks and sections of society—farmers, merchants, tradesmen. The

■ *The fate of the Tories was an unhappy one. The patriots meted out harsh punishments to those who did not flee to England or Canada.*

wealthier exiles went to London and begged for pensions from the king. Others relocated in Canada or the West Indies.

The Loyalists were caught in a difficult squeeze. The British did not trust them; after all, they were Americans. Nor could they trust the British, who after urgently soliciting their support, left them exposed to rebel retaliation. In England, the exiles found themselves treated as second-class citizens. Embittered and unwanted in America, they often found themselves just as embittered and unwanted in London.

Americans who actively supported independence saw these people as traitors. According to one patriot, "A Tory [Loyalist] is a thing whose head is in England, its body in America, and its neck ought to be stretched." In many states revolutionary governments confiscated Loyalist property. Some Loyalists were beaten, and a few were even executed. Long after the victorious Americans turned their attentions to the business of building a new republic, Loyalists remembered a comfortable, ordered world that had been lost forever at Yorktown. Theirs was a sad, often lonely, fate.

Winning the Peace

Congress appointed a splendid delegation to negotiate a peace treaty: Benjamin Franklin, John Adams, and John Jay. According to their official instructions, they were to insist only upon the recognition of the independence of the United States. On other issues, Congress ordered its delegates to defer to the counsel of the French government.

But in Paris there were grave problems. The French had formed a military alliance with Spain, and French officials announced that they could not consider the details of an American settlement until after the Spanish had recaptured Gibraltar from the British. The prospects for a Spanish victory were not good. More than anything the American representatives feared that some European intrigue might cost the United States its independence.

While the three American delegates publicly paid their respects to French officials, they secretly entered into negotiations with an English agent. These actions not only violated their instructions, they did not fool the French for a moment. French spies kept them informed of what occurred at these meetings, and while they could have protested the American breach of faith, they did not do so.

The negotiators drove a remarkable bargain. The preliminary agreement, signed on September 3, 1783, not only guaranteed the independence of the United States, it also transferred all the territory east of the Mississippi River—except Florida, which remained under Spanish sovereignty—to the new Republic. The treaty established generous boundaries on the north and south and gave the Americans important fishing rights in the North Atlantic. In exchange, Congress promised to help British merchants collect debts contracted before the Revolution and to compensate Loyalists whose land had been confiscated by the various state governments. The preliminary treaty did not take effect until after the French reached their own agreement with Great Britain, thus formally honoring the Franco-American alliance. It is hard to imagine how Franklin, Adams, and Jay could have negotiated a more favorable conclusion to the war. In the fall of 1783, the last redcoats sailed from New York City, ending 176 years of colonial rule.

The American people had waged war against the most powerful nation in Europe and emerged victorious. The treaty marked the conclusion of a colonial rebellion, but it remained for the men and women who had resisted taxation without representation to work out the full implications of republicanism. What would be the scope of the new government? What powers would be delegated to the people, the states, the federal authorities? How far would the wealthy, well-born leaders of the rebellion be willing to extend political, social, and economic rights? The war was over, but the drama of the American Revolution was still unfolding.

Recommended Reading

The revolutionary era is one of the most heavily analyzed periods of American history. Two of the more readable syntheses of this vast literature are Merrill Jensen, *The Founding of a Nation: A History of the American Revolution, 1763–1789* (1968), and Robert Middlekauff, *The Glorious Cause: The American Revolution, 1763–1789* (1982). Edmund S. Morgan, *The Birth of the Republic, 1763–1789* (1956), is a short, provocative examination of the revolutionary era. The best introduction to military history remains Howard H. Peckham, *The War for Independence: A Military History* (1958).

The literature dealing with British politics on the eve of the American Revolution is particularly rich. One important study is John Brooke, *King George III* (1974). For information on the development of political associations, see John Brewer, *Party Ideology and Popular Politics at the Accession of George III* (1976). The American interpretation of changing British politics is imaginatively discussed in Bernard Bailyn, *The Ideological Origins of the American Revolution* (1967), and Pauline Maier, *From Resistance to Revolution: Colonial Radicals and the Development of American Opposition to Britain, 1765–1776* (1972).

The most perceptive work on the events leading to the Revolution is Edmund S. and Helen M. Morgan, *The Stamp Act Crisis* (1953), a book that provides an excellent account of American society in 1765. Other studies of these difficult years are John Shy, *Toward Lexington* (1965); Rhys Isaac, *The Transformation of Virginia, 1740–1790* (1982); David Ammerman, *In the Common Cause: American Response to the Coercive Acts of 1774* (1974); and Benjamin W. Labaree, *The Boston Tea Party* (1964). Robert A. Gross, *The Minutemen and Their World* (1976) is a fine study of Concord. Edward Countryman explores the complex events in New York in *A People in Revolution: The American Revolution and Political Society in New York, 1760–1790* (1982). For information on Thomas Paine see Eric Foner, *Tom Paine and Revolutionary America* (1976).

The most detailed study of the war is Don Higginbotham, *The War of American Independence* (1971). The British side of the story is well told in Piers Mackesy, *The War for America, 1775–1783* (1964). The Loyalists are examined in Wallace Brown, *The King's Friends: The Composition and Motives of the American Loyalist Claimants* (1965), and William H. Nelson, *The American Tory* (1961). Richard B. Morris, *The Peacemakers: The Great Powers and American Independence* (1965), provides a comprehensive study of the peace negotiations.

chapter 6

THE
REPUBLICAN
EXPERIMENT

In 1785 the sons and daughters of some of Boston's wealthiest families announced the formation of a tea assembly or "Sans Souci Club." The members of this select group gathered once a week for the pleasure of good conversation, a game of cards, some dancing, and perhaps a glass of Madeira wine. These meetings outraged other Bostonians, many of them old patriots. For men like Samuel Adams, who dreamed of creating a "Christian Sparta," the club represented the worst excesses of British society. Thus the club's very existence threatened the *"republican principles"* for which Americans had so recently fought a revolution. Men who had lived through the tense years of the 1770s believed such "foolish gratifications" would erode public morality, substituting "luxury, prodigality, and profligacy" for "prudence, virtue, and economy."

However ridiculous it may now appear, this local tempest reflected deep tensions within postrevolutionary American society. Victory over the British forced people to translate abstract notions about republicanism into daily practice. The effort proved considerably more difficult than anyone had predicted in 1776. As students of classical history understood, republican government required public virtue, a commitment to self-sacrifice.

Yet during the 1780s, citizens of the new nation seemed caught up in a wild, destructive scramble for material wealth. Revolutionary leaders had boldly declared that all men were created equal, and yet black Americans languished in bondage. The patriots had condemned colonialism, and yet some Americans thought that people who settled west of the Appalachian Mountains should remain dependent upon the original thirteen states. Indeed, in 1785 it was not even clear whether the Americans would establish a strong central government or divide themselves into smaller, autonomous republics.

These challenges generated an outpouring of

political genius. At other times in American history, persons of extraordinary talent have been drawn to theology, commerce, or science, but during the 1780s, the country's intellectual leaders—Thomas Jefferson, James Madison, Alexander Hamilton, and John Adams among them—focused their creative energies on the problem of how a free people ought to govern themselves.

The Limits of Revolutionary Change

Revolution changed American society, often in ways that no one had planned. This phenomenon is not unusual. The great revolutions of modern times produced radical transformations in French, Russian, and Chinese society. By comparison, the immediate results of the American Revolution appear much tamer, less wrenching. Nevertheless, national independence compelled people to reevaluate social relations that they had taken for granted during the colonial period. However faltering their first steps, they raised fundamental questions about the meaning of equality in American society that still have not been answered to everyone's satisfactions.

Social and Political Reform

Following the war, Americans aggressively ferreted out and, with republican fervor, denounced any traces of aristocratic pretense. As colonists, they had long resented the claims that certain Englishmen made to special privilege simply because of noble birth. A society based on artificial status was contrary to republican principles.

The appearance of equality was as important as the actual achievement. In fact, the distribution of wealth in postwar America was more uneven than it had been in the mid-eighteenth century. Yet Americans attempted to root out the notion of a privileged class. States abolished laws of primogeniture and entail. In co-

lonial times these laws allowed a landholder either to pass his entire estate to his eldest son or to declare that his property could never be divided, sold, or given away. Although America had never been affected greatly by such customs, their abolition was an important symbolic blow against the idea of a landed aristocracy.

Republican ferment also encouraged many states to lower property requirements for voting. After the revolutionary experience, such a step seemed logical. The concept of a representative government was well accepted in America. These reforms, however, did not significantly expand the American electorate. Long before the Revolution, an overwhelming percentage of free males had owned enough land to vote, and few leaders at that time were willing to entertain the idea of universal manhood suffrage.

The most important changes in voting patterns were the result of western migration. As Americans moved to the frontier, they received full political representation in their state legislatures, and because new districts tended to be poorer than established coastal settlements, their inhabitants selected representatives who seemed less cultured, less well trained than those sent by eastern voters. Moreover, western delegates resented traveling so far to attend legislative meetings, and they lobbied successfully to transfer state capitals to more convenient locations.

After independence, Americans also reexamined the relationship between church and state. Republican spokesmen such as Thomas Jefferson argued in favor of the disestablishment of state churches. They insisted that rulers had no right to interfere with the free expression of an individual's religious beliefs. Nor did they believe that churches should be supported with taxpayers' monies. Although Massachusetts and Connecticut did not disestablish their Congregational churches, most of the southern states did disestablish the Anglican church. Few Americans favored irreligion or secularism, though they championed toleration.

Slave auctions (such as this one from Lewis Miller's sketchbook of a slightly later time) were an abomination to many Americans and an embarrassment to many more.

Slaves and Women in the New Republic

Revolutionary fervor even forced Americans to confront the most appalling contradiction to the republican principles—slavery. Abolitionist sentiment ran high during the 1780s, especially among the Quakers of the middle states. Americans formed groups to end slavery from Massachusetts to Virginia that included such prominent figures as Alexander Hamilton, John Jay, and Benjamin Franklin.

The attack on slavery took a number of different forms. The Vermont constitution of 1777 specifically prohibited slavery. In 1780 the Pennsylvania legislature abolished the practice. Other states followed suit. By the decade after 1800 slavery was well on the road to extinction in the northern states.

Even in the South, where blacks made up a large percentage of the population, slavery embarrassed thoughtful republicans. Some planters followed James Madison's egalitarian example and simply freed their slaves. Despite these promising beginnings, however, the southern states did not abolish slavery. The economic incentives to maintain a servile labor force, especially after the invention of the cotton gin in 1793 and the opening up of the Alabama and Mississippi frontier, over-

whelmed the abolitionist impulse. An opportunity to translate the rhetoric of the American Revolution into social practice had been lost, at least temporarily. Even Thomas Jefferson, the man who wrote the Declaration of Independence, could not bring himself to free his own slaves.

The currents of republicanism also raised the expectations of American women. For example, during this period women began to petition for divorce on new grounds. One case is particularly instructive concerning changing attitudes toward women and the family. In 1784, John Backus, an obscure Massachusetts silversmith, was hauled before a local court and asked why he beat his wife. He responded that "it was Partly owing to his Education for his father treated his mother in the same manner." The difference was that Backus' wife refused to tolerate such abuse, and she sued successfully for divorce.

The war itself presented some women with fresh opportunities to employ their talents. In 1780 Esther DeBerdt Reed founded a large, volunteer woman's organization in Philadelphia— the first of its kind in the United States—that raised over $300,000 for Washington's army. Other women ran family farms and businesses while their husbands fought the British.

Despite these scattered gains, republican

Americans had fewer entrenched barriers to overcome in the first place. Indeed, the Revolution confirmed many rights that colonial Americans had long enjoyed—broad suffrage, religious toleration, and freedom of movement. Nor was the traditional ruling class in America attacked, although new classes were soon challenging them for political and economic leadership. As one wealthy Bostonian complained in 1779, "Fellows who would have cleaned my shoes five years ago, have amassed fortunes and are riding chariots."

Experimenting with Self-Government

In May 1776 the Second Continental Congress urged the states to adopt constitutions. Rhode Island and Connecticut already had republican governments by virtue of their unique charters, and the rest of the new states soon complied. Several constitutions were frankly experimental, and some states later rewrote documents that had been drafted in the first flush of independence. But if these early constitutions were provisional, they nevertheless provided the framers of the federal Constitution of 1787 with invaluable insights into the strengths and weaknesses of government based on the will of the people.

Blueprints for State Government

Despite disagreements over details, Americans who wrote the various state constitutions shared certain political assumptions. First, they insisted upon preparing *written* documents. As colonists, they had lived under royal charters, documents that described the workings of local government in detail, and they felt comfortable with the contractual language of legal documents.

However logical the decision to produce written documents may have seemed to the Americans, it represented a major break with English practice. Political philosophers in the mother country had long boasted of Britain's

society still defined women's roles exclusively in terms of mother, wife, and homemaker. Other pursuits seemed unnatural, even threatening. It is perhaps not surprising that New Jersey, whose legislature in 1790 had voted to allow women who owned property to vote, in 1807 repealed female suffrage in the interests of "the safety, quiet, and good order and dignity of the state."

Although the Revolution did not bring about a massive restructuring of American society, it did raise issues of immense significance for the later history of the United States. Republican spokesmen insisted that equality, however narrowly defined, was an essential element of republican government. They failed to abolish slavery or institute universal manhood suffrage, true, but they vigorously articulated a set of assumptions about people's rights and liberties that challenged future generations of Americans to make good on the promise of the Revolution.

If the Revolution seems less radical than those of other nations, particularly that of France, it may be because eighteenth-century unwritten constitution, a collection of judicial reports and parliamentary statutes. Yet this highly vaunted system had not protected the colonists from oppression. It is understandable then why, after declaring independence, Americans demanded that their state constitutions explicitly define the rights of the people as well as the powers of their rulers. They desired more from public officials than simply assurances of good faith.

The authors of the state constitutions believed that men and women possessed certain natural rights over which government exercised no control whatsoever. So that future rulers—potential tyrants—would know the exact limits of their authority, these fundamental rights were carefully spelled out.

Eight state constitutions contained specific Declarations of Rights. In general, they affirmed three fundamental freedoms: religion, speech, and press. They protected citizens from unlawful searches and seizures; they upheld trial by jury. Ultimately, the best expression of this impulse is contained in the famed Bill of Rights of the federal Constitution.

In almost every state, delegates to constitutional conventions drastically reduced the power of the governor. He was allowed to make almost no political appointments, and while the state legislators closely monitored his activities, he possessed no veto over their decisions (Massachusetts being the lone exception). Most early constitutions lodged nearly all effective power in the legislature. In fact, the writers of the state constitutions were so fearful of the concentration of power in the hands of one person that they failed to realize that governors—like the representatives—were servants of a free people.

The legislature dominated early state government. Some states even questioned the need for a senate or upper house, and Pennsylvania and Georgia instituted a unicameral, or one-house, system. Many Americans believed that the lower house could handle all the state's problems. The two-house form survived the Revolution largely because it was familiar and because some persons had already begun to suspect that certain checks upon the popular will, however arbitrary they might appear, were necessary to preserve minority rights.

Defining the Will of the People

Perhaps the most significant state constitution was the one adopted by the people of Massachusetts because they hit upon a remarkable political innovation. Their state constitution was drafted by a specially elected convention of delegates, not ordinary officeholders.

John Adams served as the chief architect of the governmental framework of the state. It included a house and senate, a popularly elected governor who—unlike the chief executives of the state—possessed a veto over legislative bills, and property qualifications for officeholders as well as voters. The most striking aspect of the 1780 constitution, however, was its opening sentence: "We . . . the people of Massachusetts . . . agree upon, ordain, and establish." This powerful vocabulary would be echoed in the federal Constitution.

The state constitutions ushered a different type of person into public office. When one Virginian surveyed the newly elected House of Burgesses in 1776, he discovered that it was "composed of men not quite so well dressed, not so politely educated, nor so highly born as some Assemblies I have formerly seen." They were indeed the people's people, representative republicans. Whether this new breed of representative would be virtuous enough to safeguard the fledgling republic remained a hotly debated question.

Creating a New National Government

When the Second Continental Congress convened in 1775, the delegates found themselves waging war in the name of a country that did not yet exist. As the military crisis deepened, Congress gradually—often reluctantly—assumed greater authority over national affairs, but everyone agreed that such narrowly conceived measures were a poor substitute for a legally constituted government. The separate states could not possibly deal with the range of issues that now confronted the American people. Indeed, if independence meant anything in a world of sovereign nations, it implied the creation of a central authority capable of conducting war, borrowing money, regulating trade, and negotiating treaties.

Unenthusiastic Reception for the Articles of Confederation

The first attempt to produce a framework for national government failed miserably. Congress appointed a committee headed by John Dickinson, a lawyer who had written an important revolutionary pamphlet entitled *Letters from a Farmer in Pennsylvania*. Dickinson's plan for creating a strong central government shocked the delegates, who had assumed that the constitution would authorize a loose confederation of states.

Dickinson's plan called for equal state representation in Congress. This upset states such as Virginia and Massachusetts that were more populous than others and fueled tensions between large and small states. Also unsettling was Dickinson's recommendation that taxes be paid to Congress on the basis of a state's total population, black as well as white, a formula that angered Southerners.

Not unexpectedly, the draft that Congress finally approved in November 1777 bore little resemblance to Dickinson's original plan. The Articles of Confederation jealously guarded the sovereignty of the states. The delegates who drafted this framework shared a general republican conviction that power—especially power so far removed from the people—was inherently dangerous and that the only way to preserve liberty was to place as many constraints as possible upon federal authority.

They succeeded marvelously; Congress created a government that many people regarded as powerless. The Articles provided for a single legislative body, consisting of representatives selected annually by the state legislatures. Each state possessed a single vote in Congress.

There was no independent executive, and of course, no veto over legislative decisions. The Articles also denied Congress the power of taxation, a serious oversight in time of war. The national government could obtain funds only by asking the states for contributions, called requisitions. If a state failed to cooperate—and many did—Congress limped along without financial support. Amendments to this constitution required unanimous assent by all thirteen states. The authors of the new system apparently expected a powerless national government to handle foreign relations, military matters, Indian affairs, and interstate disputes. They most emphatically did not award Congress ownership of the lands west of the Appalachian Mountains.

Who Owns the West?

Once the new constitution had been sent to the states for ratification, the major bone of contention became the disposition of the vast, unsurveyed territory west of the Appalachians that everyone hoped the British would soon surrender. Some states, such as Virginia and Georgia, claimed land all the way from the Atlantic Ocean to the elusive "South Sea" by virtue of royal charters. People who lived in those states not blessed with vague or ambiguous royal charters seemed to be in danger of being permanently cut off from the anticipated bounty. In protest, these "landless" states stubbornly refused to ratify the Articles of Confederation. All states had sacrificed during the Revolution, they reasoned, and so all states should profit from the fruits of victory, in this case, from the sale of western lands. Marylanders were particularly vociferous, fearing depopulation by settlers in search of cheap farmland.

The states resolved this bitter controversy in 1781 as much by accident as by design. Virginia, a "landed" state, realized that her position was not without its special problems. Republicans such as Thomas Jefferson worried about expanding their state beyond the mountains; with poor transportation links, it seemed impossible to govern such a large territory effectively from Richmond. The western

Western Land Claims Ceded by the States

BRITISH NORTH AMERICA

Lake of the Woods

Lake Superior

LOWER CANADA
St. Lawrence R.

Claimed by Great Britain

MAINE (part of Mass.)

NORTHWEST

Lake Michigan
Lake Huron

UPPER CANADA

Lake Ontario

VT. Statehood 1791

N.H.

NEW YORK

MASS.

CONN.

RHODE ISLAND

Ceded by Massachusetts 1785

TERRITORY

Lake Erie

Missouri R.

Ceded by Conn. 1786

Ceded by New York 1782

Ceded by Conn. 1800

PENNSYLVANIA

NEW JERSEY

MD.

DELAWARE

D.C.

Ceded by New York 1782

Ohio R.

Ceded by Va. 1789

VIRGINIA

LOUISIANA

Ceded by Spain to France 1800

KENTUCKY Statehood 1792

Cumberland Gap

Ceded by N.C. 1790

NORTH CAROLINA

ATLANTIC OCEAN

TENNESSEE Statehood 1796

Mississippi R.

Ceded by Georgia 1802

Ceded by S.C. 1787

SOUTH CAROLINA

GEORGIA

Ceded by Spain 1795

SPANISH FLORIDA

Gulf of Mexico

Boundary of territory ceded by New York, 1782

Northwest Territory, ceded by Virginia, 1784

Other western land claims ceded by the states

0   300 Miles
0   300 Kilometers

settlers might even come to regard Virginia as a colonial power insensitive to their needs. Virginia, therefore, agreed to cede its western land claims to Congress, and the other landed states soon followed suit. These transfers established an important principle, for after 1781 there was no question that the West belonged not to the states but to the United States.

No one greeted ratification of the Articles with jubilation. Americans were still fully occupied with winning independence. In 1781 the new government began setting up a bureaucracy. It created the Departments of War, Foreign Affairs, and Finance. By far the most influential figure in the Confederation government was Robert Morris (1734–1806), a freewheeling Philadelphia merchant who was appointed the first superintendent of finance. His

91

decisions provoked controversy. Contemporaries who feared the development of a strong national government identified Morris with efforts to undermine the authority of the states and to seize the power of taxation; at least one congressional critic labeled him a "pecuniary dictator."

The Confederation's Major Achievement

Whatever Congress's weaknesses, it scored one impressive triumph. Congressional action brought order to western settlement, especially in the Northwest Territory, and incorporated frontier Americans into an expanded federal system.

In 1781, however, the prospects for success did not seem promising. For years, colonial authorities had ignored people who migrated far inland, sending neither money nor soldiers to protect them from Indian attack. Tensions between the seaboard colonies and the frontier regions had occasionally flared into violence. With thousands of men and women, most of them squatters, pouring across the Appalachian Mountains, Congress had to act quickly to avoid the past errors of royal and colonial authorities.

The initial attempt to deal with this explosive problem came in 1784. Jefferson, then serving as a member of Congress, drafted an ordinance that became a basis for later, more enduring legislation. He recommended carving ten new states out of the western lands located north of the Ohio River. He specified that each new state establish a republican form of government. When the population of a territory equaled that of the smallest state already in the Confederation, the region could apply for full statehood. In the meantime, free adult males could participate in local government, a democratic guarantee that frightened several of Jefferson's more conservative colleagues.

The impoverished Congress was eager to sell off the western territory as quickly as possible. After all, the frontier represented a source of income that did not depend upon the unreliable generosity of the states. A second ordinance, passed in 1785 and called the Land Ordinance, established an orderly process for laying out new townships and marketing public lands. After surveying and subdividing various regions, the government planned to auction off its holdings in 640-acre sections (one square mile) at prices of not less than a dollar an acre, payable in coin only. Section 16 was set aside for the support of public education and four other sections were reserved for the federal government.

Public response disappointed Congress. Surveying the lands took far longer than anticipated, and few persons possessed enough hard currency to make even the minimum purchase of 640 acres. Finally, a solution to the problem came from Manasseh Cutler, a land speculator and congressional lobbyist. He and his companions offered to purchase more than 6 million unsurveyed acres of land located in present-day southeastern Ohio by persuading Congress to accept at full face value government loan certificates that had been issued to soldiers during the Revolution. The speculators could pick up these certificates on the open market for as little as 10 percent of their face value. Like so many other get-rich-quick schemes, however, this one failed to produce the anticipated millions.

Congress also had reservations about frontier democracy. In the 1780s the West seemed to be filling up with people who, by eastern standards, were uncultured. The attitude was as old as the frontier itself. Indeed, seventeenth-century Englishmen had felt the same way about the earliest Virginians. The belief that the westerners were lawless, however, persisted, and even a sober observer like Washington insisted that the West crawled with "banditti." The Ordinance of 1784 placed the government of the territories in the hands of people about whom congressmen and speculators had second thoughts.

These various currents shaped the Ordinance of 1787, one of the final acts passed under the Confederation. This bill, also called the Northwest Ordinance, provided a new structure for government of the Northwest Territory. The plan authorized the creation of

Grid Pattern of a Township
36 sections of 640 acres (1 square mile each)

6	5	4	3	2	1
7	8	9	10	11	12
18	17	16	15	14	13
19	20	21	22	23	24
30	29	28	27	26	25
31	32	33	34	35	36

6 miles (vertical) — 6 miles (horizontal)

A Half-section   320 acres
B Quarter-section   160 acres
C Half-quarter section   80 acres
D Quarter-quarter sections   40 acres

16 — Income of one section reserved for the support of public education

between three and five territories, each to be ruled by a governor, a secretary, and three judges appointed by Congress. When the population reached 5000, voters who owned property could elect an assembly, but the decisions were subject to the governor's absolute veto. Once 60,000 persons resided in a territory, they could write a constitution and petition for full statehood. While these procedures represented a retreat from Jefferson's original proposal, the Ordinance of 1787 contained several significant features. A bill of rights guaranteed the settlers trial by jury, freedom of religion, and due process of law. In addition, this act outlawed slavery, a prohibition that freed the future states of Ohio, Indiana, Illinois, Michigan, and Wisconsin from the curse of human bondage.

By contrast, the growing settlements south of the Ohio River seemed chaotic. Between 1775 and 1784, for example, the population of what was to become Kentucky jumped from approximately 100 to 30,000 persons. In this and other southwestern regions, land speculators were an ever present problem. By 1796 the entire region south of the Ohio River had been transformed into a crazy quilt of claims and counterclaims that generated lawsuits for many years to come.

Weaknesses of the Confederation

Throughout the country, Americans became increasingly critical of the Articles of Confederation. Complaints varied from region to region, from person to person, but most disappointment reflected economic frustration. Americans had assumed that peace would restore prosperity. When such was not the case, they searched the political horizon for a reason.

Weak Congress Blamed for Economic Problems

Renewed trade with Great Britain on a large scale undermined the stability of the American economy. Specie (coins) flowed eastward across the Atlantic, leaving the United States desperately short of hard currency, and when British merchants called in their debts, thriftless American buyers often fell into bankruptcy. Critics also pointed to the government's inability to regulate trade. Southerners in particular resisted any such attempts. They protested that any control on the export of to-

■ *"Not worth a Continental" became a common oath when inflation eroded the value of the Continental currency. Currency issued by the states was equally valueless.*

bacco, rice, and cotton smacked of the Navigation Acts.

To blame the Confederation alone for the economic depression would be unfair. Nevertheless, during the 1780s many people agreed that a stronger government could somehow have softened the blow. In their rush to acquire imported luxuries, Americans seemed to have deserted republican principles, and a weak Congress was helpless to restore national virtue.

The country's chronic fiscal instability increased public anxiety. During the war, Congress printed over $200 million in paper currency, but because of an extraordinarily high rate of inflation, the rate of exchange for Continental bills soon declined to a fraction of their face value. In 1781 Congress turned to the states for help, asking them to retire the

worthless money. Instead, several states not only recirculated the continental bills, they also issued worthless currency of their own.

A heavy burden of state and national debt compounded the general sense of economic crisis. Revolutionary soldiers had yet to be paid, and the government owed money to domestic and foreign creditors. The pressure to pay these debts grew, but Congress was unable to respond. Since Congress was prohibited from taxing the American people, it required little imagination to see that the Confederation would soon default on its legal obligations unless something was done quickly.

In response, an aggressive group of men announced that they knew how to save the Confederation. The "nationalists"—led by Alexander Hamilton, James Madison, and Robert Morris—called for major constitutional reforms, the chief of which was an amendment allowing Congress to collect a 5-percent tax on imported goods. Revenues generated by the proposed Impost of 1781 would be used by the Confederation to reduce the national debt. Twelve states accepted the Impost, but Rhode Island resolutely refused to cooperate. One negative vote was enough to kill the taxing plan; amending the Articles required unanimous consent.

The nationalists sparked fierce opposition. Many Americans were apprehensive of their plans. The nationalists, for their part, regarded their opponents as economically naive and argued that a country with the potential of the United States required a complex, centralized fiscal system. But for all their pretensions to realism, the nationalists of the early 1780s were politically inept. They underestimated the depth of republican fears, and in their rush to strengthen the Articles, they overplayed their hand.

A group of extreme nationalists even appealed to the army for support. To this day, no one knows the full story of the Newburgh Conspiracy of 1783. Officers of the Continental army stationed at Newburgh, New York, worried that Congress would disband them without funding their pensions and began to lobby intensively for relief. The officers' initial efforts were harmless enough, but frustrated nationalists such as Morris and Hamilton decided that if the army exerted sufficient pressure on the government, perhaps even threatened a military takeover, then stubborn Americans might be compelled to amend the Articles.

The conspirators failed to take George Washington's integrity into account. In a surprise visit, he confronted the officers directly at Newburgh. So great was his personal influence that a few words from him ended any chance of rebellion. Washington, indeed, deserves credit for preserving civilian rule in this country. He refused to consider any scheme that contemplated using the army as a political instrument.

In April 1783 Congress proposed a second impost, but it too failed to win unanimous ratification. Even a personal appeal by Washington could not save the amendment. With this defeat, nationalists gave up on the Confederation. Morris retired from government, and Madison returned to Virginia utterly depressed by what he had witnessed.

Difficulties in Confederation Diplomacy

In foreign affairs, Congress endured further embarrassment. American negotiators had promised Great Britain that its citizens could collect debts contracted before the Revolution. The states, however, dragged their heels, and several even passed laws obstructing the settlement of legitimate prewar claims. Congress was powerless to force compliance. The British responded to this apparent provocation by refusing to evacuate troops from posts located in the Northwest Territory. A strong central government would have driven the redcoats out, but without adequate funds, the weak Congress was powerless to act.

Congress's postrevolutionary dealings with Spain were equally humiliating. That nation refused to accept the southern boundary of the United States established by the Treaty of Paris. Spanish agents schemed with southern Indian tribes to resist American expansion, and on July 21, 1784, Spain added a further insult by closing the lower Mississippi River to citizens of the United States. This last event devastated western farmers who needed free use of the Mississippi to send their crops to the world's markets. Without the river, the economic development of the entire Ohio valley was in jeopardy.

In 1785 a Spanish official, Don Diego de Gardoqui, opened talks with John Jay, a New Yorker appointed by Congress to obtain rights to navigation of the Mississippi. Jay soon discovered that Gardoqui would not compromise, but he pressed on, attempting to win concessions that would have commercially linked the United States to Spain and benefited northern traders while foregoing free navigation of the Mississippi for twenty-five years. When Congress learned of Jay's plans, it wisely terminated the negotiations with Spain.

By the mid-1780s, Congress had squandered whatever respect it may once have enjoyed. It met irregularly, and some states did not even bother to send delegates. The nation lacked a permanent capital, and Congress drifted from Philadelphia to Princeton to Annapolis to New York City, prompting one humorist to suggest that the government purchase an air balloon to allow members of Congress to "float along from one end of the continent to the other" and "suddenly pop down into any of the states they please."

Restructuring the Republic

Thoughtful Americans, especially those who had provided leadership during the Revolution, agreed that something had to be done. By 1785 the country seemed to be drifting; the buoyant optimism that had sustained revolutionary patriots had dissolved into pessimism and doubt. By 1786 Washington was asking his countrymen exactly why they had fought the Revolution.

Problems and Reform

The country's problems could be traced in part to the republicans' own ideology. More than anything else, they feared the concentration of power in the hands of unscrupulous rulers. They therefore created governments—national and state—with weak chief executives and strong assemblies. However, too many of the people who manned the State assemblies and Congress were not up to the task. The result was a government of excessive individualism where legitimate minority rights took a backseat to the desires of the majority.

Confronted with economic chaos, many states blithely churned out worthless currency, while others passed laws impeding the collection of debts. In Rhode Island the situation became absurd. State legislators made it illegal for merchants to reject Rhode Island money even though everyone knew it had no value. As Americans tried to interpret these experiences within a republican framework, they were checked by the most widely accepted political wisdom of the age. Baron de Montesquieu (1689–1755), a French political philosopher of immense international reputation, declared flatly that a republican government could not flourish in a large territory. For such a government to function properly, the people had to be able to keep a close eye on their representatives. Americans treated Montesquieu's theories as self-evident truths, and they were thus nervous about tampering with the sovereignty of the states.

James Madison rejected Montesquieu's argument, and in so doing, helped Americans to think of republican government in exciting new ways. This soft-spoken, rather unprepossessing Virginian was the most brilliant American political thinker of his generation. Based on his reading of the Scottish philosopher David Hume and others, Madison became convinced that Americans need not fear a greatly expanded republic. In fact, he believed that a republican form of government would work better in a large country than in a small one. In small states like Rhode Island, for example,

■ *Among the framers of the Constitution, James Madison, not yet forty, was the most effective advocate of a strong central government.*

legislative majorities tyrannized the propertied minority. In a large republic, these injustices could be avoided. With so many people scattered over a huge area, no one faction would be able to form an effective majority, and one powerful interest would be checked by some other equally powerful interest.

Madison did not, however, advocate a modern "interest-group" model of political behavior. Rather, he thought that the competing selfish factions would neutralize each other, leaving the business of governing the republic to the ablest, most virtuous persons that the nation could produce. In other words, the government Madison envisioned would be based on the will of the people and yet detached from their narrowly based demands. This thinking formed the foundation of Madison's most famous political essay, *The Federalist* No. 10.

A concerted movement to overhaul the Articles of Confederation began in the mid-1780s. The Massachusetts legislature asked Congress to call a convention for the purpose of revising the entire constitution. Nothing came of the suggestion until 1786 when Madison and his friends persuaded the Virginia assembly to recommend a convention to explore the creation of a unified system of "commercial regulation." Congress supported the idea. However, only five states sent delegates to the Annapolis convention. Rather than try to conduct any business, the Annapolis delegates advised Congress to hold a second meeting in Philadelphia to consider constitutional changes. Congress authorized a grand convention to gather in May 1787.

Events played into Madison's hands. Soon after the Annapolis meeting, an uprising known as Shays' Rebellion, involving several thousand impoverished farmers, shattered the peace of western Massachusetts. These farmers complained of high taxes, of high interest rates, and most of all, of a state government insensitive to their economic problems. In 1786 Daniel Shays, a veteran of the battle of Bunker Hill, and his armed neighbors closed a county courthouse where creditors were suing to foreclose farm mortgages. His band then marched to Springfield, site of a federal arsenal, but the state militia soon put down the rebellion.

Nationalists throughout the United States overreacted to news of Shays' Rebellion. From their perspective, the incident symbolized the breakdown of law and order that they had long predicted. And even more important, the event persuaded persons who might otherwise have ignored the Philadelphia meeting to participate in drafting a new constitution.

Constitutional Convention Meets in Philadelphia

In the spring of 1787 fifty-five men representing twelve states traveled to Philadelphia. Only Rhode Island refused to take part in the proceedings. The delegates were practical men: lawyers, merchants, and planters, many

of whom had fought in the Revolution and served in the Congress of the Confederation. The majority were in their thirties and forties. The gathering included George Washington, James Madison, George Mason, Robert Morris, John Dickinson, Benjamin Franklin, and Alexander Hamilton. Absent were John Adams and Jefferson, who were conducting diplomacy in Europe; Patrick Henry stayed home in Virginia because he "smelled a rat."

As soon as the convention opened on May 25, the delegates made several procedural decisions of utmost importance. First, they ruled that their discussions would be kept absolutely secret. This determination allowed delegates to speak their minds freely, without fear of criticism from people who had not actually witnessed the debates. The delegates also decided to vote by state, but to avoid the kinds of problems that had plagued the Confederation, they ruled that key proposals needed the support of only a majority instead of the nine states required in the Articles.

Madison understood that whoever sets the agenda, controls the meeting. Even before the delegates had arrived, he drew up a framework for a new federal system known as the "Virginia Plan." He wisely persuaded Edmund Randolph, Virginia's popular governor, to present this scheme to the convention on May 29. In his plan, Madison advocated a strong central government, one that could override the short-sighted local legislatures.

The Virginia Plan envisioned a national legislature consisting of two houses, one elected directly by the people, the other chosen by the first house from nominations made by the state assemblies. Representation in both houses was proportional to the state's population. The Virginia Plan provided for an executive elected by Congress. To the surprise of the states' rights supporters, the entire package carried easily, and the convention found itself discussing the details of a "a *national* Government . . . consisting of a *supreme* Legislature, Executive, and Judiciary."

On June 15, William Paterson, a New Jersey lawyer, presented a counterproposal. The New

Jersey Plan preserved the fundamental spirit of the Articles of Confederation, including the retention of a unicameral legislature. Paterson argued that his revisions, while more modest than Madison's plan, would have greater appeal for the American people. The delegates listened politely to his plan, which would have given Congress extensive new powers to tax and regulate trade, and then they soundly rejected it on June 19.

Rejection of the New Jersey Plan, however, did not clear the way for a final vote. Delegates from small states feared that Madison's plan would hurt their states. These men maintained that unless each state possessed an equal vote in Congress, the small states would find themselves at the mercy of their larger neighbors. Countering this claim, delegates from the large states argued that it was absurd to assert that Rhode Island with only 68,000 people should have the same voice in Congress as Virginia's 747,000 inhabitants.

The mood of the convention was tense. Hard work and frustration, coupled with Philadelphia's sweltering summer heat, frayed nerves. Although some members predicted that the meeting would accomplish nothing of significance, the gathering did not break up; the delegates desperately wanted to produce a constitution. On July 2 a "grand committee" of one person from each state was elected by the convention to resolve persistent differences between the large and small states.

And the grand committee did just that. It recommended that the states be equally represented in the upper house of Congress and proportionately by population in the lower house. Only the lower house could initiate money bills. The committee also decided that one member of the lower house should be selected for every forty thousand inhabitants of a state, and for this purpose, a slave was to be counted as three-fifths of a freeman. This compromise overcame the impasse between large and small states.

On July 26, the convention formed a Committee of Detail, a group that prepared a rough draft of the Constitution. When its work was done, the delegates debated each article. The task required the better part of a month.

During these sessions, the members of the convention concluded that the president, as they now called the executive, should be selected by an electoral college, a body of prominent men in each state chosen by local voters. The number of "electoral" votes held by each state equaled its number of representatives and senators. Whoever received the second largest number of votes in the electoral college automatically became vice-president. In the event that no person received a majority of the votes, the election would be decided by the lower house—the House of Representatives—with each state casting a single vote.

Delegates also armed the chief executive with a veto power over legislation as well as the right to nominate judges. Both privileges, of course, would have been unthinkable a decade earlier, but the state experiences revealed the importance of having an independent executive to maintain a balanced system of republican government. The Philadelphia convention thus telescoped into four months the process of constitutional education that had taken over four years to learn at the state level.

Hints of Future Controversy

During the final days of August, two new issues suddenly disrupted the convention. One was a harbinger of the great sectional crisis of the nineteenth century. Many northern representatives detested the slave trade and wanted to end it immediately. In order to win southern support for the Constitution, however, the northern delegates promised that the legislature would not interfere with the slave trade until 1808 (see Chapter 8).

The second issue was the absence in the Constitution of a bill of rights. Such declarations had been included in most state constitutions. Virginians like George Mason insisted that the states and their citizens needed explicit protection from possible excesses by the federal government. While many delegates sympathized with Mason's appeal, they in-

■ *Paintings like this, in which Washington appears enthroned in a radiant aura, contributed to the mythic reputations of the men who framed the Constitution at the 1787 Convention in Independence Hall, Philadelphia.*

sisted that the proposed constitution provided sufficient security for individual rights. During the hard battle over ratification the delegates to the convention may have regretted passing over the issue so lightly.

The delegates adopted an ingenious procedure for ratification. Instead of submitting the Constitution to the various state legislatures, all of which had a vested interest in maintaining the status quo, they called for the election of thirteen state conventions especially chosen to review the new federal government. Moreover, the Constitution would take effect after the assent of only nine states. There was no danger, therefore, that the proposed system would fail simply because a single state like Rhode Island withheld approval.

On September 17, thirty-nine men signed the Constitution. A few members of the convention like Mason could not support the document. Others had already gone home. Out of the three months of heat and effort a new form of government had emerged.

Battle for Ratification

Supporters of the Constitution recognized that ratification would not be easy. After all, the convention had been authorized only to revise the Articles. Instead, it produced a radical new plan that fundamentally altered relations between the states and the central government. The delegates dispatched a copy of the document to the Congress of Confederation which in turn referred it to the separate states. The fight for ratification had begun.

Federalists and Anti-Federalists

Proponents of the Constitution enjoyed great advantages over the unorganized opposition. In the contest for ratification, however, they took no chances. Their most astute move was the adoption of the label *Federalist*, a term that cleverly suggested that they stood for a confederation of states rather than for the creation of

Ratification of the Constitution

State	Date	Vote For	Vote Against
Delaware	Dec. 8, 1787	30	0
Pennsylvania	Dec. 12, 1787	46	23
New Jersey	Dec. 18, 1787	38	0
Georgia	Jan. 2, 1788	26	0
Connecticut	Jan. 9, 1788	128	40
Massachusetts	Feb. 16, 1788	187	168
Maryland	Apr. 26, 1788	63	11
South Carolina	May 23, 1788	149	73
New Hampshire	June 21, 1788	57	47
Virginia	June 25, 1788	89	79
New York	July 26, 1788	30	27
North Carolina	Nov. 21, 1789	194	77
Rhode Island	May 29, 1790	34	32

a supreme national authority. Critics of the Constitution—who tended to be somewhat poorer, less urban, and less well-educated than their opponents—cried foul, but there was little they could do. They were stuck with the name *Anti-Federalist*, an awkward term that made their cause seem far more obstructionist than it actually was.

The Federalists recruited the most prominent public figures of the day. In every state convention, speakers favoring the Constitution were more polished, better educated, more fully prepared than were their opponents. In New York the campaign to win ratification sparked publication of *The Federalist*, a remarkable series of essays written by Madison, Hamilton, and Jay during the fall and winter of 1787 and 1788. The nation's newspapers threw themselves overwhelmingly behind the new government. In fact, few journals even bothered to carry Anti-Federalist writings. Nor were Federalists above using threats and even strong-arm tactics. They were determined to win. A nation was at stake.

With so many factors working against them, the Anti-Federalists still came very near victory. Voting was exceptionally close in three large states: Massachusetts, New York, and Virginia. Apparently those who resisted ratification were not so far removed from the political mainstream as has sometimes been

suggested by scholars who dismiss the Anti-Federalists as "narrow-minded local politicians."

The Anti-Federalists spoke in the language of the Commonwealthmen (see Chapter 4). Like the extreme republicans who wrote the first state constitutions, the Anti-Federalists were deeply suspicious of political power. During the debates over ratification, they warned that public officials, however selected, would be constantly scheming to expand their authority. It seemed obvious to these critics of the Constitution that the larger the republic, the greater the opportunity for political corruption. Local voters could not possibly know what their representatives in a distant capital were doing. Anti-Federalists possessed a narrow view of representation. They argued that elected officials should reflect the character of their constituents as closely as possible. They feared that in large congressional districts, representatives would lose touch with the people and the wealthy would win the elections. Older on the average than their opponents, they recalled how aristocrats in Britain had abused their power.

Federalist speakers mocked their opponents' limited perspective. The Constitution deserved general support precisely because it ensured that future Americans would be represented by "natural aristocrats," individuals possessing greater insights, skills, and training than did the average citizen. These talented leaders, Federalists insisted, could discern the interests of the entire population. They were not tied to the selfish needs of local communities. The first ten amendments to the Constitution are the major legacy of the Anti-Federalist argument. The absence of a bill of rights troubled many people. In almost every state convention, opponents of the Constitution pointed to the need for greater protection of individual liberties and rights that people presumably possessed naturally such as freedom of religion and the right to a jury trial. To counter this complaint, Federalists pledged to present a bill of rights to Congress as soon as the Constitution was ratified.

The Constitution drew support from many

different types of people. In fact, historians have been unable to discover sharp correlations between wealth and occupation on the one hand and attitudes toward the proposed system of government on the other. In general, Federalists lived in more commercialized areas than did their opponents. Those men involved in commerce—artisans as well as merchants—tended to vote for ratification, while farmers only marginally involved in commercial agriculture frequently voted Anti-Federalist.

Despite passionate pleas from Patrick Henry and other Anti-Federalists, most state conventions quickly adopted the Constitution. Although the battle was close in several states, and although it took almost three years for Rhode Island to ratify, all the states eventually ratified the Constitution. And once the ratification process was over, Americans soon closed ranks behind the new government.

Adding a Bill of Rights

After ratification Madison and other Federalists urged passage of a bill of rights to appease able men like Mason and Edmund Randolph, who might otherwise remain alienated from the new federal system. But they proceeded with caution. Madison certainly did not want Anti-Federalists to use the bill of rights as an excuse to revise the entire Constitution or to promote a second constitution.

Madison carefully reviewed the state recommendations as well as the various declarations of rights that had appeared in the early state constitutions, and on June 8, 1789, he placed before the House of Representatives a set of amendments designed to protect individual rights from government interference. Madison told the members of Congress that the greatest dangers to popular liberties came from "the majority [operating] against the minority." A committee compressed and revised his original ideas into twelve amendments, ten of which were ratified and became known collectively as the Bill of Rights.

The Bill of Rights protects the freedoms of assembly, speech, religion, and the press; guarantees speedy trial by an impartial jury; pre-

Chronology

1776 Second Continental Congress authorizes colonies to create republican governments (May)
Eight states draft new constitutions; two others already enjoy republican government by virtue of former colonial charters

1777 Congress accepts Articles of Confederation after long debate (November)

1780 Massachusetts finally ratifies state constitution

1781 States ratify Articles of Confederation following settlement of Virginia's western land claims
British army surrenders at Yorktown (October)

1782 States fail to ratify proposed Impost tax

1783 Newburgh Conspiracy thwarted (March)
Treaty of peace signed with Great Britain (September)

1785 Land Ordinance for Northwest Territory passed by Congress

1786 Jay-Gardoqui negotiations over Mississippi navigation anger southern states
Annapolis Convention suggests second meeting to revise the Articles of Confederation (September)
Shays' Rebellion frightens American leaders

1787 Constitutional Convention convenes in Philadelphia (May)
Northwest Ordinance passed by Congress; restructures territorial government

1787–1788 The federal Constitution is ratified by all states except North Carolina and Rhode Island

1791 Bill of Rights (first ten amendments of the Constitution) ratified by states

serves the people's right to bear arms; and prohibits unreasonable searches. Other amendments deal with legal procedure. Only the Tenth Amendment addresses the states' relation to the federal system. This crucial article, designed to calm Anti-Federalists' fears, specifies that those "powers not delegated to the United States by the Constitution, nor prohibited by it to the States, are reserved to the States respectively, or to the people."

On September 25, 1789, the Bill of Rights passed both houses of Congress, and by December 15, 1791, these amendments had been ratified by three-fourths of the states. Madison was justly proud of his achievement. He had effectively secured individual rights without undermining the Constitution.

A New Beginning

By 1789 one phase of American political experimentation had come to an end. During these exciting years, the people gradually, often haltingly, learned that in a republican society they themselves were sovereign. They could no longer blame the failure of government on inept monarchs or greedy aristocrats. They bore a great responsibility. Americans had demanded a government of the people only to discover during the 1780s that in some situations the people cannot be trusted with power, that majorities can tyrannize minorities, that the best government can abuse individual rights. They had the good sense, therefore, to establish a marvelous system of checks and balances that protected the people from themselves.

The country's prospects seemed bright. Benjamin Franklin captured the national mood during the final moments of the constitutional convention. As the delegates came forward to sign the document, he observed that there was a sun carved on the back of Washington's chair. "I have . . . often in the course of the session . . . looked at the sun behind the President without being able to tell whether it was rising or setting: but now at length I have the happiness to know that it is a rising and not a setting sun."

Recommended Reading

The best general accounts of this period have been written by Merrill Jensen and Jackson Turner Main. See especially Main's *The Sovereign States, 1775–1783* (1973), and *The Anti-Federalists, Critics of the Constitution, 1781–1788* (1961). Gordon S. Wood provides a penetrating analysis in *The Creation of the American Republic, 1776–1787* (1969). The failure of Congress during the 1780s is the subject of Jack N. Rakove's monograph, *The Beginnings of National Politics: An Interpretive History of the Continental Congress* (1979), and Peter S. Onuf, *The Origins of the Federal Republic* (1983).

The changing basis of political participation is discussed in Chilton Williamson, *American Suffrage from Property to Democracy, 1760–1860* (1960). On black Americans, see Winthrop Jordan, *White over Black: American Attitudes Toward the Negro, 1550–1812* (1968), and Benjamin Quarles, *The Negro in the American Revolution* (1961). On women, see Linda K. Kerber, *Women of the Republic: Intellect and Ideology in Revolutionary America* (1980), and Mary Beth Norton, *Liberty's Daughters: The Revolutionary Experience of American Women, 1750–1800* (1980).

The early state constitutions are discussed in Willi Paul Adams, *The First American Constitutions: Republican Ideology and the Making of the State Constitutions* (1980). The Newburgh Conspiracy is covered in Richard H. Kohn, *Eagle and Sword: The Federalists and the Creation of the Military Establishment in America, 1783–1802* (1975). On the financial problems that beset the Confederation, see E. J. Ferguson, *The Power of the Purse: A History of American Public Finance, 1776–1790* (1961). The day-to-day workings of Congress are examined in H. J. Henderson, *Party Politics in the Continental Congress* (1974). A good survey of western settlement is Thomas D. Clark, *Frontier America: The Story of the Western Movement* (1959).

The best source on the Constitution is Max Farrand, ed., *Records of the Federal Convention of 1787*, 4 vols. (1911–1937). The intellectual background of the Founders is examined in Garry Wills, *Explaining America: The Federalist* (1981). To understand Madison's thinking about a large republic, see the essays in Douglass Adair, *Fame and the Founding Fathers*, edited by Trevor Colbourn (1974); and Irving Brant, *The Fourth President, A Life of James Madison* (1970).

chapter 7.

REPUBLICAN GOVERNMENT ON TRIAL, 1788-1800

While presiding over the first meeting of the United States Senate in 1789, Vice-President John Adams raised a pressing procedural question: How should the senators address George Washington, the newly elected president? Adams insisted that Washington deserved an impressive title, a designation that would lend dignity and weight to his office. Adams recommended "His Highness, the President of the United States, and Protector of their Liberties," but some senators favored "His Elective Majesty" or "His Excellency."

Washington and many other people regarded the entire debate as ridiculous. Madison believed that such a discussion befit European aristocrats more than American republicans. When the senators learned that their efforts embarrassed Washington, they dropped the topic. The leader of the new Republic would be called President of the United States. One wag, however, dubbed the portly Adams, "His Rotundity."

The comic-opera quality of this debate should not obscure the participants' seriousness. During the 1790s, decisions about the use of power, about actual governmental policies and positions, had the potential to set a lasting precedent and thus to reinforce or imperil the Revolution itself. But the question of how best to put widely shared republican principles into practice divided Americans. Public figures increasingly gravitated to Alexander Hamilton or Thomas Jefferson, the two most powerful personalities of the decade, and before Washington retired from the presidency, these loose political affiliations had hardened into open party identification, either Federalist or Republican, a development that no one in 1787 had anticipated or desired.

The process was painful and the participants often became bitter. Contemporaries associated parties with faction, with conspiratorial efforts to undermine public virtue. The United States had not yet developed the concept of loyal party opposition. In the 1790s, therefore, sensible and honorable people sometimes mistook simple disagreement over policy for treason. Since Federalists and Republicans both claimed to speak for the common good, for a revolutionary heritage, people assumed that one group or the other had to be lying. Suspicion, verging on paranoia, permeated political discussion; before the end of this difficult decade, party spokesmen advocated blatantly partisan actions that could have involved the United States in international war, shattered the Union, and destroyed constitutional liberties. Few times in this country's history has politics so fully occupied the attention of the American people.

The Young Republic Is Launched

In 1788 George Washington enjoyed great popularity throughout the nation. In America's first presidential election, he received the unanimous support of the electoral college, an achievement that no subsequent president has duplicated. John Adams was selected vice-president.

The responsibility Washington bore was as great as his popularity. The political stability of the young Republic depended in large measure on how he handled himself in office. In the eyes of his compatriots, he had been transformed into a living symbol of the new government, and during his presidency (1789–1797), he carried himself with studied dignity and reserve—never ostentatious, the embodiment of classical republican virtues. A French diplomat who witnessed Washington's first inauguration reported in awe: "He has the soul, look and figure of a hero united in him." But the adulation of Washington—however well meant—seriously affected the conduct of public affairs, for criticism of his administration was regarded as an attack on the president and by extension, on the Republic itself. During the early years of Washington's presidency, therefore, American public opinion discouraged partisan politics.

Washington created a strong, independent presidency. While he discussed pressing issues with the members of his cabinet, he left no doubt that he ultimately made policy. Moreover, the first president resisted congressional efforts to restrict executive authority, especially in foreign affairs.

The first Congress quickly established executive departments. Each department was headed by a secretary nominated by the president and serving at the president's pleasure. For the Departments of War, State, and the Treasury, Washington nominated Henry Knox, Thomas Jefferson, and Alexander Hamilton respectively. Edmund Randolph served as part-time attorney general, a position that ranked slightly lower in prestige than the head of a department. As head of the Treasury, which oversaw the collection of customs and other federal taxes, Hamilton could anticipate having several thousand political patronage jobs to dispense.

To modern Americans accustomed to a large federal bureaucracy, the size of Washington's government seems amazingly small. Jefferson, for example, ran the entire State Department with a staff of two chief clerks, two assistants, and a part-time translator. The situation in most other departments was similar. Overworked clerks scribbled madly just to keep up with the press of correspondence. Considering the workloads of men like Jefferson, Hamilton, and Adams, it is no wonder that the president had difficulty persuading able people to accept positions in the new government.

Congress also provided for a federal court system. The Judiciary Act of 1789 created a Supreme Court staffed by a chief justice and five associate justices. In addition, the statute set up thirteen district courts authorized to review the decisions of the state courts. John Jay, a leading figure in New York politics, agreed to serve as chief justice, but since federal judges in the 1790s were expected to travel hundreds of miles over terrible roads to attend sessions of the inferior courts, few persons of outstanding talent and training joined Jay on the federal bench.

Remembering the financial insecurity of the old Confederation government, the newly elected congressmen passed the tariff of 1789, a tax of approximately 5 percent on imports. The act generated considerable revenue, but it also sparked controversy. Southern planters, who relied heavily upon European imports, claimed the tariff discriminated against their interests in favor of those of northern merchants. These battle lines would re-form again and again in the years to come.

Opposing Views of the Destiny of America

Washington's first cabinet included two extraordinary personalities, Alexander Hamilton and Thomas Jefferson. Both had served the country with distinction during the Revolution, were recognized by contemporaries as men of special genius as well as high ambition,

and brought to public office a powerful vision of how the American people could achieve greatness. The story of their opposing views during the decade of the 1790s provides insight into the birth and development of political parties. It also reveals how a common political ideology, republicanism, could be interpreted in two vastly different ways, turning former friends into bitter adversaries. Indeed, the falling out of Hamilton and Jefferson reflected deep, potentially explosive, political divisions within American society.

Hamilton was a brilliant, dynamic young lawyer who had distinguished himself as Washington's aide-de-camp during the Revolution. Born in the West Indies, the child of an adulterous relationship, Hamilton employed charm, courage, and intellect to fulfill his inexhaustible ambition. He strove not for wealth but for reputation. Men and women who fell under his spell found him almost irresistible,

During the first years of Washington's administration, neither Hamilton (left) nor Jefferson recognized the full extent of their differences. But as events forced the federal government to make decisions on economic and foreign affairs, the two secretaries increasingly came into open conflict.

but to enemies, Hamilton appeared a dark, calculating, even evil, genius. He advocated a strong central government and refused to be bound by the strict wording of the Constitution. He loved America, but he admired English culture, and during the 1790s, he advocated closer commercial and diplomatic ties with Britain.

Jefferson possessed a profoundly different temperament. More reflective, he shone less brightly in society than did Hamilton. He thirsted not for power or wealth but for an opportunity to advance the democratic principles that he had stated so eloquently in the Declaration of Independence. He became secretary of state just after returning from Paris where he had witnessed the first, exhilarating moments of the French Revolution. He believed that republicanism would everywhere replace absolute monarchy and aristocratic privilege. His European experiences biased Jefferson in favor of France over Great Britain when the two nations clashed.

Both Hamilton and Jefferson insisted that they were working for the creation of a strong, prosperous republic. Rather than seeing them as spokesmen for competing ideologies, one should view Hamilton and Jefferson as different kinds of republicans who during the 1790s attempted as best they could to cope with unprecedented political challenges.

The two men did seriously disagree on precisely how the United States should fulfill its destiny. As head of the Treasury Department, Hamilton urged his fellow citizens to think in terms of bold commercial development, of farms and factories embedded within a complex financial network that would reduce the nation's reliance upon foreign trade. Because Great Britain had already established an elaborate system of banking and credit, the secretary looked to that country for economic models that might be reproduced on this side of the Atlantic.

Hamilton's pessimistic view of human nature caused him to fear total democracy. Anarchy, not monarchy, was his nightmare. The best hope for the survival of the Republic, Hamilton believed, lay with the country's monied classes. If the wealthiest people could be persuaded that their economic self-interest could be advanced by the central government, then they would strengthen it, and by so doing, bring a greater measure of prosperity to the common people. From Hamilton's perspective, there was no conflict between private greed and public good; one was the source of the other.

In almost every detail, Jefferson challenged Hamilton's analysis. The secretary of state assumed that the strength of the American economy lay not in its industrial potential, but in its agricultural productivity. He recognized the necessity of change, and while he thought that persons who worked the soil were more responsible citizens than those who labored in factories for wages, he encouraged the nation's farmers to participate in an expanding international market.

Unlike Hamilton, Jefferson expressed faith in the ability of the American people to shape policy. He had a boundless optimism in the judgment of the common folk. He instinctively trusted the people, feared that uncontrolled government power might destroy their liberties, and insisted that public officials follow the letter of the Constitution. The greatest threat to the young Republic, he argued, came from the corrupt activities of pseudo-aristocrats, persons who placed the protection of "property" and "civil order" above the preservation of "liberty." Under no circumstance did he want to mortgage the nation's future—through the creation of a large national debt—to the selfish interests of bankers, manufacturers, and speculators.

Hamilton's Grand Design

The unsettled state of the nation's finances presented a staggering challenge to the new government. Congress turned to Hamilton for a policy, and he eagerly accepted the assignment. He read deeply in abstruse economic literature, but the reports he wrote bore the unmistakable stamp of his own creative genius. The secretary synthesized a vast amount of information into an economic blueprint so complex, so innovative that even his allies were slightly baffled. Certainly, Washington never fully grasped the subtleties of Hamilton's plan.

The secretary presented his *Report on Public Credit* to Congress on January 14, 1790. His research revealed that the nation's outstanding debt stood at approximately $54 million. This sum represented various foreign and domestic obligations that the United States government had incurred during the Revolutionary War. But that was not all. The states still owed creditors approximately $25 million. During the 1780s, Americans desperate for cash had been forced to sell government loan certificates to speculators at greatly discounted prices, and it was estimated that approximately $40 million of the nation's debt was owed to twenty thousand people, only 20 percent of whom were the original creditors.

Funding and Assumption

Hamilton's *Report on the Public Credit* contained two major recommendations covering the areas of funding and assumption. First, under his plan the United States promised to fund its foreign and domestic obligations at full face value. Current holders of loan certificates, whoever they were and no matter how they obtained them, could exchange the old certificates for new government bonds bearing a moderate rate of interest. Second, the secretary urged the federal government to assume responsibility for paying the remaining state debts.

Hamilton reasoned that his credit system would accomplish several desirable goals. It would significantly reduce the power of the individual states to shape national economic policy, something Hamilton regarded as essential in maintaining a strong federal government. Moreover, the creation of a fully funded national debt signaled to investors throughout the world that the United States was now solvent, that its bonds represented a good risk. Hamilton hoped that American investment capital would remain in America, providing a source of money for commercial and industrial growth, rather than flow to Europe. In short, Hamilton invited the country's wealthiest citizens to invest in the future of the United States.

To Hamilton's great surprise, his friend Madison attacked the funding scheme in the House of Representatives. He too wanted the United States to pay its debts, but he was more concerned with the original buyers of the certificates than with the speculators who had purchased them from the hard-pressed patriots. However, far too many records had been lost since the Revolution for the Treasury Department to be able to identify all the original holders. In the end, Congress sided with Hamilton's more practical position.

Assumption unleashed even greater criticism. Hamilton's program seemed designed to reward states that had not paid their debts. In addition, the secretary's opponents in Congress became suspicious that assumption was merely a ploy to increase the power and wealth of Hamilton's immediate friends. On April 12, 1790, a rebellious House led by Madison defeated assumption.

The victory was short lived. Hamilton and congressional supporters resorted to legislative horse-trading to revive his foundering program. In exchange for locating the new federal capital on the Potomac River, a move that would stimulate the depressed economy of northern Virginia, several key congressmen who shared Madison's political philosophy changed their votes on assumption. In August Washington signed assumption and funding into law. The first element of Hamilton's design was now securely in place.

The Controversial Bank of the United States

The persistent Hamilton submitted his second report to Congress in January 1791. He proposed that the United States government charter a national bank, much like the Bank of England. This privately owned institution would be funded in part by the federal government. The bank not only would serve as the main depository of the United States government but also would issue currency acceptable in payment of federal taxes. Because of that guarantee, the money would maintain its value while in circulation.

Madison and others in Congress immediately raised a howl of protest. They feared that banks might "perpetuate a larged monied interest" in America. And what about the Constitution? That document said nothing specifically about chartering financial corporations, and they warned that if Hamilton and his supporters were allowed to stretch fundamental law on this occasion, they could not be held back in the future. On this issue, Hamilton stubbornly refused to compromise.

This intense controversy involving his closest advisers worried the president. Even though the bank bill passed Congress (February 8), Washington seriously considered vetoing the legislation on constitutional grounds. Before doing so, however, he requested written opinions from the members of his cabinet. Jefferson's rambling attack on the bank was wholly predictable; Hamilton's defense was masterful. He boldly articulated a doctrine of *implied powers*—that the "necessary and proper" clause of the Constitution (Article 1, Section 8) gave Congress more power than it specified. Neither Madison nor Jefferson had anticipated this interpretation of the Constitution. Hamilton's so-called loose construction carried the day, and on February 25, 1791, Washington signed the bank act into law.

Hamilton triumphed in Congress, but the general public looked upon his actions with growing fear and hostility. Many persons associated huge national debts and privileged banks with the decay of public virtue. They believed that Hamilton was intent upon turning the future of America over to corrupt speculators. To back-country farmers, making money without actually engaging in physical labor appeared immoral, unrepublican, and certainly, un-American. When the greed of a

former Treasury Department official led to several serious bankruptcies in 1792, people began to listen more closely to what Madison, Jefferson, and their associates were saying about growing corruption in high places.

Setback for Hamilton

In his third major report, *Report on Manufactures,* submitted to Congress in December 1791, Hamilton revealed the final details of his grand design for the economic future of the United States. This lengthy document suggested ways by which the federal government might stimulate manufacturing and thus free itself from dependency upon European imports. What was needed was direct government intervention. Hamilton argued that protective tariffs and special industrial bounties would greatly accelerate the growth of a balanced economy, and with proper planning, the United States would soon hold its own with England and France.

In Congress the battle lines were clearly drawn. Hamilton's opponents ignored his economic arguments and instead engaged him on moral and political grounds. Madison took a states' rights position and railed against the dangers of "consolidation," a process that threatened to concentrate all power in the federal government, leaving the states defenseless. Jefferson argued that the development of manufacturing entailed urbanization and cities bred every sort of vice. Other southern congressmen saw tariffs and bounties as vehicles for enriching Hamilton's northern friends at the planters' expense. The recommendations in the *Report on Manufactures* were soundly defeated in the House of Representatives.

Washington detested political squabbling. In August 1792, he begged Hamilton and Jefferson to rise above their differences. The appeal came too late. Hamilton's reports eroded the goodwill of 1788, and by the conclusion of Washington's term, neither secretary trusted the other's judgment. Their sparring had produced congressional factions, but no actual parties had yet formed with permanent organizations that engaged in campaigning.

Foreign Affairs:
A Catalyst to the
Birth of Political Parties

During Washington's second term (1793–1797), war in Europe dramatically thrust foreign affairs into the forefront of American life. Officials who had disagreed over Hamilton's economic policies now were divided by the fighting between France and Britain. Bitter feelings, inflamed emotions, and accusations of treason were common. This poisonous atmosphere spawned the formation of formal political organizations—the Federalists and Republicans. The clash between these groups developed over how best to preserve the new Republic. The Republicans advocated states' rights, strict interpretation of the Constitution, friendship with France, and vigilance against "the avaricious, monopolizing Spirit of Commerce and Commercial Man." The Federalists urged a strong national government, central economic planning, closer ties with Great Britain, and maintenance of public order, even if that meant calling out federal troops.

Threats to United States Neutrality

Great Britain treated the United States with arrogance. Contrary to the instructions of the Treaty of 1783, British troops continued to occupy military posts in the Northwest Territory. Moreover, even though 75 percent of American imports came from Great Britain, that country refused to grant the United States full commercial reciprocity.

France presented a very different challenge. In the spring of 1789, the French Revolution began, and Louis XVI was dethroned. The men who seized power were militant republicans, ideologues eager to liberate all Europe from feudal institutions. Once the Revolution was set in motion, however, the leaders lost control of the movement. Constitutional reform turned into bloody purges, and one radical group, the Jacobins, guillotined thousands of

people during the so-called Reign of Terror (October 1793–July 1794). These events left Americans confused. While those who shared Jefferson's views cheered the spread of republicanism, those who sided with Hamilton condemned French expansionism and political violence.

In the face of growing international tension, neutrality seemed the most prudent course for the United States. But the policy was easier for a weak country to proclaim than to defend. In February 1793 France declared war on Great Britain, and both countries immediately challenged the official American position on shipping: "free ships make free goods," meaning that belligerents should not interfere with the shipping of neutral carriers. To make matters worse, no one was certain whether the Franco-American Treaty of 1778 (see Chapter 5) legally bound the United States to support its old ally against Great Britain.

Both Hamilton and Jefferson wanted to avoid war. Jefferson believed that if Great Britain refused to honor America's neutrality and observe neutral shipping rights—in other words, if the Royal Navy seized American sailors—then the United States should award France special trade advantages. Hamilton thought Jefferson's scheme insane. He pointed out that Britain possessed the largest navy in the world and was not likely to be coerced by American threats. The United States, he counseled, should appease the former mother country even if that meant swallowing national pride.

A newly appointed French minister to the United States, Edmond Genêt, precipitated the first major diplomatic crisis. This unstable young man arrived in Charleston, South Carolina, in April 1793. He found considerable popular enthusiasm for the French Revolution, and heartened by this reception, he authorized privately owned American vessels to seize British ships in the name of France. Such actions clearly violated United States neutrality and invited British retaliation. When government officials warned Genêt to desist, he threatened to take his appeal directly to the American people, who presumably loved

The execution of Louis XVI by French revolutionaries served to deepen the growing political division in America. Republicans, although they deplored the excesses of the Reign of Terror, continued to support the French people. Federalists feared that the violence and lawlessness would spread to the United States.

France more than the Washington administration did.

This confrontation particularly embarrassed Jefferson, the most outspoken pro-French member of the cabinet. He condemned Genêt's imprudent actions. Washington did not wait to determine if the treaties of 1778 were still in force. Even before he had formally received the French minister, the president issued a Proclamation of Neutrality (April 22).

Jay's Treaty Divides the Nation

Great Britain failed to take advantage of Genêt's insolence. Instead, it pushed the United States to the brink of war. British forts on U.S. soil in the Northwest Territory remained a constant source of tension. In June 1793 a new element was added. The London government closed French ports to neutral shipping, and in November, its navy captured several hundred American vessels trading in

the French West Indies. Outraged members of Congress, especially those who identified with Jefferson and Madison, demanded retaliation, an embargo, a stoppage of debt payment, even war.

Before this rhetoric produced violence, Washington made one final effort to preserve peace. In May 1794 he sent Chief Justice John Jay to London to negotiate a formidable list of grievances. Jay's major objectives were removal of the British forts, payment for ships taken in the West Indies, improved commercial relations, and acceptance of the American definition of neutral rights.

Jay's mission had little chance of success, partly because Hamilton had secretly informed British officials that the United States would compromise on most issues. Jay did persuade the British to abandon their frontier posts and to allow small American ships to trade in the British West Indies, but they rejected out of hand the United States position on neutral rights. The British would continue to search American vessels on the high seas for contraband and to seize sailors suspected of being British citizens. Moreover, there would be no compensation for the ships seized in 1793 until the Americans paid British merchants for debts contracted before the Revolution. And to the particular annoyance of Southerners, not a word was said about the slaves that the British army had carried off at the conclusion of the war. While Jay salvaged the peace, he appeared to have betrayed the national interest.

News of Jay's Treaty produced an angry outcry in the national capital. Even Washington was apprehensive. He submitted the document to the Senate without recommending ratification. After an extremely bitter debate, the upper house, controlled by Federalists, narrowly accepted a revised version of the treaty (June 1795).

■ *John Jay was burned in effigy by angry mobs who viewed the terms of his agreement with Great Britain as a betrayal of American interests.*

The details of the Jay agreement soon leaked to the press. Throughout the country Jay was burned in effigy. Southerners announced they would not pay prerevolutionary debts to British merchants. And when news of the treaty reached the House of Representatives, a storm of protest broke out in that august body. Followers of Jefferson—now called Republicans—in Congress thought they could stop Jay's Treaty by withholding funds for its implementation.

But the president still had a trump card to play. He raised the possibility that the House was really contemplating his impeachment. Such an action was, of course, unthinkable, and public support quickly swung toward Washington and the Federalists, as the followers of Hamilton were called. Jay's Treaty was saved, but the division between the two parties was beyond repair.

By the time that Jay's Treaty became law (June 14, 1795), the two giants of Washington's first cabinet had retired. Late in 1793 Jefferson returned to his Virginia plantation, Monticello, where despite his separation from day-to-day political affairs, he remained the chief spokesman for the Republican party. His rival, Hamilton, left the Treasury in January 1795 to return to private life in New York City. He maintained close ties with important Federalist officials, however, and even more than Jefferson, Hamilton concerned himself with the details of party organization.

Diplomacy in the West

Before Great Britain finally withdrew its troops from the western forts in 1796, its military officers encouraged local tribes to attack settlers and traders from the United States. The Indians won several impressive victories over federal troops in the area that would become western Ohio and Indiana. But the tribes were actually more vulnerable than they realized, for when confronted with a major United States army under the command of General Anthony Wayne, they received no support from their British allies. At the battle of Fallen Timbers (August 20, 1794), Wayne's forces

Foreign Affairs: A Catalyst to the Birth of Political Parties

crushed Indian resistance in the Northwest Territory, and the tribes were compelled to sign the Treaty of Greenville, formally ceding to the United States government the land that became Ohio.

Shrewd negotiations mixed with pure luck helped secure the nation's southwestern frontier. For complex reasons having to do with the state of European diplomacy, Spanish officials in 1795 encouraged the United States representative in Madrid to discuss the navigation of the Mississippi River. Before this initiative, the Spanish government not only had closed the river to American commerce but also had incited the Indians of the region to harass United States settlers (see Chapter 6). Relations between the two countries would probably have deteriorated further had the United States not signed Jay's Treaty. The Spanish assumed—quite erroneously—that Great Britain and the United States had formed an alliance to strip Spain of its North American possessions.

To avoid this imagined disaster, officials in Madrid offered the American envoy, Thomas Pinckney, extraordinary concessions: the opening of the Mississippi, the right to deposit goods in New Orleans without paying duties, a secure southern boundary on the thirty-first parallel, and a promise to stay out of Indian affairs. An amazed Pinckney signed the Treaty of San Lorenzo (also called Pinckney's Treaty) on October 27, 1795, and in March the Senate ratified the document without a single dissenting vote.

Popular Political Culture: The Partisan Role of Newspapers and Political Clubs

More than any other event during Washington's administration, ratification of Jay's Treaty generated intense political strife. It divided Americans along party lines at a time when parties or factions were viewed as sub-

versive. Party conflict also suggested that Americans had lost the sense of common purpose that had united them during the Revolution. Politicians agreed that opposition smacked of disloyalty and therefore should be eliminated by any means—fair or foul. But who should eliminate whom? That was the question that engaged Federalists and Republicans.

More than any other single element, newspapers transformed the political culture of the United States. Americans were voracious readers, and they were well supplied with newspapers. Most of these journals were fiercely partisan. Rumor and opinion were presented as fact, and public officials were regularly dragged through the rhetorical mud. Jefferson, for example, was accused of cowardice; Hamilton vilified as an adulterer.

Even poets and essayists were caught up in the political fray. The better writers often produced party propaganda. American writers sometimes complained that the culture of the young Republic was too materialistic, too unappreciative of the subtler forms of art then popular in Europe. But it was clear that poets who ignored patriotism and politics simply did not sell well in the United States.

This decade also witnessed the birth of political clubs. Modeled on the political debating societies that sprang up in France during the early years of the French Revolution, the clubs emphasized political indoctrination. By 1794 at least twenty-four clubs were holding regular meetings. Along with newspapers, they provided the common people with highly partisan political information.

In 1794 the Federalists accused the political clubs of triggering real violence—the so-called Whiskey Rebellion. The farmers of western Pennsylvania regularly distilled their grain into whiskey, and they bitterly resented paying the federal excise tax on their product that Congress had imposed in 1791.

A minor tax revolt occurred in the Pittsburgh region in 1794, and local farmers threatened a federal excise collector with bodily harm. In response to this incident, President Washington raised thirteen thousand troops

■ *Tarring and feathering federal officials was one way in which western Pennsylvanians protested the tax on whiskey in 1794. Washington's call for troops to put down the insurrection drew more volunteers than he had been able to raise during most of the American Revolution.*

and sent them after the culprits. They found only twenty troublemakers and convicted only two, one reportedly a "simpleton" and the other insane. Washington eventually pardoned both rebels, and peace returned to the frontier.

In the national political forum, however, the Whiskey Rebellion had just begun. Washington blamed the "Republican" clubs for promoting civil unrest. Jefferson labeled the entire episode a Hamiltonian device to create an army for the purpose of intimidating Republicans. How else could one explain the administration's gross overreaction to a few disgruntled farmers? The response of both parties reveals a pervasive fear of some secret, evil design to destroy the Republic. The clubs and newspapers fanned these anxieties, convincing many government officials that the First Amendment should not be interpreted as protecting political dissent.

In September 1796 Washington published his famed "Farewell Address," formally declaring his intention to retire from the presidency. Written largely by Hamilton, who drew upon a draft by Madison, it sought to advance the Federalist cause in the forthcoming election. By waiting until September to announce his retirement, Washington denied the Republicans valuable time to organize an effective campaign. There was an element of irony in this initiative. Washington had always maintained that he stood above party. While he may have done so in the early years of his presidency, events such as the signing of Jay's Treaty and the suppression of the Whiskey Rebellion transformed him in the eyes of many Americans into a spokesman solely for Hamilton's Federalist party.

In the address, Washington issued two warnings. First, he warned his country against all political faction. Second, he counseled the United States to avoid making any permanent alliances with distant nations that had no real interest in promoting American security. If few Americans paid attention to the first part of his message, the second part guided foreign relations for many years and became the credo of later American isolationists.

Federalists in Power

The election of 1796 took place in an atmosphere of mutual distrust. Jefferson, soon to be the vice-president, believed he was running against the American representatives of British aristocracy. On their part, the Federalists were convinced that their Republican opponents wanted to hand the government over to French radicals. By modern standards, the structures of both parties and the campaign methods employed were still primitive.

During the campaign the Federalists sowed the seeds of their eventual destruction. Party stalwarts agreed that John Adams should run against the Republican candidate, Thomas Jefferson. Hamilton, however, could not leave well enough alone. From his law office in New York City, he schemed to deprive Adams of the presidency. He apparently feared that an independent-minded Adams would be difficult to manipulate. He was correct.

Hamilton exploited an awkward feature of the electoral college. In accordance with the Constitution, each elector cast two ballots, and the person who gained the most votes became president. The runner-up, regardless of party affiliation, served as vice-president. Ordinarily the Federalist electors would have cast one vote for Adams and one for Thomas Pinckney, the party's choice for vice-president. Everyone hoped, of course, that there would be no tie. Hamilton secretly urged southern Federalists to support Pinckney with their first vote, which meant throwing away an elector's second vote. The strategy backfired when New Englanders loyal to Adams heard of Hamilton's maneuvering. They dropped Pinckney, and when the votes were counted, Adams had 71, Jefferson 68, and Pinckney 59. Hamilton's treachery not only angered the new president but also heightened tensions within the Federalist party.

Adams assumed the presidency under intolerable conditions. He found himself saddled with the members of Washington's old cabinet, who regularly consulted with Hamilton behind Adams' back. But to have dismissed them summarily would have called Washington's judgment into question, and Adams was not publicly prepared to take that risk. Adams also had to work with a Republican vice-president. Adams hoped that he and Jefferson could cooperate, but partisan pressures soon overwhelmed the president's good intentions. After a short time, Adams stopped consulting Jefferson.

The XYZ Affair and Domestic Politics

Foreign affairs immediately occupied Adams' full attention. The French government regarded Jay's Treaty as an affront. By allowing Great Britain to define the condition for neutrality, the United States had in effect sided with that nation against the interests of France.

Relations between the two countries steadily deteriorated. The French dismissed Charles Cotesworth Pinckney, the United States representative in Paris, and the French minister in Philadelphia openly supported Jefferson for president in 1796. In 1797 French privateers began seizing American ships. During this period, neither country bothered to declare war, and for that reason the hostilities came to be known as the Quasi-War.

Hamilton and his friends welcomed the popular outpouring of anti-French sentiment. They counseled the president to prepare for all-out war, hoping that war would purge the United States of French influence. Adams was not persuaded to escalate the conflict. Instead he sent a three-man commission—Charles Pinckney, John Marshall, and Elbridge Gerry—to Paris in a final attempt to remove the sources of antagonism. They were instructed to obtain compensation for the ships seized by French privateers as well as release from the treaties of 1778. In exchange, the commission offered France the same commercial privileges granted to Great Britain in Jay's Treaty.

The commission was shocked by the outrageous treatment it received in France. Instead

■ *This cartoon captures the anti-French sentiment many Americans felt after President Adams disclosed the papers of the XYZ affair. America— depicted as a young maiden—is being plundered by five Frenchmen, who represent the five Directors of the French government.*

of dealing directly with Talleyrand, the French minister of foreign relations, they met with obscure intermediaries who reported that Talleyrand would not open negotiations unless he was given $250,000. In addition, the French government expected a "loan" of millions of dollars. The Americans refused to play this insulting game.

The event set off a domestic political explosion. When Adams presented the commission's official correspondence before Congress— the names of Talleyrand's lackeys were labeled X, Y, and Z—the Federalists burst out with a war cry. At last, they would be able to even old scores with the Republicans. So tense was the atmosphere that old friendships between Federalists and Republicans were shattered. As Jefferson wrote to an old colleague: "Men who have been intimate all their lives, cross the streets to avoid meeting, and turn their heads

another way, lest they should be obliged to touch their hats."

Efforts to Crush Political Dissent

In the spring of 1798 the followers of Hamilton—called High Federalists—assumed that it was just a matter of time until Adams asked Congress for a formal declaration of war. In the meantime, they pushed for a general rearmament, new fighting ships, additional harbor fortifications, and most important, a greatly expanded United States army. About the need for land forces, Adams remained understandably skeptical. He saw no likelihood of a French invasion.

The president missed the political point. The army the Federalists wanted was intended not to thwart French aggression but to stifle internal opposition. Indeed, militant Federalists used the XYZ affair as the occasion to institute what Jefferson termed the "reign of witches." Jefferson was right; the threat to Republicans was real.

During the summer of 1798 a provisional army gradually came into existence. George Washington agreed to lead the troops, but he would do so only on condition that Adams appoint Hamilton as second-in-command. Although Adams did not want to promote Hamilton to the command over others who outranked him and were more agreeable, he was not about to refuse Washington's request.

The chief of the High Federalists threw himself into the task of recruiting and supplying the troops. No detail escaped his attention. Only loyal Federalists received commissions—even Adams' son-in-law was denied a post—as Hamilton put the finishing touches on his plan to restore domestic order. The mood of the nation grew tense, and many politicians predicted that a civil war would soon erupt.

Hamilton should not have treated Adams with such open contempt. After all, without presidential cooperation, Hamilton could not fulfill his grand military ambitions. Whenever pressing questions concerning the army arose, Adams was nowhere to be found. He delayed Hamilton at every step, making it quite clear that his first love was the navy. In May 1798, the president even persuaded Congress to establish the Navy Department. Moreover, Adams steadfastly refused to ask Congress for a formal declaration of war. As the weeks passed, the American people increasingly looked upon the idle army as an expensive extravagance.

The Alien and Sedition Acts

The Federalists did not rely solely upon the army to crush political dissent. During the summer of 1798, the party's majority in Congress passed a group of bills known collectively as the Alien and Sedition Acts. The legislation authorized the use of federal courts and the powers of the presidency to silence the Republicans. The acts were born of fear and vindictiveness, and in their efforts to punish the followers of Jefferson, the Federalists created the nation's first major crisis over civil liberties.

Congress drew up three separate Alien Acts. The first, the Alien Enemies Law, vested the president with extraordinary wartime powers. On his own authority he could detain or deport foreigners who behaved in a manner he thought suspicious. Since Adams refused to ask for a declaration of war, this legislation never went into effect. The second act, the Alien Law, empowered the president to expel any foreigner from the United States simply by executive decree. While Adams did not attempt to enforce the act, the mere threat of arrest caused some Frenchmen to flee the country. The third act, the Naturalization Law was the most flagrantly political of the group. The act established a fourteen-year probationary period before foreigners could apply for full United States citizenship. This act was designed to limit the "hordes of wild Irishmen" and other immigrants who voted Republican.

The Sedition Law struck at the heart of free political exchange. It defined criticism of the United States government as criminal libel; citizens found guilty by a jury were subject to fines and imprisonment. Republicans were justly worried that the Sedition Law undermined rights guaranteed by the First Amendment. As far as the Federalists were concerned, if their opposition could be silenced, they were willing to restrict freedom of speech.

Americans living in widely scattered regions of the country soon witnessed political repression first hand. District courts staffed by Federalist appointees indicted seventeen people for criticizing the government. The most celebrated trial occurred in Vermont. A Republican congressman, Matthew Lyon, who was running for reelection, publicly accused the Adams' administration of mishandling the Quasi-War. Lyon, an Irish immigrant, had earlier angered Federalists by spitting in the eye of a Federalist congressman during a heated exchange. Now a Federalist court was pleased to have the opportunity to convict him of libel.

In the early years of the Republic, political dissent sometimes escalated to physical violence. This fistfight on the floor of Congress took place on February 15, 1798. The combatants are Republican Matthew Lyon and Federalist Roger Griswold.

But Lyon enjoyed the last laugh. While he served his term in jail, his constituents re-elected him to Congress.

As this and other cases demonstrated, the federal courts had become political tools. While the fumbling efforts at enforcement of the Sedition Law did not silence opposition—indeed, they sparked even greater criticism and created martyrs—the actions of the administration persuaded Republicans that the survival of free government was at stake.

The Republicans Appeal to the States

By the fall of 1798 Jefferson and Madison were convinced that the Federalists envisioned the creation of a police state. Some extreme Republicans such as John Taylor of Virginia recommended secession from the Union; others advocated armed resistance. But Jefferson wisely counseled against such extreme strategies. Instead, he turned to the state legislatures for help.

As the crisis deepened, Jefferson and Madison drafted separate protests known as the Virginia and Kentucky Resolutions respectively. Both statements vigorously defended the right of individual state assemblies to interpret the constitutionality of federal law. Jefferson wrote the Kentucky Resolutions in November 1798, and in an outburst of partisan anger, he flirted with a doctrine as dangerous to the survival of the United States as anything advanced by Hamilton and his High Federalist friends.

In the Kentucky Resolutions, Jefferson described the federal union as a compact. The states transferred certain explicit powers to the national government, but in his opinion, they retained full authority over all matters not specifically mentioned in the Constitution. Jefferson rejected Hamilton's broad interpretation of the "general welfare" clause. He believed that individual states had the right to nullify any law that was not specifically within the charter of the Constitution. Carried to an extreme, Jefferson's logic could have led to the break-up of the federal government. Although Madison agreed that the Alien and Sedition Acts were unconstitutional, his Virginia Resolutions were more moderate than Jefferson's Kentucky Resolutions.

The Virginia and Kentucky Resolutions must be viewed in proper historical context. They were not intended as statements of ab-

1787   Constitution of the United States signed (September)

1789   George Washington inaugurated (April)
        Louis XVI of France calls meeting of the Estates General (May)

1790   Congress approves Hamilton's plan for funding and assumption (July)

1791   Bank of the United States is chartered (February)
        Hamilton's *Report on Manufactures* rejected by Congress (December)

1793   France's revolutionary government announces a "war of all people against all kings" (February)
        Genêt affair strains relations with France (April)
        Washington issues Proclamation of Neutrality (April)
        Spread of "Democratic" clubs alarms Federalists
        Jefferson resigns as secretary of state (December)

1794   Whiskey Rebellion put down by United States Army (July-November)
        General Anthony Wayne defeats Indians at Battle of Fallen Timbers (August)

1795   Hamilton resigns as secretary of the treasury (January)
        Jay's Treaty divides the nation (June)
        Pinckney's Treaty with Spain is a welcome surprise (October)

1796   Washington publishes "Farewell Address" (September)
        John Adams elected president (December)

1797   XYZ affair poisons United States relations with France (October)

1798–1800   Quasi-War with France

1798   Congress passes the Alien and Sedition Acts (June and July)
        Provisional army is formed
        Virginia and Kentucky Resolutions protest the Alien and Sedition Acts (November and December)

1799   George Washington dies (December)

1800   Convention of Mortefontaine is signed with France, ending Quasi-War (September)

1801   House of Representatives elects Thomas Jefferson president (February)

stract principles and most certainly not as a justification for southern secession. They were pure political party propaganda. Jefferson and Madison were simply reminding American voters during a period of severe domestic tension that the Republicans offered a clear alternative to Federalist rule.

Adams' Finest Hour

In February 1799 President Adams belatedly declared his independence from the Hamiltonian wing of the Federalist party. Throughout the confrontation with France, Adams had shown little enthusiasm for war, and after the XYZ affair, the French changed their tune. Talleyrand now sent word that he was ready to negotiate in good faith. The High Federalists ridiculed this report, but Adams decided to accept this peace initiative. In February he asked the Senate to confirm William Jans Murry as United States representative to France.

In November 1799, Murry and several other negotiators arrived in France. By then Napoleon Bonaparte had come to power, but he cooperated with the Americans. Together, they drew up an agreement known as the Convention of Mortefontaine. The French refused to compensate the Americans for vessels taken during the Quasi-War, but they did declare the treaties of 1778 null and void. Moreover, the convention removed annoying French restrictions on United States commerce. Not only had Adams avoided war, he had also created an atmosphere of mutual trust that paved the way for the purchase of the Louisiana Territory. The negotiations brought Adams personal satisfaction, but they cost him reelection.

The Peaceful Revolution: The Election of 1800

On the eve of the election of 1800, the Federalists were fatally divided between the followers of both Adams and Hamilton. Once again the former secretary of the treasury attempted to rig the voting in the electoral college so that the party's vice-presidential candidate, Charles Cotesworth Pinckney, would receive more ballots than did Adams. Again the conspiracy backfired, and the Republicans carried the election.

But to everyone's surprise, the election was not resolved in the electoral college. When the ballots were counted, Jefferson and his running mate, Aaron Burr, had tied. This accident—a Republican elector should have thrown away his second vote—sent the selection of the next president to the House of Representatives, a body still controlled by members of the Federalist party.

As the House began its work on February 27, 1801, excitement ran high. Each state delegation cast a single vote, with nine votes needed to be elected. The drama dragged on for days. To add to the confusion, the ambitious Burr refused to withdraw. Finally, leading Federalists decided that Jefferson, whatever his faults, would make a more responsible president than would the shifty Burr. On the thirty-sixth ballot, Jefferson was elected. The Twelfth Amendment, ratified in 1804, saved the American people from repeating this potentially dangerous turn of events. Henceforth, the electoral college cast separate ballots for president and vice-president.

During the final days of his presidency, Adams appointed as many Federalists as possible to the federal bench. Jefferson protested the hasty manner in which these "midnight judges" were selected. One of them, John Marshall, became chief justice of the United States, a post he held with distinction for thirty-four years. But behind the last-minute flurry of activity lay bitterness and disappointment. On the morning of Jefferson's inauguration, Adams slipped away from the capital—now located in Washington—unnoticed and unappreciated.

In the address that Adams missed. Jefferson attempted to quiet partisan fears. "We are all Republicans; we are all Federalists," he declared. He did not mean that there were no longer any party differences, only that all politicians shared a deep commitment to a federal Union based upon republican ideals. Indeed, the president interpreted the election of 1800 as a fulfillment of the principles of 1776.

From a broader historical perspective, however, the election of 1800 seems noteworthy for what did not occur. There were no riots in the streets, no attempted coup by military officers, no secession from the Union, nothing except the peaceful transfer of government from the leaders of one party to those of the opposition. That in itself was a remarkable achievement.

Recommended Reading

John C. Miller, *The Federalist Era, 1789–1801* (1960), provides the best political survey of this exciting period. Forrest McDonald has reinterpreted the politics of the 1790s in *The Presidency of George Washington* (1974) and *Alexander Hamilton* (1979). See also Merrill D. Peterson, *Thomas Jefferson and the New Nation: A Biography* (1970), and Jacob Ernest Cooke, *Alexander Hamilton* (1982). Drew McCoy, *The Elusive Republic: Political Economy in Jeffersonian America* (1980), and Joyce Appleby, *Capitalism and a New Social Order: The Republican Version of the 1790s* (1984) provide important insights into the issues that divided Hamilton and Jefferson. Richard Hofstadter avoided taking sides in *The Idea of a Party System: The Rise of Legitimate Opposition in the United States, 1780–1840* (1969).

Political ideologies of this period are discussed in Lance Banning, *The Jeffersonian Persuasion: Evolution of Party Ideology* (1978), and Richard Buel, Jr., *Securing the Revolution: Ideology in American Politics, 1789–1815* (1972). The problems associated with the developing political parties are examined in William N. Chambers, *Political Parties in a New Nation: The American Experience, 1776–1809* (1963), and Noble E. Cunningham, Jr., *The Jeffersonian Republicans: The Formation of Party Organization, 1789–1801* (1957).

Detailed treatments of the major negotiations and treaty fights are Alexander De Conde, *Entangling Alliance: Politics and Diplomacy Under George Washington* (1958); Jerald A. Combs, *The Jay Treaty: Political Battleground of the Founding Fathers* (1970); and William Stinchcombe, *The XYZ Affair* (1980). The new government's attempt to restrict civil rights is covered in James Morton Smith, *Freedom's Fetters: The Alien and Sedition Laws and American Civil Liberties* (1956).

chapter 8

REPUBLICAN ASCENDANCY

British visitors often disliked Jeffersonian society. Wherever they traveled in the young Republic, they met ill-mannered people inspired with a ruling passion for liberty and equality. Charles William Janson, an Englishman who lived in the United States for thirteen years, was particularly upset by the lack of deference in American society. He remembered one woman who worked for an acquaintance of his and who refused to acknowledge that any person was her master. She told Janson: "I'd have you know, *man*, that I am no *sarvant* [sic]; none but *negers* [sic] are *sarvants.*"

This was the authentic voice of Jeffersonian republicanism—self-confident, assertive, blatantly racist, and having no intention of being relegated to low social status. The maid believed that she was her employer's equal. She may even have fostered dreams of having employees of her own some day. After all, for the men and women who believed in the vision that Jefferson and other Republicans offered, America was a land of boundless opportunity.

Yet the limits of the Jeffersonian vision were obvious even to contemporaries. The people who spoke most nobly about equality often owned slaves. It is not surprising that leaders of the Federalist party accused the Republicans, especially those who lived in the South, of hypocrisy. The race issue simply would not go away. Beneath the political maneuvering over the acquisition of the Louisiana Territory and the War of 1812 lay fundamental disagreement about the spread of slavery to the western territories.

In other areas the Jeffersonians did not fulfill even their own high expectations. As members of the opposition party during the presidency of John Adams, they insisted upon a strict interpretation of the Constitution, peaceful foreign relations, and a reduction of the role of the federal government in the lives of the average citizens. But following the election of 1800, Jefferson and his supporters discovered that unanticipated pressures, foreign and domestic, forced them to moderate these goals. Before he retired from public office, Jefferson interpreted the Constitution in a way that permitted the government to purchase the Louisiana Territory when the opportunity arose; he regulated the national economy with a rigor that would have made Alexander Hamilton blush; and he led the country to the brink of war. Some Americans praised the president's pragmatism; other felt betrayed.

Burgeoning Population and Economy

During the early decades of the nineteenth century, the population of the United States experienced substantial growth more the result of natural reproduction than immigration. The 1810 census counted 7,240,000 Americans, a jump of almost 2 million in just ten years. Of this total, approximately 20 percent were blacks. It was a young population. The largest single group in this society was children, boys and girls who were born after Washington's administration and who came of age at a time when the nation's boundaries were rapidly expanding.

Even as Americans defended the rights of individual states, they were forming strong regional identifications. In commerce and politics they perceived themselves as representatives of distinct subcultures—Southerners, New Englanders, or Westerners. Pride and defensiveness mingled together to produce sectional identities which in time became stronger than even state loyalties.

This shifting focus of attention resulted not only from an awareness of shared economic interests but also from a sensitivity to outside attacks upon slavery. Long before Jefferson died in 1826, Southerners raised the specter of secession and showed how fragile national unity was.

Peopling the West

The most striking changes occurred in the West. Before the end of the American Revolution, only Indian traders and a few hardy settlers had ventured across the Appalachians.

After 1790, however, a flood of people poured west to stake out farms on the rich soil. Pittsburgh and Cincinnati, both strategically located on the Ohio River, became important commercial ports. Congress rapidly formed new territories and admitted new states. Wherever they located, Westerners depended upon water transportation. Riverboats represented the cheapest and fastest way to get crops to market. The Mississippi River was the crucial commercial link for the entire region.

Families who moved west attempted to transplant familiar Eastern customs to the frontier. In some areas such as the Western Reserve, a narrow strip of land along Lake Erie in northern Ohio, the influence of New England remained strong. In general, however, a creative mixing of peoples of different backgrounds in a strange environment generated distinctive folkways. They developed their own heroic figures and prided themselves on their toughness, ambition, and self-confidence. Restless and excited by the challenges and opportunities of the frontier, these settlers thought little about packing up their belongings and moving further west.

Only one obstacle barred the way—Indians. Native Americans still lived in the region, and they insisted that they owned the land. The tragedy was that the Indians, many of them dependent on trade with whites and ravaged by disease and alcohol, lacked unity. Small groups allegedly representing the interests of an entire tribe sold off huge pieces of land, often for whiskey or trinkets.

These fraudulent transactions disgusted the brilliant Shawnee leaders, Tecumseh, and his brother, Tenskwatawa (known as the Prophet). These men desperately tried to revitalize tribal culture, encouraging Indians to avoid contact with whites, to resist alcohol, and most important, to hold on to their land. Frontiersmen saw Tecumseh as a threat to progress, and during the War of 1812, they shattered the Indians' dream of cultural renaissance. North and South, American settlers pushing west swept away the Indian barrier.

Well-meaning Jeffersonians did not intend to exterminate the Indians. The president talked

■ *The Prophet provided spiritual leadership for the union of Indian tribes he and his brother Tecumseh organized to resist white encroachment upon Indian lands.*

about creating a vast reservation beyond the Mississippi River. He planned to turn the Indians into yeoman farmers. But even the most enlightened thinkers of the day did not believe that the Indians possessed a culture worth preserving.

Commercial Capitalism

Before 1820 the prosperity of the United States depended primarily upon its agriculture and trade. Jeffersonian America was by no stretch of the imagination an industrial economy. Except for the cotton gin, important mechanical and chemical inventions did not appear in the fields for another generation. Southerners concentrated upon staple crops, tobacco, rice, and cotton. In the North people generally produced livestock and cereal crops. Regardless of location, however, the nation's farmers, who represented 84 percent of the population, followed a back-breaking work routine that did not differ substantially from that of their parents and grandparents. Probably the major innovation of this period was the agricultural fair, which was first introduced in hopes of improving animal breeding.

The merchant marine represented an equally important element in America's preindustrial economy. At the turn of the century ships flying the Stars and Stripes transported a large share of the world's trade. Merchants in Boston, New York, and Philadelphia received handsome profits from this commerce. Their ships provided essential links between European countries and their Caribbean colonies. This trade, along with the export of domestic staples, especially cotton, generated great fortunes. Unfortunately, the boom did not last. The success of the "carrying trade" depended in large measure upon friendly relations between the United States and the major European powers. When England and France began seizing American ships—as they both did after 1805—national prosperity suffered.

The cities of Jeffersonian America functioned chiefly as depots for international trade. Only about 7 percent of the nation's population lived in urban centers, and most of these people owed their livelihoods either directly or indirectly to the "carrying trade." Ship builders, stevedores, and artisans, as well as merchants, contributed to the shipping business. As the merchant families grew wealthy, their demand for luxury items drew a group of master craftsmen whose beautiful and intricate pieces—such as New England clocks—were perhaps the highest artistic achievement of the period.

American cities exercised only marginal economic influence upon the nation's vast hinterland. Because of the high cost of land transportation, urban merchants seldom purchased goods for export—flour and meat, for example—from a distance of more than 150 miles. The separation between rural and urban Americans was far more pronounced during Jefferson's presidency than it was after the development of canals and railroads a few decades later.

Merchants in Boston, Philadelphia, and New York (above, in 1797) grew rich off the volume of international trade that flowed through these cities, especially between 1793 and 1807. The merchant marine's crucial role in America's preindustrial economy made it worth fighting for in 1802 when the United States found itself waging an undeclared war against Morocco, Algiers, Tripoli, and Tunis (the Barbary States) over the high tributes extracted by Barbary potentates for the "protection" of American ships against seizure. War and eventual victory confirmed the importance of freedom of the seas and unrestricted commerce to the new nation.

The booming carrying trade may actually have retarded the industrialization of the United States. The lure of large profits drew investment capital—a scarce resource in a developing society—into commerce. By contrast, manufacturing seemed too risky.

Industry was not entirely forgotten, however. Samuel Slater, an English-born designer of textile machinery, did establish several cotton spinning mills in New England, but before the 1820s these plants employed only a small number of workers. Another farsighted inventor, Robert Fulton, sailed the first American steamship up the Hudson River in 1807. In time, this marvelous innovation opened new markets for domestic manufacturers, especially in the West.

Republicans in Power

The District of Columbia seemed an appropriate capital for a Republican president. At the time of Jefferson's first inauguration, Washington was still an isolated rural village. Jefferson fit comfortably into Washington society. He despised formal ceremony and sometimes shocked foreign dignitaries by meeting them in his slippers or a threadbare jacket. Reading and reflection were his primary escapes from official duties.

The president was a poor public speaker. He wisely refused to deliver annual addresses before Congress. In personal conversation, however, Jefferson exuded considerable charm. His dinner parties were major social events, and in this forum, Jefferson regaled politicians with his knowledge of literature, philosophy, and science.

Notwithstanding his commitment to the life of the mind, Jefferson was a politician to the core. He ran for the presidency in order to achieve specific goals: the reduction of the size and cost of federal government, the repeal of the obnoxious Federalist legislation such as the Alien Acts, and the maintenance of international peace. Jefferson realized that he required the full cooperation of congressional Republicans, some of whom were fiercely independent men. To accomplish his program, Jefferson developed friendships, wrote memoranda, and held intimate meetings with key Republicans. In two terms as president, Jefferson never had to veto a single act of Congress.

Jefferson carefully selected the members of his cabinet. During Washington's administration, he had witnessed—even provoked—severe infighting; as president, he nominated only those who enthusiastically supported his programs. James Madison became secretary of state, and Albert Gallatin, a Swiss-born financier who understood the complexities of the federal budget, accepted Jefferson's appointment as secretary of the treasury. Henry Dearborn, Levi Lincoln, and Robert Smith, all loyal to Jefferson, filled the other cabinet posts.

Jeffersonian Reforms

A top priority of the new government was cutting the national debt. Throughout American history, presidents have advocated such reductions, but in the twentieth century, few have achieved them. Jefferson succeeded. Both he and Gallatin associated debt with Alexander Hamilton's Federalist financial programs (see Chapter 7), measures they considered harmful to republicanism. Jefferson claimed that legislators elected by the current generation did not have the right to mortgage the future of unborn Americans.

Jefferson also wanted to diminish the activities of the federal government. He urged Congress to repeal all direct taxes. Gallatin linked federal income to the carrying trade. He calculated that the entire cost of national government could be borne by customs receipts. The only problem with Gallatin's plan was that it depended upon peaceful international relations, a factor that was not predictable.

To help pay the debt inherited from the Adams administration, Jefferson ordered substantial cuts in the national budget. He closed several embassies in Europe, slashed military spending, and during his first term, he reduced the size of the United States Army by 50 percent. In addition, he retired a majority of the navy's warships, a move he claimed promoted peace.

More than budgetary considerations prompted Jefferson's military reductions. A product of the revolutionary experience, he was deeply suspicious of standing armies. In the event of foreign attack, he reasoned, the militia would rise in defense of the Republic. To ensure that the citizen soldiers would receive professional leadership in battle, Jefferson created the Army Corps of Engineers and the military academy at West Point in 1802.

Political patronage greatly annoyed the new president. Although he controlled several hundred jobs, he refused to dismiss all the Federalists. To transform federal hiring into an undisciplined spoils system, especially at the highest levels of the federal bureaucracy, seemed to Jefferson to be shortsighted. Moderate Federalists might be converted to the Republican party, and in any case, there was a good chance that they possessed the expertise needed to run the government.

Jefferson's political moderation helped hasten the demise of the Federalist party. But the Federalists also contributed to their own decline. The party's organization was loose, and Federalist leaders refused to adopt the popular forms of campaigning that the Republicans had developed so successfully during the late 1790s. The mere prospect of flattering the common people was odious enough to drive some Federalists into political retirement.

Many of them also sensed that national expansion worked against their interests. Western states inevitably seemed to send Republican representatives to Washington. By 1805 the Federalists retained only a few states in New England and Delaware.

Faced with the imminent death of their party, younger Federalists belatedly attempted to pump life into their organization. They experimented with popular election techniques, tightened party organization, held nominating conventions, and campaigned energetically for office. But the results of these activities were disappointing. Even the younger Federalists felt it was demeaning to appeal to voters.

Louisiana Purchase

When Jefferson first took office, he was confident that Louisiana as well as Florida would eventually become part of the United States. He hoped to persuade the notoriously weak Spanish rulers to sell the territory, but failing in this, he was prepared to threaten forceable occupation.

In May 1801, however, prospects for the easy or inevitable acquisition of Louisiana suddenly darkened. Jefferson learned that Spain had secretly transferred title of the entire region to France. To make matters worse, the French ruler Napoleon Bonaparte seemed intent upon reestablishing an empire in North America. Napolean dispatched a large army to put down a rebellion in France's sugar-rich Caribbean colony, Santo Domingo. From that island stronghold in the West Indies, French troops could seize New Orleans and close the Mississippi River to American trade.

A sense of crisis enveloped Washington. Tensions increased when the Spanish officials who still governed New Orleans announced the closing of that port to American commerce (October 1802). Jefferson and his advisers assumed that the Spanish had acted upon orders from France, but despite this serious provocation, the president preferred negotiations to war. In January 1803 he asked James Monroe, a loyal Republican from Virginia, to join the American Minister, Robert Livingston, in Paris. The president instructed the two men to explore the possibility of purchasing the city of New Orleans. If Livingston and Monroe failed, Jefferson realized that he would be forced to turn to Great Britain for military assistance.

By the time Monroe joined Livingston in France, Napoleon's army in Santo Domingo had succumbed to tropical disease, and he had lost interest in establishing an American empire. Knowing nothing of these developments, the American diplomats were taken by surprise when they were offered the entire Louisiana Territory for only $15 million. At one stroke, the Americans doubled the size of the United States, although the boundaries were vague.

By 1803, when this view was painted, New Orleans was already a thriving port and an important outlet for products from the growing frontier. President Jefferson recognized the strategic location of the city and determined to buy it from France.

The American people responded enthusiastically to news of the treaty that formalized the Louisiana Purchase (May 1803). Jefferson, of course, was relieved that the nation had avoided war with France, but he worried that the treaty might be unconstitutional. The president pointed out that the Constitution did not specifically authorize the acquisition of vast new territories and the incorporation of thousands of foreign citizens. To escape this apparent legal dilemma, Jefferson proposed an amendment to the Constitution, but Napoleon's impatience for money convinced the president to forego the amendment and act quickly.

Jefferson's fears about the incorporation of this new territory were not unwarranted. The Spanish and French people who lived in the region were unfamiliar with America's customs, government, and laws. Jefferson frankly questioned whether these people would be loyal to the United States. He therefore recommended to Congress a transitional government

consisting entirely of appointed officials. Some congressmen attacked this bill as anti-republican because it imposed taxes on the citizens of Louisiana without their consent. By a narrow margin the bill passed.

In the midst of the Louisiana controversy, Jefferson dispatched a secret message to Congress requesting $2500 for the exploration of the Far West. How closely this decision was connected to the Paris negotiations is not clear. The president asked his talented private secretary, Meriwether Lewis, to discover whether the Missouri River offered a direct and practical "water communication across this continent for the purposes of commerce." Jefferson also regarded the expedition as a wonderful opportunity to collect precise data about flora and fauna. While preparing for this great adventure, Lewis' second in command, William Clark, assumed such a prominent role that the effort became known as the Lewis and Clark Expedition. Setting out from St. Louis in May 1804, the exploring party reached the Pacific Ocean in November 1805. The group returned safely the following September. The results of this expedition not only fulfilled Jefferson's scientific expectations, but also reaffirmed his faith in the future economic prosperity of the United States.

The Louisiana Purchase added to Jefferson's popularity. During his first term he had maintained the peace, reduced taxes, and expanded the boundaries of the United States. He overwhelmed Federalist Charles Cotesworth Pinckney in the election of 1804. So far, Jefferson's "revolution" had been successful.

Sources of Political Dissension

At the moment of Jefferson's greatest electoral victory, a perceptive person might have seen signs of serious division within the Republican party and within the country. The president's heavy-handed attempts to reform the federal courts stirred deep animosities. Republicans had begun sniping at other Republicans, and one leading member of the party, Aaron Burr, became involved in a bizarre plot to separate the West from the rest of the nation. Congressional debates over the future of the slave trade revealed the existence of powerful sectional loyalties and profound disagreement on the issue.

Attack on the Judges

Jefferson's controversy with the federal bench commenced the moment he first became president. The Federalists, realizing that they would soon lose control over the executive branch, passed the Judiciary Act of 1801, which expanded the federal court system. Through his "midnight" appointments, Adams filled these posts with loyal Federalists. Jefferson opposed this attempt by Federalists to maintain their political control. Even more

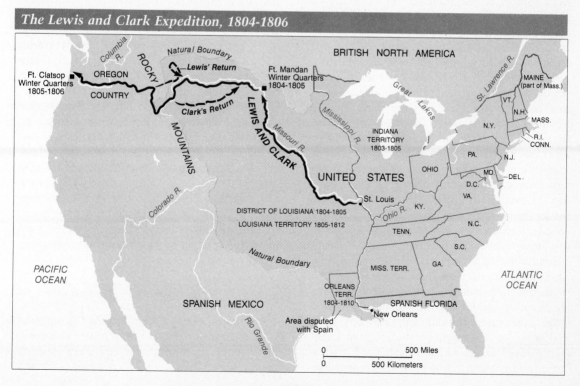

The Lewis and Clark Expedition, 1804-1806

infuriating was Adams' appointment of John Marshall as the new chief justice. Marshall was one of the few men in the country who could hold his own against Jefferson.

In January 1802 Jefferson's congressional allies called for repeal of the Judiciary Act. Although they avoided the political issues, no one doubted that their attack was politically motivated. But the Constitution held that the judges could be removed only when they were found guilty of high crimes and misdemeanors. By repealing the Judiciary Act, Congress would in effect be dismissing judges without a trial, a clear violation of their constitutional rights. Unimpressed by this argument, in March Congress voted for repeal.

While Congress debated the Judiciary Act, another battle suddenly erupted. One of Adams' "midnight" appointees, William Marbury, complained that the new administration would not give him his commission for the office of justice of the peace for the District of Columbia. He sought redress before the Supreme Court, demanding that the federal justices compel James Madison, the secretary of state, to deliver the necessary papers. In his celebrated *Marbury* v. *Madison* decision (February 1803), Marshall berated the secretary of state for withholding Marbury's commission. Nevertheless, he concluded that the Supreme Court did not possess jurisdiction over such matters. Poor Marbury was out of luck. The Republicans proclaimed victory. However, they failed to examine the logic of Marshall's decision. He had ruled that part of the earlier judiciary act on which Marbury based his appeal, the one Congress passed in 1789, was unconstitutional. Thus *Marbury* v. *Madison* set an important precedent for judicial review of federal statutes.

Neither Marbury's defeat nor repeal of the Judiciary Act placated extreme Republicans. They insisted that federal judges should be made more responsible to the will of the people. One solution, short of electing federal judges, was impeachment. Early in 1803, John Pickering, an incompetent judge from New Hampshire, presented the Republicans with a curious test case. This Federalist appointee suffered from alcoholism as well as insanity. However, Pickering had not committed any high crimes against the United States government. Ignoring such legal niceties, Jefferson's allies in the Senate impeached Pickering (March 1804), and he was removed from the bench.

Jefferson had his sights set on bigger game even before Pickering's impeachment. In the spring of 1803, he accused Samuel Chase, a justice of the Supreme Court, of delivering a treasonous speech. Republican congressmen took the hint, agreeing that Chase, who had frequently attacked Republican policies, had committed an indictable offense.

At this stage, some members of Congress expressed uneasiness. The charges drawn up against the judge were purely political. Certainly Chase had been indiscreet, accusing Republicans of threatening "peace and order, freedom and property." But his attack on the Jefferson administration hardly seemed criminal. It was clear that if the Senate convicted Chase, every member of the Supreme Court, including Marshall, might also be dismissed.

Chase's impeachment trial before the United States Senate was one of the most dramatic events in American legal history. Aaron Burr, the vice-president, organized the proceeding, and he redecorated the Senate chamber for the event. In this luxurious setting, Chase and his lawyers conducted a masterful defense. By contrast, John Randolph, the congressman who served as chief prosecutor, behaved in an erratic manner, betraying repeatedly his ignorance of relevant points of law. On March 1, 1805, the Senate acquitted the justice of all charges. This trial, too, set a valuable precedent: While most Republican senators personally disliked the arrogant Chase, they refused to expand the constitutional definition of impeachable offenses.

Critics and Conspirators

The collapse of the Federalists on the national level encouraged dissension within the Republican party. Extremists in Congress insisted upon monopolizing the president's ear, and when he listened to political moderates, they rebelled. During Jefferson's second term, these critics—labeled "Tertium Quids"—argued that the president's policies, foreign and domestic, sacrificed virtue for pragmatism. Their chief spokesmen were two members from Virginia, John Randolph and John Taylor. They both despised commercial capitalism and urged Americans to return to a simple, agrarian way of life.

The Yazoo controversy raised the Quids from political obscurity. This complex legal battle began in 1795 when a thoroughly corrupt Georgia assembly sold 35 million acres of western land, known as the Yazoo claims, to private companies at bargain prices. It soon became apparent that every member of the legislature had been bribed, and in 1796 state lawmakers rescinded the entire agreement. Unfortunately, some land had already changed hands. Jefferson inherited the entire mess when he became president. The special commission he appointed to look into the matter recommended that Congress set aside 5 million acres for buyers who had unwittingly purchased land from the discredited companies.

Randolph immediately cried foul. Such a compromise, however well-meaning, condoned fraud. Republican virtue hung in the balance. Finally, the Marshall Supreme Court ruled in *Fletcher* v. *Peck* (1810) that legislative fraud did not impair private contracts and that the Georgia assembly of 1796 did not have authority to take away lands already sold to innocent buyers. This important case upheld the Supreme Court's authority to rule on the constitutionality of state laws.

Vice-President Aaron Burr created far more serious difficulties for the president. The two men had never been close, and Burr's refusal to bow out during the election of 1800 (see Chapter 7) further strained the relationship. During Jefferson's first term, the ambitious Burr played a distinctly minor role in shaping policy.

In the spring of 1804 Burr decided to run for the governorship of New York. Although he was a Republican, he curried the favor of High Federalists who were plotting the secession of New England and New York from the Union. Alexander Hamilton frustrated Burr's efforts, however, when he described the Republican as "a dangerous man . . . who ought not to be trusted with the reins of government." Burr blamed Hamilton for his subsequent defeat and challenged his tormentor to a duel. On July 11, 1804, at Weehawken, New Jersey, the vice-president shot and killed the former secretary of the treasury. Both New York and New Jersey indicted Burr for murder. His political career lay in shambles.

In his final weeks as vice-president, Burr hatched a scheme so audacious that the people with whom he dealt could not decide whether he was a genius or a madman. Although he told different stories to different men, he evidently planned a filibustering campaign against a Spanish colony, perhaps Mexico, and he envisioned separating the western states and territories from the Union. The persuasive Burr convinced a handful of politicians and adventurers to follow him. Even James Wilkinson, commander of the United States Army in the Mississippi valley, joined Burr.

In the late summer of 1806 Burr put his ill-defined plan into action. It ended almost before it started. Wilkinson had a change of heart and denounced Burr to Jefferson. This started a general stampede, as conspirators rushed pell-mell to save their own skins. Federal authorities arrested Burr in February 1807 and took him to Richmond to stand trial for treason. Even before a jury had been called, Jefferson announced publicly that Burr's guilt was beyond question.

Jefferson spoke prematurely. The trial judge was John Marshall, who insisted upon a narrow constitutional definition of treason. He refused to hear testimony regarding Burr's supposed intentions and demanded two witnesses to each overt act of treason.

Burr, of course, had been too clever to leave this sort of evidence. While Jefferson complained bitterly about the miscarriage of justice, the jurors declared on September 1, 1807, that the defendant was "not proved guilty by any evidence submitted to us." Although Marshall had acted in an undeniably partisan manner, his actions inadvertently helped protect the civil rights of all Americans. If the chief justice had allowed circumstantial evidence into the Richmond courtroom, if he had listened to rumor and hearsay, he would have made it much easier for later presidents to use trumped-up conspiracy charges to silence legitimate political opposition.

Trying to End the Slave Trade

Slavery sparked angry debate at the Constitutional Convention of 1787. If delegates from the northern states had refused to compromise on this issue, Southerners would not have supported the new government. At the convention, the South agreed that after 1808 Congress *might consider* banning the importation of slaves into the United States. In return, the North agreed to count a slave as three fifths of a free white male, which increased southern representatives in Congress and accounted for Jefferson's 1800 presidential victory.

In an annual message sent to Congress in December 1806, Jefferson urged the representatives to prepare legislation outlawing the slave trade. During the early months of 1807, congressmen debated various ways of ending this embarrassing commerce. Although northern representatives generally favored a strong bill, southern congressmen responded with threats and ridicule. They explained to their northern colleagues that no one in the South regarded slavery as evil. It appeared naive, therefore, to expect local planters to enforce a ban on the slave trade or to inform federal agents when they spotted a smuggler.

The bill that Jefferson finally signed in March 1807 probably pleased no one. The law prohibited the importation of slaves into the United States after the new year. Whenever customs officials captured a smuggler, the slaves were turned over to state authorities and disposed of according to local custom. Southerners did not cooperate, and for many years African slaves continued to pour into southern ports. Undoubtedly Great Britain, which outlawed the slave trade in 1807, was the greatest single force in limiting the number of African slaves shipped to the United States. Ships of the Royal Navy took British—and in this case, American—laws seriously.

Failure of Foreign Policy

During Jefferson's second term (1805–1809), the United States found itself in the midst of a world at war. A brief peace in Europe ended abruptly in 1803, and the two military giants of the age, France and Great Britain, fought for supremacy on land and sea. It was a total war, an ideological war, a type of war unknown in the eighteenth century. Britain was the master of the seas, but France held clear superiority on land.

During the early stages of the war, the United States profited from European adversity. As "neutral carriers," American ships transported goods to any port in the world where they could find a buyer, and American merchants grew wealthy serving Britain and France.

Napoleon's successes on the battlefield, however, quickly strained Britain's economic resources. In response, Britain tightened its control over the seas. British warships seized American vessels engaged in trade beneficial to France, and British captains stepped up the impressment of sailors on ships flying the United States flag. Then in 1806, the British government issued a series of trade regulations known as "Orders in Council." These proclamations forbade neutral commerce with the Continent and threatened any ship that violated these orders with seizure. The declarations created what were in effect "paper blockades," for even the powerful British navy could not monitor the activities of every continental port.

Napoleon responded to Britain's commercial regulations with its own "paper blockade," called the Continental System. In the Berlin Decree of November 1806 and the Milan Decree of December 1807, he announced the closing of all continental ports to British trade and decreed that neutral vessels carrying British goods were subject to seizure. Since French armies occupied most of the territory between Spain and Germany, the decrees obviously cut the British out of a large market. Americans were caught between two conflicting systems. To please one power was to displease the other.

This unhappy turn of international events baffled Jefferson. He had assumed that civilized countries would respect neutral rights; justice obliged them to do so. Appeals to reason, however, made little impression upon states at war. Jefferson tried to negotiate with Britain, but the agreement that resulted was unacceptable to the president.

The United States soon suffered an even greater humiliation. A ship of the Royal Navy, the *Leopard,* sailing off the coast of Virginia, commanded an American warship to submit to a search for deserters (June 21, 1807). When the captain of the *Chesapeake* refused to cooperate, the *Leopard* opened fire, killing three men and wounding eighteen. The attack clearly violated the sovereignty of the United States. The American people demanded revenge.

Despite the pressure of public opinion, Jefferson played for time. He recognized that the United States was unprepared for war against a powerful nation like Great Britain. The president worried that an expensive conflict with Great Britain would quickly undo the fiscal reforms of his first term. For Jefferson, war entailed deaths, debts, and taxes, none of which he particularly relished.

Embargo Divides the Nation

Jefferson found what he regarded as a satisfactory way to deal with European predators with a policy he called "peaceable coercion." If Britain and France refused to respect the rights of neutral carriers, then the United States would keep its ships at home. Not only would this action protect them from seizure, it would also deprive the European powers of much needed American goods, especially food. Jefferson predicted that a total embargo of American commerce would soon force Britain and France to

negotiate with the United States in good faith. Congress passed the Embargo Act on December 22, 1807.

"Peaceable coercion" turned into a Jeffersonian nightmare. Americans objected strenuously to the legislation, and Jefferson had to push through a series of acts to force compliance. By the middle of 1808, Jefferson and Gallatin were involved in the regulation of the smallest details of American economic life. The federal government supervised the coastal trade and regulated the overland trade with Canada. When violations still occurred, Congress gave customs collectors the right to seize a vessel merely on suspicion of wrongdoing. Jefferson's eagerness to pursue a reasonable foreign policy blinded him to the fact that he and a Republican Congress would have to establish a police state to make it work.

Northerners hated the embargo and regularly engaged in smuggling. Persons living near Lake Champlain in upper New York State simply ignored the regulations, and they roughed up collectors who interfered with the Canadian trade. Jefferson was so determined to stop the illegal activity that he even urged the governor of New York to call out the militia. In a decision that George III might have applauded, Jefferson dispatched federal troops to overawe the citizens of New York.

New Englanders regarded the embargo as lunacy. Merchants preferred to take their chances on the high seas. Sailors and artisans were thrown out of work. The popular press maintained a constant howl of protest. One writer observed that embargo in reverse spelled "O grab me!" Opposition to the embargo caused a brief revival of the Federalist party in New England, and a few extremists suggested the possibility of state assemblies nullifying federal laws.

By 1809 the bankruptcy of Jefferson's foreign policy was obvious. The embargo never seriously damaged the British economy. Napoleon liked the embargo, since it seemed to harm Great Britain more than it did France. Finally, Republicans in Congress panicked and repealed the embargo a few days before James Madison's inauguration. Relations between the United States and the great European powers were much worse in 1809 than they had been in 1805.

Fumbling Toward War

James Madison followed his good friend Tom Jefferson into the White House. As president, Madison suffered from several personal and political handicaps. Although his intellectual abilities were great, he lacked the qualities necessary for effective leadership. His critics argued that his modest and unassuming nature revealed a weak, vacillating character.

During the election of 1808, Randolph and the Quids tried unsuccessfully to persuade James Monroe to challenge Madison's candidacy. Jefferson favored his old friend Madison. In the end, a caucus of Republican congressmen gave the official nod to Madison, the first time in American history that such a congres-

■ *Dolly Madison, a charming and vivacious woman, hosted popular informal entertainments at the White House and set the standard for future First Ladies.*

sional group controlled a presidential nomination. Although Madison won the presidency, the Federalists made impressive gains in the House of Representatives. Madison compounded his difficulties by appointing cabinet members who actively opposed his policies.

The new president inherited Jefferson's foreign policy problems. Neither Britain nor France showed the slightest interest in respecting American neutral rights. Madison's solution was to implement a weak and clumsy Non-Intercourse Act (March 1, 1809), that Congress passed at the same time it repealed the Embargo. The new bill authorized the resumption of trade between the United States and all nations of the world *except* Britain and France. Either of these countries could restore full commercial relations simply by promising to observe the rights of neutral carriers.

The British immediately took advantage of this offer. Their minister to the United States, David M. Erskine, informed Madison that the British government had modified its position on a number of sensitive commercial issues. Encouraged by these talks, Madison announced that trade with Great Britain could resume on June 10, 1809. Unfortunately, Erskine had not conferred with his superiors, who rejected the agreement out of hand. While an embarrassed Madison fumed in Washington, the Royal Navy seized the American ships that had already put to sea.

Britain's apparent betrayal led the artless Madison straight into a French trap. In May 1810 Congress passed Macon's Bill Number Two. In a complete reversal of strategy, this poorly drafted legislation reestablished trade with *both* England and France. It also contained a curious carrot-and-stick provision. As soon as either of these European states repealed restrictions upon neutral shipping, the United States government promised to halt all commerce with the other.

Napoleon spotted a rare opportunity. He announced that he would respect American neutral rights. Again, Madison acted impulsively, announcing that unless Britain repealed the Orders in Council by November, the United States would cut off all commercial re-

■ *While Tecumseh was away, Shawnee tribesmen attacked the U.S. troops led by General William Henry Harrison. Although his troops lost more men than did the Indians, Harrison claimed the victory.*

lations. Only later did Madison learn that Napoleon had no intention of living up to his side of the bargain. But humiliated by the Erskine experience, Madison decided to ignore French provocations and to pretend that the emperor was behaving in an honest manner.

Events unrelated to international commerce fueled anti-British sentiment in the newly settled parts of the United States. Westerners believed—incorrectly as it turned out—that British agents operating out of Canada had persuaded Tecumseh's warriors to resist the spread of American settlement. General William Henry Harrison, governor of the Indiana Territory, marched an army to the edge of a large Shawnee village at the mouth of Tippecanoe Creek near the banks of the Wabash River. On the morning of November 7, 1811, the American troops bested the Indians at the battle of Tippecanoe. The incident forced Tecumseh to seek British military assistance, something he probably would not have done had Harrison left him alone.

In 1811 the anti-British mood of Congress

intensified. A group of militant representatives, some of them elected to Congress for the first time in the election of 1810, announced that they would no longer tolerate national humiliation. These aggressive nationalists, many of them elected in the South and West, have sometimes been labeled the "War Hawks." Men like Henry Clay and John C. Calhoun spoke about honor and pride, as if foreign relations were some sort of duel between gentlemen. While the War Hawks were Republicans, they repudiated Jefferson's policy of peaceful coercion.

Madison surrendered to the War Hawks. On June 1, 1812, he sent Congress a message requesting a declaration of war against Great Britain. The timing of his action was peculiar. Over the preceding months, tensions between the two countries had relaxed, and the British government was suspending the Orders in Council. Because of the slowness of transatlantic communications, however, the president did not learn of this decision until Americans had already taken up arms.

Even contemporaries expressed confusion about the causes of the War of 1812. Madison's formal message to Congress listed Great Britain's violation of maritime rights, impressment of American seamen, and provocation of Indians. The War Hawks wanted war for other reasons. Some probably hoped to conquer Canada. For others the whole affair may have truly been a matter of national pride. Surprisingly, New Englanders, in whose commercial interests the war would supposedly be waged, ridiculed such chauvinism. Although Congress voted for war, the nation was clearly divided about the need to fight Britain. Madison's slim victory over De Witt Clinton, nominated by a faction of antiwar Republicans, in the election of 1812 indicated this split in America.

The Strange War of 1812

Optimism among the War Hawks ran high. However, they failed to appreciate how unprepared the country was for war, and they also refused to mobilize needed resources. The House rejected proposals for direct taxes and authorized naval appropriations only with the greatest reluctance. They did not seem to understand that a weak, highly decentralized government—the one that Jeffersonians championed—was incapable of waging an expensive war against the world's greatest sea power.

New Englanders refused to cooperate with the war effort. Throughout the war, they carried on a lucrative, though illegal, commerce with the enemy. The British government apparently believed that the New England states might negotiate a separate peace, and during the first year of the war, the Royal Navy did not bother to blockade the major northern ports.

American military operations focused initially upon the western forts, but the battles in this region demonstrated that the militia, no matter how enthusiastic, was no match for well-trained European veterans. American forces surrendered Detroit and Michilimackinac to the enemy, and poorly coordinated

marches on Niagara and Montreal accomplished nothing. On the sea, the United States did much better. In August, Captain Isaac Hull's *Constitution* defeated the *H.M.S. Guerriere* in a fierce battle, and American privateers destroyed or captured a number of British merchantmen. These victories, however, indicate that Britain was more concerned with Napoleon than the United States. As soon as peace returned to Europe in the spring of 1814, Britain redeployed its fleet and easily blockaded the tiny United States Navy.

The campaigns of 1813 revealed that conquering Canada would be more difficult than the War Hawks ever imagined. Both sides in

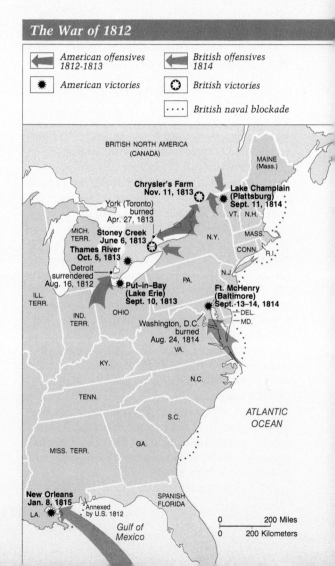

The War of 1812

← American offensives 1812-1813
← British offensives 1814
✳ American victories
✿ British victories
···· British naval blockade

BRITISH NORTH AMERICA (CANADA)

MAINE (Mass.)

Chrysler's Farm Nov. 11, 1813
Lake Champlain (Plattsburg) Sept. 11, 1814
York (Toronto) burned Apr. 27, 1813
VT. N.H.
MICH. TERR.
Stoney Creek June 6, 1813
N.Y.
MASS.
Thames River Oct. 5, 1813
CONN. R.I.
Detroit surrendered Aug. 16, 1812
N.J.
PA.
Put-in-Bay (Lake Erie) Sept. 10, 1813
Ft. McHenry (Baltimore) Sept. 13-14, 1814
ILL. TERR.
OHIO
DEL. MD.
IND. TERR.
Washington, D.C. burned Aug. 24, 1814
VA.
KY.
N.C.
TENN.
S.C.
MISS. TERR.
GA.
ATLANTIC OCEAN
New Orleans Jan. 8, 1815
SPANISH FLORIDA
LA.
Annexed by U.S. 1812
Gulf of Mexico
0   200 Miles
0   200 Kilometers

this war recognized that whoever controlled the Great Lakes controlled the West. On Lake Erie the Americans won the race for naval superiority. Oliver Hazard Perry won an important naval battle at Put-in-Bay, and General Harrison overran an army of British troops and Indian warriors at the battle of Thames River. During this engagement Tecumseh was killed. On the other fronts, however, the war went badly for the Americans.

In 1814 the British took the offensive. Following their victory over Napoleon, British strategists planned to increase pressure on three separate American fronts: the Canadian frontier, Chesapeake coastal settlements, and New Orleans. In the Canadian theater, the British suffered a setback. The American victory off Plattsburg on Lake Champlain accelerated peace negotiations, for after news of the battle reached London, the British government concluded that major land operations along the Canadian border were futile.

Throughout the year, British warships harassed the Chesapeake coast. To their surprise, the British found the region almost totally undefended, and on August 24, 1814, a small force of British marines burned the nation's capital, a victory more symbolic than strategic. Encouraged by their easy success, the British launched a full-scale attack on Baltimore (September 14). To everyone's surprise, the fort guarding the harbor held out against a heavy bombardment, and the British gave up the operation. The survival of Fort McHenry inspired Francis Scott Key to write "The Star-Spangled Banner."

The battle of New Orleans should never have occurred. The battle took place after the diplomats in Europe had concluded their peace negotiations. General Edward Pakenham, the commander of the British forces, was not aware of these negotiations, however, and on January 8, 1815, he foolishly ordered a frontal attack against General Andrew Jackson's well-defended positions. In a matter of hours, the entire British force had been destroyed. The victory not only transformed Jackson into a national folk hero, it also provided the people of the United States with a much needed source of pride. Even in military terms, the battle was significant, for if the British had managed to occupy New Orleans, they would have been difficult to dislodge regardless of the specific provisions of the peace treaty.

Hartford Convention: The Demise of the Federalists

In the fall of 1814, a group of leading New England politicians, most of them moderate Federalists, gathered in Hartford to discuss relations between the people of their region and the federal government. The delegates were angry and hurt by the Madison administration's seeming insensitivity to the economic interests of the New England states.

The men who met at Hartford on December 15 did not advocate secession from the Union. Although people living in other sections of the country cried treason, the convention delegates only recommended changes in the Constitution. Frustrated by the three-fifths clause that gave southern slaveholders a disproportionately large voice in the House, the delegates proposed that congressional representation should be calculated on the basis of the number of white males living in a state. The convention also wanted to limit each president to a single term in office, a reform that New Englanders hoped might end Virginia's monopoly of the executive mansion. And finally, to protect their region from what they saw as the tyranny of southern Republicans, the delegates insisted that a two-thirds majority was necessary before Congress could declare war, pass commercial regulations, or admit new states to the Union.

The convention's recommendations arrived in Washington at the same time as the news of the Battle of New Orleans reached the capital. Republican leaders in Congress accused the hapless New Englanders of disloyalty, and people throughout the country were persuaded that a group of wild secessionists had attempted to destroy the Union. The Hartford Convention accelerated the final demise of the Federalist party.

1800 Thomas Jefferson elected president

1801 Adams makes "midnight" appointments of federal judges

1802 Judiciary Act is repealed (March)

1803 Chief Justice John Marshall rules on *Marbury* v. *Madison* (February); sets precedent for judicial review

Louisiana Purchase concluded with France (May)

1803–1806 Lewis and Clark explore the Northwest

1804 Aaron Burr kills Alexander Hamilton in a duel (July)

Jefferson elected to second term

1805 Justice Samuel Chase acquitted by Senate (March)

1807 American warship *Chesapeake* fired upon by British *Leopard* (June)

Burr is tried for conspiracy (August-September)

Embargo Act passed (December)

1808 Slave trade is ended (January)

Madison elected president

1809 Embargo is repealed; Non-Intercourse Act passed (March)

1810 Macon's Bill Number Two reestablishes trade with Britain and France (May)

1811 Harrison defeats Indians at Tippecanoe (November)

1812 Declaration of war against Great Britain (June)

Madison elected to second term, defeating De Witt Clinton of New York

1813 Perry destroys British fleet at battle of Put-in-Bay (September)

Harrison wins again at battle of Thames River (October)

1814 Jackson crushes Creek Indians at Horseshoe Bend (March)

British marines burn Washington, D.C. (August)

Americans turn back British at Plattsburg (September)

Hartford Convention meets to recommend constitutional changes (December)

Treaty of Ghent ends War of 1812 (December)

1815 Jackson routs British at battle of New Orleans (January)

Treaty of Ghent Ends the War

On August 8, 1814, serious peace talks began in the Belgian city of Ghent. The United States sent a distinguished negotiating team: John Quincy Adams, Albert Gallatin, Henry Clay, James A. Bayard, and Jonathan Russell. The members of the British delegation were both more arrogant and more obscure. During the early weeks of negotiations, it seemed as if the Americans and English representatives were not speaking the same language, and they made little real progress.

Fatigue finally broke the diplomatic deadlock. The British government realized that no amount of military force could significantly alter the outcome of hostilities in the United States. Weary negotiators signed the Treaty of Ghent on Christmas Eve 1814. The document dealt with virtually none of the topics contained in Madison's original war message. Neither side surrendered territory; Great Britain refused even to discuss the topic of impressment. In fact, the treaty was simply an agreement to end fighting. The Senate apparently concluded that stalemate was preferable to continued conflict and ratified the treaty 35 to 0.

Most Americans thought the War of 1812 an important success. Even though the country's military accomplishments had been unimpressive, the people of the United States had been swept up in a contagion of nationalism. For many Americans, this "second war of independence" reaffirmed their faith in themselves and the revolutionary experience.

Jeffersonian Legacy

A remarkable coincidence occurred on July 4, 1826, the fiftieth anniversary of the Declaration of Independence. On that day, Thomas Jefferson died at Monticello. His last words were "Is it the Fourth?" On the same day several hundred miles to the north, John Adams also passed his last day on earth. His mind was on his old friend and sometime adversary, and during his final moments, Adams found comfort in the assurance that "Thomas Jefferson still survives."

Adams was correct. The political battles that occupied both men during their presidencies had already passed into history and were largely forgotten. But the spirit of the Declaration of Independence survived, and Jefferson's vision of a society in which "all men are created equal" challenged later Americans to make good on the promise of 1776.

Recommended Reading

The best-written and in many ways the fullest account of the first two decades of the nineteenth century remains Henry Adams' classic *History of the United States During the Administrations of Jefferson and Madison*, 9 vols. (1889–1891). A fine abridged edition has been prepared by Ernest Samuels (1967). A good general account of the period is Marshall Smelser, *The Democratic Republic, 1801–1815* (1968). Those interested in the problems that Jefferson faced as president should read Merrill D. Peterson, *Thomas Jefferson and the New Nation: A Biography* (1970), and Dumas Malone, *Jefferson and His Time*, vols. 4 and 5 (1970, 1974).

Several works focus more narrowly upon political problems: Noble E. Cunningham, Jr., *The Process of Government Under Jefferson* (1978); James Sterling Young, *The Washington Community, 1800–1828* (1966); and Robert M. Johnstone, Jr., *Jefferson and the Presidency: Leadership in the Young Republic* (1978). See also Richard E. Ellis' masterful *The Jeffersonian Crisis: Courts and Politics in the Young Republic* (1971). A good introduction to the political philosophy of the Jeffersonians is Daniel Boorstin, *The Lost World of Thomas Jefferson* (1948).

For Madison's life see Ralph Ketcham, *James Madison, A Biography* (1971). J. C. Stagg provides a full account of the War of 1812 in *Mr. Madison's War* (1983). Foreign policy problems are treated in Bradford Perkins, *Prologue to War, England and the United States, 1805–.812* (1961), and Burton Spivak, *Jefferson's English Crisis: Commerce, Embargo, and the Republican Revolution* (1979).

The economic developments of this period are the subject of several interesting studies. The most provocative is Thomas C. Cochran, *Frontiers of Change: Early Industrialization of America* (1981). Also see Stuart Bruchey, *The Roots of American Economic Growth, 1607–1861* (1965), and James A. Henretta, *The Evolution of American Society, 1700–1815: An Interdisciplinary Analysis* (1973). A good introduction to the history of the western settlements is Reginald Horsman, *The Frontier in the Formative Years, 1783–1815* (1970).

The Burr conspiracy is discussed in Milton Lomask's biography, *Aaron Burr* (1982). Problems facing the Federalist party are the subject of David Hackett Fischer, *The Revolution of American Conservatism* (1965), and Linda K. Kerber, *Federalists in Dissent: Imagery and Ideology in Jeffersonian America* (1970).

A
NATION
EMERGES

When the Marquis of Lafayette revisited the United States in 1824, he marveled at how the country had changed in the more than forty years since he had served with George Washington. The country had grown remarkably, and steam-powered boats now united the various western outposts. Everywhere Lafayette was greeted with patriotic oratory celebrating the liberty, prosperity, and progress of the new nation. Always the diplomat, Lafayette told Americans what they wanted to hear. He hailed "the immense improvements" and "admirable communications" that he had witnessed and declared himself deeply moved by "all the grandeur and prosperity of these happy United States, which, at the same time they nobly seem the complete assertion of American independence, reflect on every part of the world the light of a far superior political civilization."

There were good reasons why Americans made Lafayette's return visit the occasion for patriotic celebration and reaffirmation. Free from foreign threats, America was growing rapidly in population, size, and wealth. Its republican form of government was apparently working well. In his first inaugural address, James Monroe had anticipated Lafayette's observations. It was a speech full of national self-satisfaction. "No country was ever happier with respect to its domain," Monroe said. As for the government itself, it was so near to perfection that "in respect to it we have no essential improvements to make."

Beneath the optimism and self-confidence, however, there were undercurrents of doubt and anxiety about the future. Almost all the Founding Fathers were dead. Could their example of republican virtue and self-sacrifice be maintained in an increasingly prosperous and materialistic society? Many Americans feared the answer. And what about the place of slavery in a "perfect" democratic republic? Lafayette himself wondered why the United States had not yet extended freedom and equality to the black slaves.

But the peace following the War of 1812 did open the way for a great surge of nation-building. Transportation improvements created new markets, and advances in the processing of raw materials led to the first stirrings of industrialization. Political leadership provided little active direction for the process of growth and expansion, but an active judiciary took up part of the slack in a series of decisions that served to promote economic development and assert the priority of national over state and local interests. To guarantee the peace and security essential for internal progress, statesmen proclaimed a foreign policy designed to insulate America from external involvements. A new nation of great potential wealth and power was emerging.

Expansion and Migration

The peace concluded with Great Britain in 1815 allowed the American people to shift their attention from Europe and the Atlantic to the vast lands of North America that lay before them. Although the British had withdrawn from the region north of the Ohio, they continued to lay claim to the Pacific Northwest. Spain still possessed Florida and much of the present-day American West. Between the Appalachians and the Mississippi and in the lower Mississippi Valley settlement had already begun in earnest. Many parts of the region, however, were only sparsely settled by whites, and much good land remained in Indian hands. Diplomacy, military action (or at least the threat of it), and the western movement of vast numbers of settlers were all needed before the continent would yield up its wealth.

Extending the Boundaries

The first goal of postwar expansionists was to obtain Florida from Spain. In the eyes of the Spanish, their possession extended along the Gulf Coast to the Mississippi, but in 1812 the United States had annexed the area between the Mississippi and the Perdido rivers in what became Alabama. The remainder, known as East Florida, became the prime object of territorial ambition for President James Monroe and his energetic secretary of state, John Quincy Adams. Spanish claims west and east of the Mississippi blocked Adams' grand design for continental expansion.

General Andrew Jackson provided Adams with an opportunity to acquire the land. In 1816 United States troops touched off a conflict when they went into East Florida in pursuit of hostile Seminole Indians and the fugitive slaves that they were harboring. In April and May of 1818 Jackson exceeded his official orders and occupied East Florida. In addition, he court-martialed and executed two British subjects whom he accused of being enemy agents. Although his actions were widely criticized by government officials, no disciplinary action was taken.

Secretary Adams informed the Spanish government that the United States had acted in self-defense and that further conflict could be avoided only if East Florida was ceded to the United States. Weakened by Latin American revolutions and liberation movements, Spain was in no position to resist American bullying. Spanish minister Luis de Onís acceded. In addition to relinquishing Florida, de Onís agreed to a dividing line between Spanish and American territory that ran all the way to the Pacific, thus giving up Spain's claim to Pacific coastal areas north of California and opening a path for future American expansion. These understandings were formalized in the Adams-Onís Treaty (1819), which also became known as the Transcontinental Treaty. Great Britain and Russia still had competing claims to the Pacific Northwest, but the United States was now poised to acquire some frontage on a second ocean. Secretary Adams described the agreement on a definite boundary to the Pacific as "forming a great epoch in our history."

Interest in exploitation of the Far West continued to grow between 1810 and 1830. In 1811 a New York merchant, John Jacob Astor,

■ *Mountain men like Jim Beckwourth (left) and Indians met at an annual
"rendezvous" to trade their furs to agents of the Rocky Mountain Fur
Company for food, ammunition, and other goods. Feasting, drinking,
gambling, and sharing exploits were also part of the event. Later
generations would romanticize the hard life these men led, presenting it
as the harmonious mingling of Man and Nature.*

founded the fur trading post of Astoria at the
mouth of the Columbia River in the Oregon
country. In the 1820s and 1830s fur traders
operating out of St. Louis worked their way up
the Missouri to the northern Rockies and beyond. First they limited themselves to trading
for furs with the Indians, but eventually these
"mountain men" went after game on their
own and sold the furs to agents of the Rocky
Mountain Fur Company at an annual "rendezvous."

These colorful characters, who included
such legendary figures as Jedediah Smith, Jim
Bridger, Kit Carson, and Jim Beckwourth, accomplished prodigious feats of survival under
harsh natural conditions. Although they actually depleted the animal resources on which
the Indians depended, these mountain men
projected an image of being part of their environment rather than destroyers of it. To later
generations they typified a romantic ideal of
lonely self-reliance in harmony with unspoiled
nature.

The reports of military expeditions provided
better information about the Far West than the

tales of the mountain men, most of whom
were illiterate. The most notable of the postwar expeditions was mounted by Major Stephen S. Long in 1819–1820. Long mapped
some of the rivers of the Great Plains and endorsed the misleading view that the plains
beyond the Missouri were a "great American
desert" unfit for cultivation or settlement. The
real focus of attention between 1815 and the
1840s, therefore, was the nearer West, the rich
agricultural lands between the Appalachians
and the Mississippi that were being opened up
for settlement.

Settlement to the Mississippi

Complete occupation and exploitation of the
trans-Appalachian interior required displacing
the many Indian communities still inhabiting
that region in 1815. In the Ohio Valley and the
Northwest Territory, the Indians had already
been defeated. Consigned by treaty to reservations outside the main lines of white advance,
most of the tribes were eventually forced west
of the Mississippi. In 1831–1832 a faction of

the confederated Sac and Fox Indians under Chief Black Hawk attempted to reoccupy lands east of the Mississippi previously ceded by another tribal faction. Federal troops and Illinois state militia routed the Indians. It was the last stand of the woodland Indians of the Midwest.

Uprooting the once populous Indian communities of the Old Northwest was part of a national program for removing Indians of the eastern part of the country to an area beyond the Mississippi. Whites believed that Indians impeded "progress." Furthermore, Indians held land communally and not in private parcels: white settlers regarded this practice as an insuperable obstacle to economic development. During the Monroe era it became clear that white settlers wanted the removal of all Indians. The issue was particularly pressing in the South, where greed combined with racism to doom the Indian tribes.

In the South, as in the Old Northwest, a series of treaties negotiated between 1815 and 1830 reduced tribal holdings and provided for the eventual removal of most Indians to the trans-Mississippi West. Not all tribes left quietly. The so-called five civilized tribes—the Cherokees, Creeks, Seminoles, Choctaws, and Chickasaws—had become settled agriculturalists, and they owned good land in the South. Pressure continued to mount. When deception, bribery, and threats by the federal government failed to induce land cessions, state governments took matters into their own hands. The stage was thus set for the forced removal of the five civilized tribes to Oklahoma during the 1830s. (See Chapter 10 for a more complete discussion.)

While Indians were being driven beyond the Mississippi, settlers poured into the agricultural heartland of the United States. This movement was the most dramatic and significant phase of the great westward expansion of population and settlement that began in the early colonial period and lasted until the 1880s. In 1810 only about one seventh of the American population lived beyond the Appalachians; by 1840 more than a third did. Eight new states were added to the Union during this period. The government took care of Indian removal, but the settlers faced the difficult task of gaining a livelihood from the land.

Much of the vast acreage opened up by the western movement passed through the hands of land speculators before it reached those of the farmers and planters. After a financial panic in 1819 brought ruin to many who had purchased tracts on credit, the minimum price was lowered from $2.00 to $1.25 an acre, but full payment was required in cash. This change favored wealthy speculators who bought land at a massive rate.

Eventually most of the land did find its way into the hands of actual cultivators. In some areas squatters arrived before the official survey and formed claims associations which policed land auctions to prevent "outsiders" from bidding up the price and buying their farms out from under them. Squatters also insisted that they had the right to buy the land that they had already improved at the minimum price, a program called "preemption." In 1841 the right to farm on public lands with the assurance of a *future* preemption right was formally acknowledged by Congress.

Settlers who arrived after speculators had secured title had to deal with land barons. Fortunately for the settlers, most speculators operated on credit and were forced to obtain a quick return on their investment. They did this by selling land at a profit to settlers who had some capital and by arranging finance plans for tenants who did not. Thus the family farm or owner-operated plantation was the typical unit of western agriculture.

Since debt was common in the West, most farmers found it necessary to do more than simply raise enough food to subsist; they had to produce something for market. Most of the earliest settlement was along rivers, which provided cheap transportation. But even in more remote areas, farmers managed to get their corn, wheat, cotton, or cured meat to market. To meet the needs of farmers, local marketing centers quickly sprang up, usually at river junctions. Cities emerged seemingly overnight, and they in turn accelerated regional development.

The log cabin and split-rail fence of this typical frontier farmstead were cut from trees on the land. Other nearby trees have been burned to clear the land for farming.

The People and Culture of the Frontier

Most of the hundreds of thousands of settlers who populated the West were farmers from the seaboard states. They migrated for all sorts of reasons, but prominent among them were overpopulation, rising land prices, and declining fertility of the soil in the older regions. Most moved as family units and tried to re-create their former way of life as soon as possible. Women were often reluctant to migrate in the first place, and when they arrived in new areas, they strove valiantly to recapture the comfort and stability that they had left behind.

New Englanders carried with them their churches, schools, notions of community uplift, and Puritan ideals of hard work and self-denial. Similarly, settlers from Virginia and the Carolinas retained their devotion to family honor, personal independence, and ideas of white supremacy. In the West, differences between the North and South soon emerged.

In general, the pioneers sought out the kind of terrain and soil with which they were already familiar. People from the eastern uplands favored the hill country of the West. Piedmont and tidewater farmers and planters usually made for the lower and flatter areas.

Both groups avoided the fertile but unfamiliar prairies. Rather than being the bold and deliberate innovators of myth, the typical agricultural pioneers were deeply averse to changing their traditional habits.

Yet some adjustments were necessary simply to survive under frontier conditions. Initially, at least, a high degree of self-sufficiency was required on isolated homesteads. The settlers built their own homes and raised their own crops; they made their own clothes and manufactured their own household necessities, such as soap and candles.

But this picture of frontier self-reliance is not the whole story. Most settlers in fact found it extremely difficult to accomplish all the tasks using only family labor. A more common practice was the sharing of work by a number of pioneer families. Assembling the neighbors to raise a house, harvest wheat, or sew quilts helped turn collective work into a rare festive occasion. The jug was passed, and various contests sped the work along. Sharing the work was a creative response to the shortage of labor that also provided a source for communal solidarity. These events probably tell us more about the "spirit of the frontier" than the conventional image of the pioneer as a lonely individualist.

Restlessness and geographic mobility also characterized many of these settlers. The wandering of young Abraham Lincoln's family from Kentucky to Indiana and finally to Illinois between 1816 and 1830 was fairly typical. Improved land could be sold at a profit and the proceeds used to buy new acreage beyond the horizon where the soil was reportedly richer. Hence few early-nineteenth-century American farmers developed the kind of attachment to the land that is often associated with rural populations in other parts of the world.

Transportation and the Market Economy

It took more than the spread of settlement to bring prosperity to new areas and ensure that they would identify with older regions or with the country as a whole. Along the eastern seaboard land transportation was so primitive that in 1813 it took seventy-five days for one wagon of goods drawn by four horses to make a trip of about a thousand miles, and traveling west over the mountains meant months on the trail.

After the War of 1812 political leaders realized that national security, economic progress, and political unity were all more or less dependent on binding the nation together through a greatly improved transportation network. Accordingly, President Monroe called for a federally supported program of "internal improvements" in 1815. In the ensuing decades, the nationalist's vision of a transportation revolution was realized to a considerable extent, although the direct role of the federal government proved to be less important than anticipated.

A Revolution in Transportation: Roads and Steamboats

Americans who wished to get from place to place rapidly and cheaply needed new and improved roads. The first great federal transportation project was the building between 1811 and 1818 of the National Road between Cumberland, Maryland, on the Potomac, and Wheeling, Virginia, on the Ohio. This impressive, gravel-surfaced toll road was subsequently extended and reached Vandalia, Illinois, in 1838. Soon state governments promoted the building of other "turnpikes," as these privately owned toll roads chartered by the states were called. By about 1825 southern New England, upstate New York, much of Pennsylvania, and northern New Jersey were crisscrossed by thousands of miles of turnpikes.

But the toll roads benefited travelers more than they did transporters of bulky freight. The latter usually found that total expenses—toll plus the cost and maintenance of heavy wagons and great teams of horses—were too high to guarantee a satisfactory profit from haulage. Hence, traffic was less than anticipated, and investors were disappointed with returns. In the final analysis, turnpikes failed to link up the settled seaboard areas with the new West. What was desperately needed was a form of transportation that could inexpensively haul freight over long distances.

The fact that the United States had a great natural transportation system in its river network was one of the most significant reasons for the country's rapid economic development. The Ohio-Mississippi system in particular provided ready access to the rich agricultural areas of the interior and a natural outlet for their products. By 1815, flatboats loaded with wheat, flour, salt pork, and cotton were floating toward New Orleans. Even after the coming of the steamboat, flatboats continued to carry a major share of the downriver trade.

But the flatboat trade was necessarily a one-way traffic. A farmer from Ohio or Illinois, or someone hired to do the job, could float down to New Orleans easily enough, but there was generally no way to get back except by walking overland through rough country. Until the problem of upriver navigation was solved, the Ohio-Mississippi could not carry the manufactured goods that farmers desired in exchange for their crops.

Fortunately, a solution was readily at hand—

143

the use of steam power for river transportation. Inventor Robert Fulton improved upon an idea that many men had toyed with for years. In 1807 he successfully propelled the *Clermont* 150 miles up the Hudson River. The first steamboat launched in the West was the *New Orleans*, which made the trip from Pittsburgh to New Orleans in 1811–1812. The steamboat revolutionized the commerce of the West. By 1820, 69 steamboats with a total tonnage of 13,890 were plying western waters.

Steam transport was a great boon for farmers and merchants. It reduced costs, increased the speed of moving goods and people, and allowed a two-way commerce on the Mississippi and Ohio. Eastern manufacturers and merchants were now much more firmly linked to the interior markets.

The steamboat quickly captured the American imagination. The great paddle wheelers became luxurious floating hotels, the natural habitats of gamblers and confidence men. But the boats also had a lamentable safety record, frequently running aground, colliding, or blowing up. As a result of such accidents, the federal government began in 1838 to regulate steamboats and monitor their construction and operation. This legislation stands as the only instance in the pre-Civil War period of direct federal regulation of domestic transportation.

The Canal Boom

A transportation system based solely on rivers and roads had one enormous gap—it did not provide an economical way to ship western farm produce directly east to the growing urban market of the seaboard states. The solution offered by the politicians and merchants of the Middle Atlantic and Midwestern states was to build a system of canals to link seaboard cities directly to the Great Lakes, the Ohio, and ultimately the Mississippi.

The best natural location for a canal between a river flowing into the Atlantic and one of the Great Lakes was between Albany and Buffalo, a relatively flat stretch of 364 miles.

When the New York legislature approved of the bold project in 1817, no more than about 100 miles of canal existed in the entire United States. Credit for the enterprise belongs to New York's governor, DeWitt Clinton, who convinced the state legislature that the project could be successfully financed by issuing bonds. In 1825 the entire canal was opened with great public acclaim and celebration.

At 364 miles long, 40 feet wide, 4 feet deep, and containing 84 locks, the Erie Canal was the most spectacular engineering achievement of the young Republic. Furthermore, it was a great economic success. It reduced the cost of moving goods from Buffalo to Albany to one twelfth the previous rate. Easterners and Westerners could now buy each other's goods at a sharply reduced rate. The canal also helped to make New York City the unchallenged commercial capital of the nation.

The great success of the Erie Canal inspired other states to extend public credit for canal building. Between 1826 and 1834, Pennsylvania constructed an even longer and more elaborate canal, covering the 395 miles from Philadelphia to Pittsburgh. But the Pennsylvania Main Line Canal did not do as well as the Erie, partly because of the bottleneck that developed at the crest of the Alleghenies where canal boats had to be hauled over a high ridge on an inclined-plane railroad. Other states followed suit, and the nation's rivers and lakes were linked by an elaborate canal network.

The canal boom ended when it became apparent in the 1830s and 1840s that most of these waterways were unprofitable. State credit had been overextended, and the panic and depression of the late 1830s and early 1840s forced retrenchment. Moreover, by this time railroads were beginning to compete successfully for the same traffic, and a new phase in the transportation revolution was beginning.

But canals should not be written off as economic failures that contributed little to the improvement of transportation. Some of them continued to be important arteries up to the time of the Civil War and well beyond. Fur-

Man-made canals temporarily filled the gap in a developing transportation system of rivers and roads. This scene of the junction of the Erie and Northern canals (c. 1835) shows mules walking alongside the canal towing barges. The locks are seen in the background.

thermore, the failure of many of the canals was due solely to their inability to yield an adequate return on the money invested in them. This problem of financing tells us little or nothing about their public usefulness. Had the canals been thought of as providing a service rather than yielding a profit—in the manner, for example, of modern interstate highways—they might have maintained a high reputation for serving the economic interests of the nation. As it was, they contributed enormously to creating vital economic ties between the agricultural West and the industrializing Northeast.

Emergence of a Market Economy

The desire to reduce the costs and increase the speed of shipping heavy freight over great distances laid the groundwork for a new economic system. With the advent of steamboats and canals, Western farmers could inexpensively ship their crops both to the Northeast and New Orleans. This improved transport led to an increase in farm income and provided a stimulus for commercial agriculture.

At the beginning of the nineteenth century, the typical farming household consumed most of what it produced and sold only a small surplus in nearby markets. Most manufactured articles were produced at home. Easier and cheaper access to distant markets caused a decisive change in this pattern. Between 1800 and 1840, agricultural output increased remarkably. The rise in productivity was partly due to technological advances. Iron or steel plows proved better than wooden ones, the grain cradle replaced the scythe, and better varieties or strains of crops, grasses, and livestock were introduced. But the availability of good land and the revolution in marketing were the most important spurs to profitable commercial farming. The existence or extension of transportation facilities made distant markets available and plugged farmers into a commercial network that provided credit and relieved them of the need to do their own selling.

The emerging exchange network encouraged a movement away from diversified farming and toward regional concentration on staple crops. Wheat was the main cash crop in the North, and the center of its cultivation moved westward as soil depletion, pests, and plant diseases lowered yields in older regions. On the rocky hillsides of New England, sheep raising was displacing the mixed farming of an earlier era. But the prime example of successful staple production in this era was the rise of the cotton kingdom in the South.

A number of factors made the South the world's greatest producer of cotton. First was the great demand generated by the rise of textile manufacturing in England and, to a lesser extent, in New England. Second was the effect of the cotton gin in processing. Invented by Eli Whitney in 1793, this simple device cut the labor costs involved in cleaning short-staple cotton. Third was the availability of good land in the Southeast. Similar to the movement of the center of wheat cultivation in the North, the center of cotton growing moved steadily west from mainly South Carolina and Georgia toward the fertile plantation areas of Alabama, Mississippi, and Louisiana.

A fourth factor—the existence of slavery, which provided a flexible system of forced labor—permitted operations on a scale impossible for the family labor system of the agricultural North. Finally, the cotton economy benefited from the South's splendid natural transportation system, its great network of navigable rivers. The South had less need than other agricultural regions for artificial "internal improvements" such as canals and good roads. Planters could simply establish themselves on or near a river and ship their crops to market via natural waterways.

Commerce and Banking

As regions specialized in the growing of commercial crops, a new system of marketing emerged. During an early or pioneer stage in many areas, farmers did their marketing personally. With the growth of country towns, local merchants took over the crop near the source, bartering clothing and other manufactured goods for produce. These intermediaries shipped the farmers' crops to larger local markets such as Pittsburgh, Cincinnati, and St. Louis. Cotton growers in the South were more likely to deal directly with factors or agents in the port cities from which their crop was exported. But even in the South, intermediaries existed in such inland towns as Macon, Nashville, and Shreveport.

The extension of credit was a crucial element in the whole system. Farmers borrowed from local merchants, who received an advance of their own when they consigned the crop to a commission house or factor. The commission agents relied on credit from merchants or manufacturers at the ultimate destination, which might be Liverpool or New York City. The need for credit encouraged the growth of money and banking.

Before the revolutions in transportation and marketing, small-scale local economies could survive to a considerable extent on barter. But long-distance transactions involving credit and deferred payment required money and lots of it. Although the Constitution authorized only the federal government to issue money, in the early-to-mid-nineteenth century the government printed no paper money and produced gold and silver coins in such small quantities that it utterly failed to meet the expanding economy's need for a circulating currency.

Private or state banking institutions filled the void by issuing bank notes, promises to redeem their paper in *specie*—gold or silver—on the bearer's demand. The demand for money and credit during the economic boom after 1815 led to a vast increase in the number of state banks—from 88 to 208 in two years. The resulting flood of state bank notes caused this form of currency to depreciate well below its face value and threatened a runaway inflation. In an effort to stabilize the currency, Congress established a second Bank of the United States in 1816.

Whenever the national bank tried to enforce tight money policies by requiring that banks have adequate specie reserves to back their notes, state banks in the South and West—where national bank notes were scarce and the demand for credit was high—resisted vigorously. The result was a running battle between state and private banks and the national bank. The state banks were not as irresponsible or as out of tune with the real economic needs of their regions as they are often pictured as being. Their notes may have circulated at less than face value, but they nevertheless met a genuine need for currency and credit.

Early Industrialism

The growth of a market economy also created new opportunities for industrialists. In 1815 most manufacturing in the United States was carried on in households, in the workshops of skilled artisans, or in small mills. The factory form of production, in which supervised workers tended or operated machines under one roof, was rare. Even in the American textile industry, most of the spinning of thread and weaving, cutting, and sewing of cloth was still done by women working at home.

Most of the clothing worn by Americans was made entirely in households by female family members. But a growing proportion was produced for market, rather than direct home consumption. Under the "putting-out system" of manufacturing, merchant capitalists provided raw material to people in their own homes, picked up the finished or semifinished products, paid the workers, and took charge of distribution. The putting-out system was centered in the Northeast, and besides textiles, such items as shoes and hats were made in this manner.

The making of articles that required greater skill was mostly carried on by artisans working in small shops in towns. But in the decades after 1815, the merchants who purchased from these workers gained greater control over production. Shops expanded in size, masters tended to become entrepreneurs rather than working artisans, and journeymen often became wage earners rather than aspiring masters. At the same time, the growing market for low-priced goods led to a stress on speed, quantity, and standardization in methods of production.

A fully developed factory system emerged first in textile manufacturing. The establishment of the first cotton mills utilizing the power loom as well as spinning machinery—thus making it possible to turn fiber into cloth in a single factory—resulted from the efforts of a trio of Boston merchants, Francis Cabot Lowell, Nathan Appleton, and Patrick Tracy Jackson.

Under the name of the Boston Manufacturing Company, the associates began their Waltham operation in 1813. Their phenomenal success led to the erection of larger and even more profitable mills. The mill at Lowell became a great showplace for early American industrialization. Its large and seemingly contented work force of unmarried women residing in supervised dormitories, its unprecedented scale of operation, its successful mechanization of almost every stage of production—all captured the American middle-class imagination in the 1820s and 1830s. Other mills using similar methods sprang up throughout New England, and the region became the first important manufacturing area in the United States.

The shift away from the putting-out system to factory production changed the course of capitalistic activity in the region. Before the 1820s, New England merchants concentrated mainly on international trade. A major source of capital was the lucrative China trade carried on by fast, well-built New England vessels. When the success of Waltham and Lowell became clear, many merchants shifted their capital away from oceanic trade and into manufacturing. Politically, this meant that representatives from New England no longer advocated a low tariff that favored exporters over importers. They now became leading proponents of a high duty rate designed to protect manufacturers from foreign competition.

The development of other "infant industries" of the postwar period was less dramatic and would not come to fruition until the 1840s and 1850s. But the first stirring of an iron industry and a small arms industry was felt during this period. And although most manufacturing was centered in the Northeast, the West also experienced a modest industrial progress as the number and size of facilities such as grist mills, slaughterhouses, and tanneries increased. Distilleries in Kentucky and Ohio were particularly active.

One should not assume, however, that America had already experienced an industrial revolution by 1840. Most of the nation's labor force was still employed in agriculture; less than one out of every ten workers was directly

Technological Development, 1750–1860

(Dates refer to patent or first successful use)

Year	Inventor	Contribution	Importance/Description
1787	John Fitch	Steamboat	First successful American steamboat
1793	Eli Whitney	Cotton gin	Simplified process of separating fiber from seeds; helped make cotton a profitable staple of southern agriculture
1798	Eli Whitney	Jig for guiding tools	Facilitated manufacture of interchangeable parts
1802	Oliver Evans	Steam engine	First American steam engine; led to manufacture of high-pressure engines used throughout eastern United States
1813	Richard B. Chenaworth	Cast-iron plow	First iron plow to be made in three separate pieces, thus making possible replacement of parts
1830	Peter Cooper	Railroad locomotive	First steam locomotive built in America
1831	Cyrus McCormick	Reaper	Mechanized harvesting; early model could cut six acres of grain a day
1836	Samuel Colt	Revolver	First successful repeating pistol
1837	John Deere	Steel plow	Steel surface kept soil from sticking; farming thus made easier on rich prairies of Midwest
1839	Charles Goodyear	Vulcanization of rubber	Made rubber much more useful by preventing it from sticking and melting in hot weather
1842	Crawford W. Long	First administered ether in surgery	Reduced pain and risk of shock during operations
1844	Samuel F. B. Morse	Telegraph	Made long-distance communication almost instantaneous
1846	Elias Howe	Sewing machine	First practical machine for automatic sewing
1846	Norbert Rillieux	Vacuum evaporator	Improved method of removing water from sugar cane; revolutionized sugar industry and was later applied to many other products
1847	Richard M. Hoe	Rotary printing press	Printed an entire sheet in one motion, vastly speeded up printing process
1851	William Kelly	"Air-boiling process"	Improved method of converting iron into steel (usually known as Bessemer process because English inventor had more advantageous patent and financial arrangements)
1853	Elisha G. Otis	Passenger elevator	Improved movement in buildings; when later electrified, stimulated development of skyscrapers
1859	Edwin L. Drake	First American oil well	Initiated oil industry in the United States
1859	George M. Pullman	Pullman car	First sleeping-car suitable for long-distance travel

Source: From Freedom and Crisis: An American History, Third Edition, by Allen Weinstein and Frank Otto Gatell (1981).

involved in factory production. The revolution that did occur during these years was essentially one of distribution rather than production. The growth of a market economy of national scope was the major economic development of this period. And it was one that had vast repercussions for all aspects of American life.

The Politics of Nation-Building After the War of 1812

Geographic expansion, economic growth, and the changes in American life that accompanied them were bound in the long run to generate political controversy. Federal and state policies meant to encourage or control growth and expansion did not benefit farmers, merchants, manufacturers, and laborers equally. Conflicts inevitably arose. Northerners, Southerners, and Westerners were affected in different ways, too. But the temporary lack of a party system meant that politicians did not have to band together and offer the voters a choice of programs and ideologies. A myth of national harmony prevailed, culminating in the "Era of Good Feeling" during James Monroe's two terms as president.

Behind the facade, individuals and groups fought for advantage, as always, but without the public accountability and need for broad popular approval that a party system would have required. As a result, popular interest in national politics fell to a low ebb.

The absence of party discipline and programs did not completely immobilize the federal government. The president took important initiatives in foreign policy; Congress legislated on matters of national concern; and the Supreme Court made far-reaching decisions. The common theme of the public policies that emerged between the War of 1812 and the Age of Jackson was an awakening nationalism—a sense of American pride and purpose that reflected the events of the period.

The Republicans in Power

By the end of the War of 1812, the Federalist party was no longer a significant force in national politics, although the Republican party had adopted some of their rival's policies. Retreating from their original philosophy of states' rights and limited government, Republican party leaders now openly embraced a national bank, a protective tariff for industry, and a program of federally financed internal improvements.

In Congress, Henry Clay of Kentucky took the lead in advocating that the government take action to promote economic development. The keystone of what Clay called the "American system" was a high protective tariff to stimulate industrial growth and provide a "home market" for the farmers of the West, making the nation economically self-sufficient and free from a dangerous dependence on Europe.

In 1816 Congress took the first step toward Clay's goal by passing a tariff that raised import duties an average of 20 percent. The tariff was passed to protect American industry from British competition and received patriotic support in all sections of the country. Americans viewed the act as a move toward economic independence, a necessity to protect political independence.

Later the same year, Congress voted to establish the second Bank of the United States. Organized much like the first bank, it was a mixed public–private institution. The Bank served the government by providing a depository for its funds, an outlet for marketing its securities, and a source of redeemable bank notes that could be used for the payment of taxes or the purchase of public lands. The bank bill was opposed by state banking interests and strict constructionists, but the majority of Congress found it a necessary and proper means for promoting financial stability and meeting the constitutional responsibilities of the federal government to raise money from taxation and loans.

Legislation dealing with internal improvements made less headway in Congress. Except for the National Road, the federal government undertook no major transportation projects during the Madison and Monroe administrations. Both presidents believed that internal improvements were desirable but that a constitutional amendment was required before federal monies could legally be used for the building of roads and canals within individual states. Both men vetoed internal improvement bills. Consequently, public aid for the building of roads and canals continued to come almost exclusively from state and local governments.

Monroe as President

As had Jefferson before him, President Madison chose his own successor in 1816. James Monroe thus became the third successive Virginian to occupy the White House for a full two terms. Experienced, but stolid and unimaginative, he lacked the intellectual depth and agility of his predecessors, but he was reliable, dignified, and high-principled.

The keynote of Monroe's presidency was national harmony, which meant that he went out of his way to avoid controversy. Indeed, one newspaper writer announced that party strife was a thing of the past and that an "era of good feelings" had begun. The principal aim of Monroe's administrations was to see that these good feelings persisted. He wanted to end all sectional and economic differences and assert American power and influence on the world stage. His choice of a cabinet was well calculated to serve these purposes. His secretary of state, John Quincy Adams, was not only a diplomat of great experience and skill but also a New Englander. If recent precedent was to be followed, he would succeed Monroe as president and thus end the "Virginia dynasty." As secretary of war, Monroe chose John C. Calhoun, a leading Southerner who was at this time a fervent nationalist. To accommodate the old-line states' rights wing of the party, he appointed William C. Crawford of Georgia as secretary of the treasury.

The first challenge to Monroe's hopes for domestic peace and prosperity was the Panic of 1819, which ended the postwar boom. After a period of rampant inflation, easy credit, and massive land speculation, the Bank of the United States called in loans and demanded the immediate redemption in specie of the state bank notes in its possession. This retrenchment brought a drastic downturn in the economy, as prices fell sharply, businesses failed, and banks repossessed land bought on credit.

Congress responded slowly and weakly to the economic crisis. Monroe himself refused to exert strong leadership. He was able to remain above the battle and persuade the American public that he was in no way responsible for the state of the economy nor was he in a position to do anything about it. Unlike a modern president, Monroe could retain his full popularity during hard times.

Monroe prized national harmony even more than economic prosperity. But during his first administration a bitter controversy developed between the North and the South over the admission of Missouri to the Union. Once again Monroe remained above the battle and suffered little damage to his own prestige. It was left entirely to Congress to deal with the nation's most serious domestic political crisis between the War of 1812 and the late 1840s.

The Missouri Compromise

In 1817, the Missouri territorial assembly applied for statehood. It was clear that Missouri expected to be admitted into the Union as a slave state. Since Missouri was the first state, other than Louisiana, to be carved out of the Louisiana Purchase, the resolution of the status of slaves there would have implications for the rest of the trans-Mississippi West.

When the question came before Congress in early 1819, submerged sectional fears and anxieties came bubbling to the surface. Many Northerners resented southern control of the presidency and the three-fifths clause of the Constitution. Southerners feared for the future of what they regarded as a necessary balance of power between the sections. Up until 1819 a strict equality had been maintained by alternately admitting slave and free states. Because the North had a decisive majority in the House of Representatives, the South saw its equal vote in the Senate as essential for preservation of the balance.

In February 1819, Congressman James Tallmadge of New York introduced an amendment to the statehood bill banning further introduction of slaves into Missouri and providing for the gradual emancipation of those already there. The amendment was approved by the House but voted down by the Senate. The issue remained unresolved until a new Congress convened in December 1819. In the meantime, the measure elicited hot debate. Southern senators saw the Tallmadge amendment as an attack on the principle of equality between the states—a Northern ploy to upset the balance of power.

A separate statehood petition from the people of Maine suggested a way out of the impasse. In February 1820, the Senate voted to couple the admission of Missouri as a slave state with the admission of Maine as a free state. A further amendment was also passed prohibiting slavery in the rest of the Louisiana Purchase north of the southern border of Missouri, or above the latitude of 36°30'. The Senate's compromise then went back to the House where Henry Clay—who broke the proposal into three separate bills—adroitly maneuvered it through to narrow victory.

A major sectional crisis had been resolved. But the Missouri affair had ominous overtones for the future of North–South relations. Thomas Jefferson described the controversy as "a fire bell in the night," threatening the peace of the Union. Clearly, the subject of slavery or its extension aroused deep sectional feeling. Emotional rhetoric about morality and fundamental rights issued from both sides. If the United States were to acquire any new territories in which the status of slavery had to be determined by Congress, renewed sectional strife would be inevitable.

The Missouri Compromise

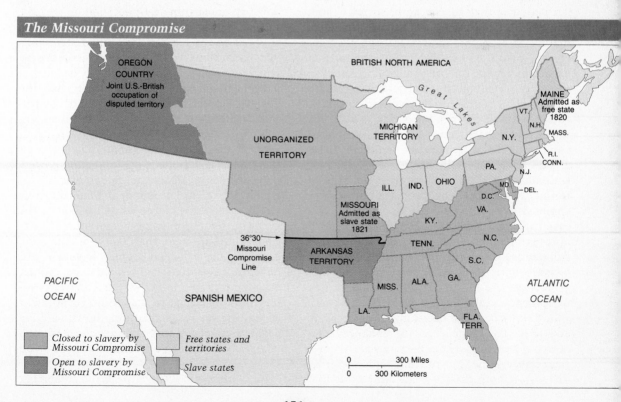

151

Postwar Nationalism and the Supreme Court

While the Monroe administration was proclaiming national harmony and congressional leaders were struggling to reconcile sectional differences, the Supreme Court was making a more substantial and enduring contribution to the growth of nationalism and a strong federal government, thanks to Chief Justice John Marshall. A Virginian, a Federalist, and a devoted disciple of George Washington, Marshall served as chief justice from 1801 to 1835, and during that entire period he dominated the Court as no other chief justice has ever done.

As the author of most of the major opinions issued by the Supreme Court during its formative period, Marshall gave shape to the Constitution and clarified the crucial role of the Court in the American system of government. He placed the protection of individual liberty, especially the right to acquire property, above the attainment of political, social, and economic equality. Ultimately he was a nationalist, believing that the strength, security, and happiness of the American people depended mainly on economic growth and the creation of new wealth. As he saw it, the Constitution existed to provide the political ground rules for a society of industrious and productive individuals who could enrich themselves while adding to the strength of the nation as a whole.

The role of the Supreme Court, in Marshall's view, was to interpret and enforce these ground rules, especially against the efforts of state legislatures to interfere with the constitutionally protected rights of individuals or combinations of individuals to acquire property through productive activity. The Court also permitted the federal government to assume broad powers so that it could fulfill its constitutional responsibility to promote the general welfare by encouraging economic development and national prosperity.

In a series of major decisions between 1819 and 1824, the Marshall Court enhanced the power of the judicial branch and used the contract clause of the Constitution (which prohibited a state from passing a law "impairing the obligations of contracts") to limit the power of state legislatures. It also strengthened the federal government by sanctioning a broad or loose construction of its constitutional powers and by clearly affirming its supremacy over the states.

In *Dartmouth College* v. *Woodward* (1819) the Marshall Court made the far-reaching determination that any charter granted by a state to a private corporation was fully protected by the contract clause. In practical terms, the Court's ruling in the Dartmouth case meant that the kind of business enterprises then being incorporated by state governments—such as turnpike or canal companies and textile manufacturing firms—could hold on indefinitely to any privileges or favors that had been granted in their original charters. The decision therefore increased the power and independence of business corporations by weakening the ability of the states to regulate them or withdraw their privileges.

About a month after the Dartmouth ruling, in March 1819, the Marshall Court handed down its most important decision. In *McCulloch* v. *Maryland* the Court ruled that a Maryland tax on the Bank of the United States was unconstitutional. The two main issues were whether Congress had the right to establish a national bank and whether a state had the power to tax or regulate an agency or institution created by Congress.

In response to the first question, Marshall set forth his doctrine of "implied powers," that the federal government could assume powers that helped it fulfill the "great object" for which it had been founded. Marshall thus struck a blow for "loose construction" of the Constitution. In answer to the second question, Marshall held that if a state had the power to tax a federal agency, it would also have the power to destroy it. Shot through the decision was the belief that the American people "did not design to make this government dependent on the states." In the continuing debate between states' righters and nationalists, the Marshall Court came down firmly on the side of the nationalists.

In *Gibbons* v. *Ogden* (1824) a steamboat

monopoly granted by the state of New York was challenged by a competing ferry service. The Supreme Court declared the New York grant unconstitutional in a move that further broadened the power of the federal government at the expense of the states by bolstering the right of Congress to regulate interstate commerce. At the same time, the Court encouraged the growth of a national market economy. The actions of the Supreme Court provide the clearest and most consistent example of the main nationalistic trends of the postwar period—the acknowledgment of the federal government's major role in promoting the growth of a powerful and prosperous America and the rise of a nationwide capitalistic economy.

Nationalism in Foreign Policy: The Monroe Doctrine

The new spirit of nationalism was also reflected in foreign affairs. The main diplomatic challenge facing Monroe after his reelection in 1820 was how to respond to the successful revolt of most of Spain's Latin American colonies after the Napoleonic wars. Henry Clay and many other Americans favored immediate recognition of the new republics, believing that their neighbors to the south were simply following the example of the United States in its own struggle for independence.

Before 1822, the administration struck a policy of neutrality. But Congress clamored for recognition. Starting in 1822 Monroe reversed his position, and during the next four years the United States officially recognized Mexico, Colombia, Chile, Argentina, Brazil, the Federation of Central American States, and Peru.

Recognizing the republics put the United States on a possible collision course with the major European powers. In 1822 Austria, Prussia, Russia, and France met in Verona and formed the "Grand Alliance," a reactionary union committed to rolling back the tides of liberalism, self-government, and national self-determination that had arisen during the French Revolution and its Napoleonic aftermath. Although the Grand Alliance did not undertake direct intervention in Latin Amer-

Chronology	
1813	Boston Manufacturing Company founds cotton mill at Waltham, Massachusetts
1815	War of 1812 ends
1816	James Monroe elected president
1818	Andrew Jackson invades Florida
1819	Supreme Court hands down far-reaching decision in Dartmouth College case and in *McCulloch* v. *Maryland* Adams-Onís treaty cedes Spanish territory to the United States Financial panic is followed by a depression lasting until 1823
1820	Missouri Compromise resolves nation's first sectional crisis Monroe reelected president unanimously
1823	Monroe Doctrine proclaimed
1824	Lafayette revisits the United States Supreme Court decides *Gibbons* v. *Ogden*
1825	Erie Canal completed; Canal Era begins

ica, it did give France the green light to invade Spain and, if so disposed, to reconquer the empire. Both Great Britain and the United States were alarmed by this prospect.

American policymakers were particularly troubled by Tsar Alexander I who was attempting to extend Russian claims on the Pacific coast of North America south to the fifty-first parallel—into the Oregon country that the United States wanted for itself. The Russian threat weighed heavily on the mind of Secretary of State Adams as he formulated foreign policy during Monroe's second term.

The threat from the Grand Alliance forced America to move closer to Great Britain, which for trading reasons favored independent Latin American countries. In August 1823 the British foreign secretary George Canning broached the possibility of joint Anglo-American action against the designs of the Alliance to the U.S. minister to Great Britain. Monroe, as well as former presidents Jefferson and Madison, welcomed the suggestion and favored open cooperation with the British.

Secretary of State Adams, however, favored a different approach. He believed that the national interest would best be served by avoiding all entanglement in European politics while at the same time discouraging European intervention in the Americas. In addition, political ambition motivated Adams, and he did not want to be labeled pro-British. He therefore advocated unilateral action by the United States rather than some kind of joint declaration with the British.

In the end, Adams managed to swing Monroe around to his viewpoint. In his annual message to Congress on December 2, 1823, Monroe included a far-reaching statement on foreign policy that was actually written mainly by Adams. What came to be known as the Monroe Doctrine solemnly declared that the United States opposed any further colonization in the Americas or any effort by European nations to extend their political systems outside of their own hemisphere. In return, the United States pledged not to involve itself in the internal affairs of Europe or to take part in European wars.

Although the Monroe Doctrine made little impression on the great powers of Europe at the time it was proclaimed, it signified the rise of a new sense of independence and self-confidence in American attitudes toward the Old World. The Doctrine also reflected the inward-looking nationalism that had arisen after the War of 1812.

The Monroe Doctrine was the capstone of an era that celebrated American strength, prosperity, and independence. Self-satisfaction, geographic expansion, and solid economic achievement were the keynotes of the age. The wider world was receding from view, but as Americans shifted their attention to internal matters the spirit of harmony and consensus that President Monroe had tried to call forth could not sustain itself. Ahead lay economic competition and political conflict. To a considerable extent these controversies involved the fruits of "progress"—the question of who would reap the benefits—or pay the price—of a growing economy and a changing society.

Recommended Reading

The standard surveys of the period between the War of 1812 and the Age of Jackson are two works by George Dangerfield—*The Era of Good Feelings* (1952) and *Awakening of American Nationalism, 1815–1828* (1965). For general accounts of the westward movement, see Ray A. Billington, *Westward Expansion* (1974), and Malcolm J. Rohrbough, *The Trans-Appalachian Frontier* (1978). On the removal of Native Americans, see Francis P. Prucha, *American Indian Policy in the Formative Years* (1962), and Dale Van Every, *Disinherited: The Lost Birthright of the American Indian* (1966). Insights into social, cultural, and economic life of settlers in the frontier areas can be derived from Frank Owsley, *Plain Folk of the Old South* (1948), and Allen G. Bogue, *From Prairie to Corn Belt* (1963). On the exploration of the trans-Mississippi West, see William H. Goetzmann, *Exploration and Empire* (1966).

Outstanding studies of economic transformation are George R. Taylor, *The Transportation Revolution, 1815–1860* (1951), and Stuart Bruchey, *Growth of the American Economy* (1975). On the development of internal waterways, see Carter Goodrich, *Government Promotion of American Canals and Railroads* (1960), and Harry N. Schieber, *Ohio Canal Era* (1969). Agricultural development is treated in Paul W. Gates, *The Farmer's Age: Agriculture, 1815–1860* (1960). On the early growth of manufacturing see Peter Termin, *Iron and Steel in Nineteenth-Century America* (1964); H. J. Habakkuk, *American and British Technology in the Nineteenth Century* (1962); and David J. Jeremy, *Transatlantic Industrial Revolution* (1981).

Insight into the politics of postwar nationalism can be derived from Shaw Livermore, Jr., *The Twilight of Federalism* (1962), and James S. Young, *The Washington Community, 1800–1828* (1966). The Marshall Court and legal-constitutional developments are covered in Robert K. Faulkner, *The Jurisprudence of John Marshall* (1968), and Morton J. Horwitz, *The Transformation of American Law, 1780–1860* (1977).

On diplomacy and the Monroe Doctrine, see Samuel F. Bemis, *John Quincy Adams and the Foundations of American Foreign Policy*, and Ernest May, *The Making of the Monroe Doctrine* (1976).

chapter 10

THE
TRIUMPH
OF DEMOCRACY

As the number of travelers, transients, and other Americans on the move in this country increased during the 1820s and 1830s, enterprising businessmen began to erect a new type of hotel to provide lodging, food, and drink on a large scale in the center of many cities. A prototype of the new hotel was the Boston Exchange Hotel with its 8 stories and 300 rooms. The "first-class" hotel became a prominent feature on the American scene—soon every commercial center in the country had a grand hotel or two to brag about.

The "democratic" mingling of the social classes in these new hotels often caused foreigners to view them as "a true reflection of American society." Their very existence showed that people were on the move geographically and socially. Among their patrons were traveling salesmen, ambitious young men seeking to establish themselves in a new city, and restless pursuers of "the main chance" not yet ready to put down roots.

Hotel managers shocked European visitors by failing to enforce traditional social distinctions among their clientele. Under the "American Plan," guests were required to pay for their meals, and everyone, regardless of class, ate at a common table. Except for unescorted women and people of color, almost anyone who could pay enjoyed the kind of personal service previously available only to a privileged class.

But the hotel culture also revealed some of the limitations of the new era of democratic ideals and aspirations. Blacks and women were excluded or discriminated against, just as they were denied the suffrage at a time when it was being extended to all white males. The genuinely poor simply could not afford to patronize the hotels and were consigned to squalid rooming houses. If the social equality *within* the hotel reflected a decline in traditional rigid class lines, the broad gulf between potential patrons and those who could not pay the rates signaled the growth of inequality based squarely on wealth rather than inherited status.

The hotel life also reflected the emergence of

democratic politics. Professional politicians of a new breed, pursuing the votes of a mass electorate, spent much of their time in hotels as they traveled about. Those elected to Congress or a state legislature often lodged and conducted political transactions in hotels. In fact, when Andrew Jackson arrived in Washington to prepare for his administration in 1829, he took residence at the new National Hotel. The hotel was more than a public and "democratic" gathering place; it was also a haven where the rising men of politics and business could find rest and privacy. In its lobbies, salons, and private rooms the spirit of an age was expressing itself.

Democracy in Theory and Practice

Historians have often viewed Andrew Jackson's coming to power—his election in 1828 and the boisterous "people's" inauguration that followed—as the critical moment when a democratic spirit took possession of American culture and public life. But that oversimplifies a very complex movement. The rise of Jackson took place in an atmosphere of ferment and a changing climate of opinion that turned America in a more democratic direction.

During the 1820s and 1830s the term *democracy* first became generally accepted as a way of describing how American institutions were supposed to work. Most of the Founders had viewed democracy as a dangerous tendency that needed to be held in check within a well-balanced republic. They believed that the general public was more likely to be ruled by passion and susceptible to unscrupulous leaders than was the cultivated elite. For champions of popular government in the Jacksonian period, however, the people were truly sovereign and could do no wrong. "The voice of the people is the voice of God" was their clearest expression of this principle.

Besides evoking this heightened sense of "popular sovereignty," the democratic im-

■ *A painting of Andrew Jackson in the heroic style by Thomas Sully. The painting shows the president as the common people saw him.*

pulse also stimulated a process of social leveling. Early Americans had usually assumed that the rich and wellborn should be treated with special respect and recognized as natural leaders of the community and guardians of its culture and values. By the 1830s the disappearance of inherited social ranks and clearly defined aristocracies or privileged groups struck European visitors as the most radical feature of democracy in America. The spirit of deference was dying in America.

"Self-made men" of lowly origins could now rise more readily to positions of power and influence. Exclusiveness and aristocratic pretension were now likely to provoke popular hostility or scorn. But economic equality, in the sense of an equitable sharing of wealth, was not part of the agenda of mainstream Jacksonianism. The watchword was equality of opportunity not equality of rewards.

The Democratic Ferment

The supremacy of democracy was most obvious in the new politics of universal manhood suffrage and mass political parties. By the 1820s, most states had removed the last remaining barriers to political participation by all white males. This change was not as radical or controversial as it would be later in nineteenth-century Europe; ownership of land was so common in the United States that a general suffrage did not mean that men without property became a voting majority.

Accompanying this broadening of the electorate was a rise in the proportion of public officials who were elected rather than appointed. More and more judges, as well as legislative and executive officeholders, were chosen by the people. As a result, a new style of politicking developed, emphasizing dramatic speeches that played to the voters' fears and concerns.

Skillful and farsighted politicians—like Martin Van Buren in New York—began in the 1820s to build stable statewide political organizations out of what had been loosely organized factions of the Jeffersonian party. Earlier politicians had regarded parties as a threat to republican virtue and had embraced them only as a temporary expedient. But in Van Buren's opinion, regular parties were an effective check on the temptation to abuse power, a tendency deeply planted in the human heart. The major breakthrough in American political thought during the 1820s and 1830s was the idea of a "loyal opposition," ready to capitalize politically on the mistakes or excesses of the "ins," without denying their right to act in the same way when the "ins" became the "outs."

Changes in the method of nominating and electing a president fostered the growth of a two-party system on the national level. By 1828 presidential electors were chosen by popular vote rather than by state legislature in all but two of the twenty-four states. The need to mobilize grass-roots support behind particular candidates required some form of national organization. When national nominating conventions made their appearance in 1831, the choice of candidates became a matter for representative party assemblies rather than congressional caucuses or ad hoc political alliances. These democratic practices generated much more widespread interest in politics. Between 1824 and 1840 the percentage of eligible voters who cast their ballot in presidential elections tripled.

Economic questions dominated the political controversies of the 1820s and 1830s. The Panic of 1819 and the subsequent depression heightened popular interest in government economic policy. Americans advanced several solutions for keeping the economy healthy. Some, especially small farmers, favored a return to a simpler and more "honest" economy without banks, paper money, and the easy credit that encouraged speculation. Others, particularly emerging entrepreneurs, saw salvation in government aid and protection for venture capital. Politicians and eventually political parties responded to these conflicting views.

The party disputes that arose over corporations, tariffs, banks, and internal improvements involved more than the direct economic concerns of particular interest groups. They were viewed in the context of republican fears of conspiracy against American liberty and equality. Charges of corruption and impending tyranny were common.

The notion that the American experiment was a fragile one, constantly threatened by power-hungry conspirators, eventually took two principal forms. For Jacksonians, it was "the money power" that endangered the survival of republicanism; for their opponents it was men like Jackson himself—alleged "rabble-rousers" who duped the electorate into ratifying high-handed and tyrannical action contrary to the true interests of the nation.

An object of increasing concern for both sides was the role of the federal government. National Republicans and later the Whigs believed the government should take active steps to foster economic growth; Jacksonians only wanted to eliminate "special privileges." How best to guarantee equality of opportunity—

whether by active governmental promotion of commerce and industry or by strict laissez-faire policies—was a hotly debated issue of the period.

For one group of dissenters, democracy took on a more radical meaning. Leaders of the workingmen's parties and trade unions condemned the growing gap between the rich and the poor resulting from early industrialization and the growth of a market economy. Society, in their view, was divided between "producers"—laborers, artisans, farmers, and small business owners who ran their own enterprises—and nonproducing "parasites"—bankers, speculators, and merchant capitalists. Their aim was to give the producers greater control over the fruits of their labor. They advocated such things as abolition of inheritance and a redistribution of land, as well as educational reforms, a ten-hour day, abolition of imprisonment for debt, and a currency system based exclusively on hard money so that workers could no longer be paid in depreciated bank notes.

Northern abolitionists and early proponents of women's rights made another kind of effort to extend the meaning and scope of democracy. Radical men and women advocated immediate emancipation for slaves and equal rights for blacks and women. But Jacksonian America was too permeated with racism and male chauvinism to listen to such reformers. In many ways, the civil and political situation of both blacks and women deteriorated during an era when white males were claiming their full democratic birthright. (See Chapter 11.)

Democracy and Society

Although some inequalities persisted or even grew during the age of democracy, they did so in the face of a growing belief that equality was the governing principle of American society. What this meant in practice was that no one could expect special privileges because of family connections. The popular hero was "the self-made man" who had climbed the ladder of success through his own efforts without forgetting his origin.

Except for southern slaveholders, wealthy Americans could not depend on a distinctive social class for domestic service. Instead of keeping "servants," they hired "help"—household workers who sometimes insisted on sharing meals with their employers. No true American was willing to be considered a member of a servant class and those engaged in domestic work considered it a temporary stopgap. Except as a euphemistic substitute for the word *slave*, the term *servant* virtually disappeared from the American vocabulary.

Another sign of equality was the decline of distinctive modes of dress for upper and lower classes. The elaborate periwigs and knee breeches worn by eighteenth-century gentlemen gave way to short hair and pantaloons, a style that was adopted by men of all social classes. Those with a good eye for detail might detect subtle differences in taste or in the quality of materials, but the casual observer could easily conclude that all Americans belonged to a single social class.

Of course Americans were not all of one social class. In fact, inequality based on control of productive resources was increasing during the Jacksonian period. The rise of industrialization was creating a permanent class of landless, low-paid wage earners in America's cities. In the rural areas there was a significant division between successful commercial farmers or planters and those who subsisted on marginal land. Nevertheless, European observers commented upon the fact that all white males were equal before the law and at the polls.

Furthermore, traditional forms of privilege and elitism were indeed under strong attack, as evidenced by changes in the organization and status of the learned professions. State legislatures abolished the licensing requirements for physicians previously administered by local medical societies. As a result, practitioners of unorthodox modes of healing were permitted to compete freely with established medical doctors. The legal profession was similarly opened up to far more people. The result was not always beneficial.

For the clergy, "popular sovereignty" meant that they were increasingly under the thumb

■ *To the untrained eye, serving girls in their day-off finery were indistinguishable from the wives and daughters of the wealthy.*

Democratic Culture

The democratic spirit also found expression in the rise of new forms of literature and art directed at a mass audience. The intonations of individual artists and writers varied considerably. But they all had one thing in common: They were aware that their audience was the broad citizenry of a democratic nation rather than a refined elite.

A mass market for popular literature was made possible by a rise in literacy and a revolution in the technology of printing. An increase in potential readers and a decrease in publishing costs led to a flood of lurid and sentimental novels, some of which became the first American best-sellers. Many of the new sentimental novels were written by and for women. Some female authors implicitly protested against their situation by portraying men in general as tyrannical, unreliable, or cruel and the women these men made miserable as resourceful individualists capable of making their own way. But the standard happy endings sustained the convention that a woman on her own is an unnatural thing, for a virtuous and protective man always turned up and saved the heroine from a truly independent life.

In the theater, melodrama became the dominant genre, involving the inevitable trio of beleaguered heroine, mustachioed villain, and a hero who arrives in the nick of time. Another favorite was the patriotic comedy in which the rustic Yankee foiled the foppish European aristocrat. Men and women of all classes went to the theater, and those in the cheap seats often openly voiced their displeasure with an actor or play.

The spirit of "popular sovereignty" expressed itself less dramatically in the visual arts, but its influence was nonetheless felt. Beginning in the 1830s, genre painting that glorified democracy came into vogue. Scenes from everyday life, usually with a comic twist; popular recreation; and electioneering activity were common motifs.

Architecture and sculpture reflected the democratic spirit in another mode; they were viewed as civic art forms meant to extol the

of the laity. Ministers had ceased to command respect merely because of their office, and to succeed in their calling, they were forced to develop a more popular and emotional style of preaching. Preachers, as much as politicians, prospered by pleasing the public.

Members of the upper class who could not adapt to the new politics and democratic rhetoric often found themselves stripped of the offices they had once held almost as a matter of right. Denied direct political power, they sought to exert influence through their control of philanthropic and charitable activities. But even in this arena, local notables were challenged by national reform movements and philanthropic organizations that employed professional traveling agents and experimented with new forms of mass appeal.

159

■ *With the Natty Bumpo series, James Fenimore Cooper became the first major American writer to use frontier settings and characters.*

The ideal of art for art's sake was utterly alien to the instructional spirit of mid-nineteenth-century American culture. The responsibility of the artist in a democratic society, it was generally assumed, was to contribute to the general welfare by encouraging virtue and proper sentiments. Only Edgar Allan Poe seemed to fit the European image of romantic genius rebelling against middle-class pieties. The most original of the antebellum poets, Walt Whitman, sought to be a direct mouthpiece for the rising democratic spirit, but his abandonment of traditional verse forms and his freedom in dealing with the sexual side of human nature left him isolated and unappreciated during his most creative years.

Jackson and the Politics of Democracy

The public figure who came to symbolize the triumph of democracy was Andrew Jackson, although he came out a loser in the presidential election of 1824. His victory four years later, his actions as president, and the great political party that formed around him refashioned national politics in a more democratic mold. It may be an exaggeration to call the whole period from the 1820s to the 1840s "the age of Jackson," but Old Hickory occupied the center of the public stage during much of that turbulent and eventful era.

The Election of 1824 and J. Q. Adams' Administration

The election of 1824 was one of the most complicated and controversial in American history. As Monroe's second term ended, the ruling Republican party was in disarray and could not agree on who should succeed to the presidency. The party's congressional caucus chose William Crawford of Georgia, an old-line Jeffersonian. But a majority of congressmen showed their disapproval of this outmoded method of nominating candidates by refusing to attend the caucus. Soon John Quincy

achievements of the Republic. In the 1820s and 1830s, the classical Greek style with its columned facades was favored for banks, hotels, and private dwellings as well as for public buildings. Similarly, sculpture was intended strictly for public admiration or inspiration, and its principal subjects were the heroes of the Republic.

Serious exponents of a higher culture and a more refined sensibility sought to reach the new public in the hope of elevating its taste or uplifting its morals. The "Brahmin poets" of New England—Henry Wadsworth Longfellow, James Russell Lowell, and Oliver Wendell Holmes—offered lofty sentiments to a receptive middle class; Ralph Waldo Emerson carried his philosophy of spiritual self-reliance to lyceums and lecture halls across the country; and great novelists like Nathaniel Hawthorne and Herman Melville experimented with the popular romantic genres. But the ironic and pessimistic view of life that permeated the fiction of these two authors clashed with the optimism of the age and their work failed to gain a large readership.

The Election of 1824

Candidate	Party	Popular Vote	Electoral Vote*
J. Q. Adams	(No party	113,122	84
Jackson	desig-	151,271	99
Clay	nations)	47,531	37
Crawford		40,856	41

No candidate received a majority of the electoral votes. Adams was elected by the House of Representatives.

Adams, Henry Clay, John C. Calhoun, and Andrew Jackson had their hats in the ring.

Initially Jackson was not given much of a chance. He was a military hero, not a national politician, and few party leaders felt that wartime victories were enough to catapult him into the White House. But after testing the waters, Calhoun withdrew and chose instead to run for vice-president. Then Crawford suffered a debilitating stroke that weakened his chances. These events made Jackson the favorite in the South. He also found favor among those in the North and West who were disenchanted with the economic nationalism of Clay and Adams.

In the election Jackson won a plurality of the electoral votes. But since he lacked the necessary majority, the contest was thrown into the House of Representatives where the legislators were to choose from among the three top candidates. Here Adams emerged victorious over Jackson and Crawford. Clay, who had just missed making the final three, provided the winning margin by persuading his supporters to vote for Adams. When Adams proceeded to appoint Clay as his secretary of state, the Jacksonians charged that a "corrupt bargain" had deprived their favorite of the presidency. Even though the charges were unproven, Adams assumed office under a cloud of suspicion.

Although he was a man of integrity and vision, Adams was an inept politician. He refused to bow to the public antipathy toward nationalistic programs and called for an expansion of governmental activity. Congress, however, had no intention of following Adams' lead.

The new Congress that was elected in 1826 was clearly under the control of men hostile to the administration and favorable to the presidential aspirations of Andrew Jackson. The main business before Congress was the tariff issue. Pressure for greater protection came not only from manufacturers but also from many farmers. The cotton-growing South—the only section where tariffs of all kinds were unpopular—was already safely in the general's camp. In order to gain popularity in other sections, Jackson tacitly lent his support to the tariff of 1828. This "tariff of abominations" was a congressional grab bag which contained substantial across-the-board increases in duties—gifts for all sections save the South. It was not, however, simply a ploy to get Jackson elected; it was in fact an early example of how special interest groups can achieve their goals in democratic politics through a process of legislative bargaining known as logrolling.

Jackson Comes to Power

The campaign of 1828 actually began early in the Adams administration. Resurrecting the corrupt bargain charge, Jackson's supporters began to organize on the state and local level. So successful were their efforts that influential state and regional leaders who had supported other candidates in 1824 now rallied behind Jackson to create a formidable coalition.

The most significant of these were Vice-President Calhoun, who now spoke for the militant states' rights sentiment of the South; Senator Martin Van Buren, who dominated New York politics through the political machine known as the Albany Regency; and two Kentucky editors, Francis P. Blair and Amous Kendall, who worked to mobilize opposition to Henry Clay and his "American system" in the West. These men and their followers laid the foundation for the first modern American political party—the Democrats. And from this time on, national parties existed primarily to engage in a contest for the presidency. Without this great prize, there would have been little incentive to create national organizations out

161

of the parties and factions developing in the states.

The election of 1828 saw the birth of a new era of mass democracy. Jackson's supporters made widespread use of such electioneering techniques as huge public rallies, torchlight parades, and lavish barbecues or picnics paid for by the candidate's organization. Personalities and mudslinging dominated the campaign, which reached its low point when Adams' supporters accused Jackson's wife Rachel of bigamy and adultery and Jackson's associates charged that Adams' wife was born out of wedlock.

What gave Jacksonians the edge was their success in portraying their candidate as an authentic man of the people, despite his substantial fortune in land and slaves. They emphasized Jackson's backwoods upbringing, military record, and common sense unclouded by a fancy education. Adams, according to Democratic propagandists, was the exact opposite—an overeducated aristocrat, more at home in the salon and the study than among the plain people. Anti-intellectualism was a potent force, and Adams never really had a chance.

The result had the appearance of a landslide for Old Hickory. But the verdict of the people was not as decisive as the returns might suggest. Although Jackson had piled up massive majorities in some of the slave states, the voters elsewhere divided fairly evenly. Furthermore, it was not clear what kind of a mandate he had won. Most of the politicians in his camp favored states' rights and limited government as against the nationalism of Adams and Clay, but the general himself had never taken a clear public stand on such issues as banks, tariffs, and internal improvements. His victory was more a triumph of image and personality than the popular endorsement of a particular set of programs.

Jackson turned out to be one of the most forceful and domineering of American presidents. His most striking character traits were an indomitable will, an intolerance of opposition, and a prickly pride that would not permit him to forgive or forget an insult or supposed act of betrayal. His violent temper had led him to fight a number of duels, and as a soldier his critics claimed he was guilty of using excessive force. His frontier background and military experiences had made him tough and resourceful but had also deprived him of the flexibility normally associated with successful politicians. Yet he generally got what he wanted.

Jackson's presidency commenced with his open endorsement of rotation of officeholders or what his critics called "the spoils system." Although he did not actually depart radically from his predecessors in the degree to which he removed federal officeholders and replaced them with his supporters, he was the first president to defend this practice as a legitimate application of democratic doctrine. He contended that the duties of public officers were simple and that any man of intelligence could readily fill the positions.

Jackson also established a new kind of relationship with his cabinet. Cabinet members became less important than they had been in previous administrations. Old Hickory regarded himself as "the direct representative of the people" and his cabinet as an interchangeable set of administrators whose sole function was to carry out the will of the chief executive. He used his cabinet members more for consultation than for policymaking, and he diluted their influence even further by relying heavily on the advice of an unofficial and confidential set of advisors known as his Kitchen Cabinet.

Midway in his first administration Jackson completely reorganized his cabinet. The apparent cause of this upheaval was the Peggy Eaton affair. Peggy O'Neale Eaton, the daughter of a Washington tavern owner, married Secretary of War John Eaton in 1829. Because of gossip about her moral character, the wives of other cabinet members refused to receive her socially. Jackson became her champion. Eventually all but one of his cabinet members resigned over the incident, and Jackson formed a fresh cabinet. Perhaps the most important consequence of the affair was that Martin Van Buren, although he resigned with the rest, also supported Peggy Eaton, and therefore won Jackson's favor.

Indian Removal

The first major policy question facing the Jackson administration concerned the fate of Native Americans. Jackson had long favored removing eastern Indians to lands beyond the Mississippi. His support of removal was no different from the policy of previous administrations. The only real issue was how rapidly and thoroughly the process should be carried out and by what means. At the time of Jackson's election, the states of Georgia, Alabama, and Mississippi were clamoring for quick action.

The greatest obstacle to voluntary relocation, however, was the Cherokee nation which held land in Georgia, Alabama, North Carolina, and Tennessee. The Cherokees not only refused to move but had instituted a republican form of government for themselves, achieved literacy in their own language, and made considerable progress toward adopting a settled agrarian way of life similar to that of southern whites. These were obviously not Indians in need of the "civilizing" benefits of the government's program, and missionaries and northeastern philanthropists argued that the Cherokee should be allowed to remain where they were.

The southern states disagreed. Georgia, Alabama, and Mississippi extended their state laws over the Cherokees, moves which defied provisions of the Constitution giving the federal government exclusive jurisdiction over Indian affairs and also violated specific treaties. Jackson, however, endorsed the state actions. His own attitude was that Indians were children when they did the whites' bidding, and savage beasts when they resisted. In his December 1829 message to Congress he advocated a new and more coercive removal policy. He denied Cherokee autonomy, asserted the primacy of states' rights over Indian rights, and called for the speedy and thorough removal of all eastern Indians to designated areas beyond the Mississippi.

Early in 1830 the president's congressional

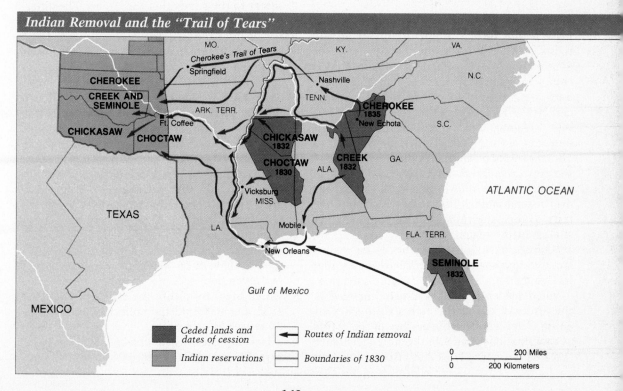

Indian Removal and the "Trail of Tears"

Ceded lands and dates of cession

Indian reservations

Routes of Indian removal

Boundaries of 1830

0   200 Miles
0   200 Kilometers

supporters introduced a bill to implement this policy. The ensuing debate was vigorous and heated, but senators and House members from the South and western border states pushed through the bill. Jackson then moved quickly to conclude the necessary treaties, using the threat of unilateral state action to bludgeon the tribes into submission. In 1832 he condoned Georgia's defiance of a Supreme Court decision (*Worcester* v. *Georgia*) that denied the right of a state to extend its jurisdiction over tribal lands. The fate of the eastern Indians was sealed.

In 1838 a stubbornly resisting majority faction of the Cherokees were rounded up by federal troops and forcibly marched to Oklahoma. This trek—known as the "Trail of Tears"—was made under such harsh conditions that almost a quarter of the Indians died on the way. A ruthless land grab, the Cherokee removal exposed the prejudiced and greedy side of Jacksonian democracy.

The Nullification Crisis

During the 1820s Southerners became increasingly fearful of federal encroachment on the rights of the states. Behind this concern, in South Carolina at least, was a strengthened commitment to the preservation of slavery and a resulting anxiety about possible uses of federal power to strike at the "peculiar institution." Hoping to keep the explosive slavery issue out of the political limelight, South Carolinians seized on another genuine grievance—the protective tariff—as the issue on which to take their stand in favor of a state veto power over federal actions that they viewed as contrary to their interests. As a staple-producing and exporting region, the South was hurt by any tariff that increased the prices for manufactured goods and threatened to undermine foreign markets by inciting counterprotection.

Vice-President John C. Calhoun emerged as the leader of the states' rights insurgency in South Carolina. After the passage of the "tariff of abominations" in 1828, the state legislature declared the new duties unconstitutional and

endorsed a lengthy disquisition—written anonymously by Calhoun—that affirmed the right of an individual state to nullify federal law. However, Calhoun and South Carolina hoped that Jackson would defend their position. In the president's position on Georgia's de facto nullification of federal treaties upholding Indian tribal rights and his veto of a major internal improvement bill (the Maysville Road in Kentucky) based upon a strict interpretation of the Constitution, South Carolinians saw room for hope.

In the meantime, a bitter personal feud developed between Jackson and Calhoun. As Calhoun lost favor with Jackson because of his position on the Eaton affair, it became clear that Van Buren would be Jackson's designated successor. The personal breech between Jackson and Calhoun colored and intensified their confrontation over nullification and the tariff.

But there were also differences of principle. Although generally a defender of states' rights and strict construction of the Constitution, Jackson opposed the theory of nullification as a threat to the survival of the Union. The differences between Jackson and Calhoun came into the open at the Jefferson Day Dinner in 1830, when Jackson offered the toast "Our Union: It must be preserved"; to which Calhoun responded: "The Union: next to Liberty most dear. May we always remember that it can only be preserved by distributing equally [its] benefits and the burdens . . . ."

In 1830 and 1831 the movement against the tariff gained strength in South Carolina. Calhoun resigned as vice-president and openly took the lead. In 1832 Congress passed a new tariff that lowered the rates slightly but retained the principle of protection. Supporters of nullification then succeeded in persuading the South Carolina state legislature to call a special convention. When the convention met in November 1832, the members voted overwhelmingly to nullify the tariffs of 1828 and 1832 and to forbid the collection of customs duties within the state.

Jackson reacted with characteristic decisiveness. He asked Congress to vote him the authority to use the army to enforce the tariff. At the same time, he sought to pacify the nullifiers somewhat by recommending a lower tariff. The Congress responded by enacting the Force Bill—which gave the president the military powers he sought—and the compromise tariff of 1833. Faced with this combination of force and compromise, South Carolina eventually rescinded the nullification ordinance. But to demonstrate that they had not conceded their constitutional position, the convention delegates concluded their deliberations by nullifying the Force Bill.

The nullification crisis revealed that Southerners would not tolerate any federal action that seemed contrary to their interests or raised doubts about the institution of slavery. The nullifiers' principle of state sovereignty implied the right of secession as well as the right to declare laws of Congress null and void. Although in many ways Jackson was a proslavery president, some far-sighted southern loyalists were alarmed by the Unionist doctrines the president propounded in his proclamation against nullification. More strongly than any previous president, he had asserted that the federal government was supreme over the states and that the Union was indivisible. What was more, he had justified the use of force against states that denied federal authority.

The Bank War and the Second Party System

Jackson's most important and controversial use of executive power was his successful attack on the Bank of the United States. "The Bank War" revealed some of the deepest concerns of Jackson and his supporters and expressed their concept of democracy in a dramatic way. It also aroused intense opposition to the president and his policies, an opposition that crystallized in a new national party—the Whigs. The destruction of the Bank and the economic disruption that followed brought to the forefront the issue of the government's relationship to the nation's financial system. Differences on this question helped to sustain the new two-party system and provided the stuff of political controversy during the administration of Jackson's handpicked successor— Martin Van Buren.

Mr. Biddle's Bank

The Bank of the United States had long been embroiled in public controversy. The South and West openly blamed it for the Panic of 1819 and the depression that followed. But after Nicholas Biddle took over the Bank's presidency in 1823, it regained public confidence. Cultured and able, Biddle probably understood the mysteries of banking and currency better than any other American of his generation. But he was arrogant and vain, as sure of his own judgment as Jackson himself.

Old-line Jeffersonians had always opposed the Bank on the grounds that its establishment was unconstitutional and it placed too much power in the hands of a small, privileged group. Its influence on the national economy was tremendous, and because of this, it was a convenient scapegoat for anything that went wrong with the economy. In an era of rising democracy, the most obvious and telling objection to the Bank was simply that it possessed great power and privilege without being under popular control.

The Bank Veto and the Election of 1832

Jackson came into office with strong reservations about banking and paper money in general. He also harbored suspicions that branches of the Bank of the United States had illicitly used their influence on behalf of his opponent in the presidential election. In his annual messages in 1829 and 1830, he called on Congress to begin discussing ways of reducing the Bank's power.

Biddle began to worry about the fate of the Bank's charter when it came up for renewal in

1836. At the same time, Jackson's Kitchen Cabinet advised him that an attack on the Bank would provide a good party issue for the election of 1832. Biddle then made a fateful blunder. He determined to seek recharter by Congress in 1832, four years ahead of schedule. Senator Henry Clay, leader of the antiadministration forces on Capitol Hill, encouraged this move because he was convinced that Jackson had chosen the unpopular side of the issue. The bill to recharter, therefore, was introduced in the House and Senate in early 1832. It passed Congress with ease.

The next move was Jackson's, and he made the most of the opportunity. He vetoed the bill and defended his action with ringing statements of principle. The Bank was unconstitutional, he said, and even worse because it was a monopoly, it violated the fundamental rights of the people in a democratic society. Jackson believed that the government should guarantee equality of opportunity, not grant privileges which gave special interests exclusive advantages.

Jackson thus called on the common people to join him in fighting the "monster" corporation. His veto message was the first to go beyond strictly constitutional arguments to deal directly with social and economic issues. Congressional attempts to override the veto failed, and Jackson resolved to take the entire issue to the people in the upcoming presidential election, which he viewed as a referendum to decide whether he or the Bank would prevail.

The 1832 election pitted Jackson against Henry Clay, standard-bearer of the National Republicans. The Bank recharter was the major issue. In the end, Jackson won a great personal triumph, garnering 219 electoral votes to 49 for Clay. As far as Old Hickory was concerned, he had his mandate.

Killing the Bank

Not content with preventing the Bank from getting a new charter, the victorious Jackson now resolved to attack it directly by removing federal deposits from Biddle's vaults. Jackson told Van Buren, "The bank . . . is trying to kill me, but I will kill it." Old Hickory regarded Biddle's opposition during the presidential race as a personal attack, part of a devious plot to destroy the president's reputation and deny him the popular approval that he deserved. As always, Jackson believed his opponents were not merely wrong but evil besides and deserved to be destroyed. Furthermore, he viewed the election result as his popular mandate to go after the Bank.

In order to remove the deposits from the Bank, Jackson had to overcome strong resistance in his own cabinet. When one secretary of the treasury refused to support the policy, he was shifted to another cabinet post. When a second balked at carrying out removal, he was replaced by Roger B. Taney, a Jackson loyalist and dedicated opponent of the Bank. Beginning in late September 1833, Taney ceased depositing government money in the Bank and began to withdraw the funds already there. The funds were then ill-advisedly placed in selected state banks. Opponents charged that the banks had been chosen for political rather than fiscal reasons and dubbed them Jackson's "pet banks."

The Bank counterattacked by calling in outstanding loans and instituting a policy of credit contraction that helped bring on an economic recession. Biddle hoped to win support for recharter by demonstrating that weakening the Bank's position would be disastrous for the economy. But all he showed, at least to the president's supporters, was that they had been right all along about the Bank's excessive power. With some justice, they blamed the economic distress on Biddle, and the Bank never did regain its charter.

Even more serious than the conflict over the Bank was the strong opposition to Jackson's fiscal policies that developed in Congress. Led by Henry Clay, the Senate approved a motion of censure against Jackson, charging him with exceeding his constitutional authority in removing the deposits. Jacksonians in the House were able to block such action, but the president was further humiliated when the Senate refused to confirm Taney as secretary of the treasury. Anti-Jacksonians were gaining in strength.

Emergence of the Whigs

The coalition that passed the censure resolution in the Senate provided the nucleus for a new national party—the Whigs. The leadership of the new party and a majority of its support came from National Republicans and ex-Federalists. But the Whigs also picked up critical backing from southern proponents of states' rights who had been upset by Jackson's stand on nullification and now saw an unconstitutional abuse of power in his withdrawal of federal deposits from the Bank of the United States. The Whig label was chosen because of its associations with both English and American revolutionary opposition to royal power and prerogatives; its rallying cry was "executive usurpation" by the tyrannical designs of "King Andrew."

The Whigs also gradually absorbed the Anti-Masonic party, a surprisingly strong northeastern political movement that exploited traditional American fears of secret societies and conspiracies. They also appealed successfully to the moral concerns of the northern middle class under the sway of an emerging evangelical Protestantism. Anti-Masons detested Jacksonianism mainly because it stood for a toleration of diverse life-styles. They believed that the government should restrict such "sinful" behavior as drinking, gambling, and breaking the Sabbath.

As the election of 1836 approached, the government's fiscal policies also provoked a localized rebellion among the urban, working-class elements of the Democratic coalition. This group favored a strict hard-money policy and condemned Jackson's transfer of federal deposits to the state banks as inflationary. Because they wanted working people to be paid in specie rather than inflated bank notes, the "Loco-Focos"—named for the matches they used for illumination when their opponents turned off the gaslights at a party meeting—went beyond opposition to the Bank of the United States

and attacked state banks as well. Seeing no basis for cooperation with the Whigs, they established the independent Equal Rights Party and nominated a separate state ticket in 1836.

Jackson himself had hard-money sentiments and probably regarded the "pet banks" solution as a temporary expedient. Nonetheless, in early 1836 he surrendered to congressional pressure and signed legislation allocating surplus federal revenues to the deposit banks, increasing their numbers and weakening federal controls over them. The result was runaway inflation, wild land speculation, and irresponsible printing of paper money. Reacting somewhat belatedly to the speculative mania he had helped to create, Jackson pricked the bubble on July 11, 1836. He issued his "specie circular" requiring that after August 15 only gold and silver would be accepted in payment for public lands. This action served to curb inflation and land speculation but did so in such a sudden and drastic way that it helped precipitate the financial panic of 1837.

The Rise and Fall of Van Buren

As his successor, Jackson chose Martin Van Buren, a master of practical politics. The Democratic National Convention of 1835 unanimously confirmed Jackson's choice. Van Buren promised to "tread generally in the footsteps of General Jackson."

The newly created Whig party, reflecting the diversity of its constituency, was unable to decide on a single standard-bearer and chose instead to run three regional candidates— Daniel Webster in the East, William Henry Harrison in the Old Northwest, and Hugh Lawson White in the South. The Whigs hoped to deprive Van Buren of enough electoral votes to throw the election into the House of Representatives where one of the Whigs might stand a chance.

This stratagem proved unsuccessful. Van Buren won a clear victory. But the election foreshadowed future trouble for the Democrats, particularly in the South. There the Whigs ran virtually even. The emergence of a

167

two-party system in the previously solid South resulted from two factors—opposition to some of Jackson's policies and the image of Van Buren as an unreliable Yankee politician.

The main business of Van Buren's administration was to straighten out the financial disorder resulting from the destruction of the Bank of the United States and the issuing of Jackson's specie circular. As he took office Van Buren was immediately faced with a catastrophic depression. The Panic of 1837 was not exclusively, or even primarily, the result of government policies. It was in fact international in scope and reflected some complex changes in the world economy that were beyond the control of American policymakers.

But the Whigs were quick to blame the state of the economy on Jacksonian finance, and the administration had to make a politically effective response. Since Van Buren and his party were committed to a policy of laissez-faire on the federal level, there was little or nothing they could do to relieve economic distress through subsidies or relief measures. But the president could at least try to salvage the federal funds deposited in shaky state banks and devise a new system of public finance that would not contribute to future panics by fueling speculation and credit expansion.

Van Buren's solution was to establish a public depository for government funds with no connections whatsoever to commercial banking. His proposal for an "independent subtreasury" aroused intense opposition from the congressional Whigs, and it was not until 1840 that it was enacted into law. In the meantime the economy had temporarily revived in 1838 only to sink again into a deeper depression the following year.

Van Buren's chances for reelection in 1840 were undoubtedly hurt by the state of the economy. But the principal reason for his defeat was that he lacked the charisma of a Jackson and was thus unable to overcome the extremely effective campaign mounted by the Whigs. The Whig party of 1840 was well-organized on a grass-roots level, and they found their own Jackson in William Henry Harrison,

A charismatic leader, a folksy man of the people—that was the image conveyed by the banners the Whig party created for the 1840 campaign of William Henry Harrison, the hero of Tippecanoe.

a military hero of advanced age, who was associated in the public mind with the battle of Tippecanoe and the winning of the West.

Harrison's views on public issues were little known, and the Whigs ran him without a platform to avoid distracting the electorate from his personal qualities. They pretended that Harrison had been born in a log cabin—actually it was a pillared mansion—and that he preferred hard cider to more effete beverages. To balance the ticket and increase its appeal in the South they chose John Tyler of Virginia, a converted states' rights Democrat, to be Harrison's running rate.

Using the slogan, "Tippecanoe and Tyler, Too," the Whigs pulled out all stops in their bid for the White House. Imitating the Jacksonian propaganda against Adams in 1828, they portrayed Van Buren as a luxury-loving aristocrat and compared him with their own homespun candidate. The Democrats tried but were unable to project Van Buren as a man of the people. Harrison won, and the Whigs gained control of both houses of Congress.

Heyday of the Second Party System

America's "second party system" came of age in the election of 1840. The rivalry of Democrats and Whigs made the two-party pattern a permanent feature of the electoral politics in the United States. During the 1840s, the two national parties competed on fairly equal terms for the support of the electorate. Allegiance to one party or the other became an important source of personal identity for many Americans and increased their interest and participation in politics.

In addition to drama and entertainment, the parties offered the voters a real choice of programs and ideologies. Whigs stood for a "positive liberal state," in which the government had the right and duty to subsidize or protect enterprises that could contribute to general prosperity and economic growth. Democrats advocated a "negative liberal state," in which government keeps its hands off the economy.

Conflict over economic issues helped determine each party's base of support. In the Whig camp were most industrialists and merchants, plus a large proportion of those farmers and planters who had adapted successfully to a market economy. Democrats appealed mainly to small farmers, workers, declining gentry, and emerging entrepreneurs who were excluded from the established commercial groups that stood to benefit most from Whig programs. But issues like the tariff could further complicate this pattern; workers in protected industries often voted Whig, while importers normally voted for the Democrats and freer trade.

Economic interest was not the only factor behind the choice of parties. Life-styles and ethnic or religious identities strongly affected party loyalties during this period. In the northern states, one way to tell the typical Whig from the typical Democrat was to see what each did on Sunday. An evangelical Protestant was likely to be a Whig. A person who belonged to a ritualized church—Catholic, Lutheran, or Episcopalian—or did not go to church at all was probably a Democrat.

The Democrats were the favored party of immigrants, Catholics, free-thinkers, backwoods farmers, and those of all classes who enjoyed traditional amusements condemned by the new breed of moral reformers. One thing that all these groups had in common was a desire to be left alone, free of restrictions on their freedom to think and behave as they liked. In general the Whigs welcomed a market economy but wished to restrain the individualism and disorder it created by enforcing cultural and moral values derived from the Puritan tradition. Most of those who sought to be "their brothers' keepers" were Whigs.

Chronology	
1824	House of Representatives elects John Quincy Adams president
1828	Congress passes "tariff of abominations" Jackson elected president over J. Q. Adams
1830	Jackson vetoes the Maysville Road bill Congress passes Indian Removal Act
1831	Jackson reorganizes his cabinet First national nominating conventions meet
1832	Jackson vetoes the bill rechartering the Bank of the United States Jackson reelected, defeating Henry Clay (National Republican candidate)
1832–1833	Crisis erupts over South Carolina's attempt to nullify the tariff of 1832
1833	Jackson removes federal deposits from the Bank of the United States
1834	Whig party comes into existence
1836	Jackson issues "specie circular" Martin Van Buren elected president
1837	Financial panic occurs, followed by depression lasting until 1843
1840	Congress passes the Independent Subtreasury Bill Harrison (Whig) defeats Van Buren (Democrat) for the presidency

Nevertheless, party conflict in Congress continued to center on national economic policy. Whigs stood firm for a loose construction of the Constitution and positive federal guidance and support for business and economic development. The Democrats persisted in their defense of strict construction, states' rights, and laissez-faire. Debates over tariffs, banking, and internal improvements remained vital and vigorous during the 1840s.

True believers in both parties saw a deep ideological or moral meaning in the clash over economic or social issues. The Democrats were the party of individualism and personal liberty. The role of government was to remove obstacles to individual rights, which could mean the right to rise economically, the right to drink hard liquor, or the right to be unorthodox in religion. The Whigs, on the other hand, were the party of community. They believed that the propertied, the well-educated, and the pious were responsible for guiding the masses toward a common good.

Each, in a sense, reflected one side of a broader democratic impulse. This Jacksonian legacy was a stress on individual freedom and ethnic or cultural tolerance (except for blacks). The Whigs perceived that in a republic, strong government could serve the general interest and further the spirit of national unity. Later generations of progressive Americans would seek to create a balance between freedom and community, liberty and order. In doing so, they would necessarily draw on both of the political cultures of the second party system.

Recommended Reading

The best general accounts of Jacksonian democracy are Arthur M. Schlesinger, Jr., *The Age of Jackson* (1945); Glyndon G. Van Deusen, *The Jacksonian Era, 1828–1848* (1959); and Edward Pessen, *Jacksonian America: Society, Personality, and Politics*, rev. ed. (1979). Alexis de Tocqueville's *Democracy in America* (2 vols., 1945) is the classic analysis of Jacksonian America by a perceptive foreign visitor.

The new political system is described in Richard P. McCormick, *The Second American Party System* (1966), and Richard Hofstadter, *The Idea of a Party System* (1970). On radical, working-class movements, see Edward Pessen, *Most Uncommon Jacksonians: The Radical Leaders of the Early Labor Movement* (1967), and Bruce M. Laurie, *Working People of Philadelphia, 1800–1850* (1980). Social manifestations of the democratic ethos are covered in Douglas T. Miller, *Jacksonian Autocracy: Class and Democracy in New York, 1830–1860*, and Joseph F. Kett, *The Formation of the American Medical Profession* (1968). On democratic culture, see David Grimstad, *Melodrama Unveiled: American Theater and Culture, 1800–1850* (1968); Neil Harris, *The Artist in American Society* (1966); and Russel B. Nye, *Society and Culture in America, 1830–1860* (1960).

The emergence of Andrew Jackson and the Democratic party is described in Samuel F. Bemis, *John Quincy Adams and the Union* (1956), and in two books by Robert V. Remini: *Martin Van Buren and the Making of the Democratic Party* (1959) and *The Election of Andrew Jackson* (1964). A good general account of Jackson's presidency is Richard B. Latner, *The Presidency of Andrew Jackson* (1979). On Jacksonian Indian Policy, see Bernard W. Sheehan, *The Seeds of Extinction: Jeffersonian Philanthropy and the American Indian*, and Michael Paul Rogin, *Fathers and Children: Andrew Jackson and the Subjugation of the American Indian* (1975). The standard work on the nullification crisis is William W. Freehling, *Prelude to Civil War* (1966).

The Bank War is discussed in Bray Hammond, *Banks and Politics in America from the Revolution to the Civl War* (1957), and Robert V. Remini, *Andrew Jackson and the Bank War* (1967). On Van Buren's administration see James C. Curtis, *The Fox at Bay: Martin Van Buren and the Presidency* (1970).

On the Whigs, see Clement Eaton, *Henry Clay and the Art of American Politics* (1957), and Daniel Walker Howe, *The Political Culture of the American Whigs* (1979). The growth of a two-party system in the South is described in William J. Cooper, Jr., *The South and the Politics of Slavery* (1978). On the cultural differences between Whigs and Democrats, see Ronald P. Formisano, *The Birth of Mass Political Parties: Michigan, 1827–1861* (1971).

chapter 11

THE
PURSUIT
OF PERFECTION

In the winter of 1830–1831 a wave of religious revivals swept the northern states. For six months in Rochester, New York, evangelist Charles G. Finney preached almost daily, emphasizing that every man or woman had the power to choose Christ and a godly life. He converted hundreds, and he urged them in turn to convert relatives, neighbors, and employees. If enough people enlisted in the evangelical crusade, Finney proclaimed, the millennium would be achieved within months.

Finney's call for religious and moral renewal fell on fertile ground in Rochester. The leading families in this bustling boom town were divided into quarreling factions, and workingmen were breaking free from the control that their employers had previously exerted over their daily lives. More vigorous standards of proper behavior and religious conformity unified Rochester's elite and increased its ability to control the rest of the community. Evangelical Protestantism provided the middle class with a stronger sense of identity and purpose.

But the war on sin was not limited to such safe ground. Before long religious and moral reformers took the logical step from individual to societal reformation. They demanded that all social and political institutions measure up to the standards of Christian perfection. They proceeded to attack such collective "sins" as the liquor traffic, war, slavery, and even government. Religiously inspired reformism cut two ways. On the one hand, it brought a measure of order and cultural unity to previously divided and troubled communities like Rochester. But it also inspired a variety of more radical movements or experiments that threatened to undermine established institutions and principles. One of these—abolitionism— would trigger political upheaval and help to bring on the Civil War.

Although both the evangelical reformers and the new democratic politicians sought popular favor and assumed that individuals were free agents capable of self-direction and self-improvement, the leaders differed in important respects. Jacksonians idealized common folk pretty much as they found them and saw no danger to the community if individuals pursued their worldly interests. Evangelical reformers, on the other hand, believed that the common people needed to be redeemed and uplifted. They did not trust a democracy of unbelievers and sinners. The Republic would be safe, they insisted, only if a right-minded minority preached, taught, and agitated until the mass of ordinary citizens was reborn into a higher life.

The Rise of Evangelicalism

American Protestantism was in a state of constant ferment during the early nineteenth century. The separation of church and state was now complete. Dissenting groups, like the Baptists and Methodists, welcomed full religious freedom because it offered a better chance to win new converts. But all pious Protestants were concerned about the spread of "infidelity"—their word for laxity in matters of faith and excessive worldliness.

Revivalism provided the best way to extend religious values and build up church membership. The Great Awakening of the mid-eighteenth century had shown the wonders that evangelists could accomplish, and the new revivalists repeated this success by increasing the proportion of the population that belonged to Protestant churches, forming voluntary organizations, and mobilizing the faithful into associations to spread the gospel and reform American morals.

The Second Great Awakening:
The Southern Frontier Phase

The Second Great Awakening began in earnest on the southern frontier around the turn of the century. Highly emotional camp meetings, organized usually by Methodists or Baptists, became a regular feature of religious life in the South and lower Midwest. On the frontier the camp meeting met social as well as religious needs. In the sparsely settled southern back-

country, for many people the only way to get baptized, married, or have a communal religious experience was to attend a camp meeting.

Rowdies and scoffers also attended. Mostly they drank whiskey, caroused, and fornicated on the fringes of the small city of tents and wagons. But sometimes they too fell into emotional fits and were converted. Evangelists loved to tell stories of such conversions or near conversions.

Camp meetings obviously provided an emotional outlet for rural people whose everyday lives were often lonely and tedious. But they could also promote a sense of community and social discipline. Conversion at a camp meeting could be a rite of passage, signifying that a young man or woman had outgrown wild or antisocial behavior and was now ready to become a respectable member of the community. But for the most part frontier revivalism remained highly individualistic. It strengthened personal piety and morality but did not stimulate organized benevolence or social reform.

The Second Great Awakening
in the North

Reformist tendencies were more evident in the distinctive kind of revivalism that originated in New England and western New York. The northern evangelists were mostly Congregationalists and Presbyterians, strongly influenced by the traditions of New England Puritanism. Their revivals, although less extravagant and emotional than those on the frontier, found fertile soil in small-to-medium-sized towns and cities. The northern brand of evangelism resulted in the formation of societies devoted to the redemption of the human race in general and American society in particular.

The reform movement began in New England as an effort to defend Calvinism against the liberal views of religion fostered by the Enlightenment. The Reverend Timothy Dwight, who became president of Yale College in 1795, and other like minds were alarmed by

■ *Frontier camp meetings in the early 1800s were attended by large crowds of people (sometimes thousands at a time) who sang, prayed, wept, and begged for divine mercy as the spirit moved them. The meetings served as an emotional outlet for rural people whose lives were lonely and tedious.*

the growing tendency to view the Diety as the benevolent master architect of a rational universe rather than as an all-powerful mysterious God. Some Congregationalist clergy reached the point of denying the doctrine of the Trinity, proclaiming themselves "Unitarians." Horrified when the Unitarians won control of the Harvard Divinity School, Dwight battled this liberal tendency by reaffirming the old Calvinist belief that man was sinful and depraved. But the harshness and pessimism of orthodox Calvinist doctrine, with its stress on original sin and predestination, had limited appeal in a Republic committed to human freedom and progress.

Dwight himself made some concessions to the spirit of the age by agreeing that human beings had a limited control over their spiritual destiny. But a younger generation of Congregational ministers reshaped New England

Puritanism to increase its appeal to people who shared the prevailing optimism about human capabilities.

The main theologian of early-nineteenth-century neo-Calvinism was Nathaniel Taylor, a disciple of Dwight. Taylor softened the doctrine of predestination and contended that every individual was a "free agent" who had the ability to overcome a natural inclination to sin. This reconciliation of original sin with "free agency" enabled the neo-Calvinists to compete successfully with the revival denominations which preached that sinners had the ability to choose salvation.

The first great practitioner of the new evangelical Calvinism was Lyman Beecher, another of Dwight's pupils. In the period just before and after the War of 1812, Beecher helped to promote a series of revivals in the Congregational churches of New England. Using his

The Rise of Evangelicalism

own homespun version of free agency, he induced thousands of churchgoers to acknowledge their sinfulness and surrender to God.

During the late 1820s Beecher was forced to confront the new and more radical form of revivalism being practiced in western New York by Charles G. Finney. Upstate New York was a seedbed for religious enthusiasms. A majority of its population were transplanted New Englanders who had left behind their close-knit village communities and ancestral churches but not their Puritan consciences. Troubled by rapid economic changes and social dislocations, they were ripe for the assurances of a new faith and a sense of moral direction.

Although he worked within the Congregational and Presbyterian churches, Finney departed radically from traditional Calvinist doctrines. In his hands, the doctrine of free agency became unqualified freewill. Indifferent to theological issues, Finney appealed strictly to emotion or to "the heart" rather than to doctrine or reason. He eventually adopted the extreme view that it was possible for redeemed Christians to be totally free of sin—to be perfect as their Father in Heaven is perfect.

Beginning in 1823, Finney conducted a series of highly successful revivals in the towns and cities of western New York. Even more controversial than his freewheeling approach to theology were the means he used to win converts. Finney sought instantaneous conversions through a variety of new methods including protracted meetings lasting all night or for several days in a row. He achieved dramatic results. Sometimes listeners fell to the floor in fits of excitement and immediately sought God's grace.

Beecher and the eastern evangelicals were disturbed by Finney's new methods and by the hysteria that they produced. They were also upset because he violated long-standing Christian tradition by allowing women to pray aloud in church. But it soon became clear that Finney was not merely stirring people to temporary peaks of excitement; he was also leaving strong and active churches behind him, and eastern opposition gradually weakened.

From Revivalism to Reform

Northern revivalists inspired a great movement for social reform. Converts were organized into voluntary associations that sought to stamp out sin and social evil and win the world for Christ. Most of the converts of northern revivalism were middle-class citizens already active in the lives of their communities. They were seeking to adjust to the bustling world of the market revolution in ways that would not violate their traditional moral and social values. Given the generally optimistic and forwardlooking attitudes of such Americans, it is understandable that a wave of conversions would lead to hopes for the salvation of the nation and the world.

In New England, Beecher and his evangelical associates were behind the establishment of a great network of missionary and benevolent societies. Foreign missionaries spread the gospel to remote parts of the world, and organizations such as the American Bible Society distributed Bibles in areas of the West where there was a scarcity of churches and clergymen. Missionaries even reached out to the many poor people in American cities.

Evangelicals formed moral reform societies as well as missions. Some of these aimed at curbing irreligious activity on the Sabbath; others sought to stamp out dueling, gambling, and prostitution. In the latter case, crusaders attempted to redeem the prostitutes as well as to curtail the activities of their patrons. Others felt that the cause of virtue would be better served by suppressing public discussion and investigation of sexual vices.

Beecher was especially influential in the temperance crusade, the most successful of the reform movements. The temperance movement was directed at a real social evil, more serious in many ways than the drug problem of today. Since the Revolution, whiskey had become the most popular American beverage. It was cheaper than milk or beer and safer than water (which was often contaminated). Per capita annual consumption of distilled beverages in the 1820s was almost triple what it is today, and alcoholism had reached epidemic proportions.

The temperance reformers viewed indulgence in alcohol as a threat to public morality. Drunkenness was seen as a loss of self-control and moral responsibility that spawned crime, vice, and disorder. Above all, it threatened the family. The main target of temperance propaganda was the husband and father who abused, neglected, or abandoned his wife and children because he was a slave to the bottle. The drinking habits of the poor and laboring classes also aroused great concern, for the "respectable" and propertied elements lived in fear that lower class mobs, crazed with drink, would attack private property and destroy social order.

Many of the evangelical reformers regarded intemperance as the greatest single obstacle to the achievement of a republic of God-fearing, self-disciplined citizens. In 1826 a group of clergymen organized the American Temperance Society to educate Americans about the evils of hard liquor. The society sent out lecturers, issued a flood of literature, and sponsored essay contests.

The campaign was enormously effective. Although it may be doubted whether large numbers of confirmed drunkards were actually cured, the movement did succeed in altering the drinking habits of middle-class Americans by making temperance a mark of respectability. Per capita consumption of hard liquor declined more than 50 percent during the 1830s.

Cooperating missionary and reform societies—collectively known as "the benevolent empire"—were a major force in American culture by the early 1830s. A new ethic of self-control and self-discipline was being instilled in the middle class that equipped individuals to confront a new world of economic growth and social mobility without losing their cultural and moral bearings.

By the 1830s the French traveler Alexis de Tocqueville could marvel at the power of Christian faith and morality in a land without an established church. It seemed to him that voluntaristic religion produced moral and law-abiding citizens without the need for governmental coercion. In religion and reform, and not in politics, many Americans saw the best and last hope for the Republic.

Domesticity and Changes in the American Family

The evangelical culture of the 1820s and 1830s influenced the family as an institution and inspired new conceptions of its role in American society. For many parents, child-rearing was viewed as essential preparation for the self-disciplined Christian life. Women—who were regarded as particularly susceptible to religious and moral influences—assumed a greater importance within the domestic circle. Home and family were glorified to such an extent that people could lose sight of the fact that a market society was weakening traditional kinship ties and setting many people adrift in an impersonal world of economic relationships.

Marriage and Sex Roles

The American family underwent major changes in the decades between the revolution and the mid-nineteenth century. One was the triumph of marriage for love. Parents now exercised even less control over their children's selection of mates than they had in the colonial period. The prompting of the heart, so important to religious conversion, was now seen as the primary factor in choosing a mate.

It seems likely, too, that relations between husbands and wives were becoming more affectionate. In the main, eighteenth-century correspondence between spouses had been formal and distant in tone. The husband, for example, rarely confessed that he missed his wife or craved her company. By the early nineteenth century first names, pet names, and terms of endearment like "honey" or "darling" were increasingly used by both sexes, and absent husbands frequently confessed that they felt lost without their mates. In return, wives assumed a more egalitarian tone and offered counsel on a wide range of subjects.

At its best, marriage had become more a matter of companionship and less an exertion of male dominance. But the change should not be exaggerated or romanticized. In law, and in cases of conflict between spouses, the husband remained the unchallenged head of the household. True independence or equality for women was impossible at a time when men held exclusive legal authority over a couple's property and children.

Such power as women exerted within the home came from their ability to affect the decisions of men who had learned to respect their moral qualities and good sense. The evangelical movement encouraged this quiet expression of feminine influence. Revivals not only gave women a role in converting men but made a feminized Christ the main object of worship. A nurturing, loving, merciful Savior, mediating between a stern father and his erring children, provided the model for woman's new role as spiritual head of the home.

Historians have described the new conception of woman's role as the "Cult of True Womanhood" or the "ideology of domesticity." Woman's place was in the home and on a pedestal. The ideal wife was a model of piety and virtue who exerted a wholesome moral and religious influence over members of the coarser sex.

The sociological reality behind the Cult of True Womanhood was an increasing division between the working lives of men and women. In the eighteenth century and earlier most economic activity had been centered in the home and nearby, and husbands and wives often worked together in a common enterprise. By early in the mid-nineteenth century this way of life was limited mainly to rural areas. In towns and cities, the rise of factories and countinghouses severed the home from the workplace. Men went forth every morning to their places of labor, leaving their wives at home to tend the house and the children. The cult of domesticity made a virtue of the fact that men were solely responsible for running the affairs of the world and building up the economy.

A new concept of sex roles justified and glorified this pattern. The "doctrine of two spheres"—set forth in novels, advice literature, and the new ladies' magazines—sentimentalized the woman who kept a spotless house, nurtured her children, and offered her husband a refuge from the heartless world of commerce and industry. From a modern point of view, it is easy to condemn the cult of domesticity as a rationalization for male dominance. But most women of the early- to mid-nineteenth century probably did not feel oppressed or degraded by the new arrangement. Women had never enjoyed equality, and the new norm of confinement to the home did not necessarily imply that women were inferior. By the standards of evangelical culture, women in the domestic sphere could be viewed as superior to men since women were in a good position to cultivate the "feminine" virtues of love and self-sacrifice and thus act as official guardians of religious and moral values.

The domestic ideology had real meaning only for relatively affluent women. Working-class wives were not usually employed outside the home during this period, but they labored long and hard within the household, often taking in washing or piece work to supplement a meager family income. Their endless domestic drudgery made a sham of the notion that women had the time and energy for the "higher things in life."

For middle-class women whose husbands earned a good income, however, freedom from industrial or farm labor offered tangible benefits. They now had the leisure to read extensively in the new literature directed primarily at housewives and to cultivate deep and lasting friendships with other women. The result was a distinctively feminine subculture emphasizing "sisterhood" or "sorority." This growing sense of solidarity with other women often bridged economic and social gaps as demonstrated when upper- and middle-class women organized societies for the relief and rehabilitation of poor or "fallen women."

For some women, the domestic ideal even sanctioned ladylike efforts to extend their sphere until it conquered the masculine world outside the home. This domestic feminism was reflected in women's involvement in crusades to stamp out such masculine sins as intemperance, gambling, and sexual vice. It was also the motivating force behind the campaign to make schoolteaching a woman's occupation.

Women attempted to make the world a better place by properly rearing their children who were captive pupils for the mother's instructions. Since women were considered particularly well qualified to transmit piety and morality to future citizens of the Republic, the cult of domesticity exalted motherhood and encouraged a new concern with childhood as the time of life when "character" was formed.

The Discovery of Childhood

The nineteenth century has been called "the century of the child." More than before, childhood was seen as a distinct stage of life requiring the special and sustained attention of parents. The family now became "child-centered," which meant that the care, nurturing, and rearing of children was viewed as the family's prime function.

New customs and fashions heralded the "discovery" of childhood. Books aimed specifically at juveniles and others providing expert advice to parents on child-rearing began to roll off the presses. The ideal family described in the advice manuals and sentimental literature was bound together by affection rather than authority. Firm discipline remained at the core of "family government," but there was a change in the preferred method of enforcing good behavior. Corporal punishment declined, partially displaced by shaming or withholding of affection. The intended result of punishment was often described as "self-government"; and to achieve it parents used guilt, rather than fear, as their main source of leverage.

Child-centered families also meant smaller families. If nineteenth-century families had remained as large as those of earlier times, it would have been impossible to lavish so much care and attention on individual offspring. Between 1800 and 1850 the average family size declined about 25 percent, beginning a long-range trend lasting to the present day.

The practice of various forms of birth control undoubtedly contributed to this demographic revolution. Ancestors of the modern condom and diaphragm were openly advertised and sold during the pre-Civil War period, but it is likely that most couples controlled family size by practicing the withdrawal method or limiting the frequency of intercourse. Abortion was also surprisingly common and was on the rise.

Parents seemed to understand that having fewer children meant that they could provide their offspring with a better start in life. Such attitudes were appropriate to a society that was beginning to shift from agriculture to commerce and industry.

Institutional Reform

The family could not carry the whole burden of socializing and reforming individuals. Children needed schooling as well as parental nurture. Some adults, too, seemed to require special kinds of attention and treatment. Seeking to extend the advantages of "family government" beyond the domestic circle, reformers worked to establish or improve public institutions that were designed to shape individual character and instill a capacity for self-discipline.

The Extension of Education

The period from 1820 to 1850 saw an enormous expansion of free public schools. The new resolve to put more children in school for longer periods reflected many of the same values that exalted the child-centered family. It was believed that formal training at a character-building institution would prepare children to make a living and bear the burdens of republican citizenship when they became adults. Purely intellectual training at school was

■ *The lessons and examples in* McGuffy's Readers *upheld the basic virtues of thrift, honesty, and charity and taught that evil deeds never went unpunished.*

regarded as less important than moral indoc-trination.

Besides being an extension of the family, the school could also serve as a substitute for it. Educational reformers were alarmed at the masses of poor and immigrant children who allegedly lacked a proper home environment. The safety of the Republic depended on schools to make up for this disadvantage.

Before the 1820s, schooling in the United States was a haphazard affair. The wealthy sent their children to private schools, and some of the poor sent their children to charity or "pauper" schools that were usually financed in part by state or local government. Between the 1820s and the 1850s, the movement for publicly supported common schools made great headway in the North and had limited success in parts of the South. In theory, the common school was an egalitarian institution providing a free basic education for children of all backgrounds.

The agitation for expanded public education began in the 1820s and early 1830s as a central demand of the workingmen's movements in eastern cities. These artisans and tradespeople viewed free schools open to all as a way of countering the growing gap between rich and poor. Middle-class reformers soon seized the initiative, shaped educational reform toward the goal of social discipline, and provided the momentum needed for legislative success.

The most influential spokesman for the common school movement was Horace Mann of Massachusetts. As a lawyer and a member of the state legislature, Mann worked tirelessly for the establishment of a state board of educa-tion and adequate tax support for local schools. His philosophy of education was based on the premise that children were clay in the hands of teachers and school officials and could be molded to a state of perfection. Like the advo-cates of child-rearing through moral influence rather than physical force, he discouraged cor-poral punishment except as a last resort. Against those who argued that school taxes violated the rights of property, Mann con-tended that private property was actually held in trust for the good of the community. Educa-tion, he stressed, saved children from drifting into lives of poverty and vice and prepared them to become good, law-abiding citizens. Mann's conception of public education as a means of social discipline converted the mid-dle and upper classes to his cause.

In practice, the new or improved public schools often alienated working-class pupils and their families rather than reforming them. Compulsory attendance laws deprived poor families of needed wage earners without guar-anteeing new occupational opportunities for those with an elementary education. Futher-more, Catholic immigrants complained quite correctly that Mann and his disciples were try-ing to impose a uniform Protestant culture on the pupils.

In addition to the "three Rs" of reading, writing, and arithmetic, the essence of what was being taught in the public schools of the mid-nineteenth century was the "Protestant ethic"—industry, punctuality, sobriety, and frugality. These were the virtues stressed in the famous McGuffey readers, which first appeared in 1836. Such moral indoctrination helped produce generations of Americans with personalities and beliefs adapted to the needs of an industrialized society. If the system did not encourage thinking for one's self, it did prepare people who could easily adjust to the regular routines of the factory or the office.

Fortunately, however, education was not limited to the schools nor devoted solely to children. Every city and almost every town or village had a lyceum, debating society, or mechanic's institute where adults of all social classes could broaden their intellectual horizons. Young Abe Lincoln, for example, sharpened his intellect and honed his debating skills as a member of such an institute in New Salem, Illinois in the early 1830s. Unlike the public schools, the lyceums and debating societies fostered independent thought and the spread of new ideas.

Discovering the Asylum

Some segments of the population were obviously beyond the reach of family government and character training provided in homes and schools. In the 1820s and 1830s, reformers became acutely aware of the dangers to society posed by an apparently increasing number of

In this 1876 woodcut, prisoners—in hand-on-shoulder lockstep—march into the dining room at Sing Sing Prison in New York. Rigid discipline and extensive rules restricting the inmates' movements, speech, and actions were thought to be important elements in reforming criminals. In most prisons, a strict silence was enforced at all times and solitary confinement was viewed as a humanitarian and therapeutic policy because it allowed prisoners to reflect on the error of their ways.

criminals, lunatics, and paupers. Their answer was to establish special institutions to provide a controlled environment in which the inmates could be reformed and rehabilitated.

In earlier times, the existence of paupers, lawbreakers, and insane persons was viewed as the consequence of divine judgment or original sin. For the most part these people were dealt with in ways that did not isolate them from local communities. But dealing with deviants in a neighborly way broke down as economic development and organization disrupted community life. At the same time, reformers were concluding that all defects of mind and character were correctable—that the insane could be cured, criminals reformed, and paupers taught to pull themselves out of destitution. The result was the discovery of the asylum.

The 1820s and 1830s saw the emergence of state-supported prisons, insane asylums, and poorhouses. New York and Pennsylvania led the way in prison reform. In theory, prisons

■ *Inmates of asylums, prisons, and almshouses could have fared worse had it not been for the considerable efforts of Dorothea Dix to publicize inhumane conditions.*

and asylums substituted for the family. The custodians were intended to act as parents by providing moral advice and training. In practice, these institutions were far different from the affectionate families idealized by the cult of domesticity. Their most prominent feature was the imposition of a rigid daily routine. The early superintendents and wardens believed that the enforcement of an inflexible and demanding set of rules and procedures would encourage self-discipline.

In retrospect, it is clear that the prisons, asylums, and poorhouses did not achieve the aims of their founders. A combination of naive theories and poor performance doomed these institutions to a custodial rather than a reformatory role. Public support was inadequate to meet the needs of the growing inmate population; the result was overcrowding and the use of brutality to keep order.

But conditions would have been even worse without the efforts of a remarkable woman—Dorothea Dix—one of the most effective of all the pre-Civil War reformers. As a direct result of her skill in publicizing the inhumane treatment prevailing in prisons, almshouses, and insane asylums, fifteen states built new hospitals and improved supervision of penitentiaries and other institutional facilities.

Reform Turns Radical

During the 1830s, internal dissension split the great reform movement spawned by the Second Great Awakening. Efforts to promote evangelical piety, improve personal and public morality, and shape character through familial or institutional discipline continued and even flourished. But bolder spirits went beyond such goals and set their sights on the total liberation and perfection of the individual. Especially in New England and the upper North, a new breed of reformers, prophets, and utopians attacked established institutions and rejected all compromise with what they viewed as a corrupt society.

Divisions in the Benevolent Empire

Early-nineteenth-century reformers were generally committed to gradually changing existing attitudes and practices in ways that would not invite conflict or disrupt the fabric of society. But by the mid-1830s a new mood of impatience and perfectionism surfaced within the benevolent societies. The Temperance Society, for example, split between radicals who insisted on a total commitment to "cold water" and moderates who were willing to overlook moderate wine and beer drinking. The same sort of division arose in the American Peace Society between those insisting on absolute pacifism and those willing to sanction "defensive wars."

The new perfectionism realized its most dramatic and important success within the antislavery movement. Before the 1830s many of the people who expressed religious and moral concern over slavery were affiliated with the American Colonization Society, a benevolent organization founded in 1817. Most colonizationists admitted that slavery was an evil, but they felt it should be eliminated only gradually and with the cooperation of slaveholders. Reflecting the power of racial prejudice, they proposed to transport freed blacks to Africa as a way of relieving southern fears that a race war would erupt if slaves were simply released from bondage and allowed to remain in America. In 1821 the society established a colony in West Africa, named it Liberia, and settled several thousand American blacks there over the next decade.

Colonization proved to be grossly inadequate as a step toward the elimination of slavery. Slaveholders rarely cooperated with the movement, and free blacks rejected the whole process. Black opposition to colonization helped persuade William Lloyd Garrison and other white abolitionists to repudiate the Colonization Society and support immediate emancipation without emigration.

Garrison launched a new and more radical antislavery movement in 1831 when he began

■ *Black leaders in the abolitionist movement included Frederick Douglass, who escaped from slavery himself and was one of the most effective voices in the anti-slavery campaign.*

to publish a journal called the *Liberator* in Boston. Most of his early subscribers were free blacks, who were also a mainstay of support for the American Anti-Slavery Society he founded in 1833. Black orators, especially escaped slaves like Frederick Douglass, were featured at anti-slavery rallies. Garrison's rhetoric was as severe as his proposals were radical. As he wrote in the first issue of the *Liberator*, "I will be as harsh as the truth and as uncompromising as justice . . . . I will not retreat a single inch—AND I WILL BE HEARD."

The Abolitionist Enterprise

The abolitionist movement, like the temperance crusade, was a direct outgrowth of the Second Great Awakening. Many leading abolitionists had undergone conversion experiences in the 1820s and were already committed to a life of Christian activism before they dedicated themselves to freeing the slaves. Several were ministers or divinity students seeking a mission in life that would fulfill their spiritual and professional ambitions.

The career of Theodore Dwight Weld exemplified the connection between revivalism and abolitionism. Influenced strongly by Charles G. Finney, Weld underwent a conversion experience in 1826. He then became an itinerant lecturer for various reform causes. By the early 1830s, his attention was focused on the moral issue raised by the institution of slavery. After a brief flirtation with the colonization movement, he became a convert to abolitionism. Traveling throughout Ohio, where he and his associates founded Oberlin College as a center for abolitionist activity, he used the the tried and true methods of the revival—fervent preaching, protracted meetings, and the call for individuals to come forth and announce their redemption—in the cause of the antislavery movement. As a result of these efforts, northern Ohio and western New York became hotbeds of abolitionist sentiment.

In general, antislavery orators and organizers enjoyed their greatest success in the smaller towns of the upper North. The typical convert came from an upwardly mobile family engaged in small business, the skilled trades, or market farming. In the cities, abolitionists sometimes encountered fierce and effective opposition. Indeed, Garrison was once almost lynched in Boston, and riots caused Weld to cancel appearances in Troy, New York.

Abolitionists who thought of taking their message to the fringes of the South had reason to pause, given the fate of the antislavery editor Elijah Lovejoy. In 1837 while attempting to defend himself and his printing press from a mob in Alton, Illinois, just across the Mississippi River from slaveholding Missouri, Lovejoy was shot and killed.

Racism was a major cause of antiabolitionist violence in the North. Rumors that abolitionists advocated or practiced interracial marriage could easily excite an urban crowd to destructive acts. Working-class whites tended to fear that economic and social competition with blacks would increase if abolitionists succeeded in freeing the slaves and making them

citizens. But a striking feature of many of the mobs was that they were dominated by "gentlemen of property and standing." Solid citizens resorted to violence, it would appear, because abolitionism threatened their conservative notions of social order and hierarchy.

By the end of the 1830s, the abolitionist movement was under great stress. Besides the burden of external repression, there was dissension within the movement. Becoming an abolitionist required an exacting conscience and unwillingness to compromise on matters of principle. These character traits also made it difficult for abolitionists to work together and maintain a united front against their opponents. Furthermore, relations between black and white abolitionists were tense. Whites tended to be condescending and paternalistic, unwilling to allow blacks to assume leadership positions or shape policy.

During the late 1830s, Garrison, the most visible spokesman for the cause, began to adopt positions that other abolitionists found extreme and divisive. He attacked government, clergy, and churches for refusing to take a strong antislavery stand, and he refused to work with any person or organization that did not fully support his crusade.

These positions alienated those members of the Anti-Slavery Society who continued to hope that organized religion and the existing political system could be influenced or even taken over by abolitionists. But it was Garrison's stand on women's rights that led to an open break at the national convention of 1840. Many of his followers separated from Garrison and his organization when the Boston editor engineered the election of a female abolitionist to the executive committee of the Anti-Slavery Society.

The schism weakened Garrison's influence within the movement. When he later repudiated the United States Constitution as a proslavery document and called for Northern secession from the Union, few antislavery people in the mid-Atlantic or midwestern states went along. Outside of New England, most abolitionists worked *within* churches and the political system. The Liberty party, organized in 1840, was their first attempt to enter the electoral arena under their own banner; it signaled a new effort to turn antislavery sentiment into political power.

Historians have debated the question of whether the abolitionist movement of the 1830s and early 1840s was a success or failure. It failed to convert a majority of Americans to its position on the evil of slavery. And in the South, it caused a strong counterreaction and helped inspire a more militant and uncompromising defense of slavery. The belief that peaceful agitation, or what abolitionists called "moral suasion," would convert slaveholders and their northern sympathizers to abolition was obviously unrealistic.

But in another sense the crusade was successful. It brought the slavery issue to the forefront of public consciousness and convinced a substantial and growing segment of the northern population that the South's peculiar institution was morally wrong and a potential danger to the American way of life. The politicians who later mobilized the North against the expansion of slavery into the territories drew strength from the reservoir of antislavery attitudes and sentiment created by the abolitionists.

From Abolitionism to Women's Rights

Abolitionism also served as a catalyst for the women's rights movement. From the beginning women were active participants in the abolitionist crusade. Some antislavery women defied conventional ideas of their proper sphere by becoming public speakers and demanding an equal role in the leadership of antislavery societies. The most famous of these were the Grimké sisters, Sarah and Angelina, who attracted enormous attention because they were the rebellious daughters of a South Carolina slaveholder.

The battle to participate equally in the antislavery crusade made a number of female abolitionists acutely aware of male dominance and oppression. For them, the same principles

■ *Elizabeth Cady Stanton, a leader of the women's rights movement, is pictured here with one of her seven children. In addition to her pioneering work for women's rights, especially women's suffrage, she lectured on family life and child care.*

that justified the liberation of the slaves also applied to the emancipation of women from all restrictions on their rights as citizens. However, not all of the antislavery men agreed with the idea of equal rights for women.

Wounded by male reluctance to extend the cause of emancipation to include women, Lucretia Mott and Elizabeth Cady Stanton organized a new and independent movement for women's rights. The high point of their campaign was the famous convention at Seneca Falls, New York, in 1848. In a "Declaration of Sentiments," the delegates condemned the treatment of women by men and demanded the right to vote and to control their own property, person, and children. Rejecting the cult of domesticity with its doctrine of separate spheres, these women and their male supporters launched the modern movement for sexual equality.

1801	Massive revival held at Cane Ridge, Kentucky
1826	American Temperance Society organized
1830–1831	Charles G. Finney evangelizes Rochester, New York
1831	William Lloyd Garrison publishes first issue of the *Liberator*
1833	Abolitionists found American Anti-Slavery Society
1836	American Temperance Society splits into factions
1836–1837	Theodore Weld advocates abolition in Ohio and upstate New York
1837	Massachusetts establishes a state board of education
	Abolitionist editor Elijah Lovejoy killed by a proslavery mob
1840	American Anti-Slavery Society splits over women's rights and other issues
1841	Transcendentalists organize a model community at Brook Farm
1848	Feminists gather at Seneca Falls, New York, and found the women's rights movement
1854	Henry David Thoreau's *Walden* published

Radical Ideas and Experiments

Hopes for individual or social perfection were not limited to reformers inspired by evangelicalism. Between the 1820s and 1850s, a great variety of schemes for human redemption came from those who had rejected orthodox Protestantism. Some were freethinkers carrying on the traditions of the Enlightenment, but most were seeking new paths to spiritual or religious fulfillment. These philosophical and religious radicals attacked established institutions, proscribed new modes of living, and founded utopian communities to put their ideas into practice.

A radical movement of foreign origin that gained a toehold in Jacksonian America was utopian socialism. In 1825–1826 the British manufacturer and reformer Robert Owen founded a community based on common and equal ownership of property at New Harmony, Indiana. About the same time Owen's associate, Frances Wright, gathered a group of slaves at Nashoba, Tennessee, and set them to work earning their freedom in an atmosphere of "rational cooperation." The rapid demise of both of these model communities suggests that utopian socialism did not easily take root in American soil.

The most successful and long-lived of the pre-Civil War utopias was established in 1848 at Oneida, New York, and was inspired by an unorthodox brand of Christian perfectionism. Its founder, John Humphrey Noyes, believed that the Second Coming of Christ had already occurred; hence, human beings could be totally free from sin and were no longer obliged to follow the moral rules that their previously fallen state had required. At Oneida, traditional marriage was outlawed, and a form of "free love" prevailed. But the choosing or changing of sexual partners was closely regulated by an elaborate set of rules. Birth control was practiced, and a couple could have children only if they seemed likely to produce healthy and intelligent offspring. The economy of the community was similarly regulated and prosperous.

Brook Farm, near Roxbury, Massachusetts, is the best remembered of the utopian experiments because of its close connection with the literary and philosophical movement known as transcendentalism. Most transcendentalists were dissatisfied with rationalistic religions but were unable to embrace evangelical Christianity because of intellectual resistance to its doctrines. Instead they sought inspiration from a philosophical and literary idealism of German origin. Their prophet was Ralph Waldo Emerson, a brilliant essayist and lecturer who preached that each individual could commune directly with a benign spiritual force that animated nature and the universe—he called it the "oversoul."

There was something self-contradictory about the notion of a transcendentalist community. Radical individualism mixed uncomfortably with the ideal of community existence. Emerson, himself an advocate of self-reliance, avoided all involvement in organized movements or associations. But the group at Brook Farm went ahead anyway and attempted to set up a community in 1841 that would provide an ideal environment for self-fulfillment. They worked the land in common, conducted an excellent school on the principle that spontaneity rather than discipline was the key to education, and allowed ample time for conversation, meditation, communion with nature, and artistic activity of all kinds. The Brook Farm experiment ended in 1849.

Another experiment in transcendental living adhered more closely to the individualistic spirit of the movement. Between 1845 and 1847, Henry David Thoreau, a young disciple of Emerson, lived by himself in the woods along the shore of Walden Pond and carefully recorded his thoughts and impressions. In a sense, he pushed the ideal of "self-culture" to its logical outcome—a utopia of one. The result was *Walden* (published in 1854), one of the greatest achievements in American literature.

Fads and Fashions

Not only venturesome intellectuals experimented with new beliefs and life-styles. Between the 1830s and 1850s, a number of fads, fashions, and medical cure-alls appeared on the scene, indicating that a large segment of the middle class was obsessed with the pursuit of personal health, happiness, and moral perfection. Dietary reformers like Sylvester Graham convinced many people to give up meat, coffee, tea, and pastries in favor of fruit, vegetables, and whole wheat bread. Amelia Bloomer advocated loose-fitting pantalettes as a healthful substitute for the elaborate structure of corsets, petticoats, and hooped skirts then in fashion. A concern with understanding and improving personal character and abilities was reflected in the craze for phrenology—a popular pseudoscience that involved studying the shape of the skull to determine natural aptitudes and inclinations.

In an age of perfectionism, even the dead could be enlisted on the side of universal reform. Seances were held in parlors all over the nation; spiritualists urged direct contact with the dead, who were viewed as having "passed on" to a purer state of being and a higher wisdom. Spirtualist beliefs were a logical outgrowth of the perfectionist dream pursued so ardently by antebellum Americans.

Pre-Civil War reform was both a criticism of American reality and a celebration of America's promise. It condemned the materialism, self-seeking, and opportunistic politics of the age. It sought, perhaps unrealistically, to purify society and politics by appealing directly to the spiritual or rational capabilities of individuals. It was long on inspirational rhetoric but somewhat short on practical programs. But it did show that pursuit of the ideal was deeply rooted in American culture.

Recommended Reading

Alice Felt Tyler, *Freedom's Ferment* (1944), gives a lively overview of the varieties of pre-Civil War reform activity. Ronald G. Walters, *American Reformers, 1815–1860* (1978), provides a modern interpretation of these movements. The best general work on revivalism is William G. McLoughlin, *Modern Revivalism* (1959). Paul E. Johnson, *A Shopkeeper's Millennium: Society and Revivals in Rochester, New York, 1815–1837* (1978), describes the impact of the revival on a single community.

Various dimensions of evangelical religion are covered in Donald G. Mathews, *Religion in the Old South* (1977); Whitney R. Cross, *The Burned-Over District* (1950); Perry Miller, *The Life of the Mind in America from the Revolution to the Civil War* (1965); and Timothy L. Smith, *Revivalism and Social Reform in Mid-Nineteenth-Century America* (1957). On the temperance movement, see Ian R. Tyrell, *Sobering Up: From Temperance to Prohibition in Antebellum America, 1800–1860* (1979).

A good introduction to the changing roles of women and the family in nineteenth-century America is Carl N. Degler, *At Odds: Women and the Family in America from the Revolution to the Present* (1980). The cult of domesticity is the subject of Barbara Welter, "The Cult of True Womanhood," *American Quarterly* 18 (1966): 217–40; Nancy F.

Cott, *The Bonds of Womanhood: "Woman's Sphere" in New England 1780–1835* (1977); and Kathryn Kish Sklar, *Catherine Beecher: A Study in American Domesticity* (1973).

On educational reform, see Lawrence Cremin, *American Education: The National Experience, 1783–1876* (1980), and Michael B. Katz, *The Irony of Early School Reform: Educational Innovation in Mid-Nineteenth Century Massachusetts* (1968). David J. Rothman, *The Discovery of the Asylum: Social Order and Disorder in the New Republic* (1971), provides a penetrating analysis of the movement for institutional reform.

Among the most significant works on the abolitionist movement are John L. Thomas, *The Liberator: William Lloyd Garrison* (1963); Bertram Wyatt-Brown, *Lewis Tappan and the Evangelical War Against Slavery* (1969); Lewis Perry, *Radical Abolitionism: Anarchy and the Government of God in* *Antislavery Thought* (1973); Robert H. Abzug, *Passionate Liberator: Theodore Dwight Weld and the Dilemma of Reform* (1980); and Lawrence J. Friedman, *Gregarious Saints: Self and Community in American Abolitionism* (1982). Leonard L. Richards, *"Gentlemen of Property and Standing": Anti-Abolition Mobs in Jacksonian America* (1970), interprets violence against the abolitionists. On the connection between abolition and women's rights, see Gerda Lerner, *The Grimké Sisters from South Carolina: Rebels Against Slavery* (1967), and Blanche Glassman Hersh, *The Slavery of Sex: Feminist Abolitionists in America* (1978).

The utopian impulse is the subject of Arthur Bestor, *Backwoods Utopias* (1950), and Michael Fellman, *The Unbounded Frame: Freedom and Community in Nineteenth-Century Utopianism* (1973).

chapter 12

MASTERS
AND SLAVES

On August 22, 1831, the worst nightmare of southern slaveholders became reality. A group of slaves in Southampton County, Virginia, rose in open and bloody rebellion. Their leader was Nat Turner, a preacher and prophet who believed that God had given him a sign that the time was ripe to strike for freedom. When white forces dispersed the rampaging slaves only forty-eight hours later, Turner's band had killed nearly sixty whites. The rebels were then rounded up and executed along with dozens of other slaves vaguely suspected of complicity. Nat Turner was the last to be captured, and he went to the gallows unrepentant, convinced that he had acted in accordance with God's will.

Southern whites were determined to prevent another such uprising. Their anxiety and determination were strengthened by the fact that 1831 also saw the emergence of a more militant northern abolitionism. Nat Turner and William Lloyd Garrison were viewed as two prongs of a revolutionary attack on the southern way of life. Afraid that abolitionist agitation might cause another revolt, Southern whites launched a massive campaign to quarantine the slaves from possible exposure to antislavery ideas and attitudes.

A new series of laws severely restricted the rights of slaves to move about, assemble without white supervision, or learn to read and write. Other laws prevented white dissenters from publicly criticizing or even questioning the institution of slavery. The South rapidly became a closed society with a closed mind. Proslavery agitators sought to create a mood of crisis and danger requiring absolute unity and single-mindedness among the white population. This embattled attitude lay behind the growth of a more militant sectionalism and inspired threats to secede from the Union if security for slaveholding seemed to require it.

The campaign for repression apparently achieved its original aim. Nat Turner's revolt was the last mass slave uprising. Slave resistance, however, did not end; it simply took other and less dangerous forms. Slaves sought or perfected other methods of asserting their humanity and maintaining their self-esteem. This heroic effort to endure slavery without surrendering to it gave rise to an Afro-American culture of lasting value.

Slavery and the Southern Economy

Slavery would not have lasted as long as it did—and Southerners would not have reacted so strongly to real or imagined threats to its survival—if an influential class of whites had not had a vital and growing economic interest in this form of human exploitation. Although forced labor had always been essential to the South's economy, between the 1790s and the Civil War, plantation agriculture expanded enormously and so did dependence on slave labor.

By the time of the Civil War, 90 percent of the South's 4 million slaves worked on plantations and farms. In the seven cotton-producing states of the lower South slaves constituted close to half of the total population and were responsible for producing 90 percent of the cotton and almost all of the rice and sugar. In the upper South whites outnumbered slaves by more than three to one and were less dependent on their labor. Thus even within the cotton kingdom there were important differences between the upper and lower South.

Economic Adjustment in the Upper South

Tobacco, the plantation crop of the colonial period, continued to be the principal slave-cultivated commodity of the upper tier of southern states during the pre-Civil War era. But markets were often depressed, and profitable tobacco cultivation was hard to sustain for very long in one place because it rapidly depleted the soil. As a result, there were continual shifts in the areas of greatest production and much experimentation with new crops and methods of farming in the older regions. The heart of tobacco cultivation moved west-

ward, so that by 1860 Kentucky had emerged as the major producer.

During the lengthy depression of the tobacco market that lasted from the 1820s to the 1850s, agricultural experimentation was widespread in Virginia and Maryland. Increased use of fertilizer, systematic rotation of tobacco with other crops, and the growth of diversified farming based on a mix of wheat, corn, and livestock contributed to a gradual revival of agricultural prosperity. Such changes increased the need for capital but reduced the demand for labor. Improvements were financed in part by selling surplus slaves in regions of the lower South where staple crop production was more profitable. The interstate slave trade was thus a godsend to the slaveholders of the upper South and a key to their survival and prosperity.

The fact that slave labor was declining in importance in the upper South meant that the peculiar institution had a weaker hold on public loyalty there than in the cotton states. Diversification of agriculture was accompanied by a more rapid rate of urban and industrial development than was occurring elsewhere in the South. As a result, Virginians, Marylanders, and Kentuckians were seriously divided on whether their ultimate future lay with the Deep South's plantation economy or with the industrializing, free labor system that was flourishing just north of their borders.

The Rise of the Cotton Kingdom

The warmer climate and good soils of the lower tier of southern states made it possible to raise crops more naturally suited than tobacco or cereals to the plantation form of agriculture and the heavy use of slave labor. Since the colonial period, rice and a special variety of fine cotton (known as "long-staple") had been grown profitably on the vast estates along the coast of South Carolina and Georgia. In lower Louisiana sugar was the cash crop, and it too required well-financed plantations and small armies of slave laborers. However, it was the rise of "short-staple" cotton as the South's

Three scenes of slave life
from the 1850s. Cotton, a
labor-intensive crop, was
well suited to a plantation
form of production. Slave
labor was used to pick, gin,
and press the master's cotton
into bales.

major crop that strengthened the hold of slavery and the plantation on the southern economy.

Short-staple cotton differed from the long-staple variety in two important ways: its bolls contained seeds that were much more difficult to extract by hand, and it could be grown almost anywhere south of Virginia and Kentucky—the main requirement was a guarantee of 200 frost-free days. The invention of the cotton gin in 1793 ended the seed extraction problem and made short-staple cotton the South's major crop. Unlike rice or sugar, cotton could

be grown on small farms as well as on plantations. But large planters enjoyed certain advantages that made them the main producers. Only relatively large operators could afford their own gins or possessed the capital to acquire the fertile bottomlands that brought the highest yields. They also had lower transportation costs because they were able to monopolize the land along the rivers and streams that were the South's natural arteries of transportation.

Cotton was well suited to a plantation form of production. The required tasks were rela-

Slavery & the Southern Economy

tively simple and could be performed by supervised gangs of unfree workers. Furthermore, there was enough work to be done in all seasons to keep the force occupied throughout the year. Cotton requires constant weeding or "chopping" while growing and can be picked over an extended period. The relative absence of seasonal variations in work needs made the use of slave laborers highly practical.

The first major cotton-producing regions were inland areas of Georgia and South Carolina. The center of production shifted rapidly westward during the nineteenth century, first to Alabama and Mississippi and then to Arkansas, northwest Louisiana, and east Texas. The rise in total production that accompanied this geographical expansion was phenomenal. In 1792 the South's output of cotton was about 13,000 bales; in 1840 it was 1,350,000 bales; and in 1860 production peaked at the colossal figure of 4,800,000 bales. Most of this cotton went to supply the booming textile industry of Great Britain.

"Cotton is king!" proclaimed a southern orator in the 1850s, and he was right. By that time, three quarters of the world's supply of cotton came from the American South, and this single commodity accounted for over half of the total dollar value of American exports. Cotton growing and the network of commercial and industrial enterprises that marketed and processed this crop constituted the most important economic interest in the United States on the eve of the Civil War. Since slavery and cotton seemed inextricably linked, it appeared self-evident to many Southerners that their peculiar institution was the keystone of national wealth and economic progress.

Despite its overall success, however, the rise of the cotton kingdom did not bring a uniform or steady prosperity to the lower South. Many planters worked the land until it was exhausted and then took their slaves westward to richer soils, leaving depressed and ravaged areas in their wake. In addition, planters were beset and sometimes ruined by fluctuations in markets and prices. The boom periods of 1815–1819 and 1832–1837 were each followed by a depression and a wave of bankruptcies. However, during the eleven years of rising output and high prices preceding the Civil War the planters gradually forgot their earlier troubles and began to imagine that they were immune to future economic disasters.

Despite the insecurities associated with cotton production, most of the time this crop represented the best chance for profitable investment that existed in the Old South. Prudent planters who had not borrowed too heavily during flush times could survive periods of depression by cutting costs and making their plantations self-sufficient. For those with worn-out land, two options existed: They could sell their land and move west or they could sell their slaves to raise capital for fertilization, crop rotation, and other improvements that could help them survive where they were. Hence planters had little incentive to seek alternatives to slavery, the plantation, and dependence on a single cash crop. From a purely economic point of view they had every reason to rally to the defense of slavery.

Slavery and Industrialization

As the sectional quarrel with the North intensified, Southerners became increasingly alarmed by their region's lack of economic self-sufficiency. Dependence on the North for capital, marketing facilities, and manufactured goods was seen as evidence of a dangerous subservience to "external" economic interests. Southern nationalists like J.D.B. DeBow, editor of the influential *DeBow's Review*, called during the 1850s for the South to develop its own industries, commerce, and shipping. But his call went unanswered. Men with capital were doing too well in plantation agriculture to risk much money in other ventures.

In the 1840s and 1850s, a debate raged among white capitalists over whether the South should use free whites or enslaved blacks as the basic labor force in the development of industry. Some leaders defended a white labor policy, arguing that factory work would provide new economic opportunities for a degraded class of poor whites. But other advocates of industrialization feared that the growth of a free working class would lead to social conflict among whites and preferred using slaves for all supervised manual labor. In practice, some factories employed slaves, others white workers, and a few even experimented with integrated work forces. As nearly as can be determined, mills that hired or purchased slave labor were just as profitable and efficient as those paying wages to whites.

It is clear, however, that the union of slavery and cotton that was central to the South's prosperity impeded industrialization and left the region dependent on a one-crop agriculture and on the North for capital and marketing. So long as plantations yielded substantial profits, there could be no major movement of slaves from agriculture to industry. If anything the trend was in the opposite direction.

The "Profitability" Issue

Some Southerners were obviously making money, and a great deal of it, using slave labor to raise cotton. But did slavery yield a good return for the great majority of slaveholders who were not large planters? Did it provide the basis for general prosperity and a relatively high standard of living for the southern population in general, or at least for the two thirds of it who were white and free? In a word, was slavery "profitable?"

For many years historians believed that slave-based agriculture was, on the average, not very lucrative. Planters' account books seemed to show at best a modest return on investment. In the 1850s, the price of slaves rose at a faster rate than the price of cotton, allegedly squeezing many operators. Some historians even concluded that slavery was a dying institution by the time of the Civil War. Profitability, they argued, depended on access to new and fertile land suitable for plantation agriculture, and virtually all such land within the limits of the United States had already been taken up by 1860. Hence slavery had

reached its natural limits of expansion and was on the verge of becoming so unprofitable that it would fall of its own weight in the near future.

A more recent interpretation holds that slavery was in fact still an economically sound institution in 1860 and showed no signs of imminent decline. During the 1850s planters could normally expect an annual return of 8 to 10 percent on capital invested. This yield was roughly equivalent to the best that could then be obtained from the most lucrative sectors of northern industry and commerce. Furthermore, it is no longer clear that plantation agriculture had reached its natural limits of expansion by 1860. Production in Texas had not yet peaked, and transportation improvements and flood control would certainly have opened up new areas for growing cotton. Those who now argue that slavery was profitable and had an expansive future have made a strong and convincing case.

But a larger question remains: What sort of economic development did a slave plantation system foster? What portion of the Southern population benefited from the system? Did it promote efficiency and progressive change? Two recent economists, Robert Fogel and Stanley Engerman, have argued that slave plantation agriculture was much more efficient than northern family farming. However, critics of this thesis contend that Fogel and Engerman's sophisticated calculations were not sophisticated enough and that there is no proof that the plantation was an internally efficient enterprise with good managers and industrious, well-motivated workers.

Other evidence suggests that small slaveholders and nonslaveholders shared only to a very limited extent in the bonanza profits of the cotton economy. Because of various insecurities—lack of credit, high transportation costs, and a greater vulnerability to market fluctuations—they had to devote a larger share of their acreage to subsistence crops than did the planters. This kept their standard of living lower than that of most northern farmers. Slaves benefited from planter profits to the extent that they were better fed, housed, and clothed than they would have been had their owners been less prosperous. But to suggest that they were better off than northern wage laborers is proslavery propaganda rather than documented fact.

The South's economic development was skewed in favor of a single route to wealth, open only to the minority possessing both a white skin and access to capital. The concentration of capital and business energies on cotton production foreclosed the kind of diversified industrial and commercial growth that would have provided wider opportunities. Thus, in comparison to the industrializing North, the South was an underdeveloped region in which neither slaves nor lower class whites had much incentive to work hard. A lack of public education for whites and the denial of even minimal literacy to slaves represented a critical failure to develop human resources. Good ground exists for concluding that the South's economy was condemned to backwardness so long as it was based on slavery.

The Slaveholding Society

If the precise effect of slavery on the South's economic life remains debatable, there is less room for disagreement concerning its impact on social arrangements and attitudes. More than any other factor, the ownership of slaves

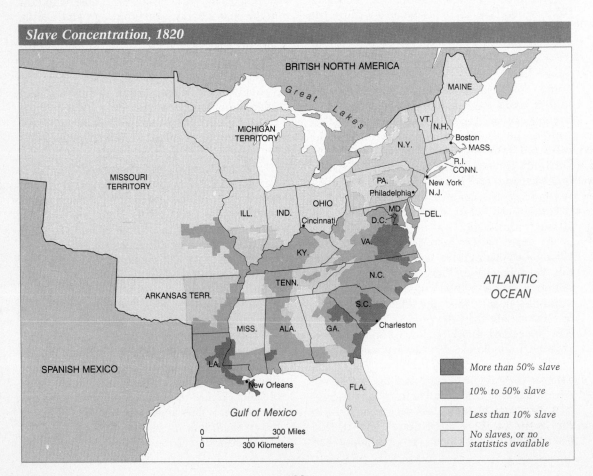

Slave Concentration, 1820

More than 50% slave

10% to 50% slave

Less than 10% slave

No slaves, or no statistics available

Masters & Slaves

determined gradations of social prestige and influence among whites. But the fact that all whites were free and that most blacks were slaves created a sharp cleavage between the races that could create the impression of a basic equality within "the master race." In the language of sociologists, inequality in the Old South was determined in two ways: by "class" and by "caste." An awareness of both systems of social ranking is necessary for an understanding of southern society.

The Planters' World

Those who know the Old South only from modern novels, films, and television programs are likely to envision a land filled with majestic plantations, courtly gentlemen, elegant ladies, and faithful retainers. It is easy to conclude from such images that the typical white Southerner was an aristocrat who belonged to a family that owned large numbers of slaves. Certainly the great houses existed, some wealthy slaveholders did maintain an aristocratic life-style, and the great planters did set the tone and values for much of the society. But this was the world of only a small percentage of slaveowners and a minuscule portion of the total white population.

In 1860 only 25 percent of all white Southerners belonged to families owning slaves. Even in the cotton belt of the Deep South, slaveholders were a minority of whites on the eve of the Civil War. Planters, defined as agri-

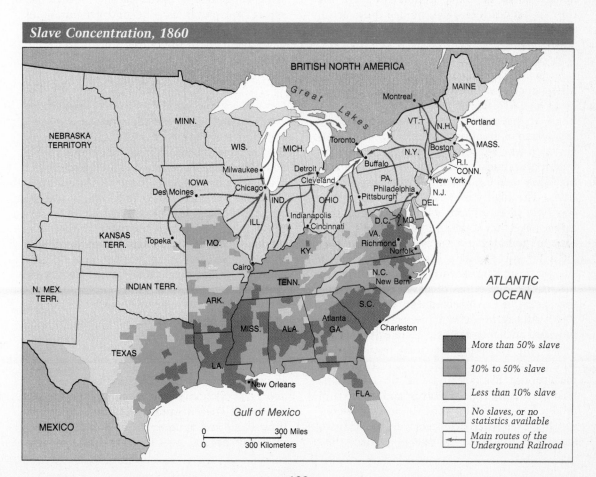

Slave Concentration, 1860

More than 50% slave

10% to 50% slave

Less than 10% slave

No slaves, or no statistics available

Main routes of the Underground Railroad

culturalists owning twenty or more slaves, were the minority of a minority. In 1860 planters and their families constituted about 12 percent of all slaveholders and less than 4 percent of the total white population of the South. But even the master of twenty to fifty slaves could rarely live up to the popular image of aristocratic grandeur. To live this sort of life a planter had to own at least fifty slaves and preferably many more. In 1860 these substantial planters comprised less than 3 percent of all slaveholders and less than 1 percent of all whites.

Contrary to legend, most of the great planters of the pre-Civil War period were self-made rather than descendants of the old colonial gentry. For example, one Irish immigrant started out with a log cabin and a few acres in upland South Carolina around 1800. By the time of his death in 1854, he had built up an estate of 2000 acres, 114 slaves, and 4 cotton gins.

As the cotton kingdom spread westward from South Carolina and Georgia to Alabama, Mississippi, and Louisiana, the men who became the wealthiest planters were even less likely to have genteel backgrounds. A large proportion of them began as hard-driving businessmen who built up capital from commerce, land speculation, banking, and even slave-trading. They then used their profits to buy plantations. The highly competitive, boom-or-bust economy of the Southwest put a greater premium on sharp dealing and business skills than on genealogy.

To be successful, a planter had to be a shrewd businessman who kept a careful eye on the market, the prices of slaves and land, and the extent of his indebtedness. Reliable "factors"—the agents who marketed the crop and provided advances against future sales—could assist him in making decisions, but a planter who failed to spend a good deal of time with his account books could end up in serious trouble. Managing the slaves and plantation production was also difficult and time-consuming, even when overseers were available to supervise day-to-day activities. Hence few

planters could be the men of leisure featured in the popular image of the Old South.

Some of the richest and most secure did aspire to live in the manner of a traditional landed aristocracy. "Big houses," elegant carriages, fancy-dress balls, and excessive numbers of house servants all reflected aristocratic aspirations. Dueling, despite some efforts to repress it, remained the standard way to settle "affairs of honor" among gentlemen. Another sign of gentility was the tendency of planters' sons to avoid "trade" as a primary or secondary career in favor of law or the military. Planters' daughters were trained from girlhood to play the piano, speak French, dress in the latest fashions, and sparkle in the drawing room or on the dance floor. The aristocratic style originated among the older gentry of the seaboard slave states, but by the 1840s and 1850s it had spread southwest as a second generation of wealthy planters began to displace the rough-hewn pioneers of the cotton kingdom.

Planters and Slaves

No assessment of the planters' outlook or "world view" can be made without considering their relations with their slaves. Planters owned more than half of all the slaves in the South and set the standards for treatment and management of them. Most of the planters liked to think of themselves as kindly and paternalistic. They tended to view slaves as perpetual children who were part of their extended patriarchal family. Paternalistic rhetoric increased greatly after abolitionists began to charge that most slaveholders were sadistic monsters. To some extent, the response was part of a defensive effort to redeem the South's reputation and self-respect.

There was, nevertheless, an element of truth in the planters' claim that their slaves were relatively well treated. Food, clothing, and shelter were normally sufficient to sustain life and labor at above a bare subsistence level; family life was encouraged and to some extent flourished; and average life expectancy, birth rate, and natural growth in population were only slightly below the average for southern whites. Certainly North American slaves of the pre-Civil War period enjoyed a higher standard of living than those in other New World slave societies.

But relatively good physical conditions for slaves do not demonstrate that planters put ethical considerations ahead of self-interest. The ban on the transatlantic slave trade in 1808 was effective enough to make the domestic reproduction of the slave force an economic necessity if the system were to be perpetuated. Slaves were also valuable property and the main tools of production for a booming economy, and it was in the interest of masters to see that their property remained in good enough condition to work hard and bear large numbers of children.

The testimony of slaves themselves and of some independent white observers suggests that masters of large plantations generally did not have close and intimate relations with the mass of field slaves. The kind of affection and concern associated with a father figure appears to have been limited mainly to relationships with a few favored house servants or other elite slaves. The field hands on large estates dealt mostly with overseers who were hired or fired on their ability to meet production quotas.

When they were being most realistic, planters conceded that the ultimate basis of their authority was force and intimidation, rather than the natural obedience due to a loving parent. Devices for inspiring fear included whipping—a common practice on most plantations—and the threat of sale away from family and friends. Planters and overseers maintained order and productivity by swift punishment for any infraction of the rules or even for a surly attitude.

Despite economic considerations, some masters inevitably yielded to the temptations of power or to their bad tempers and tortured

■
When pressed, most planters would admit that their authority was based upon force and intimidation. The female slave pictured in this scene of a New Orleans street wears a headpiece intended as punishment for some infraction of her master's rules.

or killed their slaves. Others raped slave women or forced them into sexual relationships. Slaves had little legal protection against such abuse because slave testimony was not accepted in court. Human nature being what it is, such a situation was bound to result in atrocities. As Harriet Beecher Stowe, the author of Uncle Tom's Cabin, pointed out, there was something terribly wrong with any institution that gave one human being nearly absolute power over another.

The World of the Common Whites

As we have seen, 88 percent of all slaveholders in 1860 owned fewer than twenty slaves and thus were not planters in the usual sense of the term. Of these, the great majority had fewer than ten. Many were simply farmers who used one or two slave families to ease the burden of their own labor. These slaveowners lived spartan lives; their houses were simple and their lives were hard.

For better or worse, relations between owners and their slaves were more intimate than on larger estates. Unlike planters, these families often worked in the fields alongside their slaves and sometimes ate at the same table or slept under the same roof. But such closeness did not necessarily result in better treatment. Both the best and worst of slavery could be found on these farms, depending on the character and disposition of the master. Given a choice, most slaves preferred to live on plantations because they offered the sociability, culture, and kinship of the quarters, as well as better prospects for adequate food, clothing, and shelter.

Just below the small slaveholders on the social scale was a substantial class of yeoman farmers. Contrary to another myth about the Old South, most of these people did not fit the image of the degraded, shiftless, "poor white." The majority were proud, self-reliant farmers whose way of life did not differ markedly from that of family farmers in the Midwest during the early stages of settlement.

The yeomen were mostly concentrated in the backcountry where slaves and plantations were rarely seen. The foothills or interior valleys of the Appalachians and the Ozarks were unsuitable for plantation agriculture but offered reasonably good soil for mixed farming, and long stretches of "piney barrens" along the Gulf Coast were suitable for raising livestock. In such regions slaveless farmers concentrated, giving rise to the "white counties" that complicated southern politics.

The lack of transportation facilities, more than some failure of energy or character, limited the prosperity of the yeoman. A large part of their effort was devoted to growing subsistence crops, mainly corn. Their principal source of cash was livestock, especially hogs. But since the livestock was generally allowed to forage in the woods rather than being fattened on grain, it was of poor quality and did not bring high prices or big profits to raisers.

Although they did not benefit directly from the peculiar institution, most yeomen and other nonslaveholders tolerated slavery and were fiercely opposed to abolitionism in any form. Many abolitionists could not understand the reasons for their position, for undoubtedly yeomen were hurt economically by the existence of slavery and a planter class. In addition, most yeomen were staunch Jacksonians who resented aristocratic pretensions and feared concentrations of power and wealth in the hands of the few. On issues involving representation, banking, and internal improvements yeomen sometimes voted against the planters. Why, then, did they fail to respond to antislavery appeals that called for them to strike at the real source of planter power and privilege?

One reason was that some nonslaveholders hoped to get ahead in the world, and in the South this meant acquiring slaves of their own. Just enough of the more prosperous yeomen broke into the slaveholding classes to make the dream seem believable. Planters, anxious to ensure the loyalty of nonslaveholders, strenuously encouraged the notion that every white man was a potential master.

But the main reason why most nonslaveholders went along with the proslavery leadership was their intense fear and dislike of blacks. Although they had no natural love of planters and slavery, they believed that abolitionism would lead to disaster. In part their anxieties were economic; freed slaves would compete with them for land and jobs. But their racism went deeper than this. Emancipation was unthinkable because it would remove the pride and status that automatically went along with a white skin in this acutely race-conscious society. Slavery, despite its drawbacks, served to keep blacks "in their place" and to make all whites, however poor or underprivileged they might be, feel that they were superior to somebody.

A Closed Mind and a Closed Society

Despite the tacit assent of most nonslaveholders, the dominant class never lost its fear that lower class whites would turn against slavery. They felt threatened from two sides: from the slave quarters where a new Nat Turner might be gathering his forces and from the backcountry where yeomen and poor whites might heed the call of abolitionists to rise up against planter domination. Beginning in the 1830s, the ruling element tightened their grip on Southern society and culture.

Before the 1830s, open discussion of the rights or wrongs of slavery had been possible in many parts of the South. Apologists commonly described the institution as "a necessary evil," and in the upper South there was support for colonization plans. By the end of 1832, however, all talk about emancipation had ended in the South. The argument that slavery was "a positive good"—rather than an evil slated for gradual elimination—won the day.

The "positive good" defense of slavery was an answer to the abolitionist charge that the institution was inherently sinful. The message was carried in a host of books, pamphlets, and newspaper editorials published between the 1830s and the Civil War. Who, historians have

asked, was it meant to persuade? Partly, the argument was aimed at the North. But Southerners themselves were a prime target. In popularized forms, the message was used to arouse racial anxieties that tended to neutralize antislavery sentiment among the lower classes.

The proslavery argument was based on three main propositions. The first and foremost was that enslavement was the natural and proper status for people of African descent. Blacks, it was alleged, were innately inferior to whites and suited only for slavery. Biased scientific and historical evidence was presented to support this claim. Secondly, slavery was held to be sanctioned by the Bible and Christianity—a position made necessary by the abolitionist appeal to Christian ethics. Finally, efforts were made to show that slavery was consistent with the humanitarian spirit of the nineteenth century. The plantation was seen as a sort of asylum providing guidance and care for a race that could not rule itself.

By the 1850s, the proslavery argument had gone beyond mere apology for the South and its peculiar institution and featured an ingenious attack on the free labor system of the North. According to the Virginian George Fitzhugh, the master–slave relationship was more humane than the one prevailing between employers and wage laborers in the North. Slaves had security against unemployment and a guarantee of care in old age, while free workers might face destitution and even starvation at any time. Fitzhugh believed that on the whole slave societies were more orderly, just, and peaceful than free societies.

In addition to arguing against the abolitionists, proslavery Southerners attempted to seal off their region from antislavery ideas and influences. Whites who were bold enough to criticize slavery publicly were mobbed or persecuted. One of the bravest of the Southern abolitionists, Cassius Clay of Kentucky, armed himself with a brace of pistols when he gave speeches. Clergymen who questioned the morality of slavery were driven from their pulpits, and northern travelers suspected of being abolitionist agents were tarred and feathered.

When abolitionists tried to send their literature through the mails during the 1830s, it was seized in southern post offices and publicly burned.

Such flagrant denials of free speech and civil liberties were inspired by fears that nonslaveholding whites and slaves would get the wrong ideas. Hinton R. Helper's book, *The Impending Crisis of the South*, an 1857 appeal to nonslaveholders to resist the planter regime, was suppressed with particular vigor. But the deepest fear was that slaves would hear the abolitionist talk or read antislavery literature and be inspired to rebel. Consequently, new laws were passed making it a crime to teach slaves to read and write. Free blacks, who were thought to be possible instigators of slave revolt, were denied basic civil liberties and were the object of growing surveillance and harassment.

All these efforts at thought control and internal security did not allay the fears of abolitionist subversion, lower class white dissent, and, above all, slave revolt. The persistent barrage of proslavery propaganda and the course of national events in the 1850s created a mood of panic and desperation. By this time an increasing number of Southerners had become convinced that safety from abolitionism and its associated terrors required a formal withdrawal from the Union—secession.

The Black Experience Under Slavery

Most blacks, if not most whites, experienced slavery on plantations; the majority of slaves lived on units owned by planters who had twenty or more slaves. The masters of these agrarian communities sought to ensure their personal safety and the profitability of their enterprises by using all the means—physical and psychological—at their command to make slaves docile and obedient. By word and deed, they tried to demonstrate their power, authority, and self-assumed superiority over their servants. As increasing numbers of slaves were converted to Christianity and attended white-supervised services, they were forced to hear, over and over again, that God had commanded slaves to obey their masters.

It is a great tribute to the resourcefulness and spirit of Afro-Americans that most of them resisted these pressures and managed to retain an inner sense of their own worth and dignity. When conditions were right, they openly asserted their desire for freedom and equality and showed their disdain for white claims that slavery was "a positive good." But the struggle for freedom involved more than the confrontation of master and slave; free blacks, in both the North and the South, did what they could to speed the day when all Afro-Americans would be free.

How Slaves Resisted

Open rebellion, the bearing of arms against the white oppressors, was the most dramatic and clear-cut form of slave resistance. In the period between 1800 and 1831, a number of slaves participated in revolts that showed their willingness to risk their lives in a desperate bid for liberation. In 1800, for example, a Virginia slave named Gabriel Prosser mobilized a large band of his followers to march on Richmond, but whites suppressed the uprising without any loss of white life. In 1811 another band of rebellious slaves was stopped as it moved toward New Orleans. In 1822 whites in Charleston, South Carolina, uncovered an extensive and well-planned conspiracy, organized by a free black man named Denmark Vesey, to arm the slave population and take possession of the city.

As we have already seen, the most bloody and terrifying of all slave revolts was the Nat Turner insurrection of 1831. Although it was the last slave rebellion of this kind during the pre-Civil War period, armed resistance had not ended. Hundreds of black fugitives fought in the Second Seminole War (1835–1842) alongside the Indians who had given them a haven. Many of the blacks eventually accompanied the Indian allies to the transMississippi West. Only a tiny fraction of all slaves ever took part in organized acts of violent resistance against white power. Most realized that the odds against a successful revolt were very high, and bitter experience had showed them that the usual outcome was death to the rebels. As a consequence, therefore, they characteristically devised safer or more ingenious ways to resist white dominance.

One way of protesting against slavery was to run away, and thousands of slaves showed their discontent and desire for freedom in this fashion. Although most fugitives never got beyond the neighborhood of the plantation, many escapees remained free for years by hiding in swamps or other remote areas, and a fraction made it to freedom in the North or Mexico.

For the majority of slaves, however, flight was not a real option. Either they lived too deep in the South to have any chance of reaching free soil, or they were reluctant to leave family and friends behind. The typical fugitive was a young, unmarried male from the upper South.

Slaves who did not revolt or run away often registered their opposition to their bondage in other ways. The normal way of expressing discontent was by engaging in a kind of indirect or passive resistance. Many slaves worked slowly and inefficiently, not because they were naturally lazy (as whites supposed), but as a gesture of protest or alienation. Others soundlessly voiced their protest by feigning illness or injury, stealing provisions, and committing such acts of sabotage as breaking tools, mistreating livestock, and setting barns on fire. The ultimate act of clandestine resistance was poisoning the master's food.

The basic attitude behind such actions was revealed in the folk tales that slaves passed down from generation to generation. The famous Bruh Rabbit stories showed how a small, apparently defenseless animal could overcome a bigger and stronger one through cunning and deceit. Such stories served as an allegory for the black view of the master–slave relationship. Other stories—which were not told in front of whites—openly portrayed the slave as a clever trickster outwitting the master.

The Struggles of Free Blacks

In addition to the 4 million blacks in bondage, there were approximately 500,000 free Afro-Americans in 1860, about half of them living in slave states. Whether they were in the North or in the South, "free Negroes" were treated as social outcasts and denied legal and political equality with whites. Public facilities were strictly segregated, and after the 1830s blacks in the United States could vote only in four New England states. Nowhere but in Massachusetts could they testify in court cases involving whites.

Free blacks had difficulty finding decent jobs. Most states excluded blacks entirely from public school, and the federal government barred them from the militia, the postal service, and full access to public lands. Free blacks were even denied U.S. passports; in effect they were stateless persons even before the 1857 Supreme Court ruling that no Negro could claim American citizenship.

In the South, free blacks were subject to a set of direct controls that tended to make them semi-slaves. Invariably they were required to carry papers proving their free status and their movement was strictly limited. They were excluded from certain occupations, normally prohibited from holding meetings or forming organizations, and often forced into a state of economic dependency barely distinguishable from outright slavery.

Although beset by special problems of their own, most free blacks identified with the suffering of the slaves. Many of them had once been slaves themselves or were the children of slaves: Often they had close relatives who were still in bondage. Furthermore, they knew that as long as slavery existed, their own rights were likely to be denied and even their freedom was at risk. Kidnapping or fraudulent seizure by slave-catchers was always a possibility.

Because of the elaborate system of control and surveillance, free blacks in the South were in a relatively weak position to work against slavery. The wave of repression that followed the Denmark Vesey episode revealed the dangers of revolutionary activity and the odds against success. Consequently, most free blacks found that survival depended on creating the impression of loyalty to the planter regime.

In the North, free blacks were in a better position to join the struggle for freedom. Despite all the prejudice and discrimination that they faced, they still enjoyed some basic civil liberties denied to southern blacks. They could protest publicly against slavery or white supremacy and could form associations for the advancement and liberation of Afro-Americans. Beginning in 1830, northern Afro-Americans regularly held conventions to protest the existence of human bondage.

Black newspapers, such as *Freedom's Journal*, first published in 1827, and *The North Star*, founded by Frederick Douglass in 1847, gave black writers a chance to preach their gospel of liberation to black readers. Afro-American authors also produced a stream of books and pamphlets attacking slavery, refuting racism, and advocating various forms of resistance. One of the most influential publications was David Walker's *Appeal . . . to the Colored Citizens of the World*, which appeared in 1829. Walker denounced slavery in the most vigor-

ous language possible and called for a black revolt against white tyranny.

Free blacks in the North did more than make verbal protests against racial injustice. They were also the main conductors on the fabled "underground railroad" that opened a path for fugitives of slavery. Courageous ex-slaves such as Harriet Tubman and Josiah Henson made regular forays into the slave states to lead other blacks to freedom, and many of the "stations" along the way were manned by free Negroes. In northern towns and cities, free blacks organized "vigilance committees" to protect fugitives and thwart the slave catchers. Groups of blacks even used force to rescue recaptured fugitives from the authorities. In deeds as well as words, free blacks showed their unyielding hostility to slavery and racism.

Afro-American Religion

Afro-Americans could not have resisted or even endured slavery if they had been utterly demoralized by its oppressiveness. What made the struggle for freedom possible were inner resources and patterns of thought that gave dignity to their lives and hopes for a brighter future. From the realm of culture and funda-

Harriet Tubman, on the extreme left, is shown here with some of the slaves she led to freedom on the underground railroad. Born a slave in Maryland, she escaped to Philadelphia in 1849. She is said to have helped as many as three hundred blacks to freedom. Many of them she took all the way to Canada, where they were beyond the reach of the Fugitive Slave Law.

mental beliefs blacks drew the strength to hold their heads high and look beyond their immediate condition.

Religion was the cornerstone of this emerging Afro-American culture, especially among the slaves. Black Christianity was far from being a mere imitation of white religious form and beliefs. It was rather a distinctive variant of evangelical Protestantism that incorporated elements of African religion and stressed those portions of the Bible that spoke to the aspirations of an enslaved people thirsting for freedom.

Free blacks formed the first independent black churches by seceding from white congregations that discriminated against them in seating and church governance. Out of these secessions came a variety of autonomous Baptist groups and the highly successful African Methodist Episcopal (A.M.E.) Church organized under the leadership of Rev. Richard Allen of Philadelphia in 1816. But the mass of blacks did not have access to these independent churches. Mostly they served only free blacks and urban slaves with indulgent masters.

Plantation slaves who were exposed to Christianity either attended neighboring white churches or worshipped at home. On large estates, masters or white missionaries often conducted regular Sunday services. But white-sanctioned religious activity was only a superficial part of the slaves' spiritual life. The true slave religion was practiced at night, often secretly, and was led by black preachers.

This covert slave religion was a highly emotional affair that featured singing, shouting, and dancing. In some ways the atmosphere resembled a backwoods revival meeting. But much of what went on was actually an adaptation of African religious beliefs and customs. The chanting mode of preaching—with the congregation responding at regular intervals—and the expression of religious feelings through rhythmical movements, really a form of dance, were clearly African in origin. The emphasis on sinfulness and fear of damnation that were core themes of white evangelicalism played a lesser role among blacks. For them,

religion was more an affirmation of the joy of life than a rejection of worldly pleasures and temptations.

Slave sermons and religious songs spoke directly to the plight of a people in bondage and implicitly asserted their right to be free. The most popular of all biblical subjects was the deliverance of the children of Israel from slavery in Egypt. Many sermons and songs referred to the crossing of Jordan and the arrival in the Promised Land. Other songs invoked the liberation theme in different ways. One recalled that Jesus had "set poor sinners free."

Most of the songs of freedom and deliverance can be interpreted as referring exclusively to religious salvation and the afterlife—and this was undoubtedly how slaves hoped their masters would understand them. But the slaves did not forget that God had once freed a people from slavery in this life and punished their masters. The Bible thus gave Afro-Americans the hope that they, as a people, would repeat the experience of the Israelites and be delivered from bondage. During the Civil War, observers noted that freed slaves seemed to regard their emancipation as something that was preordained and were inclined to view Lincoln as the reincarnation of Moses.

Besides being the basis for a deep-rooted hope for eventual freedom, religion helped slaves endure bondage without losing their sense of inner worth. Religious slaves sometimes regarded themselves as superior to their owners and believed that all whites were damned because of their treatment of blacks.

More important, slave religion gave blacks a chance to create and control a world of their own. Preachers, elders, and other leaders of unofficial slave congregations could acquire a sense of status within their own community that had not been conferred by whites. Although religion did not inspire slaves to open rebellion (except in the case of Nat Turner), it must be regarded as a prime source of resistance to the dehumanizing effects of enslavement. It helped create a sense of community, solidarity, and self-esteem among slaves by giving them something of their own that they found infinitely precious.

The Slave Family

The black family was the other institution that prevented slavery from becoming unendurable and utterly demoralizing. Contrary to earlier beliefs, the majority of slaves lived in two-parent households. Although slave marriages were not legally binding, many masters encouraged stable unions, and the slaves themselves apparently preferred monogamy to more casual or promiscuous relationships. The black sexual ethic valued marital fidelity, an attitude strongly influenced by Christian teaching. But slaves did not attach the same importance as whites to chastity among unmarried females. Premarital sex was tolerated, and it was common for a slave woman to bear one child out of wedlock before settling into a permanent union.

Relations between spouses and between parents and children were normally close and affectionate. Slave husbands and fathers did not, of course, have the same power and authority as free heads of families. But they did what they could, and this included supplementing the family diet by hunting, fishing, or pilfering plantation stores. Husbands and wives usually interacted on a basis of rough equality and did everything possible to relieve each other's burdens; together they taught their children how to survive slavery and plantation life.

The terrible anguish that usually accompanied the breakup of families through sale showed the depth of kinship feelings. After emancipation, thousands of freed slaves wandered about looking for spouses, children, or parents from whom they had been forcibly separated for years.

Feelings of kinship and mutual obligation extended beyond the nuclear family. Grandparents, uncles, aunts, and even cousins were known to slaves through direct contact or family lore. Nor were kinship ties limited to blood relations. When families were broken up by sale, individual members who found themselves on plantations far from home were likely to be "adopted" into new kinship networks.

What becomes apparent from studies of the slave family is that kinship provided a model for personal relationships and the basis for a sense of community. For some purposes, all the slaves on a plantation were in reality members of a single extended family. Slave culture was a family culture, and this was one of its greatest sources of strength and cohesion. Strong kinship ties, whether real or fictive, meant that slaves could depend on one another in times of trouble. The kinship network also provided a vehicle for the transmission of Afro-American folk traditions from one generation to the next. Together with slave religion, kinship gave Afro-Americans a feeling that they were members of a community, not just a collection of individuals victimized by oppression.

The sense of being part of a community was the key to black survival under slavery. Although slave culture did not normally sanction violent resistance to the slaveholder's regime, the inner world that the slaves made for themselves gave them the spiritual strength to thwart the masters' efforts to dominate their hearts and minds. After emancipation, this rich and resilient cultural heritage would continue to give meaning to the lives of Afro-Americans. When combined with the tradition of open protest created by rebellious slaves and free black abolitionists, it would inspire and sustain new struggles for equality.

Recommended Reading

Major works that take a broad view of slavery are Kenneth M. Stampp, *The Peculiar Institution: Slavery in the Ante-Bellum South* (1956), and Eugene D. Genovese, *Roll, Jordan, Roll: The World the Slaves Made* (1974).

Clement Eaton, *The Growth of Southern Civilization, 1790–1860* (1961), provides a good introduction to life in the Old South. Other general works on slavery and the Old South include Eugene D. Genovese, *The Political Economy of Slavery: Studies in the Economy and Society of the Slave South* (1965), and Leslie Howard Owens, *This Species of Property:*

Slave Life and Culture in the Old South (1976). On the economics of slavery, see Gavin Wright, *The Political Economy of the Cotton South: Households, Markets, and Wealth in the Nineteenth Century* (1978); Robert William Fogel and Stanley L. Engerman, *Time on the Cross: The Economics of American Negro Slavery*, 2 vols. (1974); and Paul A. David *et al.*, *Reckoning with Slavery: A Critical Study of the Quantitative History of American Negro Slavery* (1976). Nonagricultural slavery is examined in Robert S. Starobin, *Industrial Slavery in the Old South* (1970), and Richard C. Wade, *Slavery in the Cities* (1964).

On the society and culture of the southern white population, see W. J. Cash, *The Mind of the South* (1941); Frank L. Owsley, *Plain Folk of the Old South* (1949); Drew Gilpin Faust, *A Sacred Circle: The Dilemma of the Intellectual in the Old South, 1840–1860* (1977); and Bertram Wyatt-Brown, *Southern Honor: Ethics and Behavior in the Old South* (1982).

Proslavery consciousness is treated in William Sumner Jenkins, *Pro-Slavery Thought in the Old South* (1935). Southern dissent and efforts to repress it are well covered in Carl N. Degler, *The Other South: Southern Dissenters in the Nineteenth Century* (1974).

On slave revolts, see Vincent Harding, *There Is a River: The Black Struggle for Freedom in America* (1981), and Herbert Aptheker, *American Negro Slave Revolts* (1943). The plight of Southern free blacks is covered in Ira Berlin, *Slaves Without Masters: The Free Negro in the Antebellum South* (1974). Slave culture and community are examined in Albert J. Raboteau, *Slave Religion* (1978); Herbert G. Gutman, *The Black Family in Slavery and Freedom, 1750–1925* (1976); and Lawrence W. Levine, *Black Culture and Consciousness: Afro-American Folk Thought from Slavery to Freedom* (1977).

chapter 13

AN AGE OF EXPANSIONISM

Orators and writers, responding to the surging nationalism of the 1840s, hailed the emergence of a mood or movement known as "Young America." The rhetoric of the Young Americans was as extravagant as their ambitions. They heralded a nation on the move—onward, upward, westward. Nothing, one writer noted, could "stop the advancement of this truly democratic and omnipotent spirit of the age." This identification of Young America with the extension of democracy reveals its roots in the Jacksonianism of the previous decade; the major voices for the expansionist spirit were young Democrats seeking a new way to recapture the political magic of Old Hickory. Their current hero was a "Young Hickory," who also came out of Tennessee to become a strong president—James K. Polk.

Those who identified with this image of an adolescent nation awakening to maturity favored an aggressive foreign policy, territorial acquisitions, and rapid economic growth. They called in turn for annexation of Texas, assertion of an American claim to all of Oregon, and the appropriation of vast new territories from Mexico. They also celebrated the technological advances that would knit this new empire together, especially the telegraph and the railroad.

Young America was an intellectual as well as a political movement. During the Polk administration, "Young American" writers and critics—mostly based in New York—called for a new and distinctive national literature, free of subservience to European themes or models and expressive of the democratic spirit. Their organ was the *Literary World*, founded in 1847, and its ideals influenced two of the greatest writers the nation has ever produced—Walt Whitman and Herman Melville.

Whitman captured much of the exuberance, optimism, and expansionism of Young America. He celebrated a nation whose limits were circumscribed only by the imagination. In *Moby Dick*, Herman Melville produced a novel sufficiently original in form and conception to more than fulfill the demand of Young Americans for "a New Literature to fit the

204

New Man in the New Age." But he was too deep a thinker not to see the perils that underlay the soaring ambition and aggressiveness of the new age. In the character of Ahab, the whaling captain who brings destruction on himself and his ship by his relentless pursuit of the white whale, Melville symbolized—among other things—the dangers facing a nation that was overreaching itself by indulging its pride and exalted sense of destiny with too little concern for the moral and practical consequences.

Movement to the Far West

In the 1830s and 1840s the westward movement of population left the valley of the Mississippi behind and penetrated the Far West all the way to the Pacific. Pioneers pursued fertile land and economic opportunities beyond the existing boundaries of the United States and thus helped set the stage for the annexations and international crises of the 1840s. Some went for material gain, others for adventure, and a significant minority sought freedom from religious persecution. They carried American attitudes and loyalties with them into regions that were already occupied or at least claimed by Mexico or Great Britain. Whether they realized it or not, these pioneers were the vanguard of American expansionism.

Borderlands of the 1830s

Territorial ambition lured Americans northward as well as westward, and for a time it seemed that Canada might be a new frontier for expansionism. Conflicts over the border between America and British North America led periodically to calls for diplomatic or military action to wrest the northern half of the continent from the English. During the 1830s tensions were particularly high as Americans and Canadians wrestled over the exact location of the border between Maine and New Brunswick. Finally in 1842, Secretary of State Daniel Webster concluded an agreement with the British government, represented by Lord Ashburton. The Webster-Ashburton Treaty gave over half of the disputed territory to the United States and established a definite northeastern boundary with Canada.

On the other side of the continent, the United States and Britain both laid claim to Oregon, a vast unsettled area that lay between the Rockies and the Pacific from the forty-second parallel (the northern boundary of California) to the latitude of 54°40' (the southern boundary of Alaska). Although in 1818 the two nations had agreed to joint occupation, the Americans had strengthened their claim by acquiring Spain's rights to the Pacific Northwest in the Adams-Onis Treaty (see Chapter 9), and the British had gained effective control of the northern portion of the Oregon country. Blocking an equitable division was the reluctance on both sides to surrender access to the Columbia River basin and the adjacent territory extending north to the forty-ninth parallel (which later became the northern border of the state of Washington).

The Oregon country was virtually unpopulated before 1840, but the same could not be said of the Mexican borderlands that lay directly west of Jacksonian America. By 1827 Mexican settlements in present-day New Mexico contained about 44,000 people. To save the province from economic stagnation, the Mexican authorities decided in 1822 to encourage trade between Santa Fe, the capital of New Mexico, and the United States. They succeeded in stimulating commercial prosperity, but they also whetted expansionist appetites on the Anglo side of the border.

California in the 1820s and 1830s was a more colorful, turbulent, and fragile northward expansion of Mexican civilization. Much less populous than New Mexico—there were only about 4000 Hispanic inhabitants in 1827—California was a land of huge estates and enormous herds of cattle. At the beginning of the 1830s most of the land and the wealth of the province was controlled by the chain of twenty-one mission stations of the Catholic Church that stretched from San Diego to San Francisco.

■ *Mission San Carlos, 1839. Although the Mexican government released the Indians from forced labor on the missions when they wrenched control of vast tracts of Old California from the Church, the Indians soon found themselves bowing to the harsh rule of the* rancheros *who became the new landowners.*

In 1833 the Mexican government confiscated the Church's lands and released the Indians from semislavery, but this in fact made their plight even worse. Rather than giving the land to the 30,000 Christian Indians in California, the government awarded immense tracts to Mexican citizens. During the fifteen years that they held sway, the *rancheros* (as the large landowners were called) captured the fancy and aroused the envy of Anglo traders and visitors to California through their flamboyant life-style, superb horsemanship, and taste for violent and dangerous sports.

The easterners who conveyed to the rest of the nation a romantic image of this sun-baked land of beautiful scenery and senoritas were mostly merchants and sailors involved in the oceanic trade between Boston and California ports. By the mid-1830s, several Yankee merchants had taken up permanent residence in towns like Monterey and San Diego in order to conduct the California end of the business. The reports that they sent back about the Golden West sparked great interest in eastern business circles.

The Texas Revolution

At the same time that some Americans were trading with California, others were taking possession of Texas. After Mexico became independent in 1821, it inherited Spain's claim to Texas, which the United States recognized. Both Adams and Jackson tried to buy Texas from Mexico, but their efforts were firmly rebuffed. Beginning in the early 1820s, however, American settlers began to move into Texas at the invitation of the Mexican government.

In 1823 Mexican officials agreed to the proposal of two Americans—Moses Austin and his son Stephen F. Austin—to populate Texas by granting huge tracts of land to a few individuals who would then act as colonizing agents. American immigrants were drawn by the offer of fertile and inexpensive land, and those from the southwestern states often brought slaves with them in the hope of extending the cotton kingdom.

Friction soon developed between the Mexican government and the American colonists over such issues as the status of slavery and the Catholic Church. In 1829 Mexico formally freed all slaves under its jurisdiction, but the Texans simply ignored the decree. Mexican law also required that immigrants accept the Catholic faith, but this regulation also became a dead letter. The abuses of Mexican law grew, along with the size of the American population in Texas, and in 1830 the Mexican Congress prohibited further American immigration and importation of slaves to Texas.

But enforcement of the new law was feeble, and the flow of settlers, slaves, and smuggled goods continued virtually unabated. A long-standing complaint of the Texans was the failure of the Mexican constitution to grant them local self-government. In 1832 Texans showed their displeasure with Mexican rule by rioting in protest against the arrest of several Americans by the commander of the Galveston garrison.

Stephen F. Austin went to Mexico City in 1833 to present the Texans' grievances and seek concessions from the central government. He succeeded in having the ban against American immigration lifted but failed to win agreement for self-government. Then, as he was about to return to Texas, Austin was arrested and imprisoned for more than a year for writing a letter recommending that Texans set up a state government without Mexico City's consent.

The spark that ignited a full-scale revolt in 1835 was a comic-opera incident involving the collection of Mexican export duties in the port of Galveston. An American prankster marked a box of sawdust for export, and the angry customs official who inspected it sought to arrest the perpetrator of the joke. When his efforts were resisted by a mob of Texans, he summoned troops, and the settlers rose in rebellion.

During the revolution that followed the Texans claimed that they were fighting for freedom against a long experience of oppression. Actually, Mexican rule had not been harsh, although it was inefficient and ofttimes corrupt. Furthermore, the Texans' devotion to "liberty" did not prevent them from defending slavery against Mexico's attempt to abolish it.

Texans had done pretty much what they pleased, despite laws to the contrary and angry rumblings from south of the Rio Grande.

A more plausible justification for revolution was the Texans' fear of the future under the latest regime to be established in Mexico City. In 1834 General Antonio López de Santa Anna made himself dictator of Mexico and abolished the federal system of government. When news of these developments reached Texas late in the year, they were accompanied by rumors of the impending disenfranchisement and even expulsion of American immigrants. Influenced by these rumors, the rebels tended to ascribe sinister motives to Santa Anna's new policy of enforcing tariff regulation by military force.

When he learned that the Texans were resisting customs collections, Santa Anna sent reinforcements. By October 1835 the two sides were engaged in a war. The first phase of the fighting ended when Stephen F. Austin laid siege to San Antonio with a force of 500 men and after six weeks forced its surrender, thereby capturing most of the Mexican troops then in Texas.

The Republic of Texas

While this early fighting was going on, delegates from the American communities met in convention and after some hesitation voted overwhelmingly to declare their independence on March 2, 1836. A constitution, based closely on that of the United States, was adopted for the new Republic of Texas, and a temporary government was installed to carry on the military struggle.

Within days after Texas declared itself a republic, 4000 Mexican soldiers were in San Antonio assaulting the Alamo, an abandoned mission where 187 Texas defenders had taken refuge. The Texans literally fought to the last man, and their martyrdom gave the revolution new inspiration. A few days later another Texas detachment was surrounded and captured in an open plain near the San Antonio River and was marched to the town of Goliad where all 350 of its members were summarily

■ *After the battle of San Jacinto, its hero Sam Houston, lying wounded under a tree, accepts the surrender of Santa Anna, at left in white breeches. The man cupping his ear at right is Erastus "Deaf" Smith, a famous scout and important man in Houston's army.*

executed. The "Goliad massacre" provoked the Texas rebels to even more desperate resistance.

The main Texas army, under General Sam Houston, moved quickly to avenge these early defeats. On April 21, 1836, Houston led his force of 700 men in a daring assault on Santa Anna's encampment near the San Jacinto River. Within fifteen minutes the battle was over, the Mexican force defeated, and Santa Anna captured. The Mexican leader was marched to Velasco where he was forced to sign treaties recognizing the independence of Texas and its claim to territory all the way to the Rio Grande.

Sam Houston, the hero of San Jacinto, became the first president of the Texas republic. He sought annexation to the United States, but Andrew Jackson and others believed that domestic politics, the sectional issue of the expansion of slavery, and the possibility of a war with Mexico made such an action untenable. Congress and the Jackson administration, however, did formally recognize Texas sovereignty, and during the following decade of independence, its population soared from 30,000 to 142,000.

Trails of Trade and Settlement

After New Mexico opened its trade to American merchants, a thriving commerce developed along the trail that ran from Independence, Missouri, to Santa Fe. To protect themselves from the hostile Indians whose territory they had to cross, the traders traveled in large caravans. The federal government assisted them by providing troops when necessary and by appropriating money to purchase rights of passage from various tribes. Even so, the trip across the Cimarron desert and the southern Rockies was often difficult and hazardous. But profits from the exchange of textiles and other manufactured goods for furs, mules, and precious metals were substantial enough to make the risk worth taking.

Relations between the United States and Mexico soured following the Texas revolution, and this had a devastating effect on the Santa Fe trade. Much of the ill feeling was caused by the Texans' blundering efforts to get a piece of the Santa Fe action. After several clashes with the Texans, the Mexican government in 1842 passed a new tariff banning the importation of many of the goods sold by American merchants and prohibiting the export of gold and silver.

The famous Oregon Trail was the great overland route that brought the wagon trains of American migrants to the West Coast during the 1840s (see map). The journey took about six months; most parties departed in May, hoping to arrive in November before the great snows hit the last mountain barriers. After small groups had made their way to both Oregon and California in 1841 and 1842, a mass migration—mostly to Oregon—began in 1843. These migrants were quick to demand the extension of full American sovereignty over the Oregon country.

The Mormon Trek

Among the settlers moving west were members, known as Mormons, of the most successful religious denomination founded exclusively on American soil—the Church of Jesus Christ of Latter Day Saints. The background of the Mormon trek was a history of persecution in the eastern states. Joseph Smith, founder of Mormonism, encountered strong opposition from the time he announced a new divine revelation, in Palmyra, New York, in 1820, that foretold the restoration of a purer Christianity that had once thrived on American soil. He and his followers were determined to establish a western Zion where they could practice their faith unmolested and carry out their special mission to convert the Native Americans.

In the 1830s the Mormons established communities in Ohio and Missouri, but the former went bankrupt in the Panic of 1837 and the latter was the target of angry mobs and vigilante violence. In 1839 the Mormons found a temporary haven at Nauvoo, Illinois. But

Smith soon reported new revelations which engendered dissension among his followers and hostility from neighboring "gentiles." Most controversial was his authorization of plural marriage. In 1844 Smith was killed by a mob while being held in jail in Carthage, Illinois.

The death of Smith confirmed the growing conviction of the Mormon leadership that they needed to move further west to establish their Zion in the wilderness. In late 1845, Smith's successor, Brigham Young, decided to send a party of 1500 men to assess the chances of maintaining a colony in the vicinity of the Great Salt Lake. In 1847 Young himself arrived in Utah and sent back word to the faithful that he had found the promised land.

The Mormon community that Young established in Utah is one of the great success stories of western settlement. In contrast to the extreme individualism and disorder that characterized the mining camps and other new communities, "the state of Deseret" (as Utah was originally called) was a model of discipline and cooperation. Because of its communitarian form of social organization, its centralized gov-

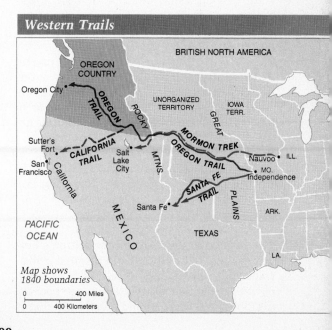

Western Trails

Map shows 1840 boundaries

0 — 400 Miles
0 — 400 Kilometers

■ *The death of Joseph Smith, founder of Mormonism, at the hands of an angry mob in 1844, convinced the Mormon leadership of the need to move further west. Thousands of Mormons set out toward Great Salt Lake from Nauvoo, Illinois, in 1846 in search of religious freedom.*

ernment, and the religious dedication of its inhabitants, this frontier society was able to expand settlement in a planned and efficient way and develop a system of irrigation that "made the desert bloom."

After Utah came under American sovereignty in 1848, the state of Deseret fought to maintain its autonomy and its custom of polygamy or "celestial marriage" against the efforts of the federal government to extend American law and set up the usual type of territorial administration. In 1857 the Mormons and the federal government almost came to blows, until President James Buchanan decided to use diplomacy rather than force.

Manifest Destiny and the Mexican War

The rush of settlers beyond the nation's borders in the 1830s and 1840s inspired politicians and propagandists to call for annexation of those areas that the migrants were occupying. Some went further and proclaimed that it was the "manifest destiny" of the United States to expand until it had absorbed all of North America, including Canada and Mexico. Such ambitions—and the policies they inspired—led to a major diplomatic confrontation with Great Britain and a war with Mexico.

Tyler and Texas

President John Tyler initiated the politics of Manifest Destiny. He was vice-president when William Henry Harrison died in office in 1841 after serving scarcely a month. Tyler was a states' rights, proslavery Virginian who had been picked as Harrison's running mate to broaden the appeal of the Whig ticket. Profoundly out of sympathy with the mainstream of his own party, he soon broke with the Whigs in Congress, who had united behind Henry Clay's nationalistic economic program. Despite the fact that he lacked a base in either of the major parties, Tyler hoped to be elected president in his own right in 1844. To accomplish this difficult feat, he needed a new issue around which he could build a following that would cut across established party lines.

In 1843 Tyler decided to put the full weight of his administration behind the annexation of Texas. He anticipated that this would be a popular move, especially in the slaveholding South, and would give him a solid base of support for the 1844 election.

To achieve his objective, Tyler enlisted the support of John C. Calhoun, the leading political defender of slavery and southern rights. Success or failure in this effort would constitute a decisive test of whether the North was willing to give the southern states a fair share of national power and adequate assurances for the future of their way of life. If antislavery sentiment succeeded in blocking the acquisition of Texas, the Southerners would at least know where they stood and begin to "calculate the value of the union."

To prepare the public mind for annexation, the Tyler administration launched a propaganda campaign in the summer of 1843. Rumors were circulated that the British were preparing to guarantee Texas independence and make a loan to that financially troubled republic in return for the abolition of slavery. Although the reports were groundless, the stories were believed and used to give urgency to the annexation cause.

The strategy of linking annexation explicitly to the interests of the South and slavery backfired politically. Northern antislavery Whigs charged that the whole scheme was a proslavery plot meant to advance the interest of one section of the nation against the other—an allegation that has more substance than most historians have been willing to acknowledge. Consequently, the Senate rejected the treaty of annexation by a decisive vote in June 1844.

The Triumph of Polk and Annexation

Tyler's initiative made the future of Texas the central issue in the 1844 campaign. But party lines held firm, and the president himself was unable to capitalize on it. Tyler tried to run as an independent, but his failure to gain significant support eventually forced him to step aside.

If the Democratic party convention had been held in 1843—as originally scheduled—ex-President Martin Van Buren would have won the nomination easily. But the convention was postponed until May 1844, and in the meantime the annexation question came to the fore. Van Buren persisted in the view he had held as president—that incorporation of Texas would arouse sectional strife and destroy the unity of the Democratic party. In an effort to keep the issue out of the campaign, Van Buren struck a gentleman's agreement with Henry Clay, the overwhelming favorite for the Whig nomination, that both of them would publicly oppose immediate annexation.

Van Buren's letter opposing annexation appeared before the Democratic convention and it cost him the nomination. Angry southern delegates invoked the rule requiring approval by a two-thirds vote. After several ballots a dark horse candidate—James K. Polk of Tennessee—emerged triumphant. A shrewd if somewhat devious politician, Polk had persuaded other presidential aspirants to stand aside by promising that he would serve only one term if elected.

Polk was an avowed expansionist, and he ran on a platform calling for the simultaneous annexation of Texas and assertion of American claims to all of Oregon. He identified himself and his party with the popular cause of turning the United States into a continental nation, an aspiration that attracted support in the North as well as in the South. The Whig nominee, Henry Clay, was basically antiexpansionist, but his sense of the growing popularity of Texas annexation among southern Whigs caused him to waffle on the issue during the campaign. This in turn cost Clay the support of a small but crucial group of northern antislavery Whigs, who defected to the abolitionist Liberty party.

Polk won the fall election by a relatively narrow popular margin. His triumph in the electoral college was secured by victories in New York and Michigan, where the Liberty party candidate, James G. Birney, had taken away enough votes from Clay to affect the outcome. Although the election was hardly a clear

Candidate	Party	Actual Vote in New York	National Electoral Vote	If Liberty Voters Had Voted Whig	Projected Electoral Vote
Clay	Whig	232,482	105	**248,294**	**141**
Birney	Liberty	15,812	0		
Polk	Democrat	237,588	170	237,588	134

mandate for expansionism, the Democrats claimed that the people were behind their aggressive campaign to extend the borders of the United States.

After the election, Congress reconvened to consider the annexation of Texas. The mood had changed as a result of Polk's victory, and leading Democratic senators were now willing to support Tyler's scheme for annexation by joint resolution of Congress. As a result, annexation was approved a few days before Polk took office.

The Doctrine of Manifest Destiny

The expansionist mood that accompanied Polk's election and the annexation of Texas was given a name and a rationale in the summer of 1845. John L. O'Sullivan, a proponent of the "Young America" movement and influential editor, charged that foreign governments were conspiring to block the annexation of Texas in an effort to thwart "the fulfillment of our manifest destiny to overspread the continent allotted by providence for the free development of our yearly multiplying millions."

Besides coining the phrase *Manifest Destiny*, O'Sullivan pointed to the three main ideas that lay behind it. One was that God was on the side of American expansionism. A second idea, implied in the phrase *free development*, was that the spread of American rule meant the extension of democratic institutions. O'Sullivan's third promise was that population growth required the outlet that territorial acquisitions would provide. Behind this notion lurked the fear that growing numbers would lead to diminished opportunities and European-type socioeconomic class divisions

if the restless and the ambitious were not given new lands to settle and exploit.

In its most extreme form, Manifest Destiny meant that the United States would someday occupy the entire North American continent; nothing less would appease its land-hungry population. The only question in the minds of fervent expansionists and "Young Americans" was whether the United States would acquire its vast new domain through a gradual, peaceful process of settler infiltration or through active diplomacy backed by force and the threat of war. The decision was up to President Polk.

Polk and the Oregon Question

In 1845 and 1846 the United States came closer to armed conflict with Great Britain than at any time since the War of 1812. The willingness of some Americans to go to war over Oregon was expressed in the Democratic rallying cry "fifty-four forty or fight." Polk fed this expansionist fever by laying claim in his inaugural address to all of the Oregon country. Privately, however, he was willing to accept the forty-ninth parallel. What made the situation so tense was that Polk was dedicated to an aggressive diplomacy of bluff and bluster.

In July 1845 Polk authorized Secretary of State James Buchanan to reply to the latest British request for terms by offering a boundary along the forty-ninth parallel. Because this did not meet the British demand for all of Vancouver Island and free navigation of the Columbia River, the British ambassador rejected the proposal out-of-hand. This rebuff infuriated Polk, who later called on Congress to terminate the agreement providing for joint occupation of the Pacific Northwest. Congress complied in April 1846.

Since abrogation of the joint agreement implied that the United States would attempt to extend its jurisdiction north to 54°40', the British government decided to take the diplomatic initiative in an effort to avert war, while at the same time dispatching warships to the Western Hemisphere in case conciliation failed. Their new proposal accepted the forty-ninth parallel as the border, gave Britain all of Vancouver Island, and provided for British navigation rights on the Columbia River. The Senate recommended that the treaty be accepted with the single change that British rights to navigate the Columbia be made temporary. It was ratified in that form on June 15.

Polk was prompted to settle the Oregon question because he now had a war with Mexico on his hands. His reckless diplomacy had brought the nation within an eyelash of being involved in two wars at the same time. American policymakers got what they wanted from the Oregon treaty, the splendid natural deepwater harbor of Puget Sound. However, by agreeing to a compromise on Oregon, Polk alienated expansionist advocates in the Old Northwest who had supported his earlier call for all of Oregon.

For many Northerners, the promise of new acquisitions of the Pacific Northwest was the only thing that made annexation of Texas palatable. They hoped that new free states could be created to counterbalance the admission of slaveholding Texas to the Union. As this prospect receded, the charge of antislavery defenders that Texas annexation was a southern plot drew more support; to Northerners Polk began to look more and more like a president concerned mainly with furthering the interests of his native region.

War with Mexico

While the United States was avoiding a war with Great Britain, it was getting into one with Mexico. Although they had recognized Texas independence in 1845, the Mexicans rejected the Lone Star Republic's unjustified claim to the unsettled territory between the Nueces River and the Rio Grande. When the United States annexed Texas and assumed its claim to the disputed area, Mexico broke off diplomatic relations and prepared for armed conflict.

Polk responded by placing troops in Louisiana on the alert and by dispatching emissary John Slidell to Mexico City. Polk hoped Slidell could resolve the boundary dispute and could persuade the Mexicans to sell New Mexico and California. Slidell's mission failed. In January 1846, Polk ordered General Zachary Taylor, commander of American forces in the Southwest, to advance well beyond the Nueces and proceed toward the Rio Grande, thus invading Mexican territory. By April, Taylor had taken up a position near Matamoras on the Rio Grande. On April 24, 1600 Mexican troops crossed the river from the south and the following day attacked a small American detachment. After learning of the incident, Taylor sent word to the president: "Hostilities may now be considered as commenced."

This news was neither unexpected nor unwelcome. Polk in fact was already preparing

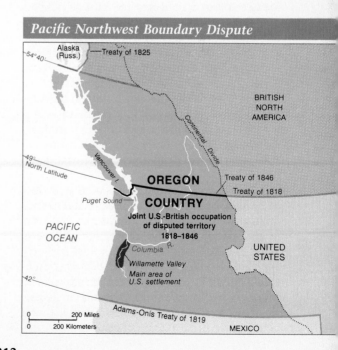

Pacific Northwest Boundary Dispute

54°40' — Alaska (Russ.) — Treaty of 1825

BRITISH NORTH AMERICA

Continental Divide

49° North Latitude

Vancouver I.

Puget Sound

PACIFIC OCEAN

OREGON COUNTRY

Treaty of 1846
Treaty of 1818

Joint U.S.-British occupation of disputed territory 1818–1846

Columbia R.

Willamette Valley
Main area of U.S. settlement

UNITED STATES

42°

0   200 Miles
0   200 Kilometers

Adams-Onis Treaty of 1819

MEXICO

213

Manifest Destiny and the Mexican War

his war message to Congress when he learned of the fighting on the Rio Grande. A short and decisive war, he had concluded, would force the cession of California and New Mexico to the United States. Thus shortly after Congress declared war on May 13, American forces under Col. Stephen Kearny captured Santa Fe and took possession of New Mexico. Kearny's troops then set off for California where Anglo settlers and a so-called exploration expedition led by Capt. John C. Fremont, aided by U. S. naval vessels, had revolted against Mexican rule. With the help of Kearny's forces, the Americans wrested control of California from Mexico.

The war lasted much longer than expected because the Mexicans refused to make peace despite a succession of military defeats. In the first major campaign of the conflict, Taylor followed up his victory in two battles fought north of the Rio Grande by crossing the river, taking Matamoras and marching on Monterrey. In September he captured this important northern city.

But Taylor's controversial decision to allow the Mexican garrison to go free and his unwillingness or inability to advance further into Mexico angered Polk and led him to adopt a new strategy for winning the war and a new commander to implement it. General Winfield Scott was ordered to prepare an amphibious attack on Vera Cruz with the aim of placing an American army within striking distance of Mexico City itself. Taylor was left to hold his position in northern Mexico, where in February 1847, he defeated a sizable Mexican army at Buena Vista. Taylor was hailed afterwards as a national hero and possible presidential material.

The decisive Vera Cruz campaign was slow to develop because of the massive and careful preparations required. But in March 1847 the main American army, now under General Scott, finally landed near that crucial port city and laid siege to it. Vera Cruz fell after eighteen days, and then Scott began his advance on Mexico City. In the most important single battle of the war, Scott met forces under General

Santa Anna at Cerro Gordo on April 17 and 18. In a well-commanded attack, Scott's forces defeated the Mexican army and opened the road to Mexico City. By August American troops were drawn up in front of the Mexican capital. After a temporary armistice, Scott ordered the massive assault that captured the city on September 14.

Settlement of the Mexican War

Accompanying Scott's army was a diplomat, Nicholas P. Trist, who was authorized to negotiate a peace treaty whenever the Mexicans decided they had had enough. Despite a sequence of American victories, however, no Mexican leader was willing to invite the wrath of an intensely proud and nationalistic citizenry by agreeing to the kind of terms Polk wanted to impose. By November, Polk was so irked by the delay that he ordered Trist to return to Washington.

Trist, to his credit, ignored Polk's instructions and continued to negotiate. On February 2, 1848, he signed a treaty that gained all the concessions he had been commissioned to obtain. The Treaty of Guadalupe Hidalgo ceded New Mexico and California to the United States for $15 million, established the Rio Grande as the border between Texas and Mexico, and promised that the United States government would assume the substantial claims of American citizens against Mexico. The Senate approved the treaty on March 10.

As a result of the Mexican War the United States gained half a million square miles of territory, including the present states of California, Utah, and New Mexico, most of Arizona, and parts of Colorado and Wyoming. But one intriguing question remains. Why, given the expansionist spirit of the age, didn't the United States take all of Mexico, as many Americans wished?

Racism and anticolonialism certainly helps to account for the decision. It was one thing to acquire thinly populated areas that could be settled by "Anglo-Saxon" pioneers. It was something else again to incorporate a large

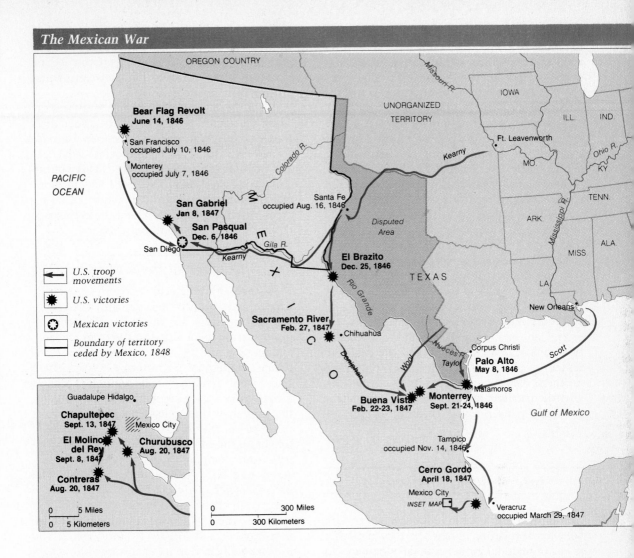

ILL.
IND.
OHIO R.
KY.
TENN.
ALA.
MISS.
LA.
ARK.
MO.
IOWA
TEXAS

population that was mainly of mixed Spanish and Indian origin. These "half-breeds," charged racist opponents of the "All Mexico" movement, could never be fit citizens of a self-governing republic. They would have to be ruled in the way that the British governed India, and the possession of colonial dependencies was contrary to American ideals and traditions.

Those actually making policy had more mundane and practical reasons for being satisfied with what was obtained at Guadalupe

Hidalgo. What they had really wanted all along were the great California harbors of San Francisco and San Diego. From these ports Americans could trade directly with the Orient and dominate the commerce of the Pacific. Once acquisition of California had been assured, policymakers had little incentive to press for more Mexican territory.

The war with Mexico divided the American public and provoked political dissension. A majority of the Whig party opposed the war in principle, arguing (correctly) that the United

States had no valid claims to the area south of the Nueces. Whig congressmen voted for military appropriations while the conflict was going on, but they constantly criticized the president for starting it. More ominous was the charge of antislavery Northerners from both parties that the real purpose of the war was to spread the institution of slavery and increase the political power of the southern states. While battles were being fought in Mexico, Congress was debating a proposal to prohibit slavery in any territories that might be acquired from Mexico. A bitter sectional quarrel over the status of slavery in new areas was a major legacy of the Mexican War.

The domestic controversies aroused by the war and the propaganda of Manifest Destiny revealed the limits of mid-nineteenth-century American expansionism and put a damper on additional efforts to extend the nation's boundaries. Concerns about slavery and race blocked further southern expansion, and the desire to remain at peace with Great Britain prevented northern expansion. After 1848, American growth usually took the form of populating and developing the vast territory already acquired.

Internal Expansionism

The expansionists of the 1840s saw a clear link between acquisition of new territory and other forms of material growth and development. In 1844 Samuel F. B. Morse perfected and demonstrated his electric telegraph. Simultaneously, the railroad was becoming increasingly important as a means of moving people and goods over great distances. Improvements in manufacturing and agricultural methods led to an upsurge in the volume and range of internal trade, and the beginnings of mass immigration were providing human resources for the exploitation of new areas and economic opportunities.

The discovery of gold in California in 1848 encouraged thousands of emigrants to move to the West Coast. The gold they unearthed spurred the national economy, and the rapid growth of population centers on the Pacific Coast inspired projects for transcontinental telegraph lines and railroad tracks.

When the spirit of Manifest Destiny and the thirst for acquiring new territory waned after the Mexican War, the expansionist impulse turned inward. The technological advances and population increase of the 1840s continued during the 1850s. The result was an acceleration of economic growth, a substantial increase in industrialization, and the emergence of a new American working class.

Triumph of the Railroad

More than anything else, it was the rise of the railroad that transformed the American economy during the 1840s and 1850s. The technology for steam locomotives came from England, and in 1830 and 1831 two American railroads began commercial operation. Although these lines were practical and profitable, canals proved to be strong competitors, especially for the freight business. Passengers might prefer the speed of trains, but the lower unit cost of freight on the canal boats prevented most shippers from changing their habits. Furthermore, states like New York and Pennsylvania that had invested heavily in canals resisted chartering a competitive form of transportation.

During the 1840s rails extended beyond the northeastern and Middle Atlantic states, and mileage increased more than threefold, reaching a total of more than 9000 miles by 1850. Expansion was even greater in the following decade, and by 1860 all the states east of the Mississippi had rail service. In addition, throughout the 1840s and 1850s, railroads cut deeply into the freight business of the canals and succeeded in driving many of them out of business.

The development of railroads had an enormous effect on the economy as a whole. Although the burgeoning demand for iron rails was initially met mainly by importation from England, that demand eventually spurred development of the domestic iron industry. Since railroads required an enormous outlay of capital, their promoters pioneered new methods for financing business enterprise. Railroad companies sold stock to the general public and helped to set the pattern for the separation of ownership and control that characterizes the modern corporation.

But the gathering and control of private capital did not fully meet the needs of the early railroad barons. State and local governments, convinced that railroads were the key to their future prosperity, loaned the railroads money, bought their stock, and actively supported their development. Despite the dominant policy of laissez-faire, the federal government became involved by surveying the routes of projected lines and providing land grants. Thus a precedent was set for the massive land grants of the post-Civil War era.

The Industrial Revolution Takes Off

While railroads were initiating a revolution in transportation, American industry was entering a new phase of rapid and sustained growth. The factory mode of production, which had originated before 1840 in the cotton mills of New England, was extended to a variety of other products. Between 1830 and 1860, wool and iron production moved toward the factory system, as did the shoemaking, firearms, clock, and sewing machine industries.

The essential features of this mode of production were the gathering of a supervised work force in a single place, the payment of cash wages to workers, the use of interchangeable parts, and manufacture by "continuous process." Within a factory setting, standardized parts, manufactured separately and in bulk, could be efficiently and rapidly assembled into a final product by an ordered sequence of continuously repeated operations. Mass production, which involved the division of labor into a series of relatively simple and repetitive tasks, contrasted sharply with the traditional craft mode of production, in which

a single worker produced the entire product out of raw materials.

New technology played an important role in the transition to mass production. Just as power looms and spinning machinery had made textile mills possible, the development of new and more reliable machines or industrial techniques revolutionized other industries. Elias Howe's invention of the sewing

Railroad Mileage, ca. 1860

Area	Miles
New England	3,660
Middle Atlantic	6,353
Old Northwest	9,592
Southeast	5,463
Southwest	4,072
Far West	1,495
Total	30,636

Source: Adapted from George R. Taylor and Irene D. Neu, The American Railroad Network, 1861 to 1890 (1956; reprint ed., Salem, N.H.: Arno, 1981).

Railroads, 1850 and 1860

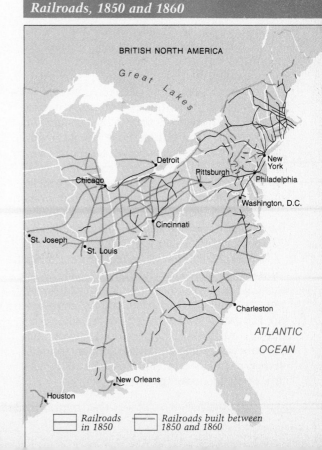

Railroads in 1850   Railroads built between 1850 and 1860

machine and Charles Goodyear's discovery of the process for the vulcanization of rubber opened the way for the mass production of a wide range of consumer items.

Perhaps the greatest triumph of American technology during the mid-nineteenth century was the development of the world's most sophisticated and reliable machine tools. Such advances as the invention of the extraordinarily accurate measuring device known as the *vernier caliper* in 1851 and the first production of turret lathes in 1854 were signs of a special American aptitude for the kind of precision toolmaking that was essential to efficient industrialization.

Progress in industrial technology and organization did not mean that the United States had become an industrial society by 1860. Agriculture retained first place both as a source of livelihood for individuals and as a contributor to the gross national product. But farming itself, at least in the North, was undergoing a technological revolution of its own. John Deere's steel plow enabled midwestern farmers to cultivate the tough prairie soils that had resisted cast iron implements, and Cyrus McCormick's mechanical reaper offered an enormous saving in the labor required for harvesting grain.

A dynamic interaction between advances in transportation, industry, and agriculture gave great strength and resiliency to the economy of the northern states during the 1850s. Railroads offered western farmers better access to eastern markets. After Chicago and New York were linked by rail in 1853, the flow of most midwestern farm commodities shifted from the North–South direction based on riverborne traffic that had still predominated in the 1830s and 1840s to an East–West pattern.

The mechanization of agriculture did more than lead to more efficient and profitable commercial farming; it also provided an additional impetus to industrialization, and its labor-saving features released manpower for other economic activities. The growth of industry and the modernization of agriculture can thus be seen as mutually reinforcing aspects of a single process of economic growth.

Mass Immigration Begins

The original incentive to mechanize northern industry and agriculture came in part from a shortage of cheap labor. Compared with the industrializing nations of Europe, the United States of the early nineteenth century was a labor-scarce economy. Since it was difficult to attract able-bodied men to work for low wages in factories or on farms, women and children were used extensively in the early textile mills, and commercial farmers had to rely heavily on the labor of their family members. Although labor-saving machinery helped ease the problem, by the 1840s and 1850s industrialization had reached a point where it needed far more unskilled workers. The growth of industrial work opportunities helped attract a multitude of European immigrants between 1840 and 1860.

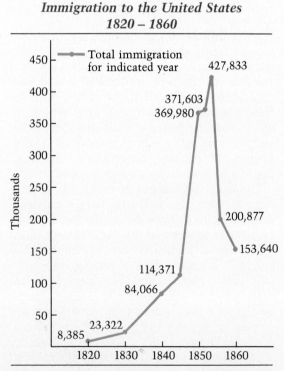

Immigration to the United States 1820 – 1860

Total immigration for indicated year

427,833
371,603
369,980
200,877
153,640
114,371
84,066
23,322
8,385

Source: U.S. Bureau of the Census, Historical Statistics of the United States, Colonial Times to 1970, *Bicentennial Edition, Washington, D.C., 1975.*

Composition of Immigration 1840 – 1860

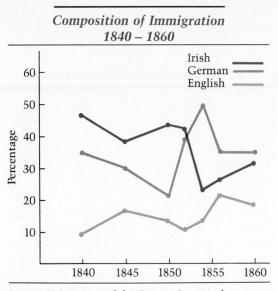

Source: U.S. Bureau of the Census, Statistical Abstract of the United States: 1982–83 (103rd edition) Washington, D.C., 1982.

Between 1820 and 1840, an estimated 700,000 immigrants arrived in the United States. During the 1840s this substantial flow suddenly became a flood. No less than 4,200,000 crossed the Atlantic between 1840 and 1860. This was the greatest influx in proportion to total population—then about 20 million—that the nation has ever experienced. The largest single source of the new mass immigration was Ireland, but Germany was not far behind.

This massive transatlantic movement had many causes; some people were "pushed" out of their homes, while others were "pulled" toward America. The great potato famine in Ireland accounted for much of the emigration from that country. Escape to America was made possible by the low fares then prevailing on sailing ships bound from England to North America. Ships involved in the timber trade carried their bulky cargoes from Boston or Halifax to Liverpool. As an alternative to returning to America partly in ballast, they packed Irish immigrants into their holds.

Because of the ports involved in the lumber trade—Boston, Halifax, Saint John's and Saint Andrews—the Irish usually arrived in Canada or the northeast states. Immobilized by poverty and a lack of skills required for pioneering in the West, most of them remained in the Northeast. Forced to subsist on low-paid menial labor and crowded into festering urban slums, they were looked down upon by most native-born Americans.

The million or so Germans who also came in the late 1840s and early 1850s were somewhat more fortunate. Most of them were also peasants, but they fled hard times rather than outright catastrophe. Unlike the Irish, they often escaped with a small amount of capital with which to make a fresh start in the New World. Many German immigrants were artisans and sought to ply their trades in cities like New York, St. Louis, Cincinnati, and Milwaukee. But a large portion of those with peasant backgrounds went back to the land. Many became successful midwestern farmers, and in general they encountered less prejudice and discrimination than the Irish.

What "pulled" most of the Irish, German, and other European immigrants to America was the promise of economic opportunity. Although a minority chose the United States because they admired its democratic political system, most immigrants were more interested in the chance to make a decent living than in voting or running for office. During times of prosperity and high demand for labor, America proved a powerful magnet to discontented Europeans.

The New Working Class

A majority of the immigrants ended up as wage workers in factories, mines, and construction camps, or as casual day laborers doing the many unskilled tasks required by urban and commercial growth. By providing a vast pool of cheap labor, they fueled and accelerated the Industrial Revolution.

In the established industries and older mill towns of the Northeast, immigrants gradually displaced the native-born workers who had predominated in the 1830s and 1840s. In the textile mills especially, native female labor

219

Internal Expansionism

1822	Santa Fe opened to American traders
1823	Earliest American settlers arrive in Texas
1830	Mexico attempts to halt American migration to Texas
1831	American railroads begin commercial operation
1834	Cyrus McCormick patents mechanical reaper
1835	Revolution breaks out in Texas
1836	Texas becomes independent republic
1837	John Deere invents steel plow
1841	President John Tyler inaugurated
1842	Webster-Ashburton Treaty fixes border between Maine and New Brunswick
1843	Mass migration to Oregon begins Mexico closes Santa Fe trade to Americans
1844	Samuel F. B. Morse demonstrates electric telegraph James K. Polk elected president on platform of expansionism
1845	Mass immigration from Europe begins United States annexes Texas John L. O'Sullivan coins slogan *Manifest Destiny*
1846	War with Mexico breaks out United States and Great Britain resolve diplomatic crisis over Oregon
1847	American conquest of California completed Mormons settle Utah American forces under Zachary Taylor defeat Mexicans at Buena Vista Winfield Scott's army captures Vera Cruz and defeats Mexicans at Cerro Gordo Mexico City falls to American invaders
1848	Treaty of Guadalupe Hidalgo consigns California and New Mexico to United States Gold discovered in California
1849	"Forty-niners" rush to California to dig for gold
1858	War between Utah Mormons and United States forces averted

was replaced by foreign male workers. Irish males, employers found, were willing to perform tasks that native-born men had generally regarded as women's work.

This trend reveals much about the changing character of the American working class. In the 1830s most male workers were artisans, while unskilled factory work was still largely the province of women and children. Both groups were predominantly of American stock. In the 1840s the proportion of men engaged in factory work increased, although the work force in the textile industry remained predominantly female. During that decade working conditions in many mills deteriorated. Management–labor relations became increasingly impersonal, and workers were driven to increase their output. Workdays of twelve to fourteen hours were common.

The result was a new upsurge of labor militancy involving female as well as male factory workers. Workers' organizations petitioned state legislatures to pass laws limiting the workday to ten hours. Some such laws were actually passed, but they turned out to be ineffective because employers could still require a prospective worker to sign a special contract agreeing to longer hours as a condition of employment.

The employment of immigrants in increasing numbers between the mid-1840s and the late 1850s made it more difficult to organize industrial workers. Impoverished fugitives from the Irish potato famine tended to have lower economic expectations and little experience with labor organizations. Consequently the Irish immigrants were willing to work for less and were not so prone to protest bad working conditions or organize into unions.

But the new working class of former rural folk did not make the transition to industrial wage labor easily or without protesting in subtle and indirect ways. Tardiness, absenteeism, drunkenness, loafing on the job, and other forms of resistance to factory discipline reflected deep hostility to the unaccustomed and seemingly unnatural routines of "continuous-process" production. The adjustment to new styles and rhythms of work was painful and took time.

By 1860 industrial expansion and immigration had created a working class of men and women who seemed destined for a life of low-paid wage labor. This reality stood in contrast to America's self-image as a land of opportunity and upward mobility. The ideal still had some validity in rapidly developing regions of the western states, but it was mostly myth when applied to the increasingly foreign-born industrial workers of the Northeast.

Both internal and external expansion had come at a heavy cost. Tensions associated with class and ethnic rivalries were only one part of the price of rapid economic development. The acquisition of new territories would soon lead to a catastrophic sectional controversy. From the late 1840s to the Civil War, the United States was a divided society in more senses than one, and the need to control or resolve these conflicts presented politicians and statesmen with a monumental challenge.

Recommended Reading

An overview of expansion to the Pacific is Ray A. Billington, *The Far Western Frontier, 1830–1860* (1956). On the impulse behind Manifest Destiny, see Frederick Merk, *Manifest Destiny and Mission in American History* (1963); Norman A. Graebner, *Empire on the Pacific: A Study in American Continental Expansionism* (1956); and Reginald Horsman, *Race and Manifest Destiny* (1981).

Other works on American penetration and settlement of the Far West include William H. Goetzmann, *Exploration and Empire: The Explorer and the Scientist in the Winning of the American West* (1966); John D. Unruh, Jr., *The Plains Across: The Overland Immigrants and the Trans-Mississippi West, 1840–1860* (1979); and Thomas O'Dea, *The Mormons* (1957). The politics and diplomacy of expansionism are treated in David M. Pletcher, *The Diplomacy of Annexation: Texas, Oregon, and the Mexican War* (1973), and Frederick Merk, *The Monroe Doctrine and American Expansion, 1843–1849* (1966). On the Mexican War, see Otis A. Singletary, *The Mexican War* (1960), and John H. Schroeder, *Mr. Polk's War: American Opposition and Dissent* (1973).

Economic developments of the 1840s and 1850s are well covered in George R. Taylor, *The Transportation Revolution, 1815–1860* (1952); Albert Fishlow, *American Railroads and the Transformation of the Ante-Bellum Economy* (1965); Douglass C. North, *The Economic Growth of the United States, 1790–1860* (1961); and Merritt Roe Smith, *Harpers Ferry Armory and the New Technology* (1977).

For insight into immigration, see Oscar Handlin, *Boston Immigrants: A Study in Acculturation*, rev. ed. (1959), and Marcus L. Hansen, *The Atlantic Migration, 1607–1860* (1976). Important recent works that deal with the working-class experience include Herbert G. Gutman, *Work, Culture, and Society in Industrializing America* (1976); Thomas Dublin, *Women At Work: The Transformation of Work and Community in Lowell, Massachusetts, 1826–1860* (1979); and Alan Dawley, *Class and Community: The Industrial Revolution in Lynn* (1976).

chapter 14

THE SECTIONAL CRISIS

On May 22, 1856, Representative Preston Brooks of South Carolina suddenly appeared on the floor of the Senate. He was looking for Charles Sumner, the antislavery senator from Massachusetts who had recently given a speech condemning the South for plotting to extend slavery to the Kansas Territory. When he found Sumner seated at his desk, Brooks proceeded to batter him over the head with a cane. Sumner made a desperate effort to rise, ripped his bolted desk from the floor, and then collapsed.

Sumner was so badly injured by the assault that he could not return to the Senate for three years. In parts of the North that were up in arms against the expansion of slavery, he was hailed as a martyr to the cause of "free soil." Brooks, denounced in the North as a bully, was lionized by his fellow Southerners and won reelection without opposition.

These contrasting reactions show how bitter sectional antagonism had become by 1856.

Sumner spoke for the radical wing of the new Republican party, which was making a bid for national power by mobilizing the North against the alleged aggressions of "the slave power." Southerners viewed the very existence of this party as an insult to their section of the country and a threat to its vital interests. Many Southerners believed that Sumner and his political friends were plotting against their way of life. By 1856, therefore, the sectional cleavage that would lead to the Civil War was already corroding the foundations of national unity.

The crisis of the mid-1850s came only a few years after the elaborate compromise of 1850 had seemingly resolved the dispute over the future of slavery in the territories acquired as a result of the Mexican War. The renewed agitation over the extension of slavery was set in motion by the Kansas-Nebraska Act of 1854. This legislation revived the sectional conflict and led to the emergence of the Republican party. From that point on, a dramatic series of events heightened the mood of sectional confrontation and destroyed the prospects for a new compromise. The caning of Charles Sumner was one of these events, and violence on the Senate floor foreshadowed violence on the battlefield.

The Compromise of 1850

During the late 1840s the leaders of the two major national parties, each with substantial followings in both the North and the South, had a vested interest in resolving the sectional crisis. Furthermore, the less tangible features of sectionalism—emotion and ideology—were not yet as divisive as they would later become. Hence a fragile compromise was achieved through a kind of give-and-take that would not be possible after the emergence of strong sectional parties in the mid-1850s.

The Problem of Slavery in the Mexican Cession

The Founders, who were generally opposed to slavery, had attempted to exclude the slavery issue from national politics as the price of uniting states committed to slavery and those in the process of abolishing it. The Constitution gave the federal government no definite authority to regulate or destroy the institution where it existed under state law. Thus it was easy to condemn slavery in principle but very difficult to develop a practical program to eliminate it without defying the Constitution.

Radical abolitionists saw this problem clearly and resolved it by rejecting the law of the land in favor of a "higher law" prohibiting human bondage. But during the 1840s the majority of Northerners showed that while they disliked slavery, they also detested abolitionism. They were inclined to view slavery as a backward institution and slaveholders as power-hungry aristocrats. But they regarded the Constitution as a binding contract be-

tween slave and free states and were likely to be prejudiced against blacks and reluctant to accept large numbers of them as free citizens. Consequently, they saw no legal or desirable way to bring about emancipation within the southern states.

However, the Constitution had not predetermined the status of slavery in *future* states. Congress had the right to require the abolition of slavery as the price of admission into the Union. An effort to use this power had led to the Missouri crisis of 1819–1820 (see Chapter 9). The resulting Missouri Compromise line was designed to decide future cases and maintain a rough parity between slave and free states. Slavery was thus allowed to expand with the westward movement of the cotton kingdom but was discouraged or prohibited above the line of 36°30'.

This tradition of providing both the free North and the slave South with opportunities for expansion and the creation of new states broke down when new territories were wrested from Mexico in the 1840s. Many Northerners were unwilling to see California and New Mexico as well as Texas admitted into the Union as slave states. Since it was generally assumed in the North that Congress had the power to prohibit slavery in new territories, a movement developed in Congress to do just that.

The Wilmot Proviso Launches the Free-Soil Movement

The "free-soil" crusade began in August 1846, only three months after the start of the Mexican War, when Congressman David Wilmot, a Pennsylvania Democrat, proposed an amendment to the military appropriations bill that would ban slavery in any territory that might be acquired from Mexico.

Wilmot spoke for a large number of northern Democrats who felt neglected and betrayed by the policies of the Polk administration. Reductions in tariff duties and Polk's veto of an internal improvement bill upset many Democrats. Still others felt betrayed because Polk had gone back on his pledge to obtain "all of Oregon" up to 54°50' and then had proceeded to wage war to win all of Texas. This twist in the course of Manifest Destiny convinced northern expansionists that the South and its interests were dominating the party and the administration.

Nevertheless, these pioneer free-soilers had a genuine interest in the issue actually at hand—the question of who would control and settle the new territories. Combining an appeal to racial prejudice with opposition to slavery as an institution, Wilmot demanded that the new territories be opened only for white people. He wanted to give the common folk of the North a fair chance by excluding unfair competition with slavery and blacks from territory obtained in the Mexican cession.

Northern Whigs backed Wilmot's Proviso because they shared his concern about the outcome of an unregulated competition between slave and free labor in the territories. Many of the northern Whigs had opposed the annexation of Texas and the Mexican War. If expansion was inevitable, they were determined that it should not be used to increase the power of the slave states.

In the first House vote on the Wilmot Proviso, party lines crumbled and were replaced by a sharp sectional cleavage. After passing the House, the Proviso was blocked in the Senate by a combination of southern influence and Democratic loyalty to the administration. When the appropriation bill went back to the House without the Proviso, the administration's arm-twisting succeeded in changing enough northern Democratic votes to defeat the Proviso.

Popular Sovereignty and the Election of 1848

After a futile attempt was made to extend the Missouri Compromise line to the Pacific—a proposal that was unacceptable to Northerners because most of the Mexican cession lay south of the line—a new approach was devised that appealed especially to Democrats. Its main proponent was Senator Lewis Cass of Michigan, an aspirant for the party's presidential nomination. He wanted to leave the determination of the status of slavery in a territory to the actual settlers. From the beginning this proposal contained an ambiguity that allowed it to be interpreted differently in the North and the South. For northern Democrats "squatter sovereignty"—or "popular sovereignty" as it was later called—meant that settlers could vote slavery up or down at the first meeting of a territorial legislature. For the southern wing of the party, it meant that a decision would only be made at the time a convention drew up a constitution and applied for statehood. It was in the interest of national Democratic leaders to leave this ambiguity unresolved for as long as possible.

Congress failed to resolve the future of slavery in the Mexican cession in time for the election of 1848. The Democrats nominated Cass on a platform of squatter sovereignty. The Whigs evaded the question by running war hero General Zachary Taylor without a platform. Northern Whigs favoring restrictions on the expansion of slavery took heart from the general's promise not to veto any territorial legislation passed by Congress. Southern Whigs supported Taylor because the general was a southern slaveholder.

Northerners who strongly supported the Wilmot Proviso were attracted by a third party movement. The Free-Soil party nominated former President Van Buren to carry their banner. Support for the Free-Soilers came mostly from Democrats and Whigs who opposed either the extension of slavery into the territories or the growing influence of the South in national politics. The founding of the Free-Soil party was the first significant effort to create a broadly based sectional party addressing itself to voters' concerns about the extension of slavery.

After a noisy and confusing campaign, Taylor came out on top, winning a majority of the electoral votes in both the North and the South. The Free-Soilers failed to carry a single state but were strong enough to run second behind Taylor in New York, Massachusetts, and Vermont.

Taylor Takes Charge

Once in office, Taylor devised a bold plan to decide the fate of slavery in the Mexican cession. He tried to engineer the immediate admission of California and New Mexico to the Union as states, thus bypassing the territorial stage entirely and eliminating the whole question of the status of slavery in the federal domain. This proposal made practical sense in regard to California which was filling up rapidly with settlers drawn there by the lust for gold. Under the administration's urging, Californians convened a constitutional convention and applied for admission to the Union as a free state. In underpopulated New Mexico, it proved impossible to get a statehood movement off the ground.

Instead of resolving the crisis, President Taylor's initiative only worsened it. Fearing that New Mexico as well as California would choose to be a free state, Southerners of both parties accused the president of trying to impose the Wilmot Proviso in a new form. The prospect that only free states would emerge from the entire Mexican cession inspired serious talk of secession.

In Congress, Senator John C. Calhoun of South Carolina saw a chance to achieve his long-standing goal of creating a southern voting bloc that would cut across regular party lines. He warmly greeted each new sign of southern discontent and sectional unity. In the fall and winter of 1849–1850 several southern states agreed to participate in a convention, to be held in Nashville in June, where grievances could be aired and demands made. For an increasing number of southern political leaders the survival of the Union would depend on the North's response to southern demands.

Forging a Compromise

When it became clear that the president would not abandon or modify his plan in order to ap-
pease the South, independent efforts began in Congress to arrange a compromise. Hoping once again to play the role of "great pacificator," Senator Henry Clay of Kentucky offered a series of resolutions meant to restore sectional harmony. On the critical territorial question, his solution was to admit California as a free state and organize the rest of the Mexican cession with no explicit prohibition of slavery. He also sought to resolve a major boundary dispute between New Mexico and Texas by granting the disputed region to New Mexico while compensating Texas through federal assumption of its state debt. As a concession to the North on another issue—the existence of slavery in the District of Columbia—he recommended prohibiting the buying and selling of slaves in the nation's capital. Finally, he called for more vigorous enforcement of the fugitive slave law.

Clay proposed the plan in February 1850, but it received a mixed reception. One obstacle was President Taylor's firm resistance to the proposal; another was the difficulty of getting congressmen to vote for it in the form of a single package or "omnibus bill." The logjam was broken in July. President Taylor died and was succeeded by Millard Fillmore, who favored the compromise. Also, a decision was made to abandon the omnibus strategy in favor of a series of measures that could be voted on separately. After the breakup of the omnibus bill, Democrats led by Senator Stephen A. Douglas replaced the original Whig sponsors as leaders of the compromise movement and maneuvered the separate provisions of the plan through Congress.

As finally approved, the Compromise of 1850 differed somewhat from Clay's original proposals. The popular sovereignty principle was included in the bills organizing New Mexico and Utah as the price of Democratic support. In addition, half of the compensation to Texas for giving up its claims to New Mexico was paid directly to holders of Texas bonds.

Abolition of the slave trade in the District of Columbia and a new fugitive slave law were also enacted. According to the provisions of

In the Senate chamber, its balconies overflowing with spectators, Henry Clay pleads for passage of the Compromise of 1850. John C. Calhoun (standing third from right) was by this time mortally ill; his speech denouncing the compromise was read by Senator James Mason of Virginia. Daniel Webster (seated at left with his head resting on his hand), himself ailing, argued in favor of the compromise plan.

the latter act, suspected fugitives were now denied a jury trial, the right to testify in their own behalf, and other minimal constitutional rights. As a result, there were no effective safeguards against false identification and the kidnapping of blacks who were legally free.

The compromise passed because its key measures were supported by both northern Democrats and southern Whigs. No single bill was backed by a majority of the congressmen from both sections and doubts persisted over the value or workability of a "compromise" that was really more like a cease-fire.

Yet the Compromise of 1850 did serve for a time as a basis for sectional peace. Southern moderates had carried the day, but southern nationalism was qualified at best. Southerners demanded strict northern adherence to the compromise, especially the Fugitive Slave Law, as a price for keeping threats of secession suppressed. In the North, the compromise received even greater support. By 1852,when the Democrats endorsed the compromise in their platform and the Whigs acceded to it in theirs, it appeared that sharp differences on the slavery issue had once again been banished from national politics.

Political Upheaval, 1852–1856

The second party system—Democrats versus Whigs—survived the crisis over slavery in the Mexican cession, but in the long run the compromise of 1850 may have weakened it. Although both national parties had been careful during the 1840s not to take stands on the slavery issue that would alienate their supporters in either section of the country, they had in fact offered voters alternative ways of dealing with the question. Democrats had endorsed headlong territorial expansion with the promise of a fair division of the spoils between slave and free states. Whigs had generally opposed annexation or acquisitions that were likely to bring the slavery question to the fore and threaten sectional harmony. Each strategy could be presented to southern voters as a good way to protect slavery and to Northerners as a good way to contain it.

The consensus of 1852 meant that the parties had to find other issues on which to base their distinctive appeals. Their failure to do so encouraged voter apathy and a disenchantment with the major parties. When the Democrats sought to revive the Manifest Destiny issue in 1854, they inadvertently reopened the explosive issue of slavery in the territories. By this time, the Whigs were too weak and divided to respond with a policy of their own, and a purely sectional free-soil party—the Republicans—gained prominence. The collapse of the second party system released sectional agitation from the earlier constraints imposed by the competition of strong national parties.

The Party System in Crisis

The presidential campaign of 1852 was singularly devoid of major issues. Both parties ignored the slavery question. Some Whigs tried to revive interest in nationalistic economic policies; but with business thriving under the Democratic program of laissez-faire, such proposals sounded empty and unnecessary.

Another tempting issue was immigration. Many Whigs were upset by the massive influx from Europe, partly because most of the new arrivals were Catholics, and the Whig following was largely evangelical Protestant. In addition, immigrants voted overwhelmingly Democratic. The Whig leadership was divided on whether to compete for the immigrant vote or to seek restrictions on immigrant voting rights.

The Whigs nominated General Winfield Scott of Mexican War fame who supported the faction that resisted nativism and sought to broaden the appeal of the party. However, Scott and his supporters were unable to break the Democratic grip on the immigrant vote, and some nativist Whigs apparently sat out the election to protest their party's disregard of their cultural prejudice.

But the main cause for Scott's crushing defeat was the support he lost in the South when he allied himself with the northern antislavery wing of the party, led by Senator William Seward of New York. The Democratic candidate, Franklin Pierce of New Hampshire, was a colorless nonentity compared to his rival, but he easily swept the Deep South and edged out

Scott in most of the free states. The outcome revealed that the Whig party was in deep trouble because it lacked a program that would distinguish it from the Democrats and would appeal to voters in both sections of the country.

Despite their overwhelming victory in 1852, the Democrats also had reasons for anxiety about the loyalty of their supporters. Voter apathy was strong, and Democratic leaders were placed in the uncomfortable position of having to appeal to both northern free-soilers and southern slaveholders.

The Kansas-Nebraska Act Raises a Storm

In January 1854, Senator Stephen A. Douglas proposed a bill to organize the territory west of Missouri and Iowa. Since this region fell within the area where slavery had been banned by the Missouri Compromise, Douglas hoped to head off southern opposition and keep the Democratic party united by disregarding the compromise line and setting up the territorial government in Kansas and Nebraska on the basis of popular sovereignty.

Douglas wanted to organize the area quickly because he was a strong supporter of the expansion of settlement and commerce. He hoped that a railroad would soon be built to the Pacific with Chicago (or another midwestern city) as its eastern terminus. A long controversy over the status of slavery in the Kansas-Nebraska area would delay the building of a railroad through the territory. Moreover, by trying to revive the spirit of Manifest Destiny he hoped to strengthen the Democratic party and enhance his chances of becoming president.

The price of southern support, Douglas soon discovered, was the addition of an amendment explicitly repealing the Missouri Compromise. He reluctantly agreed. Although the bill then made its way through Congress, it split the Democratic party. A manifesto of "independent Democrats" denounced the bill as "a gross violation of a sacred pledge." For many Northerners, the Kansas-Nebraska Act was an

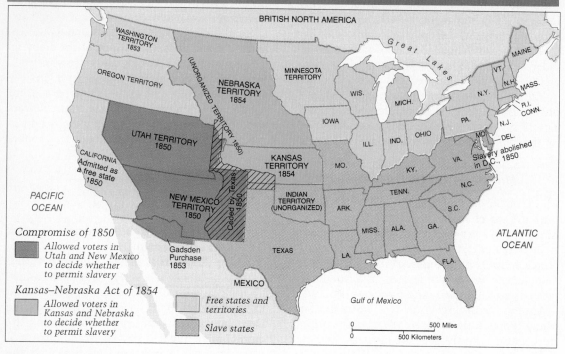

abomination because it appeared to permit slavery in an area where it had previously been prohibited. More than ever, Northerners were receptive to the theme that there was a conspiracy to extend slavery.

Douglas' bill had a catastrophic effect on the prospects for sectional harmony. It repudiated a compromise that many in the North regarded as a binding sectional compact. In defiance of the whole compromise tradition, it made a concession to the South on the issue of slavery extension without providing an equivalent concession to the North. From now on, northern sectionalists would be fighting to regain what they had lost, while Southerners would be battling just as furiously to maintain rights already conceded.

The act also destroyed what was left of the second party system. The already weakened Whig party totally disintegrated when its congressional representation split cleanly along sectional lines on the Kansas-Nebraska issue.

The Democratic party survived, but northern desertions and southern gains resulting from recruitment of proslavery Whigs destroyed its sectional balance and placed the party under firm southern control.

Finally, the furor over Kansas-Nebraska doomed the efforts of the Pierce administration to revive an expansionist foreign policy. Pierce and Secretary of State William Marcy were committed to acquiring Cuba from Spain. But Northerners interpreted the administration's plan, made public in a memorandum known as the "Ostend Manifesto," as an attempt to create a "Caribbean slave empire." The resulting storm of protest forced Pierce and his cohorts to abandon their scheme. The only tangible result of the southern expansionist dream of the 1850s was the purchase for $10 million of a 30,000 square-mile slice of Mexican territory south of the Gila River (the Gadsden Purchase, 1853). This acquisition rounded out the contiguous continental United States.

An Appeal to Nativism: The Know-Nothing Episode

The collapse of the Whigs created the opening for a new political party. The anti-Nebraska sentiment of 1854 suggested that such a party might be organized on the basis of northern opposition to the extension of slavery to the territories. Before such a prospect could be realized, however, an alternative emerged in the form of a major political movement based on hostility to immigrants. For a time, it appeared that the Whigs would be replaced by a nativist party rather than an antislavery one.

Massive immigration of Irish and Germans (see Chapter 13), most of whom were Catholic, led to increasing tensions between ethnic groups during the 1840s and early 1850s. Protestants were suspicious and distrustful of the Catholics, whom they viewed as bearers of an alien culture. Nativist agitators charged that immigrants were agents of a foreign despotism, based in Rome, that was bent on overthrowing the American Republic.

Political nativism first emerged during the 1840s in the form of local "American" parties protesting immigrant influence in cities like New York and Philadelphia. These organizations were often secretive, and one group instructed its members to answer questions about their organization with the reply, "I know nothing." The political objective of the Know-Nothings was to extend the period of naturalization in order to undercut immigrant voting strength and to keep aliens in their place.

In 1854–1855 the movement surfaced as a major political force, calling itself the American party. Most of its backing came from Whigs looking for a new home, but it also attracted some ex-Democrats. Know-Nothingism also appealed to native-born workers fearful of competition from low-paid immigrants. Others supported the party simply as an alternative to the Democratic party.

The success of the new party was so dramatic that it was compared to a hurricane. In 1854 and 1855 Know-Nothings won control of a number of state governments, ranging from Massachusetts to Maryland to Texas. By late 1855 the Know-Nothings showed every sign of displacing the Whigs as the nation's second party.

Yet, almost as rapidly as it had arisen, the Know-Nothing movement collapsed. Its demise in 1856 is one of the great mysteries of American political history. Certainly as a national party it was unable to mend the deep sectional divisions over the question of slavery in the territories. Less clear is why Know-Nothings failed to become the major opposition party to the Democrats in the North. Political nativism probably contained the seeds of its own extinction. Know-Nothingism was in part a grass-roots protest against professional politicians. Most of the movement's spokesmen and elected officials were neither professional politicians nor established community leaders. Thus their very inexperience was a major source of their original attraction to voters and a factor in the movement's decline.

Furthermore, the Know-Nothings were never a real party. Because of the lack of organizational discipline and experienced leadership, the Know-Nothings were unable to make use of their power. Once voters discovered that the Know-Nothings also *did* nothing, they recovered from their antipolitical binge and looked for more competent leadership.

Kansas and the Rise of the New Republicans

The new Republican party was an outgrowth of the anti-Nebraska sentiment of 1854. The Republican name was first used in midwestern states to attract free-soil Democrats who refused to march under the Whig banner or even support any candidate for high office who called himself a Whig.

When the Know-Nothing party split over the Kansas-Nebraska issue in 1856, most of the northern nativists went over to the Republicans. Although Republicans were more concerned with "the slave power conspiracy" than any alleged "Popish plot," nativists did not have to abandon their religious prejudices; the party had the distinct flavor of evangelical Protestantism. On the local level Republicans sometimes supported causes that reflected an anti-immigrant or anti-Catholic bias—such as defense of Protestant Bible-reading in schools and opposition to state aid for parochial education.

Unlike the Know-Nothings, the Republican party was led by seasoned professional politicians, men who had earlier been prominent Whigs or Democrats. Good organizers, they built up an effective party apparatus in an amazingly short time. By early 1856 the new party was well established throughout the North and was preparing to make a serious bid for the presidency.

Underlying the rapid growth of the Republican party was the strong and growing appeal of its position on slavery in the territories. Republicans viewed the unsettled West as a land of opportunities, a place to which the ambitious and hard-working could migrate in the hope of improving their social and economic position. But if slavery was permitted to expand, the rights of "free labor" would be denied. Republicans emphasized that slave labor was unfair competition and retarded the commercial and industrial development of a region. They envisioned a West that was free and white.

Although passage of the Kansas-Nebraska Act raised the territorial issues and gave birth to the Republican party, it was the turmoil associated with attempts to implement popular sovereignty in Kansas that kept the issue alive and enabled the Republicans to increase their following throughout the North. In Kansas a bitter, violent contest was waged for control of the territorial government between transplanted New Englanders and Midwesterners who were militantly free-soil and slaveholding settlers from Missouri. Joining the slaveholders were proslavery residents of Missouri who crossed over the border to vote illegally in territorial elections. In the first territorial election, slavery was wholeheartedly endorsed.

Settlers favoring free soil were already a majority of the actual residents of the territory when the fraudulently elected legislature stripped them of their civil rights. To defend themselves and their convictions, they took up arms and established a rival territorial government under a constitution that outlawed slavery.

A small-scale civil war then broke out between the two regimes, culminating in May 1856 when proslavery adherents raided the free-state capital at Lawrence. Portrayed in Republican propaganda as "the sack of Lawrence," the incursion resulted in substantial property damage but no loss of life. In reprisal, antislavery zealot John Brown and several followers murdered five proslavery settlers in cold blood. During the next few months, a hit-and-run guerrilla war raged between free-state and slave-state factions.

The national Republican press had a field day with the events in Kansas, exaggerating the extent of the violence but correctly pointing out that the Pierce administration was favoring rule by a proslavery minority over a free-soil majority. Since the "sack of Lawrence" occurred at about the same time that Charles Sumner was assaulted on the Senate floor, the Republicans launched their 1856 campaign under the twin slogans, "Bleeding Kansas and Bleeding Sumner." The image of an evil and aggressive "slave power" South proved a potent device for arousing northern sympathies and winning votes.

Sectional Division in the Election of 1856

The Republican nominating convention revealed the strictly sectional nature of the new party. With no delegates from the deep South in attendance, the Republicans called for a congressional prohibition of slavery in all territories. The nominee was John C. Frémont, the western explorer who had helped in the conquest of California during the Mexican war.

The Democrats nominated James Buchanan of Pennsylvania who had a long career in public service. Their platform endorsed popular sovereignty. The American party, a Know-Nothing remnant that survived mainly as the rallying point for anti-Democratic conservatives in the border states and parts of the South, chose ex-President Millard Fillmore as its standard-bearer and received the backing of those northern Whigs who hoped to revive the tradition of sectional compromise.

The election was really two separate races—one in the North between Frémont and Buchanan and the other in the South between Fillmore and Buchanan. With strong southern support and victories in four crucial northern states, Buchanan won. But the Republicans did remarkably well for a party that was scarcely more than a year old. Frémont swept the upper North with substantial majorities and won a larger proportion of the northern popular vote than either of his opponents. Since the free states had a substantial majority in the electoral college, a future Republican candidate could win the presidency simply by overcoming a slim Democratic edge in the lower North.

In the South the results of the election brought a momentary sense of relief tinged with deep anxiety about the future. For Southerners, the very existence of a sectional party committed to restricting the expansion of slavery constituted an insult to their way of life. They felt threatened. Only the continued success of a unified Democratic party under southern influence or control could maintain sectional balance and "southern rights."

The House Divided, 1857–1860

The sectional quarrel deepened and became virtually "irreconcilable" in the years between the elections of 1856 and 1860. A series of incidents provoked one side or the other, heightened the tension, and ultimately brought the crisis to a head. Behind the panicky reaction to public events lay a growing sense that the North and South were so different in culture and so opposed in basic interests that they could no longer coexist in the same nation.

Cultural Sectionalism

Signs of cultural and intellectual cleavage had appeared well before the triumph of sectional politics. As early as the mid-1840s, the slavery issue split the Baptist and Methodist churches into northern and southern wings. Instead of unifying Americans around a common Protestant faith, the churches became nurseries of sectional discord. Increasingly, northern preachers and congregations denounced slaveholding as a sin, while most southern church leaders rallied to a biblical defense of the peculiar institution and became influential apologists for the southern way of life. Both in the North and the South, ministers helped to turn political questions into moral issues and reduced the prospects for a compromise.

American literature also became sectionalized during the 1840s and 1850s. Southern men of letters such as William Gilmore Simms and Edgar Allen Poe wrote proslavery polemics, and lesser writers penned novels which glorified southern civilization at the expense of northern society. In the North, prominent men of letters—Emerson, Thoreau and others—expressed strong antislavery sentiments in prose and poetry.

Literary abolitionism reached a climax in 1852 when Harriet Beecher Stowe published *Uncle Tom's Cabin*, a novel that sold more than 300,000 copies in a single year and fixed in the northern mind the image of the slaveholder as a brutal Simon Legree. Much of its emotional impact came from the book's portrayal of slavery as a threat to the family and the cult of domesticity. When the saintly Uncle Tom was sold away from his adoring wife and children, Northerners shuddered with horror and some Southerners felt a painful twinge of conscience.

Southern defensiveness gradually hardened into cultural and economic nationalism. Southerners encouraged the use of proslavery textbooks, induced young men of the planter class to stay in the South for higher education, and sought to develop their own industry and commerce. Almost without exception, prominent southern educators and intellectuals of the late 1850s rallied behind the idea of a southern nation.

The Dred Scott Case

When James Buchanan was inaugurated on March 7, 1857, the dispute over the legal status of slavery in the territories was an open door through which sectional fears and hatreds could enter the political arena. Buchanan hoped to close that door by encouraging the Supreme Court to render a broad decision that would resolve the constitutional issue once and for all.

The Court was then about to render its decision in the case of *Dred Scott* v. *Sanford.* The case involved a Missouri slave whose owner had taken him to the Wisconsin Territory during the 1830s but then returned him to Missouri. After his master's death, Dred Scott sued for his freedom on the grounds that he had lived for many years in an area where slavery had been outlawed by the Missouri Compromise. The Court, headed by Chief Justice Roger B. Taney, made several rulings in the case. First, it held that a slave was not a citizen and therefore had no right to sue in federal courts. Second, and more important for the general issue of slavery, the Court ruled that even if Scott had been a legitimate plaintiff, he would not have won his case. His residence in the Wisconsin Territory established no right to freedom because Congress had no power to prohibit slavery there. The Missouri Compromise was thus declared unconstitutional and so, implicitly, was popular sovereignty—the main plank in the Republican platform.

In the north, and especially among Republicans, the Court's verdict was viewed as the latest diabolical act of the "slave power conspiracy." Five of the six justices who voted in the majority, Northerners argued, were proslavery Southerners. Furthermore, the fact that Buchanan had played a role in the decision was widely known, and it was suspected that he had conspired with the justices in response to pressure from the prosouthern wing of the Democratic party.

Republicans denounced the decision as "the greatest crime in the annals of the republic"; but they managed to avoid open defiance of the Supreme Court's authority by denying that the justices had formally decided the territorial question. According to their interpretation of what the Court had done, the overthrow of the Missouri Compromise was *obiter dicta*, a judicial opinion that was not binding because it had not been necessary to decide the case at hand. Although their reasoning was faulty, it served to reassure the moderates in the party that they were not violating the law of the land by demanding a congressional ban on slavery in the territories. The decision actually helped the Republicans build support since it lent credence to their claim that an aggressive slave power was dominating all branches of the federal government and attempting to use the Constitution to achieve its own ends.

The Lecompton Controversy

While the Dred Scott case was being decided, leaders of the proslavery faction in Kansas concluded that the time was ripe to draft a constitution and seek admission to the Union as a slave state. Since settlers with free-state views were now an overwhelming majority in the territory, the success of the plan required a rigged, gerrymandered election for convention delegates. When it became clear that the election was fixed, the free-staters boycotted it. The resulting constitution, drawn up at Lecompton, was certain to be rejected by Congress if a fairer election were not held.

To resolve the issue, supporters of the constitution decided to permit a vote on the slavery provision alone, giving the electorate the narrow choice of allowing or forbidding the future importation of slaves. Since there was no way to vote for total abolition, the free-state majority again resorted to boycott, thus allowing ratification of a constitution that protected existing slave property and placed no restriction on importations. In a second referendum, proposed by the free-staters and boycotted by the proslavery forces, the Lecompton constitution was overwhelmingly rejected.

The Lecompton constitution was such an obvious perversion of popular sovereignty that Stephen A. Douglas spoke out against it. But the Buchanan administration tried to push it through Congress in early 1858. The resulting debate was bitter and sometimes violent. The bill to admit Kansas into the Union as a slave state passed the Senate but was defeated in the House.

The Lecompton controversy seriously aggravated the sectional quarrel. The issue strengthened Republicans' belief that the Democratic party was dominated by Southerners, and at the same time it split the Democratic party between the followers of Douglas and the backers of Buchanan.

For Douglas the affair was a disaster; it destroyed his hopes of uniting the Democratic party and defusing the slavery issue through the application of popular sovereignty. In practice, popular sovereignty was an invitation to civil war. Furthermore, the Dred Scott decision protected Southerners' rights to own human property in federal territories. For his stand against Lecompton, Douglas was denounced as a traitor in the South, and his hopes of being elected president were greatly diminished.

■ *Abraham Lincoln, shown here in his first full-length portrait. Although Lincoln lost the contest for the Senate seat in 1858, his participation in the Lincoln-Douglas debates established his reputation as a rising star of the Republican party.*

Debating the Morality of Slavery

Douglas' more immediate problem was to win reelection to the Senate from Illinois in 1858. Here he faced surprisingly tough opposition from Republican candidate Abraham Lincoln, who set out to convince the voters that Douglas could not be relied upon to oppose consistently the extension of slavery.

In the famous speech that opened his campaign, Lincoln tried to distance himself from his opponent by taking a more radical position. He argued, " 'a house divided against itself cannot stand.' I believe this government cannot

endure, permanently half *slave* and half *free.*" He then described the chain of events between the Kansas-Nebraska Act and the Dred Scott decision as evidence of a plot to extend slavery, and he tried to link Douglas to that proslavery conspiracy by pointing to his rival's unwillingness to take a stand on the morality of slavery. Lincoln demanded that slavery be considered a moral, and not simply a political, issue.

In the subsequent series of debates that focused national attention on the Illinois senatorial contest, Lincoln hammered away at the theme that Douglas was a covert defender of slavery because he was not a principled opponent of it. Douglas responded by accusing Lincoln of endangering the Union by his talk of putting slavery on the path to extinction. Lincoln denied that he was an abolitionist but readily admitted that he, like the Founders, opposed any extension of slavery.

In the debate at Freeport, Illinois, Lincoln questioned Douglas on how he could reconcile popular sovereignty with the Dred Scott decision. Douglas responded that slavery could not exist without supportive legislation to sustain it and that territorial legislatures could simply refrain from passing a slave code if they wanted to keep it out. Coupled with his anti-Lecompton stand, Douglas' "Freeport Doctrine" hardened southern opposition to his presidential ambitions.

Douglas' most effective debating point was to charge that Lincoln's moral opposition to slavery implied a belief in racial equality. Lincoln, facing an intensely racist electorate, vigorously denied this charge and affirmed his commitment to white supremacy. He would grant blacks the right to the fruits of their own labor while denying them the "privileges" of citizenship. This was an inherently contradictory position, and Douglas made the most of it.

Although republican candidates for the state legislature won a majority of the popular votes, the Democrats carried more counties and thus were able to send Douglas back to the Senate. Lincoln lost an office, but he won respect in Republican circles throughout the country. By stressing the moral dimension of the slavery question and undercutting any possibility of fusion between Republicans and Douglas Democrats, he had sharpened his party's ideological focus and had stiffened its backbone against any temptation to compromise the free-soil position.

The South's Crisis of Fear

After Kansas became a free territory instead of a slave state in August 1858, slavery in the territories became a symbolic issue rather than a practical and substantive one. The remaining unorganized areas in the Rockies and northern Great Plains were unlikely to attract slaveholding settlers. Nevertheless, Southerners continued to demand the "right" to take their slaves into the territories, and Republicans persisted in denying it to them. Although they repeatedly promised not to interfere with slavery where it already existed, the Republicans did not gain the trust of the Southerners, who interpreted the Republicans' unyielding stand against the extension of slavery as a threat to southern rights and security.

A chain of events in late 1859 and early 1860 turned southern anxiety about northern attitudes and policies into a "crisis of fear." The first of these incidents was John Brown's raid on Harpers Ferry, Virginia, in October 1859. Brown was a fervent abolitionist with the appearance of an Old Testament prophet. He believed he was God's chosen instrument "to purge this land with blood" and eradicate the sin of slaveholding. On October 16, he led a small band of men across the Potomac River from his base in Maryland and seized the federal arsenal and armory in Harpers Ferry.

Brown's aim was to arm the local slave population and commence a guerrilla war from havens in the Appalachians that would eventually extend to the plantation regions of the lower South. But the neighboring slaves did not rise up to join him, and his plan failed. In the fight with U.S. marines that followed, ten of Brown's men were killed or mortally wounded, along with seven of the townspeople and soldiers who opposed them.

The wounded Brown and his remaining followers were put on trial for treason against the state of Virginia. The subsequent investigation produced evidence that several prominent northern abolitionists had approved of Brown's plan and had raised money for his preparations. This revelation seemed to confirm southern fears that abolitionists were actively engaged in fomenting slave insurrection. Southerners were further stunned by the outpouring of sympathy and admiration for Brown in the North. His actual execution on December 2 completed Brown's elevation to the status of a martyred saint of the antislavery cause.

Although Republican politicians were quick to denounce John Brown for his violent methods, Southerners interpreted the wave of northern sympathy as an expression of the majority opinion and the Republicans' "real" attitude. In the southern mind, abolitionists, Republicans, and Northerners were taking on one face. Within the South, the raid and its aftermath touched off a frenzy of fear. Southerners became increasingly vigilant for any sign of attack on their way of life, whether from without or from within.

Brown was scarcely in his grave when another set of events put southern nerves on edge. Next to abolitionist-abetted rebellions, the slaveholding South's greatest fear was that the nonslaveholding majority would turn against the master class and that the solidarity of southern whites would crumble. Hinton Rowan Helper's *Impending Crisis of the South,* which called upon lower class whites to resist planter dominance and abolish slavery in their own interest, was regarded by slaveholders as even more seditious than *Uncle Tom's Cabin.* They feared the spread of "Helperism" among poor whites almost as much as the effect of "John Brownism" on the slaves.

The Republican candidate for Speaker of the U.S. House of Representatives, John Sherman of Ohio, had endorsed Helper's book as a campaign document. Southern congressmen threatened secession if Sherman was elected, and feelings became so heated that some House members began to carry weapons on the floor of the chamber. A more moderate Republican was elected, and the impasse over the speakership was resolved, but the contest helped persuade Southerners that the Republicans were committed to stirring up class conflict among southern whites. The identification of Republicans with Helper's ideas may have been decisive in convincing many conservative planters that a Republican president in 1860 would be intolerable.

1846	David Wilmot introduces proviso banning slavery in the Mexican cession
1848	Free-Soil party is founded
	Zachary Taylor (Whig) elected president, defeating Lewis Cass (Democrat) and Martin Van Buren (Free-Soil)
1849	California seeks admission to the Union as a free state
1850	Congress debates sectional issues and enacts Compromise of 1850
1852	Harriet Beecher Stowe publishes *Uncle Tom's Cabin*
	Franklin Pierce (Democrat) elected president by a large majority over Winfield Scott (Whig)
1854	Congress passes Kansas-Nebraska Act, repealing Missouri Compromise
	Republican party founded in several northern states
	Anti-Nebraska coalitions score victories in congressional elections in the North
1854–1855	Know-Nothing party achieves stunning successes in state politics
1854–1856	Free-state and slave-state forces struggle for control of Kansas Territory
1856	Preston Brooks assaults Charles Sumner on Senate floor
	James Buchanan wins presidency despite strong challenge in the North from John C. Frémont
1857	Supreme Court decides Dred Scott case and legalizes slavery in all territories
1858	Congress refuses to admit Kansas to Union under the proslavery Lecompton constitution
	Lincoln and Douglas debate
1859	John Brown raids Harpers Ferry, is captured and executed
1859–1860	Fierce struggle takes place over election of a Republican as Speaker of the House (December–February)
1860	Republicans nominate Abraham Lincoln for presidency (May)
	Democratic party splits into northern and southern factions with separate candidates and platforms (June)
	Lincoln wins the presidency over Douglas (northern Democrat), Breckinridge (southern Democrat), and Bell (Constitutional Unionist)

The Election of 1860

The Republicans, sniffing victory and generally unaware of the depth of southern feeling against them, met in Chicago on May 16 to nominate a presidential candidate. The initial front-runner, Senator William H. Seward of New York, proved unacceptable because of his reputation for radicalism and his long record of strong opposition to the nativist movement. What a majority of the delegates wanted was a less controversial nominee who could win two or three of the northern states that had been in the Democratic column in 1856. Abraham Lincoln met their specifications: He was considered more moderate than Seward and had kept his personal distaste for Know-Nothingism to himself. In addition, his rise to prominence from humble beginnings embodied the Republican ideal of equal opportunity for all.

The platform, like the nominee, was meant to broaden the party's appeal in the North. Although a commitment to halt the expansion of slavery remained, economic matters received more attention than they had in 1856. The platform called for a high protective tariff, free homesteads, and federal aid for internal improvements. The platform was cleverly designed to bring most ex-Whigs into the Republican camp while also accommodating enough renegade Democrats to give the party a solid majority in the northern states.

The Democrats failed to present a united front against this formidable challenge. When the party first met in the sweltering heat of Charleston in late April, Douglas was unable to win the nomination because of southern opposition. He did succeed in getting the convention to endorse popular sovereignty as its slavery platform, but the price was a walkout by southern delegates who favored a federal slave code for the territories.

Unable to agree on a nominee, the convention adjourned to reconvene in Baltimore in June. When the pro-Douglas force won most of the contested seats, another and more massive southern walkout took place. The result was a fracture of the Democratic party. The delegates who remained nominated Douglas, reaffirming their commitment to popular sovereignty; the southern bolters convened elsewhere to nominate John Breckinridge of Kentucky on a platform pledging federal protection of slavery in the territories.

By the time the campaign got underway, four parties were running presidential candidates. In addition to the Republicans, the Douglas Democrats, and the "Southern Rights" Democrats, a remnant of conservative Whigs and Know-Nothings nominated John

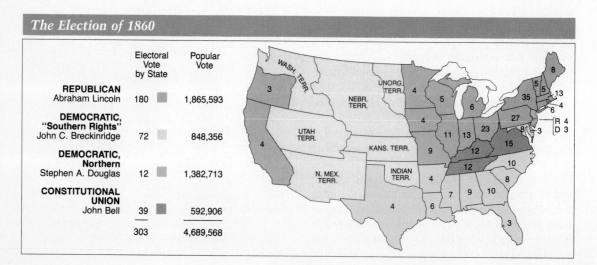

The Election of 1860

	Electoral Vote by State	Popular Vote
REPUBLICAN Abraham Lincoln	180	1,865,593
DEMOCRATIC, "Southern Rights" John C. Breckinridge	72	848,356
DEMOCRATIC, Northern Stephen A. Douglas	12	1,382,713
CONSTITUTIONAL UNION John Bell	39	592,906
	303	4,689,568

Bell of Tennessee under the banner of the Constitutional Union party. Taking no explicit stand on slavery in the territories, Bell and his backers tried to represent the spirit of sectional compromise. In effect, the race became separate two-party contests in each section: In the North the real choice was between Lincoln and Douglas, and in the South the only candidates with a fighting chance were Breckenridge and Bell.

When the results came in, the Republicans had achieved a stunning victory. By gaining the electoral votes of all the free states except a fraction of New Jersey's, Lincoln won a decisive majority. The Republican strategy of seeking power by trying to win the majority section was brilliantly successful. Less than 40 percent of those who went to the polls throughout the nation actually voted for Lincoln, but his support in the North was so solid that he would have won in the electoral college even if his opponents had been unified behind a single candidate.

Most Southerners saw the results of the election as a catastrophe. A candidate and a party with no support in their own section had won the presidency on a platform viewed as insulting to southern honor and hostile to vital southern interests. For the first time in history, southern interests were in no way represented in the White House. Rather than accept permanent minority status in American politics and face the threat to black slavery and white "liberty" that was bound to follow, the political leaders of the lower South launched a movement for immediate secession from the Union.

Explaining the Crisis

Generations of historians have searched for the underlying causes of the crisis leading to the disruption of the Union but have failed to agree on an answer. Some have stressed the clash of economic interests between agrarian and industrializing regions. But this interpretation does not reflect the way people at the time expressed their concerns. The main issues in the sectional debates of the 1850s were whether slavery was right or wrong and whether it should be extended or contained. In the face of these issues, all economic considerations pale. Indeed, there was no necessity for producers of raw materials to go to war with those who marketed and processed them.

Another group of historians have blamed the crisis on "irresponsible" politicians and agitators on both sides of the Mason-Dixon line. Public opinion, they argue, was whipped into a frenzy over issues that competent statesmen could have resolved. But this viewpoint has been sharply criticized for failing to acknowledge the depths of feeling that could be aroused by the slavery question and for underestimating the obstacles to a peaceful solution.

The dominant modern view is that the crisis was rooted in profound ideological differences over the morality and utility of slavery as an institution. Most interpreters are now agreed that the conflict stemmed from the fact that the South was a slave society and was determined to stay that way, while the North was equally committed to a free labor system. It is hard to imagine that secessionism would have developed if the South had followed the North's example and abolished slavery in the postrevolutionary period.

Nevertheless, the existence or nonexistence of slavery will not explain why the crisis came when it did and in the way that it did. Why did the conflict become "irreconcilable" in the 1850s and not earlier or later? Why did it take the form of a political struggle over the future of slavery in the territories? Adequate answers to both questions require an understanding of political developments that were not directly caused by tensions over slavery.

By the 1850s, the established Whig and Democratic parties were in trouble because they no longer offered the voters clear-cut alternatives on the economic issues that had been the bread and butter of politics during the heyday of the second party system. This situation created an opening for new parties and issues. The Republicans used the issue of slavery in the territories to build the first successful sectional party in American history. They called for "free soil" rather than freedom for blacks because abolitionism conflicted with the northern majority's commitment to white supremacy and its respect for the original constitutional compromise that established a hands-off policy toward slavery in the southern states.

If politicians seeking new ways to mobilize an apathetic electorate are seen as the main instigators of sectional crisis, the reason why certain appeals were more effective than others must still be explained. Why did the slavery extension issue arouse such strong feelings in the two sections during the 1850s? After all, the same issues had arisen earlier and had proved adjustable.

Ultimately, therefore, the crisis of the 1850s must be understood as having a deep social and cultural as well as a purely political one. The North and South had diverged significantly in basic beliefs and values between the 1820s and the 1850s. In the free states, the rise of reform-minded evangelicalism had given a new sense of moral direction and purpose to a rising middle class adapting to the new market economy (see Chapter 11). In much of the South, the slave plantation system prospered, and the notion that white liberty and equality depended on having enslaved blacks to do menial labor became more deeply entrenched.

When politicians appealed to sectionalism during the 1850s, therefore, they could evoke conflicting views of what constituted a good society. The South—with its allegedly idle masters, degraded unfree workers, and shiftless poor whites—seemed to a majority of Northerners to be in flagrant violation of the Protestant work ethic and the ideal of open competition. From the dominant southern point of view, the North was a land of hypocritical money-grubbers who denied the obvious fact that dependent laboring classes—especially racially inferior ones—had to be kept under the kind of rigid control that only slavery could provide. Once these contrary views of the world had become the main themes of political discourse, sectional compromise was no longer possible.

Recommended Reading

The best general account of the politics of the sectional crisis is David M. Potter, *The Impending Crisis, 1848–1861* (1976). A provocative new analysis of the party system in crisis is Michael F. Holt, *The Political Crisis of the 1850s* (1978). The most thorough discussion of the events leading up to the Civil War is Allan Nevins, *The Ordeal of the Union*, vols. 1–4 (1947–1950). On southern responses to the events of the crisis period, see Avery Craven, *The Growth of Southern Nationalism 1848–1861* (1953), and William L. Barney, *The Road to Secession* (1972).

For the first phase of the sectional controversy, see Holman Hamilton, *Prologue to Conflict: The Crisis and Compromise of 1850* (1964). The rise of antislavery politics in the 1840s and 1850s is described in Richard Sewell, *Ballots for Freedom: Antislavery Politics in the United States, 1837–1860* (1976); Eric Foner, *Free Soil, Free Labor, Free Men: The Ideology of the Republican Party before the Civil War* (1970); and Eugene H. Berwanger, *The Frontier Against Slavery: Western Anti-Negro Prejudice in the Slavery Extension Controversy* (1967).

On nativism, see Ray Allen Billington, *The Protestant Crusade, 1800–1860* (1938) and Carleton Beales, *Brass Knuckles Crusade: The Great Know-Nothing Conspiracy* (1960). Major biographical studies of key participants in the crisis of the 1850s include Robert W. Johannsen: *Stephen A. Douglas* (1973); David Donald, *Charles Sumner and the Coming of the Civil War* (1960); and Don E. Fehrenbacher, *Prelude to Greatness: Lincoln in the 1850s* (1962). Another book by Don E. Fehrenbacher, *The Dred Scott Case: Its Significance in American Law and Politics* (1978), is the definitive work on the subject.

On the Lincoln-Douglas rivalry, see Harry V. Jaffa, *Crisis of the House Divided: An Interpretation of the Lincoln-Douglas Debates* (1959), and George B. Forgie, *Patricide in the House Divided: A Psychological Interpretation of Lincoln and His Age* (1979). On John Brown and his raid, see Stephen B. Oates, *To Purge This Land with Blood: A Biography of John Brown* (1970).

Perspectives on the intellectual and cultural aspects of the sectional conflict can be derived from William R. Taylor, *Cavalier and Yankee: The Old South and American National Character* (1961); John McCardell, *The Idea of a Southern Nation: Southern Nationalists and Southern Nationalism, 1830–1860* (1979); and Paul C. Nagel, *One Nation Indivisible: The Union in American Thought* (1964).

chapter 15

SECESSION
AND THE
CIVIL WAR

President Abraham Lincoln was striking in appearance—at six feet four inches in height, he seemed even taller because of his disproportionately long legs and his habit of wearing a high silk "stovepipe" hat. His career prior to taking up residence in the White House in 1860 was less remarkable than his person, however. A look at his previous experience certainly provided no guarantee that he would one day tower over most of our other presidents in more than physical height.

Born to poor and illiterate parents on the Kentucky frontier in 1809, Lincoln received a few months of formal schooling in Indiana after the family moved there in 1816. But mostly he educated himself, reading and re-reading a few treasured books by firelight. In 1831, when the family migrated to Illinois, he left home to make a living for himself. After failing as a merchant, he found a path to success in law and politics. Lincoln combined exceptional political and legal skills with a down-to-earth, humorous way of addressing jurors and voters. He became a leader of the Whig party in Illinois and one of the most sought after of the lawyers who rode the central Illinois judicial circuit.

The high point of his political career as a Whig was one term in Congress (1847–1849), but he alienated much of his constituency by opposing the Mexican War and wisely chose not to run for reelection. In 1848 he campaigned vigorously and effectively for Zachary Taylor, but the new president failed to appoint Lincoln to a patronage job he coveted. Disappointed by his political fortunes, Lincoln retired from active politics and concentrated on building his law practice.

The Kansas-Nebraska Act of 1854, with its advocacy of popular sovereignty, provided Lincoln with an opportunity to reconcile his driving ambition for political success with his personal convictions. Lincoln had long believed that slavery was an unjust institution that should be tolerated only to the extent that the Constitution and the tradition of sectional compromise required. Attacking Douglas' plan on popular sovereignty, Lincoln threw in his lot with the Republicans and assumed leadership of the new party in Illinois. He attracted national attention in his bid for Douglas' Senate seat in 1858, and happened to have the right qualifications when the Republicans chose a presidential nominee in 1860.

After Lincoln's election provoked southern secession and plunged the nation into the greatest crisis in its history, there was understandable skepticism about his qualifications in many quarters. After all, the former rail-splitter from Illinois had never been a governor, senator, cabinet officer, or high-ranking military officer. But some of his training as a prairie politician would prove extremely useful in the years ahead.

Lincoln had shown himself adept at the art of party leadership, which meant being able to accommodate various factions and define party issues and principles in a way that would encourage unity and dedication to the cause. Holding the Republican party together by persuasion and patronage was essential to unifying the nation by force, and Lincoln succeeded in doing both.

Another reason for Lincoln's effectiveness as a war leader was that he identified wholeheartedly with the northern cause and could inspire others to make sacrifices for it. In his view, the issue in the conflict was nothing less than the survival of the kind of political system that gave men like himself a chance for high office. For Lincoln, a government had to be strong enough to maintain its own existence and guarantee equality of opportunity.

The Civil War tested America's ability to preserve its democratic form of government in the face of domestic foes. It put on trial the very principle of democracy at a time when most European nations had rejected political liberalism and accepted the view that popular government would inevitably collapse into anarchy. As Lincoln put it in the Gettysburg Address, the only cause great enough to justify the enormous sacrifice of life on the battlefields was the struggle to preserve the democratic ideal, or to ensure that "government of

the people, by the people, and for the people, shall not perish from the earth."

The Storm Gathers

Lincoln's election provoked the secession of seven states of the Deep South but did not lead immediately to armed conflict. Before the sectional quarrel turned from a cold war into a hot one, two things had to happen: A final effort to defuse the conflict by compromise and conciliation had to fail, and the North needed to develop a firm resolve to maintain the Union by military action. Both of these developments may seem inevitable to us, but for most of those living at the time it was not clear until the guns blazed at Fort Sumter that the sectional crisis would have to be resolved on the battlefield.

The Deep South Secedes

South Carolina, which had long been in the forefront of southern rights and proslavery agitation, was the first state to leave the Union (December 20, 1860). The constitutional theory behind secession was that the Union was a "compact" among sovereign states, each of which could withdraw from the Union by a vote of a convention similar to the one that had ratified the Constitution in the first place. The South Carolinians justified seceding at this time by charging that "a sectional party" had elected a president hostile to slavery.

In other states of the cotton kingdom there was similar outrage at Lincoln's election but less certainty about how to respond to it. Some Southerners, labeled "cooperationists," believed the South should respond as a unit, after holding a southern convention. South Carolina's unilateral action, however, set a precedent.

When conventions in six other states of the Deep South met during January 1861, delegates favoring immediate secession were everywhere in the majority. By February 1, seven states had removed themselves from the Union—South Carolina, Alabama, Mississippi, Florida, Georgia, Louisiana, and Texas. In the upper South, however, calls for immediate secession were unsuccessful; majority opinion in Virginia, North Carolina, Tennessee and Arkansas did not subscribe to the view that Lincoln's election was a sufficient reason for breaking up the Union.

Delegates from the Deep South met in Montgomery, Alabama, on February 4 to establish the Confederate States of America. Relatively moderate leaders dominated the proceedings and defeated or modified some of the pet schemes of a radical faction composed of extreme southern nationalists. Voted down were proposals to reopen the Atlantic slave trade, to count *all* slaves in determining congressional representation, instead of three-fifths, and to prohibit the admission of free states to the new Confederacy.

The resulting provisional constitution was surprisingly similar to that of the United States. Most of the differences merely spelled out traditional southern interpretations of the federal charter: The central government was denied the authority to impose protective tariffs, subsidize internal improvements, or interfere with slavery in the states, and was required to pass laws protecting slavery in the territories. As provisional president and vice-president, the convention chose Jefferson Davis of Mississippi and Alexander Stephens of Georgia, men who had previously resisted secessionist agitation.

The moderation shown in Montgomery resulted in part from a desire to win support for the cause of secessionism in the reluctant states of the upper South. But it also revealed that extremists had never succeeded in getting a majority behind them. Most Southerners were staunchly proslavery but had been opposed to dissolving the Union and repudiating their traditional patriotic loyalties so long as there had been good reasons to believe that slavery was safe from northern interference.

The panic following Lincoln's election destroyed that sense of security; but it was clear from the actions of the Montgomery convention that the goal of the new converts to secessionism was not to establish a slaveholders'

reactionary utopia. They only wished to recreate the Union that existed before the rise of the Republican party, and they opted for secession only when it seemed clear that separation was the only way to achieve their aim. Some optimists even predicted that all of the North except New England would eventually join the Confederacy.

Secession and the formation of the Confederacy thus amounted to a very conservative and defensive kind of "revolution." The only justification for southern independence upon which a majority could agree was the need for greater security for slavery and the social relations that institution entailed.

The Failure of Compromise

While the Deep South was opting for independence, moderates in the North and the border slave states were trying to devise a compromise that would stem the secessionist tide before it could engulf the entire South. In Congress, Senator John Crittenden of Kentucky presented a plan that served as the focus for discussion. Crittenden advocated extending the Missouri Compromise line to the Pacific to guarantee the protection of slavery in the southwestern territories. He also recommended a constitutional amendment that would forever prohibit the federal government from abolishing or regulating slavery in the states.

Initially, congressional Republicans showed some willingness to give ground and take these proposals seriously. However, Republican support quickly vanished when Lincoln sent word from Springfield that he was adamantly opposed to the extension of the compromise line. With Lincoln opposing the plan, Republicans voted against the compromise in committee. When the senators and congressmen of the seceding states also voted against the plan, it was doomed to defeat.

Some historians have blamed Lincoln and the Republicans for causing unnecessary war by rejecting a compromise that would have appeased southern pride without providing any practical opportunity for the expansion of slavery. But it is quite possible that the secessionists, who wanted slavery protected in *all* territories, would not have been satisfied even if the Republicans had approved the plan.

Furthermore, Lincoln and his followers had what they considered to be very good reasons for not making territorial concessions. They mistakenly believed that secessionism reflected a minority opinion in the South and that a strong stand would win the support of southern Unionists and moderates. In addition, Lincoln took his stand on free-soil seriously. He did not want to give slaveholders any chance to enlarge their domain.

And the War Came

By the time of Lincoln's inauguration, seven states had seceded, formed an independent confederacy, and seized most federal forts and other installations in the Deep South without firing a shot. Lincoln's predecessor, James Buchanan, rejected the right of secession, but refused to use coercion to maintain federal authority. Many Northerners agreed with his stand.

The collapse of compromise efforts narrowed the choice to peaceful separation or war between the sections. By early March, the tide of public opinion was beginning to shift in favor of strong action to preserve the Union. Even in the business community sentiment mounted in favor of a coercive policy.

In his inaugural address, Lincoln called for a cautious and limited use of force. He would defend federal forts and installations not yet in Confederate hands but would not attempt to recapture the ones already taken. He thus tried to shift the burden for beginning hostilities to the Confederacy. As Lincoln spoke, only four military installations within the seceded states were still held by United States forces. The most important and vulnerable of these installations was Fort Sumter inside Charleston harbor. The Confederacy demanded the surrender of the garrison, and shortly after taking office, Lincoln was informed that Sumter could not hold out much longer without reinforcements and supplies.

After some initial indecision and opposition from his cabinet, Lincoln decided to reinforce the fort, and he so informed the governor of South Carolina on April 4. The Confederacy regarded the sending of provisions as a hostile act and began shelling the fort near dawn on April 12. After forty hours of bombardment, the commander of the Union forces surrendered, and the Confederate flag was raised over Fort Sumter. The South had won a victory but had also assumed responsibility for firing the first shot.

On April 15, Lincoln proclaimed that an insurrection existed in the Deep South and called upon the militia of the loyal states to provide 75,000 troops for short-term service to put it down. Two days later, a Virginia convention voted to join the Confederacy. Within the next five weeks, Arkansas, Tennessee, and North Carolina followed suit. Lincoln's policy of coercion forced them to choose sides, and they opted to join the other slave states in the Confederacy.

In the North, the firing on Sumter evoked strong feelings of patriotism and dedication to the Union. Like many other Northerners, Stephen A. Douglas, Lincoln's former political rival, pledged his full support for the crusade against secession and literally worked himself to death rallying midwestern Democrats behind the government. Everyone assumed that the war would be short and not very bloody; it remained to be seen whether Unionist fervor could be sustained through a long and costly struggle.

The entire Confederacy comprised only eleven of the fifteen states in which slavery was lawful. In the border slave states of Maryland, Delaware, Kentucky, and Missouri, secession was thwarted by a combination of local Unionism and federal intervention. By taking care to respect Kentucky's neutrality, using martial law ruthlessly in Maryland, and stationing regular troops in Missouri, Lincoln kept these crucial border states in the Union.

Hence the Civil War was not, strictly speaking, a struggle between slave and free states. More than anything else, conflicting views on the right of secession determined the ultimate

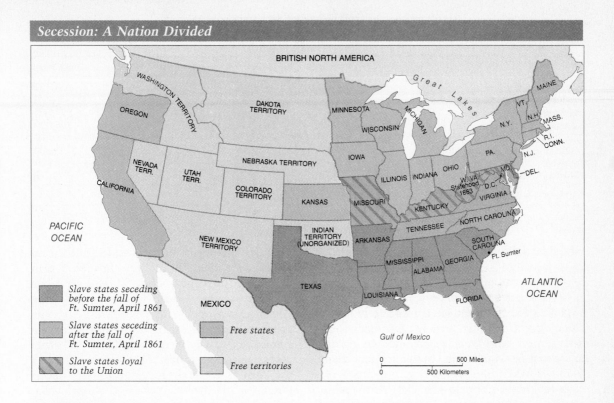

BRITISH NORTH AMERICA

Slave states seceding before the fall of Ft. Sumter, April 1861

Slave states seceding after the fall of Ft. Sumter, April 1861

Slave states loyal to the Union

Free states

Free territories

---

division of states and the choices of individuals in areas where sentiment was divided. General Robert E. Lee, for example, was neither a defender of slavery nor a southern nationalist. But he followed Virginia out of the Union because he was the loyal son of a "sovereign state." Although concern about the future of slavery had driven the Deep South to secede in the first place, the war was seen less as a struggle over slavery than as a contest to determine whether the Union was indivisible.

Adjusting to Total War

The Civil War was a "total war" because the North could achieve its aims of restoring the Union only if the South was so thoroughly defeated that its separatist government was overthrown. It was a long war because the Confederacy put up "a hell of a fight" before it would agree to be put to death. A total war is a test of societies, economies, and political systems as well as a battle of wits between generals and military strategists.

Prospects, Plans, and Expectations

If the war was to be decided by sheer physical strength, then the North had an enormous edge in population, industrial capacity, and railroad mileage. Nevertheless, the South also had some advantages. To achieve its aim of independence, the Confederacy needed only to defend its own territory successfully. The North, on the other hand, had to invade and conquer the South. Consequently, the Confederacy faced a less serious supply problem, had a greater capacity to choose the time and place of combat, and could take advantage of familiar terrain and a friendly civilian population.

The nature of the war meant that southern leaders could define their cause as defense of their homeland against a Yankee invasion. It seemed doubtful in 1861 that Northerners

Resources of the Union and the Confederacy, 1861
(Figures in thousands)

	Union	Confederacy
Population	23,000	8,700*
Real and personal property	$11,000,000	$5,370,000
Banking capital	$330,000	$27,000
Capital investment	$850,000	$95,000
Manufacturing establishments	110	18
Value of production (annual)	$1,500,000	$155,000
Industrial workers	1,300	110
Railroad mileage	22	9

*40 percent were slaves (3,500)

Source: From Freedom and Crisis: An American History, *Third Edition, by Allen Weinstein and Frank Otto Gatell (1981).*

would be willing to make an equal sacrifice for the relatively abstract principle that the Union was sacred and perpetual.

Confederate optimism on the eve of the war was also fed by other—and more dubious—calculations. It was widely assumed that Southerners who were accustomed to riding and shooting would make better soldiers than Yankees. When most of the large proportion of high-ranking officers in the U.S. Army who were of southern origin resigned to accept Confederate commands, Southerners confidently anticipated that their armies would be better led. Finally, Southerners assumed that if external help was needed, England and France would come to their aid.

Both sides based their strategies on their advantages. The choice before President Davis, who assumed personal direction of the Confederate military effort, was whether to stay on the defensive or seek a sudden and dramatic victory by invading the North. He chose to wage an essentially defensive war in the hope that the North would soon tire of the blood and sacrifice and allow the Confederacy to go its own way.

Northern military planners had greater difficulty in working out a basic strategy, and it took a good deal of trial and error before there was a clear sense of what had to be done. Some optimists believed that the war could be won quickly and easily by sending an army to capture the Confederate capital of Richmond, scarcely a hundred miles from Washington.

The early battles in Virginia ended this casual optimism. Other Northerners favored a plan called the "anaconda policy." Like a great boa constrictor, the North would squeeze the South into submission by blockading the southern coasts, seizing control of the Mississippi, and cutting off supplies of food and other essential commodities. This plan pointed to the West as the main focus of military operations.

Eventually Lincoln decided on a two-front war. He would keep the pressure on Virginia while at the same time authorizing an advance down the Mississippi valley. He also attached great importance to the coastal blockade and expected naval operations to seize the ports through which goods entered and left the Confederacy. His basic plan of applying pressure and probing for weaknesses at several points simultaneously was a good one because it took maximum advantage of the northern superiority in manpower and material. But it required better military leadership than the North possessed at the beginning of the war and took a painfully long time to put into effect.

Mobilizing the Home Front

The North and South faced very similar problems in trying to create the vast support systems needed by armies in the field. At the beginning of the conflict, both sides had more volunteers than could be armed and outfitted.

But as it became clear that hopes for a short and easy war were false, the pool of volunteers began to dry up. To resolve this problem, the Confederacy passed a conscription law in April 1862, and the Union edged toward a draft in July when Congress gave Lincoln the power to assign manpower quotas to each state and resort to conscription if they were not met.

To produce the materials of war, both governments relied mainly on private industry. In the North, especially, the system of contracting with private firms and individuals to supply the army often resulted in corruption, inefficiency, and "shoddy" goods. But the North's economy was strong at the core, and by 1863 its factories and farms were producing more than enough to provision the troops without significantly lowering the living standards of the civilian population.

The southern economy was much less adaptable to the needs of total war. Dependent on the outside world for most of its manufactured goods before the war, the Union blockade forced the southern government to sponsor a crash program to produce its own war materials and to encourage private enterprise. Astonishingly, the Confederate Ordinance Bureau succeeded in producing or procuring sufficient armaments to keep southern armies well supplied throughout the conflict.

Southern agriculture, however, failed to meet the challenge. Planters were reluctant to switch from cotton to foodstuffs, and the South's internal transportation system was inadequate. Its limited rail network was designed to link plantation regions to port cities rather than connect food-producing areas with centers of population. And when northern forces penetrated parts of the South, they created new gaps in the system. To supply the troops, the Confederate commissary resorted to impressment of agricultural produce, a policy so fiercely resisted by farmers and local politicians that it eventually had to be abandoned. By 1863 civilians in urban areas were rioting to protest food shortages.

Another challenge faced by both sides was how to finance an enormously costly struggle. Neither side was willing to resort to the heavy taxation that was needed to maintain fiscal integrity. Americans, it seems, were more willing to die for their government than to pay for it. Besides floating loans and selling bonds, both treasuries deliberately inflated the currency by printing large quantities of paper money that could not be redeemed in gold and silver. Runaway inflation was the inevitable result. But the problem was much less severe in the North, because of the overall strength of its economy and willingness of its citizens to buy bonds and pay taxes.

The Confederacy was hampered from the outset by a severe shortage of readily disposable wealth that could be tapped for public purposes. Land and cotton could not easily be turned into rifles and cannons, and the southern treasury had to accept payments "in kind." As a result, Confederate "assets" eventually consisted mainly of bales of cotton that were unexportable because of the blockade. As the Confederate government fell deeper and deeper into debt and printed more and more paper money, its rate of inflation soared out of sight.

Political Leadership: Northern Success and Southern Failure

Total war also forced political adjustment, and both the Union and the Confederacy had to face the question of how much democracy and individual freedom could be permitted when military success required an unprecedented exercise of governmental authority. Since both constitutions made the president commander in chief of the army and navy, Lincoln and Davis took actions that would have been regarded as arbitrary or even tyrannical in peacetime.

Lincoln was especially bold in assuming new executive powers. After the fighting started at Fort Sumter, he expanded the regular army and advanced public money to private individuals without authorization by Congress. On April 27, 1861, he declared martial law, which enabled the military to arrest and detain without trial civilians suspected of aiding the enemy, and suspended the writ of habeas corpus in the area between Philadelphia and Washington. This latter action was deemed necessary because of mob attacks on Union troops passing through Baltimore. In September 1862 Lincoln extended this authority to all parts of the United States where "disloyal" elements were active. He argued that preservation of the Union justified such actions.

For the most part, however, the Lincoln administration showed restraint and tolerated a broad spectrum of political dissent. "Politics as usual" persisted to a surprising degree. Anti-administration newspapers were allowed to criticize the president and his party almost at will, and opposition to Lincoln's programs was freely voiced in Congress.

Jefferson Davis proved to be a less effective war leader than Lincoln. He defined his powers as commander in chief narrowly and literally, which meant that he assumed personal direction of the armed forces but left policymaking for the mobilization and control of the civilian population primarily to the Confederate Congress. Unfortunately, Davis overestimated his capacities as a strategist and lacked the tact to handle field commanders who were as proud and testy as he was.

Davis' greatest failing, however, was his lack of initiative and leadership in dealing with the problems of the home front. He devoted little attention to a deteriorating economic situation that caused great hardship and sapped Confederate morale. In addition, although the South had a much more serious problem of internal division and disloyalty than the North, he chose to be extremely cautious in his use of martial law.

As the war dragged on, Davis' political and popular support eroded. He was opposed and obstructed by state governors who resisted conscription and other Confederate policies that violated the tradition of states' rights. The Confederate Congress and southern newspapers similarly criticized Davis' policies. His authority was further undermined because he did not even have an organized party behind him. As a result, it was difficult to mobilize the support required for hard decisions and controversial policies.

Early Campaigns and Battles

The first campaign of the war was a minor triumph for the Union, as forces under General George McClellan succeeded in driving Confederate troops out of western Virginia during May and June 1861. McClellan's victory ensured that this region of predominantly Unionist sentiment remained under northern control; out of it came the new "loyal" state of West Virginia, organized and admitted to the Union in 1863.

But the war's first major battle was a disaster for northern arms. Against his better judgment, General Winfield Scott responded to the "On to Richmond" clamor and ordered poorly trained Union troops under General Irvin McDowell to advance against the Confederate forces gathered at Manassas Junction, Virginia. They attacked the enemy position near Bull Run Creek on July 21. Confederate forces held the line against the northern assault until reinforcements arrived and then counterattacked. The routed northern forces quickly broke ranks and fled toward Washington and safety.

The humiliating defeat at Bull Run led to a shake-up of the northern high command. The man of the hour was George McClellan, who first replaced McDowell and then became general in chief when Scott was eased into retirement. A cautious disciplinarian, McClellan spent the fall and winter drilling his troops and whipping them into shape, much to the anxiety of a more and more impatient Lincoln.

Before McClellan moved, Union forces in the West won some important victories. In February 1862, a joint military-naval operation, commanded by General Ulysses S. Grant, captured Fort Henry on the Tennessee River and Fort Donelson on the Cumberland. The Confederate army was forced to withdraw from Kentucky and middle Tennessee, amassing its western forces at Corinth, Mississippi. The Union army slowly followed, but on April 6, the South launched a surprise attack. In the battle of Shiloh, one of the bloodiest of the war, only the timely arrival of reinforcements prevented the annihilation of Union troops backed up against the Tennessee River. After a

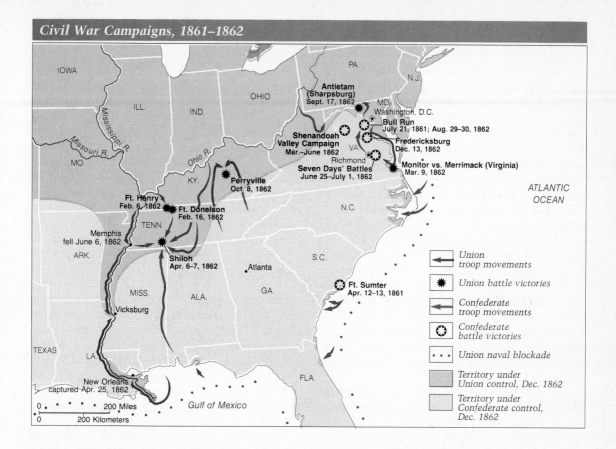

second day of fierce fighting, the Confederates retreated to Corinth, leaving the enemy forces battered and exhausted.

Although the military effort to seize control of the Mississippi Valley was temporarily halted at Shiloh, the Union navy soon contributed dramatically to the pursuit of that objective. On April 26 a fleet coming up from the Gulf captured the port of New Orleans. The occupation of New Orleans, besides securing the mouth of the Mississippi, climaxed a series of naval and amphibious operations around the edges of the Confederacy that provided strategically located bases for the northern blockade. The last serious challenge to the North's naval supremacy ended on March 9, 1862, when the Confederate ironclad vessel *Virginia* (originally the U.S.S. *Merrimack*) was driven back by the *Monitor*, an armored and turreted Union gunship.

Successes around the edges of the Confederacy did not relieve northern frustration at the inactivity or failure of Union forces on the eastern front. Finally, at Lincoln's insistence, McClellan started toward Richmond. He moved his forces by water to the peninsula southeast of the Confederate capital and began his march toward Richmond in early April 1862. By late May, his forces had pushed to within twenty miles of Richmond. There he stopped, awaiting the additional troops that he expected Lincoln to send.

These reinforcements were not forthcoming because the president felt that they were needed to defend Washington. While McClellan was inching his way up the peninsula, a relatively small southern force under General Thomas J. "Stonewall" Jackson was on the rampage in the Shenandoah valley. When it appeared by late May that Jackson might be

247

Adjusting to Total War

poised to march east and attack the Union capital, Lincoln decided to withhold troops from McClellan.

If McClellan had moved more boldly and decisively, he probably could have captured Richmond with the forces he had. But a combination of faulty intelligence reports and his own natural caution led him to falter in the face of what he wrongly believed to be superior numbers. At the end of May, the Confederates under Joseph E. Johnston took the offensive when they discovered that McClellan's army was divided on either side of the Chickahominy River. In the battle of Seven Pines, McClellan was barely able to withstand the assault. During the battle, General Johnston was severely wounded; succeeding him in command of the Confederate Army of Northern Virginia was native Virginian and West Point graduate Robert E. Lee.

Toward the end of June, Lee began an all-out effort to expel McClellan from the outskirts of Richmond. In a series of battles that lasted seven days, the two armies clawed at each other indecisively. Nevertheless, McClellan decided to retreat down the peninsula to a more secure base. This backward step convinced Lincoln that the peninsula campaign was an exercise in futility.

On July 11 Lincoln appointed General Henry W. Halleck to be the new general in chief and through him ordered McClellan to withdraw his army from the peninsula to join a force under General John Pope that was preparing to move on Richmond by an overland route. Before the ever cautious McClellan could reach Pope, however, the Confederates attacked the overland army near Bull Run. In a battle superbly commanded by Lee, Pope was forced to retreat to Washington, where he was stripped of his command.

Lee proceeded to lead his exuberant troops on an invasion of Maryland, in the hope of isolating Washington from the rest of the North. McClellan caught up with him at Antietam, near Sharpsburg, and the bloodiest one-day battle of the war ensued. The result was a draw, but Lee was forced to fall back south of the Potomac. McClellan was slow in pursuit, and Lincoln blamed him for letting the enemy escape.

Convinced that McClellan was fatally infected with "the slows," Lincoln once again sought a more aggressive general and put Ambrose E. Burnside in command of the Army of the Potomac. Aggressive but rather dense, Burnside's limitations were disastrously revealed at the battle of Fredericksburg, Virginia, on December 13, 1862, when he launched a deadly charge against a Confederate uphill position. The range and accuracy of small arms fire made such a charge utter folly. Thus ended a year of bitter failure for the North on the eastern front.

The Diplomatic Struggle

The critical period of Civil War diplomacy was 1861–1862, when the South was making every effort to induce major foreign powers to recognize its independence and break the Union blockade. The hope that England and France could be persuaded to involve themselves in the war on the Confederate side stemmed from the fact that these nations depended on the South for three-quarters of their cotton supply.

The Confederate commissioners sent to England and France in May 1861 succeeded in gaining recognition of southern "belligerency," which meant that the new government could claim some of the international rights of a nation at war, such as purchasing and outfitting privateers in neutral ports. As a result, Confederate raiders, built and armed in British shipyards, devastated northern shipping to such an extent that insurance costs eventually forced most of the American merchant marine off the high seas for the duration of the war.

In the fall of 1861 the Confederate government dispatched James M. Mason and John Slidell to be its permanent envoys to England and France respectively and instructed them to push for full recognition of the Confederacy. They took passage on the British steamer *Trent*, which was stopped and boarded in international waters by a United States warship. Mason and Slidell were taken into custody by the Union captain, causing a diplomatic crisis that nearly led to war between England and the United States. After several weeks of international tension, Lincoln and Secretary of State William H. Seward made the prudent decision to allow the Confederates to proceed to their destinations.

These envoys may as well have stayed at home; they failed in their mission to obtain full recognition of the Confederacy from either England or France. The anticipated cotton shortage was slow to develop, for the bumper crop of 1860 had created a large surplus in British and French warehouses. For a time in the fall of 1862, French ruler Napoleon III toyed with the idea of recognition, but he refused to act without British support. British leaders feared that recognition would lead to a war with the United States; the American minister to Great Britain, Charles Francis Adams, knew well how to play on those fears. Only if the South won decisively on the battlefield, would Britain be willing to risk the dangers of recognition and intervention.

The cotton famine finally hit in late 1862, causing massive unemployment in the British textile industry. But, contrary to southern hopes, public opinion did not force the government to abandon its neutrality and use force to break the Union blockade. Influential interest groups, which actually benefited from the famine, provided the crucial support for continuing a policy of nonintervention. Among these groups were owners of large cotton mills who had made bonanza profits on their existing stocks and were happy to see weaker competitors go under while they awaited new sources of supply. By early 1863 cotton from Egypt and India put the industry back on the track toward full production. Other obvious beneficiaries of nonintervention were manufacturers of wool and linen textiles, munition-makers who supplied both sides, and shipping interests who profited from the decline of American competition on the world's sea lanes. Since the British economy as a whole gained more than it lost from neutrality, it is not surprising that there was little effective pressure for a change in policy.

By early 1863, when it was clear that "King Cotton Diplomacy" had failed, the Confederacy broke off formal relations with Great Britain. For the European powers, the advantages of getting involved in the conflict were not worth the risk of a war with the United States. Independence for the South would have to be won on the battlefield.

Fight to the Finish

The last two and a half years of the struggle saw the implementation of more radical war measures. The most dramatic and important of these was the North's effort to follow through on Lincoln's decision to free the slaves and bring the black population into the war on the Union side. The tide of battle turned in the summer of 1863, but the South continued to resist valiantly for two more years, until finally overcome by the sheer weight of the North's advantages in manpower and resources.

The Coming of Emancipation

At the beginning of the war, when the North still hoped for a quick and easy victory, only dedicated abolitionists favored turning the struggle for the Union into a crusade against slavery. But as it became clear how hard it was going to be to subdue the "rebels," congressional and public sentiment developed for striking a fatal blow at the South's economic and social system by freeing its slaves.

Although Lincoln favored freedom for blacks as an ultimate goal, he was reluctant to commit his administration to a policy of immediate emancipation. In the fall of 1861 and again in the spring of 1862, he disallowed the orders of field commanders who sought to free slaves in areas occupied by their forces, thus angering the strongly antislavery Republicans known as "Radicals." Lincoln's caution stemmed from an effort to avoid alienating Unionist elements in the border slave states and from his own preference for a gradual, compensated form of emancipation.

Lincoln was also aware that one of the main obstacles to any program leading to emancipation was the strong racial prejudices of most whites in the North and the South. Since he was pessimistic about the prospects of equality for blacks in the United States, Lincoln coupled his moderate proposals with a plea for government subsidies to support the voluntary "colonization" of free blacks outside the United States, and he actively sought places that would accept them.

But the slaveholding states that remained loyal to the Union refused to endorse Lincoln's gradual plan, and the failure of Union arms in the spring and summer of 1862 increased the public clamor for striking directly at the South's peculiar institution. Responding to political pressure, on September 22, 1862, Lincoln issued his preliminary Emancipation Proclamation. Had he failed to act, he would have split the Republican party, most of whose members favored emancipation. The proclamation gave the Confederate states one hundred days to give up the struggle without losing their slaves.

When there was no response from the South and no enthusiasm in Congress for Lincoln's gradual, compensated plan, the president on January 1, 1863, declared that all slaves in those areas under Confederate control "shall be . . . thenceforward, and forever free." He justified the final proclamation as an act of "military necessity" sanctioned by the war powers of the president and authorized the enlistment of freed slaves in the Union army. The language and tone of the document had "all the grandeur of a bill of lading," and made it clear that blacks were being freed for reasons of state and not out of humanitarian conviction.

Despite its uninspiring origin and limited application—it did not extend to loyal slave states or occupied areas—the proclamation did enunciate the abolition of slavery as a war aim. It also accelerated the breakdown of slavery as a labor system. As word spread among the slaves that emancipation was now official policy, larger numbers of them were inspired to run off and seek the protection of approaching northern armies. Approximately one-quarter of the slave population gained freedom during the war under the terms of the Emancipation Proclamation and thus deprived the South of an important part of its agricultural work force.

The Black Role in the War

Almost 200,000 Afro-Americans, most of them newly freed slaves, eventually served in the Union armed forces and made a vital contribution to the North's victory. Although they were enrolled in segregated units under white officers, initially paid less than their white counterparts, and used disproportionately for garrison duty or heavy labor behind the lines, "blacks in blue" fought heroically in several major battles during the last two years of the war.

Wartime freed slaves who avoided military service were often conscripted to serve as contract wage laborers on cotton plantations owned or leased by "loyal" white planters within the occupied areas of the Deep South. Abolitionists protested that the coercion used by military authorities to get blacks back into the cotton fields amounted to slavery in a new form, but those in power argued that the necessities of war and the northern economy required such "temporary" arrangements. To some extent, regimentation of the freedmen within the South was a way of assuring racially prejudiced Northerners that emancipation would not result in an influx of black refugees to their region of the country.

The heroic performance of Afro-American troops and the easing of northern anxieties about massive black migration led to a deepening commitment to emancipation as a permanent and comprehensive policy. Realizing that his proclamation had a shaky constitutional foundation, Lincoln pressed for a Constitutional amendment outlawing involuntary servitude. After supporting its inclusion as a central plank in the Republican platform of 1864, Lincoln used all his influence to win congressional approval for the new Thirteenth Amendment. The cause of freedom for blacks

■ *The 54th Massachusetts Colored Regiment charging Fort Wagner, South Carolina, July 1863. The 54th was the first black unit recruited during the war. Charles and Lewis Douglass, sons of abolitionist Frederick Douglass, both served with this regiment.*

and the cause of the Union had at last become one and the same. Lincoln, despite his earlier hesitations and misgivings, had earned the right to go down in history as "the great emancipator."

The Tide Turns

By early 1863 the Confederate economy was in shambles, and its diplomacy had collapsed. The social order of the South was also showing signs of severe strain. Masters were losing control of their slaves, and nonslaveholding whites were becoming disillusioned with the hardships of a war that some of them described as a "rich man's war and a poor man's fight." Yet the North was slow to capitalize on the South's internal weaknesses; it had its own serious morale problems. The long series of defeats on the eastern front had engendered war weariness, and the new policies that "military necessity" forced the government to adopt encountered fierce opposition.

Although popular with Republicans, emancipation was viewed by most Democrats as a betrayal of northern war aims. Racism was a main ingredient in their opposition to freeing blacks. Especially in the Midwest, Democrats used the backlash against the proclamation to win political support. The Enrollment Act of March 1863, which provided for outright conscription, provoked a violent response from those unwilling to "fight for the niggers" and too poor to buy exemption from the draft. A series of antidraft riots culminated in the bloodiest domestic disorder in American history—the New York riot of July 1863. A New York mob, composed mainly of Irish-American laborers, burned the draft office, the homes of leading Republicans, and an orphanage for black children. At least 120 people died before federal troops restored order.

To fight dissension and "disloyalty," the government used its martial law authority to arrest the alleged ringleaders. Patriotic private organizations also issued a barrage of propaganda aimed at what they believed was a vast secret conspiracy to undermine the northern war effort. Historians disagree about the real extent of covert and illegal antiwar activity, but militant advocates of "peace at any price"— popularly known as Copperheads—were certainly active in some areas, especially among the immigrant working classes of large cities and in southern Ohio, Indiana, and Illinois.

The only effective way to overcome the disillusionment that fed the peace movement was to start winning battles and thus convince the northern public that victory was assured. But before this could happen the North suffered one more humiliating defeat on the eastern front. In early May 1863, Union forces under General Joseph Hooker were routed at Chancellorsville, Virginia, by a much smaller Confederate army masterfully led by Robert E. Lee.

In the West, however, a major Union triumph was taking shape. For over a year, General Ulysses S. Grant had been trying to put his forces in position to capture Vicksburg, Mississippi, the almost inaccessible Confederate bastion that stood between the North and control of the Mississippi River. Finally, in late March 1863, he crossed the river north of the city and moved his forces to a point south of it, where he joined up with naval forces that had run the Confederate batteries mounted on Vicksburg's high bluffs. In one of the boldest campaigns of the war, Grant crossed the river, deliberately cutting himself off from his sources of supply, and marched into the interior of Mississippi. Living off the land and out of communication with an anxious and perplexed Lincoln, his troops won a series of victories and advanced on Vicksburg from the east. After unsuccessfully assaulting the city's defenses, Grant settled down for a siege on May 22.

In an effort to turn the tide of the war, President Davis approved Robert E. Lee's plan for an all-out invasion of the Northeast. Although this plan provided no hope for relieving Vicksburg, it might lead to a dramatic victory that would more than compensate for loss of the Mississippi stronghold. Lee's army crossed the Potomac in June and kept going until it reached Gettysburg, Pennsylvania. There Lee confronted a Union army that had taken up strong defensive positions on Cemetery Ridge and Culp's Hill.

On July 2 a series of Confederate attacks failed to dislodge General George Meade's troops from the high ground they occupied. The following day Lee faced the choice of retreating to protect his lines of communication or launching a final, desperate assault. With more boldness than wisdom, he chose to make a direct attack on the strongest part of the Union line. The resulting charge on Cemetery Ridge was disastrous; advancing Confederate soldiers dropped like flies under the barrage of Union artillery and rifle fire.

Retreat was now inevitable, and Lee withdrew his battered troops to the Potomac, only to find that the river was at flood stage and could not be crossed for several days. For some reason, Meade failed to follow up his victory with a vigorous pursuit, and Lee was allowed to escape a trap that could have resulted in his annihilation. Vicksburg fell to Grant on July 4, the same day that Lee began his withdrawal, and Northerners rejoiced at the twin Independence Day victories. The Union had secured control of the Mississippi and had at last won a major battle in the East. But Lincoln's joy turned to frustration when he learned that his generals had missed the chance to capture Lee's army and bring a quick end to the war.

Last Stages of the Conflict

Later in 1863 the North finally gained control of the middle South, an area where indecisive fighting had been going on since the beginning of the conflict. The main Union target was Chattanooga, "the gateway to the Southeast." In September Union forces maneuvered the Confederates out of the city but were in turn eventually surrounded and besieged there by southern forces. After Grant arrived from Vicksburg to take command, the encirclement was broken by daring assaults upon the Con-

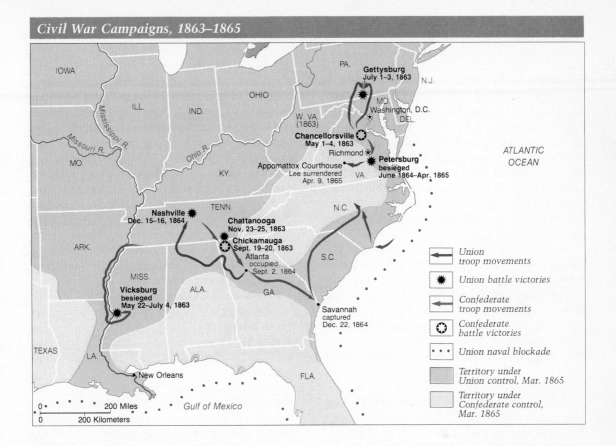

Union troop movements

Union battle victories

Confederate troop movements

Confederate battle victories

Union naval blockade

Territory under Union control, Mar. 1865

Territory under Confederate control, Mar. 1865

federate positions on Lookout Mountain and Missionary Ridge. As a result of its success in the battle of Chattanooga, the North was poised for an invasion of Georgia.

Grant's victories in the West earned him promotion to general in chief of all the Union armies. After assuming that position in March 1864, he ordered a multipronged offensive to finish off the Confederacy. The main movements were a march on Richmond under his personal command and a thrust by the western armies, now led by General William T. Sherman, in the direction of Atlanta and the heart of Georgia.

In May and early June, Grant and Lee fought a series of bloody battles in northern Virginia that tended to follow a set pattern. Lee would take up an entrenched position in the path of the invading force, and Grant would attack it, sustaining heavy losses but also inflicting cas-

ualties that the shrinking Confederate army could ill afford. When his direct assault had failed, Grant would move to his left, hoping in vain to maneuver Lee into a less defensible position. After losing about 60,000 men, Grant decided to change his tactics and moved his army to the south of Richmond. There he drew up before Petersburg, a rail center that linked Richmond to the rest of the Confederacy; after failing to take it by assault, he settled down for a siege.

The siege of Petersburg was a long-drawn-out affair, and the resulting stalemate in the East caused northern morale to plummet during the summer of 1864. Lincoln was facing reelection, and his failure to end the war dimmed his prospects. Although nominated with ease in June, Lincoln confronted growing opposition within his own party, especially from radicals who disagreed with his apparently lenient approach to the future restoration of seceded states to the Union.

The Democrats seemed in a good position to capitalize on Republican divisions and make a strong bid for the White House. Their platform appealed to war weariness by calling for a cease-fire followed by negotiations to reestablish the Union. The party's nominee, General George McClellan, announced that he would not be bound by the peace plank and would pursue the war. But he promised to end the conflict soon because he would not insist on emancipation as a condition for reconstruction. By late summer Lincoln believed he would probably be defeated.

Northern military successes changed the political outlook. Sherman's invasion of Georgia went well. On September 2, Atlanta fell, and northern forces occupied the hub of the Deep South. The news unified the Republican party behind Lincoln. The election in November was almost an anticlimax; Lincoln won 212 of a possible 233 electoral votes and 55 percent of the popular vote. The Republican cause of "liberty and Union" was secure.

The concluding military operations revealed the futility of further southern resistance. Sherman marched almost unopposed through Georgia to the sea, destroying nearly everything of possible military or economic value in a corridor 300 miles long and 60 miles wide. The Confederate army that had opposed him at Atlanta moved northward into Tennessee, where it was defeated and almost destroyed by Union forces at Nashville in mid-December. Sherman captured Savannah on December 22. He then turned north and marched through the Carolinas, intending to join up with Grant at Petersburg.

While Sherman was tearing up the Carolinas, Grant finally ended the stalemate at Petersburg. When Lee's starving and exhausted army tried to break through the Union lines, Grant renewed his attack and forced the Confederates to abandon Petersburg and Richmond on April 2, 1865. A week later, Lee recognized that further fighting was pointless and surrendered his army at Appomattox Courthouse on April 9.

But the joy of the victorious North turned to sorrow and anger when actor John Wilkes Booth assassinated Abraham Lincoln at Ford's Theater in Washington on April 14. Although Booth had a few accomplices, popular theories that the assassination was the result of a vast conspiracy involving Confederate leaders or (according to another version) Radical Republicans have never been substantiated and are extremely implausible. The man who had spoken at Gettysburg of the need to sacrifice for the Union cause had himself given "the last full measure of devotion." Four days after Lincoln's death the only remaining Confederate force of any significance, the troops under Joseph E. Johnston who had been opposing Sherman in North Carolina, laid down their arms. The Union was saved.

Effects of the War

The nation that emerged from four years of total war was not the same America that had split apart in 1861. The war had claimed nearly 640,000 young men, and the widows and sweethearts they left behind temporarily increased the proportion of unmarried women in the population. Some members of this generation of involuntary "spinsters" sought new opportunities for making a living or serving the community that went beyond the purely domestic roles previously prescribed for women.

At enormous human and economic cost, the nation had emancipated 4 million Afro-Americans from slavery, but it had not yet resolved that they should be equal citizens. At the time of Lincoln's assassination, most northern states still denied blacks equality under the law and the right to vote. Whether the North would extend more rights to southern freedmen than it had granted to its own "free Negroes" was an open question.

The impact of the war on white working people was also unclear. Those in the industrializing parts of the North had suffered and lost ground economically because prices had risen much faster than wages during the conflict. But Republican rhetoric stressing "equal opportunity" and the "dignity of labor" raised hopes that the crusade against slavery could be broadened into a movement to improve the lot of working people in general. Foreign-born workers had additional reason to be optimistic; the fact that so many immigrants had fought and died for the Union cause had—for the moment—weakened nativist sentiment and encouraged ethnic tolerance.

What the war definitely decided was that the federal government was supreme over the states and had a broad grant of constitutional authority to act on matters affecting "the general welfare." The southern principle of state sovereignty and strict construction died at Appomattox, and the United States was on its way to becoming a true nation-state with an effective central government. Although the states retained many powers and the Constitution placed limits on what the national government could do, the war ended all questions about where ultimate authority rested.

A broadened definition of federal powers had its greatest impact in the realm of economic policy. During the war, Republican-dominated Congresses passed a rash of legislation designed to give encouragement and direction to the nation's economic development. Taking advantage of the absence of southern opposition, Republicans rejected the pre-Civil War tradition of laissez-faire and enacted a Whiggish program of active support for business and agriculture. In 1862 Congress passed a high protective tariff, approved a homestead act intended to encourage settlement of the West by providing free land to settlers, granted huge tracts of public land to railroad companies to support the building of a transcontinental railroad, and gave the states land for the establishment of agricultural colleges. The following year, Congress set up a national banking system. The notes that the national banks issued became the country's first standardized and reliable circulating currency.

These wartime achievements added up to a decisive and permanent shift in the relationship between the federal government and private enterprise. The Republicans took a limited government that did little more than seek

Chronology

1860 South Carolina secedes from the Union (December)

1861 Rest of Deep South secedes: Confederacy is founded (January–February)
Fort Sumter is fired upon and surrenders to Confederate forces (April)
Upper South secedes (April–May)
South wins first battle of Bull Run (July)

1862 Grant captures Forts Henry and Donelson (February)
Farragut captures New Orleans for the Union (April)
McClellan leads unsuccessful campaign on the peninsula southeast of Richmond (March–July)
South wins second battle of Bull Run (August)
McClellan stops Lee at battle of Antietam (September)
Lincoln issues preliminary Emancipation Proclamation (September)
Lee defeats Union army at Fredericksburg (December)

1863 Lincoln issues final Emancipation Proclamation (January)
Lee is victorious at Chancellorsville (May)
North gains major victories at Gettysburg and Vicksburg (July)
Grant defeats Confederate forces at Chattanooga (November)

1864 Grant and Lee battle in northern Virginia (May–June)
Atlanta falls to Sherman (September)
Lincoln is reelected president, defeating McClellan (November)
Sherman marches through Georgia (November–December)

1865 Congress passes Thirteenth Amendment abolishing slavery (January)
Grant captures Petersburg and Richmond
Lee surrenders at Appomattox (April)
Lincoln assassinated by John Wilkes Booth (April)
Remaining Confederate forces surrender (April–May)

to protect the marketplace from the threat of monopoly and changed it into an activist state that promoted and subsidized the efforts of the economically industrious and ambitious.

The most pervasive effect of the war on northern society was to encourage an "organizational revolution." Aided by government policies, venturesome businessmen took advantage of the new national market created by military procurement to build larger firms that could operate across state lines; some of the huge corporate enterprises of the post-war era began to take shape. Philanthropists also developed more effective national associations. Both the men who served in the army and those men and women who supported them on the home front became accustomed to working in large, bureaucratic organizations of a kind that had scarcely existed before the war. The result was that an individualistic society of small producers began to be transformed into the more highly organized and "incorporated" America that would emerge during the Gilded Age.

Recommended Reading

Two general surveys of the Civil War era stand out among the vast number that have been published: J. G. Randall and David Donald, *The Civil War and Reconstruction*, 2nd ed. (1969), and James M. McPherson, *Ordeal by Fire: The Civil War and Reconstruction* (1981). An excellent shorter account is David Herbert Donald, *Liberty and Union* (1978). The best one-volume introduction to the military side of the conflict is Bruce Catton, *This Hallowed Ground* (1956). A brilliant study of the writings of those who experienced the war is Edmund Wilson, *Patriotic Gore: Studies in the Literature of the American Civil War* (1962).

For detailed accounts of the war, see Allan Nevins, *The War for the Union*, 4 vols. (1959–1971), and Bruce Catton, *Centennial History of the Civil War*, 3 vols. (1961–1965). The Confederate experience is well covered in Clement Eaton, *A History of the Southern Confederacy* (1954); Emory M. Thomas, *The Confederate Nation: 1861–1865* (1979); and Frank E. Vandiver, *Their Tattered Flags: The Epic of the Confederacy* (1970).

Lincoln's career and wartime leadership are treated in two excellent biographies: Benjamin P. Thomas, *Abraham Lincoln* (1954) and Stephen B.

Oates, *With Malice Toward None: The Life of Abraham Lincoln* (1977). The most detailed works on Lincoln's stewardship of the Union cause are James G. Randall, *Lincoln the President*, 4 vols. (1945–1955, vol. 4 completed by Richard N. Current), and Carl Sandburg's less reliable *Abraham Lincoln: The War Years*, 4 vols. (1939).

Events leading up to the outbreak of hostilities are covered in Kenneth M. Stampp, *And the War Came: The North and the Sectional Crisis* (1950), and David M. Potter, *Lincoln and His Party in the Secession Crisis*, 2nd ed. (1962). The literature on military commanders, campaigns, and battles is enormous, but mention must be made of Douglas Southall Freeman's outstanding works on southern generalship: *R. E. Lee: A Biography*, 4 vols. (1934–1935), and *Lee Lieutenants*, 3 vols. (1942–1944). On the common soldier's experience of the war, see two books by Bell I. Wiley: *The Life of Johnny Reb* (1943) and *The Life of Billy Yank* (1952).

Major works on northern politics during the war include Hans Trefousse, *The Radical Republicans: Lincoln's Vanguard for Racial Justice* (1969); David Donald, *Charles Sumner and the Rights of Man* (1970); and Joel Sibley, *A Respectable Minority: The Democratic Party in the Civil War Era* (1977). On legal and constitutional issues, see James G. Randall, *Constitutional Problems under Lincoln*, rev. ed. (1961), and Harold M. Hyman, *A More Perfect Union: The Impact of the Civil War and Reconstruction on the Constitution* (1973).

On the cultural impact of the war, see George M. Fredrickson, *The Inner Civil War: Northern Intellectuals and the Crisis of the Union* (1965); Daniel Aaron, *The Unwritten War: American Writers and the Civil War* (1973); and James H. Morehead, *American Apocalypse: Yankee Protestants and the Civil War* (1978).

For an understanding of the South's internal problems, see Frank Owsley, *States Rights in the Confederacy* (1925); Curtis A. Amlund, *Federalism in the Southern Confederacy* (1966); and Bell I. Wiley, *The Plain People and the Confederacy* (1934).

Emancipation and the role of blacks in the war are the subject of a number of excellent studies, including Benjamin Quarles, *The Negro in the Civil War* (1953) and *Lincoln and the Negro* (1962); Bell I. Wiley, *Southern Negroes, 1861–1865* (1938); James M. McPherson, *The Struggle for Equality: Abolitionists and the Negro in the Civil War and Reconstruction* (1964); LaWanda Cox, *Lincoln and Black Freedom* (1981); Willie Lee Rose, *Rehearsal for Reconstruction: The Port Royal Experiment* (1964); and Herman Belz, *A New Birth of Freedom: The Republican Party and Freedmen's Rights, 1861–1866* (1976).

chapter 16

THE
AGONY OF
RECONSTRUCTION

D.W. Griffith's *Birth of a Nation* (1915), an early epic film about the Civil War and Reconstruction, presents a simplistic interpretation of that period. The villains are vindictive northern politicians, corrupt carpetbaggers, and ignorant ex-slaves lusting both for power over their former masters and the sexual conquest of white women.

Lincoln is depicted as a wise statesman who would have spared the South the horrors of black rule had not his assassination given power to a vengeful Republican congressman, meant to represent Thaddeus Stevens. Under the urging of his mulatto mistress, the congressman hatches a devilish plot to oppress and humiliate the white South. The fruits of this scheme are revealed in a scene portraying the South Carolina state legislature as a mob of grinning, barefooted blacks.

The melodramatic plot features two climactic episodes. In the first a southern maiden throws herself from a cliff to escape the embraces of a "renegade Negro," and in the second the Ku Klux Klan rescues the daughter of a northern Republican from a forced marriage with a mulatto politician. The message is unmistakable—the Klan saved the South and white civilization from a fate worse than death.

The picture of Reconstruction presented in *Birth of a Nation* developed from the image projected by the southern leaders who had overthrown Radical rule in the 1870s and then proceeded to put blacks "in their place" by stripping them of rights supposedly guaranteed by the Fourteenth and Fifteenth Amendments. Over the next forty years many Northerners became persuaded that their forebears made a terrible mistake in trying to enforce equal rights for blacks after the Civil War.

From the 1890s to the 1940s, most professional historians subscribed to this view. They described Reconstruction as a "tragic era" when misguided or opportunistic northern politicians had enfranchised a black population obviously unfit for citizenship. Although such black scholars as W.E.B. DuBois disagreed vehemently with the view as early as the 1930s, it was not until the 1950s and 1960s that the majority of Reconstruction historians rejected the exaggerations, distortions, and racist assumptions of this image.

Retelling the story of Reconstruction from a modern perspective does not require setting up a new myth of saintly Radical Republicans, model black officeholders, and totally vicious southern whites to replace the stereotypes in *Birth of a Nation*. Mixed motives, hypocrisy, blunders, and corruption were important aspects of the complex drama that unfolded between the end of the Civil War and the final collapse of Reconstruction in 1877. But there was another side, involving the heroic struggle of blacks and their white allies to achieve racial justice and equality against overwhelming odds. The tragedy of Reconstruction was not that it was wrong but that it failed.

The President Versus Congress

The problem of how to reconstruct the Union in the wake of the South's military defeat was one of the most difficult challenges ever faced by American policymakers. The Constitution provided no firm guidelines, and once emancipation became a northern war aim, the problem was compounded by a new issue: How far should the federal government go to secure freedom and civil rights for 4 million former slaves?

The debate that evolved led to a major political crisis. Advocates of a minimal Reconstruction policy favored quick restoration of the Union with no protection for the freed slaves beyond the prohibition of slavery. Proponents of a more radical policy wanted readmission of the southern states to be dependent on guarantees that "loyal" men would replace the Confederate elite and that blacks would acquire some of the basic rights of American citizenship. The White House favored the minimal approach, while Congress came to endorse the more radical policy. The resulting struggle between Congress and the chief executive was the most serious clash between two branches of government in the nation's history.

Wartime Reconstruction

Tension between the president and Congress over how to reconstruct the Union began during the war. Although Lincoln did not set forth a final and comprehensive plan, he did indicate that he favored a lenient and conciliatory policy toward Southerners who would give up the struggle and repudiate slavery. In December 1863 he offered a full pardon to all Southerners (with the exception of certain classes of Confederate leaders) who would take an oath of allegiance to the Union and acknowledge the legality of emancipation. Once 10 percent or more of the voting population of any occupied state had taken the oath, they were authorized to set up a loyal government. By 1864 Louisiana and Arkansas had established fully functioning Unionist governments.

Lincoln's policy was meant to shorten the war by offering a moderate peace plan. It was also intended to further his emancipation policy by insisting that the new governments abolish slavery. When constitutional conventions operating under the 10 percent plan in Louisiana and Arkansas dutifully abolished slavery in 1864, emancipation came closer to being irreversible.

But Congress was unhappy with the president's reconstruction experiments and in 1864 refused to seat the Unionists elected to the House and Senate from Louisiana and Arkansas. A minority of congressional Republicans— the strongly antislavery Radicals—favored strong protection for black civil rights and provision for their enfranchisement as a precondition for the readmission of southern states. A larger group of moderates also opposed Lincoln's plan, but they did so primarily because they did not trust the repentant Confederates who would play a major role in the new governments.

Also disturbing Congress was a sense that the president was exceeding his authority by using executive powers to restore the Union. Lincoln operated on the theory that secession, being illegal, did not place the Confederate states outside the Union in a constitutional sense. Since individuals and not states had defied federal authority, the president could use his pardoning power to certify a loyal electorate, which could then function as the legitimate state government. The dominant view in Congress, however, was that the southern states had definitely withdrawn from the Union and that it was up to Congress to decide when and how they would be readmitted.

After refusing to recognize Lincoln's 10 percent governments, Congress passed a Reconstruction bill of its own in July 1864. Known as the Wade-Davis bill, this legislation required that 50 percent of the voters must take an oath of future loyalty before the restoration process could begin. Once this had occurred, those who could swear that they had never willingly supported the Confederacy could vote in an election for delegates to a constitutional convention. Lincoln exercised a pocket veto by refusing to sign the bill before Congress adjourned, angering many Congressmen.

Congress and the president remained stalemated on the Reconstruction issue for the rest of the war. During his last months in office, however, Lincoln showed a willingness to compromise. But he died without clarifying his intentions, leaving historians to speculate on whether his quarrel with Congress would have worsened or been resolved. Given Lincoln's past record of political flexibility, the best bet is that he would have come to terms with the majority of his party.

Andrew Johnson at the Helm

Andrew Johnson, the man suddenly made president by an assassin's bullet, attempted to put the Union back together on his own authority in 1865. But his policies eventually put him at odds with Congress and the Republican party and provoked a serious internal crisis in the system of checks and balances among the branches of the federal government.

Johnson's approach to Reconstruction was shaped by his background. Born in dire poverty in North Carolina, he migrated as a young man to eastern Tennessee where he made his living as a tailor. Although poorly educated, he was an effective stump speaker who railed against

■ *Nearly insurmountable problems with a Congress determined to enact its own Reconstruction policy plagued Andrew Johnson through his presidency. Impeached in 1868, he escaped conviction by a single vote.*

the planter aristocracy. A Jacksonian Democrat, he became the political spokesman for Tennessee's nonslaveholding whites. He advanced from state legislator to congressman to governor and in 1857 was elected to the United States Senate.

When Tennessee seceded in 1861, Johnson was the only senator from a Confederate state who remained loyal to the Union and continued to serve in Washington. But his Unionism did not include antislavery sentiments or friendship for blacks. He wished that "every head of family in the United States had one slave to take the drudgery and menial service off his family."

During the war, while acting as military governor of Tennessee, Johnson implemented Lincoln's emancipation policy as a means of destroying the power of the hated planter class rather than as a recognition of black humanity. He was chosen as Lincoln's running mate in

1864 in order to broaden the appeal of the ticket. No one expected that this southern Democrat and fervent white supremacist would ever become president.

Some Radical Republicans initially welcomed Johnson's ascent to the nation's highest office. Like the Radicals themselves, he was loyal to the Union and believed that ex-Confederates should be severely treated. He seemed more likely than Lincoln to punish southern "traitors" and prevent them from regaining political influence. Only gradually did Johnson and the Republican majority in Congress drift apart.

The Reconstruction policy that Johnson initiated on May 29, 1865, created some uneasiness among the Radicals, but most other Republicans were willing to give it a chance. Johnson placed North Carolina and eventually other states under appointed provisional governors chosen from among prominent southern politicians who had opposed the secession movement and had rendered no conspicuous service to the confederacy. They were then responsible for calling constitutional conventions to elect "loyal" officeholders. Johnson's plan was especially designed to prevent his longtime adversaries—the planter class—from participating in the reconstruction of southern state governments.

Johnson urged the conventions to declare the ordinances of secession illegal, repudiate the Confederate debt, and ratify the Thirteenth Amendment abolishing slavery. After governments had been reestablished under constitutions meeting these conditions, the president assumed that the process of Reconstruction would be complete and that the ex-Confederate states would regain their full rights under the Constitution.

Many congressional Republicans were troubled by the work of the southern conventions, which balked at fully implementing Johnson's recommendations. Furthermore, in no state was even limited black suffrage approved. Johnson, however, seemed eager to give southern white majorities a free hand in determining the civil and political status of freed slaves.

Republican uneasiness turned to disillusionment and anger when the state legislatures elected under the new constitutions proceeded to pass "Black Codes" subjecting the former slaves to a variety of special regulations and restrictions on their freedom. Especially troubling were vagrancy and apprenticeship laws that forced blacks to work and denied them a choice of employers. To Radicals, the Black Codes looked suspiciously like slavery under a new guise.

The growing rift between the president and Congress came into the open in December when the House and Senate refused to seat the recently elected southern delegation. Instead of endorsing Johnson's work and recognizing the state governments he had called into being, Congress established a joint committee, chaired by William Pitt Fessenden of Maine, to review Reconstruction policy and set further conditions for readmission of the seceded states.

Congress Takes the Initiative

The struggle over how to reconstruct the Union ended with Congress doing the job all over again. The clash between Johnson and Congress was a matter of principle and could not be reconciled. Johnson's stubborn and prideful nature did not help his political cause. But the root of the problem was that he disagreed with the majority of Congress on what Reconstruction was supposed to accomplish. An heir of the Democratic states' rights tradition, he wanted to restore the prewar federal system as quickly as possible.

Most Republicans, however, believed that the North would be cheated of the full fruits of victory if the old southern ruling class were to regain regional power and national influence by devising new ways to subjugate blacks. (Since emancipation had nullified the three-fifths clause of the Constitution, all blacks were now to be counted in determining representation. Consequently, the Republicans worried about increased southern strength in Congress and the electoral college.) Congress thus sought a reconstruction policy that would limit the political role of ex-Confederates and provide some protection for black citizenship.

Except for a few extreme Radicals, Republican leaders were not convinced that blacks were inherently equal to whites. They were convinced, however, that all citizens should have the same basic rights and opportunities. Principle coincided easily with political expediency; southern blacks were likely to be loyal to the Republican party that had emancipated them and thus increase that party's political power in the South.

The disagreement between the president and Congress became irreconcilable in early 1866 when Johnson vetoed two bills that had passed with overwhelming Republican support. One, the Freedmen's Bureau Bill, extended the life of the agency charged with providing former slaves with relief, legal help, and educational and employment assistance. The second, a civil rights bill, was intended to nullify the detested Black Codes and guarantee "equal benefit of all laws."

The vetoes shocked moderate Republicans who had expected Johnson to accept these relatively modest measures. Congress promptly passed the Civil Rights Act over Johnson's veto, signifying that the president was now hopelessly at odds with most of the congressmen from what was supposed to be his own party.

Johnson soon revealed that he intended to abandon the Republicans and place himself at the head of a new conservative party uniting the small minority of Republicans who supported him with a reviving Democratic party that was rallying behind his Reconstruction policy. As the elections of 1866 neared, Johnson stepped up his criticism of Congress.

Meanwhile, the Republican majority on Capitol Hill passed the Fourteenth Amendment. This, the most important of our constitutional amendments, gave the federal government responsibility for guaranteeing equal rights under the law to all Americans. The major section defined national citizenship for the first time as extending to "all persons born

■ *The First Reconstruction Act, passed in 1867, was based on the false assumption that once blacks had the vote, they would be able to protect themselves from whites who tried to deny them their rights.*

or naturalized in the United States." The states were prohibited from abridging the rights of American citizens and could not "deprive any person life, liberty, or property, without due process of law; nor deny to any person . . . equal protection of the laws." The amendment was sent to the states with an implied understanding that Southerners would be readmitted to Congress only if their states ratified it.

The congressional elections of 1866 served as a referendum on the Fourteenth Amendment. With the support of Johnson, all the southern states except Tennessee rejected the amendment. But bloody race riots in Memphis and New Orleans and maltreatment of blacks throughout the South made it painfully clear that southern state governments were failing abysmally to protect the "life, liberty, or property" of the ex-slaves.

Johnson further weakened his cause by taking the stump on behalf of candidates who supported his policies. His undignified speeches and his inflexibility enraged northern voters.

The Republican majority in Congress increased to a solid two thirds in both houses, and the radical wing of the party gained strength at the expense of moderates and conservatives.

Congressional Reconstruction Plan Enacted

Congress was now in a position to implement its own plan of Reconstruction. In 1867 it passed a series of acts that reorganized the South on a new basis. Generally referred to as "Radical Reconstruction," these measures actually represented a compromise between genuine Radicals and the more moderate elements within the party.

Consistent Radicals, such as Charles Sumner of Massachusetts and Thaddeus Stevens of Pennsylvania, wanted to shape southern society before readmitting ex-Confederates to the Union. Their program required an extended period of military rule, confiscation and redistribution of large landholdings among freedmen, and federal aid for schools that would educate blacks for citizenship. But the majority of Republican congressmen found such a program unacceptable because it broke with American traditions of federalism and regard for property rights.

The First Reconstruction Act, passed over Johnson's veto on March 2, 1867, did place the South under military rule—but only for a short period. The act opened the way for the readmission of any state that framed and ratified a new constitution providing for black suffrage. Since blacks (but not ex-Confederates) were allowed to participate in this process, Republi-

Reconstruction Amendments, 1865–1870

Amendment	Main Provisions	Congressional Passage (⅔ majority in each house required)	Ratification Process (¾ of all states including ex-Confederate states required)
13	Slavery prohibited in United States	January 1865	December 1865 (twenty-seven states, including eight southern states)
14	1. National citizenship extended; federal government given responsibility for guaranteeing equal rights	June 1866	Rejected by twelve southern and border states, February 1867
	2. State representation in Congress reduced proportionally to number of voters disenfranchised		Radicals make readmission of southern states hinge on ratification
			Ratified July 1868
	3. Former Confederates denied right to hold office		
15	Explicit prohibition of denial of franchise because of race, color, or past servitude	February 1869	Ratification required for readmission of Virginia, Texas, Mississippi, Georgia
			Ratified March 1870

cans thought they had found a way to ensure that "loyal men" would dominate the new governments.

"Radical Reconstruction" was based on the false assumption that once blacks had the vote, they would have the power to protect themselves against the efforts of white supremacists to deny them their rights. The Reconstruction Acts thus signaled a retreat from the true Radical position that a sustained use of federal authority was needed to complete the transition from slavery to freedom and prevent the resurgence of the South's old ruling class.

Even so, congressional Reconstruction did have a radical aspect. It strongly endorsed black suffrage. The principle that even the poorest and most underprivileged should have access to the ballot box was a noble and enlightened one. The problem was how to enforce it under conditions then existing in the postwar South.

The Impeachment Crisis

President Johnson was unalterably opposed to the congressional Reconstruction program, and he did everything within his power to prevent its full implementation. Congress responded by passing laws designed to limit presidential authority over Reconstruction matters. One of these measures was the Tenure of Office Act, requiring Senate approval for the firing of cabinet officers and other officials whose appointment had needed the consent of the Senate. Another measure sought to limit Johnson's authority to issue orders to military commanders.

Johnson objected vigorously to these restrictions on the grounds that they violated the constitutional doctrine of the separation of powers. Faced with Johnson's opposition, some congressmen began to call for his impeachment. When Johnson tried to discharge Secretary of War Edwin Stanton—the only Radical in his cabinet—the pro-impeachment forces gained in strength.

In January 1868 Johnson ordered General Grant to take over Stanton's job as head of the War Department. But Grant had his eye on the Republican presidential nomination and refused to defy Congress. Johnson then appointed General Lorenzo Thomas. Faced with this apparent violation of the Tenure of Office Act, the House voted overwhelmingly to impeach the president, and he was placed on trial before the Senate.

Johnson narrowly avoided conviction and removal from office when the impeachment effort fell one vote short of the necessary two thirds. This outcome resulted in part from a skillful defense. Responding to the charge that Johnson had deliberately violated the Tenure of Office Act, the defense contended that the law did not apply to the removal of Stanton because he had been appointed by Lincoln.

The prosecution was more concerned that Johnson had abused the powers of his office in an effort to sabotage the congressional Reconstruction policy. Obstructing the will of the legislative branch, they claimed, was sufficient grounds for conviction. The Republicans who broke ranks to vote for acquittal feared that removal of a president for essentially political reasons would threaten the constitutional balance of powers and open the way to legislative supremacy over the executive.

The impeachment episode helped create an impression in the public mind that the Radicals were ready to turn the Constitution to their own use to gain their objectives. But the evidence of congressional ruthlessness and illegality is not as strong as most historians used to think. Modern legal scholars have found merit in the Radicals' claim that their actions did not violate the Constitution.

The failed impeachment effort was an embarrassment to congressional Republicans, but the episode did ensure that Reconstruction in the South would proceed as the majority in Congress intended. During the trial Johnson helped influence the verdict by pledging to enforce the Reconstruction Acts, and he held to this promise during his remaining months in office.

Reconstruction in the South

The Civil War left the South devastated, demoralized, and destitute. Slavery was dead, but what this meant for future relationships between whites and blacks was still in doubt. Most whites were determined to restrict the freedmen's rights, and many blacks were just as set on achieving real independence. For blacks the acquisition of land, education, and the vote seemed the best means of achieving their goal. The thousands of Northerners who went south after the war for economic or humanitarian reasons hoped to extend Yankee "civilization" to what they viewed as a barbarous region. For most of them this reformation required the aid of the freedmen.

The struggle of these groups to achieve their conflicting goals bred chaos, violence, and instability. It was not the ideal setting for an experiment in interracial democracy. When the federal government's support of reform faltered, the forces of reaction and white supremacy were unleashed.

Social and Economic Adjustments

The Civil War scarred the southern landscape and wrecked its economy. Many plantations were ruined and several major cities—including Atlanta and Richmond—were gutted by fire. Most factories were dismantled or destroyed, and long stretches of railroad were torn up.

Nor was there adequate investment capital for rebuilding. The substantial wealth represented by Confederate currency and bonds had melted away, and emancipation of the slaves had divested the propertied classes of their most valuable and productive assets. According to some estimates, the South's per capita wealth in 1865 was only about half what it had been in 1860.

Recovery could not even begin until a new labor system replaced slavery. The lack of capital hindered the rebuilding of plantations, and most Americans assumed that Southern pros-

perity would depend on plantation grown cotton. In addition, southern whites believed that blacks would work only under compulsion, and freedmen resisted labor conditions that recalled slavery.

Blacks strongly preferred to be small independent farmers rather than plantation laborers. For a time they had reason to hope that the federal government would support their ambitions. Some forty-acre land grants were given by federal authorities to freedmen. By July 1865, 40,000 black farmers were at work on 300,000 acres of what they thought would be their own land.

But the dream of "forty acres and a mule" was not to be realized. Neither President Johnson nor most Congressmen favored an effective program of land confiscation and redistribution. Consequently, the vast majority of blacks in physical possession of small farms failed to acquire title and were left with little or no prospect of becoming landowners.

For most ex-slaves no alternative remained except to return to the white-owned cotton fields. By mid to late 1865 the majority of freedmen had accepted this fate. The most common form of agricultural employment in 1865 and 1866 was a contract labor system. Under this system workers committed themselves for a year in return for fixed wages. Although blacks occasionally received help from the Freedmen's Bureau, more often than not they were worked hard and paid little, and the contracts normally protected the employers more than the employees.

Unhappy with gang labor and constant white supervision, blacks demanded sharecropper status—in other words, the right to work a small piece of land independently in return for a fixed share of the crop produced on it, usually one half. Many landowners accepted this arrangement because it did not require much capital and forced the tenant to share the risks of crop failure or a fall in cotton prices.

Blacks initially viewed sharecropping as a step up from wage labor in the direction of landownership. But during the 1870s this form of tenancy evolved into a new kind of servitude. Croppers had to live on credit until their cotton was sold, and planters or merchants seized the chance to "provision" them at high prices and exorbitant rates of interest. Soon croppers discovered that debts multiplied faster than profits. Furthermore, various methods were eventually devised to bind indebted tenants to a single landlord for extended periods, and a system of virtual peonage resulted.

Blacks in towns and cities found themselves living in an increasingly segregated society. Through legal and illegal methods, they were separated from whites in most public places and often forced to use separate facilities. Most hotels, restaurants, and other privately owned establishments catered only to whites. When black-supported Republican governments came to power in 1868, some of them passed civil rights acts requiring equal access to public facilities, but little effort was made to enforce the legislation. Some forms of racial separation were not openly discriminatory, and blacks accepted and even endorsed them. For the first time, blacks could organize all-black churches, an opportunity that had been denied to them during slavery. They tolerated segregated schools.

The upshot of all forms of racial separation was to create a divided society, one in which blacks and whites lived much of the time in separate worlds. But there were two exceptions to this pattern: One was at work, where blacks necessarily dealt with white employers; the other was in the political sphere, where blacks sought to exercise their rights as citizens of a democracy.

Political Reconstruction in the South

The state governments that emerged in 1865 had little or no regard for the rights of the freed slaves. Some of their codes made black unemployment a crime and limited the rights of blacks to own property or engage in occupations other than those of servant or laborer. Although federal authorities attacked these codes, private violence and discrimination against blacks continued on a massive scale. Hundreds, perhaps thousands, of blacks were murdered by organized terror groups as well as by acts of individual whites in 1865–1866, and few of the perpetrators were brought to justice.

The imposition of military rule in 1867 was designed in part to protect former slaves from violence and intimidation, but the task was beyond the capacity of the few thousand troops stationed in the South. When new constitutions were approved and states readmitted to the Union under the congressional plan in 1868, the problem became more severe. Armed white supremacists used violent terrorism to discourage blacks from voting and to crush the new Republican regimes.

Hastily organized in 1867, the southern Republican party dominated the constitution making of 1868 and the regimes that came out of it. The party was an attempted coalition of three social groups: businessmen seeking aid for economic development, poor white farmers, and blacks. Although all three groups had different goals, their opposition to the old planter ruling class appeared to give them a solid basis for unity.

To be sure, the coalition faced difficulties even within their own ranks. Small farmers of the yeoman class had a bred-in-the-bone resistance to black equality. And conservative businessmen questioned costly measures for the elevation or relief of the lower classes of either race. In some states, astute Democratic politicians exploited these divisions, thus weakening the Republican coalition and opening the way for the overthrow of Radical rule.

But during the relatively brief period when they were in power in the South, the Republicans chalked up some notable achievements. They established (on paper at least) the South's first adequate systems of public education, democratized state and local government, and appropriated funds for an enormous expansion of public services and welfare responsibilities. They also sought to foster economic development by subsidizing the construction of railroads and other internal improvements.

These activities were often accompanied by

■ *This Currier & Ives engraving shows the first black senator (H. R. Revels, Miss.) and first six black representatives (B. S. Turner, Ala.; Robert C. De Large, S.C.; J. T. Wells, Fla.; J. H. Long, Ga.; and J. H. Rainey and R. B. Elliott, S.C.) to serve in the U.S. Congress.*

inefficiency, waste, and corruption. State debts and tax burdens rose enormously, mainly because governments had undertaken heavy new responsibilities, but partly as a result of waste and graft. In short, the radical regimes brought needed reforms to the South, but they were not always model governments.

Southern corruption, however, was not exceptional, nor was it a special result of the extension of suffrage to uneducated blacks, as critics of Radical Reconstruction have claimed. It was part of a national pattern during an era when private interests considered buying government favors a part of the cost of doing business, and many politicians expected to profit by obliging them. The Louisiana governor who pocketed $100,000 in a single year on an $8000 salary was apparently a small-time operator compared to Boss Tweed of New York, whose notorious "Ring" was accused of stealing more than was embezzled in all the southern states combined.

Blacks bore only a limited responsibility for the dishonesty of the Radical governments because they never controlled a state government and held few major offices. The biggest grafters were opportunistic whites—some of the most notorious were carpetbaggers but others were native Southerners. Some black legislators went with the tide and accepted "loans" from those railroad lobbyists who would pay most for their votes, but the same men could usually be depended upon to vote the will of their constituents on civil rights or educational issues. Contrary to myth, the small number of blacks elected to state or national office during Reconstruction demonstrated on the average more integrity and competence than their white counterparts. Most were fairly well educated, having been free Negroes or unusually privileged slaves before the war. Many battled tirelessly to promote the interests of their race. It was unfortunate that Democratic critics of Radical Reconstruction were able to capitalize on racial prejudice and persuade many Americans that "good government" was synonymous with white supremacy.

The Age of Grant

Ulysses S. Grant was the only president between Jackson and Wilson to serve two full and consecutive terms (1869–1877). But unlike other chief executives so favored by for-

The Agony of Reconstruction

tune and the electorate, Grant is commonly regarded as a failure. His administration was riddled with corruption, and his southern policy failed to achieve its goals. Faced with the demands of the presidency, Grant found that he had no strong principles to guide him except loyalty to old friends and politicians. But the problems he faced seemed insoluble. A president with a clearer sense of duty and purpose might have done little better.

Retreat from Reconstruction

The Republican effort to make equal rights for blacks the law of the land culminated in the Fifteenth Amendment, ratified in 1870, which prohibited any state from denying a citizen the right to vote because of race, color, or previous condition of servitude. Much to the displeasure of advocates of women's rights, however, the amendment made no provision for female suffrage. And states could still limit male suffrage by imposing literacy tests, property qualifications, or poll taxes allegedly applying to all racial groups; such devices would eventually be used to strip southern blacks of the right to vote. But the makers of the amendment did not foresee this result.

The Grant administration was charged with enforcing the amendment and protecting black voting rights in the reconstructed states. Since survival of the Republican regimes depended on black support, political partisanship dictated federal action, even though the North's emotional and ideological commitment to black citizenship was waning.

Between 1868 and 1872, the main threat to southern Republican regimes came from the Ku Klux Klan and other secret societies bent on restoring white supremacy by intimidating blacks who sought to exercise their political rights. A grass-roots vigilante movement, not a centralized conspiracy, the Klan thrived on local initiative and gained support from whites of all social classes. Its secrecy, decentralization, popular support, and utter ruthlessness made it very difficult to suppress. Blacks who voted ran the risk of being verbally intimidated, whipped, or even murdered.

These methods were first used effectively in the presidential election of 1868. Terrorism by white supremacists cost Grant the electoral votes of Louisiana and Georgia. In Louisiana political violence claimed hundreds of lives, and in Arkansas more than two hundred Republicans were assassinated. Thereafter, Klan terrorism was directed mainly at Republican state governments. Virtual insurrections broke out in Arkansas, Tennessee, North Carolina, and parts of South Carolina. In Tennessee, North Carolina, and Georgia, Klan activities helped undermine Republican control, thus allowing the Democrats to come to power in all those states by 1870.

Faced with the violent overthrow of the southern Republican party, Congress and the Grant administration were forced to act. A series of laws passed in 1870–1871 sought to enforce the Fifteenth Amendment by providing federal protection for black suffrage and authorizing use of the army against the Klan. Although the "Ku Klux Klan" or "Force" Acts did not totally destroy the Klan, the enforcement effort was vigorous enough to put a damper on hooded terrorism and ensure relatively fair and peaceful elections in 1872.

Radical Reconstruction in the South was obviously tottering by 1872, and further outbreaks of violence helped bring its total collapse. The surviving Republican governments were riddled by factionalism and tainted by charges of corruption; the northern public became increasingly disenchanted with federal intervention on behalf of these regimes. By 1875, Grant was no longer willing to use federal force to protect blacks and Republican regimes in the South.

Spoilsmen Versus Reformers

One reason Grant found it increasingly difficult to take strong action to protect southern Republicans was the charge by reformers that his administration was propping up bad governments in the South for personal and partisan advantage. And in some cases, the charges held a measure of truth.

The Republican party in the Grant era was

rapidly losing the idealism and high purpose associated with the crusade against slavery. By the beginning of the 1870s, men who had been the conscience of the party had been replaced by a new breed of Republicans, such as Senator Roscoe Conkling of New York, whom historians have dubbed "spoilsmen" or "politicos." More often than not, Grant sided with the spoilsmen of his party.

During Grant's first administration, an aura of scandal surrounded the White House but did not directly implicate the president. In 1869 the financial buccaneer Jay Gould enlisted the aid of a brother-in-law of Grant to further his incredible scheme to corner the gold market. Gould failed in the attempt, but he did manage to come away with a huge profit.

Grant's first-term vice-president, Schuyler Colfax of Indiana, was directly involved in the notorious Crédit Mobilier scandal. Crédit Mobilier was a construction company that actually served as a fraudulent device for siphoning off profits that should have gone to the stockholders of the Union Pacific Railroad, which was the beneficiary of massive federal land grants. In order to forestall government inquiry into this arrangement, Crédit Mobilier stock was distributed to influential congressmen. The whole business came to light just before the campaign of 1872.

Republicans who could not tolerate such corruption or had other grievances against the administration broke with Grant in 1872 and formed a third party committed to "honest government" and "reconciliation" between the North and the South. The "Liberal Republicans," led initially by such high-minded reformers as Senator Carl Schurz of Missouri, endorsed reform of the civil service to curb the corruption-breeding patronage system and advocated strict laissez faire economic policies—which meant low tariffs, an end to government subsidies for railroads, and hard money.

The Liberal Republicans' national convention nominated Horace Greeley, editor of the respected *New York Tribune*. This was a curious and divisive choice since Greeley was at odds with the founders of the movement on

the tariff question and indifferent to civil service reform. The Democrats also endorsed Greeley, mainly because he promised to end Radical Reconstruction. Greeley, however, failed to attract strong popular support and was soundly defeated by Grant.

Grant's second administration bore out the reformers' worst suspicions about corruption in high places. In 1875 the public learned that federal revenue officials had conspired with distillers to defraud the government of millions of dollars in liquor taxes. Grant's private secretary, Orville E. Babcock, was indicted as a member of the "Whiskey Ring" and was saved from conviction only by the president's personal intercession. The next year, Grant's Secretary of War William E. Belknap was impeached by the House after an investigation revealed that he had taken bribes for the sale of Indian trading posts. He avoided conviction in the Senate only by resigning from office before his trial.

There is no evidence that Grant profited personally from any of the misdeeds of his subordinates. Yet he is not entirely without blame for the corruption of his administration. He failed to take action against the malefactors, and, even after their guilt had been clearly established, he tried to shield them from justice.

Rise of the Money Question

In 1868 the question of how to manage the nation's currency and more specifically what to do about "greenbacks"—paper money issued during the war—competed with Reconstruction and spoilsmen issues for public attention. Defenders of "sound" money, mostly financial interests in the East, wanted the greenbacks withdrawn from circulation and Civil War debts redeemed in specie payments (silver and gold). Opponents of this hard-money policy and the resulting deflation of the currency, mainly credit-hungry Westerners and expansionist-minded manufacturers, wanted to keep greenbacks in circulation. Both political parties had hard- and easy-money factions, preventing the money question from becoming a heated presidential election issue in 1868 and 1872.

But the Panic of 1873, which brought much of the economy to its knees, led to agitation to inflate the currency by issuing more paper money. Debt-ridden farmers, who would be the backbone of the greenback movement for years to come, now joined the easy-money clamor for the first time. Responding to the money and credit crunch, Congress moved in 1874 to authorize a modest issue of new greenbacks, but Grant vetoed the bill. In 1875, Congress enacted the Specie Resumption Act, which provided for a gradual reduction of greenbacks leading to full resumption of specie payment by 1879. The act was interpreted as deflationary, and farmers and workers, who were already suffering from deflation, reacted with dismay and anger.

The Democratic party could not capitalize adequately on these sentiments because of the influence of its own hard-money faction, and in 1876 an independent Greenback party entered the national political arena. Greenbackers kept the money issue alive through the next decade.

Reunion and the New South

By 1876 Republicans held on to only three southern states—South Carolina, Louisiana, and Florida. Partly because of Grant's hesitant and inconsistent use of presidential power but mainly because the northern electorate would no longer tolerate military action to sustain Republican governments and black voting rights, Radical Reconstruction was falling into total eclipse. Its end in 1877 opened the way to a reconciliation of North and South. But the costs of reunion were high for less privileged groups in the South. The civil and political rights of blacks, left unprotected, were stripped away by white supremacist regimes. Lower class whites saw their interests sacrificed to those of capitalists and landlords. Despite the rhetoric hailing a prosperous "New South,"

Chronology

1863	Lincoln sets forth 10 percent Reconstruction plan
1864	Wade-Davis Bill passes Congress, is pocket-vetoed by Lincoln
1865	Johnson moves to reconstruct the South on his own initiative
	Congress refuses to seat representatives and senators elected from states reestablished under presidential plan (December)
1866	Congress passes Fourteenth Amendment (June)
	Republicans increase their congressional majority in the fall elections
1867	First Reconstruction Act is passed over Johnson's veto (March)
1868	Johnson is impeached; he avoids conviction by one vote (February–May)
	Grant wins presidential election, defeating Horatio Seymour
1869	Congress passes Fifteenth Amendment, granting blacks the right to vote
1870–1871	Congress passes Ku Klux Klan Acts to protect black voting rights in the South
1872	Grant reelected president, defeating Horace Greeley, candidate of Liberal Republicans and Democrats
1873	Financial panic plunges nation into depression
1875	Congress passes Specie Resumption Act "Whiskey Ring" scandal exposed
1876–1877	Disputed presidential election resolved in favor of Republican Hayes over Democrat Tilden
1877	"Compromise of 1877" results in end to military intervention in the South and fall of the last Radical governments

the region remained poor and open to exploitation by northern business interests.

The Compromise of 1877

The election of 1876 pitted Rutherford B. Hayes of Ohio, an honest Republican governor, against Governor Samuel J. Tilden of New

York, a Democratic reformer. Honest government was apparently the electorate's highest priority. When the returns came in, Tilden had clearly won the popular vote and seemed likely to win a narrow victory in the electoral college. But the result was placed in doubt when the returns from the three southern states still controlled by the Republicans were contested. If Hayes were to be awarded these three states, plus one contested electoral vote in Oregon, Republican strategists realized, he would triumph in the electoral college by a single vote.

The outcome of the election remained undecided for months. To resolve the impasse, Congress appointed a special electoral commission of fifteen members to determine who would receive the votes of the disputed states. The commission split along party lines and voted 8 to 7 to award Hayes the disputed states. But this decision still had to be ratified by both houses of Congress, and in the House there was strong Democratic opposition.

To ensure Hayes' election, Republican leaders negotiated secretly with conservative southern Democrats, some of whom seemed willing to abandon their opposition if the last troops were withdrawn and "home rule" was restored to the South. Vague pledges of federal support for southern railroads and internal improvements were made, and Hayes assured southern negotiators that he had every intention of ending Reconstruction. Eventually an informal bargain, dubbed the "Compromise of 1877" was struck.

With southern Democratic acquiescence, the opposition was overcome and Hayes took the oath of office. He immediately ordered the army not to resist a Democratic takeover in South Carolina and Louisiana. Thus fell the last of the Radical governments, and the entire South was firmly under the control of white Democrats.

The New South

The men who led the crusade against Radical Reconstruction in the South and came to power after it fell are usually referred to as the "Redeemers." They were predominantly upper class in origins and loyalties. But unlike the ruling class of the Old South, most Redeemers favored commerce and industry over agrarian interests.

The ideology of the Redeemers rested on two bases—white supremacy and industrial progress. White supremacy was the principal rallying cry that brought them to power; evoking the specter of "black domination" kept them in control of southern state governments. The gospel of industrial progress served to mask Redeemer policies that favored employers over workers, landlords over tenants, and creditors over debtors. It also opened the doors to northern capital and encouraged absentee ownership of important segments of the southern economy.

The new governments were more economical than those of Reconstruction, mainly because they cut back drastically on appropriations for schools and other needed public services. But they were scarcely more honest. Embezzlement of public funds and bribery of

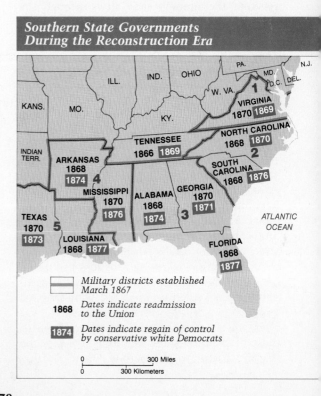

Southern State Governments During the Reconstruction Era

Military districts established March 1867

1868 Dates indicate readmission to the Union

1874 Dates indicate regain of control by conservative white Democrats

0 ___ 300 Miles
0 ___ 300 Kilometers

Supreme Court Decisions Affecting Black Civil Rights, 1875–1900

Hall v. *DeCuir* (1878)	Struck down Louisiana law prohibiting racial discrimination by "common carriers" (railroads, steamboats, buses). Court declared the law a "burden" on interstate commerce, over which states had no authority.
United States v. *Harris* (1882)	Declared Federal laws to punish crimes such as murder and assault unconstitutional. Such crimes declared to be the sole concern of local government. Court ignored the frequent racial motivation behind such crimes in the South.
Civil Rights Cases (1883)	Struck down Civil Rights Act of 1875. Congress may not legislate on civil rights unless a *state* passes a discriminatory law. Court declared the Fourteenth Amendment silent on racial discrimination by private citizens.
Plessy v. *Ferguson* (1896)	Upheld Louisiana statute requiring "separate but equal" accommodations on railroads. Court declared that segregation is *not* necessarily discrimination.
Williams v. *Mississippi* (1898)	Upheld state law requiring a literacy test to qualify for voting. Court refused to find any implication of racial discrimination in the law. Using such laws, southern states rapidly disenfranchised blacks.

public officials continued at an alarming extent.

The Redeemer regimes of the late 1870s and 1880s badly neglected the interests of small white farmers. Whites, as well as blacks, were suffering from the notorious "crop lien" system, which gave local merchants who advanced credit at high rates of interest during the growing season the right to take possession of the harvested crop on terms that buried farmers deeper and deeper in debt. As a result, increasing numbers of whites lost title to their homesteads and were reduced to tenancy.

But the greatest hardships imposed by the new order were reserved for blacks. The Redeemers had pledged, as part of the Compromise of 1877, that they would respect the rights of blacks as set forth in the Fourteenth and Fifteenth amendments. But when blacks tried to vote Republican in the "redeemed" states, they encountered renewed violence and intimidation. Moreover, white Democrats now controlled the election machinery. By the 1890s blacks were virtually disfranchised throughout the South.

The dark night of racism that fell on the South after Reconstruction seemed to unleash all the baser impulses of human nature. Between 1889 and 1899 an average of 187 blacks were lynched every year for alleged offenses against white supremacy. Those convicted of petty crimes against property were often little better off; many were condemned to be leased out to private contractors whose brutality rivaled that of the most sadistic slaveholders. Finally, the dignity of blacks was cruelly affronted by the wave of Jim Crow (strict segregation) laws passed in the 1890s.

The North and the federal government did little or nothing to stem the tide of racial oppression in the South. A series of Supreme Court decisions between 1878 and 1898 gutted the Reconstruction amendments and the legislation passed to enforce them, leaving blacks virtually defenseless against political and social discrimination.

At the same time, the wounds of the Civil War were healing for white Americans. "Reunion" became a cultural and political reality. But whites could come back together only because Northerners had tacitly agreed to give Southerners a free hand in their efforts to reduce blacks to a new form of servitude. It was the Afro-Americans of the South who paid the heaviest price for sectional reunion and reconciliation.

Recommended Reading

Two excellent short accounts of what happened during Reconstruction are Kenneth Stampp, *The Era of Reconstruction, 1865–1877* (1965), and John Hope Franklin, *Reconstruction: After the Civil War* (1961). W.E.B. DuBois, *Black Reconstruction in America, 1860–1880* (1935), a longer and more detailed study, remains brilliant and provocative. The latest reconsiderations of Reconstruction issues can be found in J. Morgan Kousser and James M. McPherson, eds., *Region, Race and Reconstruction: Essays in Honor of C. Vann Woodward* (1982). Morton Keller, *Affairs of State: Public Life in Late Nineteenth Century America* (1977), provides a splendid analysis of American government and politics during Reconstruction and afterward.

For an understanding of the conflict between the president and Congress, see Eric L. McKitrick, *Andrew Johnson and Reconstruction, 1865–1867* (1960), and Michael Les Benedict, *A Compromise of Principle: Congressional Republicans and Reconstruction* (1974). On Constitutional issues, Stanley I. Kutler, *Judicial Power and Reconstruction Politics* (1968), and Harold M. Hyman, *A More Perfect Union: The Impact of the Civil War and Reconstruction on the Constitution* (1973) are especially useful.

Michael Perman's two books, *Reunion Without Compromise: The South and Reconstruction, 1865–1868* (1973) and *The Road to Redemption: Southern Politics, 1869–1879* (1984), deal effectively with southern politics in the postwar years. On the activities of the Freedmen's Bureau, see William McFeeley, *Yankee Godfather: General O. O. Howard and the Freedmen* (1968), and Donald G. Nieman, *To Set the Law in Motion: The Freedmen's Bureau and Legal Rights for Blacks, 1865–1868* (1979).

The changing situation of blacks in the postwar South is treated in Leon Litwack, *Been in the Storm So Long: The Aftermath of Slavery* (1979); Harold O. Rabinowitz, *Race Relations in the Urban South, 1865–1890* (1977); and C. Vann Woodward, *The Strange Career of Jim Crow*, 3rd rev. ed. (1974). Economic adjustments are analyzed in Lawrence N. Powell, *New Masters: Northern Planters During the Civil War and Reconstruction* (1980), and Roger L. Ransom and Richard Sutch, *One Kind of Freedom: The Economic Consequences of Emancipation* (1977).

A provocative study of American labor during the Reconstruction period is David Montgomery, *Beyond Equality: Labor and the Radical Republicans, 1861–1872* (1967). The best introduction to the Grant era is William S. McFeeley, *Grant: A Biography* (1981).

Studies of the decline and fall of Reconstruction include C. Vann Woodward, *Reunion and Reaction*, rev. ed. (1956) and Keith I. Polakoff, *The Politics of Inertia* (1977). C. Vann Woodward, *Origins of the New South, 1877–1913* (1951) remains the standard work on the post-Reconstruction South, but see also Paul M. Gaston, *The New South Creed* (1970); Jonathan M. Weiner, *Social Origins of the New South: Alabama, 1860–1885* (1978); and J. Morgan Kousser, *The Shaping of Southern Politics: Suffrage Restriction and the Establishment of the One-Party South* (1974).

APPENDIX

The Declaration of Independence

In Congress, July 4, 1776

The Unanimous Declaration
of the thirteen United States of America,

When, in the course of human events, it becomes necessary for one people to dissolve the political bonds which have connected them with another, and to assume, among the powers of the earth, the separate and equal station to which the laws of nature and of nature's God entitle them, a decent respect to the opinions of mankind requires that they should declare the causes which impel them to the separation.

We hold these truths to be self-evident: That all men are created equal; that they are endowed by their Creator with certain unalienable rights; that among these are life, liberty, and the pursuit of happiness; that, to secure these rights, governments are instituted among men, deriving their just powers from the consent of the governed; that whenever any form of government becomes destructive of these ends, it is the right of the people to alter or to abolish it, and to institute new government, laying its foundation on such principles, and organizing its powers in such form, as to them shall seem most likely to effect their safety and happiness. Prudence, indeed, will dictate that governments long established should not be changed for light and transient causes; and accordingly all experience hath shown that mankind are more disposed to suffer, while evils are sufferable, than to right themselves by abolishing the forms to which they are accustomed. But when a long train of abuses and usurpations, pursuing invariably the same object, evinces a design to reduce them under absolute despotism, it is their right, it is their duty, to throw off such government, and to provide new guards for their future security. Such has been the patient sufferance of these colonies; and such is now the necessity which constrains them to alter their former systems of government. The history of the present King of Great Britain is a history of repeated injuries and usurpations, all having in direct object the establishment of an absolute tyranny over these states. To prove this, let facts be submitted to a candid world.

He has refused his assent to laws, the most wholesome and necessary for the public good.

He has forbidden his governors to pass laws of immediate and pressing importance, unless suspended in their operation till his assent should be obtained; and, when so suspended, he has utterly neglected to attend to them.

He has refused to pass other laws for the accommodation of large districts of people, unless those people would relinquish the right of representation in the legislature, a right inestimable to them, and formidable to tyrants only.

He has called together legislative bodies at places unusual, uncomfortable, and distant from the depository of their public records, for the sole purpose of fatiguing them into compliance with his measures.

He has dissolved representative houses repeatedly, for opposing, with many firmness, his invasions on the rights of the people.

He has refused for a long time, after such disolutions, to cause others to be elected; whereby the legislative powers, incapable of annihilation, have returned to the people at large for their exercise; the state remaining, in the mean time, exposed to all the dangers of invasions from without and convulsions within.

He has endeavored to prevent the population of these states; for that purpose obstructing the laws for naturalization of foreigners; refusing to pass others to encourage their migration hither, and raising the conditions of new appropriations of lands.

He has obstructed the administration of justice, by refusing his assent to laws for establishing judiciary powers.

He has made judges dependent on his will alone, for the tenure of their offices, and the amount and payment of their salaries.

He has erected a multitude of new offices, and sent hither swarms of officers to harass our people and eat out their substance.

He has kept among us, in times of peace, standing armies, without the consent of our legislatures.

He has affected to render the military independent of, and superior to, the civil power.

He has combined with others to subject us to a jurisdiction foreign to our constitution, and unacknowledged by our laws, giving his assent to their acts of pretended legislation:

For quartering large bodies of armed troops among us;

For protecting them, by a mock trial, from punishment for any murder which they should commit on the inhabitants of these states;

For cutting off our trade with all parts of the world;

For imposing taxes on us without our consent;

For depriving us, in many cases, of the benefits of trial by jury;

For transporting us beyond seas, to be tried for pretended offenses;

For abolishing the free system of English laws in a neighboring province, establishing therein an arbitrary government, and enlarging its boundaries, so as to render it at once an example and fit instrument for introducing the same absolute rule into these colonies;

For taking away our charters, abolishing our most valuable laws, and altering fundamentally the forms of our governments;

For suspending our own legislatures, and declaring themselves invested with power to legislate for us in all cases whatsoever.

He has abdicated government here, by declaring us out of his protection and waging war against us.

He has plundered our seas, ravaged our coasts, burned our towns, and destroyed the lives of our people.

He is at this time transporting large armies of foreign mercenaries to complete the works of death, desolation, and tyranny already begun with circumstances of cruelty and perfidy scarcely paralleled in the most barbarous ages, and totally unworthy the head of a civilized nation.

He has constrained our fellow-citizens, taken captive on the high seas, to bear arms against their country, to become the executioners of their friends and brethren, or to fall themselves by their hands.

He has excited domestic insurrection among us, and has endeavored to bring on the inhabitants of our frontiers the merciless Indian savages, whose known rule of warfare is an undistinguished destruction of all ages, sexes, and conditions.

In every stage of these oppressions we have petitioned for redress in the most humble terms; our repeated petitions have been answered only by repeated injury. A prince, whose character is thus marked by every act which may define a tyrant, is unfit to be the ruler of a free people.

Nor have we been wanting in our attentions to our British brethren. We have warned them, from time to time, of attempts by their legislature to extend an unwarrantable jurisdiction over us. We have reminded them of the circumstances of our emigration and settlement here. We have appealed to their native justice and magnanimity; and we have conjured them, by the ties of our common kindred, to disavow these usurpations, which would inevitably interrupt our connections and correspondence. They, too, have been deaf to the voice of justice and of consanguinity. We must, therefore, acquiesce in the necessity which denounces our separation, and hold them, as we hold the rest of mankind, enemies in war, in peace friends.

We, therefore, the representatives of the United States of America, in General Congress assembled, appealing to the Supreme Judge of the world for the rectitude of our intentions, do, in the name and by the authority of the good people of these colonies, solemnly publish and declare, that these United Colonies are, and of right ought to be, FREE AND INDEPENDENT STATES; that they are absolved from all allegiance to the British crown, and that all political connection between them and the state of Great Britain is, and ought to be, totally dissolved; and that, as free and independent states, they have full power to levy war, conclude peace, contract alliances, establish commerce, and do all other acts and things which independent states may of right do. And for the support of this declaration, with a firm reliance on the protection of Divine Providence, we mutually pledge to each other our lives, our fortunes, and our sacred honor.

JOHN HANCOCK
and fifty-five others

The Constitution of the United States of America

We the People of the United States, in Order to form a more perfect Union, establish Justice, insure domestic Tranquility, provide for the common defence, promote the general Welfare, and secure the Blessings of Liberty to ourselves and our Posterity, do ordain and establish this Constitution for the United States of America.

Article I.

Section 1

All legislative Powers herein granted shall be vested in a Congress of the United States, which shall consist of a Senate and House of Representatives.

Section 2

The House of Representatives shall be composed of Members chosen every second Year by the People of the several States, and the Electors in each State shall have the Qualifications requisite for Electors of the most numerous Branch of the State Legislature.

No Person shall be a Representative who shall not have attained to the Age of twenty five Years, and been seven Years a Citizen of the United States, and who shall not, when elected, be an Inhabitant of that State in which he shall be chosen.

Representatives and direct Taxes shall be apportioned among the several States which may be included within this Union, according to their respective Numbers, *which shall be determined by adding to the whole Number of free Persons, including those bound to Service for a Term of Years, and excluding Indians not taxed, three fifths of all other Persons.*[1] The actual Enumeration shall be made within three Years after the first Meeting of the Congress of the United States, and within every subsequent Term of ten Years, in such Manner as they shall be Law direct. The Number of Representatives shall not exceed one for every thirty Thousand, but each State shall have at Least one Representative; *and until such enumeration shall be made, the State of New Hampshire shall be entitled to chuse three, Massachusetts eight, Rhode-Island and Providence Plantations one, Connecticut five, New York six, New Jersey four, Pennsylvania eight, Delaware one, Maryland six, Virginia ten, North Carolina five, South Carolina five, and Georgia three.*

When vacancies happen in the Representation from any State, the Executive Authority thereof shall issue Writs of Election to fill such Vacancies.

The House of Representatives shall chuse their Speaker and other Officers; and shall have the sole Power of Impeachment.

Section 3

The Senate of the United States shall be composed of two Senators from each State, *chosen by the Legislature thereof,* for six Years; and each Senator shall have one Vote.

Immediately after they shall be assembled in Consequence of the first Election, they shall be divided as equally as may be into three Classes. The Seats of the Senators of the first Class shall be vacated at the Expiration of the second Year, of the second Class at the Expiration of the fourth Year, and of the third Class at the Expiration of the sixth Year so that one third may be chosen every second Year; and if Vacancies happen by Resignation, or otherwise, during the Recess of the Legislature of any state, the Executive thereof may make temporary Appointments until the next Meeting of the Legislature, which shall then fill such Vacancies.[2]

No Person shall be a Senator who shall not have attained to the Age of thirty Years, and been nine Years a Citizen of the United States, and who shall not, when elected, be an Inhabitant of that State for which he shall be chosen.

The Vice President of the United States shall be President of the Senate, but shall have no Vote, unless they be equally divided.

The Senate shall chuse their other Officers, and also a President *pro tempore,* in the Absence of the Vice President, or when he shall exercise the Office of President of the United States.

The Senate shall have the sole Power to try all Impeachments. When sitting for that Purpose, they shall be on Oath or Affirmation. When the President of the United States is tried the Chief Justice shall preside: And no Person shall be convicted whithout the Concurrence of two thirds of the Members present.

Judgment in Cases of Impeachment shall not extend further than to removal from Office, and disqualification to hold and enjoy any Office of honor, Trust or Profit under the United States: but the Party convicted

[1] "Other Persons" being black slaves. Modified by Amendment XIV, Section 2.

[2] Provisions changed by Amendment XVII.

A–3

shall nevertheless be liable and subject to Indictment, Trial, Judgment and Punishment, according to Law.

Section 4

The Times, Places and Manner of holding Elections for Senators and Representatives, shall be prescribed in each State by the Legislature thereof; but the Congress may at any time by Law make or alter such Regulations, except as to the Places of chusing Senators.

The Congress shall assemble at least once in every Year, and such Meeting *shall be on the first Monday in December, unless they shall by Law appoint a different Day.*[3]

Section 5

Each House shall be the Judge of the Elections, Returns and Qualifications of its own Members, and a Majority of each shall constitute a Quorum to do Business; but a smaller Number may adjourn from day to day, and may be authorized to compel the Attendance of absent Members, in such Manner, and under such Penalties as each House may provide.

Each House may determine the Rules of its Proceedings, punish its Members for disorderly Behaviour, and, with the Concurrence of two thirds, expel a Member.

Each House shall keep a Journal of its Proceedings, and from time to time publish the same, excepting such Parts as may in their Judgment require Secrecy; and the Yeas and Nays of the Members of either House on any question shall, at the Desire of one fifth of those Present, be entered on the Journal.

Neither House, during the Session of Congress, shall, without the Consent of the other, adjourn for more than three days, nor to any other Place than that in which the two Houses shall be sitting.

Section 6

The Senators and Representatives shall receive a Compensation for their Services, to be ascertained by Law, and paid out of the Treasury of the United States. They shall in all Cases, except Treason, Felony and Breach of the Peace, be privileged from Arrest during their Attendance at the Session of their respective Houses, and in going to and returning from the same; and for any Speech or Debate in either House, they shall not be questioned in any other Place.

No Senator or Representative shall, during the Time for which he was elected, be appointed to any civil Office under the Authority of the United States, which shall have been created, or the Emoluments whereof shall have been encreased during such time; and no Person holding any Office under the United States, shall be a Member of either House during his Continuance in Office.

[3] Provision changed by Amendment XX, Section 2.

Section 7

All Bills for raising Revenue shall originate in the House of Representatives; but the Senate may propose or concur with Amendments as on other Bills.

Every Bill which shall have passed the House of Representatives and the Senate, shall, before it become a Law, be presented to the President of the United States; If he approve he shall sign it, but if not he shall return it, with his Objections to that House in which it shall have originated, who shall enter the Objections at large on their Journal, and proceed to reconsider it. If after such Reconsideration two thirds of that House shall agree to pass the Bill, it shall be sent, together with the Objections, to the other House, by which it shall likewise be reconsidered, and if approved by two thirds of that House, it shall become a Law. But in all such Cases the Votes of both Houses shall be determined by yeas and Nays, and the Names of the Persons voting for and against the Bill shall be entered on the Journal of each House respectively. If any Bill shall not be returned by the President within ten Days (Sundays excepted) after it shall have been presented to him, the Same shall be a Law, in like Manner as if he had signed it, unless the Congress by their Adjournment prevent its Return, in which Case it shall not be a Law.

Every Order, Resolution, or Vote to which the Concurrence of the Senate and House of Representatives may be necessary (except on a question of Adjournment) shall be presented to the President of the United States; and before the Same shall take Effect, shall be approved by him, or being disapproved by him, shall be repassed by two thirds of the Senate and House of Representatives, according to the Rules and Limitations prescribed in the Case of a Bill.

Section 8

The Congress shall have Power To lay and collect Taxes, Duties, Imposts and Excises, to pay the Debts and provide for the common Defence and general Welfare of the United States; but all Duties, Imposts and Excises shall be uniform throughout the United States;

To borrow Money on the credit of the United States;

To regulate Commerce with foreign Nations, and among the several States, and with the Indian Tribes;

To establish an uniform Rule of Naturalization, and uniform Laws on the subject of Bankruptcies throughout the United States;

To coin Money, regulate the Value thereof, and of foreign Coin, and fix the Standard of Weights and Measures;

To provide for the Punishment of counterfeiting the Securities and current Coin of the United States;

To establish Post Offices and post Roads;

To promote the Progress of Science and useful Arts, by securing for limited Times to Authors and Inventors the exclusive Right to their respective Writings and Discoveries;

To constitute Tribunals inferior to the supreme Court;

To define and punish Piracies and Felonies committed on the high Seas, and Offences against the Law of Nations;

To declare War, grant Letters of Marque and Reprisal, and make Rules concerning Captures on Land and Water;

To raise and support Armies, but no Appropriation of Money to that Use shall be for a longer Term than two Years;

To provide and maintain a Navy;

To make Rules for the Government and Regulation of the land and naval Forces;

To provide for calling forth the Militia to execute the Laws of the Union, suppress Insurrections and repel Invasions;

To provide for organizing, arming, and disciplining, the Militia, and for governing such Part of them as may be employed in the Service of the United States, reserving to the States respectively, the Appointment of the Officers, and the Authority of training the Militia according to the discipline prescribed by Congress;

To exercise exclusive Legislation in all Cases whatsoever, over such District (not exceeding ten Miles square) as may, by Cession of particular States, and the Acceptance of Congress, become the Seat of the Government of the United States, and to exercise like Authority over all Places purchased by the Consent of the Legislature of the State in which the Same shall be, for the Erection of Forts, Magazines, Arsenals, dock-Yards, and other needful Buildings;—And

To make all Laws which shall be necessary and proper for carrying into Execution the foregoing Powers, and all other Powers vested by this Constitution in the Government of the United States, or in any Department or Officer thereof.

Section 9

The Migration or Importation of such Persons as any of the States now existing shall think proper to admit, shall not be prohibited by the Congress prior to the Year one thousand eight hundred and eight, but a Tax or duty may be imposed on such Importation, not exceeding ten dollars for each Person.

The Privilege of the Writ of Habeas Corpus shall not be suspended, unless when in Cases of Rebellion or Invasion the public Safety may require it.

No Bill of Attainder or ex post facto Law shall be passed.

No Capitation, or other direct, Tax shall be laid, unless in Proportion to the Census or Enumeration herein before directed to be taken.

No Tax or Duty shall be laid on Articles exported from any State.

No Preference shall be given by any Regulation of Commerce or Revenue to the Ports of one State over those of another: nor shall Vessels bound to, or from, one State, be obliged to enter, clear, or pay Duties in another.

No Money shall be drawn from the Treasury, but in Consequence of Appropriations made by Law; and a regular Statement and Account of the Receipts and Expenditures of all public Money shall be published from time to time.

No Title of Nobility shall be granted by the United States: And no Person holding any Office of Profit or Trust under them, shall, without the Consent of the Congress, accept of any present, Emolument, Office, or Title, of any kind whatever, from any King, Prince, or foreign State.

Section 10

No State shall enter into any Treaty, Alliance, or Confederation; grant Letters of Marque and Reprisal; coin Money; emit Bills of Credit; make any Thing but gold and silver Coin a Tender in Payment of Debts; pass any Bill of Attainder, ex post facto Law, or Law impairing the obligation of Contracts, or grant any Title of Nobility.

No State shall, without the Consent of the Congress, lay any Imposts or Duties on Imports or Exports, except what may be absolutely necessary for executing its inspection Laws: and the net Produce of all Duties and Imposts, laid by any State on Imports or Exports, shall be for the Use of the Treasury of the United States; and all such Laws shall be subject to the Revision and Controul of the Congress.

No State shall, without the Consent of Congress, lay any Duty of Tonnage, keep Troops, or Ships of War in time of Peace, enter into any Agreement or Compact with another State, or with a foreign Power, or engage in War, unless actually invaded, or in such imminent Danger as will not admit of delay.

Article II.

Section 1

The executive Power shall be vested in a President of the United States of America. He shall hold his Office during the Term of four Years, and, together with the Vice President, chosen for the same Term, be elected, as follows:

Each State shall appoint, in such Manner as the Legislature thereof may direct, a Number of Electors, equal to the whole Number of Senators and Representatives to which the State may be entitled in the Congress: but no Senator or Representative, or Person holding an Office of Trust or Profit under the United States, shall be appointed an Elector.

The Electors shall meet in their respective States, and vote by Ballot for two Persons, of whom one at least shall not be an Inhabitant of the same State with themselves. And they shall make a List of all the Persons voted for, and of the Number of Votes for each; which List they shall sign and certify, and transmit sealed to the Seat of the Government of the United States, directed to the President of the Senate. The President of the Senate shall, in the Presence of the Senate and House of Representatives, open all the Certificates, and the Votes shall then be counted. The Person having the greatest Number of Votes shall be the President, if such Number be a Majority of the whole Number of Electors appointed; and if there be more than one who have such Majority, and have an equal Number of Votes, then the House of Representatives shall immediately chuse by Ballot one of them for President; and if no Person have a Majority, then from the five highest on the List the said House shall in like Manner chuse the President. But in chusing the President, the Votes shall be taken by States, the Representation from each State having one Vote; A quorum for this Purpose shall consist of a Member or Members from two thirds of the States, and a Majority of all the States shall be necessary to a Choice. In every Case, after the Choice of the President, the Person having the greatest Number of Votes of the Electors shall be the Vice President. But if there should remain two or more who have equal Votes, the Senate shall chuse from them by Ballot the Vice President.[4]

The Congress may determine the Time of chusing the Electors, and the Day on which they shall give their Votes; which Day shall be the same throughout the United States.

No person except a natural born Citizen, *or a Citizen of the United States, at the time of the Adoption of this Constitution,* shall be eligible to the Office of President; neither shall any Person be eligible to that Office who shall not have attained to the Age of thirty five Years, and been fourteen Years a Resident within the United States.

In Case of the Removal of the President from Office, or of his Death, Resignation, or Inability to discharge the Powers and Duties of the said Office, the Same shall devolve on the Vice President, and the Congress may by Law provide for the Case of Removal, Death, Resignation or Inability, both of the President and Vice President, declaring what Officer shall then act as President, and such Officer shall act accordingly, until the Disability be removed, or a President shall be elected.

The President shall, at stated Times, receive for his Services, a Compensation, which shall neither be encreased nor diminished during the Period for which he shall have been elected, and he shall not receive within that period any other Emolument from the United States, or any of them.

Before he enter on the Execution of his Office, he shall take the following Oath or Affirmation:—"I do solemnly swear (or affirm) that I will faithfully execute the Office of President of the United States, and will to the best of my Ability, preserve, protect and defend the Constitution of the United States."

Section 2

The President shall be Commander in Chief of the Army and Navy of the United States, and of the Militia of the several States, when called into the actual Service of the United States; he may require the Opinion, in writing, of the principal Officer in each of the executive Departments, upon any Subject relating to the Duties of their respective Offices, and he shall have Power to grant Reprieves and Pardons for Offences against the United States, except in Cases of Impeachment.

He shall have Power, by and with the Advice and Consent of the Senate, to make Treaties, provided two thirds of the Senators present concur; and he shall nominate, and by and with the Advice and Consent of the Senate, shall appoint Ambassadors, other public Ministers and Consuls, Judges of the supreme Court, and all other Officers of the United States, whose Appointments are not herein otherwise provided for, and which shall be established by Law: but the Congress may by Law vest the Appointment of such inferior Officers, as they think proper in the President alone, in the Courts of Law, or in the Heads of Departments.

The President shall have Power to fill up all Vacancies that may happen during the Recess of the Senate, by granting Commissions which shall expire at the End of their next Session.

Section 3

He shall from time to time give to the Congress Information of the State of the Union, and recommend to their Consideration such Measures as he shall judge necessary and expedient; he may, on extraordinary Occasions, convene both Houses, or either of them, and in Case of Disagreement between them, with Respect to the Time of Adjournment, he may adjourn them to such Time as he shall think proper; he shall receive Ambassadors and other public Ministers; he shall take Care that the Laws be faithfully executed, and shall Commission all the Officers of the United States.

Section 4

The President, Vice President and all civil Officers of the United States, shall be removed from Office on Impeachment for, and Conviction of, Treason, Bribery or other high Crimes and Misdemeanors.

[4] Provisions superseded by Amendment XII.

Article III.

Section 1

The judicial Power of the United States, shall be vested in one supreme Court, and in such inferior Courts as the Congress may from time to time ordain and establish. The Judges, both of the supreme and inferior Courts, shall hold their offices during good Behaviour, and shall, at stated Times, receive for their Services, a Compensation, which shall not be diminished during their Continuance in Office.

Section 2

The judicial Power shall extend to all Cases, in Law and Equity, arising under this Constitution, the Laws of the United States, and Treaties made, or which shall be made, under their Authority;—to all Cases affecting Ambassadors, other public Ministers and Consuls;—to all Cases of admiralty and maritime Jurisdiction;—to Controversies to which the United States shall be a Party;—to Controversies between two or more States;— *between a State and Citizens of another State;[5]*— between Citizens of different States, —between Citizens of the same State claiming Lands under Grants of different States, and between a State, or the Citizens thereof, and foreign States, Citizens or Subjects.

In all Cases affecting Ambassadors, other public Ministers and Consuls, and those in which a State shall be Party, the supreme Court shall have original Jurisdiction. In all the other Cases before mentioned, the supreme Court shall have appellate Jurisdiction, both as to Law and Fact, with such Exceptions, and under such Regulations as the Congress shall make.

The Trial of all Crimes, except in Cases of Impeachment, shall be by Jury; and such Trial shall be held in the State where the said Crimes shall have been committed, but when not committed within any State, the Trial shall be at such Place or Places as the Congress may by Law have directed.

Section 3

Treason against the United States, shall consist only in levying War against them, or in adhering to their Enemies, giving them Aid and Comfort. No person shall be convicted of Treason unless on the Testimony of two Witnesses to the same overt Act, or on Confession in open Court.

The Congress shall have Power to declare the Punishment of Treason, but no Attainder of Treason shall work Corruption of Blood, or Forfeiture except during the Life of the Person attainted.

Article IV.

Section 1

Full Faith and Credit shall be given in each State to the public Acts, Records, and judicial Proceedings of every other State. And the Congress may by general Laws prescribe the Manner in which such Acts, Records and Proceedings shall be proved, and the Effect thereof.

Section 2

The Citizens of each State shall be entitled to all Privileges and Immunities of Citizens in the several States.

A Person charged in any State with Treason, Felony, or other Crime, who shall flee from Justice, and be found in another State, shall on Demand of the executive Authority of the State from which he fled, be delivered up, to be removed to the State having Jurisdiction of the Crime.

No Person held to Service or Labour in one State, under the Laws thereof, escaping into another, shall, in Consequence of any Law or Regulation therein, be discharged from such Service or Labour, but shall be delivered up on Claim of the Party to whom such Service or Labour may be due.

Section 3

New States may be admitted by the Congress into this Union; but no new State shall be formed or erected within the Jurisdiction of any other State; nor any State be formed by the Junction of two or more States, or Parts of States, without the Consent of the Legislatures of the States concerned as well as of the Congress.

The Congress shall have Power to dispose of and make all needful Rules and Regulations respecting the Territory or other Property belonging to the United States; and nothing in this Constitution shall be so construed as to Prejudice any Claims of the United States, or of any particular States.

Section 4

The United States shall guarantee to every State in this Union a Republican Form of Government, and shall protect each of them against Invasion; and on Application of the Legislature, or of the Executive (when the Legislature cannot be convened) against domestic violence.

Article V.

The Congress, whenever two thirds of both Houses shall deem it necessary, shall propose Amendments to this Constitution, or, on the Application of the Legislatures of two thirds of the several States, shall call a Convention for proposing Amendments, which, in ei-

---

[5] Clause changed by Amendment XI.

ther Case, shall be valid to all Intents and Purposes, as Part of this Constitution, when ratified by the Legislatures of three fourths of the several States, or by Conventions in three fourths thereof, as the one or the other Mode of Ratification may be proposed by the Congress; Provided *that no Amendment which may be made prior to the Year One thousand eight hundred and eight shall in any Manner affect the first and fourth Clauses in the Ninth Section of the first Article;* and that no State without its Consent, shall be deprived of its equal Suffrage in the Senate.

Article VI.

All Debts contracted and Engagements entered into, before the Adoption of this Constitution, shall be as valid against the United States under this Constitution, as under the Confederation.

This Constitution, and the Laws of the United States which shall be made in Pursuance thereof; and all Treaties made, or which shall be made, under the Authority of the United States, shall be the supreme Law of the Land; and the Judges in every State shall be bound thereby, any Thing in the Constitution or Laws of any State to the Contrary notwithstanding.

The Senators and Representatives before mentioned, and the Members of the several State Legislatures, and all executive and Judicial Officers, both of the United States and of the several States, shall be bound by Oath or Affirmation, to support this Constitution; but no religious Test shall ever be required as a Qualification to any Office of public Trust under the United States.

Article VII.

The Ratification of the Conventions of nine States, shall be sufficient for the Establishment of this Constitution between the States so ratifying the Same.

done in Convention by the Unanimous Consent of the States present the Seventeenth Day of September in the Year of our Lord one thousand seven hundred and Eighty seven and of the Independence of the United states of America the Twelfth[6] IN WITNESS whereof We have hereunto subscribed our Names,

GEORGE WASHINGTON,
President and Deputy from Virginia
and thirty-seven others

---

[6] The Constitution was submitted on September 17, 1787, by the Constitutional Convention, was ratified by the conventions of several states at various dates up to May 29, 1790, and became effective on March 4, 1789.

Amendments to the Constitution

Amendment 1

Congress shall make no law respecting an establishment of religion, or prohibiting the free exercise thereof; or abridging the freedom of speech, or of the press; or the right of the people peaceably to assemble, and to petition the Government for a redress of grievances.

Amendment II

A well regulated Militia being necessary to the security of a free State, the right of the people to keep and bear Arms, shall not be infringed.

Amendment III

No Soldier shall, in time of peace be quartered in any house, without the consent of the Owner, nor in time of war, but in a manner to be prescribed by law.

Amendment IV

The right of the people to be secure in their persons, houses, papers, and effects, against unreasonable searches and seizures, shall not be violated, and no Warrants shall issue, but upon probable cause, supported by Oath or affirmation, and particularly describing the place to be searched, and the persons or things to be seized.

Amendment V

No person shall be held to answer for a capital, or otherwise infamous crime, unless on a presentment or indictment of a Grand Jury, except in cases arising in the land or naval forces, or in the Militia, when in actual service in time of War or public danger; nor shall any person be subject for the same offense to be twice put in jeopardy of life or limb; nor shall be compelled in any criminal case to be a witness against himself, nor be deprived of life, liberty, or property, without due process of law; nor shall private property be taken for public use, without just compensation.

Amendment VI

In all criminal prosecutions, the accused shall enjoy the right to a speedy and public trial, by an impartial jury of the State and district wherein the crime shall have been committed, which district shall have been previously ascertained by law, and to be informed of the nature and cause of the accusation; to be confronted with the witnesses against him; to have compulsory process for obtaining witnesses in his favor, and to have the Assistance of Counsel for his defence.

Amendment VII

In Suits at common law, where the value in controversy shall exceed twenty dollars, the right of trial by jury shall be preserved, and no fact tried by a jury, shall be otherwise re-examined in any Court of the United States, than according to the rules of the common law.

Amendment VIII

Excessive bail shall not be required, nor excessive fines imposed, nor cruel and unusual punishments inflicted.

Amendment IX

The enumeration in the Constitution, of certain rights, shall not be construed to deny or disparage others retained by the people.

Amendment X

The powers not delegated to the United States by the Constitution, nor prohibited by it to the States, are reserved to the States respectively, or the people.[7]

[7] The first ten amendments were all proposed by Congress on September 25, 1789, and were ratified and adoption certified on December 15, 1791.

Amendment XI

The Judicial power of the United States shall not be construed to extend to any suit in law or equity, commenced or prosecuted against one of the United States by Citizens of another State, or by Citizens or Subjects of any Foreign State.[8]

Amendment XII

The Electors shall meet in their respective states, and vote by ballot for President and Vice-President, one of whom, at least, shall not be an inhabitant of the same state with themselves; they shall name in their ballots the person voted for as President, and in distinct ballots the person voted for as Vice-President, and they shall make distinct lists of all persons voted for as President, and of all persons voted for as Vice-President, and of the number of votes for each, which lists they shall sign and certify, and transmit sealed to the seat of the government of the United States, directed to the President of the Senate;—The President of the Senate shall, in the presence of the Senate and House of Representatives, open all the certificates and the votes shall then be counted;—The person having the greatest number of votes for President, shall be the President, if such number be a majority of the whole number of Electors appointed; and if no person have such majority, then from the persons having the highest numbers not exceeding three on the list of those voted for as President, the House of Representatives shall choose immediately, by ballot, the President. But in choosing the President, the votes shall be taken by states, the representation from each state having one vote; a quorum for this purpose shall consist of a member or members from two-thirds of the states, and a majority of all the states shall be necessary to a choice. And if the House of Representatives shall not choose a President whenever the right of choice shall devolve upon them, before *the fourth day of March* next following, then the Vice-President shall act as President, as in the case of the death or other constitutional disability of the President.—The person having the greatest number of votes as Vice-President, shall be the Vice-President, if such number be a majority of the whole number of Electors appointed, and if no person have a majority, then from the two highest numbers on the list, the Senate shall choose the Vice-President; a quorum for the purpose shall consist of two-thirds of the whole number of Senators, and a majority of the whole number shall be necessary to a choice. But no person constitutionally ineligible to the office of

President shall be eligible to that of Vice President of the United States.[9]

Amendment XIII

Section 1
Neither slavery nor involuntary servitude, except as a punishment for crime whereof the party shall have been duly convicted, shall exist within the United States, or any place subject to their jurisdiction.

Section 2
Congress shall have power to enforce this article by appropriate legislation.[10]

Amendment XIV

Section 1
All persons born or naturalized in the United States, and subject to the jurisdiction thereof, are citizens of the United States and of the State wherein they reside. No State shall make or enforce any law which shall abridge the privileges or immunities of citizens of the United States; nor shall any State deprive any person of life, liberty, or property, without due process of law; nor deny to any person within its jurisdiction the equal protection of the laws.

Section 2
Representatives shall be apportioned among the several States according to their respective numbers, counting the whole number of persons in each State, excluding Indians not taxed. But when the right to vote at any election for the choice of electors for President and Vice-President of the United States, Representatives in Congress, the Executive and Judicial officers of a State, or the members of the Legislature thereof, is denied to any of the male inhabitants of such State, being twenty-one years of age, and citizens of the United States, or in any way abridged, except for participation in rebellion, or other crime, the basis of representation therein shall be reduced in the proportion which the number of such male citizens shall bear to the whole number of male citizens twenty-one years of age in such State.

Section 3
No person shall be a Senator or Representative in Congress, or elector of President and Vice President, or

[8] Proposed by Congress on March 4, 1794, and declared ratified on January 8, 1798.

[9] Proposed by Congress on December 9, 1803; declared ratified on September 25, 1804; supplemented by Amendments XX and XXIII.

[10] Proposed by Congress on January 31, 1865; declared ratified on December 18, 1865.

hold any office, civil or military, under the United States, or under any State, who, having previously taken an oath, as a member of Congress, or as an officer of the United States, or as a member of any State legislature, or as an executive or judicial officer of any State, to support the Constitution of the United States, shall have engaged in insurrection or rebellion against the same, or given aid or comfort to the enemies thereof. But Congress may by a vote of two-thirds of each House, remove such disability.

Section 4
The validity of the public debt of the United States, authorized by law, including debts incurred for payment of pensions and bounties for services in suppressing insurrection or rebellion, shall not be questioned. But neither the United States nor any State shall assume or pay any debt or obligation incurred in aid of insurrection or rebellion against the United States, or any claim for the loss or emancipation of any slave; but all such debts, obligations and claims shall be held illegal and void.

Section 5
The Congress shall have power to enforce, by appropriate legislation, the provisions of this article.[11]

Amendment XV

Section 1
The right of citizens of the United States to vote shall not be denied or abridged by the United States or by any State on account of race, color, or previous condition of servitude.

Section 2
The Congress shall have power to enforce this article by appropriate legislation.[12]

Amendment XVI

The Congress shall have power to lay and collect taxes on incomes, from whatever source derived, without apportionment among the several States, and without regard to any census or enumeration.[13]

Amendment XVII

The Senate of the United States shall be composed of two Senators from each State, elected by the people thereof, for six years; and each Senator shall have one vote. The electors in each State shall have the qualifications requisite for electors of the most numerous branch of the State legislatures.

When vacancies happen in the representation of any State in the Senate, the executive authority of such State shall issue writs of election to fill such vacancies: *Provided,* That the legislature of any State may empower the executive thereof to make temporary appointments until the people fill the vacancies by election as the legislature may direct.

This amendment shall not be so construed as to affect the election or term of any Senator chosen before it becomes valid as part of the Constitution.[14]

Amendment XVIII

Section 1
After one year from the ratification of this article the manufacturer, sale, or transportation of intoxicating liquors within, the importation thereof into, or the exportation thereof from the United States and all territory subject to the jurisdiction thereof for beverage purposes is hereby prohibited.

Section 2
The Congress and the several States shall have concurrent power to enforce this article by appropriate legislation.

Section 3
This article shall be inoperative unless it shall have been ratified as an amendment to the Constitution by the legislatures of the several States, as provided in the Constitution, within seven years from the date of the submission hereof to the States by the Congress.[15]

Amendment XIX

The right of citizens of the United States to vote shall not be denied or abridged by the United States or by any State on account of sex.

Congress shall have power to enforce this article by appropriate legislation.[16]

---

[11] Proposed by Congress on June 13, 1866; declared ratified on July 28, 1868.
[12] Proposed by Congress on February 26, 1869; declared ratified on March 30, 1870.
[13] Proposed by Congress on July 12, 1909; declared ratified on February 25, 1913.

[14] Proposed by Congress on May 13, 1912; declared ratified on May 31, 1913.
[15] Proposed by Congress on December 18, 1917; declared ratified on January 29, 1919; repealed by Amendment XXI.
[16] Proposed by Congress on June 4, 1919; declared ratified on August 26, 1920.

Amendment XX

Section 1

The terms of the President and Vice President shall end at noon on the 20th day of January, and the terms of Senators and Representatives at noon on the 3d day of January, of the years in which such terms would have ended if this article had not been ratified; and the terms of their successors shall then begin.

Section 2

The Congress shall assemble at least once in every year, and such meeting shall begin at noon on the 3d day of January, unless they shall by law appoint a different day.

Section 3

If, at the time fixed for the beginning of the term of the President, the President elect shall have died, the Vice President elect shall become President. If a President shall not have been chosen before the time fixed for the beginning of his term, or if the President elect shall have failed to qualify, then the Vice President elect shall act as President until a President shall have qualified; and the Congress may by law provide for the case wherein neither a President elect nor a Vice President elect shall have qualified, declaring who shall then act as President, or the manner in which one who is to act shall be selected, and such person shall act accordingly until a President or Vice President shall have qualified.

Section 4

The Congress may by law provide for the case of the death of any of the persons from whom the House of Representatives may choose a President whenever the right of choice shall have devolved upon them, and for the case of the death of any of the persons from whom the Senate may choose a Vice President whenever the right of choice shall have devolved upon them.

Section 5

Sections 1 and 2 shall take effect on the 15th day of October following the ratification of this article.

Section 6

This article shall be inoperative unless it shall have been ratified as an amendment to the Constitution by the legislatures of three-fourths of the several States within seven years from the date of its submission.[17]

Amendment XXI

Section 1

The eighteenth article of amendment to the Constitution of the United States is hereby repealed.

Section 2

The transportation or importation into any States, Territory, or possession of the United States for delivery or use therein of intoxicating liquors, in violation of the laws thereof, is hereby prohibited.

Section 3

This article shall be inoperative unless it shall have been ratified as an amendment to the Constitution by conventions in the several States, as provided in the Constitution, within seven years from the date of the submission hereof to the States by the Congress.[18]

Amendment XXII

Section 1

No person shall be elected to the office of the President more than twice, and no person who has held the office of President, or acted as President, for more than two years of a term to which some other person was elected President shall be elected to the office of the President more than once. But this Article shall not apply to any person holding the office of President when this Article was proposed by the Congress, and shall not prevent any person who may be holding the office of President, or acting as President, during the term within which this Article becomes operative from holding the office of President or acting as President during the remainder of such term.

Section 2

This article shall be inoperative unless it shall have been ratified as an amendment to the Constitution by the legislatures of three-fourths of the several States within seven years from the date of its submission to the States by the Congress.[19]

Amendment XXIII

Section 1

The District constituting the seat of Government of the United States shall appoint in such manner as the Congress shall direct:

---

[17] Proposed by Congress on March 2, 1932; declared ratified on February 6, 1933.

[18] Proposed by Congress on February 20, 1933; declared ratified on December 5, 1933.

[19] Proposed by Congress on March 24, 1947; declared ratified on March 1, 1951.

A number of electors of President and Vice President equal to the whole number of Senators and Representatives in Congress to which the District would be entitled if it were a State, but in no event more than the least populous State; they shall be in addition to those appointed by the States, but they shall be considered, for the purposes of the election of President and Vice President, to be electors appointed by a State; and they shall meet in the District and perform such duties as provided by the twelfth article of amendment.

Section 2

The Congress shall have power to enforce this article by appropriate legislation.[20]

Amendment XXIV

Section 1

The right of citizens of the United States to vote in any primary or other election for President or Vice President, for electors for President or Vice President, or for Senator or Representative in Congress, shall not be denied or abridged by the United States or any state by reason of failure to pay any poll tax or other tax.

Section 2

The Congress shall have the power to enforce this article by appropriate legislation.[21]

Amendment XXV

Section 1

In case of the removal of the President from office or his death or resignation, the Vice President shall become President.

Section 2

Whenever there is a vacancy in the office of the Vice President, the President shall nominate a Vice President who shall take the office upon confirmation by a majority vote of both houses of Congress.

Section 3

Whenever the President transmits to the President pro tempore of the Senate and the Speaker of the House of Representatives his written declaration that he is unable to discharge the powers and duties of his office,

and until he transmits to them a written declaration to the contrary, such powers and duties shall be discharged by the Vice President as Acting President.

Section 4

Whenever the Vice President and a majority of either the principal officers of the executive departments or of such other body as Congress may by law provide, transmit to the President pro tempore of the Senate and the Speaker of the House of Representatives their written declaration that the President is unable to discharge the powers and duties of his office, the Vice President shall immediately resume the powers and duties of the office as Acting President.

Thereafter, when the President transmits to the President pro tempore of the Senate and the Speaker of the House of Representatives his written declaration that no inability exists, he shall resume the powers and duties of his office unless the Vice President and a majority of either the principal officers of the executive department or of such other body as Congress may by law provide, transmit within four days to the President pro tempore of the Senate and the Speaker of the House of Representatives their written declaration that the President is unable to discharge the powers and duties of his office. Thereupon Congress shall decide the issue, assembling within 48 hours for that purpose if not in session. If the Congress, within 21 days after receipt of the latter written declaration, or, if Congress is not in session, within 21 days after Congress is required to assemble, determines by two-thirds vote of both houses that the President is unable to discharge the powers and duties of his office, the Vice President shall continue to discharge the same as Acting President; otherwise, the President shall resume the powers and duties of his office.[22]

Amendment XXVI

Section 1

The right of citizens of the United States, who are 18 years of age or older, to vote shall not be denied or abridged by the United States or any state on account of age.

Section 2

The Congress shall have the power to enforce this article by appropriate legislation.[23]

---

[20] Proposed by Congress on June 16, 1960; declared ratified on April 3, 1961.
[21] Proposed by Congress on August 27, 1962; declared ratified on January 23, 1963.

[22] Proposed by Congress on July 6, 1965; declared ratified on February 10, 1967.
[23] Proposed by Congress on March 23, 1971; declared ratified on June 30, 1971.

Choosing the President

Presidential Election Year	Elected to Office			
	President	Party	Vice President	Party
1789	George Washington		John Adams	Parties not yet established
1792	George Washington		John Adams	Federalist
1796	John Adams	Federalist	Thomas Jefferson	Democratic-Republican
1800	Thomas Jefferson	Democratic-Republican	Aaron Burr	Democratic-Republican
1804	Thomas Jefferson	Democratic-Republican	George Clinton	Democratic-Republican
1808	James Madison	Democratic-Republican	George Clinton	Democratic-Republican
1812	James Madison	Democratic-Republican	Elbridge Gerry	Democratic-Republican
1816	James Monroe	Democratic-Republican	Daniel D. Tompkins	Democratic-Republican
1820	James Monroe	Democratic-Republican	Daniel D. Tompkins	Democratic-Republican
1824	John Quincy Adams Elected by House of Representatives because no candidate received a majority of electoral votes.	National Republican	John C. Calhoun	Democratic
1828	Andrew Jackson	Democratic	John C. Calhoun	Democratic
1832	Andrew Jackson	Democratic	Martin Van Buren	Democratic

Major Opponents		Electoral Vote		Popular Vote
For President	Party			
		Washington	69	Electors selected by state legislatures
		J. Adams	34	
George Clinton	Democratic-Republican	Washington	132	Electors selected by state legislatures
		J. Adams	77	
		Clinton	50	
Thomas Pinckney	Federalist	J. Adams	71	Electors selected by state legislatures
Aaron Burr	Democratic-Republican	Jefferson	68	
		Pinckney	59	
John Adams	Federalist	Jefferson	73	Electors selected by state legislatures
Charles Cotesworth Pinckney	Federalist	J. Adams	65	
Charles Cotesworth Pinckney	Federalist	Jefferson	162	Electors selected by state legislatures
		Pinckney	14	
Charles Cotesworth Pinckney	Federalist	Madison	122	Electors selected by state legislatures
George Clinton	Eastern Republican	Pinckney	47	
De Witt Clinton	Democratic-Republican (antiwar faction) and Federalist	Madison	128	Electors selected by state legislatures
		Clinton	89	
Rufus King	Federalist	Monroe	183	Electors selected by state legislatures
		King	34	
		Monroe	231	Electors selected by State legislatures
		J. Q. Adams	1	
Andrew Jackson	Democratic	J. Q. Adams	84	113,122
Henry Clay	Democratic-Republican	Jackson	99	151,271
		Clay	37	47,531
William H. Crawford	Democratic-Republican	Crawford	41	40,856
John Quincy Adams	National Republican	Jackson	178	642,553
		J. Q. Adams	83	500,897
Henry Clay	National Republican	Jackson	219	701,780
William Wirt	Anti-Masonic	Clay	49	482,205
		Wirt	7	100,715
		*Floyd (Ind. Dem.)	11	*Delegates chosen by South Carolina legislature

Presidential Election Year	Elected to Office			
	President	*Party*	*Vice President*	*Party*
1836	Martin Van Buren	Democratic	Richard M. Johnson First and only Vice President elected by the Senate (1837), having failed to receive a majority of electoral votes.	Democratic
1840	William Henry Harrison	Whig	John Tyler	Whig
1844	James K. Polk	Democratic	George M. Dallas	Democratic
1848	Zachary Taylor	Whig	Millard Fillmore	Whig
1852	Franklin Pierce	Democratic	William R. King	Democratic
1856	James Buchanan	Democratic	John C. Breckinridge	Democratic
1860	Abraham Lincoln	Republican	Hannibal Hamlin	Republican
1864	Abraham Lincoln	National Union/Republican	Andrew Johnson	National Union/Democratic
1868	Ulysses S. Grant	Republican	Schuyler Colfax	Republican
1872	Ulysses S. Grant	Republican	Henry Wilson	Republican
1876	Rutherford B. Hayes Contested result settled by special election commission in favor of Hayes	Republican	William A. Wheeler	Republican

Major Opponents		Electoral Vote		Popular Vote
For President	*Party*			
Daniel Webster	Whig	Van Buren	170	764,176
Hugh L. White	Whig	W. Harrison	73	550,816
William Henry Harrison	Anti-Masonic	White	26	146,107
		Webster	14	41,201
		*Mangum (Ind. Dem.)	11	*Delegates chosen by South Carolina legislature
Martin Van Buren	Democratic	W. Harrison	234	1,274,624
James G. Birney	Liberty	Van Buren	60	1,127,781
Henry Clay	Whig	Polk	170	1,338,464
James G. Birney	Liberty	Clay	105	1,300,097
		Birney	—	62,300
Lewis Cass	Democratic	Taylor	163	1,360,967
Martin Van Buren	Free-Soil	Cass	127	1,222,342
		Van Buren	—	291,263
Winfield Scott	Whig	Pierce	254	1,601,117
John P. Hale	Free-Soil	Scott	42	1,385,453
		Hale	—	155,825
John C. Fremont	Republican	Buchanan	174	1,832,955
Millard Fillmore	American (Know-Nothing)	Fremont	114	1,339,932
		Fillmore	8	871,731
John Bell	Constitutional Union	Lincoln	180	1,865,593
Stephen A. Douglas	Democratic	Breckinridge	72	848,356
John C. Breckinridge	Democratic	Douglas	12	1,382,713
		Bell	39	592,906
George B. McClennan	Democratic	Lincoln	212	2,218,388
		McClellen	21	1,812,807
		*Eleven secessionist states did not participate		
Horatio Seymour	Democratic	Grant	286	3,598,235
		Seymour	80	2,706,829
		*Texas, Mississippi, and Virginia did not participate		
Horace Greeley	Democratic and Liberal Republican	Grant	286	3,598,235
		Greeley	80*	2,834,761
Charles O'Conor	Democratic	*Greeley died before the Electoral College met. His electoral votes were divided among the four minor candidates.		
James Black	Temperance			
Samuel J. Tilden	Democratic	Hayes	185	4,034,311
Peter Cooper	Greenback	Tilden	184	4,288,546
Green Clay Smith	Prohibition	Cooper	—	75,973

Presidential Election Year	Elected to Office			
	President	Party	Vice President	Party
1880	James A. Garfield	Republican	Chester A. Arthur	Republican
1884	Grover Cleveland	Democratic	Thomas A. Hendricks	Democratic
1888	Benjamin Harrison	Republican	Levi P. Morton	Republican
1892	Grover Cleveland	Democratic	Adlai E. Stevenson	Democratic
1896	William McKinley	Republican	Garret A. Hobart	Republican
1900	William McKinley	Republican	Theodore Roosevelt	Republican
1904	Theodore Roosevelt	Republican	Charles W. Fairbanks	Republican
1908	William Howard Taft	Republican	James S. Sherman	Republican
1912	Woodrow Wilson	Democratic	Thomas R. Marshall	Democratic
1916	Woodrow Wilson	Democratic	Thomas R. Marshall	Democratic
1920	Warren G. Harding	Republican	Calvin Coolidge	Republican

Major Opponents		Electoral Vote		Popular Vote
For President	*Party*			
Winfield S. Hancock	Democratic	Garfield	214	4,446,158
James B. Weaver	Greenback	Hancock	155	4,444,260
Neal Dow	Prohibition	Weaver	—	305,997
James G. Blaine	Republican	Cleveland	219	4,874,621
John P. St. John	Prohibition	Blaine	182	4,848,936
Benjamin F. Butler	Greenback	Butler	—	175,096
		St. John	—	147,482
Grover Cleveland	Democratic	B. Harrison	233	5,447,129
Clinton B. Fisk	Prohibition	Cleveland	168	5,537,857
Alson J. Streeter	Union Labor			
Benjamin Harrison	Republican	Cleveland	277	5,555,426
James B. Weaver	Populist	B. Harrison	145	5,182,600
John Bidwell	Prohibition	Weaver	22	1,029,846
William Jennings Bryan	Democratic, Populist, and National Silver Republican	McKinley	271	7,102,246
		Bryan	176	6,492,559
Joshua Levering	Prohibition			
John M. Palmer	National Democratic			
William Jennings Bryan	Democratic and Fusion Populist	McKinley	292	7,218,039
		Bryan	155	6,358,345
Wharton Barker	Anti-Fusion Populist	Woolley	—	209,004
Eugene V. Debs	Social Democratic	Debs	—	86,935
John G. Woolley	Prohibition			
Alton B. Parker	Democratic	T. Roosevelt	336	7,626,593
Eugene V. Debs	Socialist	Parker	140	5,082,898
Silas C. Swallow	Prohibition	Debs	—	402,489
		Swallow	—	258,596
William Jennings Bryan	Democratic	Taft	321	7,676,258
		Bryan	162	6,406,801
Eugene V. Debs	Socialist	Debs	—	420,380
Eugene W. Chafin	Prohibition	Chalfin	—	252,821
William Howard Taft	Republican	Wilson	435	6,296,547
Theodore Roosevelt	Progressive (Bull Moose)	T. Roosevelt	88	4,118,571
		Taft	8	3,486,720
Eugene V. Debs	Socialist			
Eugene W. Chafin	Prohibition			
Charles E. Hughes	Republican	Wilson	277	9,127,695
Allen L. Benson	Socialist	Hughes	254	8,533,507
J. Frank Hanly	Prohibition			
Charles W. Fairbanks	Republican			
James M. Cox	Democratic	Harding	404	16,133,314
Eugene V. Debs	Socialist	Cox	127	9,140,884
		Debs	—	913,664

Presidential Election Year	Elected to Office			
	President	Party	Vice President	Party
1924	Calvin Coolidge	Republican	Charles G. Dawes	Republican
1928	Herbert C. Hoover	Republican	Charles Curtis	Republican
1932	Franklin D. Roosevelt	Democratic	John N. Garner	Democratic
1936	Franklin D. Roosevelt	Democratic	John N. Garner	Democratic
1940	Franklin D. Roosevelt	Democratic	Henry A. Wallace	Democratic
1944	Franklin D. Roosevelt	Democratic	Harry S Truman	Democratic
1948	Harry S. Truman	Democratic	Alben W. Barkley	Democratic
1952	Dwight D. Eisenhower	Republican	Richard M. Nixon	Republican
1956	Dwight D. Eisenhower	Republican	Richard M. Nixon	Republican
1960	John F. Kennedy	Democratic	Lyndon B. Johnson	Democratic
1964	Lyndon B. Johnson	Democratic	Hubert H. Humphrey	Democratic
1968	Richard M. Nixon	Republican	Spiro T. Agnew	Republican
1972	Richard M. Nixon	Republican	Spiro T. Agnew	Republican
1976	Jimmy Carter	Democratic	Walter Mondale	Democratic
1980	Ronald Reagan	Republican	George Bush	Republican
1984	Ronald Reagan	Republican	George Bush	Republican

Major Opponents		Electoral Vote		Popular Vote
For President	*Party*			
John W. Davis	Democratic	Coolidge	382	15,717,553
Robert M. LaFollette	Progressive	Davis	136	8,386,169
		LaFollette	13	4,814,050
Alfred E. Smith	Democratic	Hoover	444	21,391,993
Norman Thomas	Socialist	Smith	87	15,016,169
Herbert C. Hoover	Republican	F. Roosevelt	472	22,809,638
Norman Thomas	Socialist	Hoover	59	15,758,901
Alfred M. Landon	Republican	F. Roosevelt	523	27,752,869
William Lemke	Union	Landon	8	16,674,665
Wendell L. Willkie	Republican	F. Roosevelt	449	27,263,448
		Willkie	82	22,336,260
Thomas E. Dewey	Republican	F. Roosevelt	432	25,611,936
		Dewey	99	22,013,372
Thomas E. Dewey	Republican	Truman	303	24,105,182
J. Strom Thurmond	States' Rights Democratic	Dewey	189	21,970,065
		Thurmond	39	1,169,063
Henry A. Wallace	Progressive	H. Wallace	—	1,157,326
Adlai E. Stevenson	Democratic	Eisenhower	442	33,936,137
		Stevenson	89	27,314,649
Adlai E. Stevenson	Democratic	Eisenhower	457	35,585,245
		Stevenson	73	26,030,172
Richard M. Nixon	Republican	Kennedy	303	34,227,096
		Nixon	219	34,108,546
		H. Byrd (Ind. Dem.)	15	—
Barry M. Goldwater	Republican	Johnson	486	43,126,584
		Goldwater	52	27,177,838
Hubert H. Humphrey	Democratic	Nixon	301	31,770,237
George C. Wallace	American Independent	Humphrey	191	31,270,533
		G. Wallace	46	9,906,141
George S. McGovern	Democratic	Nixon	520	46,740,323
		McGovern	17	28,901,598
		Hospers (Va.)	1	—
Gerald R. Ford	Republican	Carter	297	40,830,763
Eugene McCarthy	Independent	Ford	240	39,147,793
		E. McCarthy	—	756,631
Jimmy Carter	Democratic	Reagan	489	43,899,248
John B. Anderson	Independent	Carter	49	35,481,435
Ed Clark	Libertarian	Anderson	—	5,719,437
Walter Mondale	Democratic	Reagan	525	54,451,521
David Bergland	Libertarian	Mondale	13	37,565,334

Cabinet Members for Each Administration

The Washington Administration

Secretary of State	Thomas Jefferson	1789–1793
	Edmund Randolph	1794–1795
	Timothy Pickering	1795–1797
Secretary of Treasury	Alexander Hamilton	1789–1795
	Oliver Wolcott	1795–1797
Secretary of War	Henry Knox	1789–1794
	Timothy Pickering	1795–1796
	James McHenry	1796–1797
Attorney General	Edmund Randolph	1789–1793
	William Bradford	1794–1795
	Charles Lee	1795–1797
Postmaster General	Samuel Osgood	1789–1791
	Timothy Pickering	1791–1794
	Joseph Habersham	1795–1797

The John Adams Administration

Secretary of State	Timothy Pickering	1797–1800
	John Marshall	1800–1801
Secretary of Treasury	Oliver Wolcott	1797–1800
	Samuel Dexter	1800–1801
Secretary of War	James McHenry	1797–1800
	Samuel Dexter	1800–1801
Attorney General	Charles Lee	1797–1801
Postmaster General	Joseph Habersham	1797–1801
Secretary of Navy	Benjamin Stoddert	1798–1801

The Jefferson Administration

Secretary of State	James Madison	1801–1809
Secretary of Treasury	Samuel Dexter	1801
	Albert Gallatin	1801–1809
Secretary of War	Henry Dearborn	1801–1809
Attorney General	Levi Lincoln	1801–1805
	Robert Smith	1805
	John Breckinridge	1805–1806
	Caesar Rodney	1807–1809

Postmaster General	Joseph Habersham	1801
	Gideon Granger	1801–1809
Secretary of Navy	Robert Smith	1801–1809

The Madison Administration

Secretary of State	Robert Smith	1809–1811
	James Monroe	1811–1817
Secretary of Treasury	Albert Gallatin	1809–1813
	George Campbell	1814
	Alexander Dallas	1814–1816
	William Crawford	1816–1817
Secretary of War	William Eustis	1809–1812
	John Armstrong	1813–1814
	James Monroe	1814–1815
	William Crawford	1815–1817
Attorney General	Caesar Rodney	1809–1811
	William Pinkney	1811–1814
	Richard Rush	1814–1817
Postmaster General	Gideon Granger	1809–1814
	Return Meigs	1814–1817
Secretary of Navy	Paul Hamilton	1809–1813
	William Jones	1813–1814
	Benjamin Crowninshield	1814–1817

The Monroe Administration

Secretary of State	John Quincy Adams	1817–1825
Secretary of Treasury	William Crawford	1817–1825
Secretary of War	George Graham	1817
	John C. Calhoun	1817–1825
Attorney General	Richard Rush	1817
	William Wirt	1817–1825
Postmaster General	Return Meigs	1817–1823
	John McLean	1823–1825
Secretary of Navy	Benjamin Crowninshield	1817–1818
	Smith Thompson	1818–1823
	Samuel Southard	1823–1825

The John Quincy Adams Administration

Secretary of State	Henry Clay	1825–1829
Secretary of Treasury	Richard Rush	1825–1829
Secretary of War	James Barbour	1825–1828
	Peter Porter	1828–1829
Attorney General	William Wirt	1825–1829
Postmaster General	John McLean	1825–1829
Secretary of Navy	Samuel Southard	1825–1829

The Jackson Administration

Secretary of State	Martin Van Buren	1829–1831
	Edward Livingston	1831–1833
	Louis McLane	1833–1834
	John Forsyth	1834–1837
Secretary of Treasury	Samuel Ingham	1829–1831
	Louis McLane	1831–1833
	William Duane	1833
	Roger B. Taney	1833–1834
	Levi Woodbury	1834–1837
Secretary of War	John H. Eaton	1829–1831
	Lewis Cass	1831–1837
	Benjamin Butler	1837
Attorney General	John M. Berrien	1829–1831
	Roger B. Taney	1831–1833
	Benjamin Butler	1833–1837
Postmaster General	William Barry	1929–1835
	Amos Kendall	1835–1837
Secretary of Navy	John Branch	1829–1831
	Levi Woodbury	1831–1834
	Mahlon Dickerson	1834–1837

The Van Buren Administration

Secretary of State	John Forsyth	1837–1841
Secretary of Treasury	Levi Woodbury	1837–1841
Secretary of War	Joel Poinsett	1837–1841
Attorney General	Benjamin Butler	1837–1838
	Felix Grundy	1838–1840
	Henry D. Gilpin	1840–1841
Postmaster General	Amos Kendall	1837–1840
	John M. Niles	1840–1841
Secretary of Navy	Mahlon Dickerson	1837–1838
	James Paulding	1838–1841

The William Harrison Administration

Secretary of State	Daniel Webster	1841
Secretary of Treasury	Thomas Ewing	1841
Secretary of War	John Bell	1841
Attorney General	John J. Crittenden	1841
Postmaster General	Francis Granger	1841
Secretary of Navy	George Badger	1841

The Tyler Administration

Secretary of State	Daniel Webster	1841–1843
	Hugh S. Legaré	1843
	Abel P. Upshur	1843–1844
	John C. Calhoun	1844–1845
Secretary of Treasury	Thomas Ewing	1841
	Walter Forward	1841–1843
	John C. Spencer	1843–1844
	George Bibb	1844–1845
Secretary of War	John Bell	1841
	John C. Spencer	1841–1843
	James M. Porter	1843–1844
	William Wilkins	1844–1845
Attorney General	John J. Crittenden	1841
	Hugh S. Legaré	1841–1843
	John Nelson	1843–1845
Postmaster General	Francis Granger	1841
	Charles Wickliffe	1841
Secretary of Navy	George Badger	1841
	Abel P. Upshur	1841
	David Henshaw	1843–1844
	Thomas Gilmer	1844
	John Y. Mason	1844–1845

The Polk Administration

Secretary of State	James Buchanan	1845–1849
Secretary of Treasury	Robert J. Walker	1845–1849
Secretary of War	William L. Marcy	1845–1849
Attorney General	John Y. Mason	1845–1846
	Nathan Clifford	1846–1848
	Isaac Toucey	1848–1849
Postmaster General	Cave Johnson	1845–1849

| Secretary of Navy | George Bancroft | 1845–1846 |
| | John Y. Mason | 1846–1849 |

| Secretary of Interior | Robert McClelland | 1853–1857 |

The Taylor Administration

Secretary of State	John M. Clayton	1849–1850
Secretary of Treasury	William Meredith	1849–1850
Secretary of War	George Crawford	1849–1850
Attorney General	Reverdy Johnson	1849–1850
Postmaster General	Jacob Collamer	1849–1850
Secretary of Navy	William Preston	1849–1850
Secretary of Interior	Thomas Ewing	1849–1850

The Fillmore Administration

Secretary of State	Daniel Webster	1850–1852
	Edward Everett	1852–1853
Secretary of Treasury	Thomas Corwin	1850–1853
Secretary of War	Charles Conrad	1850–1853
Attorney General	John J. Crittenden	1850–1853
Postmaster General	Nathan Hall	1850–1852
	Sam D. Hubbard	1852–1853
Secretary of Navy	William A. Graham	1850–1852
	John P. Kennedy	1852–1853
Secretary of Interior	Thomas McKennan	1850
	Alexander Stuart	1850–1853

The Pierce Administration

Secretary of State	William L. Marcy	1853–1857
Secretary of Treasury	James Guthrie	1853–1857
Secretary of War	Jefferson Davis	1853–1857
Attorney General	Caleb Cushing	1853–1857
Postmaster General	James Campbell	1853–1857
Secretary of Navy	James C. Dobbin	1853–1857

The Buchanan Administration

Secretary of State	Lewis Cass	1857–1860
	Jeremiah S. Black	1860–1861
Secretary of Treasury	Howell Cobb	1857–1860
	Philip Thomas	1860–1861
	John A. Dix	1861
Secretary of War	John B. Floyd	1857–1861
	Joseph Holt	1861
Attorney General	Jeremiah S. Black	1857–1860
	Edwin M. Stanton	1860–1861
Postmaster General	Aaron V. Brown	1857–1859
	Joseph Holt	1859–1861
	Horatio King	1861
Secretary of Navy	Isaac Toucey	1857–1861
Secretary of Interior	Jacob Thompson	1857–1861

The Lincoln Administration

Secretary of State	William H. Seward	1861–1865
Secretary of Treasury	Samuel P. Chase	1861–1864
	William P. Fessenden	1864–1865
	Hugh McCulloch	1865
Secretary of War	Simon Cameron	1861–1862
	Edwin M. Stanton	1862–1865
Attorney General	Edward Bates	1861–1864
	James Speed	1864–1865
Postmaster General	Horatio King	1861
	Montgomery Blair	1861–1864
	William Dennison	1864–1865
Secretary of Navy	Gideon Welles	1861–1865
Secretary of Interior	Caleb B. Smith	1861–1863
	John P. Usher	1863–1865

The Andrew Johnson Administration

Secretary of State	William H. Seward	1865–1869
Secretary of Treasury	Hugh McCulloch	1865–1869
Secretary of War	Edwin M. Stanton	1865–1867
	Ulysses S. Grant	1867–1868
	Lorenzo Thomas	1868
	John M. Schofield	1868–1869

Attorney General	James Speed	1865–1866
	Henry Stanbery	1866–1868
	William M. Evarts	1868–1869
Postmaster General	William Dennison	1865–1866
	Alexander Randall	1866–1869
Secretary of Navy	Gideon Welles	1865–1869
Secretary of Interior	John P. Usher	1865
	James Harlan	1865–1866
	Orville H. Browning	1866–1869

The Grant Administration

Secretary of State	Elihu B. Washburne	1869
	Hamilton Fish	1869–1877
Secretary of Treasury	George S. Boutwell	1869–1873
	William Richardson	1873–1874
	Benjamin Bristow	1874–1876
	Lot M. Morrill	1876–1877
Secretary of War	John A. Rawlins	1869
	William T. Sherman	1869
	William W. Belknap	1869–1876
	Alphonso Taft	1876
	James D. Cameron	1876–1877
Attorney General	Ebenezer Hoar	1869–1870
	Amos T. Ackerman	1870–1871
	G. H. Williams	1871–1875
	Edwards Pierrepont	1875–1876
	Alphonso Taft	1876–1877
Postmaster General	John A. J. Creswell	1869–1874
	James W. Marshall	1874
	Marshall Jewell	1874–1876
	James N. Tyner	1876–1877
Secretary of Navy	Adolph E. Borie	1869
	George M. Robeson	1869–1877
Secretary of Interior	Jacob D. Cox	1869–1870
	Columbus Delano	1870–1875
	Zachariah Chandler	1875–1877

The Hayes Administration

Secretary of State	William B. Evarts	1877–1881
Secretary of Treasury	John Sherman	1877–1881
Secretary of War	George W. McCrary	1877–1879
	Alex Ramsey	1879–1881
Attorney General	Charles Devens	1877–1881
Postmaster General	David M. Key	1877–1880
	Horace Maynard	1880–1881

Secretary of Navy	Richard W. Thompson	1877–1880
	Nathan Goff, Jr.	1881
Secretary of Interior	Carl Schurz	1877–1881

The Garfield Administration

Secretary of State	James G. Blaine	1881
Secretary of Treasury	William Windom	1881
Secretary of War	Robert T. Lincoln	1881
Attorney General	Wayne MacVeagh	1881
Postmaster General	Thomas L. James	1881
Secretary of Navy	William H. Hunt	1881
Secretary of Interior	Samuel J. Kirkwood	1881

The Arthur Administration

Secretary of State	F. T. Frelinghuysen	1881–1885
Secretary of Treasury	Charles J. Folger	1881–1884
	Walter Q. Gresham	1884
	Hugh McCulloch	1884–1885
Secretary of War	Robert T. Lincoln	1881–1885
Attorney General	Benjamin H. Brewster	1881–1885
Postmaster General	Timothy O. Howe	1881–1883
	Walter Q. Gresham	1883–1884
	Frank Hatton	1884–1885
Secretary of Navy	William H. Hunt	1881–1882
	William E. Chandler	1882–1885
Secretary of Interior	Samuel J. Kirkwood	1881–1882
	Henry M. Teller	1882–1885

The First Cleveland Administration

Secretary of State	Thomas F. Bayard	1885–1889
Secretary of Treasury	Daniel Manning	1885–1887
	Charles S. Fairchild	1887–1889
Secretary of War	William C. Endicott	1885–1889
Attorney General	Augustus H. Garland	1885–1889

Postmaster General	William F. Vilas	1885–1888
	Don M. Dickinson	1888–1889
Secretary of Navy	William C. Whitney	1885–1889
Secretary of Interior	Lucius Q. C. Lamar	1885–1888
	William F. Vilas	1888–1889
Secretary of Agriculture	Norman J. Colman	1889

The Benjamin Harrison Administration

Secretary of State	James G. Blaine	1889–1892
	John W. Foster	1892–1893
Secretary of Treasury	William Windom	1889–1891
	Charles Foster	1891–1983
Secretary of War	Redfield Proctor	1889–1891
	Stephen B. Elkins	1891–1893
Attorney General	William H. H. Miller	1889–1891
Postmaster General	John Wanamaker	1889–1893
Secretary of Navy	Benjamin F. Tracy	1889–1893
Secretary of Interior	John W. Noble	1889–1893
Secretary of Agriculture	Jeremiah M. Rusk	1889–1893

The Second Cleveland Administration

Secretary of State	Walter Q. Gresham	1893–1895
	Richard Olney	1895–1897
Secretary of Treasury	John G. Carlisle	1893–1897
Secretary of War	Daniel S. Lamont	1893–1987
Attorney General	Richard Olney	1893–1895
	James Harmon	1895–1897
Postmaster General	Wilson S. Bissell	1893–1895
	William L. Wilson	1895–1897
Secretary of Navy	Hilary A. Herbert	1893–1897
Secretary of Interior	Hoke Smith	1893–1896
	David R. Francis	1896–1897
Secretary of Agriculture	Julius S. Morton	1893–1897

The McKinley Administration

Secretary of State	John Sherman	1897–1898
	William R. Day	1898
	John Hay	1898–1901
Secretary of Treasury	Lyman J. Gage	1897–1901
Secretary of War	Russell A. Alger	1897–1899
	Elihu Root	1899–1901
Attorney General	Joseph McKenna	1897–1898
	John W. Griggs	1898–1901
	Philander C. Knox	1901
Postmaster General	James A. Gary	1897–1898
	Charles E. Smith	1898–1901
Secretary of Navy	John D. Long	1897–1901
Secretary of Interior	Cornelius N. Bliss	1897–1899
	Ethan A. Hitchcock	1899–1901
Secretary of Agriculture	James Wilson	1897–1901

The Theodore Roosevelt Administration

Secretary of State	John Hay	1901–1905
	Elihu Root	1905–1909
	Robert Bacon	1909
Secretary of Treasury	Lyman J. Gage	1901–1902
	Leslie M. Shaw	1902–1907
	George B. Cortelyou	1907–1909
Secretary of War	Elihu Root	1901–1904
	William H. Taft	1904–1908
	Luke E. Wright	1908–1909
Attorney General	Philander C. Knox	1901–1904
	William H. Moody	1904–1906
	Charles J. Bonaparte	1906–1909
Postmaster General	Charles E. Smith	1901–1902
	Henry C. Payne	1902–1904
	Robert J. Wynne	1904–1905
	George B. Cortelyou	1905–1907
	George von L. Meyer	1907–1909
Secretary of Navy	John D. Long	1901–1902
	William H. Moody	1902–1904
	Paul Morton	1904–1905
	Charles J. Bonaparte	1905–1906
	Victor H. Metcalf	1906–1908
	Truman H. Newberry	1908–1909
Secretary of Interior	Ethan A. Hitchcock	1901–1907
	James R. Garfield	1907–1909
Secretary of Agriculture	James Wilson	1901–1909
Secretary of Labor and Commerce	George B. Cortelyou	1903–1904
	Victor H. Metcalf	1904–1906
	Oscar S. Straus	1906–1909
	Charles Nagel	1909

The Taft Administration

Secretary of State	Philander C. Knox	1909–1913
Secretary of Treasury	Franklin MacVeagh	1909–1913
Secretary of War	Jacob M. Dickinson Henry L. Stimson	1909–1911 1911–1913
Attorney General	George W. Wickersham	1909–1913
Postmaster General	Frank H. Hitchcock	1909–1913
Secretary of Navy	George von L. Meyer	1909–1913
Secretary of Interior	Richard A. Ballinger Walter L. Fisher	1909–1911 1911–1913
Secretary of Agriculture	James Wilson	1909–1913
Secretary of Labor and Commerce	Charles Nagel	1909–1913

The Wilson Administration

Secretary of State	William J. Bryan Robert Lansing Bainbridge Colby	1913–1915 1915–1920 1920–1921
Secretary of Treasury	William G. McAdoo Carter Glass David F. Houston	1913–1918 1918–1920 1920–1921
Secretary of War	Lindley M. Garrison Newton D. Baker	1913–1916 1916–1921
Attorney General	James C. McReynolds Thomas W. Gregory A. Mitchell Palmer	1913–1914 1914–1919 1919–1921
Postmaster General	Albert S. Burleson	1913–1921
Secretary of Navy	Josephus Daniels	1913–1921
Secretary of Interior	Franklin K. Lane John B. Payne	1913–1920 1920–1921
Secretary of Agriculture	David F. Houston Edwin T. Meredith	1913–1920 1920–1921
Secretary of Commerce	William C. Redfield Joshua W. Alexander	1913–1919 1919–1921
Secretary of Labor	William B. Wilson	1913–1921

The Harding Administration

Secretary of State	Charles E. Hughes	1921–1923
Secretary of Treasury	Andrew Mellon	1921–1923
Secretary of War	John W. Weeks	1921–1923
Attorney General	Harry M. Daugherty	1921–1923
Postmaster General	Will H. Hays Hubert Work Harry S. New	1921–1922 1922–1923 1923
Secretary of Navy	Edwin Denby	1921–1923
Secretary of Interior	Albert B. Fall Hubert Work	1921–1923 1923
Secretary of Agriculture	Henry C. Wallace	1921–1923
Secretary of Commerce	Herbert C. Hoover	1921–1923
Secretary of Labor	James J. Davis	1921–1923

The Coolidge Administration

Secretary of State	Charles E. Hughes Frank B. Kellogg	1923–1925 1925–1929
Secretary of Treasury	Andrew Mellon	1923–1929
Secretary of War	John W. Weeks Dwight F. Davis	1923–1925 1925–1929
Attorney General	Henry M. Daugherty Harlan F. Stone John G. Sargent	1923–1924 1924–1925 1925–1929
Postmaster General	Harry S. New	1923–1929
Secretary of Navy	Edwin Denby Curtis D. Wilbur	1923–1924 1924–1929
Secretary of Interior	Hubert Work Roy O. West	1923–1928 1928–1929
Secretary of Agriculture	Henry C. Wallace Howard M. Gore William M. Jardine	1923–1924 1924–1925 1925–1929
Secretary of Commerce	Herbert C. Hoover William F. Whiting	1923–1928 1928–1929
Secretary of Labor	James J. Davis	1923–1929

The Hoover Administration

Secretary of State	Henry L. Stimson	1929–1933
Secretary of Treasury	Andrew Mellon Ogden L. Mills	1929–1932 1932–1933

Secretary of War	James W. Good	1929
	Patrick J. Hurley	1929–1933
Attorney General	William D. Mitchell	1929–1933
Postmaster General	Walter F. Brown	1929–1933
Secretary of Navy	Charles F. Adams	1929–1933
Secretary of Interior	Ray L. Wilbur	1929–1933
Secretary of Agriculture	Arthur M. Hyde	1929–1933
Secretary of Commerce	Robert P. Lamont	1929–1932
	Roy D. Chapin	1932–1933
Secretary of Labor	James J. Davis	1929–1930
	William N. Doak	1930–1933

The Franklin D. Roosevelt Administration

Secretary of State	Cordell Hull	1933–1944
	E. R. Stettinius, Jr.	1944–1945
Secretary of Treasury	William H. Woodin	1933–1934
	Henry Morgenthau, Jr.	1934–1945
Secretary of War	George H. Dern	1933–1936
	Henry A. Woodring	1936–1940
	Henry L. Stimson	1940–1945
Attorney General	Homer S. Cummings	1933–1939
	Frank Murphy	1939–1940
	Robert H. Jackson	1940–1941
	Francis Biddle	1941–1945
Postmaster General	James A. Farley	1933–1940
	Frank C. Walker	1940–1945
Secretary of Navy	Claude A. Swanson	1933–1940
	Charles Edison	1940
	Frank Knox	1940–1944
	James V. Forrestal	1944–1945
Secretary of Interior	Harold L. Ickes	1933–1945
Secretary of Agriculture	Henry A. Wallace	1933–1940
	Claude R. Wickard	1940–1945
Secretary of Commerce	Daniel C. Roper	1933–1939
	Harry L. Hopkins	1939–1940
	Jesse Jones	1940–1945
	Henry A. Wallace	1945
Secretary of Labor	Frances Perkins	1933–1945

The Truman Administration

Secretary of State	James F. Byrnes	1945–1947
	George C. Marshall	1947–1949
	Dean G. Acheson	1949–1953

Secretary of Treasury	Fred M. Vinson	1945–1946
	John W. Snyder	1946–1953
Secretary of War	Robert P. Patterson	1945–1947
	Kenneth C. Royall	1947
Attorney General	Tom C. Clark	1945–1949
	J. Howard McGrath	1949–1952
	James P. McGranery	1952–1953
Postmaster General	Frank C. Walker	1945
	Robert E. Hannegan	1945–1957
	Jessee M. Donaldson	1947–1953
Secretary of Navy	James V. Forrestal	1945–1947
Secretary of Interior	Harold L. Ickes	1945–1946
	Julius A. Krug	1946–1949
	Oscar L. Chapman	1949–1953
Secretary of Agriculture	Clinton P. Anderson	1945–1948
	Charles F. Brannan	1948–1953
Secretary of Commerce	Henry A. Wallace	1945–1946
	W. Averell Harriman	1946–1948
	Charles W. Sawyer	1948–1953
Secretary of Labor	Lewis B. Schwellenbach	1945–1948
	Maurice J. Tobin	1948–1953
Secretary of Defense	James V. Forrestal	1947–1949
	Louis A. Johnson	1949–1950
	George C. Marshall	1950–1951
	Robert A. Lovett	1951–1953

The Eisenhower Administration

Secretary of State	John Foster Dulles	1953–1959
	Christian A. Herter	1959–1961
Secretary of Treasury	George M. Humphrey	1953–1957
	Robert B. Anderson	1957–1961
Attorney General	Herbert Brownell, Jr.	1953–1958
	William P. Rogers	1958–1961
Postmaster General	Arthur E. Summerfield	1953–1961
Secretary of Interior	Douglas McKay	1953–1956
	Fred A. Seaton	1956–1961
Secretary of Agriculture	Ezra T. Benson	1953–1961
Secretary of Commerce	Sinclair Weeks	1953–1958
	Lewis L. Strauss	1958–1959
	Frederick H. Mueller	1959–1961
Secretary of Labor	Martin P. Durkin	1953
	James P. Mitchell	1953–1961
Secretary of Defense	Charles E. Wilson	1953–1957
	Neil H. McElroy	1957–1959
	Thomas S. Gates, Jr.	1959–1961

Secretary of Health, Education and Welfare	Oveta Culp Hobby	1953–1955
	Marion B. Folsom	1955–1958
	Arthur S. Flemming	1958–1961

The Kennedy Administration

Secretary of State	Dean Rusk	1961–1963
Secretary of Treasury	C. Douglas Dillon	1961–1963
Attorney General	Robert F. Kennedy	1961–1963
Postmaster General	J. Edward Day	1961–1963
	John A. Gronouski	1963
Secretary of Interior	Stewart L. Udall	1961–1963
Secretary of Agriculture	Orville L. Freeman	1961–1963
Secretary of Commerce	Luther H. Hodges	1961–1963
Secretary of Labor	Arthur J. Goldberg	1961–1962
	W. Willard Wirtz	1962–1963
Secretary of Defense	Robert S. McNamara	1961–1963
Secretary of Health, Education and Welfare	Abraham A. Ribicoff	1961–1962
	Anthony J. Celebrezze	1962–1963

The Lyndon Johnson Administration

Secretary of State	Dean Rusk	1963–1969
Secretary of Treasury	C. Douglas Dillon	1963–1965
	Henry H. Fowler	1965–1969
Attorney General	Robert F. Kennedy	1963–1964
	Nicholas Katzenbach	1965–1966
	Ramsey Clark	1967–1969
Postmaster General	John A. Gronouski	1963–1965
	Lawrence F. O'Brien	1965–1968
	Marvin Watson	1968–1969
Secretary of Interior	Stewart L. Udall	1963–1969
Secretary of Agriculture	Orville L. Freeman	1963–1969
Secretary of Commerce	Luther H. Hodges	1963–1964
	John T. Connor	1964–1967
	Alexander B. Trowbridge	1967–1968
	Cyrus R. Smith	1968–1969
Secretary of Labor	W. Willard Wirtz	1963–1969

Secretary of Defense	Robert F. McNamara	1963–1968
	Clark Clifford	1968–1969
Secretary of Health, Education and Welfare	Anthony J. Celebrezze	1963–1965
	John W. Gardner	1965–1968
	Wilbur J. Cohen	1968–1969
Secretary of Housing and Urban Development	Robert C. Weaver	1966–1969
	Robert C. Wood	1969
Secretary of Transportation	Alan S. Boyd	1967–1969

The Nixon Administration

Secretary of State	William P. Rogers	1969–1973
	Henry A. Kissinger	1973–1974
Secretary of Treasury	David M. Kennedy	1969–1970
	John B. Connally	1971–1972
	George P. Shultz	1972–1974
	William E. Simon	1974
Attorney General	John N. Mitchell	1969–1972
	Richard G. Kleindienst	1972–1973
	Elliot L. Richardson	1973
	William B. Saxbe	1973–1974
Postmaster General	Winton M. Blount	1969–1971
Secretary of Interior	Walter J. Hickel	1969–1970
	Rogers Morton	1971–1974
Secretary of Agriculture	Clifford M. Hardin	1969–1971
	Earl L. Butz	1971–1974
Secretary of Commerce	Maurice H. Stans	1969–1972
	Peter G. Peterson	1972–1973
	Frederick B. Dent	1973–1974
Secretary of Labor	George P. Shultz	1969–1970
	James D. Hodgson	1970–1973
	Peter J. Brennan	1973–1974
Secretary of Defense	Melvin R. Laird	1969–1973
	Elliot L. Richardson	1973
	James R. Schlesinger	1973–1974
Secretary of Health, Education and Welfare	Robert H. Finch	1969–1970
	Elliot L. Richardson	1970–1973
	Casper W. Weinberger	1973–1974
Secretary of Housing and Urban Development	George Romney	1969–1973
	James T. Lynn	1973–1974
Secretary of Transportation	John A. Volpe	1969–1973
	Claude S. Brinegar	1973–1974

The Ford Administration

Secretary of State	Henry A. Kissinger	1974–1977
Secretary of Treasury	William E. Simon	1974–1977
Attorney General	William Saxbe	1974–1975
	Edward Levi	1975–1977
Secretary of Interior	Rogers Morton	1974–1975
	Stanley K. Hathaway	1975
	Thomas Kleppe	1975–1977
Secretary of Agriculture	Earl L. Butz	1974–1976
	John A. Knebel	1976–1977
Secretary of Commerce	Frederick B. Dent	1974–1975
	Rogers Morton	1975–1976
	Elliot L. Richardson	1976–1977
Secretary of Labor	Peter J. Brennan	1974–1975
	John T. Dunlop	1975–1976
	W. J. Usery	1976–1977
Secretary of Defense	James R. Schlesinger	1974–1975
	Donald Rumsfeld	1975–1977
Secretary of Health, Education and Welfare	Casper Weinberger	1974–1975
	Forrest D. Mathews	1975–1977
Secretary of Housing and Urban Development	James T. Lynn	1974–1975
	Carla A. Hills	1975–1977
Secretary of Transportation	Claude Brinegar	1974–1975
	William T. Coleman	1975–1977

The Carter Administration

Secretary of State	Cyrus R. Vance	1977–1980
	Edmund Muskie	1980–1981
Secretary of Treasury	W. Michael Blumenthal	1977–1979
	G. William Miller	1979–1981
Attorney General	Griffin Bell	1977–1979
	Benjamin R. Civiletti	1979–1981
Secretary of Interior	Cecil D. Andrus	1977–1981
Secretary of Agriculture	Robert Bergland	1977–1981
Secretary of Commerce	Juanita M. Kreps	1977–1979
	Philip M. Klutznick	1979–1981
Secretary of Labor	F. Ray Marshall	1977–1981
Secretary of Defense	Harold Brown	1977–1981
Secretary of Health Education and Welfare	Joseph A. Califano	1977–1979
	Patricia R. Harris	1979
Secretary of Health and Human Services	Patricia R. Harris	1979–1981
Secretary of Education	Shirley M. Hufstedler	1979–1981
Secretary of Housing and Urban Development	Patricia R. Harris	1977–1979
	Moon Landrieu	1979–1981
Secretary of Transportation	Brock Adams	1977–1979
	Neil E. Goldschmidt	1979–1981
Secretary of Energy	James R. Schlesinger	1977–1979
	Charles W. Duncan	1979–1981

The Reagan Administration

Secretary of State	Alexander M. Haig	1981–1982
	George Shultz	1982–
Secretary of Treasury	Donald Regan	1981–1985
	James Baker	1985–
Attorney General	William French Smith	1981–1985
	Edwin Meese	1985–
Secretary of Interior	James Watt	1981–1983
	William P. Clark	1983–1985
	Donald Hodel	1985–
Secretary of Agriculture	John Block	1981–
Secretary of Commerce	Malcolm Baldrige	1981–
Secretary of Labor	Raymond Donovan	1981–1985
	William Brock	1985–
Secretary of Defense	Casper Weinberger	1981–
Secretary of Health and Human Services	Richard Schweiker	1981–1983
	Margaret Heckler	1983–1985
Secretary of Education	Terrel Bell	1981–1985
	William J. Bennett	1985–
Secretary of Housing and Urban Development	Samuel Pierce	1981–
Secretary of Transportation	Drew Lewis	1981–1983
	Elizabeth Dole	1983–
Secretary of Energy	James Edwards	1981–1982
	Donald Hodel	1982–1985
	John Herrington	1985–

Supreme Court Justices

Name	Terms of Service[1]	Appointed by	Name	Terms of Service[1]	Appointed by
John Jay	1789–1795	Washington	George Shiras, Jr.	1892–1903	B. Harrison
James Wilson	1789–1798	Washington	Howell E. Jackson	1893–1895	B. Harrison
John Rutledge	1790–1791	Washington	Edward D. White	1894–1910	Cleveland
William Cushing	1790–1810	Washington	Rufus W. Peckham	1896–1909	Cleveland
John Blair	1790–1796	Washington	Joseph McKenna	1898–1925	McKinley
James Iredell	1790–1799	Washington	Oliver W. Homes	1902–1932	T. Roosevelt
Thomas Johnson	1792–1793	Washington	William R. Day	1903–1922	T. Roosevelt
William Paterson	1793–1806	Washington	William H. Moody	1906–1910	T. Roosevelt
John Rutledge[2]	1795	Washington	Horace H. Lurton	1910–1914	Taft
Samuel Chase	1796–1811	Washington	Charles E. Hughes	1910–1916	Taft
Oliver Ellsworth	1796–1800	Washington	Willis Van Devanter	1911–1937	Taft
Bushrod Washington	1799–1829	J. Adams	Joseph R. Lamar	1911–1916	Taft
Alfred Moore	1800–1804	J. Adams	**Edward D. White**	1910–1921	Taft
John Marshall	1801–1835	J. Adams	Mahlon Pitney	1912–1922	Taft
William Johnson	1804–1834	Jefferson	James C. McReynolds	1914–1941	Wilson
Brockholst Livingston	1807–1823	Jefferson	Louis D. Brandeis	1916–1939	Wilson
Thomas Todd	1807–1826	Jefferson	John H. Clarke	1916–1922	Wilson
Gabriel Duval	1811–1835	Madison	**William H. Taft**	1921–1930	Harding
Joseph Story	1812–1845	Madison	George Sutherland	1922–1938	Harding
Smith Thompson	1823–1843	Monroe	Pierce Butler	1923–1939	Harding
Robert Trimble	1826–1828	J. Q. Adams	Edward T. Sanford	1923–1930	Harding
John McLean	1830–1861	Jackson	Harlan F. Stone	1925–1941	Coolidge
Henry Baldwin	1830–1844	Jackson	**Charles E. Hughes**	1930–1941	Hoover
James M. Wayne	1835–1867	Jackson	Owen J. Roberts	1930–1945	Hoover
Roger B. Taney	1836–1864	Jackson	Benjamin N. Cardozo	1932–1938	Hoover
Philip P. Barbour	1836–1841	Jackson	Hugo L. Black	1937–1971	F. Roosevelt
John Cartron	1837–1865	Van Buren	Stanley F. Reed	1938–1957	F. Roosevelt
John McKinley	1838–1852	Van Buren	Felix Frankfurter	1939–1962	F. Roosevelt
Peter V. Daniel	1842–1860	Van Buren	William O. Douglas	1939–1975	F. Roosevelt
Samuel Nelson	1845–1872	Tyler	Frank Murphy	1940–1949	F. Roosevelt
Levi Woodbury	1845–1851	Polk	**Harlan F. Stone**	1941–1946	F. Roosevelt
Robert C. Grier	1846–1870	Polk	James F. Byrnes	1941–1942	F. Roosevelt
Benjamin R. Curtis	1851–1857	Fillmore	Robert H. Jackson	1941–1954	F. Roosevelt
John A. Campbell	1853–1861	Pierce	Wiley B. Rutledge	1943–1949	F. Roosevelt
Nathan Clifford	1858–1881	Buchanan	Harold H. Burton	1945–1958	Truman
Noah H. Swayne	1862–1881	Lincoln	**Frederick M. Vinson**	1946–1953	Truman
Samuel F. Miller	1862–1890	Lincoln	Tom C. Clark	1949–1967	Truman
David Davis	1862–1877	Lincoln	Sherman Minton	1949–1956	Truman
Stephen J. Field	1863–1897	Lincoln	**Earl Warren**	1953–1969	Eisenhower
Salmon P. Chase	1864–1873	Lincoln	John Marshall Harlan	1955–1971	Eisenhower
William Strong	1870–1880	Grant	William J. Brennan, Jr.	1956–	Eisenhower
Joseph P. Bradley	1870–1892	Grant	Charles E. Whittaker	1957–1962	Eisenhower
Ward Hunt	1873–1882	Grant	Potter Stewart	1958–1981	Eisenhower
Morrison R. Waite	1873–1882	Grant	Byron R. White	1962–	Kennedy
John M. Harlan	1877–1911	Hayes	Arthur J. Goldberg	1962–1965	Kennedy
William B. Woods	1881–1887	Hayes	Abe Fortas	1965–1970	Johnson
Stanley Matthews	1881–1889	Garfield	Thurgood Marshall	1967–	Johnson
Horace Gray	1882–1902	Arthur	**Warren E. Burger**	1969–	Nixon
Samuel Blatchford	1882–1893	Arthur	Harry A. Blackmun	1970–	Nixon
Lucius Q. C. Lamar	1888–1893	Cleveland	Lewis F. Powell, Jr.	1971–	Nixon
Melville W. Fuller	1888–1910	Cleveland	William H. Rehnquist	1971–	Nixon
David J. Brewer	1890–1910	B. Harrison	John Paul Stevens	1975–	Ford
Henry B. Brown	1891–1906	B. Harrison	Sandra Day O'Connor	1981–	Reagan

Chief Justices in bold type

1 The date on which the justice took his judicial oath is here used as the date of the beginning of his service, for until that oath is taken he is not vested with the prerogatives of his office. Justices, however, receive their commissions ("letters patent") before taking their oath—in some instances, in the preceding year.

2 Acting Chief Justice; Senate refused to confirm appointment.

Credits

2 Rare Book Division, New York Public Library, Astor, Lenox and Tilden Foundations 5 By permission of the Folger Shakespeare Library 9 Museo de America, Madrid/Photo MAS 10 *La Salle Crossing Lake Michigan on the Ice;* George CATLIN; National Gallery of Art, Washington, D.C., Paul Mellon Collection, 1965 13 By permission of the Folger Shakespeare Library 14 Reproduced by Courtesy of the Trustees of the British Museum 21 Courtesy A. H. Robins Company 22 National Portrait Gallery, Smithsonian Institution, Washington, D.C. 25 Courtesy, American Antiquarian Society 28 The I.N. Phelps Stokes Collection of American Historical Prints, Prints Division, New York Public Library, Astor, Lenox and Tilden Foundations 31 Courtesy, Museum of Fine Arts, Boston. Bequest of Maxim Karolik 36 Massachusetts Historical Society 37 Rare Book Division, New York Public Library, Astor, Lenox and Tilden Foundations 42 Courtesy, American Antiquarian Society 43 Abby Aldrich Rockefeller Folk Art Center 47 Shelburne Museum, Inc. 53 Courtesy, The Henry Francis du Pont Winterthur Museum 55(l) The Library Company of Philadelphia 55(r) The Historical Society of Pennsylvania 58 The Trustees of Sir John Soane's Museum 61 Newberry Library, Chicago 66 Library of Congress 67 Colonial Williamsburg Photograph 72 Library of Congress 75 Lexington Historical Society 77(l) By courtesy of the National Portrait Gallery, London 77(r) Library of Congress 82 Copyright Yale University Art Gallery 83 Library of Congress 87 Abby Aldrich Rockefeller Folk Art Center, Gift of Dr. and Mrs. Richard M. Kain in memory of George Hay Kain 88 New York State Historical Association, Cooperstown 94(both) Smithsonian Institution 96 Library of Congress 99, 105(both) Independence National Historical Park, Eastern National Park and Monument Association 110 Bibliotheque Nationale, Paris/Giraudon 111 New York State Historical Association, Cooperstown 113 From *Our First Century* 115 Courtesy of Lilly Library, Indiana University, Bloomington 117, 122 Library of Congress 123(t) Courtesy of the New-York Historical Society, New York City 123(b) Department of the Navy 126 Chicago Historical Society 132 Pennsylvania Academy of the Fine Arts, Harrison Earl Fund Purchase 133 Library of Congress 140(l) The State Historical Society of Colorado 140(r) Denver Public Library, Western History Department 142 The Hudson's Bay Company 145 Courtesy of the New-York Historical Society, New York City 156 In the Collection of The Corcoran Gallery of Art, Gift of William Wilson Corcoran 159 Culver Pictures 168 Mattatuck Museum, Waterbury, Connecticut 173 The Whaling Museum, New Bedford, Mass. 178 Newberry Library, Chicago 179, 180 Bettmann Archive 181 Library of Congress 183 Picture Collection, New York Public Library, Astor, Lenox and Tilden Foundations 189(tl,tr) *Harper's New Monthly Magazine* 189(br) *Ballou's Pictorial* 195 The Historic New Orleans Collection, 533 Royal Street 200 Sophia Smith Collection, Smith College 206 Library of Congress 208 Texas State Capitol 210 The Newberry Library, Chicago 226 Courtesy of the New-York Historical Society, New York City 223, 251, 259 Library of Congress 261 *Harper's Weekly*, November 16, 1867 266 Library of Congress

Index

Freemen in American colonies, 26, 40
Free Soil movement, Lincoln's stand
on, 242
Free Soil party, 222–225; Republican
party as, 227, 230, 234
Fremont, John C., 214, 230–231
French and Indian War, 61, 63–64, 68
French Revolution in 1789, 106, 109
Frobisher, Martin, 15
Frontier, people and culture of, 142–
143
Fugitive slave law of 1850, 225–226.
See also Dred Scott v. Sanford (1857)
case
Fulton, Robert, 143–144
Fundamental Constitution of Carolina,
32

■

Gadsden Purchase (1853), 228
Gage, Thomas, 74, 75, 78, 81
Gallatin, James, 124, 136
Gardoqui, Don Diego de, 95
Garrison, William LLoyd, 181–183, 187
Gates, Horatio, 79, 81
Genêt, Edmond, 109–110
George I (King of England), 60
George II (King of England), 63
George III (King of England), 67, 73–78
Georgia colony, 61, 74
Georgian architecture, 52
Germain, Lord George, 79
German immigration: in mid–1800s,
219; to Pennsylvania, 51–52
Gerry, Elbridge, 114
Gettysburg, battle of, 252
Ghent, Treaty of (1814), 136
Gibbons v. Ogden (1824) case, 152–153
Gilbert, Sir Humphrey, 14–16
Gilded Age, 256
Glorious Revolution, in Great Britain,
47–48
Gold: and Cartier, 10; and the Con-
quistadores, 7–9; discovery of, in Cal-
ifornia, 216
Goliad massacre, 207–208
Goodyear, Charles, 148$_{t.1}$, 217–218
Gordon, Thomas, 58
Gould, Jay, 268
Grand Alliance of European monarchs,
153
Grant, Ulysses S., 266–269; corruption
under, 267–268; in election of 1872,
268; as general, 246, 252–254; as
president, 266–269; war department
leadership turned down by, 263
Grasse, Comte de, 82
Great Awakening, in 1700s, 54–55–57,
65, 68, 172
Great Awakening, Second, 172–175,
180–183; and abolitionist movement,
181–183; Northern, 172, 174; South-
ern frontier phase of, 172; and the
Temperance crusade, 174–175, 181
Great Britain: American debts to, following Revolution, 95; and the
American Revolution, 67–84; claim

to Northwest Territory of, 205; conditions in, leading to emigration, 18;
Confederate efforts to involve, in
Civil War, 248–249; confrontation
with, over Oregon territory, 212–213;
confrontation with, over Texas territory, 210–212, 216; constitution of,
and American government, 57–59,
65; Glorious Revolution in, 47–48;
and the Grand Alliance, 153; Ireland
colonized by, 14–15; legislation of,
colonial reaction to. *See* Legislation,
British, colonial reaction to; and Native Americans, 133; North America
explored by, 11–16; North American
colonization by, 19–33. *See also*
Americas; American colonies; Protestantism of, 11–13; Reformation in,
11–14; and slave trade, 130; textile
industry of, and American cotton,
190; trade with, by American colonies, 44–47, 53–54; trade with, resumed after American Revolution,
93; and the Treaty of Ghent, 136; and
U. S. Neutrality in early 1800s, 132–
134; U. S. relations with, in late
1700s, 109–111, 114–116; and the
War of 1812, 134–136; at war with
France in 1803, 130–131; wars with
France of, in America, 60–64, 81, 114–
117
Great Salt Lake, 209
Great Wagon Road, 54
Greeley, Horace, 268
Greenback party, 269
Greenbacks, after the Civil War, 268–
269
Greene, Nathanael, 82
Greenville, Treaty of (1795), 112
Grenville, George, 69–72
Grenville, Sir Richard, 15–16
Griffith, D. W., 257
Grimké sisters, Sarah and Angelina,
183
Guadalupe Hidalgo, Treaty of (1848),
214–215

■

Hakluyt, Richard, 16, 19–20
Halleck, Henry W., 248
Hall v. Cuir (1878), 271$_{t.1}$
Hamilton, Alexander: as abolitionist,
87; Adams (John) opposed to, 114–
118; and Bill of Rights, 101–102; at
Constitutional Convention, 97; constitutional reforms of, 94–95; death
of, 129; and election of 1796, 114;
and federalism, 100–101, 103–104;
and the *Federalist*, 100; and foreign
affairs, 109–111, 114; Grand Design
of, 106–108, 124; Jefferson opposing,
105–106; and Nationalists, 94–95; as
secretary of the treasury, 104–108;
Washington advised by, 108, 113
Hancock, John, 73
Harper's Ferry, Virginia, raid on, 234–
235

Harrison, William Henry, 133, 135,
167–168, 210
Hartford Convention, 135
Harvard College, 37
Harvard Divinity School, 173
Hawthorne, Nathaniel, 160
Hayes, Rutherford B., 269–270
Headright, 22
Helper, Hinton R., 198, 235–236
Henry VII (King of England), 5–6, 11–
13
Henry VIII (King of England), 11–12
Henry, Patrick, 70–71, 74, 97, 101
Henson, Josiah, 200
Hessian mercenaries in the Revolution-
ary War, 77, 79
Hillsborough, Lord, 72
Historia de las Indias (Fra Bartolomé
de Las Casas), 8
Hoe, Richard M., 148$_{t.1}$
Holmes, Oliver Wendall, 160
Hooker, Joseph, 252
Hooker, Thomas, 27
Hotels in 1800s, 155–156
House of Burgesses, in Virginia, 22–23,
40, 45, 70–71, 89
Houston, Sam, 208
Howe, Elias, 148$_{t.1}$, 217–218
Howe, Sir William, 78–79, 81
Hudson, Henry, 28
Huguenots, 12
Hume, David, 96
Hutchinson, Anne, 27
Hutchinson, Thomas, 73–74

■

Ideology of domesticity, 176–177, 180,
183
Immigrants: and Know-Nothing move-
ment, 229; as workers, 219–221
Immigration: to America in 1700s, 51–
52; to Americas, reasons for, 18–19;
mass, beginnings of, in mid–1800s,
216, 218–219; to Mexican border-
lands, in 1830s, 205–206
Impeachment efforts: Belknap, 268;
Chase, 128; Johnson (Andrew), 262;
Pickering, 128
The Impending Crisis of the South
(Helper), 198, 235–236
Implied powers doctrine, 152
Impost tax of 1781, 94
Indentured servants in American colo-
nies, 22, 24, 39–41. *See also* Slavery
Independent sub-treasury bill, 168
Indians. *See* Native Americans
Industrialization: early, and a market
economy, 147–148; and education in
mid–1800s, 179; and slavery, 190–
191; and social class in 1800s, 158
Industrial Revolution: and a new
American working class, 219–221; in
U. S., in mid–1800s, 216–218
Inflation during the Civil War, 245
Insane asylums in 1800s, 179–180
Institutional reform in early 1800s,
177–180

constitutions in, 88–89; taxation proposals during, 94; trade with England in, 93–94; voting pattern changes in, 86, 88; women in, rising expectations of, 87–88; women in, status of, 87–88; See also Articles of Confederation; Constitution, U. S.; Constitutional Congress

Presidential elections: 1796, 114; 1800, 118–119; 1804, 127; 1808, 132; 1812, 134; 1816, 150; 1820, 150, 153; 1824, 160–161, 161t.1; 1828, 161–162; 1832, 165–166; 1836, 167; 1840, 168–169; 1844, 210–211; 1848, 224–225; 1852, 227; 1856, 230–231; 1860, 236–237; 1864, 253–254; 1868, 266–269; 1872, 266–269; 1876, 269–270

Primogeniture, abolished after American Revolution, 86

The Principall Navigation, Voyages, and Discoveries of the English Nation (Hakluyt), 16

Princeton University, 57

Printing press, rotary, invention of, 148t.1

Prisons in 1800s, 179–180

Proclamation of Neutrality, 110

Proclamation of 1763, 69

Prohibitory Act (1775), 69t.1, 76

Prophet, The. *See* Tenskwatawa

Proslavery propaganda, 197–198

Prosser, Gabriel, 198

Protestant Association, 48

Protestant ethic, 179

Protestantism: and the American (Know-Nothing) party, 229; in England and Europe, 11–13, 18–19; and English nationalism, 13; in Maryland, 48; and radical ideas and experiments, 184–185; and revivalism in America, 56–57, 171–172; and sectionalism based on slavery, 231; *See also* Evangelicalism; Puritans; Reformation; Protestant

Protestantism, evangelical: and black Christianity, 201; and reform movement, 172–173; rise of, 172–175; and Whig party, 167, 171–172

Prussia and the Grand Alliance, 153

Public schools, 177–179

Pullman, George M., 148t.1

Pullman car, invention of, 148t.1

Puritanism, history of, 25–26

Puritans: in Massachusetts Bay colony, 25–27, 46–47; in New Netherland colony, 28–29, religion of, 25–26; in westward migration, 142

"Putting-out system" of manufacturing, 147

Quakers: in the Jersey colonies, 29; in the Pennsylvania colony, 30–31; and slavery question in postrevolutionary America, 87

Quartering Act (1765), 69t.1

Quasi-War, between France and U. S. in late 1700s, 114, 116, 118

Quebec Act, 74

Queen Anne's War, 60

Quids, 128–129

Racial discrimination: and antiabolitionist violence in North, 182; after Civil War, 257–258, 260–261, 264–267, 269–272. *See also* Jim Crow laws; and the Mexican War, 214–215; and slavery, 196–197, 250–252, 254

Racism in the South, 270–272

Race riots in 1866, 261

Radicalism of social reform in 1800s, 180–185

Radical Reconstruction, 258, 262–263, 265–270

Railroads: importance of, in mid-1800s, 216–218, 227; replacing canals, 216

Raleigh, Sir Walter, 15–16

Rancheros, 206

Randolph, Edmund, 97, 101, 104

Randolph, John, 128–129, 132

Reaper, mechanical, invention of, 148t.1, 218

Reconstruction, 257–272; in *Birth of a Nation*, 257–258; collapse of, 258; Congressional position on, 258–264; constitutional amendments during (1865–1870), 250–251, 257, 260–261, 262t.1, 267, 271; corruption during, 265; economy of South during, 264–271; during Grant administration, 266–269; historical views of, 257–258; Johnson (Andrew) versus Congress over, 259–263; Johnson (Andrew), policy of, during, 260–263; Lincoln versus Congress over, 258–259; Lincoln, policy of, during, 258–259; money question during, 268–269; political, in South, 265–266; proposals for, during Civil War, 258–259; and racism, 257–258, 265–267, 270–272; Radical, 258, 262–263, 265–270; retreat from, 267; and reunion, in New South, 269–272; social adjustments during, 264–271; in the South, 264–266

Reconstruction Acts, 262–263

Reconstruction amendments, to U. S. Constitution (1865–1870), 250–251, 257, 260–261, 262t.1, 267, 271

"Redeemers" in New South, 270–272

Reed, Esther De Berdt, 87

Reform: institutional, 1800s, 177–180; political, 86; radical, 184–185; social. *See* Families; Social reform; Women

Reformation, Protestant, 11–14

Regional identification in early 1800s, 121

Reign of Terror in France, 109

Religion: in American colonies, 23–32, 54, 55–57; of black Americans, 201; in England, 11–14, 18–19; in Maryland colony, 19, 23–24; of Native Americans, 3; in New England colo-

nies, 55–57; and party choice, in 1840s, 169; sectionalism of, prior to Civil War, 231; of slaves, 200–201; in Spain, 6, 8

Religious revivalism: in the 1700s, 56–57; in 1830s, 171–172; Great Awakening as, 54, 55–57; leading to reform, 171–186; role of women in, 176; Second Great Awakening as, 172–174

Relocation of Native Americans, 141, 163–164

Renaissance, and exploration of the Americas, 5–6

Report on Manufactures (Hamilton), 108

Report on Public Credit (Hamilton), 107

Republicanism following American Revolution, 95–99; and a Bill of Rights, 99, 101–102; and the Constitution, 97–102; problems and reform in, 96–97; and slavery, 98; on trial, 103–119

Republican party: ascendency of, 227, 229–231; Civil War blamed on, 241–242; Dred Scott decision denounced by, 232; in election of 1860, 236–237, 254; as Free Soil party, 227, 230, 234; in Grant era, 266–268; National, 166–167. *See also* Whig party; New. *See* New Republican Party; in power, 1850s, 229–235; radical wing of, mid-1800s, 222; and sectionalism in 1856, 230–231; and slavery issue, 232–235; in South, during Reconstruction, 265–268

Republican party of Jefferson: dissension in, early 1800s, 127–130; and Embargo Act of 1807, 131; versus Federalists, in late 1700s, policies of, 103, 105, 109–117; Federalists oppressing, late 1700s, 109–111; in power, early 1800s, 123–127, 148–149

Resources of the Union and the Confederacy, for the Civil War, 244t.1

Reunion in New South, 269–272

Revenue Act of 1764. *See* Sugar Act

Revere, Paul, 75

Revivalism. *See* Religious revivalism

Revolutionary War. *See* American Revolution

Revolver, invention of, 148t.1

Rhode Island colonies, 27–28, 46–47

Richmond campaign, 247–248, 253

Rights: Bill of, 89, 98–99, 101–102. *See also* Constitutional amendments; civil. *See entries beginning with* Civil rights; equal. *See* Equality; *entries beginning with* Civil rights guaranteed by state constitutions, 89; states'. *See* States' rights

Rillieux, Norbert, 148t.1

Rivers, as transportation system in 1800s, 143–144

Roads, in early 1800s, 143, 149

Roanoke, Virginia, colony, 15–16, 19, 21

Rochambeau, Comte de, 82

Rockingham, Lord, 71
Rocky Mountain Fur Co., 140
Rolfe, John, 21
Rubber, vulcanization of, invention of, 148$_{t.1}$, 217–218
Russell, Jonathan, 136
Russia and the Grand Alliance, 153
Rutgers University, 57
Ryswick, Treaty of (1697), 60

■

St. Augustine, 9
Salem village, witchcraft terror in, 47–48
Sandys, Sir Edwin, 21–22
San Lorenzo, Treaty of (1795), 112
Sans Souci Club, 85
Santa Ana, Antonie López de, 207–208, 214
Santa Fe trade, in mid–1800s, 208–209
Schurz, Carl, 268
Scotch-Irish immigration to American colonies, 51–52
Scott, Winfield, 214, 227, 246
Scrooby Separatists, 24
Secession of southern states before the Civil War, 237, 240–243; early thinking about, 121; and Lincoln's election in 1860, 240
Second Continental Congress, 76, 88–97; economic problems blamed on, 93–95; foreign affairs difficulties of, 95; national government created by, 89–93; state constitutions urged by, 88–89; western land sales by, 90–92; See also Articles of Confederation
Second Great Awakening. See Great Awakening, Second
Second party system, 165, 167–170, 226–228
Second Seminole War, and blacks, 198
Sectionalism prior to Civil War, 222–238; cultural, 231–232; 1857–1860, 231–237; in election of 1856, 230–231; issues in, 237; in literature, 231; in religion, 231; over slavery, 222–237
Sedition law, 116–117
Segregation of black Americans. See Jim Crow laws; Racial discrimination after Civil War
Separation, racial, after Civil War, 264–265
Separatists, 24
Servitude in American colonies, 22, 24, 38–40
Seven Pines, battle of, 248
Seven Years' War, 68, 80. See also French and Indian War
Seward, William, 227, 236, 249
Sewing machine, invention of, 148$_{t.1}$, 217–218
Sex roles, changing, in 1800s, 175–177
Sharecroppers, black Americans as, 264–265
Shays, Daniel, 97
Shays' Rebellion, 97
Shenandoah Valley, 52

Sherman, John, 235
Sherman, William T., 253–254
Sherman's march to the sea, 253–254
Shiloh, battle of, 246–247
Simms, William Gilmore, 231
Slavery: and abolitionist movement, 181–183. See also Abolitionist movement; and agriculture, 188–196; in American colonies, 22, 35, 39–44, 61–62. See also Indentured servants in American colonies; after American Revolution, 87–88; arguments for, 197–198; black experience under, 198–203; and the Catholic church, 206–207; and the Constitution, 223; as issue at Constitutional Convention of 1787, 98–99; and cotton production in the South, 145–146, 188–196; in a democracy, place of, 138; and expansion to Texas, 206; freedmen as fighting, 199–200; and Fugitive Slave Law of 1850, 225–226; and industrialization, 190–191; and Kansas-Nebraska Act, 222–223, 227–230, 233–234; legality of, in Dred Scott case, 232–234; Manifest Destiny and issue of, 211–213, 215–216; in Mexican cession, 224–225; in Mexican War, 215–216; Mexico's attempt to abolish, 206–207; and the Missouri Compromise, 150–151, 223–224, 227–228, 232; morality of, debated by Lincoln and Douglas, 233–234, 237; in new states, movement for prohibiting, 216, 222–233; and the nullification crisis, 164–165; political parties and issue of, 233–237; "positive good" defense of, 197; in postrevolutionary America, 87–88; profitability of, debate over, 191–192; prohibition of, by amendment to U. S. Constitution, 262$_{t.1}$; and racism, 196–197, 250–252, 254; Republican party opposed to, 232–235; resisted by slaves, 198–199; secession, and issue of, 241–243; sectionalism over, prior to Civil War, 222–237; social effects of, 192–198; and the Southern economy, 188–196; in territories, as symbolic issue, 234–235; and tobacco-growing, 188; See also Civil War
Slaves: Afro-American culture of, 200–201; Afro-American religion of, 200–201; experience of, 198–202; family life of, 202–203; kinship network of, 202–203; life expectancy of, 43; literacy of, 198; marriages of, 202–203; and passive resistance, 199; and planters, relationships of, 194–196; population of, by Civil War, 188; rebellions of, 43–44, 187, 198–199; religion of, 200–201; resistance by, 198–199; runaway, as means of resistance, 199; and servants, 158; on small farms, 196; at time of Revolutionary War, 76; trade in, outlawed, 130; treatment of, by masters, 194–196; and the underground railroad, 200
Slave trade: and the Confederate States of America, 241; in the District of

Columbia, 225; issue of, in the Constitution, 98; attempt to outlaw, under Jefferson, 130
Slidell, John, 213, 248–249
Sloughter, Henry, 48
Smith, Adam, 44
Smith, Jedediah, 140
Smith, John, 21
Smith, Joseph, 209
Smith, Sir Thomas, 21
Social adjustments during Reconstruction, 264–271
Social reform: after American Revolution, 86; in 1800s, 171–172, 174–177, 180–185
Social structure: in Chesapeake colonies, 39–40; in colonial New England, 38–39; in 1600s, 40
Society, American, in early 1800s: classes and ranking in, 35–49, 156, 158–159, 192–198, 199–200; equality in, 155, 158; Jacksonian democracy, and changes in, 156–163, 169–170; slaveholding affecting, 192–198; See also Social reform
Society of Friends. See Quakers
Sons of Liberty, 71–72
South, the: agriculture in, 142, 145–146, 188–191, 193–196, 245, 248–249, 264–265. See also Cotton production in South; Tobacco-growing; black Americans in, 264–267. See also Jim Crow laws; Racial discrimination; Slaves; in Civil War. See Civil War; Confederate States of America (Confederacy); cotton production in. See Cotton production in the South; "crisis of fear" in, 234–237; Deep. See Deep South; dueling in, 194; economy of, 264–265; Lower, and cotton, 188–190; New, 269–272; versus North, prior to Civil War. See Sectionalism, prior to Civil War; and North, reconciliation of, 269–272. See also Reconstruction; Old, 192–203; planters in, 193–196; poor whites in, 196–197; Reconstruction in, 264–266. See also Reconstruction; repression of slaves in, 187; secession of, 211, 240–241, 243; Second Great Awakening in, 172; as a slaveholding society, 193–198; social adjustments during Reconstruction in, 264–265; social order of, 251; Upper, economy in, during pre-Civil War era, 188, 197; yeomen farmers in, 196–197
South Carolina: and Fort Sumter, 242; and secession, 240
Southern colonies, population of, 1720–1760, 51$_{t.1}$
Southern Rights Democrats, 236–237
Spain: and American policy following the Revolution, 95; and the Americas, 6–10; armada of, defeated, 14; claim to Texas by, 206; colonization of Americas by, 6–10; dealings with, after the American Revolution, 95; explorations in Americas by, 6–10; France allied with, in wars in America, 61; lands relinquished by in

I–10

election of 1836, 167; in election of 1844, 211; in election of 1848, 224–225; as president, 167–168; as senator, 161–162
Vernier caliper, 218
Vesey, Denmark, 198–200
Vespucci, Amérigo, 7
Vicksburg, battle of, 252
Vikings, 5
Virginia, cession of western land by, 90–91
Virginia colony, 15–16, 19–24, 40–46
Virginian Company, 20–23
Virginia (Confederate ship), 247
Virginia dynasty, 150
Virginia House of Burgesses, 22–23, 40, 45, 70–71, 89
Virginia Plan, 97
Virginia Resolution of Thomas Jefferson, 117–118
Virginia Resolves, 70–71
Voting after American Revolution, pattern changes in, 86
Voting rights for black Americans, problems attaining, 271–272. *See also* Suffrage

■

Wade-Davis bill, 259
Walden (Thoreau), 184
Walker, David, 200
War of Austrian Succession. *See* King George's War
War of 1812, 134–136; and Native Americans, 122; peace following, 138–139, 143; politics of nation-building after, 148–153
War Hawks in 1811–1812, 133–135
War of the League of Augsburg. *See* King William's War
War of Spanish Succession. *See* Queen Anne's War
Warfare in American colonies, 59–64; Braddock's defeat, 62; French and Indian War, 63–64; King William's and Queen Anne's Wars, 60–62
Washington, George: at Constitutional Convention of 1787, 97; as Continental Army commander, 78–82, 95, 116; at Continental Congress of 1774, 74–75; domestic policy of, 111–113;

Farewell Address of, 113; foreign policy of, 109–112; in French and Indian War, 64; Hamilton influencing, 108, 113; as militia commander, 116; Newburgh Conspiracy thwarted by, 94–95; and political party birth, 104; as president, 102, 103–105, 108–112
Washington, D. C., burning of, 135
Wayne, Anthony, 112
Webster, Daniel, 167, 205
Webster-Ashburton Treaty, 205
Weld, Theodore Dwight, 182
West, the: agriculture in, early 1800s, 142–146, 218; battles for, late 1700s, 111–112; and British troops, 111–112, 133; Continental Congress selling lands of, 92–93; culture of, 142–143; Far, expansion to, 205–210; Far, exploitation of, in early 1800s, 139–140; Lewis and Clark's explorations of, 125–126; population shifts to, in early 1800s, 121–122, 141–143; settling of, early 1800s, 121–122, 140–143; settling of, mid–1800s, 208–210; slavery in, Republican party opposed to, 232, 235; state claims in lands of, 90–92; trade in, mid–1800s, 208–209
West Indies as importer of American goods, 53
West Point, creation of, 125
West Virginia, establishment of, 246
Whig party, 165, 167–170; and Compromise of 1850, 226; and Democratic party, rivalry of, 169–170; and election of 1848, 224–225; and election of 1852, 227; and Abraham Lincoln, 239; make-up of, 169–170, 227; and Manifest Destiny, 210–211; and the Mexican War, 215–216; as a new national party, 167–168; weakening and demise of, 227–229, 231; and Wilmot Proviso, 224
Whigs in English Parliament, 67–68
Whiskey Rebellion, 112–113
Whiskey Ring, 268
Whitefield, George, 56–57
White supremacists after the Civil War, 260–261, 265, 267, 269–272
Whitman, Walt, 160, 204
Whitney, Eli, 146, 148t.1
Wilkinson, James, 129
William and Mary (King and Queen of England), 47–48
Williams, Roger, 27

Williams v. Mississippi (1898) case, 271t.2
Wilmot, David, 223
Wilmot Proviso, 223–225
Winthrop, John, 25–27, 35
Witchcraft terror in Salem, 47–48
Wolfe, James, 63–64
Woman suffrage, 267
Women: in abolitionist movement, 158, 183; Civil War affecting, 254; and domesticity, changes in, in 1800s, 175–177; and evangelical protestantism, 174; and factory work, 219–220; in Georgia, 61–62; in post-revolutionary America, 87–88; rising expectations of, 87–88; rights of, in American colonies, 38; roles of, in 1800s, 175–177; status of, in 1820s and 1830s, 158; status of, and women's rights in mid–1800s, 182–183; traditional work of, 219–221; working, in mid–1800s, 219–220
Women's rights movement: after Civil War, 267; in mid–1800s, 182–183
Worcester v. Georgia case, 164
Working class, American, emergence of, 216, 219–221
Workingmen's movements and education, 178
Workingmen's parties, 158
Working women in mid–1800s, 219–220
Wright, Frances, 184

■

XYZ Affair with France, 114–116, 118

■

Yale College, 172
Yazoo controversy, 129
Yeomen farmers: Native Americans as, 122; in New England, 38, 40; and Republican party after Civil War, 265; in Revolutionary War, 78; and slavery, issue of, 196
Young, Brigham, 209
Young America movement, 204–205, 212

Legal Writing
and Other Lawyering Skills

ASPEN PUBLISHERS

Legal Writing
and Other Lawyering Skills

Fifth Edition

Nancy L. Schultz
Professor, Chapman University School of Law

Louis J. Sirico, Jr.
Professor of Law and Director, Legal Writing Program
Villanova Law School

Wolters Kluwer
Law & Business

AUSTIN   BOSTON   CHICAGO   NEW YORK   THE NETHERLANDS

Aspen Publishers
Attn: Permissions Department
76 Ninth Avenue, 7th Floor
New York, NY 10011-5201

To contact Customer Care, e-mail customer.care@aspenpublishers.com, call 1-800-234-1660, fax 1-800-901-9075, or mail correspondence to:

Aspen Publishers
Attn: Order Department
PO Box 990
Frederick, MD 21705

Printed in the United States of America.

1 2 3 4 5 6 7 8 9 0

ISBN 978-0-7355-9402-9

Schultz, Nancy L.
    Legal writing and other lawyering skills / Nancy L. Schultz, Louis J. Sirico, Jr. — 5th ed.
        p. cm.
    Includes bibliographical references and index.
    ISBN 978-0-7355-9402-9
    1.   Legal composition. 2.   Oral pleading — United States. I.   Sirico, Louis J. II.   Title.
    KF250.S38 2010
    808'.06634 — dc22

                                                                        2010013520

About Wolters Kluwer Law & Business

Wolters Kluwer Law & Business is a leading provider of research information and workflow solutions in key specialty areas. The strengths of the individual brands of Aspen Publishers, CCH, Kluwer Law International and Loislaw are aligned within Wolters Kluwer Law & Business to provide comprehensive, in-depth solutions and expert-authored content for the legal, professional and education markets.

CCH was founded in 1913 and has served more than four generations of business professionals and their clients. The CCH products in the Wolters Kluwer Law & Business group are highly regarded electronic and print resources for legal, securities, antitrust and trade regulation, government contracting, banking, pension, payroll, employment and labor, and healthcare reimbursement and compliance professionals.

Aspen Publishers is a leading information provider for attorneys, business professionals and law students. Written by preeminent authorities, Aspen products offer analytical and practical information in a range of specialty practice areas from securities law and intellectual property to mergers and acquisitions and pension/ benefits. Aspen's trusted legal education resources provide professors and students with high-quality, up-to-date and effective resources for successful instruction and study in all areas of the law.

Kluwer Law International supplies the global business community with comprehensive English-language international legal information. Legal practitioners, corporate counsel and business executives around the world rely on the Kluwer Law International journals, loose-leafs, books and electronic products for authoritative information in many areas of international legal practice.

Loislaw is a premier provider of digitized legal content to small law firm practitioners of various specializations. Loislaw provides attorneys with the ability to quickly and efficiently find the necessary legal information they need, when and where they need it, by facilitating access to primary law as well as state-specific law, records, forms and treatises.

Wolters Kluwer Law & Business, a unit of Wolters Kluwer, is headquartered in New York and Riverwoods, Illinois. Wolters Kluwer is a leading multinational publisher and information services company.

SUMMARY OF CONTENTS

CONTENTS

Chapter 5
Introduction to Legal Analysis

Chapter 6
Purpose, Context, and Structure

Chapter 7
Make Your Main Themes Stand Out

Chapter 8
Help the Reader to Understand You

Chapter 9
Meeting the Client

Chapter 10
Introduction to the Memo

Chapter 11
The Memo: Heading, Issue, and Conclusion

Chapter 12
Practice with Drafting Memos: Headings, Issues, and Conclusions

Chapter 23
Writing Pretrial Motions

Chapter 24
Introduction to Writing Briefs

Chapter 25
Appellate Process and Standard of Review

Chapter 26
The Appellate Brief: The Introductory Parts

Chapter 27
The Appellate Brief: Statement of Facts; Summary of Argument

Chapter 28
Practice in Writing the Statement of Facts and Summary of Argument

Chapter 29
The Appellate Brief: Argument and Conclusion

Chapter 30
Basic Principles of Oral Communication

Chapter 31
The Appellate Argument

Appendices

Index

We have used the materials in this book to teach legal writing and analysis to students at Villanova Law School, George Washington University Law School, and Chapman University School of Law. We wish to thank them for all they have taught us about teaching the subject. Most of the sample documents in this book are the products of our students. The names of the authors of documents reproduced in the appendices appear with their documents.

CHAPTER 1

Overview

§ 1.01. INTRODUCTION

To be a successful lawyer, you must write and speak effectively. In your profession, you will spend much of your time crafting legal documents and speaking with clients, courts, and other lawyers. In this book, we help you learn some of the skills you will need to be a lawyer. You will learn how to draft memoranda, opinion letters, pleadings, and briefs. You also will learn about client counseling, negotiations, and how to make oral arguments in court. You will master an approach that emphasizes precision, good organization, and plain English. By learning to communicate clearly, you will increase your effectiveness as a lawyer.

Our educational philosophy is to teach you how to write and argue in a traditionally accepted style. As you gain experience, you will develop a style that reflects your personality and particular strengths. At this stage, however, you should learn the standard method as a foundation for later growth.

This chapter gives you an overview of the book. It briefly discusses the legal system and legal analysis and then describes the major types of legal writing. It also explains our approach to writing style, discusses citation form, and introduces the lawyering skills you need to learn.

§ 1.02. THE LEGAL SYSTEM AND LEGAL ANALYSIS

Before you can make legal arguments or draft legal documents, you need to learn about the American legal system and about accepted methods of legal analysis. You need to learn more than television and the movies have taught you. You also need to unlearn some of what they have taught you.

Television and the movies offer a simplified view of the law. Though they frequently portray trials, they rarely show lawyers engaging in legal research and drafting documents. The media spend little time on pretrial proceedings and on courts that hear appeals from trial decisions. The media almost never tell us that this country has many court systems: every state has its own courts, and the federal government has not only the United States Supreme Court, but also trial courts, appeals courts, and various specialized courts.

The media also fail to offer even a glimpse of how lawyers construct legal arguments. Though television and the movies frequently present arguments based on common sense, they do not show how these arguments must be stylized to become legal arguments that judges will find persuasive.

Legal analysis is not particularly difficult or different from other methods of reasoning. Nonetheless, you must expend considerable effort to become good at it. In this book, we teach you about the legal system and legal reasoning. Over the next several years, these subjects will occupy much of your time. Becoming proficient in the methods outlined in this introduction will aid you in your other courses.

§ 1.03. TYPES OF LEGAL WRITING

1. The Case Brief

A case brief is a summary of a court opinion. As a student, you undoubtedly are writing case briefs in most of your courses. Writing the brief helps you prepare for class. During class, the brief serves as an accessible set of notes on the case. Chapter 4 offers help in reading and briefing cases.

The word "brief" has another meaning. It also refers to the written argument that a lawyer presents to a court deciding a case. See Section 1.03[6].

2. The Memorandum

By "memorandum" or "memo" we mean the interoffice memorandum. It discusses the law concerning a client's legal problem and predicts how a court or other body would decide the issue presented. The memo, then, is essential in determining how to proceed. The writer of the memo first must research the law thoroughly and then explain how it supports his or her conclusion. In legal practice, memos may take many forms, as we discuss later in the book.

The word "memorandum" sometimes is used to describe the written argument that a lawyer presents to a court or an administrative agency. The lawyer may write this type of memo to support or oppose a pretrial motion, to summarize the argument in a trial or administrative hearing, or to support the client's argument before an appellate court. In the latter case, most courts would call the document a brief. In all cases, the document is similar to a brief in that its goal is to persuade rather than to summarize the law. See Section 1.03[6].

3. The Client Opinion Letter

The client opinion letter advises the client how the law applies to a particular problem and suggests a course of action. The lawyer should explain any legal concepts in lay language.

4. Pleadings

Pleadings are the written papers that a lawyer serves on the opposing side and files with the court to begin litigation. In a noncriminal case, for example, the plaintiff's lawyer files a complaint asserting that the client has suffered a legal wrong and that the defendant is liable. The defendant's lawyer files an answer and may file a counterclaim asserting claims against the plaintiff. Other pleadings may also be filed.

Complaints are the first opportunity the lawyer has to state the case in writing. They must be drafted clearly and precisely, and establish sufficient facts to support the alleged cause of action or the court may refuse to hear the case and dismiss the complaint.

5. Motions

Before, during, or after trial, a lawyer may file a motion asking the court to deal with a particular issue. For example, the defendant's lawyer might move to dismiss the plaintiff's claim and argue that even if all the plaintiff's assertions are true, the defendant still would not be liable. Motions are persuasive documents and should follow the principles of advocacy writing. There are very few universal rules that govern the format of motions, so you will need to learn the procedures that are followed in your jurisdiction and in the law office where you work.

6. The Brief

By "brief," we mean the appellate brief. It is the written document that the lawyer submits to the court when the client's case is on appeal. It includes a factual explanation of the case and an argument based on detailed legal analysis of relevant cases and other authorities as well as fairness and social policy concerns. Some courts call the brief a memorandum. See Section 1.03[2]. "Brief" also refers to the written argument that the attorney presents at the pretrial or trial level.

Different courts have different rules for the format of the brief. In this book, you will learn a standard form that you can easily adjust to meet the requirements of a particular court.

§ 1.04. WRITING STYLE

This book is about writing and speaking like a lawyer. A lawyer should write and speak clearly, concisely, and forcefully. So should other professionals. Our profession faces a particular problem: it has inherited a tradition of poor writing. Many of the court opinions in your casebooks offer sad examples of this tradition. If the judges had written the opinions clearly, you would understand the decisions better and spend less time reading and briefing them.

Lawyers frequently justify lapses in comprehensibility by emphasizing the need to convey highly technical information and complex ideas. We reject such excuses. As a lawyer, you can write and speak clearly. Lawyers and scholars concerned with this matter agree. Current books and articles make clear that short sentences and plain English are the trend. Rambling sentences and legalese are out. You may recognize this philosophy if you have read *The Elements of Style* by Strunk and White[1] and *On Writing Well* by William Zinsser.[2]

Some first-year students are shocked when they receive their writing assignments back from the writing instructor. They find their papers covered with red-penned criticisms. Often the real shock comes to students who always believed they were excellent writers. In undergraduate school, they received praise and good grades and gained confidence in their ability. For them, legal writing seems to be a totally new form of writing.

Throughout this book, we use the written work of our students to provide good and bad examples of legal writing. The bad examples were written by intelligent, capable students. Most of the students came to law school confident about their writing abilities. They discovered they had more lessons to learn if they were to be good legal writers. They mastered those lessons and improved their legal writing style.

Your pre-law writing experience may not be a valid predictor of your initial performance in legal writing. Legal writing can be equally difficult for students of all backgrounds.

You may have been an English major who wrote brilliant essays or poetry for years. You may experience strong feelings of hurt and discouragement if you receive a paper that the writing instructor has torn apart. The instructor then gently tries to lessen the pain by explaining that you now are learning a new and very different method of writing. It is best for you to accept this fact now, before you hand in your first assignment.

On the other hand, you may have been an accounting or science major in undergraduate school with little writing experience and with many fears about legal writing. You may be delighted to discover that you can write very well in the legal setting.

We do not claim that the writing style we teach is superior to all other writing styles. Many great works of literature conform to other styles. Much good journalism lacks the precision that we demand. We make only one claim: the writing style that we teach is the best style for legal writing.

Many lawyers cling to the old ways. Some of your future employers may be among them, and you may have to compromise if you cannot persuade them to give you a free hand. But the tide is turning. Your efforts at communicating clearly will pay off. Judges, clients, and other lawyers will be more likely to understand you. They will also find you more persuasive. Lawyers who refuse to abandon verbosity and jargon may find themselves viewed as dinosaurs in a modern world.

---

1. William Strunk & E.B. White, *The Elements of Style* (4th ed., Allyn & Bacon 2000).

2. William Zinsser, *On Writing Well* (30th ann. ed., Harper 2006). A number of books urge lawyers to write in plain English. They include Irwin Alterman, *Plain and Accurate Style in Court Papers* (ALI-ABA 1987); Gertrude Block, *Effective Legal Writing* (5th ed., Foundation Press 1999); Louis J. Sirico, Jr. & Nancy L. Schultz, *Persuasive Writing for Lawyers and the Legal Profession* (2d ed., LexisNexis 2001); Richard Wydick, *Plain English for Lawyers* (5th ed., Carolina Academic Press 2005).

§ 1.05. CITATION FORM

As a lawyer, you will rely heavily on constitutions, statutes, prior cases, and other authorities. To cite authority means to refer to specific statutes, cases, and the like when you prepare an analysis of a legal point or make a legal argument. You may cite authority to provide important information, to support your argument, or to acknowledge adverse authority that you must distinguish or contest.

When you cite authority in a written document, you must include enough information so that the reader can make an initial decision about the authority's importance. For example, the reader may find it important to know how old a case is, whether the court is a local one, and whether the court is prestigious. You also must include enough information to enable the reader to find the authority in the library or online. For a case, a successful library search requires knowing the case's name, the set of books in which it appears, the volume, and the page number. A successful online search requires knowing the case name, jurisdiction, and date.

Two competing manuals set out rules on what information you must include in a citation and what format you should use. They are the *ALWD Citation Manual* (created by the Association of Legal Writing Directors and Darby Dickerson) and *The Bluebook: A Uniform System of Citation* (published by a small group of law reviews). Fortunately, for most citations that you will use in a first-year law course, the citation rules of both manuals are virtually the same. However, the *ALWD Citation Manual* is much more student oriented and much easier to understand than the *Bluebook*. *The ALWD Citation Manual* is used in first-year legal writing courses in the majority of United States law schools, and it is the manual we follow for citations used in this book.

§ 1.06. COMMUNICATIONS SKILLS

1. Client Interviewing and Counseling

Lawyers have occasion to generate written documents only if they have clients to represent. You must be able to convince a potential client that you are the right person to handle the important and delicate matter that he or she proposes to hand over to your keeping. You will be able to do this if you plan your interviews to maximize the likelihood that you will get all necessary information and be able to accurately assess the client's problem and develop appropriate options for resolving it. You will have satisfied clients and lots of work if you can help clients to resolve their legal dilemmas in ways that meet their needs and take their goals and priorities into account. To be able to do this consistently requires skill and practice. We will introduce you to some of the fundamental skills and concepts that underlie this vital work. We will also explain how research and writing relate to client representation.

2. Negotiation

The vast majority of legal problems are resolved outside of court. Negotiation is a critical lawyering skill. In this book, we introduce you to some issues of fundamental importance to effective negotiation—preparation, information exchange, keeping track of concessions, and the tone and style of the negotiation. We discuss both adversarial and problem-solving "win/win" strategies for negotiating. You will discover that negotiating is a very human process, with few rules and lots of psychology. You will also discover that good legal research and writing skills make you a more effective negotiator and lawyer.

3. Oral Argument

Lawyers make oral arguments before legislatures and administrative bodies and in courts. In this book, you will learn specifically how to make an oral argument when a court is hearing your client's case on appeal. In an appellate court, you submit your written argument in a brief, and you also may get the opportunity to address the court in oral argument.

Appellate argument differs in style from college debate and other speaking occasions. A formal etiquette governs what you say and how you say it. By using this book, you will learn when to sit, when to stand, how to begin your argument, and the like. You also will learn how to structure your argument, what to emphasize, and how to answer questions. In addition, you will learn how to be persuasive.

Learning effective legal writing and oral advocacy is a demanding and exciting task. We wish you well.

Learning About the Legal System

§ 2.01. THE LEGAL SYSTEM AND LEGAL WRITING

Much of the legal writing you will do in your career will involve analyzing legal problems. To analyze a legal problem, you must understand the sources of our law and their relationships to each other. You must also understand the workings of our legal system. This chapter provides a broad introduction to our court system, the common law, and statutory law and interpretation. Once you understand these aspects of the legal process, you will be able to evaluate a legal problem properly and prepare an accurate and well-reasoned legal analysis.

§ 2.02. SOURCES OF LAW AND THEIR HIERARCHY

There are three primary categories of law: constitutions, statutes, and common law. The Constitution of the United States and the 50 state constitutions set out the structure and powers of government, protect individual liberties, and define the reach of statutory authority. Statutes are passed by legislatures and govern a host of areas ranging from crime to social security benefit levels. The common law is the law judges make when they rule on cases. When a case is decided, it becomes a precedent for future similar legal conflicts in the same jurisdiction.[1]

An applicable constitutional provision, statute, or common law rule always governs the outcome of a legal problem. The existing case law will assist you in interpreting the statute or constitutional provision in the context of your particular case. When there is no relevant constitutional provision or statute, as there often is not, the common law is the sole source of authority for evaluating and resolving your case.

---

1. The word "jurisdiction" means different things in different contexts. Here we use it to refer to the geographic area or court system in which a case is decided. It can also mean the power of a court to hear a case, as in "personal jurisdiction" (jurisdiction/power over a party) or "subject matter jurisdiction" (jurisdiction/power over the issue presented to the court).

§ 2.03. THE COURT SYSTEM

Two court systems operate simultaneously in the United States: the state court system and the federal court system. In both the state and federal court systems there are two types of courts: trial courts and appellate courts. The following is an overview of each system.

1. The State Courts

Each of the 50 states has a court system. Although the structure of that system differs from state to state, it is always hierarchical. There are trial courts, often an intermediate appellate court, and a court of last resort—the tribunal at the top tier of the court system. In addition, there may be numerous other courts that perform specialized roles, such as small claims courts, juvenile courts, and housing courts.

A trial court is presided over by one judge, and may or may not include a jury. The function of a trial court is to determine the facts by evaluating the evidence in a case and to arrive at a decision by applying the law to the facts. Trial courts at the state level may be divided into courts of limited jurisdiction and courts of general jurisdiction. Pursuant to the provisions of the state constitution and state laws, courts of limited jurisdiction rule on certain specific matters such as violations of criminal law. Courts of general jurisdiction are empowered to hear a broader range of civil and criminal matters and often also review appeals from courts of limited jurisdiction.

From the decision of a trial court, the losing party may appeal to the next level, the appellate court. The appeal is heard by a panel of three to five judges, of whom a majority must agree on a particular result. That result forms the basis of the court's opinion deciding the case. The appellate court evaluates the lower court's decision and determines whether it committed any legal error that would warrant reversing or modifying the decision or ordering a new trial. The decision of the appellate court may be appealed to the state's highest court, which often has discretion to choose the cases it will hear. The decisions of the courts of last resort are final, and there is no further appeal of state law issues.

This diagram of the California courts illustrates a typical state court system, though you will find that states name their courts differently—for example, New York calls its court of last resort the Court of Appeals rather than the Supreme Court.

California Court Structure

CALIFORNIA COURT SYSTEM

SUPREME COURT

COURT OF
APPEAL
(6 courts of appeal)

SUPERIOR COURT
(58 trial courts,
which handle
all criminal cases, all
civil cases, appeals of
small claims cases &
civil cases worth
$25,000 or less,
appeals of
misdemeanor- cases)

Source: Superior Court of California County of Santa Clara, Self Service Center, Overview of the State Court System, http://www.scselfservice.org/home/overview.htm.

2. The Federal Courts

The Constitution and certain federal statutes establish the federal courts and empower them to hear certain kinds of cases. Federal courts hear all cases that arise under federal law, such as those involving the United States Constitution or federal statutes, disputes between two states, or cases in which the United States is a party.

Like the state systems, the federal court system is divided into trial courts, appellate courts, and a court of last resort. The trial courts are called district courts. Each state has at least one district court, and that court's jurisdiction is limited to the territory of its district. In a district court case, a judge sits with or without a jury, depending on the nature of the case and the wishes of the parties.

The intermediate appellate courts in the federal system are called the United States courts of appeals. The courts of appeals hear appeals from the district courts located in the same circuit. A circuit is a designated geographical area usually encompassing several states. The United States is divided geographically into thirteen circuits. Eleven of these circuit courts are identified by number, for example, the United States Court of Appeals for the Third Circuit. There is also the United States Court of Appeals for the District of Columbia and the United States Court of Appeals for the Federal Circuit, which hears appeals in patent cases, certain international trade cases, and some cases involving damage claims against the United States. Usually, three judges sit on a panel to decide a particular case, and at least two must agree for a decision to be reached.

The Supreme Court of the United States, consisting of the Chief Justice and eight Associate Justices, is the highest court in the federal system. The Court hears a limited number of cases from the courts of appeals and, on certain issues, from the district courts and the highest state courts. The Court must accept review of certain types of cases, but these are rare. Typically the Court selects which cases it will hear by issuing a writ of certiorari. Cases heard by the Supreme Court generally involve new or unresolved questions of federal law affecting people throughout the country and interpretations of federal statutes or the United States Constitution.

This diagram illustrates the federal court hierarchy:

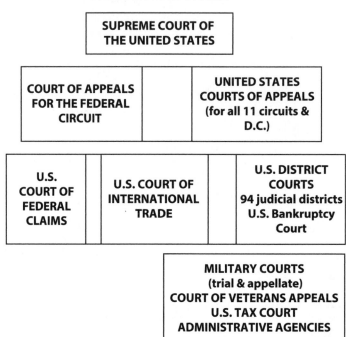

FEDERAL COURT SYSTEM

SUPREME COURT OF THE UNITED STATES

COURT OF APPEALS FOR THE FEDERAL CIRCUIT		UNITED STATES COURTS OF APPEALS (for all 11 circuits & D.C.)

U.S. COURT OF FEDERAL CLAIMS	U.S. COURT OF INTERNATIONAL TRADE	U.S. DISTRICT COURTS 94 judicial districts U.S. Bankruptcy Court

MILITARY COURTS (trial & appellate) COURT OF VETERANS APPEALS U.S. TAX COURT ADMINISTRATIVE AGENCIES

§ 2.04. THE COMMON LAW

The phrase "common law" refers to legal principles created and developed by the courts independent of legislative enactments. It is the body of law judges create when they decide cases. The doctrine of stare decisis mandates that a court follow these common law precedents. Under our system of precedent, however, courts must follow only those precedents that are mandatory or have binding authority. Case law that is not binding is often referred to as persuasive authority.

1. Mandatory Authority

Mandatory authority is authority that you must rely on because it binds the court in your jurisdiction. It is unethical to omit from a legal argument mandatory authority that is adverse to your client's interests.

When you are presented with a legal problem, you research the statutory and case law of the controlling jurisdiction to resolve that problem. If there is an applicable statute, the court is bound to follow that statute as previously interpreted by the courts. If there is no statute, you will look for case law that is binding on the court where the case is pending.

A precedent becomes binding on a court if (1) the case was decided by that court or a higher court in the same jurisdiction, and (2) the material facts of the pending case and the decided case, as well as the legal reasoning applicable to the two cases, are indistinguishable. For example, a state trial court is bound by the decisions of that state's intermediate appellate courts and its highest court. A federal district court is bound by the decisions of the court of appeals of the circuit in which the district court is situated and the decisions of the Supreme Court. District courts are not bound by the decisions of other district courts or by those of the courts of appeals of other circuits. The courts of appeals are bound by their own decisions and those of the Supreme Court. They are not bound by the decisions of other courts of appeals.

Suppose you are arguing a case in a jurisdiction and your research discloses a case from a higher court in the same jurisdiction with identical material facts and applicable reasoning. The material facts are the facts the court actually relies upon in reaching the decision. The court you are before is bound by the holding of the previous case; the earlier case is "on point" with your case. The holding is the court's decision on the issue before it. All other discussion of tangential issues is called dicta and is not binding. You will rarely, if ever, have a case that is directly "on point" with your case—most cases will be distinguishable on some material basis.

2. Persuasive Authority

Sometimes your research will show that your jurisdiction has neither a statute nor legal precedent to govern your case. You must then rely on persuasive authority to help analyze the issue. Persuasive authority is non-mandatory legal authority. It is authority that may persuade a court to decide a certain way but does not require a particular decision. Persuasive authority includes:

- Primary authority that does not control your case because the rules are not directly applicable or the relevant facts are distinguishable. For example, assume that in a particular case a court finds that the defendant was liable for assault for brandishing a real gun at plaintiff. This holding may not apply to a subsequent case in which a defendant brandishes what is obviously a toy gun at a plaintiff.
- Secondary authority, such as treatises, hornbooks, or law review articles, which present only authors' viewpoints about law but are not themselves the law.
- Dicta in court opinions, which are discussions that are explanatory, but not necessary, to the decisions. For example, the court in the gun assault case may suggest that brandishing a knife also can constitute an assault. An actual case involving brandishing of a knife, however, may not involve an assault unless all the circumstances create that offense. The victim, for example, may have felt no real threat from the defendant's brandishing the knife, and therefore no assault occurred. The court deciding the knife case will not be constrained by the suggestion in the earlier case that brandishing a knife may be an assault.
- Precedents from other states that have decided your issue are persuasive authority. In the federal system, precedents from other district courts and other courts of appeals are persuasive authority.

3. The Weight of Authority

When you draft your legal papers for the court, you must decide which cases to include in your discussion to present the most compelling argument. Certain cases will be more persuasive than others. How persuasive a case is, that is, what weight it carries, depends on a number of factors, including:

(a) The level of the court. The decision of a higher court is more authoritative than that of a lower court.

(b) Factual similarity. When the cases you cite have facts similar to your case, their value as precedent increases.

(c) The year of the decision. A more recent opinion is more useful than one that is dated.

(d) The judge. Look for an opinion written by the judge presiding over your case or by a judge with a good reputation.

(e) Majority decisions. Language from a majority decision carries more weight than that from a concurring or dissenting opinion.

(f) The state in which the court deciding the case sits.

(i) Geographic proximity. A case from a state that is relatively close geographically is often more helpful than one from a state that is far away.

(ii) Certain states, like New Jersey, are often at the forefront of emerging case law.

(g) The number of other courts that have cited the case approvingly; that is, a developing trend in the law.

§ 2.05. STATUTES AND THEIR INTERPRETATION

1. The Supremacy of the Legislature and the Legislative Process

Under our system of government, the United States Congress and the state legislatures are the supreme lawmakers, subject only to the limitations of the federal and state constitutions. Therefore, statutes provide the binding rules of decision that courts must follow. Statutes prevail over common law if there is a conflict between the two. Here is a brief discussion of how statutes come into being.

A member of Congress introduces a bill in either the House or the Senate.[2] It is then referred to the appropriate committee, which conducts hearings and issues a report. There is discussion of the bill on the floor, and a vote is taken. If it passes, it goes to the other chamber, where it goes through a similar process. If different versions of the bill are passed by the House and Senate, the bill may be sent to a conference committee for resolution of the differences. Finally, it goes to the President for signature or veto. If the President vetoes the bill, Congress may try to "override" the veto with a two-thirds majority vote, meaning they can pass it anyway if they get enough votes. Otherwise, the President's veto means the bill will not become law.

---

2. For our purposes, we simply note that the processes in the federal and state systems are similar.

In finished form, state and federal statutes usually have certain parts: a preamble, which may include a statement of policy or purpose; a definition section, which attempts to define the significant words used in the statute; the substantive provisions; and any procedural provisions. Consider the following Maryland statute:

MD. CRIM. CODE ANN. § 10-701. "Flag" defined

In this subtitle, "flag" includes any size flag, standard, color, ensign, or shield made of any substance or represented or produced on any substance, that purports to be a flag, standard, color, ensign, or shield of the United States or of this state.

MD. CRIM. CODE ANN. § 10-702. Scope of subtitle

This subtitle does not apply to:

(1) an act allowed by the statutes of the United States or of this State, or by the regulations of the armed forces of the United States; or

(2) a document or product, stationery, ornament, picture, apparel or jewelry that depicts a flag without a design or words on the flag and this is not connected with an advertisement.

MD. CRIM. CODE ANN. § 10-703. Marked flag and merchandise

Scope of section

(a) This section applies to a flag of the United States or of this State, or a flag that is authorized by law of the United States or of this State.

Prohibited—Advertising marking

(b) For exhibition or display, a person may not place or cause to be placed a work, figure, mark, picture, design or advertisement of any nature on a flag.

Prohibited—Public display of marked flag

(c) A person may not publicly exhibit a flag with a word, figure, mark, picture, design, or advertisement printed, painted, or produced on or attached to the flag.

Prohibited—Merchandise marked with flag

(d) A person may not publicly display for sale, manufacture, or otherwise, or sell, give, or possess for sale or for use as a gift or for any other purpose, an article of merchandise or receptacle on which a flag is produced or attached to advertise, decorate, or make the merchandise.

Penalty

(e) A person who violates this section is guilty of a misdemeanor and on conviction is subject to a fine not exceeding $500.

MD. CRIM. CODE ANN. § 10-704. Mutilation

Prohibited

(a) A person may not intentionally mutilate, deface, destroy, burn, trample, or use a flag:

(1) in a manner intended to incite or produce an imminent breach of the peace; and

(2) under circumstances likely to incite or produce an imminent breach of the peace.

Penalty

(b) A person who violates this section is guilty of a misdemeanor and on conviction is subject to imprisonment not exceeding 1 year or a fine not exceeding $1,000 or both.

MD. CRIM. CODE ANN. § 10-705. Construction of subtitle

This subtitle shall be construed to carry out its general purpose and to make uniform the laws of the states that enact it.

MD. CRIM. CODE ANN. § 10-706. Short title

This subtitle may be cited as the Maryland Uniform Flag Law.

As you see, while the Maryland statute has no preamble, it does have a definition section and substantive and procedural sections, including penalty and construction provisions.

2. The Relationship Between Statutory Law and Common Law

After the applicable constitutional provisions, enacted statutes are the highest authority in a jurisdiction. The courts are bound by them. A legislature may enact a statute that overrules or modifies existing common law. It may enact a common law rule into a statute. Courts, however, rule on whether statutes are constitutional.

When deciding a case governed by a statute, the court must decide how to apply and enforce that statute. Courts rely on certain aids in interpreting the meaning of a statute. You will rely on those same aids in urging the court to adopt a particular construction.

Most statutes are deliberately drafted in broad language because they are written to establish a principle rather than to solve a specific problem. The general language serves as the basis for common law development of the statute by the courts. It is the court's application of a statute to particular cases that gives meaning to the statute's language and provides guidance for future cases.

To interpret broad and ambiguous statutory language, courts look to the following for guidance:

- The actual language of the statute, (i.e., the words chosen by the legislature).
- The context within the statute. What is the subject or purpose of other headings or sections in the same statute? What language do complimentary statutes contain? Is there a statutory statement of legislative purpose? Legislatures

sometimes attempt to avoid ambiguity problems by including statements of legislative purpose as a preamble to the statute itself.

- The legislative history of the statute. A statute's legislative history provides information to the court about the legislature's intent in adopting the statute. It consists of the "official comments," the floor debate, the committee reports, and the committee hearings. Unfortunately, on a state level, the legislative history is often nearly nonexistent, and on every level it may be very difficult to obtain.
- Administrative interpretations by the agency charged with administering the statute. They occasionally provide a more specific indication of the statute's meaning. For example, the Food and Drug Administration issues regulations and interpretations of statutes governing the food and drug industries; the Federal Communications Commission issues regulations and interpretations governing cable and television, among other communications services, and the Department of Transportation issues regulations and interpretations governing all the various forms of transportation, such as trains.
- The interpretation of other courts. A court will consider how courts at a higher level, the same level, or even a lower level have applied the statute.
- The broader context of the statute. What kinds of events were taking place that caused the legislation to be created? What goals were to be furthered by enacting the statute? If a statute overrules common law or tries to fill in a gap in the common law, understanding the problems that led to the enactment can help define the scope of the statute.
- The common law. When a statute codifies existing common law, the body of cases that developed the common law rule provides highly useful guidance.
- A comparison with similar statutes of other jurisdictions.
- Scholarly interpretations, if available.

Courts sometimes also look to canons of statutory construction. These are maxims intended to provide guidance. However, courts are free to disregard them. Here are the most commonly used canons:

1. The "plain meaning rule." In construing a statute, the court shall not deviate from its literal meaning except as required by internal context or the need to avoid absurd results.

2. The rule of "negative implication." When the legislature has covered a certain subject in a statute, it must have intended to exclude everything not mentioned.

3. The principle of construing penal statutes narrowly.

4. The principle of construing statutes in derogation of the common law narrowly.

Although some canons of interpretation have themselves been adopted by statute,[3] as a rule they reflect common sense and do not provide technical help

---

3. A Pennsylvania statute states:

RULE OF STRICT AND LIBERAL CONSTRUCTION

Statutes in derogation of common law—

(a) The rule that statutes in derogation of the common law are to be strictly construed, shall have no application to the statutes of this Commonwealth enacted finally after September 1, 1937.

in construing a statute. As between the available aids to interpretation, courts will more likely be persuaded by intrinsic factors such as the statute's language and "plain meaning" than by extrinsic factors such as legislative history.

3. The Roles of the Court and the Legislature—An Illustration

The question of whether flag burning is permissible has been addressed by the legislature and courts in turn. It provides an excellent illustration of the interaction between the two in the context of statutory interpretation.

The Texas Penal Code stated:

Desecration of Venerated Object.

    (a) A person commits an offense if he intentionally or knowingly desecrates:
        (1) a public monument;
        (2) a place of worship or burial;
        (3) a state or national flag.
    (b) For purposes of this section, "desecrate" means deface, damage or otherwise physically mistreat in a way that the actor knows will seriously offend one or more persons likely to observe or discover his action.

Tex. Penal Code Ann. § 42.09 (West 1989).[4]

While the Republican National Convention was taking place in Dallas in 1984, Gregory Lee Johnson participated in a political demonstration that included the public burning of an American flag. He was convicted of desecrating a flag in violation of Texas law. This conviction was affirmed by a Texas district court of appeals, but was subsequently reversed by the Texas Court of Criminal Appeals. The United States Supreme Court granted certiorari.

Texas claimed its interest in preventing breaches of the peace justified Johnson's conviction under the statute. In fact, however, there was no breach of the peace. The Supreme Court heard the case on appeal and observed that Texas was essentially making the argument that an "audience that takes serious offense at particular expression is necessarily likely to disturb the peace and that the

---

Provisions subject to strict construction—

(b) All provisions of a statute of the classes hereafter enumerated shall be strictly construed:
    (1) Penal provisions.
    (2) Retroactive provisions.
    (3) Provisions imposing taxes.
    (4) Provisions conferring the power of eminent domain.
    (5) Provisions exempting persons and property from taxation.
    (6) Provisions exempting property from the power of eminent domain.
    (7) Provisions decreasing the jurisdiction of a court of record.
    (8) Provisions enacted finally prior to September 1, 1937 which are in derogation of the common law.

Provisions subject to liberal construction—

(c) All other provisions of a statute shall be liberally construed to effect their objects and to promote justice.

1 Pa. Cons. Stat. Ann. § 1928.
4. This statutory section now relates to cruelty to animals.

expression may be prohibited on this basis." *Texas v. Johnson*, 491 U.S. 397, 408 (1989). The Court also found that the asserted state interest in "preserving the flag as a symbol of nationhood and national unity" could not survive the scrutiny imposed on state actions that attempt to regulate speech content protected by the First Amendment. *Id.* at 420.

The federal flag burning statute in effect at the time of the *Texas v. Johnson* ruling stated:

Desecration of the flag of the United States; penalties

(a) Whoever knowingly casts contempt upon any flag of the United States by publicly mutilating, defacing, defiling, burning, or trampling upon it shall be fined not more than $1,000 or imprisoned for not more than one year, or both.

(b) The term "flag of the United States" as used in this section, shall include any flag, standard, colors, ensign, or any picture or representation of either, or of any part or parts of either, and of any substance or represented on any substance, of any size evidently purporting to be either of said flag, standard, colors, or ensign of the United States of America, or a picture or a representation of either, upon which shall be shown the colors, the stars and the stripes, in any number of either thereof, or of any part or parts of either, by which the average person seeing the same without deliberation may believe the same to represent the flag, standards, colors, or ensign of the United States of America.

(c) Nothing in this section shall be construed as indicating an intent on the part of Congress to deprive any State, territory, possession, or the Commonwealth of Puerto Rico of jurisdiction over any offense over which it would have jurisdiction in the absence of this section.

18 U.S.C. § 700 (1989).

Congress responded to the *Texas v. Johnson* case by removing the "casts contempt" language from subsection (a) of the statute, reasoning that now the flag burning prohibition was not content-based. The revised statute read, in relevant part:

AN ACT

To amend section 700 of title 18, United States Code, to protect the physical integrity of the flag.

Be it enacted by the Senate and House of Representatives of the United States of America in Congress assembled,

This Act may be cited as the "Flag Protection Act of 1989".
SEC. 2. CRIMINAL PENALTIES WITH RESPECT TO THE PHYSICAL INTEGRITY OF THE UNITED STATES FLAG.

(a) In General—Subsection (a) of section 700 of title 18, United States Code, is amended to read as follows:

(a)(1) Whoever knowingly mutilates, defaces, physically defiles, burns, maintains on the floor or ground, or tramples upon any flag of the United States shall be fined under this title or imprisoned for not more than one year, or both.

(2) This subsection does not prohibit any conduct consisting of the disposal of a flag when it has become worn or soiled.

(b) Definition.—Section 700(b) of title 18, United States Code, is amended to read as follows:

(b) As used in this section, the term 'flag of the United States' means any flag of the United States, or any part thereof, made of any substance, of any size, in a form that is commonly displayed.

18 U.S.C. §700 (Supp. II 1990).

Shortly after the passage of the revised Flag Protection Act, Shawn Eichman and two friends set several United States flags on fire on the steps of the United States Capitol during a political demonstration. Their protest was, in part, intended to demonstrate their objection to the newly enacted statute. In *United States v. Eichman*, 496 U.S. 310 (1990), the Supreme Court found that the revised language failed to make the statute constitutional.

Although the Flag Protection Act contained no explicit content-based limitation on prohibited conduct, it was nevertheless clear that the Government's asserted interest was related to the suppression of free expression and concerned with the content of such expression. The Government's interest in protecting the physical integrity of a privately owned flag rests upon a perceived need to preserve the flag's status as a symbol of our Nation and certain national ideals. But the mere disfigurement of a particular manifestation of the symbol, without more, does not diminish or otherwise affect the symbol itself in any way. For example, the secret destruction of a flag in one's own basement would not threaten the flag's recognized meaning. Rather, the Government's desire to preserve the flag as a symbol of certain national ideals is implicated only when a person's treatment of the flag communicates a message to others that is inconsistent with those ideals.

Moreover, the precise language of the Act's prohibitions confirmed Congress's interest in the communicative impact of flag destruction. The Act criminalized the conduct of anyone who knowingly mutilated, defaced, physically defiled, burned, maintained on the floor or ground, or trampled upon any flag. Each of the specified terms—with the possible exception of "burns"—unmistakably connotes disrespectful treatment of the flag and suggests a focus on those acts likely to damage the flag's symbolic value. And the explicit exemption for disposal of worn or soiled flags protected certain acts traditionally associated with patriotic respect for the flag.

Although Congress cast the Flag Protection Act in somewhat broader terms than the Texas statute at issue in *Johnson*, the Act still suffered from the same fundamental flaw: it suppressed expression out of concern for its likely communicative impact. *United States v. Eichman*, 496 U.S. 310, 312-326 (1990).

It is clear that Congress wanted to enact a law that prohibited flag burning. However, it seems equally clear that regardless of the form of such a statute, it most likely would not survive a constitutional challenge. Reread the Maryland flag burning statute at the beginning of this section. Is it possible that the Maryland legislature has drafted a statute that would survive constitutional scrutiny? The statutory language suggests that the statute will be enforced only when the circumstances surrounding the flag burning are likely to create a breach of the peace.

As you see, enacted statutes have no meaning or effect until they are interpreted by the courts and applied in context. Statutory analysis is an important function of our court system.

CHAPTER 3

Research Strategy

§ 3.01. INTRODUCTION

For purposes of this discussion, we assume that you have already learned or are learning how to use specific materials in the library. The goal of this chapter is to teach you how to integrate your knowledge of the materials in the library with what we are teaching you about legal writing and analysis.

In other words, once you have your writing assignment in hand, how do you approach the research process? Where do you start? How many places do you look? How do you balance book and computer research? When do you stop? How do you keep track of your research so that you don't end up covering the same ground repeatedly? We will take up each question in turn, using the Paul Trune problem presented in Chapter 5. The issue in the case is whether Mr. Trune can bring a civil action for false imprisonment. Before continuing, go to Section 5.04 and read the facts of the case.

As we go through this discussion, do not be concerned if you see angles that are not discussed here. Our approach shows you how one person might effectively research this particular problem. If you see other approaches, try them; you may find that they work for you, or you may find that they were not included because they were unproductive.

§ 3.02. WHERE DO YOU START?

As you begin the research process, identify the key legal terminology that will help you access the appropriate research sources. If you are unfamiliar with the area of law presented by the research problem, begin your research with a secondary resource that discusses the broad legal principles and rules that govern the area. Examples of such sources include hornbooks, treatises, and legal encyclopedias. If you do have some knowledge of the field, you can go directly to sources of primary authority such as digests and annotated statutes.[1] We will discuss the use of each of these resources in Mr. Trune's case.

---

1. If you are researching a question that might be the subject of a law review article, that would be an excellent place to start. Law review articles will give you a head start on primary source research, as well

1. Statutes

Many law students reflexively think of statutes when beginning research tasks. If you are researching a problem in an area that is likely to have been addressed by a legislature, that is not a bad reflex to have. When you are unfamiliar with the law in your jurisdiction, begin by determining whether there is a relevant statute. Is there a false imprisonment statute in Wisconsin? Section 940.30 of the Wisconsin Statutes, governing false imprisonment, provides that "[w]hoever intentionally confines or restrains another without the person's consent and with knowledge that he or she has no lawful authority to do so is guilty of a Class H felony."

Before you start searching the annotations under § 940.30 for helpful cases, read the statute carefully. The question you have been asked is whether Paul Trune can bring a *civil* action for false imprisonment. You are researching false imprisonment as a tort, not a crime. Thus, the statute's characterization of false imprisonment as a felony should tip you off that the statute does not apply to your client's situation, and you should ignore it.

2. Treatises

If you are researching an area such as tort law that tends to be governed almost exclusively by common law decisions, how do you begin your research? The answer depends in large part on how familiar you are with the subject matter of your research project. If you know the elements of false imprisonment and are familiar with the key terminology, you probably can begin with the relevant digests. If you don't, however, you will need some background information about the topic first. For that, you should consult a secondary source such as a treatise.

In a treatise, you can read generally about the applicable legal principles as well as begin to identify specific cases. Dobbs, *The Law of Torts* (West 2000) is one of the primary treatises in the area of tort law. If you look on pages 67-75, you will find an explanation of the tort of false imprisonment. You will also see some Wisconsin cases in the footnotes: *Drabek v. Sabley*, 31 Wis. 2d 184, 142 N.W.2d 798 (1966) (p. 69, n. 16; p. 71, n. 18; p. 73, n. 4); *Herbst v. Wuennenberg*, 83 Wis. 2d 768, 266 N.W.2d 391 (1978) (p. 70, n. 12; p. 71, nn. 17 and 19); and *Dupler v. Seubert*, 69 Wis. 2d 373, 230 N.W.2d 626 (1975) (p. 71, nn. 16 and 17). *Herbst* and *Dupler* are discussed at length in Chapter 5.

3. Restatements

Another good source of general rules, at least in areas of the law for which they exist, are the Restatements. Although the Restatements are not the law, unless the courts in your jurisdiction have adopted the relevant provisions, they are often persuasive. In any event, the Restatements provide a good discussion of basic principles, with examples of how those principles can be applied. The Appendix volumes contain relevant cases, so you can determine whether the courts in your

---

as an idea of arguments that can be made on your topic. You can find law review articles by using a published index to periodicals or by doing an online search.

jurisdiction have cited the Restatement. If a Restatement provision applies to your case, do not overlook this resource as you search for applicable law.

First consult the general index at the end of the pertinent Restatement (i.e., Torts, Contracts, etc.). The general index will direct you to the appropriate volume, which will include a more detailed index. False imprisonment is covered in §§ 35-45 of the Restatement (Second) of Torts. The applicable language of many of these sections is quoted in the decisions discussed in Chapter 5, so we have not reproduced it here.

If you look in the Appendix volumes, which are organized chronologically, you will find annotations of cases from various states. The Restatement is cited extensively in both *Herbst* and *Dupler*, so you should not be surprised to find the *Herbst* case in the appropriate Appendix volume. If you check earlier volumes of the Appendix, you will also find *Dupler*. If you check later volumes, you will find other Wisconsin cases. Remember that you must check several volumes to be sure you have discovered all of the relevant authority.

4. Legal Encyclopedias

Finally, legal encyclopedias are another good source of general rules and a good starting point for finding primary authority. If you have found a good treatise, you may not need to check an encyclopedia as well. Looking in an encyclopedia may also be unnecessary if there is an applicable Restatement, at least if the Restatement has been adopted in your jurisdiction. If, however, you have not located any other resources that can help you learn the basic rules and terminology of your field of inquiry, encyclopedias should do the job. Until you become comfortable with legal research and the resources available to you, you may want to check more than one source anyway, to be sure you genuinely understand the legal issues involved and to see if the different sources contain different types of useful information.

If your state publishes its own legal encyclopedia, start there. In this discussion, we will take on the slightly more difficult task of trying to find Wisconsin precedent in the general encyclopedias, *Corpus Juris Secundum* and *American Jurisprudence*; the research procedures, however, are the same. If you look in volume 32 of *American Jurisprudence 2d*, at the start of the chapter on false imprisonment, you will find an outline that breaks the topic of false imprisonment into analytical elements. As you scan the outline, Part B, "Elements," should look like a good place to start. More specifically, section 2, dealing with the basic elements of confinement, should look particularly interesting. The subsections will give you a general discussion of what constitutes sufficient restraint.

The next step is to look for cases in your jurisdiction that demonstrate how the courts have applied those concepts. When you look under sections 10-20, however, you will find that only footnote 65 cites a Wisconsin case: *Weiler v. Herzfeld-Phillipson Co.*, 208 N.W. 599 (Wis. 1926) (holding that there is no false imprisonment where a supervisor interrogates an employee suspected of dishonesty in the supervisor's office for a lengthy period; the court pointed out that the employee was being compensated for the time and was under the direction of the employer so long as she remained an employee). An examination of the pocket part discloses no additional Wisconsin cases. The case you have found will get you started on the question of what constitutes false imprisonment in Wisconsin, but given its age, you should try to find something a little more recent.

An examination of volume 35 of *Corpus Juris Secundum* will yield a similar outline. Part B, "Manner and Character of Restraint," again dealing with the basic requirements of restraint, should look like a good place to start. In the main volume, you will find one Wisconsin case: *Herbst v. Wuennenberg* (§ 15, n. 6, and § 17, n. 11). (*Herbst* is discussed in Chapter 5.)

§ 3.03. OTHER RESOURCES

1. Digests

Now that you have a greater familiarity with the elements of false imprisonment and have identified a few cases to read, you can move on to the digests, which will not give you general descriptions of the law but will probably give you more cases. Again, you should use a state digest if your state has its own, but you can also look in West's regional digests. In the *North Western Digest 2d*, you will find an outline for false imprisonment. Assuming that your primary goal is to determine what the cases have to say about the sufficiency of restraint as an element of false imprisonment, you should find notes 5 and 6 relevant. Here are the Wisconsin cases contained in the annotations under those key numbers:

Johnson v. Ray, 99 Wis. 2d 777, 299 N.W.2d 849 (1981)
Drabek v. Sabley, 31 Wis. 2d 184, 142 N.W.2d 798 (1966)
Schaidler v. Mercy Medical Center of Oshkosh, Inc., 209 Wis. 2d 457, 563 N.W.2d 554 (1997)
Peters v. Menard, Inc., 224 Wis. 2d 174, 589 N.W.2d 395 (1999)
Miller v. Wal-Mart Stores, Inc., 219 Wis. 2d 250, 580 N.W.2d 233 (1998)
Herbst v. Wuennenberg, 83 Wis. 2d 768, 266 N.W.2d 391 (1978)
Hainz v. Shopko Stores, Inc., 121 Wis. 2d 168, 359 N.W.2d 397 (1984)

At least two of these Wisconsin cases are familiar, but several new ones appear also. The advantage of the digests over the treatises and encyclopedias is that the digests provide brief general descriptions of the cases, which you can use to decide whether you want to read any particular case in full. In making this decision, always remember that such a short description of the case cannot possibly alert you to every aspect of the decision that might be useful, and that these "squibs" are occasionally inaccurate.

Even so, you can often use the annotations to eliminate cases that have no relevance to the situation you are researching. For example, if you look at the descriptions of *Johnson, Schaidler, Miller,* or *Hainz,* you should conclude that you are not likely to find anything helpful in those cases because the facts are so different as to make it difficult to compare the cases. Given that you have other cases that outline the general requirements for making a claim of false imprisonment, you do not need these cases for any general language they might contain.

An examination of the pocket part to the digest will reveal no new Wisconsin cases, so you should start to feel fairly confident that you have now identified the most relevant and up-to-date precedent on your issue. Also note that you are starting to see some of the same cases repeatedly, which is a good sign—it means that you are finding the limits of the legal universe in which you are operating.

2. A.L.R. and Legal Periodicals

If you wish to be especially thorough and to find out what others have written on your topic, you might want to consult other sources, such as the *American Law Reports* (A.L.R.), the *Current Law Index*, or one of the indexes to legal periodicals. For a topic as straightforward as this one, involving an intentional tort that has been reasonably well defined by the courts, such additional research will probably not be necessary. If you were doing this research in a firm, at a client's expense, you would almost certainly not go to such lengths. While you are in law school, however, and are still learning the law with the luxury of enough time to fully investigate all potentially helpful options, you might want to at least take a quick look at these kinds of supportive resources. If you happen to come across an annotation or law review article specifically on your topic, you might even *save* time on your research.

If you did look at the A.L.R. index, you would find brief descriptions of a number of annotations on specific aspects of false imprisonment. And, if you searched the *Current Law Index* for false imprisonment, you would again find brief descriptions of articles on specific aspects of the topic. The *Current Law Index* is organized chronologically, so you might have to check several volumes for relevant articles. The vast majority of articles and annotations listed in these sources deal with criminal false arrest and imprisonment; the few that have any civil or tort implications do not appear to be relevant. You can use your judgment as to whether you would read any of these annotations or articles, but again, if you were doing this research at a client's expense, you should consider whether the expenditure of the time required would be cost-effective, given the likely benefits of the research.

§ 3.04. COMPUTER RESEARCH

1. Traditional Legal Research Sources

Most law schools provide free access to LexisNexis and Westlaw.[2] LexisNexis and Westlaw can be used most efficiently when you have enough of an understanding of the legal terminology that you can frame a search that will retrieve only relevant cases. For example, if you search a database of Wisconsin state cases using "false imprisonment," you will retrieve 688 cases on LexisNexis and 692 cases on Westlaw.[3]

When a client is paying for your time on the computer, you simply cannot read through hundreds of cases. Even if a client is not paying, it makes no sense to go screen by screen through all those cases when a glance through an encyclopedia or a digest will let you know much faster whether you need to read the cases in their entirety. In all likelihood, the vast majority of the cases do not deal substantively

---

2. Your school may also have subscriptions to other legal research services, such as Loislaw, which can be accessed at http://www.loislaw.com.

3. As of November 2009.

with false imprisonment, or they may involve criminal charges or aspects of the tort that are not at issue in your case.

Do not use the specific facts of your case to narrow your search. It is highly unlikely that you will find other cases involving fact patterns just like yours, and your real concern is to find cases dealing with the same issues that your case raises. For example, you could narrow your search by adding the concept "farmer" to your search request, which will get you 21 cases on LexisNexis and 20 cases on Westlaw. However, you should know by now that it does not really matter that the defendant is a farmer, and such a search will only exclude helpful cases from your review.

As you narrow your search, focus on terminology that will call up cases dealing with the elements of the tort with which you are concerned. Your primary concern in Mr. Trune's case is whether there was sufficient restraint to make out that element of the tort. Thus, you might try a terms and connectors search along the lines of "false imprisonment and restrain! w/20 suffic!", which will yield 60 cases on Westlaw and 15 on LexisNexis. If you perform the search, you will note that at least some of these cases look very familiar. You can also try a natural language search to see what you find.

Many other websites offer access to legal sources; some are free, others are not. Try searching yourself to see what you find, or consult your legal writing instructor or law librarian to see what other sources they recommend. LexisNexis and Westlaw are very expensive to use in practice, so you should not assume that you will be able to do all of your research using those services once you are out of law school.

2. Not Purely Legal Resources

You no doubt already have experience researching online using Google or other search engines. For that reason, we do not discuss here all the sources available; we merely suggest one or two sources that may be helpful.

Google Scholar is a free research engine that produces surprisingly good legal research results, at least for some users. If you input a search, Google Scholar will come up with cases on the topic, plus citations to the cases in articles. It does not have an updating feature, so you cannot tell whether the case is still good law, and the cases come up without headnotes or other features available on LexisNexis and Westlaw that can lead you to other relevant sources. Law librarians and legal writing instructors who have tried searches on Google Scholar report both pleasant surprise about the speed and accuracy of the results and concern about the lack of some familiar and helpful features. If you search for civil cases on false imprisonment in Wisconsin on Google Scholar, you will come up with 10 cases, but none of them are the cases we use in Chapter 5.

You probably are familiar already with Wikipedia, especially since it appears in so many search results. Wikipedia can be very helpful for finding general information on a topic or as a launching pad for research in a particular area. We do not recommend it for formal legal research, however, because any Wikipedia user can add information on the site. As a result, you cannot guarantee the accuracy or reliability of the information you find there.

As when using other research tools, it is always a good idea to check your research by trying multiple sources. The information that comes up repeatedly is likely to be the most helpful and reliable.

3. Books versus Computers—How Do You Decide?

Many practicing attorneys report frustration and disappointment at what they see as inadequate research training and skills on the part of recent law graduates. Many law students assume that everything worth finding can be found on the Internet. However, the Internet is not always the answer—it may be inefficient, excessively costly, and unable to give you what you need. One senior attorney points out that Internet research has two major shortcomings—it cannot work with concepts or analogies, both of which are critical to legal analysis.[4] Sometimes using the books in the library leads to faster and more accurate results. You may even find key cases in the books that would not have turned up in a computer search. Sometimes this is the result of what we call the "inspiration factor." As you are scanning an outline in an encyclopedia, digest, or annotated code, you may see a heading that will lead you to important cases, but it may not use the words you would have thought of for a computer search.

All in all, the safest approach often is to try both book and computer research. You should start with the books, to gain familiarity with the relevant concepts and to use visual scanning to see connections and terminology that may not have occurred to you just sitting at your computer. Turn to the computer when you have narrowed your research sufficiently to choose the best search terms or when you are ready to look for specific cases and statutes.

§ 3.05. UPDATING YOUR RESEARCH

Always update your research, not only to make sure the cases you plan to build your argument on are good law, but also to see whether there are any subsequent cases that might be even more helpful. Updating services such as Shepard's or KeyCite can be just as useful as case finders as they are citators. Updating online is much more efficient than using the Shepard's volumes in the law library, but you should use whatever updating tools you are taught in your legal writing class. The important thing is to make sure that you are relying on the most recent authoritative sources and are not going to embarrass yourself by citing a case that has been overruled or is otherwise no longer good law.

§ 3.06. WHEN DO YOU STOP?

Perhaps the most frustrating element of legal research for those who are learning it is knowing when to stop. In their zeal to leave no stone unturned, fledgling lawyers tend to explore every conceivable alternative, to look in every resource

---

4. Scott Stolley, *The Corruption of Legal Research*, For Def. 39 (Apr. 2004).

book the library has to offer, and to read every case that even mentions the type of cause of action at issue in the case they are researching. Telling you that you will develop instincts that will help you avoid wasting time in the library or online (which you will) may offer some long-term comfort, but it will not get you through those frustrating early efforts. Thus, we offer a few guidelines that should help streamline your first research efforts.

1. Look for the Most On-Point Cases First

Students sometimes try to identify the entire universe of available case law before beginning to read the decisions and then read all the decisions in no particular order. You will save yourself time and effort, and conclude your research sooner, if you identify the most useful cases right from the start and then read them before you go on. Identify these cases by looking for factual similarities or statements of holdings that sound like they could easily apply to your case.

Shepardizing these close cases, and reading cases cited in the decisions that support propositions important to you, should allow you to narrow the scope of your subsequent research. Using these cases as a jumping-off point will eliminate the need to read cases that do no more than outline general principles without offering useful applications to your situation.

2. Stop When You Come Full Circle

One of the surest signs that you should stop looking for new cases is repeatedly coming across citations to the same cases in different sources. Thus, if you find the same cases in the digest and the encyclopedia, even when you are researching different key words, you can be confident that you have identified the most relevant case law. Focus any additional research on leads provided by those key cases.

3. Do Not Follow Every Lead

One of the most common problems encountered by students is the frustration that comes from realizing that you have wasted valuable time reading cases that have only the most tangential relevance to your situation. Often, this is the result of deciding to read a case of possible but questionable relevance, then discovering a citation to an even more tenuously related decision, following up on that one too, and perhaps going on to follow the chain even further afield. While you do not want to miss any genuinely useful authority, you must constantly remind yourself what your case is really about.

To avoid these trips down blind alleys, draft a one-page outline of your tentative analysis and keep it with you at all times. By regularly referring to the outline, you will keep focused on the real issue in your case. If you are not ready to draft an outline, find another way to stay focused, for example, keeping with you any written information that you have about your assignment.[5] Creative analysis of

---

5. If you do end up reading irrelevant cases, avoid the temptation to find a way to work them into your written product anyway, just to show your instructor (or your supervisor) how much work you

problems is to be encouraged, but if you are finding it difficult to connect the product of your research to your main issue, imagine how difficult it will be for your reader!

Even when you stay focused, sometimes you will not find cases on point, but only cases tenuously related to the topic of your research. In this predicament, your only recourse is to read many cases in search of the few that contain some useful language or fact patterns. All you can do is try to analogize these cases to yours, either factually or by looking at the underlying legal or policy issues.

Finally, if you believe that you are spending an inordinate amount of time researching, consider whether you might be procrastinating. Students are often afraid to begin writing. Let's face it: it's no easy task to put your ideas and research findings into some logical order, and then craft them into sentences, paragraphs, and pages. Spending time on research can be justified, but once you pass the point where it is really productive, move on. Writing can actually be fun, if you give it a chance!

§ 3.07. HOW DO YOU KEEP TRACK?

To avoid wasting time later, spend time early on creating a research path. When you consult a digest or encyclopedia and find a relevant case, copy down the case's full name and citation. This way, you will not spend valuable time tracking down missing parts of citations or pulling cases off the shelves only to discover that you have already read and rejected them.

When you read the case, make a note next to the citation that indicates whether it was helpful or not, and whether you plan to return to it or cite it in your written analysis. Most of us find that making copies of useful cases is a good way to keep track of them and to make sure that we have all the necessary information for citation purposes. The problems tend to arise in losing track of the cases we decide not to use, and it is worth a few extra minutes of your time to make a complete record of your research process.

Whenever your notes get disorganized, it is worth stopping to make a clean list of useful cases and rejected cases. This way, you will not have to wonder whether you have already read a case.

§ 3.08. RESEARCH CHECKLIST

The following checklist will remind you of basic sources and approaches as you research a project. You will not need to follow each step for every assignment, but the checklist should enable you to consciously reject a step or resource rather than forgetting its existence.

I. Process
- Start with secondary sources such as treatises and encyclopedias if you need to learn the fundamental rules that govern your area of the law.

---

did. You will only frustrate the reader by overwhelming him or her with useless information, and you may make him or her wonder whether you really understood the issue at all.

- Look for an applicable statute if you think there might be one, but be sure the statute actually applies before reading any annotated cases.
- Go to the digests when you know the key words that will help you identify relevant cases.
- Use computer sources as appropriate, depending on cost, efficiency, and your understanding of the subject matter.
- Update your research, and check the validity of the sources you intend to rely on.
- Read on-point cases first, Shepardize them, and read cited decisions on important points. Don't follow tenuous leads.
- Stop when you see the same cases repeatedly.
- Keep a research path.

II. Sources
- Statutes
- Treatises and hornbooks
- Restatements
- Encyclopedias
- Digests
- Computer-assisted legal research (if it is cost-effective and you know the key words)
- Shepard's, KeyCite, AutoCite (use as a case finder, not just to check whether a case is good law)
- A.L.R.
- Periodicals
- Other sources, such as looseleaf services, that might apply to different types of problems

CHAPTER 4

How to Brief a Case

§ 4.01. WHAT IS A BRIEF?

1. Briefing Is Taking Notes

In your first year of law school, your professors will expect you to brief the cases that they assign. The word "brief" has two meanings in law. A brief is a written argument that an attorney submits to a court deciding a case. A brief also is a summary of a court opinion. In your initial law school classes and in this chapter, your concern is with this second type of brief.

Because briefing is new to you and because law school is also new, you may think that briefing is very different from anything you have done before. If you examine the task closely, however, you will discover that it is a very familiar one.

Briefing a case is taking notes on the case. By this time, you are a veteran at taking notes on what you read. You probably started taking notes in high school or college. Briefing a case seems different because it is a highly structured method of taking notes. It requires you to identify various parts of a case and summarize them.

2. The Purposes of Briefing

Briefing has two purposes. First, it helps you to focus on the important aspects of the case. A court opinion may ramble on page after page. Your brief, however, will be no longer than one or two pages. Briefing forces you to get to the heart of the case to grapple with the essentials.

Second, briefing helps you prepare for class and serves as a source of reference during class. You cannot brief a case properly unless you understand it. Briefing ensures that you understand the case before you discuss it in class. During class, you will find yourself referring to your brief. The discussion in a law school class goes far beyond what the brief contains. Your professor uses a court opinion only as a springboard to a sophisticated treatment of legal doctrine and legal process. Without the sort of understanding of basic aspects of a case that briefing demands, you will not get off the springboard and will fail to gain what the class has to offer.

Your case briefs are your personal notes. Your professors are not going to grade them. They probably never will read them unless you ask for assistance.

Few students refer to their briefs when preparing for exams. View your briefs as your private study tools for class preparation.

Because you will not be handing in your briefs to your professors and will not use them at semester's end, you may be tempted not to brief cases. Briefing can be time consuming, and your time is limited. We strongly encourage you to stay with briefing at least for the first few months of law school.

At the initial stage of your legal education, you should brief all assigned cases. As your grasp of the law grows, you will switch to writing short summaries or even writing notes in the margins of your casebooks. For now, however, brief your cases diligently. Briefing will help you understand what is going on in class, not always an easy task.

§ 4.02. HOW TO BRIEF

1. The Format

The typical brief includes the name of the case, its citation, the important facts in the case, the case's procedural status, the issue in the case, the court's holding, and the court's reasoning.

Different professors may ask you to brief cases in different ways. We offer you a typical format for a case brief. If a professor asks for a slightly different format, be sure to oblige him or her. You will find that despite deviations in format, all professors want you to abstract essentially the same information.

2. Parts of the Brief

a. An Exercise

Here is an exercise to help you learn about briefing cases. After reading the trial court's opinion in *Conti v. ASPCA* (which you may read again in your property course), go back and take notes on it. You need not follow any particular format. Just take notes as if you were taking notes on a college reading assignment. Following the case is a brief of the case. Please do not read it until after you have completed taking notes.

As you read the opinion, note its format, the typical format for this sort of opinion. It begins with the name of the case, with the plaintiff's name coming first. It then lists citations, which tell you what library books contain the opinion. Next is the name of the judge who wrote the opinion. Finally comes the text of the opinion. It contains the facts of the case, the court's reasoning, and the court's decision.

Conti v. Aspca

77 Misc. 2d 61, 353 N.Y.S.2d 288 (Civ. Ct. 1974)

MARTIN RODELL, Judge.

Chester is a parrot. He is fourteen inches tall, with a green coat, yellow head and an orange streak on his wings. Red splashes cover his left shoulder. Chester is a show parrot, used by the defendant ASPCA in various educational exhibitions presented to groups of children.

On June 28, 1973, during an exhibition in Kings Point, New York, Chester flew the coop and found refuge in the tallest tree he could find. For several hours the defendant sought to retrieve Chester. Ladders proved to be too short. Offers of food were steadfastly ignored. With the approach of darkness, search efforts were discontinued. A return to the area on the next morning revealed that Chester was gone.

On July 5th, 1973 the plaintiff, who resides in Belle Harbor, Queens County, had occasion to see a green-hued parrot with a yellow head and red splashes seated in his backyard. His offer of food was eagerly accepted by the bird. This was repeated on three occasions each day for a period of two weeks. This display of human kindness was rewarded by the parrot's finally entering the plaintiff's home, where he was placed in a cage.

The next day, the plaintiff phoned the defendant ASPCA and requested advice as to the care of the parrot he had found. Thereupon the defendant sent two representatives to the plaintiff's home. Upon examination, they claimed that it was the missing parrot, Chester, and removed it from the plaintiff's home.

Upon refusal of the defendant ASPCA to return the bird, the plaintiff now brings this action in replevin.

The issues presented to the Court are twofold: One, is the parrot in question truly Chester, the missing bird? Two, if it is in fact Chester, who is entitled to its ownership?

The plaintiff presented witnesses who testified that a parrot similar to the one in question was seen in the neighborhood prior to July 5, 1973. He further contended that a parrot could not fly the distance between Kings Point and Belle Harbor in so short a period of time, and therefore the bird in question was not in fact Chester.

The representatives of the ASPCA were categorical in their testimony that the parrot was indeed Chester, that he was unique because of his size, color and habits. They claimed that Chester said "hello" and could dangle by his legs. During the entire trial the Court had the parrot under close scrutiny, but at no time did it exhibit any of these characteristics. The Court called upon the parrot to indicate by name or other mannerisms an affinity to either of the claimed owners. Alas, the parrot stood mute.

Upon all the credible evidence the Court does find as a fact that the parrot in question is indeed Chester and is the same parrot which escaped from the possession of the ASPCA on June 28, 1973.

The Court must now deal with the plaintiff's position that the ownership of the defendant was a qualified one and upon the parrot's escape, ownership passed to the first individual who captured it and placed it under his control.

The law is well settled that the true owner of lost property is entitled to the return thereof as against any person finding same. (*In re Wright's Estate*, 15 Misc. 2d 225, 177 N.Y.S.2d 410) (36A C.J.S. Finding Lost Goods § 3).

This general rule is not applicable when the property lost is an animal. In such cases the Court must inquire as to whether the animal was domesticated or ferae naturae (wild).

Where an animal is wild, the owner can only acquire a qualified right of property which is wholly lost when it escapes from its captor with no intention of returning.

Thus in *Mullett v. Bradley*, 24 Misc. 695, 53 N.Y.S. 781, an untrained and undomesticated sea lion escaped after being shipped from the West to the East Coast.

The sea lion escaped and was again captured in a fish pond off the New Jersey Coast. The original owner sued the finder for its return. The court held that the sea lion was a wild animal (ferae naturae), and when it returned to its wild state, the original owner's property rights were extinguished.

In *Amory v. Flyn*, 10 Johns. (N.Y.) 102, plaintiff sought to recover geese of the wild variety which had strayed from the owner. In granting judgment to the plaintiff, the court pointed out that the geese had been tamed by the plaintiff and therefore were unable to regain their natural liberty.

This important distinction was also demonstrated in *Manning v. Mitcherson*, 69 Ga. 447, 450-451, 52 A.L.R. 1063, where the plaintiff sought the return of a pet canary. In holding for the plaintiff the court stated, "To say that if one has a canary bird, mocking bird, parrot, or any other bird so kept, and it should accidentally escape from its cage to the street, or to a neighboring house, that the first person who caught it would be its owner is wholly at variance with all our views of right and justice."

The Court finds that Chester was a domesticated animal, subject to training and discipline. Thus the rule of ferae naturae does not prevail and the defendant as true owner is entitled to regain possession.

The Court wishes to commend the plaintiff for his acts of kindness and compassion to the parrot during the period that it was lost and was gratified to receive the defendant's assurance that the first parrot available would be offered to the plaintiff for adoption.

Judgment for defendant dismissing the complaint without costs.

———

Now that you have completed reading the case and taking notes on it, compare your notes with a typical brief of the case.

Conti (pl.) v. Aspca (def.)
77 Misc. 2d 61, 353 N.Y.S.2d 288 (Civ. Ct. 1974)

FACTS: ASPCA owned Chester, a show parrot. On June 28, he escaped to a tree and def. could not retrieve him. The next day, he disappeared. On July 5, pl. found Chester and enticed him to his home. ASPCA learned about this and took Chester back. Pl. brought replevin action. (There was a question whether the parrot really was Chester, but the court decided he was, based on the evidence.)

PROCEDURE: Action for replevin. Court dismissed the complaint, in def.'s favor. (Note: This is a trial court decision.)

ISSUE: Whether, when a domesticated animal escapes, ownership passes to the person who next captures it.

HELD: The parrot here is a domesticated animal (no discussion). When a domesticated animal escapes, ownership remains with original owner.

ANALYSIS: The owner of a wild animal (*ferae naturae*) loses ownership when it escapes with no intention of returning. This rule does not apply to domesticated animals (animals that have been trained and disciplined). They are treated as lost property, and ownership remains with the original owner. The court fails to state a rationale explicitly, but cites the *Manning* case: a contrary holding would contradict "all our views of right and justice." The court relies on three cases:

Mullett: A sea lion is treated as ferae naturae. Upon escape, the new captor gains ownership.

Amory: Court treats wild geese as tamed and therefore unable to gain their natural liberty.

Manning: Escaped pet canary is treated as a domesticated animal and as belonging to the original owner.

––––––

Your notes probably contain most of the information that the sample brief contains. The organization, however, may be quite different. You can see how the briefing format forces you to focus on essential information and state it concisely in a logical order. Now let us use the *Conti* case and the sample brief to examine the parts of a brief.

b. Name of the Case

Copy the name of the case. When you determine which party is the plaintiff and which is the defendant and, on appeal, which is the appellant or petitioner and which is the appellee or respondent, write down this information as well. Some opinions are written in a way that makes these vital facts difficult to discover. In *Conti*, the plaintiff's name comes first, but in some cases it comes second. If you fail to write down which litigant is which, you may forget this information at a crucial moment in class.

c. Citation

The citation contains the information that you need to find the case in the library. If you do not know how to use a cite to find a case, you will learn very shortly. Most casebooks offer abridged versions of cases. Your curiosity sometimes will lead you to search for the complete case in the library. If you have the cite in your brief, you will not have to return to your casebook to find it when you head for the library.

d. Facts of the Case

Write down the facts that you think were important to the court in deciding the case as well as any additional facts that are important to you. Court opinions often contain pages of facts. You would be wasting time and paper if you were to copy them. You want only the essential facts. If you read the entire case before you begin to brief it, you will have a much better sense of which facts are the essential ones. If you fail to read the case first, you run the risk of getting mired in a complex set of facts and writing pages of useless information.

The *Conti* case has relatively few essential facts. These facts are that Chester, a domesticated parrot, flew away from its owner, the ASPCA, and ultimately landed in the home of Conti, who now claims ownership. Chester's height and coloring are not significant. These characteristics would be significant if the opinion focused on whether Conti's parrot really was Chester. Therefore you need not write down Chester's description. The details of Chester's escape and ultimate welcome at the Conti household also are not essential. We know we can disregard this information because we have read the rest of the case.

e. Procedure
Answer three questions:

(1) *Who is suing whom for what?* In *Conti*, the answer is clear.

(2) *What is the legal claim?* Here, the plaintiff is suing in replevin. In some other case, a plaintiff might sue for breach of contract, false imprisonment, negligence, relief granted by a statute, or on one of many other grounds. If you come across a word like "replevin" and do not know its meaning, look it up in a dictionary. "Replevin" tells us that Conti was asking the court to order the ASPCA to return the bird to him. If you did not know the meaning of replevin, you might have thought that Conti might have been satisfied to receive the dollar value of the bird.

(3) *How did the lower court rule in the case?* It heard the arguments, considered the evidence, and rendered the decision. The trial court wrote the *Conti* opinion. Therefore we have no decision by an even lower court. Suppose Conti was dissatisfied with the court's decision and appealed to a higher court, which decided the case and issued a written opinion. If we were briefing that opinion, we would note in our brief that the court below had dismissed Conti's complaint.

f. Issue
The issue is the legal question that the court must decide in order to reach its conclusion. In *Conti*, the issue is whether the owner of a domesticated animal loses ownership when it escapes and someone else captures it. Sometimes a court opinion will state the issue explicitly. Sometimes it will state the issue only implicitly and leave you the task of articulating it explicitly.

The *Conti* court states the issue in a very shorthanded way: "[I]f it is in fact Chester, who is entitled to its ownership?" We are ignoring the court's, first issue—whether the parrot is Chester—because the court finds the issue uncontroversial and quickly decides it without analysis. You must flesh out the issue in order to state it in more general terms. The issue deals not just with a parrot named Chester, but with any domesticated animal that escapes and undergoes capture under similar circumstances. Ultimately the court must decide the case on the basis of a general rule applicable to similarly situated individuals and animals.

How narrowly or broadly you phrase the issue is, in part, a matter of taste. In the sample brief, we phrase the issue broadly:

Whether, when a domesticated animal escapes, ownership passes to the person who next captures it.

Another lawyer might phrase it more narrowly—that is, more tailored to the facts of the specific case:

Whether, when a domesticated parrot escapes, ownership passes to the person who next captures it.

Still another lawyer might phrase it even more narrowly:

> Whether the finder of Chester, an escaped parrot, owns it when the parrot was a domesticated animal that the ASPCA trained and disciplined and used in educational exhibitions.

In our experience, beginning law students frame issues too narrowly or too broadly. When they frame an issue too narrowly, they focus too much on the facts of the case and fail to understand that it applies to a broad range of cases. When they frame an issue too broadly, they fail to appreciate how important the specific facts of a case are to the court deciding it.

Learning to frame an issue is an art that takes time to learn. Your professors will give you guidance in mastering the art. They also will let you know how narrowly or broadly they want you to frame issues in their respective courses.

g. Holding

The holding is the court's decision and thus its resolution of the issue in the case. It usually requires rephrasing the issue from a question to a declarative sentence. In *Conti*, the holding is:

> When a domesticated animal escapes, ownership remains with the original owner.

As with framing issues, different professors will have individual preferences on how broadly or narrowly they want you to state the holding.

h. Analysis

Explain the court's reasoning in reaching its decision. Again, reading the case before you brief it will save you an enormous amount of time. Understanding the court's reasoning is not always easy. Sometimes the reasoning will be unclear or contain gaps in its logic or require the reader to discern what the court is saying only implicitly. These defects and similar ones often will be the subject of class discussion.

A court frequently explains that its decision furthers important social policy. In your brief, identify these policy considerations. In *Conti*, the court quotes an earlier decision to the effect that a contrary holding would contradict "all our views of right and justice." If the *Conti* court had written a more expansive opinion, it might have stated that its holding protected the right of property ownership because it forbids an individual to casually seize and keep the property of another.

Court decisions often include dicta. Dicta are discussions of law that are not necessary to the court's decision in the case before it. The singular of "dicta" is "dictum." The discussion of the *Conti* court about the rule to follow when an undomesticated animal escapes is dictum. The court's discussion of that situation is not essential to deciding the case of a domesticated parrot that escapes. It is a wise practice to note dicta in your brief.

Be sure to read any footnotes. Most cases appearing in law school casebooks are edited versions. The editor has omitted most footnotes. If the editor has retained a footnote, he or she believes that it is important to the student's understanding of the case. A footnote sometimes contains the key to the case.

Do not ignore dissenting and concurring opinions. Again, if an editor retains a dissent or concurrence, he or she has done so for a reason. Do not be surprised if your professor asks you if you agree with the majority or the dissent. If you fail to brief the dissent, you probably will be unable to answer the question.

i. More Sample Briefs

Here are two additional briefs of the *Conti* case. Each differs slightly from the sample brief we have studied. Our purpose is to show you that there is not just one way to brief a case. Just as different people take notes in different ways, different people brief cases in different ways. In each, however, the essential information is the same.

First Sample Brief

Conti v. Aspca
77 Misc. 2d 61, 353 N.Y.S.2d 288 (Civ. Ct. 1974)

FACTS: on June 28, 1973, the ASPCA's parrot, Chester, flew away. On July 5, Conti (Pl.) found a bird the court determined was Chester in his backyard. Conti caged the parrot and called the ASPCA for information on parrot care. The ASPCA (Def.) suspecting the parrot was Chester went and took the parrot from Conti. Def. refused to return the parrot to Pl.

PROCEDURE: Trial court decision on a replevin action. Replevin is an action where a person seeks to recover possession of particular goods.

ISSUE: Who has rightful possession of an escaped parrot originally owned by one party and recaptured by another?

HELD: Ownership of a domesticated parrot does not terminate upon escape, but continues as against the one who recaptures the escaped animal.

ANALYSIS: The true owner of lost property is entitled to its return. Ownership of a wild animal (ferae naturae) ends when it escapes and returns to its natural liberty. A domesticated animal (one that has been trained and disciplined) is treated as lost property and is subject to return upon recapture.

In determining whether the parrot was domesticated or wild, the court considered three cases and three guidelines. *Mullet* found an untrained sea lion to be ferae naturae. *Amory* held geese that had been trained were domesticated. *Manning* determined extinguishing ownership of a pet canary was "wholly at variance with all our views of right and justice." Chester had been trained, disciplined and was like a canary. Ownership continued to be held by the ASPCA because Chester was domesticated.

Second Sample Brief

Conti v. Aspca
77 Misc. 2d 61, 353 N.Y.S.2d 288 (Civ. Ct. 1974)

FACTS: Defendant ASPCA conducted a demonstration with a parrot named Chester during which the bird escaped. A week later, a parrot with markings and colorings similar to Chester's appeared in plaintiff's yard and remained with the plaintiff for two weeks before being caged. The ASPCA removed the bird after plaintiff called for advice about its care. ASPCA claimed the bird was Chester and belonged to the organization.

PROCEDURE: Action for replevin—plaintiff wants the bird back.

ISSUE: Court identified two issues: 1. Whether the bird is actually Chester; and 2. Who gets him?

HELD: ASPCA gets the bird because: 1. The court found that the bird was Chester; and 2. As a domesticated animal, Chester does have a true owner, whose rights are not lost when the bird escapes.

ANALYSIS: The key issue in determining ownership was whether the rule of ferae naturae applied. This rule states that an owner acquires only qualified rights in a wild animal that are extinguished if the animal escapes. The court found that Chester was subject to training and discipline and therefore was not wild.

3. Problem

Here is another case that many of you will read during your first year in law school. Please brief it. Following the opinion are three sample briefs of the case. Compare your brief to them. Please do not read these briefs until you have written your own. If you ignore this instruction, you will learn far less.

As you read the opinion, note that it is an appellate opinion. The trial court decided in favor of the defendant, and the plaintiff has appealed to the appropriate appeals court, here, the Massachusetts Supreme Judicial Court.

Note also the format of the opinion. It begins with the name of the case. Here, the first name is McAvoy, the name of the plaintiff, who is now the appellant. Though some courts put the name of the appellant first, others do not necessarily do so. In each case, you need to check. Next is the citation you need to find the case in the library. Then come the facts of the case and, then, the name of the justice who wrote the opinion. Most of the time, the name of the judge appears before the statement of the facts. In virtually all appellate cases, several judges decide the case, and one judge writes the opinion. Here, Justice Dewey had that task. After the opinion discusses the case, it gives the court's ruling. In this case, the court overruled the plaintiff's exceptions and upheld the decision of the trial court. Exceptions are the grounds on which the plaintiff sought the appeal.

McAvoy v. Medina
93 Mass. (11 Allen) 548 (1866)

[Tort action to recover sum of money found by plaintiff in defendant's shop.]

At the trial in the superior court, before Morton, J., it appeared that the defendant was a barber, and the plaintiff, being a customer in the defendant's shop, saw and took up a pocketbook which was lying upon a table there, and said, "See what I have found." The defendant came to the table and asked where he found it. The plaintiff laid it back in the same place and said, "I found it right there." The defendant then took it and counted the money, and the plaintiff told him to keep it, and if the owner should come to give it to him; and otherwise to advertise it; which the defendant promised to do. Subsequently the plaintiff made three demands for the money, and the defendant never claimed to hold the same till the last demand. It was agreed that the pocketbook was placed upon the table by a transient customer of the defendant and accidentally left there, and was first seen and taken up by the plaintiff, and that the owner had not been found.

The judge ruled that the plaintiff could not maintain his action, and a verdict was accordingly returned for the defendant; and the plaintiff alleged exceptions, (Citations omitted.)

DEWEY, J. It seems to be the settled law that the finder of lost property has a valid claim to the same against all the world except the true owner, and generally that the place in which it is found creates no exception to this rule. 2 Parsons on Con. 97. *Bridges v. Hawkesworth*, 7 Eng. Law 7 Eq. R. 424.

But this property is not, under the circumstances, to be treated as lost property in the sense in which a finder has a valid claim to hold the same until called for by the true owner. This property was voluntarily placed upon a table in the defendant's shop by a customer of his who accidentally left the same there and has never called for it. The plaintiff also came there as a customer, and first saw the same and took it up from the table. The plaintiff did not by this acquire the right to take the property from the shop, but it was rather the duty of the defendant, when the fact became thus known to him, to use reasonable care for the safe keeping of the same until the owner should call for it. In the case of *Bridges v. Hawkesworth* the property, although found in a shop, was found on the floor of the same, and had not been placed there voluntarily by the owner, and the court held that the finder was entitled to the possession of the same, except as to the owner. But the present case more resembles that of *Lawrence v. the State*, 1 Humph (Tenn.) 228, and is indeed very similar in its facts. The court there makes a distinction between the case of property thus placed by the owner and neglected to be removed, and property lost. It was there held that "to place a pocketbook upon a table and to forget to take it away is not to lose it, in the sense in which the authorities referred to speak of lost property."

We accept this as the better rule, and especially as one better adapted to secure the rights of the true owner.

In view of the facts of this case, the plaintiff acquired no original right to the property, and the defendant's subsequent acts in receiving and holding the property in the manner he did; does not create any. Exceptions overruled.

First Sample Brief

McAvoy v. Medina
93 Mass. (11 Allen) 548 (1866)

FACTS: Pl. customer found a pocketbook lying on a table in def.'s barbershop. Def. agreed to hold it in case the owner returned. The owner never showed up and apparently was a transient customer. Def. refused to give pocketbook to pl.

PROCEDURE: Pl. brought tort action to recover money in the pocketbook. T.C.: Pl. could not maintain the action; verdict for def. Pl. appeals. Ct. here affirms (exceptions overruled).

ISSUE: Does the finder have a valid claim to property that the owner voluntarily placed in a given location and forgot to retrieve (i.e. property that the owner mislaid)?

HELD: No.

ANALYSIS: The finder of lost property has a valid claim to it as against all but the true owner. But property that is voluntarily placed somewhere, like the table in the barbershop, and accidentally left behind is not lost property. The finder has no right to it. The owner of the location has the duty to take reasonable care of the property until the owner calls for it. This rule is better adapted to secure the rights of the true owner.

Second Sample Brief

McAvoy v. Medina
93 Mass. (11 Allen) 548 (1866)

FACTS: McAvoy (P) was a customer in Medina's (D's) barbershop. P found a pocketbook containing money on a table in the shop. P & D agreed (at least at the time of trial) that it was placed on the table and accidentally left by a transient customer. P left the pocketbook with D who promised to advertise it. No one claimed it, and D refused to give P the money found in it.

PROCEDURE: P appeals from the trial court, which found he could not maintain a tort action for the value of the money.

ISSUE: Whether the finder of property determined to be accidentally left has the same property right as the finder of lost property.

HOLDING: The finder of mislaid or forgotten property acquires no right to the property found against the shop owner where the article was left.

ANALYSIS: Property voluntarily placed and accidentally left in a shop does not give the finder a valid claim against all but the true owner. A shop owner has the responsibility to use due care for the property until the true owner returns. Creating a property interest in the shop owner supports its return to its proper owner.

The court uses *Bridges* and *Lawrence* to show that finding the property in the shop is not the determinative factor. The distinction is between deciding if it is lost (*Bridges*—found on the floor), in which case the finder gets it, and finding if it is mislaid or forgotten (*Lawrence*—found on a table).

Third Sample Brief

McAvoy v. Medina
93 Mass. (11 Allen) 548 (1866)

FACTS: Plaintiff McAvoy saw a purse on a table in def.'s barbershop and asked def. to give it to the owner or to advertise it. When the owner did not show up to claim the purse, pl. demanded it.

PROCEDURE: Action in tort to recover money. Pl. appeals from lower court verdict for def.

ISSUE: If the purse is not treated as lost, but as accidentally left behind, would the finder be entitled to keep it if the true owner does not show up?

HELD: Pl.'s appeal was denied (exceptions overruled). The court held that the purse would not be treated as lost under the circumstances and thus pl. acquired no right to the property.

ANALYSIS: The court relied on *Lawrence v. State* in which the court distinguished between property "placed by the owner and neglected to be removed" and property lost. The court felt that treating the mislaid property differently and giving it to the owner of the location created a rule that was "better adapted to secure the rights of the true owner."

§ 4.03. BEYOND BRIEFING

Briefing is just the beginning of preparing for class. Once you brief a case, you need to think about the opinion critically. You will spend most of your time in class evaluating the opinion rather than merely restating what the court said. By the time class is over, you may decide that you disagree with the court. After a class on the *Conti* case, you still may agree with the outcome, but you may question at least some of the court's reasoning. In a class on the *McAvoy* case, you may learn that the trend among courts is to reject its holding. Here are three questions to help you think about the cases you have briefed.

(1) *Do you agree with the court's holding and reasoning?* Does the logic flow? Does the court rely on assumptions—explicit or implicit—with which you disagree? Do you agree with the social policies that the court purports to further?

(2) *Would you use the court's holding to decide a case with similar, but not identical, facts?* In *Conti*, suppose Chester was an untamed wolf instead of a tamed parrot? Suppose he was a tiger that escaped from the zoo? Would the court still find for the ASPCA, even though the animal was undomesticated? Would you?

(3) *Why did my professor and the casebook's editor select this case?* What larger lessons are they trying to teach? Why are *Conti* and *McAvoy* usually near the beginning of property casebooks, as opposed to the middle or end? If you think about each case as part of a series of cases that you are studying, do you see a big picture in addition to a series of narrow rules?

Exercise

Pick a case that you have briefed for one of your classes. Ask your professor to read it and suggest ways to improve it. You will discover that most professors will be very willing to spend the time with you.

Introduction to Legal Analysis

§ 5.01. INTRODUCTION

Largely because of the adversary system, American legal analysis has at its core the common law doctrine of stare decisis, which means "to stand with things decided." In other words, earlier cases are precedents whose holdings determine the outcome of later cases. Constitutions, statutes, and other sources of law are frequently the bases of court decisions. Courts must determine the meaning of these law sources as they apply to specific situations. Thus, analysis of case precedent forms the core of legal analysis, and legal analysis is primarily applying court-made law to the facts of the current case. In every case, lawyers on opposite sides will be using the same facts and law, but hoping to persuade the court to reach diametrically opposed conclusions.

There are three steps for developing a legal argument:

1. Determine all legal authority, or general rules, applicable to your case.
2. Apply this legal authority to the facts of your particular case.
3. Draw a conclusion based on the legal authority that you have applied to your case.

For example:

Step One General Rule:	A lawyer may not knowingly make a false statement of material fact or law to a tribunal.
Step Two Particular Case:	Sandra North is a lawyer, and she knows that an important case she wanted to rely on in her brief has just been overruled.
Step Three Conclusion:	Sandra North must not rely on the overruled case in her brief because that would be a false statement of material law.

The next two sections discuss legal authority and how to use deductive reasoning to apply authority to your case.

§ 5.02. ARGUING DEDUCTIVELY

Legal analyis frequently relies on deductive reasoning. When you argue deductively, you take three steps:

1. apply a general rule (of law), which usually derives from a particular statute or case but also may derive from a variety of different sources,
2. to a particular case, and
3. draw a conclusion.

For example:

General Rule: All teachers are cruel and heartless.
Particular Case: John Doe is a teacher.
Conclusion: John Doe is cruel and heartless.

In a legal argument, the general rule is the relevant legal authority; the particular case is the facts of your case; and the conclusion is the result reached by applying the legal authority to the facts.
For example:

The general rule is a court decision stating that all golfers have a legal duty to avoid injuring other golfers, and a golfer fulfills this duty by yelling "fore" when hitting a golf ball. In this particular case John Doe is a golfer. Therefore, the conclusion is that John Doe has a duty to avoid injuring other golfers, and he can fulfill this duty by yelling "fore" when he hits a golf ball.

When broken into its components, the deductive reasoning applied here looks like this:

General Rule: All golfers have a legal duty to avoid injuring other golfers and can fulfill this duty by yelling "fore" when hitting golf balls.
Particular Case: John Doe is a golfer.
Conclusion: John Doe has a legal duty to avoid injuring other golfers and can fulfill this duty by yelling "fore" when hitting golf balls.

In your legal writing or other law school classes, you will probably learn about IRAC (Issue, Rule, Application/Analysis, Conclusion), or some other version of the acronym (CRAC, CIRAC, etc.). You will also hear this acronym when you start preparing for your bar exam, and you may hear it from practicing attorneys. It is the formulation of deductive reasoning that has been most commonly used in law schools for many years.

Almost all approaches to legal analysis use some form of what we teach you here—identify your issue and rule, apply the rule to your case, and state your conclusion. Most teachers and supervisors in law offices will also tell you to state your conclusion up front, which leads to CRAC or CIRAC. Whatever it is called in your classroom or office, the basic premise remains the same—use a structure that contains the essential elements of legal analysis and that presents those elements clearly for your reader to follow.

1. Limitations

Deductive reasoning is only a framework or a starting point for formulating a legal argument. It does not always dictate the outcome of a case with great precision and may only give you a "ballpark" prediction of what the outcome of your case should be. Remember that the party on the other side of the case also will apply deductive reasoning, using the same facts and law, to arrive at a very different conclusion about the case. Deductive reasoning is only as valid as your interpretation of the general rule and your application of that rule to the particular case.

For example, with regard to the case above, suppose you found the general rule in a California case, but New York law governs your case and does not follow the California rule. If New York law is settled, it controls; that is, if New York law specifically holds that yelling "fore" is not required, the California case has no precedential value. If it is unsettled, then the California rule is, at best, persuasive authority. Thus, if New York courts have said only that golfers must take "reasonable steps" to avoid injuring other golfers, you might want to argue that the California rule is more specific and should be adopted.

With regard to the same case, suppose John Doe the golfer is a child. Or suppose he was incapable of yelling "fore," either because he could not speak or he speaks a foreign language. These differences in the facts might make your authority non-mandatory and maybe not even persuasive.

If the general rule is very broad or very narrow, or if your understanding of how the rule applies to the particular case is in some way not totally accurate, your conclusion may not be persuasive to a court. Reasoning deductively is not always as easy as it appears, but it is still a useful framework for legal logic.

2. Maximizing the Use of Deductive Reasoning

To use deductive reasoning for legal argument, you must:

1. Be sure that your general statement, or rule of law, is correct by analyzing all relevant law and predicting accurately the rule you think the court will apply to your case.
2. Be sure that your statement of the facts in the particular case is accurate and does not ignore anything that might alter application of the general rule.
3. Be sure that your application of the rule to your facts is thorough and fair, taking into account all relevant analogies and distinctions.
4. Be sure that your final conclusion follows logically from the rule and facts.

If there are several issues in your case, you should apply deductive reasoning to each issue separately, again taking great care as to your interpretation of what the law is and its application to your own situation. One issue may contain many sub-issues, each of which requires a separate application of deductive reasoning.

3. Application

When writing your argument with deductive analysis, we recommend that you always state your conclusion first because readers of legal writing do not want to be left waiting in suspense for the conclusion. After you state the conclusion, identify the key issue and the applicable rule, and present the relevant legal authority. Next apply the legal authority to the facts of your case. Finally, restate the conclusion you have drawn from your analysis.

Here is a brief example of this form of analysis:

Conclusion:	The defendant here had a duty to shout "fore" to the plaintiff.
Issue:	The key issue is when a golfer has a duty to yell "fore" when hitting a golf ball in the direction of another golfer on an adjacent fairway.
Major Premise: *(Relevant legal* *authority or* *rule)*	In *Allen v. Pinewood Country Club, Inc.*, 292 So. 2d 786, 789 (La. App. 1974), the court held that golfers have a duty to yell "fore" if they hit a golf ball and another golfer on a different fairway is standing in the ball's line of flight. The court found that all golfers have a duty of reasonable care and must avoid injuring other golfers. *Id.* To fulfill this duty, a golfer must give timely and adequate warning to other golfers in the golf ball's line of flight. *Id.* Therefore, a golfer has a duty to yell "fore" when hitting a golf ball that veers toward another fairway and a golfer on the other fairway is standing in the ball's line of flight. *Id.*
Particular Case: *(Applying the* *relevant legal* *authority to the* *facts)*	Under *Allen*, the defendant in the present case had a duty to yell "fore" to the plaintiff. The defendant hit a golf ball from the fairway of the sixth hole. The ball hooked toward the fairway of the fifth hole. The plaintiff was standing on the fairway of the fifth hole and was in the direct line of flight of the golf ball hit by the defendant. Therefore, the facts of the present case fall squarely within the holding in *Allen*.
Conclusion:	Since the defendant hit a golf ball that hooked toward the plaintiff who was on an adjacent fairway and was in the direct line of flight of the golf ball, the defendant had a duty to shout "fore" to the plaintiff.

The conclusion at the end is not just a simple paraphrase of the conclusion at the beginning. It should be developed more fully and should include the relevant, concrete facts of the case.

§ 5.03. APPLYING THE LAW TO THE FACTS

As you may have surmised from the preceding discussion, a legal argument is meaningless unless you apply the relevant legal authority directly to the facts of your case. The most important aspect of legal argument is taking the general rule of law and applying it to the particular situation. Applying the law to the facts makes your argument concrete and tells the court how you think it should resolve your case. The rest of this chapter shows you in detail how to do this. After a brief overview of the process, you will see a legal analysis of an issue arising out of a case similar to the *McAvoy v. Medina* case presented in Chapter 4. We will then proceed step-by-step through two examples of legal analysis, one relying solely on cases and one adding statutory construction to the mix. As we go along, you will be asked to write out the analysis that follows from the discussion.

1. The Basic Approach

The single most important thing to remember about legal analysis is that completeness is everything. The goal is not to arrive at an answer as quickly as possible, but to lay out, in what often seems like excruciating detail, how you got from the question to the answer. In most cases, if a thought goes through your head that helps you arrive at a conclusion, it should appear on the paper. Readers of legal analysis, generally busy practitioners and judges, do not want to work at analyzing the problem while they read. They want to pick up the document you have submitted, read through it quickly, and understand instantly how you reached every conclusion you present.

How does this process work? Assume you have been asked to predict the outcome of a particular client's situation. You have identified the relevant case law and are preparing to write out an analysis that explains how the case law applies to your client's situation. Until you become comfortable with this analytical process and develop your own personal style, you should go through the following steps *in writing*. First, brief the cases you will be analyzing. Summarize the facts, holding, and rationale of each decision. Find and identify the rule of law applied by the court in each case. Add the procedural history, if it is relevant to the discussion.

Once you have the building blocks, try to formulate a general principle or principles that explain the decisions reached by the courts. Are they applying the same rules? If the courts seem to be arriving at the same end by different routes, compare and evaluate the various approaches. If the courts arrive at different results, try to figure out what distinguishes the cases. Are the facts different? Are the courts trying to implement different policies?

When you have figured out why the courts reached the decisions they did, look for analogies between the decided cases and the case you have been asked to analyze. Compare the facts. Identify the policy or policies behind the decisions, and try to decide what outcome that policy would mandate in your case. By policy, we mean the societal interest or goal that is served by the decision. Look at the equities—did the courts seek out the "fair" result, and what would that be in your case? How do these policy and equity arguments relate to the legal rules announced or applied by the courts?

After you have gone through these steps, it is time to begin writing out your analysis. When you do, *integrate* your analysis of your case with your discussion of the decided cases. Integration means you do not present all of the relevant law and then discuss its application to your case. An effective legal analysis will make comparisons between the decided cases and the case being discussed wherever appropriate, whether those comparisons are of facts, applicable policies, or equities. You want to synthesize the existing law and your client's situation by demonstrating how they fit together, and by explaining how what has happened in the past will or should inform the decisions of those faced with the current situation.

2. An Example of Legal Analysis

This section will present a sample legal analysis of a question regarding whether a piece of property was "lost" or "mislaid," and thus who can claim ownership of it. First, reread the *McAvoy v. Medina* case from Chapter 4. Assume that the only other relevant authority is the following case:

Durfee v. Jones
11 R.I. 588 (1877)

July 21, 1877. DURFEE, C.J. The facts in this case are briefly these: In April, 1874, the plaintiff bought an old safe and soon afterwards instructed his agent to sell it again. The agent offered to sell it to the defendant for ten dollars, but the defendant refused to buy it. The agent then left it with the defendant, who was a blacksmith, at his shop for sale for ten dollars, authorizing him to keep his books in it until it was sold or reclaimed. The safe was old-fashioned, of sheet iron, about three feet square, having a few pigeon-holes and a place for books, and in back of the place for books a large crack in the lining. The defendant shortly after the safe was left, upon examining it, found secreted between the sheet-iron exterior and the wooden lining a roll of bills amounting to $165, of the denomination of the national bank bills which have been current for the last ten or twelve years. Neither the plaintiff nor the defendant knew the money was there before it was found. The owner of the money is still unknown. The defendant informed the plaintiff's agent that he had found it, and offered it to him for the plaintiff; but the agent declined it, stating that it did not belong to either himself or the plaintiff, and advised the defendant to deposit it where it would be drawing interest until the rightful owner appeared. The plaintiff was then out of the city. Upon his return, being informed of the finding, he immediately called on the defendant and asked for the money, but the defendant refused to give it to him. He then, after taking advice, demanded the return of the safe and its contents, precisely as they existed when placed in the defendant's hands. The defendant promptly gave up the safe, but retained the money. The plaintiff brings this action to recover it or its equivalent.

The plaintiff does not claim that he acquired, by purchasing the safe, any right to the money in the safe as against the owner; for he bought the safe alone, not the safe and its contents. See *Merry v. Green*, 7 M. & W. 623. But he claims that as between himself and the defendant his is the better right. The defendant, however, has the possession, and therefore it is for the plaintiff, in order to succeed in his action, to prove his better right.

The plaintiff claims that he is entitled to have the money by the right of prior possession. But the plaintiff never had any possession of the money, except, unwittingly, by having possession of the safe which contained it. Such possession, if possession it can be called, does not of itself confer a right. The case at bar is in this view like *Bridges v. Hawkesworth*, 15 Jur. 1079; 21 L.J.Q.B. 75 A.D. 1851; 7 Eng. L. & Eq. 424. In that case, the plaintiff, while in the defendant's shop on business, picked up from the floor a parcel containing bank notes. He gave them to the defendant for the owner if he could be found. The owner could not be found, and it was held that the plaintiff as finder was entitled to them, as against the defendant as owner of the shop in which they were found. "The notes," said the court, "never were in the custody of the defendant nor within the protection of his house, before they were found, as they would have been if they had been intentionally deposited there." The same in effect may be said of the notes in the case at bar; for though they were originally deposited in the safe by design, they were not so deposited in the safe, after it became the plaintiff's safe, so as to be in the protection of the safe as *his* safe, or so as to affect him with any responsibility for them. The case at bar is also in this respect like *Tatum v. Sharpless*, 6 Phila. 18. There it was held, that a conductor who had found money which had been lost in a railroad car was entitled to it as against the railroad company.

The plaintiff also claims that the money was not lost but designedly left where it was found, and that therefore as owner of the safe he is entitled to its custody. He refers to cases in which it has been held, that money or other property voluntarily laid down and forgotten is not in legal contemplation lost, and that of such money or property the owner of the shop or place where it is left is the proper custodian rather than the person who happens to discover it first. *State v. McCann*, 19 Mo. 249; *Lawrence v. The State*, 1 Humph. 228; *McAvoy v. Medina*, 11 Allen, 549. It may be questioned whether this distinction has not been pushed to an extreme. See *Kincaid v. Eaton*, 98 Mass 139. But, however that may be, we think the money here, though designedly left in the safe, was probably not designedly put in the crevice or interspace where it was found, but that, being left in the safe, it probably slipped or was accidentally shoved into the place where it was found without the knowledge of the owner, and so was lost, in the stricter sense of the word. The money was not simply deposited and forgotten, but deposited and lost by reason of a defect or insecurity in the place of deposit.

The plaintiff claims that the finding was a wrongful act on the part of the defendant, and that therefore he is entitled to recover the money or to have it replaced. We do not so regard it. The safe was left with the defendant for sale. As seller he would properly examine it under an implied permission to do so, to qualify him the better to act as seller. Also under the permission to use it for his books, he would have the right to inspect it to see if it was a fit depository. And finally, as a possible purchaser he might examine it, for though he had once declined to examine it, the defendant, having found in the safe something which did not belong there, might we think, properly remove it. He certainly would not be expected either to sell the safe to another, or to buy it himself without first removing it. It is not pretended that he used any violence or did any harm to the safe. And it is evident that the idea that any trespass or tort had been committed did not even occur to the plaintiff's agent when he was first informed of the finding.

The general rule undoubtedly is, that the finder of lost property is entitled to it as against all the world except the real owner, and that ordinarily the place where it is found does not make any difference. We cannot find anything in the circumstances of the case at bar to take it out of this rule. We give the defendant judgment for costs.

Here are the facts of the case to be analyzed.

Fact Pattern: Lost or Mislaid?

While collecting books for reshelving, P., an employee at a law library, discovered a black valise lying on its side on the floor between two bookshelves. He picked up the valise and brought it to the circulation desk, where he searched the contents for some identification of the owner.

A few days later, D., a student at the law school, came to the circulation desk to find a black valise she had lost. P. showed D. the found valise. D. said that it looked like her case but wished to check the contents to be sure. P. agreed and opened the valise for D.

While examining the contents, D. discovered a secret compartment that contained a diamond engagement ring. D. pocketed the ring, leaving her name with P. in case the original owner should turn up, and left the library. P. followed, requesting that D. return the ring to the valise. D. refused. P. now sues for return of the ring.

D. claims that the ring was lost, so D., as finder, is entitled to it unless the real owner claims it. P. claims that the ring was intentionally left in the secret compartment and, as a result, was not "lost" in a legal sense. P. insists that he is a custodian of the mislaid property and is entitled to keep the ring unless the real owner claims it.

Analysis

The principal issues to be addressed in this case are whether either the ring or the valise fits the legal definition of "lost," and thus whether D. could legally have "found" the ring. Although the valise was "lost," and the ring was not, D. does not have a legal claim to custody of either one.

The rule that "the finder of lost property is entitled to it as against all the world except the real owner," *Durfee v. Jones*, 11 R.I. 588 (1877), applies to the valise. P. found the valise lying on its side, in a manner and in a place suggesting it was not left there intentionally. Consequently, P. acquired a legal interest in the valise analogous to the interest acquired by the plaintiff in the *Durfee* case when he purchased a safe containing money that had slipped into a crevice inside the safe. Durfee did not find the money while the safe was in his possession. The defendant legally acquired custody of the safe from Durfee, found the money, removed it and then returned the safe. Durfee sought the return of the money as well, but the court held that the money had not been intentionally placed into the crevice and was thus "lost." Therefore the defendant had title to the money, subject only to the title of the true owner. The only difference between the interests of Durfee and P. is that Durfee was entitled to the safe against all others whereas P. is only entitled to the valise if the original owner does not turn up.

Conversely, if the original owner places property in a particular location, intending to retrieve it, the finder is not entitled to the property but is expected to "use reasonable care for the safe keeping of [the property] until the owner should call for it." *McAvoy v. Medina*, 93 Mass. (11 Allen) 548 (1866). In that case the owner of a shop was held to have the obligation to keep a pocketbook left on a table by a customer. The plaintiff "found" the pocketbook and later attempted to obtain custody of the money inside it from the defendant shopkeeper, but the court rejected the plaintiff's claim.

These cases lead to the conclusion that an individual who acquires possession of a piece of personal property assumes only a custodial interest over any property intentionally hidden inside it. In the present case, D. cannot argue that the position of the ring within the valise was the product of some accident, as was the location of the money in *Durfee*. The ring had been deliberately placed in a secret compartment in order that it be protected. Since P., as finder, was entitled to the valise, D. could not lay claim to anything intentionally hidden within it, even if P. did not know of its existence.

Even if D. could legally "find" the ring, P. gave D. leave to look inside the valise solely to determine the identity of its owner. D. did not have to search for secret compartments to see if it was her case. The court in *Durfee* indicates that a finder must have at least implied permission to examine the property. In the present case, P. opened the case so that D. could check to see if it belonged to her. P. did not give D. permission to conduct an exhaustive search of the lining, and there was nothing inherent in the determination of whether it was D.'s valise that would have implied permission to do so.

Thus, P. may claim the valise against all but the true owner, but has only a custodial interest in the ring. D. has no claim whatsoever to either the valise or the ring.

§ 5.04. CASE ANALYSIS

Now that you have seen what the final product looks like, we will break the process into its component parts so you can learn how to produce a good legal analysis when you are assigned to do so. Assume that you are an associate in a law firm and a partner has presented you with the following situation:

> A few days ago, a business client of ours came to us with a personal problem. Paul Trune, an auditor for the Internal Revenue Service, was making a pilgrimage to Baraboo, Wisconsin, to visit the birthplace of the Ringling Bros. & Barnum & Bailey Circus. Unfortunately, while on the way to Baraboo, Paul became quite lost and ended up driving down some unknown Wisconsin back road with an overheating radiator. Paul was forced to pull off the road next to a stretch of woods. He grabbed an empty bottle that he kept in the car for such emergencies and began walking in search of water. After a mile or so, the woods gave way to a clearing in which there was a well. Paul looked around for a farmhouse or any other building, but he didn't see any. Seeing no fences or signs either, Paul walked up to the well to take some water.
>
> Just as Paul was raising the bucket from the bottom of the well, he heard a voice ring out behind him. Paul turned to see a farmer gesticulating wildly and yelling at him about "trespassing." As the farmer got closer, Paul saw he had a dead, bloody rabbit in his left hand and a rifle slung around his back. The farmer then bellowed at Paul that he "knew how to take care of trespassers," and ordered him to start walking in the direction of a small hill. Seeing that the farmer had a gun and the ability to use it, and given the man's irate state, Paul decided that it was best not to say anything and just obey.
>
> Once at the crest of the hill, Paul saw a small farmhouse and barn below. The farmer marched Paul into the barn and told him to wait until he called the sheriff. The farmer

closed the door to the barn, but didn't lock it. Paul feared for his safety so he stayed put. After about two hours in the barn, with no sign of the farmer or a sheriff, Paul peeked outside. Not seeing the farmer anywhere in sight, he took off.

Paul now wishes to know if he has a cause of action against the farmer for the intentional tort of false imprisonment.

Next, assume that there are only two cases in Wisconsin that address the tort of false imprisonment. Here they are, in relevant part:

Dupler v. Seubert
69 Wis. 2d 373, 230 N.W.2d 626 (1975)

OPINION: WILKIE, C.J. This is a false imprisonment action. On April 23, 1971, plaintiff-appellant Ethel M. Dupler was fired from her job with the defendant-respondent Wisconsin Telephone Company. She was informed of her discharge during an hour-and-a-half session with her two superiors, defendants-respondents Keith Peterson and Helen Seubert, who, Dupler claims, falsely imprisoned her during a portion of this time period. A jury found that Peterson and Seubert did falsely imprison Dupler and fixed damages at $7,500. The trial court gave Dupler the option of accepting a lower amount—$500—or a new trial on the issue of damages. The option was not exercised, judgment for $500 was entered, and Mrs. Dupler appeals. We reverse and remand for a new trial on the issue of damages, but give plaintiff-appellant an option to accept $1,000 damages in lieu of a new trial.

Dupler had worked for the telephone company as a customer service representative since 1960. At approximately 4:30 on April 23rd, Seubert asked Dupler to come to Peterson's office. When all three were inside, sitting down, with the door closed, Seubert told Dupler the telephone company would no longer employ her and that she could choose either to resign or be fired. Dupler testified that she refused to resign and that in the conversation that followed, Peterson discussed several alternatives short of dismissal, all of which had been considered but rejected.

At approximately 5 o'clock, Dupler testified, she began to feel sick to her stomach and said "You have already fired me. Why don't you just let me go." She made a motion to get up but Peterson told her to sit down in "a very loud harsh voice." Then, Dupler testified, she began to feel violently ill and stated "I got to go. I can't take this any more. I'm sick to my stomach. I know I'm going to throw up." She got up and started for the door but Seubert also arose and stood in front of the door. After Dupler repeated that she was sick, Seubert allowed her to exit, but followed her to the ladies' washroom, where Dupler did throw up. Following this, at approximately 5:25, Seubert asked Dupler to return to Peterson's office where she had left her purse to discuss the situation further. Dupler testified that she went back to the office and reached for her purse; Seubert again closed the door and Peterson said [in] a loud voice, "Sit down. I'm still your boss. I'm not through with you." At approximately 5:40 Dupler told Peterson her husband was waiting for her outside in a car and Peterson told her to go outside and ask her husband to come inside. Dupler then went outside and explained the situation to her husband who said, "You get back in there and get your coat and if you aren't right out I'll call the police." Dupler returned to Peterson's office and was again told in a loud tone of voice to sit down. She said Seubert and Peterson were trying to convince her to resign rather than be fired and again reviewed the alternatives that had been considered. Dupler then said: "What's the sense of all this. Why keep torturing me. Let me go. Let me go." She stated that Peterson replied, "No, we still aren't finished. We have a lot of things to discuss, your retirement pay, your vacation, other things." Finally, at approximately 6 o'clock Peterson told Dupler they could talk further on the phone or at her house, and Dupler left. When asked why she had stayed in Peterson's office for such a long time, Dupler replied:

> Well, for one thing, Helen, Mrs. Seubert, had blocked the door, and tempers had been raised with all the shouting and screaming, I was just plain scared to make an effort. There were two against one.

Peterson and Seubert did not dispute that Dupler had been fired on April 23rd, or that the conference lasted from 4:30 to 6 p.m., or that Dupler became very upset and sick to her stomach and had to leave to throw up. Peterson admitted that Dupler had asked to leave and that he requested that she stay and continue talking so she could indicate whether she wished to resign or be fired. Seubert said Dupler did not so indicate until "within three minutes of her leaving." Both denied that any loud or threatening language had been used, or that Dupler was detained against her will. Peterson said neither he nor Seubert even raised their voices. He said the session was so lengthy because Dupler continued to plead for another chance, and to request reasons for the dismissal.

The jury found that both Peterson and Seubert falsely imprisoned Dupler and fixed her damages at $7,500. At the same time, the jury found that Dupler's co-plaintiff husband was not entitled to any damages. It found that Peterson and Seubert had not acted maliciously and thus did not award any punitive damages. . . .

The issue raised by a motion for review filed by defendants-respondents is: Is the jury's verdict, finding that Dupler was falsely imprisoned, supported by the evidence?

The essence of false imprisonment is the intentional, unlawful, and unconsented restraint by one person of the physical liberty of another. In *Maniaci v. Marquette University*, the court adopted the definition of false imprisonment contained in sec. 35 of the Restatement of Torts 2d, which provides in part:

False Imprisonment
    (1) An actor is subject to liability to another for false imprisonment if
        (a) he acts intending to confine the other or a third person within boundaries fixed by the actor, and
            (b) his act directly or indirectly results in such a confinement of the other, and
            (c) the other is conscious of the confinement or is harmed by it.

Secs. 39 and 40 provide that the confinement may be caused by physical force or the threat of physical force, and the comment to sec. 40 indicates the threat may either be express, or inferred from the person's conduct. As Prosser comments:

Character of Defendant's Act

The restraint may be by means of physical barriers, or by threats of force which intimidate the plaintiff into compliance with orders. It is sufficient that he submits to an apprehension of force reasonably to be understood from the conduct of the defendant, although no force is used or even expressly threatened. . . . This gives rise, in borderline cases, to questions of fact, turning upon the details of the testimony, as to what was reasonably to be understood and implied from the defendant's conduct, tone of voice and the like, which seldom can be reflected accurately in an appellate record, and normally are for the jury.

This is precisely such a case and we conclude that the record contains sufficient evidence from which the jury could have concluded that Mrs. Dupler was intentionally confined, against her will, by an implied threat of actual physical restraint. She testified that defendant Peterson ordered her in a loud voice to remain seated several times, after she expressed the desire to leave. She reported being "berated, screamed and hollered at," and said the reason she did not just walk out of the room was that "Mrs. Seubert had blocked the door, and tempers had been raised with all the shouting and screaming, I was just plain scared to make an effort. There were two against one." The jury obviously believed Mrs. Dupler's rather than the defendants' account of what transpired, as it had the right to do, and we conclude her testimony was sufficient to support the jury's verdict.

Herbst v. Wuennenberg
83 Wis. 2d 768, 266 N.W.2d 391 (1978)

OPINION: Abrahamson, J. Carol Wuennenberg appeals from a judgment entered by the trial court on a jury's special verdict finding that she falsely imprisoned Jason A. Herbst, Ronald B. Nadel, and Robert A. Ritholz ("plaintiffs"). Because there is no credible evidence to sustain a finding of false imprisonment, we reverse the judgment and order the cause remanded so that plaintiffs' complaint can be dismissed and judgment entered in favor of Wuennenberg.

I

In April 1975, plaintiffs initiated a civil action charging Wuennenberg with false imprisonment, malicious prosecution, and abuse of process. Plaintiffs' cause of action for false imprisonment arose from an incident which took place on September 19, 1974 in the vestibule of a three-unit apartment building owned and lived in by Wuennenberg and located within the district which Wuennenberg represented as alderperson in the city of Madison. Plaintiffs' causes of action for malicious prosecution and abuse of process arose from trespass actions brought against the plaintiffs by the city of Madison after Wuennenberg had registered a complaint about the September 19, 1974 incident.

On September 19, 1974, the plaintiffs were comparing the voter registration list for the City of Madison with names on the mailboxes in multi-unit residential dwellings in Wuennenberg's aldermanic district. Plaintiffs' ultimate purpose was to "purge the voter lists" by challenging the registrations of people whose names were not on mailboxes at the addresses from which they were registered to vote.

The plaintiffs and Wuennenberg gave somewhat differing accounts of the incident which gave rise to the action for false imprisonment, but the dispositive facts are not in dispute.

According to Ritholz, whose version of the incident was corroborated by Herbst and Nadel, when the plaintiffs reached Wuennenberg's house at approximately 4:30 p.m. they entered unannounced through the outer door into a vestibule area which lies between the inner and outer doors to Wuennenberg's building. The plaintiffs stood in the vestibule near the mailboxes, which were on a wall in the vestibule approximately two feet inside the front door to the building. Neither he nor the other plaintiffs touched the mailboxes, stated Ritholz; he simply read the names listed for Wuennenberg's address from a computer printout of the registered voters in Wuennenberg's district, and the others checked to see if those names appeared on the mailboxes.

When they were half way through checking, testified Ritholz, Wuennenberg entered the vestibule from an inner door and asked plaintiffs what they were doing. Ritholz replied that they were working for the Republican party, purging voter lists. According to Ritholz, Wuennenberg became very agitated and told the plaintiffs that she did not want them in her district. "At first she told us to leave," testified Ritholz, "and we agreed to leave, but she very quickly changed her mind and wanted to know who we were. Since we already agreed to leave, we didn't think this was necessary."

After the plaintiffs had refused to identify themselves to her, Wuennenberg asked them whether they would be willing to identify themselves to the police. Ritholz replied that they would be willing to do so. Nonetheless, testified Ritholz, he would have preferred to leave, and several times he offered to leave. Both Nadel and Herbst, who agreed that Ritholz was acting as spokesman for the group, testified to Ritholz's statement to Wuennenberg that the plaintiffs were willing to identify themselves to the police.

Subsequently, Wuennenberg's husband came to the vestibule to see what was going on, and Wuennenberg asked him to call the police. About this time Wuennenberg moved from the inner door to a position in front of the outer door. According to Nadel, Wuennenberg blocked the outer door by "standing there with her arms on the pillars to the door to block our exit." The plaintiffs agreed that Wuennenberg had not threatened or intimidated them and that they neither asked her permission to leave nor made any attempt to get her to move away from the doorway. When asked why he had not attempted to leave the vestibule, each of the plaintiffs answered, in effect, that he assumed he would have had to push Wuennenberg out of the way in order to do so.

The plaintiffs waited in the vestibule, stated Ritholz, until the police came some five minutes later. They gave their names and explained their errand to a police officer who told them that they were not doing anything wrong and that they could continue checking the mailboxes in the district.

Wuennenberg testified that she and her husband were in their living room watching television and reading the paper when she heard the plaintiffs enter her vestibule. She came to the inner door, noted Herbst with his hands on the mailboxes, and asked the plaintiffs if she could be of any assistance to them. Ritholz answered "No." She next asked if they were looking for someone in the building. Ritholz again answered "No." ... Ritholz ... stated that the plaintiffs were election officials, volunteering their services. At this point, stated Wuennenberg, she told the plaintiffs that it did not seem proper for citizen volunteers to be interfering with mailboxes and that she considered the plaintiffs to be trespassing on her property. Ritholz, speaking in "an authoritative tone," replied that the vestibule to Wuennenberg's building was "just like a public street" and that he had a right to be there.

After Ritholz told Wuennenberg that the plaintiffs would not identify themselves to her, but that they would identify themselves to the police, Wuennenberg's husband came out to see what was happening. She explained and then told him, "It looks like you'll have to call the police." Her husband looked at the plaintiffs, and they "nodded their approval to this."

After her husband left to call the police, testified Wuennenberg, she positioned herself in front of the outer doorway because she could watch for the arrival of the police from that vantage and because "I didn't want someone trying to run away at that point." She stated she did not brace her arms against the door frame. She would not have made any effort to stop the plaintiffs had they attempted to leave, stated Wuennenberg, because, "I'm not physically capable of stopping anybody."

Plaintiffs' causes of action for false imprisonment, abuse of process, and malicious prosecution were tried before a jury. At the close of the evidence, the trial court granted Wuennenberg's motion for a directed verdict on the causes of action for malicious prosecution and abuse of process but denied Wuennenberg's motion for a directed verdict on the cause of action for false imprisonment.

The jury returned a special verdict finding that Wuennenberg had falsely imprisoned the plaintiffs and awarded Herbst, Nadel and Ritholz a total of $1,500 in actual damages. The jury found that Wuennenberg's acts had not been malicious and thus declined to award punitive damages.

II

We reiterate the rule which this court must follow in reviewing the record to determine if the jury verdict is supported by the evidence: A jury verdict will not be upset if there is any credible evidence which under any reasonable view fairly admits of an inference supporting the findings. The evidence is to be viewed in the light most favorable to the verdict. A jury cannot base its findings on conjecture and speculation. We hold that the evidence adduced in the case before us does not support a finding that the plaintiffs were falsely imprisoned, and accordingly we reverse the judgment of the trial court.

The action for the tort of false imprisonment protects the personal interest in freedom from restraint of movement. The essence of false imprisonment is the intentional, unlawful, and unconsented restraint by one person of the physical liberty of another. *Dupler v. Seubert*, 69 Wis. 2d 373, 381, 230 N.W.2d 626 (1975). There is no cause of action unless the confinement is contrary to the will of the "prisoner." It is a contradiction to say that the captor imprisoned the "prisoner" with the "prisoner's" consent. Harper & James, The Law of Torts sec. 3.7, p. 227 (1956).

In *Maniaci v. Marquette University*, 50 Wis. 2d 287, 295, 184 N.W.2d 168 (1971) and in *Dupler v. Seubert, supra*, 69 Wis. 2d at 381, we adopted the definition of false imprisonment given by the Restatement of Torts, Second, sec. 35:

> (1) An actor is subject to liability to another for false imprisonment if
> (a) he acts intending to confine the other or a third person within boundaries fixed by the actor, and
> (b) his act directly or indirectly results in such a confinement of the other, and
> (c) the other is conscious of the confinement or is harmed by it.

After review of the record we conclude that the evidence is not sufficient to support the conclusion that Wuennenberg's acts "directly or indirectly [resulted] in . . . a confinement of the [plaintiffs]," a required element of the cause of action.

The Restatement lists the ways in which an actor may bring about a "confinement": "by actual or apparent physical barriers" [Sec. 38, Comment *a*]; "by overpowering physical force, or by submission to physical force" [Sec. 39]; "by submission to a threat to apply physical force to the other's person immediately upon the other's going or attempting to go beyond the area in which the actor intends to confine him" [Sec. 40]; "by submission to duress other than threats of physical force, where such duress is sufficient to make the consent given ineffective to bar the action" (as by a threat to inflict harm upon a member of the other's immediate family, or his property) [Sec. 40A]; "by taking a person into custody under an asserted legal authority" [Sec. 41].

The plaintiffs do not contend that confinement was brought about by an actual or apparent physical barrier, or by overpowering physical force, or by submission to duress, or by taking a person into custody under an asserted legal authority. The parties agree that the central issue is whether there was confinement by threat of physical force and thus argue only as to the applicability of section 40 of the Restatement, which we cited and applied in *Dupler v. Seubert*, 69 Wis. 2d at 382. Section 40 provides:

§ 40. Confinement by Threats of Physical Force

The confinement may be by submission to a threat to apply physical force to the other's person immediately upon the other's going or attempting to go beyond the area in which the actor intends to confine him.

The comments to section 40 provide that a person has not been confined by "threats of physical force" unless by words or other acts the actor "threatens to apply" and "has the apparent intention and ability to apply" force to his person.[1]

---

1. Restatement of Torts, Second, Section 40, Comments:

a. Under the rule stated in sec. 35, the actor's threat may be by words as well as by other acts. It is not necessary that he do any act actually or apparently effectual in carrying a threat into

It is not a sufficient basis for an action for false imprisonment that the "prisoner" remained within the limits set by the actor. Remaining within such limits is not a submission to the threat unless the "prisoner" believed that the actor had the ability to carry his threat into effect.[2]

Dean Prosser comments on the elements of false imprisonment as follows:

Character of Defendant's Act

The restraint may be by means of physical barriers, or by threats of force which intimidate the plaintiff into compliance with orders. It is sufficient that he submits to an apprehension of force reasonably to be understood from the conduct of the defendant, although no force is used or even expressly threatened. The plaintiff is not required to incur the risk of personal violence by resisting until it actually is used. It is essential, however, that the restraint be against the plaintiffs will; and if he agrees of his own free choice to surrender his freedom of motion, as by remaining in a room or accompanying the defendant voluntarily, to clear himself of suspicion or to accommodate the desires of another, rather than yielding to the constraint of a threat, then there is no imprisonment. This gives rise, in borderline cases, to questions of fact, turning upon the details of the testimony, as to what was reasonably to be understood and implied from the defendant's conduct, tone of voice and the like, which seldom can be reflected accurately in an appellate record, and normally are for the jury.

As plaintiffs state in their brief, the question before this court is whether there is any credible evidence which supports a conclusion that the plaintiffs did not

---

immediate execution. It is enough that he threatens to apply and has the apparent intention and ability to apply force to the other's person immediately upon the other's attempting to escape from the area within which it is the actor's intention to confine him.

b. The submission must be made to a threat to apply the physical force immediately upon the other's going or attempting to go beyond the area within which the threat is intended to confine him. Submission to the threat to apply physical force at a time appreciably later than that at which the other attempts to go beyond the given area is not confinement.

c. Submission to threats. The other must submit to the threat by remaining within the limits fixed by the actor in order to avoid or avert force threatened to the other. The other's remaining within such limits is not a submission to the threat unless the other believes that the actor has the ability to carry his threat into effect unless prevented by the other's self-defensive action or otherwise, and that it is, therefore, necessary to remain within these limits in order to escape or avert the violence threatened.

d. It is not necessary that the force threatened be such that a reasonable man would submit to confinement rather than sustain the harm threatened; it is sufficient that the actor threatens physical force with the intention of confining the other and that the other submits to the threat.

2. Other commentators have agreed that submission must be to an apprehension of force and that a voluntary submission to a request does not constitute an imprisonment. For example, Harper and James have stated that:

. . . In ordinary practice, words are sufficient to constitute an imprisonment, if they impose a restraint upon the person and the party is accordingly restrained; for he is not obligated to incur the risk of personal violence and insult by resisting until actual violence is used. . . . *If the plaintiff voluntarily submits there is no confinement, as where one accused of crime voluntarily accompanies his accusers for the purpose of proving his innocence.* And where no force is used, submission must be by reason of an apprehension of force or other unlawful means, *mere moral persuasion not being sufficient.* 1 Harper & James, *Torts* sec. 3.8 (1956).

consent to the confinement and that they remained in the vestibule only because Wuennenberg indicated by standing in the doorway that she had "the apparent intention and ability to apply" force to their persons should they attempt to leave. We have reviewed the record, and we find that it does not support this conclusion. Ritholz testified that Wuennenberg had not verbally threatened the plaintiffs, and since none of the plaintiffs asked Wuennenberg to step aside, it could be no more than speculation to conclude that Wuennenberg would not only have refused this request but also would have physically resisted had the plaintiffs attempted to leave. At best, the evidence supports an inference that plaintiffs remained in the vestibule because they assumed they would have to push Wuennenberg out of the way in order to leave. This assumption is not sufficient to support a claim for false imprisonment.

We do not intend to suggest that false imprisonment will not lie unless a "prisoner" attempts to assault his captor or unless he fails to make such attempt only because he fears harm. The plaintiffs in the case at bar were not required to obtain their freedom by taking steps dangerous to themselves or offensive to their reasonable sense of decency or personal dignity. See Restatement of Torts, Second, sec. 36. At a minimum, however, plaintiffs should have attempted to ascertain whether there was any basis to their assumption that their freedom of movement had been curtailed. False imprisonment may not be predicated upon a person's unfounded belief that he was restrained. *White v. Levy Brothers*, 306 S.W.2d 829, 830 (Ky. 1957). *Cf. Riggs National Bank v. Price*, 359 A.2d 25 (D.C. App. 1976).

. . . Plaintiffs were not "berated, screamed, and hollered at"; they outnumbered Wuennenberg three-to-one; and they gave no testimony to the effect that they were frightened of Wuennenberg or that they feared she would harm them.

Viewed in the light most favorable to plaintiffs, the evidence shows that the plaintiffs were willing to identify themselves to the police, but that they would have preferred to leave Wuennenberg's premises. It is not a sufficient basis for an action for false imprisonment that the plaintiffs remained on the premises although they would have preferred not to do so. Because plaintiffs did not submit to an apprehension of force, they were not imprisoned.

Judgment reversed, and cause remanded with directions to the trial court to enter judgment in favor of Wuennenberg dismissing plaintiffs' complaint.

———

You are now faced with something of a dilemma. You have only two cases, and they reach opposite conclusions. You must decide which case is more like Mr. Trune's situation, and why. If you feel strongly that Mr. Trune's case is more like either *Herbst* or *Dupler*, try to figure out why. Identify the key facts, and the rule that makes those facts relevant.

Alternatively, you may have noted similarities (and differences) to both cases, and may be thinking that Mr. Trune's case could go either way. If so, welcome to the reality of law practice! In our adversary system, there will always be lawyers on both sides of a case, using the same facts and law to argue for opposite results. Your job is to make your argument more persuasive than the other side's.

Exercise

1. Identify the issue(s) in *Herbst* and *Dupler*.
2. State the rule each court applies.
3. Write down the relevant facts from each case.
4. Write down the holdings of both cases.
5. Write out the rationales for both decisions.
6. Identify the policy or policies served by the decisions.
7. Decide whether the results are fair, in a purely equitable sense. Why or why not?
8. Identify the similarities and differences between *Herbst* and *Dupler* and Mr. Trune's case.

Now you must make a prediction. Will Mr. Trune be able to make out a case of false imprisonment? Why or why not? One of the most difficult ideas to get used to is that it almost does not matter which way you answer these questions. There is no right or wrong answer, only strong or weak analysis. Even so, you should still try to reach a conclusion about the most likely result. It is almost never enough merely to describe the applicable precedents; your reader will want you to predict the most likely result when those precedents are compared to the case under consideration.

Once you choose a position, you should be prepared to explain it. Identify factual analogies, previous applications of legal rules, and policy and equity considerations that make your predicted result seem likely. You should start with a statement of the applicable legal rule as presented by the courts, explain how that rule has been applied in the past and why, and then explain how it applies to your case.

The structure of your analysis will depend on the type of question you are discussing. In our case, dealing with the tort of false imprisonment, the courts tend to break the tort down into specific elements that must be satisfied. See *Dupler* and *Herbst* excerpts. Where the decisions give you this kind of structure, use it. The format of your analysis should generally track the format of the analysis presented by the courts. It is always easier for a reader to process a message if it is structured in a familiar manner.

If you structure your analysis by elements, instead of case by case, you will probably find that you discuss each case more than once. You can avoid redundancy by presenting the facts and any other relevant aspects of the case in detail the first time you cite the case, and then referring to the case subsequently using a shorthand form, offering detail only on the portion(s) of the case on which you are relying at that point in the discussion.

You should discuss the application of each element to your case at the same time you discuss the application of that element to previously decided cases. Do not wait until you have discussed all the elements to go back and try to explain all at once how the elements apply to your case. If you save all of your application for the end, you force the reader to remember too much at once. It is much easier to deal with one element at a time, and to thoroughly understand the application of that one element, both to the decided cases and to the case being discussed.

In a truly good legal analysis, you will not stop at supporting the result you think is most likely. You will also identify, explain, and respond to the arguments likely to be made by the other side. You do not want to make better or more persuasive opposing arguments than are likely to be made by opposing counsel, but you must deal with any arguments you *know* must be made on behalf of the other party. A good lawyer understands that there are two sides to almost every argument and acknowledges the legitimacy of the other side, while at the same time explaining why the preferred result is more likely. Consider: Are the factual differences between the adverse authority and your case more significant than the factual similarities? Are the policy goals behind the rule better served by a decision along the lines you advocate? Is fairness better served by the result you have predicted? These are the questions you must answer if your legal analysis is to be considered complete and persuasive.

Exercise

Write out a full analysis of Mr. Trune's case in essay form. Can he make out a case for false imprisonment? Why or why not? What is the applicable rule? What do the decided cases hold? What are the reasons for those decisions? What policies are served by the decisions? How are the facts of those cases similar or dissimilar to Mr. Trune's case? How do those factual similarities or dissimilarities affect the rationales for the decisions and the policy goals being served? Why is the result you predict equitable? What are the arguments on the other side? Why are they less persuasive than the arguments in support of the result you advocate? (Remember, you should reach a conclusion regarding the most likely result in Mr. Trune's case.) If you answer all of these questions, you will be well on your way to writing good legal analysis.

§ 5.05. STATUTORY ANALYSIS

Here is another example, this time adding the variable of a statute that must be interpreted and applied to the client's situation. These are your facts:

I was visited today by the son of an old client who found himself in a bit of trouble over the weekend. Apparently there was a gathering of Vietnam veterans at the Vietnam Veterans' Memorial on the Mall [in Washington, D.C.] on Saturday. This young man, R. Abel Rowser, chose this occasion to protest what he sees as continuous U.S. aggression against weaker powers around the world. Wearing a sign on his back that said "Vietnam, Iraq, Afghanistan—NO MORE!!!," he climbed to the top of the wall, pulled out an American flag, poured kerosene on it, and ignited it.

Mr. Rowser says that he truly believed that most Vietnam veterans would agree with him that U.S. military involvement in places such as Iraq and Afghanistan is a mistake. He believes that the Vietnam experience should have taught us to keep our noses out of other people's business. He used the flag burning to get their attention and then fully expected to lead a rally and perhaps even a march on the White House in support of his position. We may, perhaps, question his grip on reality, but I honestly believe that his description of his intent is sincere.

Mr. Rowser's recollection of what happened after he burned the flag is a bit fuzzy, perhaps because he was running for his life at the time, but he recalls a great deal of yelling and shouting. Several of the gathered veterans apparently started running in his direction in a manner that led him to believe he may have made an error in judgment, and he took off. He escaped, so there were no face-to-face confrontations with any of the veterans.

Mr. Rowser is also not entirely clear about what was happening when he arrived, but he thinks it may have been some sort of religious service. There was a man standing at the front of the crowd wearing a clerical collar, and the group was singing something.

Please read the D.C. disorderly conduct statute and the applicable cases and let me know whether you think the statute applies to Mr. Rowser's conduct under these circumstances.

This is the relevant statute:

§ 22-1121. Disorderly conduct.[1]

Whoever, with intent to provoke a breach of the peace, or under circumstances such that a breach of the peace may be occasioned thereby: (1) Acts in such a manner as to annoy, disturb, interfere with, obstruct, or be offensive to others; (2) congregates with others on a public street and refuses to move on when ordered by the police; (3) shouts or makes a noise either outside or inside a building during the nighttime to the annoyance or disturbance of any considerable number of persons; (4) interferes with any person in any place by jostling against such person or unnecessarily crowding him or by placing a hand in the proximity of such person's pocketbook, or handbook, or handbag; or (5) causes a disturbance in any streetcar, railroad car, omnibus, or other public conveyance, by running through it, climbing through windows or upon the seats or otherwise annoying passengers or employees, shall be fined not more than $250 or imprisoned not more than 90 days, or both.

Assume that the only relevant cases are these two (edited here to include only those parts of the discussion useful for our purposes).

Rodgers v. United States and District of Columbia
290 A.2d 395 (D.C. 1972)

OPINION: Hood, Chief Judge: In a concurrent trial before a judge and jury, the judge found appellant guilty of disorderly conduct, and the jury found him guilty of destruction of property but acquitted him of assault. Appellant makes a feeble attack on the destruction of property conviction, but we find no merit in it. His attack on the disorderly conviction requires more consideration.

Appellant was arrested following a series of incidents which occurred in and around the Crampton Auditorium on the Howard University campus. On that night a blues concert was being held in the auditorium outside of which a large crowd had gathered.

Appellant, who had no ticket, made numerous attempts to gain entry to the concert. He first presented an invalid press pass which was not accepted. He then

---

1. This statute is currently codified at D.C. Code § 22-1321.

repeatedly attempted to enter the auditorium by carrying instruments for band members. This ploy also failed. Appellant then attempted to enter through the basement accompanied by a large group of people. He finally kicked the glass out of a portion of one of the doors in the main entrance. In the course of attempting to gain entry appellant sought the assistance of the crowd outside by shouting obscenities at the campus policemen inside the auditorium and by threatening to kick down one of the doors if the crowd would follow. These activities continued for approximately 2 hours until three members of the University Special Police Force approached appellant, placed him under arrest after a scuffle and turned him over to the Metropolitan Police Department.

Appellant attacks his disorderly conduct conviction on four grounds. He first claims the information was insufficient. The information, filed under D.C. Code 1967, § 22-1121, the pertinent part of which is set out below, charged that appellant did:

> . . . under circumstances such that a breach of the peace might be occasioned thereby act in a manner as to annoy, disturb, interfere with, obstruct and be offensive to others by *loud boisterous [conduct] and fighting* in violation of Section 22-1121(1) of the District of Columbia Code.

It is appellant's contention that the information is insufficient in that it fails to charge that he engaged in any activity with an intent to provoke a breach of the peace or under circumstances which threaten a breach of the peace. We disagree. This court has held that an intent to provoke a breach of the peace is not an essential element in the proof of disorderly conduct. *Sams v. District of Columbia*, D.C. App., 244 A.2d 479 (1968); *Rockwell v. District of Columbia*, D.C. Mun. App., 172 A.2d 549 (1961). It has likewise been held that proof of an actual breach of the peace is not required under § 22-1121. *Stovall v. District of Columbia*, D.C. App., 202 A.2d 390 (1964); *Scott v. District of Columbia*, D.C. Mun. App., 184 A.2d 849 (1942). It is sufficient that the alleged conduct be under circumstances such that a breach of the peace might be occasioned thereby.

Appellant further contends that the evidence presented at trial was not sufficient to support his conviction. It is argued that the conviction should be reversed because appellant's "conviction is unsupported by any evidence to show . . . that anyone other than the police were annoyed or disturbed." We disagree. Appellant was not convicted merely for conduct which was annoying or disturbing to the policemen present, but rather, he was convicted for disorderly conduct carried out under circumstances whereby a breach of the peace might have been occasioned.

The Supreme Court in *Cantwell v. Connecticut*, 310 U.S. 296 (1940), concluded that not only violent acts but acts and words likely to produce violence on the part of others were included within the purview of breach of the peace. Here we have evidence of a course of action including both acts and words which can be said to be likely to produce violence among some or all of a crowd estimated at between 300 and 400 persons. Appellant's conduct over the 2-hour period with which we are concerned included several instances falling within the purview of § 22-1121 which may be deemed disorderly conduct. In examining his conduct as to interfering with others, it is readily apparent that appellant's conduct interfered with the orderly progression of events related to attendance at a concert where such attendance was limited to those persons holding valid tickets, a requirement which appellant did not meet at any time during the course of the evening. The record plainly reveals numerous attempts by appellant to gain entry into the auditorium. Each attempt invoked counterefforts by the special police whose task it was to maintain order during the concert. These actions on the part of the appellant were obstructive to persons holding valid tickets.

By their very nature appellant's actions would tend to slow down and even halt orderly ingress to the auditorium. The holders of valid tickets, seeking orderly admission, have a right to peaceful enjoyment of the concert without unwarranted disturbances by trespassers. It is these same ticket holders to whom appellant's actions would be patently offensive, as well as annoying and disturbing. *Heard v. Rizzo*, 281 F. Supp. 720, 741 (E.D. Pa. 1968), *aff'd*, 392 U.S. 646 (1968).

Rockwell v. District of Columbia
172 A.2d 549 (D.C. 1961)

HOOD, Associate Judge. Appellant, the leader of the American Nazi Party, was arrested for disorderly conduct on July 3, 1960, after rioting and fighting broke out at a rally he and his followers were holding in the park area at Ninth Street and Constitution Avenue, N.W. While awaiting trial on that charge he was again arrested for disorderly conduct on July 24, 1960, this time at Judiciary Square during the course of another outdoor gathering which he was attempting to address.

The two informations were consolidated for trial without a jury, and appellant was found guilty on both charges. He appeals the two convictions claiming that his freedom of speech, as guaranteed by the First Amendment, was obstructed by the arrests for disorderly conduct; that he was unable to obtain service of process on key defense witnesses; and that a certain letter he offered in evidence was wrongfully excluded by the trial court.

At trial the evidence revealed the following circumstances leading to the arrests. On July 3, 1960, appellant and his followers held a rally at Ninth Street and Constitution Avenue, N.W. At about 2:00 p.m. appellant began to speak from a platform within a roped-off area. Standing inside the enclosure were appellant's followers, some of whom wore red swastika armbands. Numbering 100 to 300 people, the audience outside the enclosure included many opponents of appellant's theories and party. Fourteen members of the U.S. Park Police were also in the audience, though only eight of them were in uniform. The spectators greeted appellant's opening words with hissing, booing and derisive chanting, the noise at times growing so loud that appellant could not be heard. This turmoil continued for about an hour and a half until suddenly an unknown number of spectators breached the enclosure and attacked appellant and his followers. As the fighting began the police moved in and arrested appellant, all of his followers and apparently some of the spectators who had participated in the attack.

During the trial there was a great deal of prosecution testimony concerning appellant's reaction to the crowd noises interrupting his speech. Witnesses testified that at different times they heard appellant shouting [various negative and offensive comments regarding Jews]. . . .

One Government witness also stated that at one point appellant started shouting, "Jews, Jews, sick—dirty Jews, filthy Jews . . . ," and shortly thereafter the spectators broke through the ropes and attacked appellant and his followers. Another prosecution witness testified that in the course of his speech appellant referred "to the Jewish race as traitors; or labeled the race as traitorous to our country."

Conceding he impatiently shouted, "Dirty Jews. Rotten Jews. Miserable Jews. Shut up, Jews. Go on and yell, Jews," appellant denied he made the other statements attributed to him. He stated he had been forewarned of possible disorder by Government officials and had done all in his power to prevent trouble, short of refusing to exercise his constitutional right of free speech. Even during the course of his speech he sent several of his men to warn the police that the crowd was getting dangerously unruly. According to appellant, the police replied to his warning by informing his men that the way to restore order was for appellant to stop talking.

On the second occasion that appellant was arrested he was conducting another rally in Judiciary Square. This time appellant—his followers in two ranks directly behind him—began to address an audience of about fifty people. As soon as appellant began his speech the spectators started to heckle him. Appellant responded by calling them "Jews" and "cowards," thereby increasing the intensity of the badgering from the audience. According to one prosecution witness, appellant "sort of lost his temper, and he turned around, and he says, 'Go get 'em, boys.' " At the command appellant's followers with their arms folded in front of them moved into the audience. One spectator was struck under the chin, and as a result appellant and his men were arrested for disorderly conduct.

Denying that anyone in the audience had been assaulted, appellant explained his actions on July 24 by referring to the near riot on July 3. Conscious that more trouble was to be expected if he spoke again, he had trained his men to move out into the audience at the first sign of possible disorder. Apparently these men were to surround hecklers and shout back at them, all the time under strict orders to keep their arms folded in front to avoid any suggestion of an invitation to combat. As to the command he gave on July 24, appellant testified he merely said, "First and second squads move out," which was the signal for his men to go into the audience in the manner described above. . . .

The conviction that grew out of the July 24 charge of disorderly conduct does not even raise a constitutional question. It is clear from the record that appellant ordered his followers into a hostile audience to stop the heckling that was interrupting his speech. Under the circumstances we cannot conceive of a better way to cause disorder than that adopted by appellant. Whether appellant intended that result is not controlling. An assault on one of the spectators did occur as a direct result of appellant's command to his followers to move into the audience and the trial court could without error convict appellant of disorderly conduct. . . .

. . . Appellant, however, was charged and convicted under a statute which reads in part as follows: "Whoever, with intent to provoke a breach of the peace, or under circumstances such that a breach of the peace may be occasioned thereby . . . ." Code 1951, § 22-1121, Supp. VIII. It is clear that the language quoted is to be read disjunctively, and that one lacking an intent to be disorderly may nevertheless be guilty of the charge if his conduct is "under circumstances such that a breach of the peace may be occasioned thereby . . . ." The only question the trial court had to decide was did appellant's statements constitute disorderly conduct under the circumstances of July 3. As we have indicated, we believe there was sufficient evidence for the trial court to answer as it did.

Affirmed.

———

While both *Rockwell* and Mr. Rowser's case have fairly obvious free speech implications, confine your analysis to the question of whether Mr. Rowser's actions amount to disorderly conduct. Any time you are analyzing a legal question involving a statute, you should begin with an analysis of the language of the statute itself. The relevant language of the D.C. disorderly conduct statute seems to be the following:

> Whoever, with intent to provoke a breach of the peace, or under circumstances such that a breach of the peace may be occasioned thereby: (1) Acts in such a manner as to annoy, disturb, interfere with, obstruct, or be offensive to others. . . .

Look at the statute and be sure you understand why we have chosen this language.

Did Mr. Rowser intend to provoke a breach of the peace? Does that matter? Why or why not? What do the cases say on this point?

Did Mr. Rowser act under circumstances likely to occasion a breach of the peace? How do you know? Can you answer this question without reference to the decided cases?

Exercise

1. Identify the issue(s) in the *Rodgers* and *Rockwell* cases.
2. Identify the statutory language applied by the court in each case.
3. Identify the relevant facts of each case.
4. State the holdings of those cases.
5. Describe the rationales of those cases.
6. Identify the policy or policies served by the decisions.
7. Decide whether the results are equitable. Why or why not?
8. Identify the similarities and differences among the *Rodgers* case, the *Rockwell* case and Mr. Rowser's situation. Consider facts, issues, policies, and equitable issues.

Now go through the same process you went through with Mr. Trune's case. What is the most likely outcome? Why? Have you identified the arguments on both sides? (Be careful here—since both of the decided cases find disorderly conduct, many people have a tendency to find it automatically in Mr. Rowser's case as well.) How will you structure your discussion? Since there are no elements here, you may find it useful to deal briefly with the intent question first, then analyze the decided cases in detail in the context of whether they took place under circumstances likely to cause a breach of the peace, comparing Mr. Rowser's situation to each case as you go along.

If another approach seems more logical to you, try it—you will find that your written product is better and more persuasive if you structure it in a way that makes sense to you. Many students make the mistake of trying to copy examples or to write the way someone else writes. Use your own instincts, while observing the guidelines discussed here and following any instructions offered in your legal writing class.

Exercise

Write out, in essay form, your analysis of Mr. Rowser's case. Predict whether he will be convicted of disorderly conduct and justify your prediction, using both the language of the statute and the decided cases. Focus on important facts, and use policy and equity arguments where appropriate. Don't forget to discuss and analyze the arguments on the other side, explaining why you find them less persuasive.

§ 5.06. LEGAL ANALYSIS CHECKLIST

Until you have performed enough legal analyses that the process becomes second nature to you, you might want to refer to this checklist to be sure you have not left out any important steps that your reader will be expecting to see in your written product. There is no magic format that will work in every context or for every style, so you will have to experiment until you find the right structure for you, the case you are addressing, and the particular audience for the document. Nevertheless, any good legal analysis must contain the following information, presented in some logical order.

— Make your prediction. Your written analysis should begin with a statement of your ultimate conclusion.
— Identify the rule that governs your case and cite to its source, whether statutory or common law.
— Identify the structure of your argument, using elements of a tort, statutory requirements, or any other method that will help the reader understand how your ideas relate to each other.
— Identify the key facts of your case.
— Discuss the facts, holdings, and rationales of all important relevant cases.
— Compare the facts of those cases with the facts of your case and explain why the courts' rationales apply or do not apply. Do not forget to argue the equities of the case or the policies behind the courts' decisions, if such arguments are helpful to your position.
— Identify any persuasive adverse authority or arguments likely to be presented by the other side. Explain why your predicted result is the better outcome. Be careful here; remember not to make arguments that are better than opposing counsel is likely to make.
— Summarize the key points in your argument. Persuade the reader of the overall strength of your position by reminding him or her of the highlights of what you have presented.

CHAPTER 6

Purpose, Context, and Structure

§ 6.01. INTRODUCTION

In their eagerness to get on with the writing process, many writers forget to think about the "big picture" aspects of what they are writing about. If you consciously address the elements of purpose, context, and structure *before* you start constructing sentences and paragraphs, your finished product will be much more polished and comprehensible. This chapter will discuss each in turn and offer strategies for incorporating this kind of thinking into your writing process.

§ 6.02. PURPOSE

It seems fairly obvious to say that you should understand why you are writing a document before you begin putting words on paper. Surprisingly, many writers are so anxious to get their ideas into concrete form that they do not stop to think about what the document must accomplish and what the intended reader needs from the document. Here are two key questions to ask yourself before you begin writing (or, for that matter, before you begin researching):

- For whom am I writing this?
  - Client (consider education, level of sophistication about legal matters, anxiety level, stage of case, nature and length of relationship between you and client)
  - Supervising attorney (consider what you know about expectations based on your and others' previous experiences)
  - Judge (consider what you know about judge, level of court, stage of proceeding)
- What am I trying to accomplish?
  - Answer a specific question (keep that question in mind at all times and be sure you actually answer it)
  - Advise reader generally on the state of the law in a particular area (consider why reader needs information and tailor presentation to what you know about that need)

— Persuade reader to adopt a particular course of action (Do you want your client to do something? Do you want the trial court to grant or deny a motion? Do you want the appellate court to affirm or reverse the trial court? Do you want opposing counsel to respond to a settlement offer?)

Your answers to these two questions should go a long way toward dictating the structure and tone of the final document. For example, a letter to a client who wants to know if she has a malpractice claim will have very little in common with a motion for summary judgment to the trial judge on that same claim. If you keep the intended audience and goal in mind at all times, you should be able to avoid the trap of going on at great length about issues the reader does not care about, or simply has no need to think about. Likewise, you will be sure that you actually do address the issue or issues that are of primary importance to the reader.

§ 6.03. CONTEXT

Context is closely related to purpose, but it encompasses a few additional elements. In addition to remembering for whom you are writing and what you need to accomplish, you need to consider the forum in which you are writing. Is this a memo in a law office? A brief to a court (trial or appellate)? A letter to a client? Each type of document involves different expectations regarding format, tone, amount and type of information, and writing style. A brief to a court will be presented in a very formal tone and must conform to fixed and specific rules regarding format, while the tone and format of a letter to a client are more flexible. An office memorandum should be presented in a tone and format that is consistent with the expectations of the particular office in which it is written.

We will discuss several different types of documents in this book, but if you need to draft a document not covered in this book, you should find similar documents intended for the same or a similar audience, and learn whatever you can about the contextual expectations. Read the samples, ask questions (preferably of the intended reader, if possible), and look at any written guidelines, such as court rules, that may govern the final product.

§ 6.04. STRUCTURE

The structure of a document is much like the foundation and framework of a building. Both need to be carefully constructed, and, if done well, both will strengthen and define the finished product. All of the many aspects of the structure of a written piece require conscious thought and strategic planning. We will discuss structural issues such as outlining and the placement of arguments, and signaling tools such as road map paragraphs, thesis sentences, and transitions. We will also briefly touch on the placement of authorities and different types of argument within an argument or discussion. Because we do discuss the specifics of particular types of documents in later chapters, the approach here will be to present more general rules that should guide your preparation every time you write.

1. Outlining

For most people, the really important thing to know about an outline is that you should do one.[1] There is no formula for outlining that will work for everyone. What is crucial is that you sit down before you begin to write and plan the flow of your discussion. Here are some considerations you should take into account in that planning process:

- What are the key points to be analyzed?
- How many points do you need to make?
- What is the most logical order in which to make those points?
- How do the different parts of your discussion relate to each other?
- Which are your strongest and weakest points?
- How does the legal authority you intend to rely on fit into your arguments? Are there different cases or statutes on each point, or do you need to use the same authority to support several arguments?

Once you have done enough research to get a preliminary idea of the types of arguments you need to make, you should make a sketchy outline. There is no need to write out full sentences in the outline at this point; you will most likely be identifying only the major points to be made. You should keep this preliminary outline with you as you continue your research and analysis. It will help to keep you focused as you sort through the available authority.

You may find that the initial outline is incomplete or that it does not present the parts of the discussion in the most logical order. You should be flexible enough to recognize this and to adjust your outline in any way and as many times as seems appropriate. Even in the midst of writing, you may need to rethink your outline and restructure your presentation.

When you have collected all the authority you intend to rely upon, go back to your outline and "plug in" the authorities. Decide which cases or statutes are most helpful on particular points, and add them to the outline in the appropriate places. Then organize the authorities into the proper order.

As you finalize the outline, you may want to flesh out your major points. You can do this by writing them out in full sentences and by adding subpoints. Some writers need to, and should, construct very detailed outlines, while others can write just as efficiently with less thorough guidance. Regardless of your approach, do not forget to identify the purpose, audience, and context of your document before constructing your final outline. *Now* you are ready to begin writing.

---

1. We say "for most people" because there are those who can construct a perfectly coherent, logical discussion every time they sit down to write. If you are one of those rare people, the extra step of creating an outline may not be a terribly useful or efficient way to spend time. For most of us, however, whether we are writing memos, briefs, or law school exams, making the effort to outline the structure of our argument before we flesh it out in full paragraph form is the only way to ensure that the final product is a sensible, focused communication to the intended reader. This is true even though outlining is a more natural process for some than for others. There may be writers for whom it is a sufficiently foreign way of thinking as to be almost counterproductive, but in the context of legal writing it is usually a necessary, if difficult, endeavor, because it is the only way to ensure that our ideas will be communicated in a way that is useful to our busy readers.

Keep your outline in front of you at all times during the writing process. This will keep you from trying to make all of your points at once or in the order they occur to you as you are writing, which may or may not be the order that makes the most sense. Also, referring to the outline when you are struggling to develop a point may help you understand how that point relates to the rest of the document, which may sometimes be enough to get the writing process back on track.

If the outlining approach discussed here does not work for you, there are alternatives. You can create a very general heading-only outline, write up the discussion, and then rearrange sections of the discussion as necessary. You can write the sections in a different order than set forth in the outline if one or two points are giving you particular trouble. Starting with the easier section or sections will at least get the writing process started, and you may then discover that the difficult sections become more manageable. You also can write without an outline to get the ideas down on paper and then superimpose an outline on the discussion after you have written it, to be certain your final structure makes sense.

Let's go back to the lost ring case discussed in Chapter 5 and outline the analysis in Section 5.03. Remember that there are many ways to outline any discussion, but here is one approach.

I. Was the valise lost?
  A. *Durfee*—definition and rule for lost property
  B. *McAvoy*—definition and rule for mislaid property
II. Was the ring lost?

[Note that you will only apply the rules here since you have already defined them in Section I, and it would be unnecessary in such a short document to repeat your discussion of the cases]

III. Who gets the ring?

  Durfee—finder must have permission to examine property

This is obviously a very simple discussion, and the outline is likewise simple. You can apply the same process and principles to a much more complex discussion, and it will give you a clearer picture of where the document is going and what it will accomplish when you are finished.

Exercise

Select a memorandum from Appendix I in the back of the book and outline the discussion.

2. Deciding on a Structural Strategy

One of the decisions about structure you need to make as you begin writing is the order in which you will present the arguments. Sometimes there will be an inherently logical approach to ordering the arguments; for example, if you are discussing a tort or statute that sets forth specific elements that must be, or always are, discussed in a particular order, you should order your discussion accordingly.

The false imprisonment problem discussed in Chapter 5 presents just such a situation. Both cases rely on the Restatement (Second) of Torts, which presents the elements in a specific order: (1) intent to confine, (2) actual confinement, and (3) consciousness of confinement. In this situation, it is easier and more likely to meet the expectations of your reader to follow this structure. However, do not feel that you must devote equal time to each element. If there is a genuine issue as to whether one or two elements are present in your case, while the other element or elements are clearly satisfied, you can allude only briefly to the elements not at issue and devote the bulk of your analysis to the elements in dispute. If you are writing an advocacy document, most experts will advise you to start with your strongest argument. This is good strategic advice, as long as it does not create a conflict with the type of inherent order discussed above, and so long as it does not cause you to make the argument in an order that does not make logical sense.

Some people will also advise you to end your discussion on a strong note, so that you leave a favorable impression with the reader. Again, if you can do so logically, this is sound advice. If you have not already guessed, this strategic approach to ordering your arguments will leave your weaker points in the middle of the discussion, where they are most likely to be forgotten.

For a concrete example of strategic structuring of an argument, look at the following outlines of an argument from two appellate briefs on opposite sides of the same issue. The issue addressed by both briefs is whether a decedent's estate can bring a tort action against the hospital that employed the decedent. The decedent was murdered while working at the hospital on the late shift. The hospital sought to bar the claim by arguing that the only available remedy lay in the applicable workers' compensation statute. The crux of the argument was whether a statutory exception to the exclusivity of the workers' compensation remedy applied.

In the hospital's brief, the statutory argument is outlined as follows in the table of contents:

I. WORKERS' COMPENSATION SHOULD BE THE EXCLUSIVE REMEDY FOR INJURIES SUSTAINED BY AN EMPLOYEE IN THE COURSE OF HER EMPLOYMENT FROM AN ATTACK BY A THIRD PERSON WHEN NO RELATIONSHIP BETWEEN THE THIRD PERSON AND EMPLOYEE EXISTED PRIOR TO THE ATTACK.
   A. *Workers' Compensation Is Intended to Be the Sole Remedy for Injuries Sustained in the Course of One's Employment.*
   B. *The Attack upon Charla Louis Was Not for Reasons Personal Within the Meaning of the Workers' Compensation Act and Is Only Compensable Through Workers' Compensation.*

Here is the outline of the statutory argument from the Estate's perspective:

I. THE ESTATE OF A HOSPITAL EMPLOYEE WHO WAS ATTACKED AND MURDERED WHILE WORKING, BY AN ASSAILANT WITH PERSONAL MOTIVATION TO COMMIT SEXUAL ASSAULT, IS NOT LIMITED BY THE REMEDIES OF THE WORKERS' COMPENSATION ACT.
   A. *An Exception Provided by the Act Disallows Compensation for All Personally Motivated Assaults by Third Parties.*

B. *The Fact that the Victim Was Present on the Premises of the Employer as Required by Her Job Does Not Limit Recovery to that Provided by the Act When the Third Party Attack Is Personally Motivated.*
   1. Preexisting personal animosity is not dispositive or even highly indicative of the assailant's motivation since his motivation at the time of attack is at issue.
   2. The nature of sexual assault indicates personal motivation in the form of anticipated sexual gratification; rape is not usually motivated by work-related activity.
C. *An Employee Who Is Not Required by Her Job to Have Personal Contact with the Public Does Not Assume the Risk of Personal Assault so as to Bring Sexual Assault by a Third Party Under the Provisions of the Act.*

The exception is most helpful to the Estate, and you will notice that it appears prominently in the outline of the estate's argument—as the first subpoint of the argument. While the Hospital's argument deals with the issues raised by the exception, it is not even mentioned explicitly in the outline, thus diminishing its apparent importance. The first point in the Hospital's argument is the exclusive nature of the workers' compensation remedy.

In addition to thinking strategically about the order in which you present your arguments, you should consider how much space you will devote to each argument. A reader is likely to assume that an argument that occupies a substantial amount of room is important. Why would a writer spend a lot of time and effort developing a point that is of only passing significance? No writer would, unless that writer got so caught up in developing a tangential or tenuous analogy that the writer lost sight of the need to do a cost-benefit analysis during the writing process. Ask yourself whether the amount of time and space you spend on an argument is proportional to the persuasive impact the argument will have in the context of your overall presentation. If not, consider whether the argument can be edited substantially, or perhaps cut altogether.

3. Roadmaps, Topic Sentences, and Transitions

It is not enough to have a structure for your document. You must let the reader know what that structure is. If the reader knows up front where the document is going and gets messages along the way that help to orient him or her, the document will be easier to read and the analysis will seem more logical and possibly even more persuasive.

The simplest way to orient the reader early on is to provide a "roadmap" paragraph. This introductory paragraph highlights the most significant parts of your analysis and states your ultimate conclusion. At the risk of abusing our analogy, by identifying the destination and the major landmarks at the beginning of the journey, you make the trip easier and more comfortable for the traveler.

A roadmap paragraph can be very explicit, as is this paragraph:

> The Estate's action is premised on a negligence theory of liability. However, as the court emphasized in *Murphy v. Penn Fruit Co.*, 274 Pa. Super. 427, 418 A.2d 480 (1980), negligence is not established by the mere happening of an attack on the decedent.

Id. at 432, 418 A.2d at 483. The Estate must plead and prove each element of the tort to establish liability. The necessary elements to maintain a negligence action are a duty or obligation recognized by the law, requiring the actor to conform to the standard required; a failure to conform to the standard required; a causal connection between the conduct and the resulting injury; and actual loss or damage resulting to the interests of another. *Morena v. South Hills Health System,* 501 Pa. 634, 642, 462 A.2d 680, 684 (1983), quoting Prosser, *Law of Torts,* § 30 at 143 (4th ed. 1971). Each of these elements will be examined in turn as they apply to the facts of this case.

You can also take a slightly less detailed approach, as the writer of this memo does:

> Ms. Holmes was falsely imprisoned by Dean James. Dean James had probable cause to question Ms. Holmes about the materials found in her locker, but he acted unreasonably in confining Ms. Holmes and causing her to miss her exam. Dean James's conduct was without legal justification, and the confinement was therefore unlawful.

Both examples inform the reader of the writer's ultimate conclusion, and provide information about how the argument will progress. That is all a road map paragraph needs to do.

Topic sentences and transitions are the landmarks that let readers know where in the discussion they are at any given point. The first sentence of any paragraph should give the reader a clue as to what the rest of the paragraph will be about. As a general rule, a single paragraph should not develop more than one idea, and the purpose of that first, or topic, sentence is to identify that idea. We discuss paragraph construction in greater detail in Chapter 7.

As you shift between the major points you identified in the roadmap paragraph, make a conscious effort to put distinct transitions between them. Sometimes the transitions will be as simple as an introductory sentence that identifies the element you are about to discuss, as you will see if you look at the first memo about false imprisonment in Appendix I.

Exercise

Choose one of the remaining memos in Appendix I, and identify all thesis sentences and transitions. Are there any paragraphs that do not begin with topic sentences signaling what the paragraph is about? If so, does this cause confusion or frustration as you try to pull the central idea from each paragraph? If not, it may be that the topic has been implicitly signaled in some other way. Do the transitions act as landmarks that relate back to the roadmap? Does this help you, as a reader, understand the progression of the discussion and where you are in the analysis at any particular point?

4. Organizing Within Arguments

Thus far, we have explored ways of structuring your document at the "macro" level—outlining the progression of the discussion, choosing the order in which to present your points, and making your organizational scheme apparent to the reader. In this section, we will discuss organization at a more "micro" level. How do you decide where to present authorities within an argument or part of a discussion, and how much space do you devote to each? How do you integrate law, policy, and equity arguments? The answer is that you apply the same principles we discussed earlier, that is, you start with the stronger authorities and arguments, and devote proportionally more space to them as well.

How do you know which authorities are strongest? We discussed the different types and weight of authority in Chapter 2. Here is a summary that should help:

1. On-point decisions by higher courts in your jurisdiction are binding and should be featured conspicuously. If such decisions go against you, first look for a relevant way to distinguish them, pointing out differences between the facts or policies at issue in those cases and your case. If they cannot be distinguished, you need to deal with them in other ways, perhaps by arguing that they were wrongly decided or that times have changed sufficiently that a new rule is called for. Unless such adverse decisions are truly dispositive of your case, you can still place them strategically in the middle of your argument, using the more prominent beginning and ending positions for authority that is more helpful to you.

2. Decisions by lower courts in your jurisdiction are very persuasive and should also be given appropriate space and position. The same rules about distinguishing or otherwise dealing with adverse authority apply.

3. Recent decisions are generally more persuasive than older decisions, all other things being equal (i.e., if the facts in the older decision are significantly more analogous to your case, you might want to spend more time on the older decision).

4. Federal decisions interpreting state law are persuasive and should be given some attention if they fill in gaps in the state decisions or articulate the rationale for the state decisions particularly clearly. Unless you have no better authority, you do not want to use disproportionate amounts of space on such decisions.

5. Decisions from other jurisdictions and secondary authorities are only as persuasive as you make them. This almost inevitably means that you will have to devote considerable space to making analogies or articulating policy justifications for adopting rules from such sources. If you have no other authority, perhaps because the question you are addressing is a novel one in your jurisdiction, it may be worth your effort to do so. You may be able to discover and argue a developing trend in the law that supports adoption of the rule you advocate. If, however, you have other authority that the reader is likely to find more useful, you should think twice about using valuable space and reader energy on such subordinate points. Remember that the reader is likely to equate the time needed to develop and understand an argument with the importance of that argument, so make your decisions accordingly.

5. Placement of Policy and Equity Arguments

Keep your strategic sense working on the question of integrating law, policy, and equity arguments as well. As you learned in Chapter 5, policy arguments are based on societal goals that would be served by the result you seek, and equity arguments are based on notions of general fairness as applied to the particular facts of your case. Remember that courts of law are essentially conservative institutions, bound to a large extent by precedent and notions of stare decisis. This means that you should feature your legal arguments in the prominent positions and devote more time to them. Policy and equity arguments are supportive and will seem more persuasive if they are closely tied to your legal arguments. Therefore, on any given point, you should start with your legal arguments and authorities, and then follow immediately with related and reinforcing policy and equity arguments.

If you do not have on-point authority to support your position, you may be able to find authority to support pure policy arguments. Think about other areas of the law that have important similarities to yours and that serve the same policy goals. Look for cases in those areas that have similar facts and the result you want. Policy arguments should generally be given more prominence than purely equitable, fact-based arguments. While equitable arguments are useful, and judges generally like to feel that they are being fair in rendering their decisions, you do not want to devote a lot of time to such arguments or lead off with them, unless you have nothing else.

§ 6.05. CONTEXT AND STRUCTURE CHECKLIST

— Identify and articulate the goal of your document.
— Identify your audience and any expectations you know or suspect that audience has for your document.
— Outline the major points you need to make in the document to accomplish your goal.
— Fill in details such as legal authorities and revise the outline as necessary as you go along.
— Make sure you start and end with a strong point, to the extent logic permits.
— Organize your legal authorities according to the appropriate hierarchy, giving more space to more persuasive authorities.
— Organize your legal, policy, and equity arguments so that the more persuasive arguments receive greater prominence in terms of both position and space.
— Write your roadmap paragraph and check your document for transitions and thesis sentences that will let the reader know where in the analysis you are and where the analysis is going.

CHAPTER 7

Make Your Main Themes Stand Out

§ 7.01. INTRODUCTION

Sometimes we read a court opinion, a memo, or an appellate brief and do not understand its message until we reach the end. After we finish reading the document, we think about the conclusion and try to synthesize all the information and analysis that we have read. As we synthesize, we may find ourselves returning to earlier paragraphs in the document and puzzling over them. If we think about this process of digesting information, we probably will conclude that it is inefficient and creates the risk that the reader will misunderstand the message that the writer seeks to convey. When it comes to writing, we may conclude, there must be a better way.

There is a better way. From the very beginning of the document, let the reader know what your message is. Instead of waiting until the end to pull the rabbit out of the hat, make your main themes stand out throughout the document. Let the reader know where you are going.

To accomplish this task, apply three principles: make the outline of your argument or discussion stand out; put your conclusions first; and write well-organized paragraphs.

First, as suggested in Chapter 6, make an outline of your writing. An outline will clarify your organization for you, and your reader will benefit because of it. Because your first draft is never your best work, you should revise your outline and your writing several times.

Second, in any legal document, put your conclusions at the beginning of your writing. At the outset, the reader wants to know your conclusions about the law as applied to the facts of your case. Although you may well decide to recapitulate your conclusion at the end, the end is not the place to state your conclusion for the first time.

Third, write well-organized paragraphs. Within your document, paragraphs are major units of discourse. If the reader easily grasps the idea of each paragraph, follows the discussion of that idea, and can make a smooth transition to the idea in the next paragraph, he or she will understand your message.

§ 7.02. MAKE THE OUTLINE OF YOUR ARGUMENT OR DISCUSSION STAND OUT

As we discussed in Chapter 6, to make the outline of your argument or discussion[1] stand out, you should begin with an outline. Many students are not accustomed to making outlines of their writing in advance. They write first and outline later. For most people, this approach just does not work. Make an outline.

Your initial outline is a simple listing of the major points in your discussion or argument. As your research and analysis progress, you can develop a more comprehensive outline using full sentences. You also may decide to reorganize your outline.

Here is part of a sample sentence outline in an appellate brief concerning a case that takes place in Pennsylvania. The plaintiff in the case is attempting to take ownership of a property from the owner who has a deed to that property. Under Pennsylvania law a trespasser can gain ownership of property by possessing it for twenty-one years and performing certain acts of ownership. The doctrine is called "adverse possession."

Sample Sentence Outline:

I. SMITH HAS ACQUIRED SUFFICIENT INTEREST IN THE DISPUTED TRACT OF LAND TO ENTITLE HIM TO OWN THE LAND BY ADVERSE POSSESSION.
   A. *Smith's Possession of the Disputed Tract of Land Has Been Actual, Continuous, Visible, Notorious, Exclusive, Distinct, and Hostile for the Statutory Period of Twenty-One Years as Required to Satisfy the Elements of Adverse Possession.*
   1. Because Smith intends to hold this land for himself and has manifested his intention by many acts of possession, his decision to discontinue one act, grazing sheep, during the requisite period does not break the continuity of his possession.

Here is another example. In this case, two workers had a verbal dispute that was work related. Six months later, they engaged in a personal fight during working hours. One of the workers was injured and now seeks recovery under the Pennsylvania Workers' Compensation Act. An outline for part of a memorandum on the case might look like this:

Sample Sentence Outline:

I. BECAUSE THE FIGHT WAS PURELY PERSONAL, THE INJURED WORKER CANNOT RECOVER UNDER THE ACT.
   A. As interpreted by case law, the Act excludes injuries arising when the attacker acts for purely personal reasons.
   B. As interpreted by case law, the Act is remedial and should be liberally construed in favor of the injured worker.

---

1. The word "argument" here means arguing your client's case in a brief that goes to the court. You will learn more about writing effective briefs in Chapters 24-29. The word "discussion" here means an objective discussion of the law, without argument, in legal memoranda and client letters. You will learn more about writing effective memoranda and client letters in Chapters 10-16.

C. Nonetheless, all similar cases permitting recovery were over work-related issues with no mention of personal matters.

D. In light of the case law, the earlier dispute is too remote to permit describing the fight as work related. Therefore the injured worker probably will lose.

To complete this outline, you would fill it out by including throughout some information about the cases that you plan to discuss.

To make the outline of the argument stand out, you should follow it in your writing. With the outline in hand, you should find that you will write more easily. If you run into difficulties, you may decide that your outline is faulty and that you need to revise it.

After you turn your outline into a draft, do not let the first draft be your final writing. First-year students face many time pressures and often want to save time by not revising their writing. Many students who receive lower grades in legal writing than they expected readily admit, "Well, I didn't revise my writing. I wrote only one draft."

The usual reason the student gives is lack of time. Lawyers face just as many time pressures. Bear in mind that you will be working for clients when you become a lawyer, and your best writing is never the first draft. Your rule of thumb should be to go through at least three drafts, if not more. Make the time to go through as many revisions as necessary to make your final product the best it can be.

Once you have written a first draft, go back over it and make sure it follows your outline perfectly. If you find that the outline is forcing you to organize your discussion in an awkward way, revise your outline.

Structure your discussion so that your organization is clear to the first-time reader. In this book you will learn and relearn many rules that will help you achieve this goal. As you go through your revisions, make sure you apply each rule.

§ 7.03. PUT YOUR CONCLUSION FIRST

A conclusion is usually at the end of a writing. To make your theme stand out, however, put it at the beginning. Depending on what you are writing, you may find it desirable to also recapitulate it at the end.

The basic rule of expository writing is:

Tell your readers what you are going to say.
Say it.
Tell them what you just said.

Tell your reader your conclusion at the outset. Then discuss the rationale for your conclusion. Then remind the reader of the conclusion you have justified in your discussion.

The reader wants to know, right up front, what the law is as applied to the given situation and does not want to be "held in suspense" until the end of the memorandum, brief, or letter. You are not writing a mystery novel!

Do not make the reader wait until the end to see where you are going. If you think your writing will become repetitive, you are right. Some repetition is necessary to make your point.

The following is an edited excerpt from a student's legal memorandum. In this sample, the student stated the conclusion at the beginning of the discussion and provided an emphatic recapitulation at the end.

> In this case, a court should hold the minor operator of a rider mower to an adult standard of care because the fourteen-year-old's operation of the mower was a dangerous activity that adults normally perform. Courts generally require a minor to exercise the same standard of care that would be exercised under similar circumstances by a reasonably careful minor of the same age, intelligence, and experience. Nonetheless, they make an exception in the case of motor vehicles.
>
> In two cases involving the operation of motor vehicles by minors, the Supreme Court of Arkansas decided to hold minor operators to an adult standard of care. In one decision the court required an adult standard of care from a fifteen-year-old boy who was riding a motorcycle on a public street. *Harrelson v. Whitehead*, 365 S.W.2d 868 (Ark. 1963). In a second decision the court held that a fourteen-year-old boy operating a farm tractor in a cotton field should adhere to the same standard of care as a reasonably careful adult. *Jackson v. McCuiston*, 448 S.W.2d 33 (Ark. 1969). In *Jackson*, the court recognized that applying an adult standard of care to a minor who operates a motor vehicle is "an exception to our general rule that a minor owes that degree of care which a reasonably careful minor of his age and intelligence would exercise under similar circumstances." . . .
>
> The court should impose an adult standard of care on a minor operator of a rider mower. This activity requires an adult standard of care for the safety of the operator as well as for the safety of anyone else in the vicinity. The exception to the general rule is justified because rider mowers are inherently dangerous, and adults normally operate them. A minor who undertakes the operation of a dangerous adult activity in the business world of adults cannot avoid the standard of care of a reasonably careful adult.

Some lawyers would call the first paragraph of this excerpt a "thesis paragraph," because it states the conclusion and indicates how the writer reaches it. More specifically, in stating the conclusion, it presents the issue in concrete terms by using the facts of the case and justifies the conclusion by identifying the applicable rule, statute, or case precedent and briefly explaining how it applies.

Putting the conclusion first creates a roadmap in the reader's mind. Because the reader knows where the writer is going, the reader finds the discussion more meaningful from the outset. As readers, we find nothing more frustrating than plodding through a legal memorandum or brief that does not give us this roadmap. Without it, we find ourselves silently asking, "Now where is this writer taking me?"

Even though the student stated the conclusion at both the beginning and end of the discussion, the discussion is not too repetitive. The writer tells you what the conclusion is, explains the rationale for the conclusion, and then restates the conclusion at the end as justified by the discussion. You do not have to guess at the outset where the writer is taking you—there is no mystery here.

Note that the writer's conclusion at the end does not simply repeat the conclusion at the beginning. Instead, it makes clear the justification for the court decisions. Often the conclusion at the end will be more concrete or more emphatic than the conclusion at the beginning. Frequently, it will contain new information or a new insight.

Sometimes you will decide not to place a conclusion at the end because you find it superfluous. In such instances, the conclusion is so dominant throughout the discussion that you see no need to repeat it. Still, do not let your ending trail off. End with some emphasis, perhaps by using a pithy sentence, a compelling example that justifies your conclusion, or a suggestion on what to do next.

Compare the following edited excerpt from another memorandum on the same subject with the one above:

> Courts have tended for the past twenty years to create exceptions to the general rule governing minors' responsibility for their negligent actions. In this society with rapid technological change, courts have faced the necessity of changing many rules to keep up with the use of sophisticated equipment in the form of farm machinery, automobiles, and the like. Public policy has compelled these changes in the interest of safety in a changing world.
>
> Although minors have had to adhere to a minor's standard of care, exceptions have evolved. Today's minors operate very sophisticated equipment, and public policy requires a higher standard of care from them. Minors do have accidents as a result of their handling sophisticated equipment, and safety requires that they be responsible to a greater extent than they were in the past.

The writer gives you no idea at the outset what the memorandum will conclude. After reading two paragraphs, you have no idea what this memorandum will say about the case involved. The main theme does not stand out. In comparison, the first sample memorandum excerpt requires only a quick glance for the reader to know what the writer's conclusion is.

At the outset, always let the reader know what your conclusion is. Then explain that conclusion within the context of the discussion. Finally, if desirable, present a recapitulation at the end.

§ 7.04. WRITE EFFECTIVE PARAGRAPHS

In making your main theme stand out, you must pay attention to how you present and develop ideas. You present and develop them within your primary units of discourse: sentences and paragraphs. In this section, we discuss writing effective paragraphs. You will learn how to present the idea in a paragraph, how to develop that idea, how to give the paragraph unity and direction, and how to connect sentences and paragraphs so that your analysis flows smoothly.

1. Use Topic Sentences

Every paragraph should present one major idea. In most paragraphs, you will first present that idea in one sentence or in a group of sentences called topic sentences. (Most of the time, you will use one topic sentence.) These sentences provide the topic for the discussion that goes on in the rest of the paragraph.

Here is an example of a paragraph with a topic sentence in its most typical location, the very beginning. The writer is arguing against a court decision that upholds a statute as constitutional.

> The majority defines the right at stake too narrowly and treats the developmentally challenged as second class citizens with second-class rights. No legislature would even consider drafting a provision like § 4693(c) and applying it to legally competent adults. Just as with the legally competent, individuals like D.T. must enjoy their fundamental liberty and privacy rights if they are to develop to their maximum economic, intellectual, and social levels.

In this paragraph, the topic sentence clearly states the point. The rest of the paragraph develops the point by explaining why the writer disagrees with the majority.

Here is the same paragraph with the sentences arranged in a different order:

> No legislature would even consider drafting a provision like § 4693(c) and applying it to legally competent adults. The majority defines the right at stake too narrowly and treats the developmentally challenged as second-class citizens with second-class rights. Just as with the legally competent, individuals like D.T. must enjoy their fundamental liberty and privacy rights if they are to develop to their maximum economic, intellectual, and social levels.

This paragraph is unsatisfactory because the topic sentence is in the wrong place. A paragraph works well when the topic sentence states the idea and the remaining sentences develop that idea. Here, the paragraph begins with the development, then states the topic, and then continues the development. In its original form, the paragraph succeeds because it begins with the conclusion and then develops it.

Instead of being at the beginning of the paragraph, the topic sentence can be at the end. In this instance, the paragraph builds to a conclusion. Here is an example:

> Just as with the legally competent, individuals like D.T. must enjoy their fundamental liberty and privacy rights if they are to develop to their maximum economic, intellectual, and social levels. Their development, however, is frustrated by § 4693(c). No legislature would even consider drafting a similar provision and applying it to legally competent adults. By upholding this statute, the majority defines the right at stake too narrowly and treats the developmentally challenged as second-class citizens with second-class rights.

You often will write this type of a paragraph as an introductory or concluding paragraph to a document or to a large section of a document. In these locations, readers frequently prefer a paragraph that builds to a conclusion. However, in other locations, be cautious about putting the topic sentence at the end. As you know, readers normally like conclusions to come first and therefore like topic sentences at the beginning.

Consider this paragraph:

> The State and the independent counsel for D.T. filed identical motions requesting the Probate Court to dismiss the parents' petition. They argued that § 4693(c) bars the relief requested and that it is constitutional. The court granted the motions and dismissed the petition. On appeal, the Superior Court issued a brief per curiam opinion affirming the Probate Court's opinion.

This paragraph lacks an explicit topic sentence. Nonetheless, we know the theme of the paragraph: the procedural history of the case. As the paragraph illustrates, sometimes a paragraph has no topic sentence.

You can omit a topic sentence when the general idea of the paragraph is clear to the reader. In a sense, the idea is present by implication. Narrative paragraphs are the most typical example.

Although you sometimes can forgo a topic sentence, do not be too quick to do so. Readers like topic sentences because they make a paragraph's theme unambiguous. Err on the side of including topic sentences.

2. Write Cohesive Paragraphs

Although writing a good topic sentence will go a long way toward making your theme stand out, you also must make certain that the discussion part of your paragraph supports and develops the topic sentence. When the topic sentence and the discussion work together, your paragraph will have unity and direction.

a. Write Focused Discussion Sections

In different paragraphs, the discussion sections serve different purposes. For example, the discussion section may offer an example to illustrate the point of the topic sentence, elaborate on the topic sentence, furnish a logical argument supporting the point of the topic sentence, or provide a narrative that the topic sentence introduces. In each case, the discussion section discusses the idea in the topic sentence and focuses the reader's attention on it.

In the next paragraph, the discussion section offers an example. The topic sentence tells us that a court has declined to apply strict liability when the plaintiff is an expert in dealing with a potentially dangerous product. The discussion section discusses one case in which the court refused to find strict liability for this reason.

> The Washington Supreme Court has refused to extend strict liability to cases in which expert handlers suffer injury while working with a potentially dangerous product. For example, in *Spellmeyer v. Weyerhauser*, 544 P.2d 107 (1975), a longshoreman was injured when a bale of wood pulp fell on him. According to the court, strict liability was inappropriate because only expert loaders and carriers were required to deal with the bale. The court found that because of the plaintiff's status as such an expert, the policy considerations favoring strict liability were too diluted to be persuasive. *Id.* at 110.

Here is a paragraph in which the discussion section elaborates on the topic sentence:

> In *Seary v. Chrysler Corp.*, 609 P.2d 1382 (Wash. 1980), the Washington Supreme Court refined the *Spellmeyer* holding to permit some expert handlers to successfully invoke strict liability. In *Seary*, a worker, an expert handler, was injured while loading a truck chassis onto a convoy trailer. He was operating a temporary device that was placed on the chassis specifically for the purpose of moving and unloading. The court imposed strict liability on the manufacturer of the temporary device, but only because the expert handler was the device's intended ultimate user. *Id.* at 1385. Although the court extended strict liability to an expert handler, it still limited the doctrine to situations in which a finished product is not safe for its intended use.

In this paragraph, the topic sentence tells us that a court used a case to refine its holding in an earlier case. The rest of the paragraph tells us about the new case and how the court used it to clarify its position on strict liability.

In the next paragraph, the discussion section presents a logical argument in support of the proposition in the topic sentence.

> When the user of a product is an expert in the care and handling of such products, the product is not unreasonably dangerous if the manufacturer fails to furnish instructions on its care and handling. By definition, an expert handler knows how to handle and move a wide variety of products. The handler possesses the experience, knowledge, and judgment necessary to protect himself or herself. Although, presumably, a significant percentage of products do not come to the docks equipped with loading instructions, it would be absurd to term all these products unreasonably dangerous to their handlers.

Note that the sentences in the discussion section appear in a carefully arranged sequence. The writer thought out the argument and made it one step at a time. If we were to rearrange the sentences in the discussion group, we would upset the logical order and seriously weaken the argument.

In the next paragraph, the discussion section provides a narrative that the topic sentence introduces.

> The injury occurred when the longshoremen attempted to load two steel drafts onto a barge. After both drafts arrived at the dock, the loaders safely loaded them onto the barge by using a sling of chain steel suspended from a shoreside crane. The loaders then determined that the drafts would fit better if loaded in the opposite direction. Therefore, they directed the crane operator to rehoist the drafts above the barge. Despite the availability of a nearby forklift and the obvious danger posed by the weight of the drafts, the loaders swung the drafts around in midair. The drafts collided with the forklift, slipped free from the sling, and crushed Mr. Smyth under their combined weight.

In this paragraph, the topic sentence tells you that the rest of the paragraph is going to describe the circumstances of the accident. When you read the paragraph, you may have thought that the topic sentence provided you with some help, but that it was not essential to your understanding. As discussed in Section 7.04[1], in narratives, topic sentences are not always necessary. The reader usually knows the idea of the paragraph—to tell the story. The theme of the paragraph is implicit.

b. Avoid Extraneous Sentences

In writing the discussion section, make sure that all the material in the discussion relates to the topic sentence.

Consider this paragraph:

> Because the plaintiff failed to employ a sheriff to serve the garnishment writ on the defendant, the service was ineffective. Rule 402(a) permits a plaintiff to make service without a sheriff only when the plaintiff makes service within the Commonwealth. Because the plaintiff chose to make service at the defendant's Illinois office, Rule 402(a) cannot be successfully invoked. The plaintiff requests the court to overlook any error in service because plaintiff could have served the writ at the defendant's office in the Commonwealth.

In this paragraph, the first sentence is the topic sentence. It states that the plaintiff's service of process was ineffective because the plaintiff failed to employ a sheriff. The discussion section provides the supporting argument. It gives us the rule for when a plaintiff can make service without a sheriff and explains why that rule does not apply here. However, the last sentence of the paragraph is not part of that discussion. Instead of supporting the argument in the topic sentence, it puts forth the plaintiff's argument why the court should accept the service as valid. Although this sentence is about service of process, it does not directly relate to the topic sentence and is not part of the argument in the discussion section. As a result, it detracts from the unity and direction of the paragraph. It belongs in another paragraph.

Consider this paragraph:

> The discovery rule would not excuse the Johnsons from failing to satisfy the two-year statute of limitations. Under the rule, the statute would have begun running when the Johnsons should have known all the relevant facts. Although they had this knowledge shortly after their child's birth, they did not bring their action for another four years. However, the Johnsons could prevail under another exception to the two-year statute of limitations: the concealment exception. This exception tolls the statute of limitations when the defendant's fraud or concealment causes the plaintiff to relax his or her vigilance or fail to inquire further. In the present case, fraud and concealment were present and lulled the Johnsons into a false sense of security. Therefore the exception should apply.

The point of the topic sentence is that the discovery rule will not assist the Johnsons. We would expect the discussion section to explain why the discovery rule does not apply here. The first part of the discussion section satisfies our expectations. However, in the middle of the paragraph, the discussion shifts to the concealment rule. The rest of the paragraph fails to support the point of the topic sentence. Therefore, it belongs in a separate paragraph. In fact, the last four sentences of the paragraph should stand by themselves as a separate paragraph.

As the last two examples demonstrate, each paragraph can present only one central idea. Every sentence in the paragraph should deal directly with that idea. The focus on a single idea is what gives the paragraph unity and direction. Sentences that focus on some other idea are extraneous and must be omitted or placed in a different paragraph.

3. When Necessary, Use Transitions and Repeat Words

If the reader does not find a connection between the ideas within paragraphs and among paragraphs, he or she will not follow your analysis or argument. You create continuity by arranging your ideas in a logical or chronological order and by using transitional words—"for example," "however," "therefore," "in addition," "consequently," "in contrast," and "moreover"—and repeating words and ideas that you have used in earlier sentences and paragraphs. Here, we focus on transitions and repetition.

This paragraph illustrates how to use transitions and repetition:

> *The Supreme Court of Puerto Rico* has adopted the principle that rights and liabilities in tort must be determined according to the law of the jurisdiction having dominant contacts with the parties and the occurrence. *By adopting this approach, the court* has accepted the approach of the Restatement (Second) of Torts, which calls for applying the law of the state with the most significant relationship to the parties and the event. *The court thus* appears to conform to the Restatement's assertion that, in a personal injury case, a court should choose the law of the state where the injury occurred, unless another state's relationship to the injury is more significant.

The italicized words provide continuity between the sentences. The first sentence introduces the court. The remaining sentences make repeated references to the court and force the reader to remember that the paragraph is focusing on the Puerto Rico Supreme Court's resolution of a legal issue. The first four words of the second sentence refer back to the idea in the first sentence and let the reader know that the second sentence builds on the first. The third sentence contains the transitional word "thus" and tells the reader that the third sentence reaches a conclusion based on the preceding sentences. Repetition and transitions thus give this paragraph cohesiveness.

The sample paragraph contains only one transitional word, "thus." As you work on your writing, you will discover that when you place your sentences in the proper sequence and repeat words and ideas that you introduced earlier, you will not need to clutter up your sentences with a large number of transitional words.

You also may have been concerned that the subject of every sentence in the paragraph is the same. You may have been taught that if you begin sentences with the same subject, you will bore the reader. Yet, you probably did not realize the repetition the first time you read the paragraph, and you probably did not become bored. Concern over excessive repetition is greatly exaggerated. Using the same subject for a series of sentences usually gives legal writing great continuity.

We will use the next paragraph to learn about transitions between paragraphs.

> Ms. Joseph should be able to make out a prima facie case for disparate treatment. To make out her case, she must persuade the court that there is sufficient evidence to

prove four elements: (1) that she belongs to a protected class; (2) that she applied for an available position for which she was qualified; (3) that she was rejected; and (4) that after the rejection, the employer continued to seek applicants. She should be able to provide sufficient evidence to establish these elements. First, as a woman, she is a member of a protected class. Second, she applied for a position as a firefighter for which she was fully qualified. Third, she was rejected under circumstances that give rise to an inference of discrimination. Fourth, after she was rejected, the city continued to seek applicants.

Suppose the writer believes that it is necessary to elaborate on Ms. Joseph's evidentiary proof for each of the elements. The writer then might follow this paragraph with four paragraphs, one for each element. The first of these paragraphs might begin: "As for the first element. . . ." The second might begin: "As for the second element. . . ." In each case, the new paragraph begins with a repetition of relevant words from the first paragraph.

Suppose the writer does not believe that these four paragraphs are needed and wishes to move directly to the defendant's response. The writer might begin the second paragraph with this sentence: "If Ms. Joseph establishes her prima facie case, the defendant has the opportunity to rebut the presumption of discrimination." The first clause in the sentence repeats the idea in the preceding paragraph. It thus connects the paragraphs. Alternatively, the writer might begin the second paragraph with this sentence: "However, the defendant should not necessarily admit defeat." By using "however," a transitional word, the writer connects the paragraphs. As you can see, repetition and transitional words also are tools for connecting paragraphs.

Exercise

Here is a sequence of three paragraphs. Please rearrange the sentences to make the paragraphs more effective. You may move sentences from one paragraph to another and, if necessary, revise the sentences slightly.

Since two years have passed since the last permissible filing date, the statute of limitations, strictly read, would bar the action. Although this state's law normally imposes a two-year statute of limitations for personal injuries, the Johnsons still may be able to bring an action for wrongful birth. In medical malpractice cases, the courts have recognized an exception called the "discovery rule." The rule does not require the plaintiff to know that the physician was negligent. This exception may apply to the Johnsons' action.

In applying the rule, the courts use a three-pronged test. The discovery rule applies to plaintiffs in medical malpractice actions. Under the rule, when the plaintiff cannot reasonably ascertain the existence of an injury, the statute of limitations does not begin to run until the injury's existence is known or discovered or becomes knowable or discoverable through the exercise of due diligence.

The statute begins to run when the plaintiff knows or, through reasonable diligence, should know of: (1) his or her injury (2) the operative cause of the injury; and (3) the causal relationship between the injury and the operative.

CHAPTER **8**

Help the Reader to Understand You

§ 8.01. INTRODUCTION

In this book you will learn to write documents such as legal memoranda for internal use in a law office, briefs for the courts' use in deciding your cases, and opinion letters for distribution to your clients.

Each form of legal writing has only one goal: to inform the reader in a clear and concise way. Help the reader out in every way you can. You should not try to impress your reader with your lawyering skills and language, but tell your reader your interpretation of the law in clear language.

Always assume that

1. the senior attorney who reads your internal legal memorandum may know little or nothing about the law as applied to the current case;
2. the judge who reads your brief may know little or nothing about the law as applied to the current case; and
3. the client who reads your opinion letter probably knows little or nothing about the law as applied to the current case.

Chapter 7 explained how to make your theme stand out. It thus explained one method of helping your reader to understand your writing. In this chapter you will learn other, often more subtle, methods for expressing your points clearly in writing.

Writing clearly, briefly, and precisely requires attention to detail. Many law students and young lawyers learn this lesson the hard way. A poor choice of words or a badly constructed sentence here and there really makes a difference.

We have organized this chapter into three topics: general advice, sentence structure, and sentence content. We also have included exercises to help you apply what you have learned.

§ 8.02. GENERAL ADVICE

1. Get to the Point

If you do not get to the point immediately, you will lose your reader at the outset. The reader is most often a very busy person who does not have the time or patience to ferret out what you are trying to say.

In Chapter 7 you learned one of the best ways of getting to the point: State your conclusions first. Suppose a senior attorney asks you to write a memo to address how the courts in your state would resolve a particular dispute. In the course of your research, you may learn a historical lesson on how the relevant law developed. In the relevant cases, you also may come across dozens of pithy quotations. You also may summarize dozens of cases. You may be tempted to begin your memo with a historical essay, fill the remainder with quotations, and include a series of paragraphs each furnishing a mini-brief of each case you read. However, before you fall into these traps, remember your assignment. The senior attorney asked you to answer a specific question. Instead of loading your memo with irrelevant information, include only information that answers the question.

First, state your conclusion. Then, state the controlling rule or holding in your jurisdiction and explain how the courts have applied the rule to cases with facts similar to yours. Distinguish adverse cases with different facts. Include your historical information, your quotations, and your cases only to the extent that they help you answer the question that you were asked. In other words, get to the point. Use information only to help you explain your point.

2. Use Concrete Language

Your writing should paint a picture in the reader's mind. You will not paint this picture unless you use concrete language and avoid abstractions. Do not try to achieve a lofty tone in legal writing. Your goal should be just the opposite. Follow these rules:

(1) Use the simplest language possible, as if you are telling a story orally.
(2) Use language the reader is least likely to have to look up in a dictionary.
(3) Use words that describe things in concrete terms.

Test your writing for concrete language and simplicity by reading it aloud. Does it sound interesting? Better still, read your writing to a nonlawyer, or a nonlaw student. Does that person understand it completely?

These examples illustrate how to change abstract to concrete language:

Bad: On the day the defendant's automobile collided with the minor, the precipitation level was very high, and the automobile hydroplaned.

Better: On the day Ms. Smith's car hit Sally Jones, it was raining hard and the car skidded off the road.

———

Bad: The landlord had an obligation to secure the premises by preventing the entry of the criminal element into the domicile.

Better: The landlord should have provided adequate locks and windows on the doors to the apartment.

———

Bad: Mr. Jones committed his signature to writing on the document conveying the real estate to the new record title holder.

Better: Mr. Jones signed the deed to the land, transferring it to Ms. Smith.

––––

Bad: The assailant brandished the weapon in the air at the victim, inflicting severe emotional distress and injuries to his person.

Better: The robber waved a gun at Mr. Jones, frightening him and severely gashing his forehead.

––––

In each of the examples, abstract language became concrete language, and complex concepts became clear pictures.

Look at each sentence you write and check to see whether you have used the simplest, most direct language possible. This instruction may appear contrary to what you think you should be learning at the professional school level. The poor writing you often see in case opinions reinforces the assumption that you should use complicated words and phrases and write abstractly. But this sort of writing is the opposite of what you should strive for. Only by writing simply and clearly can you communicate your ideas effectively.

3. Use the Active Voice

This rule is one of the hardest for writers to follow. Read the following examples:

Passive Voice: Mary was hit by Sarah.

Active Voice: Sarah hit Mary.

Passive Voice: The ball was thrown by Jeff.

Active Voice: Jeff threw the ball.

In the passive voice examples, the sentences focus on the objects of the action (Mary and the ball). The subject or actor in each sentence (Sarah and Jeff) that does something to the object takes a secondary role. In the active voice, the subject appears before the verb. It may be helpful to diagram the first example:

	(object)	(verb)	(preposition)	(subject)
(Passive)	Mary	was hit	by	Sarah
(Active)	(object)	(verb)		(subject)
	Sarah	hit		Mary

The more powerful, compelling way to express ideas in English is to use the active voice. There will be times when the passive voice is necessary, and there is no better way to express what you have said. But most of the time you can eliminate it with a little time and effort.

A few examples from legal writing may illustrate the effectiveness of the active voice. Suppose you are a district attorney prosecuting a criminal case. Which of the following would sound more persuasive in your brief for the case?

Passive Voice: The victim was hit by the defendant. Then she was raped by the defendant and shoved into the trunk of his car.

Active Voice: The defendant hit the victim, raped her, and shoved her into the trunk of his car.

The sentence in the active voice is more forceful. It makes a declarative statement, emphasizes the defendant's actions, and implies knowledge and purpose on the defendant's part.

Suppose you represent Mr. Smith in a case in which he claims a parcel of land. Which of the following would sound more persuasive in your brief for the case?

Passive Voice: Mr. Smith's intentions were evidenced by the facts that the land was occupied by him, the land was used by his sheep for grazing, and the land was used by him for planting crops.

Active Voice: Mr. Smith showed his intentions by occupying the land, using it for sheep grazing, and farming it.

Use of the active voice connotes concrete actions by Mr. Smith. The active voice also helps eliminate some unnecessary words to streamline the sentence.

Passive Voice: It was found by the court that the defendant was guilty, and he was sentenced to three years in prison.

Active Voice: The court found the defendant guilty and sentenced him to three years in prison.

———

Passive Voice: Title was quieted in Mr. Smith by the court, and Mr. Jones was found to no longer own the land.

Active Voice: The court quieted title in Mr. Smith and found that Mr. Jones no longer owned the land.

———

Passive Voice: The defendant was frisked by the detective, and this frisk turned up a loaded semi-automatic pistol, which was forcibly taken from his person.

Active Voice: The detective frisked the defendant, and this frisk turned up a loaded semi-automatic pistol, which the detective forcibly took from the defendant.

It is often difficult to eliminate the passive voice from writing. The best method is to go over your last draft, sentence by sentence, and read each sentence again for only one purpose—to eliminate the use of passive voice. As you find each use of passive voice, ask yourself, "Would converting this to active voice improve this sentence, and if so, how can I do that?"

———

Once you have learned how to eliminate passive voice, then you will begin to learn when you can use it effectively in certain situations. For example, the following passage by the famous lawyer Clarence Darrow depends on the passive voice (italicized) for dramatic effect:

> I don't believe in man's tinkering with the work of God. I don't believe that you and I can say in the light of heaven that, if we *had been born* as he *was born,* if our brains *had been molded* as his *was molded,* if we *had been surrounded* as he *has been surrounded,* we might not have been like him.[1]

In this example, Darrow is using the passive voice to put emphasis on the verbs. One way to emphasize a word or phrase is to place it at the end of a sentence or clause. Here, Darrow places the verbs in these positions. If he used the active voice, he would have been unable to place the verbs in these positions. The desire to emphasize the verbs prevailed over any disadvantages of using the passive voice.

4. Avoid Legalese

Lawyers and judges too often use the jargon of the law, "legalese," in their writing. The frequent use of legalese is unnecessary and can result in unclear writing. You should avoid legalese not only because it results in ambiguity, but also because you may not yet fully understand the meanings of legal terms. Legal dictionaries do not always explain the full meanings of those terms. You will have opportunities to use the new language you are learning, but try to suppress the urge to overuse it in your writing.

A true story might be helpful here. Many first-year students love to use the word "dicta." They use "dicta" proudly and profusely in writing assignments. One student had been using the word in writing assignments throughout his first year of law school. At the end of the year, he told his professor that it was only then that he realized the full meaning of the word.

This student had used a dictionary definition of the term but, because of his limited experience, he did not understand precisely what that word meant. The word "dicta" refers to language in a court opinion that is unnecessary to the holding of a case. However, the student had been using the term to refer to

———

1. Clarence Darrow, in defense of William D. Haywood for the murder of ex-governor Frank Steunenberg of Idaho, on the night of December 30, 1905. From G. J. Clark, *Great Sayings by Great Lawyers* (Vernon Law Book Co., 1926).

actual holdings on issues other than those he had researched for his own research projects. He had not understood the term and had applied it too broadly.

Aside from this practical reason for not using legalese, the most important reason to avoid it is that you must write clearly, and use of legalese defeats this purpose. Legalese has developed over many centuries and stems from several languages—notably, Latin, French, and Old and Middle English. Very little legalese is plain, simple, modern English that everyone can understand.

However, do not avoid using necessary terms of art, which you cannot replace with everyday words. The term "assault," for example, is a term of art; and you cannot use another term such as "hit" to replace it. "Proximate cause" is a term you will learn, and you should not attempt to find a substitute for it. "Exigent circumstances" is a term in criminal procedure that has its own special meaning, and you should not attempt to simplify it. Aside from certain terms of art such as these, you can eliminate most legalese from your writing.

Do not strive to impress your reader with your newly learned legalese. Strive to impress your reader with your ability to communicate effectively.

Examples

Legalese: The parties agree only to the terms and conditions set forth *herein*.

Plain Language: The parties agree only to the terms and conditions *in this agreement*.

———

Legalese: The plaintiff *instituted legal proceedings* against the defendant.

Plain Language: The plaintiff *sued* the defendant.

———

Legalese: In the event that the defendant defaults on her obligation, she will *forfeit* her rights.

Plain Language: If the defendant defaults on her obligation, she will *lose* her rights.

———

Legalese: Subsequent to his decision, the judge changed his mind.

Plain Language: After his decision, the judge changed his mind.

———

Legalese: She is to pay him $10,000 *per annum*.

Plain Language: She is to pay him $10,000 *a year*.

The examples show that you can substitute simple words and phrases for most of the terms and phrases that are peculiar to the law. Always read over your final draft of a legal document to purge it of all legalese.

5. Define Technical Terms

In the last subsection, you learned that you should avoid legalese. However, at times you cannot escape the use of technical terms. If you must use a technical term, define it immediately so you are sure the reader understands it. Of course, always consider your audience. Use your judgment when you decide whether the reader will understand the terms you use. A lawyer or judge may understand certain terms that a client would not understand. If you decide that it is necessary to define a term for your readers, either you can follow the term with a parenthesized definition, or you can define the term with a phrase or a sentence.

The following are examples of how to define technical terms in your writing:

- Mr. Barnes filed suit against Mr. Ewing to quiet title in the land. To "quiet title" means to ask the court to decide who owns the land.
- Mr. Barnes filed a suit against Mr. Ewing claiming adverse possession of the land. By invoking adverse possession, Mr. Barnes claimed he had gained ownership of Mr. Ewing's land by conducting certain acts with regard to the land for a certain time period.
- The defendant argued that a parent-child testimonial privilege should apply in this case. She argued that the court should not allow her son to testify against her in court because of the family relationship.
- Mr. Kramden argued that the insurance company's employee had apparent authority to bind the company. "Apparent authority" means that the insurance company represented to the public that the employee could make promises that the company must keep.
- The court ruled that the child should adhere to an adult standard of care (that is, that the child should have acted as a reasonable adult under the circumstances).

Never assume that your reader, whether another attorney or a judge, knows the meaning of every technical term you use. You do not want to insult your reader's intelligence, but you do not want to confuse your reader either.

6. Write in the Appropriate Tone

Much of what you have learned thus far may appear to work against using any formality in legal writing. Nevertheless, legal writing is formal writing. Although you must strive for simplicity, clarity, and brevity, you still must achieve the appropriate tone.

Setting the appropriate tone in your writing is where you can be "lawyerly" and sound "like a lawyer." Later in this chapter, you will learn the mechanics of tone at the word and phrase level—you will learn to avoid colloquialisms and contractions and not to personalize your writing with first ("I," "we") and second ("you") person pronouns. Learning those mechanics will help you write in the appropriate tone.

The tone in legal writing is similar to that in good business writing. Some helpful hints:

1. Do not use colloquialisms or slang.
2. Do not use contractions.
3. Do not personalize your writing.

4. Do not sound "preachy" or take the "soapbox" approach (see Chapter 13, §§ 13.03 [4], [5]).

5. Do be serious. Legal documents are serious matters, and your clients have serious concerns. Legal documents are generally not the place for humor or lightness.

Although the cases you read in your casebooks may not always be the best examples of good legal writing, they usually illustrate the tone you should set in your writing. They are usually good examples for you to study.

Exercises

The following exercises give you an opportunity to put into practice some of the rules that we have just covered. Identify the errors and, to the extent possible, rewrite the sentences to eliminate those errors. You may have some difficulty rewriting some of the sentences as the original author would have because they are taken out of context. Do the best you can. For these exercises, you may assume facts not given if they are necessary.

(1) Although Pennsylvania does not provide for depositions in these circumstances, other state and the federal courts call for depositions. In *United States v. Linton*, 502 F. Supp. 878 (D. Or. 1980), the court stressed that where testimony can be adequately secured by deposition, an incarcerated witness should not be further detained. In *Linton* the witness had been in jail for two months. At that time the trial was postponed. The court held that this was an "exceptional circumstance," and that it was "in the interest of justice that his testimony be taken by deposition." *Id.* at 879. The court delineated a comprehensive method of deposition-taking that includes videotaped examinations and cross-examinations.

Therefore, considering that Pennsylvania statute and case law strongly indicate material witnesses may not be held indefinitely, that the brothers were not afforded counsel to challenge their incarceration, and that deposition is a viable alternative to incarceration, the Fernandez brothers should be released from jail.

(2) The said canine caught the minor child's (Sally's) hand in his mouth, inflicting an injury that required ten sutures.

(3) The patient listed his unhealthy habits as the consumption of tobacco and alcoholic beverages and a lack of physical activity.

(4) The Texaco signs were put up by Bi-Rite Oil Company, which is Butterbaugh's distributor out of Monroeville and is independent of Texaco; the signs were provided by Bi-Rite free of charge.

(5) A criminal complaint was filed against defendant by the district attorney on November 5, 2009, charging the defendant with indecent assault. A preliminary hearing was scheduled by the district magistrate on November 14, 2009, but the hearing was not held because the defendant was not ready. Another hearing was scheduled for November 21, 2009, but was continued by the magistrate because a government witness was unavailable. The preliminary hearing was rescheduled for November 26, 2009, but was continued by the magistrate because defendant's attorney was unavailable. Finally, on December 10, 2009, a preliminary hearing was held by a district magistrate, and a prima facie case was

established by the district attorney at that time. On December 12, 2009, the magisterial transcript was sent to the court by the clerk and was received by the district attorney on December 19, 2009. The information was filed on January 14, 2010, and the date for arraignment was set for January 22, 2010, on which date arraignment occurred.

(6) FINDINGS OF FACT

(1) The aforesaid respondent, [ ], Esq., is an attorney admitted to practice law in the Commonwealth of Pennsylvania, and his last place of business was located at [ ].

(2) Subsequent to February 2008, respondent's wife died suddenly, leaving him with two minors to care for.

(3) The sudden demise of respondent's spouse resulted in extreme mental trauma and shock to respondent thereafter.

(4) Respondent entered a period of severe depression and began heavy consumption of alcohol at or about the time of his wife's demise.

(5) Subsequent to March 2009, respondent attempted suicide and was in a state of severe psychotic depression.

(6) The suicide attempt closely paralleled the first anniversary of his wife's demise.

(7) During the period following his wife's death, and at all times material herein, respondent suffered an impairment of judgment and a diminished mental capacity.

(8) During the period of impaired judgment and diminished mental capacity, respondent committed the wrongful acts hereinafter set forth.

(9) All conditions precedent and contained in the aforesaid Agreement of Sale have been met, have been waived by defendant's aforesaid conduct or have been prevented by the defendant's aforesaid conduct.

(10) The court requested further investigation as to whether decedent was ever married or had issue. Mr. Lochner questioned, *inter alia,* whether decedent's father, Robert F. Atkinson, was in fact the uncle of Franklin A. Allen, and mentioned other possible discrepancies in the family tree. Mr. Lochner's correspondence was referred to the trustee ad litem. Franklin A. Allen died testate on March 19, 2010.

(11) In that case, where plaintiff sued a bank for conversion of checks payable to plaintiff which were paid over alleged forged endorsements to plaintiff's bookkeeper, the bank's joinder of plaintiff's accounting firm alleging negligence in permitting the embezzlement may be properly dismissed since the theory of such joinder was distinct and unrelated to the theory of plaintiff's original complaint. Moreover, the defendant and additional defendant are not joint tortfeasors.

(12) This court should not allow the lower court's decision to stand. You have a duty to protect kids from dangerous people like the defendant. You also have a duty to support the cops, who work hard to catch people like the defendant. If you don't overturn the lower court's decision in this case, you'll negate everything we prosecutors work for. The defendant didn't even provide an excuse for her actions. Our case against her should be the winner here.

§ 8.03. STRUCTURE

When you put sentences together, the most important guideline is to limit each sentence to one thought. Plan your sentences before you commit them to paper. After several weeks of intensive research and thought about a problem, you may find yourself trying to say too much too quickly. The result can be long, rambling, almost "stream of consciousness" strings of words that obscure the central idea. Here are some ways to avoid this result.

1. Write Short Sentences

The easiest way to keep your writing clear and readable is to write short sentences. The basic sentence includes a subject, a verb, and usually an object. In most cases those elements are all you need to express a single idea. Choose your words with care and work to communicate rather than impress. You then should have no trouble writing short, precise sentences, and your reader will understand you quickly and easily.

Bad: In this case, there was no public controversy involving the concert because the concert affected only its small number of participants, and even if there was plaintiff did not thrust himself to the forefront of the controversy—he was involuntarily drawn into it either by virtue of his position as promoter of the concert or by the defendant's cablecast.

Better: In this case no public controversy involving the concert existed. The concert affected only its small number of participants. If a public controversy existed, plaintiff did not thrust himself into it. He was involuntarily drawn into it, either because of his position as the concert's promoter or because of the defendant's cablecast.

Bad: The court in its opinion, however, found that the record indicated that hospital security was "more lax than it could have been," sufficiently so that the court decided to hold the hospital liable based solely on the issues of law presented in the pleadings, and on the facts as revealed in the deposed testimony of the hospital's own employees.

Better: However, the court found that, according to the record, hospital security was "more lax than it could have been." Therefore, it held the hospital liable solely on the pleadings and on the facts revealed in the depositions of the hospital's employees.

Bad: Appellant's failure to respond to the motion, however, goes to the heart of the suit, and, if he is allowed to ignore proper procedure, the judicial process will be threatened with paralysis as the court will be unable to determine when it is appropriate to assume no response will be forthcoming from appellant.

Better: Appellant did not respond to the motion. This failure goes to the heart of the suit, because it paralyzes the judicial process. When a court does not know whether a litigant plans to respond to a pleading, it is unable to proceed.

The repairs to these sentences took several forms: dividing the long sentence into several smaller sentences, removing unnecessary phrases, and rewording sentences to make them more direct. Correcting one long sentence occasionally results in a longer discussion. It is an acceptable result to have more words and sentences if the final product is clearer.

Not all the revised sentences are short one-clause sentences. Legal writing does not look like the text of a book for grade school children. If you need to use a complex sentence, use it. First, however, try to reduce your ideas to short sentences that flow.

2. Put the Parts of Your Sentence in a Logical Order

One of the most common errors writers make is failing to put sentences together in a logical sequence.

Bad: First, this court properly dismissed plaintiff's claim for fraud since plaintiff's injury, the job loss, was due to the use of information by the employer supplied by the defendant and not due to the defendant's alleged misrepresentation.

Better: First, this court properly dismissed plaintiff's claim for fraud since plaintiff's job loss was not due to the defendant's alleged misrepresentation, but rather to the employer's use of information that the defendant supplied.

Comment: Rewriting this sentence as at least two shorter sentences would be an even greater improvement.

The problem stems from "stream of consciousness" writing. Sometimes thoughts make perfect sense in a certain order in your mind but become confusing when you write them. The problem generally results from not planning sentences and trying to put too many ideas into too few words.

Avoid confusing sentences by taking the time to read what you have just written. Put yourself in the reader's shoes. Will the reader understand the sentence easily? Will the reader understand it more easily if you place the ideas in a different sequence, perhaps a sequence more chronological or logical?

The best way to catch logical errors is to put the writing aside for a while and read it later when you have greater objectivity. Then, be willing to revise it. One of the writer's hardest tasks is to proofread with a willingness to make substantial changes. It also is one of the most profitable.

Here is another example.

Bad: Any disposition of property to a third person who had notice of the pendency of the matrimonial action or who paid wholly inadequate consideration for such property may be deemed fraudulent and declared void.

Better: A court can declare fraudulent and void any disposition of property to a third person when the third person knew that a matrimonial action was pending or when that person paid wholly inadequate consideration for the property.

3. Avoid Intrusive Phrases and Clauses

Writers sometimes burden their sentences with clauses and phrases that are not needed to convey the main idea. These inserts break the sentence flow and create difficulty for the reader. Intrusive phrases appear when writers rush onto paper the many thoughts cluttering their minds.

Bad: While the Third Circuit test is on its face similar, it can lead to results such as the issue at bar, that are inconsistent with the limited public figure status determination by this Court in *Gertz*.

Better: While the Third Circuit test is facially similar to this Court's, it can lead to results that are inconsistent with this Court's definition of limited purpose public figure in *Gertz*.

Comment: The rewrite eliminates the intrusive phrase "such as the issue at bar." Awkward phrases "on its face" and "status determination" become the simpler words "facially" and "definition." To clarify the comparison between the tests of the two courts, the writer inserted "this Court's" in two appropriate locations.

Bad: The Third Circuit erred in determining plaintiff was a limited purpose public figure, because in reality, under the approach taken by the United States Supreme Court, plaintiff at best would be classified as an involuntary public figure at the extreme.

Better: The Third Circuit erred in determining that plaintiff was a limited purpose public figure. Under the Supreme Court's approach, plaintiff is an involuntary public figure at best.

Comment: The rewrite eliminated the intrusive phrase "in reality." The passive "could be classified as" became "is." For further clarification, the long sentence became two shorter sentences.

Bad: With keeping the above in mind, the court of appeals notes that Plaintiff thrust himself into the public eye by actively seeking publicity for the event.

Better: As the court of appeals noted, plaintiff thrust himself into the public eye by actively seeking publicity for the event.

Comment: The phrase eliminated, "with keeping the above in mind," could almost be described as "throat clearing" before getting to the point.

Writers occasionally use intrusive phrases as a substitute for more detailed analysis. Avoid phrases like "such as the issue at bar" in the first example. Instead, make the comparison in a clear and concrete way. Other phrases, such as those removed from the second and third examples, serve no useful purpose and may create confusion.

4. Use Full Sentences

The occasional result of convoluted phrasing and writing too fast is a sentence that is not a sentence at all. Here are some examples:

- The estate failed to meet its evidentiary burden because sufficient evidence from which the trial court could have reasonably concluded that the decedent's death was the result of preexisting animosity between the assailant and the decedent.
- A position that this Court soundly rejected in *Gertz*.
- The way in which the average person viewing the statement in its intended circumstances is of critical import.

5. Use Parallel Structure

Maintain a consistent structure when joining phrases or clauses. Writers sometimes change verb tenses or use different introductory words for clauses that require the same word.

Bad: The hospital owes its invitees reasonable protection or to warn its invitees to the potential acts of third parties.

Better: The hospital owes its invitees reasonable protection or a warning about the potential acts of third parties.

Comment: The writer shifted from the noun "protection" to the verb "to warn" when discussing what the hospital owed its invitees. Using two nouns makes the sentence correct and comprehensible.

———

Bad: The plaintiff did not allege that the defendant acted specifically for the plaintiff to lose his job, but rather acted to induce the plaintiff's cooperation.

Better: The plaintiff did not allege that the defendant acted with the specific intent to have the plaintiff lose his job. He alleged only that the defendant acted to induce plaintiff's cooperation.

Comment: The failure to include some form of the verb "allege" in both parts of the sentence made the original sentence difficult to understand. Dividing the sentence into two shorter sentences clarifies it further. However, the final version still takes some effort for the reader to understand. Although revising complicated sentences makes them easier to understand, it does not remove the inherent complexity of the underlying idea. We can improve comprehensibility, but the reader still may have to do some work.

———

Bad: The security guard had no recollection of checking the laundry room doors before the murder and he also did not check the doors to the medical records office to see if they were locked.

Better: The security guard did not recollect checking the laundry room doors or the doors to the medical records office before the murder to see if they were locked.

Comment: In the first version, the combination of "had no recollection of checking" and "he also did not check" makes the sentence more complicated than it needs to be.

———

Bad: The definition established three criteria: there must exist a public controversy, into which an individual has become voluntarily or involuntarily involved for the purpose of assuming special prominence in the resolution of that issue within the controversy.

Better: The definition established three criteria: (1) a public controversy must exist; (2) the individual must become involved in that controversy voluntarily or involuntarily; and (3) the individual must intend to assume special prominence in the resolution of the controversy.

Comment: When providing a list, make sure the elements of the list are immediately apparent to the reader.

As you can see, mistakes involving parallel structure often center around verbs. Writers either use too many verbs in different forms or do not repeat the necessary verbs when they should.

§ 8.04. CONTENT

This section focuses on choosing the right words. Make sure that you choose the words that express your idea most precisely. Your words also must be appropriate for your medium of communication and your audience. They should be more formal and technical for briefs and memoranda and less formal for letters to clients. Writers sometimes choose words that obscure meaning, that are inappropriate for their intended audience, and, occasionally, that do not mean what the writers intended. Careful attention to your own writing will help you avoid these problems.

1. Use Positives Rather Than Negatives

If you emphasize the positive and avoid qualifiers, the reader probably will understand you better. Your writing also will set a tone that encourages the reader to agree with you. If you sound as if you believe what you are saying, the reader will be more likely to believe you.

Sometimes a negative word or phrase is necessary to express an idea precisely or to emphasize a point. However, use care to prevent a negative from making your message unclear or incorrect. Some writers use negatives when they are unnecessary or inappropriate. Occasionally, a writer will commit that unpardonable sin that our first grammar teachers warned us against—the double negative.

Here is an example of an awkward use of negatives:

> The district court exercised its discretion in allowing seventeen days to pass before treating our opponent's nonresponse as not contesting the motion.

The sentence conveys the same idea but is easier to understand if phrased as follows:

> When our opponent failed to respond, the district court exercised its discretion in allowing seventeen days to pass before treating the motion as uncontested.

Another aspect of using positive rather than negative language is the avoidance of qualifying words. Students and lawyers are sometimes less than totally confident in their positions. They reflect their insecurity in their choice of words. Avoid phrases like "it would seem," "it would appear," and "we would argue." These phrases are rarely necessary. They may even highlight areas of your argument that are particularly vulnerable.

2. Avoid Ambiguous Words and Phrases

Students and young lawyers have a natural desire to "sound like lawyers." They sometimes use ambiguous words or phrases that obscure the intended meaning but sound more "professional." Sometimes you will want to obscure the exact meaning of your message, such as when you make an argument that is less than airtight, but normally you should strive for clarity and ease of understanding. In the following examples, the writers failed to convey their meaning clearly. It is therefore not possible to rewrite the sentences in "better" form.

Bad: In such cases as *Hutchinson* and *Wolston*, this Court stressed that it is not the quantity of the relationship of the individual to the media but also the quality to which the individual subjects himself to the public.

Comment: Although there are several problems with this sentence, one of the most glaring is that the words "quantity" and "quality" are virtually meaningless. Although, in this context, these words may have a particular meaning for the writer, they do not have the same meaning for the reader. In trying to set up a stylistic contrast, the writer leaves the reader at a loss in trying to determine what the writer means.

———

Bad: However, as stated earlier in reference to access to the media, this would be inconsistent with this Court in the position taken in *Time* for much of the same rationale.

Comment: The writer is trying to reinforce a point made earlier without actually making the point again. The result is an almost indecipherable sentence that requires the reader to do far too much work. If you need to repeat yourself or to refer to an earlier point and explain it briefly, do so.

————

Bad: Plaintiff, for the most part, pleaded only conclusions that, while they may indicate that the end result of defendant's actions was outrageous conduct, do not indicate facts that show that his actions were outrageous conduct in themselves.

Comment: The writer repeats the phrase "outrageous conduct" but gives the reader no clue to what it means. The writer must provide more information.

————

Bad: Defendant's interview with plaintiff did not constitute the severity of an ultimatum found in *Richette.*

Bad: The defendant did not constitute an employee.

Comment: The misuse of the word "constitute" in the examples above represents the affinity some writers have for words they do not quite understand. When in doubt, use a dictionary or use simpler words that express the same idea. For example, the writer could reword the second sentence above to say "[T]he defendant was not an employee."

3. Avoid Colloquialism

Although we often hear that we should write the way we speak, certain words and phrases should rarely find their way onto paper. You can rely on common sense to identify language that is inappropriate for a written document. For example, you should not say that a court has "come up with" a particular definition. You also should avoid contractions such as "can't," "don't," and "won't." They are too conversational for the vast majority of written documents you will prepare. Here is an example from a student brief that demonstrates language you should avoid:

> While these matters might be interesting to some people, the events of a small loosely run beauty pageant would hardly make a dent in the priority list of the public at large. Most people don't know when the pageant is held and a great number don't really care.

4. Do Not Personalize

Some writers cannot resist the temptation to refer either to themselves or to their readers with pronouns such as "I," "we," "our," or "you." These words may be appropriate for this book, but they are not appropriate in formal legal writing. Phrases such as "we submit," "I believe," or "our position is" only weaken your argument by reminding the reader that you are making arguments. When writing a brief or memorandum, make your arguments sound like statements of law rather than statements of personal opinion. A judge or a senior attorney may not care about your personal opinion. That judge or attorney wants to know what the law is and how it applies to your case.

When referring to the court to which a brief is addressed, use "this court." In a memorandum, you may refer to a senior attorney as "you," but many attorneys consider the pronoun too informal even for interoffice memoranda. It is safer to avoid its use. You also should avoid the more formal and often awkward "one."

5. Avoid Excessive Variation

Many students learn to use a different word every time they refer to the same person or thing. Using different words and phrases to refer to the same thing serves the laudable goal of preventing the reader from getting bored by repetition. Excessive variation, however, backfires. It is unaesthetic and sometimes comical. It also creates confusion when the writer uses inaccurate words rather than repeating accurate ones.

Legal terms of art offer an example. In torts, "standard of care" has a precise meaning that many court decisions have developed. If you use the phrase "standard of negligence" rather than repeat the term of art, the educated legal reader will not understand what you are saying. Excessive variation creates ambiguity.

In the following example, confusion results because the writer uses different words to refer to the same litigants.

> According to the record, Sam Spade had never before met the plaintiff. Although the plaintiff alleges that Mr. Spade already possessed some information about the plaintiff, there is no indication of any reason why this information might lead our client to maliciously intend to injure the appellant or to inflict losses upon him.

You might think that this excerpt mentions four people. It actually mentions two. "Sam Spade" and "our client" are the same person, as are "plaintiff" and "appellant."

In summary, the lessons are twofold. First, avoid boring the reader with repetition. Be creative, but do not overdo it. Second, be repetitive rather than imprecise or confusing.

Exercises

The following exercises are sentences taken from student briefs and memos. They give you an opportunity to put into practice some of the principles discussed above. Identify the errors and, to the extent possible, rewrite the sentences to eliminate those errors. You may have some difficulty rewriting some of the sentences as the author would have since they are taken out of context. Do the best you can.

(1) However, since the issue has been raised it has become necessary to demonstrate that even though a second motion to dismiss was not required, by submitting a letter of request to the judge and providing opposing counsel with a copy

of the letter, the judge correctly found that the letter was sufficient to comply with all applicable rules of procedure regarding motions.

(2) The fundamental principle of the Fourth Amendment is ensuring "one's privacy against arbitrary intrusions by the police," *Wolf v. Colorado*, 338 U.S. 25, 27 (1949), and "intended as a restraint upon the activities of sovereign authority, and was not intended to be a limitation upon other than governmental agencies. . . ." *Burdeau v. McDowell*, 256 U.S. 465, 475 (1921).

(3) Taking into consideration the Pennsylvania Rules of Civil Procedure, which limit the amount of time in which an affirmative request for a jury trial must be made and the rulings of the courts in these cases concerning the implications of failing to file for a jury trial at all, it would be difficult, after not requesting a jury trial within the past 30 days and the trial date approaching so soon, to convince the court to allow Olive Holmes's case to be heard by a jury.

(4) The question thus is whether our client's promise that she would return to talk to the police signified voluntary willingness to be confined, or whether the Dean's refusal to allow her to leave is a detaining force sufficient from which she has no legal obligation to resist in order to prove lack of consent.

(5) In *Medico*, the court held that a press defendant could relieve itself of liability without establishing the truth of the substance of the statement reported by claiming the fair report privilege when its publication contains matters of public concern and is based on acts of the executive or administrative officials or governmental reports.

(6) Ms. Holmes can establish the tort of false imprisonment against the Law School due to the fact that Ms. Holmes's nonconsensual confinement by the school dean can be predicated as false imprisonment since Ms. Holmes was exonerated of the charge establishing the basis for the school dean's confinement of Ms. Holmes.

(7) The security guard deposed that the assailant entered the hospital through the emergency room when he confronted him about an hour before the murder and that there was no other security guard on duty who was monitoring the emergency entrance.

(8) Insofar as the court moved for a summary judgment in the Estate's favor based on the evidence in the depositions, it decided that a negligent breach of duty was shown as a matter of law and that the only reasonable inference was that its negligence, and not the criminal act of the assailant, was the proximate, legal cause of plaintiff's death.

(9) The state's patient-physician privilege imputes such information as being highly confidential and personal.

(10) The key issue to be determined is whether the Law School's answer to the complaint for false imprisonment is the last pleading directed to such issue or whether the dean's answer to the Law School's third party complaint for indemnification is not the last pleading directed to that issue, but only to the issue of indemnity.

(11) Nor is there liability if the plaintiff fails to show that the private matter of the alleged publicity is not of legitimate public concern.

Meeting the Client

§ 9.01. INTRODUCTION

You may wonder why we talk about client interviewing and counseling in a text about legal research and writing. We do this because we want you to always remember why you research and write. Almost all lawyering work is done in the service of clients (except for government lawyers such as prosecutors, although in some sense "the people" are their clients). Keep this in mind, even when you are not working for real clients.

Most first-year legal writing programs introduce the idea that the information lawyers work with comes from clients. Some programs stage interviews for students to observe, while others allow the students to actually do the interviewing. Others do not require you to actually interview someone to get the information you need to write your memorandum or other legal writing assignments. Even if you get the facts that form the basis of your assignments from a piece of paper, you should remember that in the real world, legal research and writing are based on the information provided by clients, which may be incomplete, self-serving, or confusing.

We offer this introduction to the process of gathering information from clients to better prepare you to get the information you need to research and write documents that will provide the best possible assistance to your clients.

§ 9.02. PURPOSE OF THE INITIAL INTERVIEW

As you plan for the initial interview with a client, ask yourself what you need to accomplish in that interview. Remember that the client is not a walking, talking legal problem, but a living, breathing human being with feelings, goals, and priorities, who happens to have a current problem that may have some legal dimensions. Of course you do need to ascertain the scope of the problem that brings the client to you, but you need to find out more than the legally relevant facts. You need to understand the client. What kind of person is the client? What does he or she hope to accomplish by coming to see a lawyer?

You also need to lay the groundwork for a working relationship. Clients need to feel comfortable with you. They need to be able to trust that you will handle the problem appropriately and with sensitivity. Since the only way you will be able to make a living as a lawyer is if clients retain you, you must sell yourself. In most cases, you do not sell yourself best by overselling yourself. You sell yourself best by creating trust, by opening the channels of communication in both directions, and by conveying confidence and competence.

Remember that this is also a business relationship. It is sometimes difficult to bring up the subject of money when a client is presenting you with what may be the most pressing and difficult situation in his or her life at that moment. If you do not address the business aspects of the relationship early on, however, you open yourself up to the very real possibility of misunderstandings and unnecessary problems later. Although this may sound obvious, you need to get a clear commitment from the client to hire you before you begin working on the client's behalf.

The client will also likely want an initial assessment of the legal situation. Clients frequently ask questions such as "What are my rights?" "Can he do that?" "How can I get my money back?" "Will I have to go to jail?" Because you are a lawyer, clients expect you to have the answers to those questions. As you go through law school, you learn that there are far more questions than answers, and that you have to do research before you can answer most questions. One of the most delicate tasks to accomplish with a new client is to let the client know that you need more information, both factual and legal, before you can give an accurate answer to the problem. At the same time, you should try to give the client some idea of what might happen. What are some available dispute resolution options? How does the legal system treat these kinds of problems? Can you provide a preliminary assessment of the client's problem based on your existing legal knowledge?

§ 9.03. PLANNING THE INITIAL INTERVIEW

Here are some goals for an initial interview with a client:

- Get the facts.
- Get to know the client.
- Understand the client's feelings, goals and priorities.
- Begin building trust.
- Explain your fees.
- Get hired.
- Offer a preliminary assessment of the problem.

You cannot accomplish these tasks without a plan. This is not the type of conversation where you can just sit back and see where it goes. As you gain more experience, you will develop a pattern for approaching interviews that allows you to accomplish your goals, but at first you must consciously structure your approach to the conversation. Plan a strategy for building trust, getting information, getting the client to retain you, and beginning to address the client's problem. It is probably a good idea to have a written form of some kind in front of you that reminds you of the various components of the initial interview. The rest of this chapter offers advice on how to structure the initial interview so you do not forget any critical steps.

§ 9.04. GREETING THE CLIENT

It may sound artificial to suggest that you plan your greeting to the client. However, as we all know, first impressions are frequently lasting impressions, and you should consider whether you want the client's first impression of you to be that you are cold, calculating, and money-hungry, or that you are a considerate, caring human being. You will be easier to confide in if you spend a bit of time in casual conversation about neutral topics such as the weather or traffic or similar "elevator" conversation. It may seem awkward and forced, particularly at first, but it does allow the client to settle down, assess the surroundings, and prepare to discuss more difficult topics. If you seem comfortable and genuinely interested in a relaxed approach to the conversation, usually the client will follow your lead. You will find it easier to get information if the tension level in your office is low.

Be careful about accomplishing your atmospheric goal by commenting on any aspect of the client's appearance. Besides being a bit personal, you never know what might be a sensitive subject. For example, if the client is coming to you about a divorce, you may start the interview off on exactly the wrong note by commenting on what a beautiful diamond ring she is wearing.

§ 9.05. PREPARATORY EXPLANATION

It is generally a good idea to offer a roadmap of the interview before you start questioning the client. You might ask whether the client has ever seen a lawyer before, as a means of gauging what the client's expectations are likely to be. If the client has never seen a lawyer before, it is a good idea to outline the procedure you intend to follow during the interview. For example, explain how long the interview is likely to last, what your goals are, that you will be asking questions and taking notes, that the client will have a chance to ask questions, that you will try to begin developing options for resolving the client's problem, and that you will discuss the likely cost of handling the problem. You may also want to remind the client of your ethical obligations relating to confidentiality.

If the client has seen a lawyer before, it is a good idea to get a feel for whether that was a positive or negative experience. If the client comes in skeptical or suspicious about lawyers because of a previous bad experience, it is helpful for you to know that sooner rather than later. If the client has had prior negative experience with attorneys, your goal is to persuade the client that you are a valuable ally, not a necessary evil. You can best do this by taking the time to show the client that you care about him or her as a whole person, not just as a legal problem or a source of money.

§ 9.06. GETTING THE CLIENT'S PERSPECTIVE

As lawyers, we frequently are in a hurry to find out what the legal problem is. We are trained in law school to spot issues, to sift through the facts presented until we find the ones that matter, and then offer an analysis of how the law applies to those facts. That is only a small part of what you must accomplish with a client. Avoid the temptation to become impatient when the client seems to ramble or starts talking about feelings. You cannot adequately represent a client without knowing how the client feels about the problem, what the client hopes to accomplish in coming to see you, and what the client's priorities are.

You will be tempted to substitute your own value system for the client's, causing you to think about how you would handle the problem if it were yours. It is not your problem, and you must never lose sight of that fact, even if the client tries to hand you the problem. Clients frequently come to you and ask "What should I do?" The only good answer to that question is the one the client arrives at after being given a full understanding of the likely consequences of different approaches. Your job is to inform the client so that he or she can make a decision based on his or her own value system. You will do this more effectively if you understand the client's perspective on the problem.

1. Getting Started

The easiest way to begin the interview is to ask a simple, open question such as, "What brings you here today?" Or "How can I help you?" Let the client know that you want to hear the story in his or her own words and then let the client tell it. Resist the temptation to break in with constant questions. If you are afraid you will forget to ask about a needed detail, jot it down. If you derail the client's story with questions, you may end up missing key facts or elements in the story. Do not try to put legal labels on the client's problem too soon: "Oh, this is a contracts problem." If you do that you will start focusing on questions you were trained to ask about contracts, and you may never find out that the client has also brought you a tax problem and a criminal problem, or you may find out at a time and in a manner that is awkward and difficult.

If the client has difficulty knowing where to start, you might suggest a time frame. "Start at the beginning." "What event made you decide to come see a lawyer?" If the client offers unhelpful generalizations such as "I have a problem with my partner," then you want to try a few direct questions to get the story going. "Do you mean a business partner?" "What kind of business do you have?" "Does the problem relate to the business?" Once the client gets into the story, stop the questions and let the client talk.

2. Keeping Track

It is difficult to balance your need to keep track of information the client is giving you with the client's need to feel that you are listening. You will probably want to take some notes, but try not to spend the entire session staring at your legal pad as you write. Eye contact is a very important part of the conversation, not only for the client but for you. You may gain valuable clues to the client's personality and sensitive aspects of the problem by watching the nonverbal channels of communication. If you can, listen for a while and then write down only the most important aspects of the story. Jot down details such as names and dates, but don't try to record every word the client says. If you do not think that you will be able to accurately remember the client's message if you wait too long, ask the client if you may record the conversation. Having a tape recording will free you to really concentrate on the client's message and the way it is being communicated.

3. Getting the Details

You do need some details. You need detailed information about the client, including addresses and phone numbers so that you will be able to contact him or her throughout your handling of the matter. You may also need names, addresses, and phone numbers of other individuals who are involved in the matter or who may be potential witnesses. You need dates, times, places, and relevant documents. Thus you will need to ask focused, closed questions at some point in the interview. Try not to interrogate the client. If the client becomes defensive, you will likely not get information you need. It is a good idea to explain to the client why you need so much information. You may also want to have a written questionnaire for the client to take home, at least for cases such as divorce or bakruptcy, where you need a great deal of detail about personal and financial matters.

Try to get a chronological version of events. Ask for the sequence of events, and ask for dates. Find out who else is involved, and who else knows what is going on. Find out if there are any documents you need to look at and if the client can get them for you. It is a good idea to recap the client's story, perhaps several times, depending on the complexity of the story and the organization (or lack of organization) of the information provided. Telling the client what you have understood lets the client know that you were listening, and often provides an opportunity to get additional information. You may discover that you got some aspect of the story wrong, or your recap may prompt the client to fill in gaps in the story.

You will also need information the client may not think to give you because the client does not know it is important. Clients do not know the law or may have incorrect ideas about what the law says. Therefore they may have a different idea of what information is relevant than you do. They may also have personal reactions or priorities that give them a different sense of what is relevant or important. For example, it may be very important to the client that you understand that he was treated disrespectfully, while that fact may have no legal significance. Do not dismiss facts that the client thinks are important, but stay focused enough to get the facts you need.

The client may be embarrassed about certain facts; the client wants you to think that he or she is a good person and has a good case, so there may be a temptation not to tell you about things that reflect negatively on the client's character or the case. Remind the client that what is said to you will be kept in confidence (subject to certain exceptions such as information relating to imminent harm to another, which you may disclose), and that you can provide the best possible representation only if you have the full story. It is frequently a good idea to ask the client what the other party is likely to say about the situation. This allows the client to give you necessary and possibly damaging information without having to acknowledge its accuracy or validity.

4. Goals and Priorities

We have emphasized the need to get the client's perspective on the problem and potential solutions. How do you accomplish this? The simplest way is to ask: "What would you like to see happen?" "If you had to choose between X and Y, which would you choose?" The client may not have thought about the answers to these questions, assuming that you would tell him or her what to do or what would happen next. Do not succumb to the temptation to do that; explain the importance of understanding the client's wants and needs to your representation. If you do not accomplish this important step, you may very well present the client with what you think is a very good settlement offer, only to have the client reject it because it does not meet some fundamental need you were unaware of. For example, in a defamation case, if you think the client wants as much money as possible but it turns out the primary concern is the client's reputation, you may get a good monetary settlement but not push for an apology or retraction or some other measure that might rehabilitate the client's damaged reputation. These are the kinds of misunderstandings that lead to malpractice actions.

§ 9.07. PRELIMINARY ASSESSMENT OF THE CLIENT'S PROBLEM

You should try to offer a preliminary assessment of the client's problem, at least to the extent of determining whether it is an appropriate situation for legal intervention. Some problems simply do not lend themselves to legal solutions (some neighborhood or family disputes come to mind), or you may find that the client presents a problem you are not qualified or do not wish to handle. If so, you should tell the client that. If you think the client presents a problem with potential, you need to be honest about your expertise in the area. There is no shame in needing to do research or further investigation before deciding how to proceed with a matter, and you need to develop the confidence to present this need for further inquiry as part of your competence rather than something you need to apologize for. You should, however, share with the client any judgments you are able to make about likely actions or events that might resolve the client's problem, and you should offer some assessment of the likelihood that the client's goals can be met. You should also be very clear that these assessments are preliminary and may very well change as additional facts and law are discovered.

§ 9.08. DEVELOPING OPTIONS

Once you have preliminarily assessed the client's problem, you may begin a discussion of options to be pursued. For example, you can try to get a sense of whether the client is interested in litigating the matter or prefers a more amicable and informal resolution such as negotiation or mediation. You should take any nonlegal concerns of the client (such as a desire for an apology or to redeem his reputation) into account in developing the options, and you should encourage the client to participate in this process with you. Has the client thought about desirable outcomes, and possibly even ways to accomplish them? As you begin to develop options, explore the likely consequences of pursuing each option. What are the advantages and disadvantages? How likely is it that the option will actually work out? For example, if the dispute involves a lot of anger or other negative emotions on both sides, a quick and amicable negotiated resolution is unlikely.

§ 9.09. FEES

As we said previously, you must deal with the subject of money. There are several ways to structure fee agreements. You may bill your time at an hourly rate or charge a flat fee. In an appropriate case, where you are hoping to recover a sum of money for the client, you may take your fee out of the recovery. This is called a contingent fee because you will not get paid if the client does not recover. Many jurisdictions require that you present the client with a written statement of your fees at the outset of the relationship, at least in matters where you intend to charge a contingent fee.

You should put in writing your entire agreement with the client about the scope of your representation, including fees. This is called a retainer agreement. Even if it is not required, it demonstrates good business sense to agree in writing with the client what you will and will not do. In addition, signing the agreement will bring home to the client the necessity of paying the fee.

Most clients understand that this is a business relationship, and they will be relieved to get that part of the transaction out of the way. All you have to sell is your time and expertise, and you should not be embarrassed about that fact. If a client genuinely cannot pay or wants to work out a contingency arrangement, you will have to decide whether this is an appropriate case to handle on a reduced-fee or pro bono basis, or whether any possible recovery justifies the contingency fee. Regardless of the fee arrangement you work out, you should present it to the client in writing and get it signed, so that it is clear from the outset what you will be charging and what the client has agreed to pay.

When do you bring up the subject of money? It is not advisable to start the interview by talking about fees. This is partly because you will only reinforce negative stereotypes of "moneygrubbing" lawyers by doing so, and partly because you cannot possibly assess the most appropriate fee structure or the likely ultimate cost to the client without having some sense of what the problem is. We advise you to get the client's story and begin the assessment process before you get to the subject of fees. The beginning of the discussion regarding your client's legal and nonlegal options is a very logical point at which to bring up the subject of cost.

Remember that the client's ultimate cost concern will be the total amount of money needed to resolve the problem, so do not simply quote your hourly rate, if that is how you propose to charge the client. Try to estimate the likely total cost of the case, always remembering (and telling the client) that the final cost will depend on many factors that you may not be able to anticipate right now, such as the stubbornness of the other side, whether the other party hires a lawyer who likes to generate lots of paper and drag things out, the difficulty of finding necessary witnesses and evidence, and the like. At a minimum provide an estimate of the cost of handling the initial stage(s) of the matter. For example, tell the client how long it will take you to conduct preliminary research and generate a letter explaining the situation to the client or to other involved parties.

§ 9.10. CLOSING THE INTERVIEW

At the end of the interview, it can be very easy to simply end the conversation and say good-bye. This may be the most important point in the interview for the client's long-term confidence in you, if you handle it correctly. Clients' most frequent complaint about their lawyers is that lawyers do not keep them informed about the process. Clients who are insecure about the status of their case and who do not understand the steps in the process may make frequent phone calls to get answers. Nervous clients may make phone calls anyway, but well-informed clients should be less likely to contact their attorneys when there is nothing happening in the case that justifies contact.

Do not let the client leave without carefully explaining what happens next, when it will happen, and whose responsibility it is. If you are going to contact the attorney for the other side, tell the client when you will do so, and when you will let the client know about any response you receive. Give the client some "homework." This may sound odd, but if there is a way the client can help with the case, perhaps by retrieving documents or phone numbers, you give the client some measure of control over a difficult problem, which is usually reassuring. Handling the end of the interview in a concrete way gives the client confidence in you and gives you specific and immediate goals to achieve on behalf of the client.

Remember that you must also formalize the attorney-client relationship and confirm that the client wants you to handle the matter. If the client has not decided to hire you, do not agree to do any work for the client, unless the terms and conditions under which you will do some work are clearly specified, preferably in writing. Set a time frame within which the client must decide to hire you or you will close the file. This should help to reduce the possibility of misunderstandings about whether you were hired, the scope of your representation, and any deadlines involved. The best possible scenario is that you give the client a written retainer agreement that includes fees, and it is signed on the spot, or the client agrees to return it to you within a few days.

Exercise

Here is a draft intake form for an interview with a client who is coming to see you about a personal injury case. The only thing you know before the interview is that the injury is the result of an automobile accident. What would you add to this form? Is there another approach to structuring the interview that makes more sense to you? How will you begin the interview? What kinds of questions will you start with? What kinds of details will you need? What do you need to know about the law of your jurisdiction (e.g., is yours a comparative or contributory negligence jurisdiction)? What sorts of documents might be available that will help you prepare the case? What sorts of fee agreements might be appropriate? Write out your answers to these questions and redraft the form so you could actually use it effectively during the interview.

Client Intake Form

Name:
Address:
Phone number(s):
E-mail address:
Client's description of events:

Date of accident:

Other parties:

Potential witnesses:

Client's stated goal(s):

Fee structure discussed and agreed to:

§ 9.11. CLIENT INTERVIEW CHECKLIST

— Planning the initial interview: How will you get necessary information? What topics do you need to cover? Do you have fee agreements ready to be executed?

— Greeting the client: How might you best put the client at ease? Does the client seem nervous or eager to get down to business?

— Preparatory explanation: Roadmap the interview; talk about process and confidentiality.

— Getting the client's perspective: Ask about the client's goals and priorities. Let the client tell the story his or her own way! Ask what the client would like to see happen.

— Preliminary assessment: Is this problem appropriate for legal action? Is it a problem you are qualified or prepared to handle? How much additional legal or factual research do you need to do?

— Developing options: Is this matter headed for litigation, or can it be resolved amicably? What ideas does the client have for resolving the problem? What are the advantages and disadvantages of pursuing various options?

— Fees: What fee structure is appropriate for handling this case? Did you get a written fee agreement signed? Did you give the client an estimate of the likely total cost of the matter?

— Closing the interview: Was it clear what will happen next, when it will happen, and whose responsibility it is? Did you ask the client to provide you with any information or documents? Does the client understand the immediate plan of action?

CHAPTER 10

Introduction to the Memo

§ 10.01. WHAT IS A MEMO?

The memorandum of law, or memo, is an internal office document. It is a research tool that analyzes the law as it applies to the facts of a client's case and offers an unbiased evaluation.[1] A memo includes both helpful and damaging information. It suggests solutions to a legal problem or predicts the outcome of a dispute. It is the precursor to informed decision making about a case.

The memo is the most basic of legal documents and is essential to the practice of law. During the course of your legal career, you likely will write a multitude of memos for more senior attorneys. Memos will vary in length and in topic. They will also serve as a gauge of your ability to analyze and present a legal problem. Once you master this type of writing, you will draft other kinds of legal documents with greater skill and ease.

This chapter introduces you to the memo. It describes the purposes of a memo, the parts of a memo, and the hallmarks of a well-written memo. Chapters 11, 12, 13, and 14 focus on the parts of a memo in more detail and demonstrate how to draft each section effectively.

§ 10.02. THE PURPOSES OF A MEMO

The purpose of a memo is to provide a realistic analysis of the law as it applies to the facts of the client's case. That analysis will be the basis for giving advice or making decisions about the case.

A memo can serve many purposes. Its purpose determines how extensive the research should be, what the nature of the analysis should be, and how it should be written. The memo should be written to serve the specific purpose for which it was requested. By way of example, an attorney may use a memo to

- evaluate the merits of a case;
- decide whether to settle or try a case;

---

1. This chapter concerns interoffice memos only. There also are memoranda of law that are submitted to the court. They are more akin to briefs and should not be confused with the office memo.

117

- decide whether to accept a case;
- inform the reader of the status of the law;
- present recommendations as to how to proceed with a case;
- conclude that more information is needed to properly evaluate the case;
- identify the legal theories applicable to the case;
- decide whether to file any motions;
- prepare for trial;
- form the legal foundation of motions, pleadings, and briefs;
- prepare a contract, will, settlement agreement, or corporate papers;
- prepare for negotiations; or
- prepare for an appeal.

The memos you prepare during the course of a case will provide a convenient summary of the facts, issues, legal theories, and arguments involved in the case. You and any other attorneys on the case will refer to them to refresh your memories as the case progresses.[2]

§ 10.03. THE PARTS OF A MEMO

The memo is a structured document that is divided into distinct but related sections. Each section is labeled and performs a particular function. Memos do not use a universal format or a mandatory order in which their parts appear. Many law firms, corporate legal departments, and government offices prescribe a standard form. You should find out whether your office uses a standard format or, if not, whether the attorney for whom you are preparing the memo prefers a certain format. Although there are many variations in the structure of a memo, the following format is widely used:

1. Heading
2. Brief statement of the issue to be discussed
3. Conclusion
4. Brief statement of the facts
5. Discussion of the pertinent authorities

Appendix I contains sample memoranda. Please review those memoranda in conjunction with this chapter.

1. The Heading

The heading indicates the type of document, the person to whom the memorandum is addressed, the person who wrote it, its date, and its subject matter, in the following form:

---

2. Many law firms index and file the memoranda of law prepared by their attorneys. These memos are a valuable asset. A question may arise in a pending case that a previous memo already addresses. The attorney need only update the research in the memo. This procedure saves the attorney time and the client money.

MEMORANDUM

TO:
FROM:
DATE:
SUBJECT: (or RE:)

2. The Issue

The issue, sometimes called the question presented, frames the legal question to be resolved by the memo. If there is more than one issue or several subparts to an issue, number each issue and subpart separately. The issue section of the memo informs the reader of the scope of the memo. A memo should not go beyond the scope of the issue.

3. The Conclusion

The conclusion, sometimes called the short answer, provides a complete, but brief, answer to the issue. At times an attorney will refer only to the conclusion, at least initially. The conclusion includes a concise statement of the reasons for your conclusion. It also orients the reader to the general thrust of the discussion. The conclusion does not contain a detailed discussion of how you reached the conclusion. Citations to authority and cross-references to the body of the memo are inappropriate. In a memo that discusses more than one issue, number the conclusions to reflect the issues to which they refer.

4. The Facts

This section requires a clear and concise statement of the facts relevant to the legal analysis presented by the memo. The facts let the reader know what happened. The purpose of the memo is to evaluate the soundness of a particular legal position given certain facts. Therefore, present the facts objectively and include both favorable and unfavorable information. Include all the facts that you will raise in the discussion section.

5. The Discussion

The discussion section is the heart of the memo. In it you analyze the pertinent legal authorities and apply them to the facts of the problem. If there is more than one issue, address each issue separately. The discussion, like the facts, should be objective, not argumentative. Evaluate both helpful and damaging authorities. At the end of the discussion, summarize the findings presented by the memo.

§ 10.04. THE HALLMARKS OF A WELL-WRITTEN MEMO

The purpose of a memo is to inform and explain. If your memo bears the hallmarks enumerated below, it will achieve this dual purpose.

1. Thorough Research

Thoroughly research the question you are assigned. Evaluate the law you find within the context of the facts of your case. Find and analyze all of the pertinent legal authorities, those that are helpful to your case and those that are damaging, to it. Do not cite or rely on any authority without critically reading it yourself. Treatises and encyclopedias state the law only in general terms. Look up the cases on which they rely. Never rely on headnotes to cases. Remember that major decisions about the case will be made based on your memorandum, and that incomplete or inaccurate research will have far-reaching implications.

2. Good Judgment

Be certain that the memorandum you prepare is what the assigning attorney wants. When you are given the assignment, be sure you understand what purpose the memo is to serve, when it is to be submitted, and how detailed it should be. Also be certain that you understand the question that you are to research. Even if the initial instructions are clear, problems may arise later. As your research progresses, the issue may take on a different focus, unanticipated questions may arise, or additional facts may become important. Return to the assigning attorney and resolve these problems. But use good judgment. Do not trouble the attorney with questions you should be able to resolve yourself or with the help of one of your peers.

3. Objective Analysis

A memo must be objective. This is as crucial as it is simple. Your analysis of the legal authorities must be realistic and comprehensive. Examine your own arguments. Evaluate those you anticipate from opposing counsel. Consider the issues from every perspective. Honestly and thoroughly assess the strengths and weaknesses of your position. A memo is not the forum for persuasion, or for advocacy. Major choices and decisions will be made on the basis of the memo you write. Those choices and decisions can be made intelligently only on the basis of an objective memo. Indeed, the client's interests would not be served if the appraisal of his position were anything less than scrupulously realistic and objective.

4. Clear Writing Style

A memo is a complete and independent document. Another attorney who reads it should be able to fully understand the matter and make a decision. The memo memorializes, for all future readers of the file, the reasons those handling the case chose a particular course of action. By now you have read enough cases in your classes to appreciate the importance of writing style. Any poorly written legal document leads to confusion and uncertainty. A memo should be precise, accurate, and well-organized to explain a legal question effectively.

a. Good Organization

The foundation of a good memo is careful, detailed organization. The memo must be organized and written so that your thoughts are clearly presented and precisely stated. Skillful writing, thoughtful analysis, and clear presentation will be wasted unless your work is organized intelligently. The reader should not have to work at comprehending your discussion. No one reads memos for entertainment. Your legal analysis and your approach to the problem should be apparent from your organization. Make the reader's task as easy as possible.

As with other types of legal writing, memo writing requires a particular organizational framework. State your conclusions first. Follow them with your reasoning. Use mechanical aids such as headings and subheadings to help you organize the memo.

As we discussed in Chapter 6, outlining is a necessary organizational technique and one that will save you time. Outlining forces you to develop your analysis one step at a time and will expose the gaps in your discussion. Chapters 11, 12, 13, and 14 will instruct you in the principles of organization as they apply to each section of the memo.

b. Write for the Reader

Analyze and consider the problem and your memo in detail. Remember that your primary audience is the attorney who requested it. You are not writing for yourself.

Include all of the facts that you were given when you were assigned the problem. Do not assume that because the assigning attorney is familiar with the matter, he or she will remember exactly what you were told. You must include every fact you rely on in your analysis.

Explain the significance of the legal authorities in the context of the facts of the problem. Be certain that your concisions do not appear without the benefit of the analysis that preceded them. Your discussion must progress logically. Carefully and clearly guide the reader through the memo. One way to do this, as you learned in Chapter 7, is to provide the reader with a "roadmap," a guide to the discussion contained in the memo.

The memo is the end product of your exploration of the problem and its implications. Put yourself in the position of the person for whom you are writing the memo. Ask yourself whether your memo provides that person with a thoughtful analysis of the problem. Only when you are satisfied that the memo is complete, that it fully answers the question put to you, and that it is your best work, should you submit it.

c. Precision and Clarity

To communicate your thoughts effectively, you must be precise and clear. You have been asked to resolve a concrete problem. Make certain that you provide a concrete answer and specific reasons for it. Be precise about the facts and the law, but do not miss the forest for the trees. Make it clear why the authorities you rely on are relevant. Do not just tell the reader that they are pertinent. Show how those authorities apply to your case. Draw the conclusions yourself. When reading your memo, the reader should fully understand it and should be satisfied with your resolution of the problem.

5. Creativity

Your memo should present a comprehensive and organized analysis of the law in the context of the facts of your client's problem. On occasion, it might also display some legal creativity in regard to your recommendation for further action. When you are researching and writing the memo, be alert for alternative theories or creative approaches to the problem. Because you are the one who is most immersed in the issue and who is most aware of its permutations, you are the ideal person to provide a fresh perspective. Manifesting such creativity will demonstrate your initiative, even where your theory may ultimately not be workable.

6. Correct Citation Format

Your memo must include citations to the authorities on which you rely. Moreover, the cites must be complete, accurate, and in proper citation form. Correct citation form is important for at least two reasons. First, sloppy and incomplete citations give the reader cause to suspect that the substance of your analysis is equally weak. Second, if you include an inaccurate citation in the memo, you probably will copy that citation in subsequent documents that rely on the memo's research. Simply put, bad citations can haunt you and create an extremely negative impression of your work.

CHAPTER 11

The Memo: Heading, Issue, and Conclusion

As you learned in Chapter 10, the memo is a structured document that is divided into distinct sections. Each section has a label and performs a particular function. In Chapters 11, 12, 13, and 14, you will learn how to write each of these sections.

§ 11.01. THE HEADING

The heading uses the following format to set out the most basic information about the memo.

MEMORANDUM

To:	Leslie O'Brien-Wallace
FROM:	Michael R. North
DATE:	August 7, 2003
RE:	*Smith v. Lapp*; file no. 56432-007; Recovery for negligent infliction of emotional distress under Pennsylvania law.

The centered heading indicates that the document is a memorandum. "TO" indicates the person to whom the memorandum is addressed. "FROM" indicates who wrote the memorandum. Although practices vary from one office to the next, the recipient and the sender of the memo are usually referred to by their full names. Occasionally the tone is more formal and titles are used, for example, Ms./Miss/Mrs. O'Brien-Wallace and Mr. North. Do not include job titles such as senior partner or associate after the name of the recipient or sender.

"DATE" indicates the date you submitted the memo. Including the date is important. Any reader of the memo must be able to assume that the research and analysis contained in the memo are accurate and complete as of the date of the memo. The law, however, may have changed by the time you or another attorney next refer to the memo. The date will advise the reader whether the research requires updating.

"RE" indicates the subject matter of the memo. You may also see "SUBJECT" used instead of "RE." Include the case name, or the client name if no case is pending, and the office file number. Describe briefly and broadly the legal question the memo addresses. Because most case files contain a large number of documents, including numerous memoranda, this information will make it easy to locate a particular memorandum in the future. In addition, the explanation of the subject matter facilitates indexing and filing of the memorandum for general research purposes so that it may be used for future reference in other cases.

Suppose for purposes of illustration that you have just been called into the office of a more senior attorney and given the following facts.

> Wilbur Smith has retained the firm to file suit for injuries he sustained in an automobile accident. Mr. Smith also would like the firm to file suit on behalf of his fourteen-year-old daughter, Edna. Edna witnessed the automobile accident. The accident occurred on June 10, 2007. Mr. Smith had volunteered to take Edna to school. At 8:00 a.m. Mr. Smith dropped Edna off at school and drove away, intending to go to the grocery store. Edna waved good-bye to her uncle and turned to talk to some friends. As she was walking through the schoolyard with her friends, Edna heard a loud crash, followed by an explosion. When she turned to see what had happened, Edna saw that a car had collided with her father's car at an intersection one block away from the school. Her father's car was on fire. Edna ran to the scene of the accident. By the time she arrived, her father had been pulled from his car. Edna saw that her father had been severely burned and that he had a large gash on his forehead. Ever since the accident, Edna has suffered from recurring nightmares, a debilitating fear of automobiles, and chronic stomach problems. These conditions did not exist prior to the accident. An investigation of the accident disclosed that Mrs. Donna Lapp, the driver of the other car, had run a red light while intoxicated.

You have been asked to research whether, under these facts, Edna can make out a cause of action for negligent infliction of emotional distress under Pennsylvania law. The sample heading at the beginning of this section incorporates the information that would be required in the heading of the memo concerning this case.

Before writing the heading for your memo, review a few recent memos prepared by other attorneys in your office to determine the preferred style. You may find that there are minor variations from the format we describe.

§ 11.02. THE ISSUE

The memo begins with the issue section, also called the question presented. The issue section of the memo states the legal question presented in your case. Here is an example of an issue concerning the *Smith* case:

> Whether, under Pennsylvania law, a daughter who witnesses the aftermath of an automobile accident involving her father from a block away can recover for negligent infliction of emotional distress when she arrives at the scene and observes his severe injuries.

Here is another equally acceptable way to frame the issue:

> Under Pennsylvania law, can a daughter recover for negligent infliction of emotional distress if she is one block away when an automobile accident involving her father

occurs and, immediately after the accident, arrives at the scene and observes her father's severe injuries?

The issue section informs the reader of the scope of the memo. The scope of the memo should never exceed the scope of the issue. Frame the question precisely. Failure to do so will mislead the reader about the limits of your discussion and analysis.

Identifying the issue is the foundation of effective analysis. On some occasions, the attorney who requests the memo will identify the issue clearly for you. More often, you will be able to identify the precise issue only after you have thoroughly researched and thoughtfully analyzed the problem. For this reason, finalize your draft of the issue only after you have written the discussion section of the memo.

To frame an issue, you must do two things. First, identify the precise rule of law. Second, identify the key facts. Key facts are legally significant facts. Key facts are those facts that determine whether and how a particular rule of law applies to your situation. These facts are of crucial importance to the outcome of the case. Once you have fully researched the law within the context of your facts, you can determine which facts are key. Finally, after identifying the precise rule of law and the key facts, draft the issue to ask whether the rule of law applies under the particular facts of your case.

Consider the following examples of poorly phrased issues, and ask yourself what the writers have done incorrectly:

Whether a bystander to an accident can recover for negligent infliction of emotional distress under Pennsylvania law.

Whether a bystander at an automobile accident will be able to bring a tort action to recover for negligent infliction of emotional distress.

Whether, under current Pennsylvania law, a bystander at an automobile accident can successfully bring a tort action for negligent infliction of emotional distress.

Comment: Although the writers properly identified the ultimate legal question, they failed to include the key facts. The reader is left to wonder about the circumstances that prompted the question. The reader should understand the question without having to refer to the facts section. If you fail to include key facts, you will draft an abstract question, a question without context. The writers of two of the issues include a reference to Pennsylvania law. When possible, state the jurisdiction since the law may vary dramatically from one state to the next.

———

Whether a daughter who witnesses the aftermath of an accident involving her father will be able to state a cause of action for negligent infliction of emotional distress.

Comment: The writer of this issue omitted one very significant fact: the daughter's distance from the accident. The writer should also have included a reference to Pennsylvania law as the controlling jurisdiction.

———

Whether Edna can recover damages for negligent infliction of emotional distress as a result of witnessing an accident involving Mr. Smith.

Comment: When including the key facts in your issue, avoid identifying any of the people, places, or things in your case by proper name. Names may have no meaning to your reader because the facts section of your memo does not come until later. Even if you, the author of the memo, return to the file after the case has been dormant, you may not recall who all the players are. Instead of using proper names, use general categories to describe the people, places, or things in the issue.

———

The issue should consist of a concise, one-sentence question. The issue usually starts with "whether" and should call for a yes or no in response. The issue also may begin with an interrogative such as "is" or "can." Be certain that your issue is precise and complete. Do not, however, draft a question that is so complex, lengthy, and awkward that your reader cannot follow it. Ask yourself whether the rule of law is stated clearly and succinctly. Examine your facts and critically evaluate which are essential to the issue. Do not generalize because you will risk distorting the issue.

A memo can address several questions. The questions might be distinct or related and can consist of several individual questions or a question with subparts. Writing and rewriting the questions and their subparts often promotes a more thorough understanding of the problem. Generally, the more specifically the question is phrased, the more precisely it will be understood. Do not, however, divide the issue into so many questions and subquestions that the reader will become confused. Do not use a single subquestion. If the question is divided into subparts, there must be at least two subparts.

Do not forget that the memo is an informative document that realistically evaluates your client's position. Adopt an objective, nonpartisan tone. Even if a key fact is unfavorable to your client's position, you must include it. Do not draft a question to suggest a certain answer. Avoid advocacy in issue writing.

Here are two good examples of issue statements. They come from different cases:

Under the Pennsylvania Workers' Compensation Act, can an employee recover for injuries that he sustained in a personal fight with a coworker during working hours when, six months earlier, he had a work-related dispute with the same coworker?

Under New Jersey law, can the parents of a child born with Down's syndrome rely on the "discovery rule" or the "concealment exception" to bring an action for wrongful birth two years after the statute of limitations has run when:

A. before the birth, their physician stated that amniocentesis would detect any genetic defects in the fetus;

B. the mother underwent amniocentesis; and

C. after the birth, the physician stated that the amniocentesis had not detected Down's syndrome, even though he knew that the technician had made errors in performing the test and had arrived at an incorrect result?

These issues are well written. Both include the legal question and the facts that are key, according to the case law. The questions are precise and objective. They advise the reader of the scope and focus of the memo. As the samples demonstrate, there is no one correct way to draft an issue. Simply be certain that your issue contains all of the necessary elements, that you have framed it succinctly and accurately, and that you have made it comprehensible.

§ 11.03. THE CONCLUSION

The conclusion, sometimes called the brief answer or short answer, provides a short answer to each question that the issue section poses. In addition to answering the question, this section includes a concise statement of the reasoning that supports the conclusion. The conclusion section provides immediate answers to the questions that the memo raises.

The conclusion section immediately follows the issue section. For that reason, some attorneys begin with a direct response to each of the questions, such as "yes," "no," "probably," "probably not," and "maybe." Because few things in the law are ever absolutely clear, and because a noncommittal answer adds little to a well-written conclusion, we prefer memoranda without this type of response. Nevertheless, opinions and practices vary; therefore, be alert to the preferences of those for whom you are working.

In writing the conclusion section, accommodate the reader. In a memo discussing more than one issue, identify each conclusion with a number corresponding to the issue to which it refers. Be certain that each answer is self-contained. While each answer should contain a succinct explanation of the reasoning that supports your conclusion, do not discuss the details of your analysis. Do not include citations to cases, statutes, regulations, or other types of authority on which you rely. Only on the rare occasion when an authority is dispositive of the question, should you note it in the conclusion. Relegate all suppositions and hypotheses to the discussion section.

You may find it helpful to draft the conclusion after you have drafted the issue and written the discussion. Drafting these sections will force you to understand fully the reasons for your conclusion. Writing the conclusion is a two-step process. First, begin the conclusion by restating your issue as a declarative sentence. Second, add a brief explanation of the reasoning supporting your conclusion. The conclusion should be ten to fifteen lines.

Consider again the facts of the Smith matter, the illustrative case for this chapter. Then, please review the following sample conclusions from student memoranda.

Under Pennsylvania law, a daughter will be able to recover damages for negligent infliction of emotional distress if the emotional distress was foreseeable to the defendant. The factors determining foreseeability include: (1) whether the plaintiff was near the scene of the accident, (2) whether the shock resulted from the direct emotional impact upon the plaintiff from the sensory and contemporaneous observance of the accident, and (3) whether the plaintiff and the victim were closely related.

Comment: The writer has done only part of the job. This conclusion sets out the elements of the test that a plaintiff must meet to recover. The recitation of the law is correct. The conclusion, however, fails to answer the question.

———

A Pennsylvania court would hold that the bystander at the automobile accident could recover for negligent infliction of emotional distress because such emotional distress was reasonably foreseeable.

Comment: Strictly speaking, the writer has answered the question and provided a succinct explanation of the reason for the answer. The conclusion, however, lacks key facts. When the issue is devoid of key facts, the conclusion is often similarly defective. Key facts are as critical to a conclusion as they are to an issue. While you need not reiterate every key fact in your conclusion, include enough facts to give the conclusion context and meaning. Legal conclusions are based on interpretations of facts in the context of the applicable law.

———

Edna will be allowed to recover for her emotional distress because of her close proximity to the accident, her shock as a result of the perception of the accident, and her relationship with Mr. Smith.

Comment: The writer has answered the question and summarized the reasons for it. The writer's use of proper names, however, deprives the reader of the ability to identify the players and their roles.

A daughter bystander can recover for negligent infliction of emotional distress because the emotional distress was reasonably foreseeable to the defendant. Pennsylvania, in *Sinn v. Burd*, 486 Pa. 146, 404 A.2d 672 (1979), adopted a three-step test to evaluate whether the emotional distress was foreseeable: (1) whether the plaintiff stood near the scene of the accident, (2) whether the emotional impact and distress followed sensory observance of the accident, and (3) whether the plaintiff and the victim were closely related. The daughter stood only one block from the accident. The daughter saw her father immediately before the event, heard the event, and saw the scene and her father immediately after the event. The father/daughter relationship is a close relationship. All elements of the test are therefore satisfied and a claim for negligent infliction of emotional distress is made out.

Comment: In the conclusion, do not set out the governing standard, or the applicable law, in such detail. Do not apply the law to your facts. Application in the conclusion section is usually ineffective because it is too general. It can be misleading because it is usually incomplete. If the attorney reading the conclusion develops a misimpression, you are responsible. Do not condense your analysis. The discussion section should be the sole source of analysis. Provide only the answer and a brief statement of your reasoning. This conclusion is too long given the nature of the question. Moreover, citations to authority are improper in the conclusion.

Here are two good conclusions:

(1) A Pennsylvania court would allow a daughter who witnessed an automobile accident involving her father from one block away to recover for negligent infliction of emotional distress because: (1) she was near the location of the accident, (2) her shock was a result of her direct sensory perception of the accident, and (3) she is closely related to the victim.

(2) A Pennsylvania court would permit a daughter who heard a car accident involving her father from a block away and who then immediately witnessed his severe injuries to recover for negligent infliction of emotional distress.

As with the issue, there is no one correct way to write a conclusion. Be certain that you answer the question and that you provide a brief statement of the reasoning that supports that answer, as the writers of the above two samples have done.

Writing good conclusions and issues is difficult. If you follow the principles that have been discussed, review the sample memoranda in Appendix I, and practice by writing and rewriting your conclusions and issues, you will soon master the task.

Practice with Drafting Memos: Headings, Issues, and Conclusions

In this chapter, we offer you four exercises to help you learn how to draft the initial parts of an interoffice memo. The exercises should help you develop attention to formalities and precision in writing and thinking.

§ 12.01. EXERCISE I

Suppose a more senior attorney, Dewey D. Delaney, has called you into his office and told you the following:

The Firm has recently been retained by Jack Montagne to file suit against Asten Lift Company, Ltd. ("Asten"), a manufacturer of double and triple chair ski lifts based in Colorado. The file number is 98876-001. The basis of the suit he seeks to bring is an accident that occurred on Devil's Mountain, located in Pennsylvania. The accident involved his stepsister, Monica Gordon, who was thrown out of a triple chair lift and killed when a cable broke. Due to the circumstances of the accident, I think we might be able to state a cause of action for negligent infliction of emotional distress.

The facts of the case as I understand them are as follows. Jack, who is apparently an avid skier, took a ski vacation last winter with his stepsister, Monica. The two went to Devil's Mountain, as I said, where they rented a chalet for two weeks. Every morning they would have a quick breakfast, step outside, snap on their skis and ski the one hundred yards to the base of the mountain and the Diamond Triple Chair Lift, which would take them to the midpoint of the mountain. From there they would ride the Devil Triple Chair Lift (the "Devil Chair") to the peak. Once at the peak, they would separate, Jack to ski the wide open "bowls" on the back of the mountain and Monica to ski the trails on the face of the mountain. However, they had a standing agreement to meet for lunch at one o'clock at Tipler's, the restaurant at the top of the Devil Chair. They had consistently followed this schedule for seven days, and would not have deviated from it on the eighth day but for the accident.

On the day of the accident, Jack was standing near the top of the Devil Chair waiting for Monica and enjoying the sunshine. It was 12:50 p.m. Waiting for her there had become his habit. Ever since their first day on the mountain she had timed her skiing so that her last run before lunch was down Go Devil, the trail which wound back and forth under the Devil Chair, and ended at the midpoint. A run down Go Devil would take approximately half an hour. Then she would take the Devil Chair back to the top and Tipler's, a ride that took approximately twenty-five minutes. Jack had met her at the top of the chairlift every day, and she had consistently arrived within five minutes of the appointed time. Jack had been scanning the skiers as they came into view for about five minutes when he heard a loud noise that sounded like a large branch breaking off of a tree. The lift slowed to a stop and the chairs rolled back approximately 25 feet. Then, as Jack and those around him watched in horror, a wave raced up the cable, abruptly pulling the chairs ten or twelve feet up into the air and dropping them again just as suddenly. The chairs had no safety bar and Jack, who could see approximately ten percent of the chairs from his vantage point, saw people hurled out of their chairs and to the ground, which he knew was at times a 35 foot drop. Some skiers were miraculously able to hold on and remain in the chairs.

Jack could think only of Monica, who he knew had been riding the lift but who might now be lying injured or dead on the mountain. Jack started down the mountain, frantically seeking Monica in her polka-dotted ski jacket. Other skiers and the ski patrol were rushing to help those who had been thrown to the ground. Screams and moans filled the air and while some skiers writhed in pain, others seemed not to move at all. Dark blotches of blood stained the snow.

When he had gone approximately one hundred yards down the mountain, Jack still had not seen his stepsister and the trail wound away from the lift. He was almost frantic with fear and worry. Abandoning the trail to continue his search, Jack skied down directly under the chair. As he made his way through the crunchy snow and around the rocks, Jack reassured the skiers lying on the ground and those clinging to the chairs that help was en route, but he did not stop. Then he saw her. She lay on the ground, perfectly still, near a large rock. Jack took off his skis and made his way to her side. She made no sound. As he held her, he saw the gash and the blood caked to the back of her head. Her pulse was weak and irregular. Jack covered her with his jacket. Within ten minutes help arrived, and Monica was taken down to the base of the mountain in a stretcher. Jack never left her side. Within minutes of reaching the makeshift emergency center she died of head injuries sustained in the fall. She had never regained consciousness. Less than four minutes had passed from the moment Jack witnessed the skiers being thrown from their chairs and the moment he reached Monica.

Since the accident, Jack has had recurring nightmares, has suffered severe depression, and has experienced significant weight loss. He has been under continuing medical supervision for these conditions, none of which afflicted him prior to the accident.

Jack and Monica had been close since his mother and her father were married when he was 16 and she was 15. Both were only children who had longed for a sibling. At the time of the accident, both were in graduate school in Philadelphia. They talked often and met regularly for meals. Ever since Monica's father had died three years ago, and Jack's mother six months later, the two had taken a skiing vacation around Christmas and New Years so that they could spend the holidays together.

Suppose you are to prepare a memo on whether Jack Montagne could successfully state a cause of action for negligent infliction of emotional distress.

1. Write the heading of the memo.
2. Review the material in Chapter 11 on the Smith case, the illustrative case in this chapter, and:
   a. identify the key facts in the Montagne case;
   b. write the issue as it would appear in the memo;
   c. write the conclusion as it would appear in the memo.

§ 12.02. EXERCISE II

Patricia Brennan, your supervising attorney, has written you this note, which tells you about one of her cases (file no. 1945-9) and asks you to draft some sections of a memo:

We are representing the Jefferson City Transit Authority, which is the defendant in a false imprisonment case. I need your help in drafting an interoffice memo on a particular issue in the case. I will use the memo in discussing the case with other lawyers in our firm. I also will use it in preparing my arguments.

Here are the facts. June 20 of this year was the last day of school for the term at Hamilton Junior High. At the end of the day, a large group of students from that school boarded a bus owned by our client and driven by its employee, William Duer. One of the student-passengers was 15-year-old Jack Jay. On that day, the students were in exuberant and ultimately unruly. A number of students broke windows, ceiling panels, advertising poster frames, and dome lights. At this point, we do not know if Jack Jay was one of the vandals.

After several unsuccessful attempts to establish order on the bus, Duer stopped the bus, inspected the damage, and announced that he was taking the students to the local police station. He then resumed driving and bypassed several normal stops on the way to his announced destination. As he turned one corner, several students jumped out of a side window at the rear of the bus. As he turned the next corner (New York Road and Federalist Avenue), Jay positioned himself to jump out the window. However, as the bus turned, the right rear wheels hit the curb, and Jay either jumped or fell to the street. The right rear wheels then rolled over Jay's midsection and caused him serious injuries.

Jay and his father John have begun a legal action in the state of Madison to recover damages for false imprisonment. As you know, in our jurisdiction, to succeed in a claim for false imprisonment, the plaintiff must prove that (1) the defendant intended to confine the plaintiff, (2) the plaintiff was conscious of the confinement, (3) the plaintiff did not consent to the confinement, and (4) the confinement was not otherwise privileged. I plan on a defense of justification: a restraint or detention is not unlawful if it is reasonable under the circumstances and in time and manner, and is imposed for the purpose of preventing another from inflicting personal injuries or interfering with property in one's lawful possession or custody or damaging that property.

Jack Jay is seeking damages for mental anguish and bodily injuries. His father is seeking damages for loss of services and medical expenses.

Even if the court or jury rejects the defense of justification and find that there was false imprisonment, we still may have a defense against damage awards. Even if a person is falsely imprisoned, that person still has a duty to use reasonable care in trying to extricate himself or herself from the unlawful detention. Here, we will argue that Jack Jay placed himself in an unreasonably perilous position when he tried to leave a moving vehicle by placing himself in the bus window.

I would like your help in getting started on one of the memos for this case, the memo concluding that even if there is false imprisonment, no damages should be awarded. Please limit your work on this memo to the issue of defense against damages in the case of false imprisonment. Other memos will deal with other issues.

I would like you to draft the three initial parts of the memo: the heading, the issue, and the conclusion.

§ 12.03. EXERCISE III

Patricia Brennan, your supervising attorney is pleased with your work on the memo concerning the ability to Jack Jackson to recover damages for false imprisonment. She is so pleased that she gives you another assignment. Here is her note to you:

> Thanks so much for your work on the Jay case. Now I need more help. I asked another associate to draft the beginning of a memo on another aspect of the case: whether justification would be a successful defense to false imprisonment under the facts of this case. At this point, I am assuming that the memo will conclude that justification would be a successful defense here. I was not pleased with what I received. Here is a copy of the heading, issue and conclusion. I would be appreciative if you would revise them. I do not want to create a conflict between you and the associate, so please leave his name on it as author and do not include your name. I will make sure you get credit for the work. Here is the draft:
>
> FROM: Mike Smith
>
> TO: Patti
>
> DATE: (Supply the date you completed revising this memo.)
>
> RE: *Jay v. Jefferson City Transit Authority*; file no. 1945-9; Justification Defense to False Imprisonment

ISSUE:

Under the law of the State of Madison, can Jack sue for false imprisonment when he jumped out of the school bus window after the bus driver started driving the school bus to the police station when the students started acting up?

CONCLUSION:

When students on the school bus are acting up and breaking things, the bus driver has the right to turn them over to the police. This defense is called justification, and it is a good defense against false imprisonment.

§ 12.04. EXERCISE IV

Laura Johann, the mid-level associate who supervises you, has e-mailed you the following memo:

Hi. I hope you can give me a hand on a difficult case. Let me start by asking you to read this memo from our client, Attorney Kathy Clare:

> In early December, William Silton telephoned me at my office and told me that he was suffering from cancer and wanted to write a will that would pass his estate to his brother Jack. He said that he was estranged from his other brother Jim and wanted to make sure that none of his estate would go to Jim. At no time did Mr. Silton tell me that he was in immediate danger of dying or that he wanted to execute the will by a certain date.
>
> On January 15, I mailed the will and related documents to Mr. Silton. A few days later, I learned that Mr. Silton had been injured in a car accident and was now in a nursing home. The documents reached him on January 23. On January 25, I was informed that Mr. Silton was in a rapidly deteriorating condition and was anxious to sign the will. I brought the will to Mr. Silton on February 1. Mr. Silton reiterated his testamentary intent. However, he wanted to change the contingent beneficiary. In other words, in case his brother Jack predeceased him, he wanted his estate to go a charity as the contingent beneficiary. He had changed his mind on which charity to designate. I told Mr. Silton that I would revise the will and get back to him.
>
> On February 4, I returned to the nursing home with the revised will. When I spoke with Mr. Silton, I determined that he lacked the competence to sign the will and returned to my office. On February 16, Mr. Silton died. Because he died without a will, his estate passed to his heirs according to this state's intestacy statute. Thus, his two brothers (including Jim) and a nephew each gained a share of his estate.

Now, Jack Silton is suing Kathy for malpractice. He claims she was negligent in failing to have Mr. Silton sign the will promptly and to advise him on February 1 of the risk of dying without a will if he did not sign the document as drafted at that meeting. Thus, he argues that Kathy had a duty to insure that the will was executed promptly under the circumstances, that the duty extended to him as the intended beneficiary, and that the breach of that duty injured him financially.

The estate involved here is quite large, and, therefore, this is a big case. My partner asked me to draft an in-house memo on the primary legal issue. I am having trouble drafting the issue. I wonder if you could give me a hand by suggesting a well-phrased issue. I really appreciate your help.

How would you draft the issue?

CHAPTER 13

The Memo: Facts and Discussion

§ 13.01. FACTS

When you receive an assignment to write a memo, either the attorney tells you the facts of the case or you go through the case file to get the facts. Once you know the facts, you must determine which of those facts belong in the memo's facts section. Include only those facts that affect the outcome of your analysis, and enough background facts to allow the reader to understand the analytically significant facts.

To determine which facts are analytically significant, research the relevant legal authority. As you read the cases, identify the facts upon which the courts rely in reaching their holdings. After you complete your research, determine which facts in your case are analogous to the important facts in the decided cases. Also determine which of your facts are distinguishable from important facts in adverse holdings. Include those facts in the facts section. Include the facts even if you think the reader knows them.

The facts section must be objective. Include facts that are both favorable and unfavorable to your case. Just as you analyze adverse case law in the discussion section, you must include unfavorable facts in the facts section.

Organize the facts section logically so that the reader understands what happened. The most logical organization is a chronological organization. A chronological organization is also an objective organization because it emphasizes no one fact or set of facts.

Make the facts section clear, concise, and complete. After you write the facts section, read it again and streamline it by eliminating all unnecessary facts. Do not make your reader hunt through the facts section to find the relevant facts. At the same time, make certain you have included all relevant facts. If you discuss a fact in the discussion section of your memo, it should also appear in the facts section.

Here is an example of how to write a facts section. In order to write a facts section, you must get the facts from the client and analyze those facts in light of the relevant legal authority.

Here are all of the facts provided by the client:

On June 10, 2007, Edna Smith witnessed an automobile accident in which her father, Wilbur Smith, was injured. Edna suffered and has continued to suffer emotional distress as a result of witnessing that accident.

On the day of the accident, Mr. Smith drove Edna to school. Edna's mother usually drove her to school, but her mother was sick. Edna attended Central High School and was a ninth grader.

Mr. Smith drove a 1991 Honda Civic. He was a good driver and had never received any speeding tickets.

Mr. Smith dropped Edna off at school at 8:00 a.m. and drove away to get some groceries for Edna's mother. Edna waved good-bye and turned, to talk to her friends, Gertrude Jones and Florence Kramer.

Shortly thereafter, Edna heard a loud crash. She turned around and saw that a car had crashed into her father's car in an intersection located one block from the school. Her father's car was on fire.

By the time she arrived at the accident, her father had been pulled from the burning car. She saw that he was severely burned and had a large gash on his forehead.

Mrs. Donna Lapp was the driver of the car that hit Mr. Smith. She was intoxicated at the time of the accident and ran a red light.

Edna now suffers from recurring nightmares, a debilitating fear of automobiles and chronic stomach problems. None of these conditions existed prior to the accident.

Here is a synopsis of the governing case law:

1. *Sinn v. Burd,* 486 Pa. 146, 404 A.2d 672 (1979).

In *Sinn,* the court held that a bystander at an automobile accident has a valid cause of action for negligent infliction of emotional distress if the injury to the bystander is reasonably foreseeable to the defendant. The court formulated a three-part foreseeability test to determine whether the bystander's injury was reasonably foreseeable:

a. whether the bystander was located near the scene of the accident,
b. whether the shock resulted from a direct emotional impact upon the bystander from sensory and contemporaneous observance of the accident, as contrasted with learning of the accident from others after its occurrence, and
c. whether the bystander and the victim were closely related.

2. *Anfuso v. Smith,* 15 Pa. D. & C.3d 389 (Northampton Co. 1980).

In *Anfuso,* the court held that a mother, who was inside her home when she heard a car accident occur outside and rushed out to see her daughter injured in the accident, could recover for negligent infliction of emotional distress. The court applied the *Sinn v. Burd* three-part test to determine whether the mother's injury was foreseeable. The court found that the first part of the test was satisfied because the mother was sufficiently near the scene of the accident even though she was inside her house and the accident occurred on the street. The court further found that the second part of the test was satisfied because the mother heard the accident happen and then ran out and witnessed her daughter's injuries. The mother, therefore, had a sensory and contemporaneous observance of the event rather than learning about it from others. Finally, the court found that the third part of the test was satisfied because a mother-daughter relationship is a sufficiently close relationship.

3. *Brooks v. Decker*, 512 Pa. 365, 516 A.2d 1380 (1986).

In *Brooks*, the court held that a father did not have a valid cause of action for negligent infliction of emotional distress because he did not witness the car accident in which his son was injured, nor did he hear the accident. Instead, he merely saw his injured son lying on the ground after the accident occurred.

4. *Bliss v. Allentown Public Library*, 497 F. Supp. 487 (E.D. Pa. 1980).

In *Bliss*, the court held that a mother who heard a metal sculpture fall on her child but did not see it fall had a sensory and contemporaneous observance of the event. The mother thus satisfied the second part of the *Sinn v. Burd* test to recover for negligent infliction of emotional distress.

5. *Blanyar v. Pagnotti Enters.*, 451 Pa. Super. 269 (1996).

In *Blanyar*, the court held that a cousin could not recover for negligent infliction of emotional distress after watching his cousin drown since the cousin was not a member of the victim's immediate family.

6. *Mazzagatti v. Everingham*, 512 Pa. 266, 516 A.2d 672 (1986).

In *Mazzagatti*, the court held that a mother could not recover for negligent infliction of emotional distress after learning about the accident from another person through a telephone call. The court recognized that the prior knowledge serves as a buffer against the mother observing the full impact of the accident.

MODEL FACTS SECTION

On June 10, 2007, Edna Smith's father, Wilbur Smith, drove her to school. He dropped her off at the school at 8:00 a.m. and then drove away. Edna turned to talk to some friends.

At an intersection located one block from the school, Donna Lapp, the defendant, ran a red light and crashed into Mr. Smith's car. Edna did not see the accident occur, but she heard it. Edna turned around and saw the accident scene. She could see that her father's car was on fire.

By the time she arrived at the accident, her father had been pulled from the burning car. She saw that he was severely burned and had a large gash on his forehead.

Edna now suffers from recurring nightmares, a debilitating fear of automobiles, and chronic stomach problems. None of these conditions existed prior to the accident.

In the above example, the writer included only the facts that are relevant under the applicable case law and enough background facts so that the reader can understand what happened to Edna. For example, since distance from the accident is an important factor under *Sinn v. Burd,* the writer described Edna's distance from the accident. The writer eliminated extraneous facts, such as the year of the car Mr. Smith was driving and the names of Edna's friends. The writer included all of the unfavorable facts, such as the fact that Edna did not see the accident. Finally, the writer organized the facts clearly and logically by stating them in chronological order.

Here is an example of a bad facts section. Compare it with the model facts section.

> Edna Smith suffers from severe emotional distress as a result of witnessing an automobile accident. The accident was the fault of Donna Lapp. In the accident, Edna's father, Wilbur Smith, was horribly injured and he almost died.
>
> The accident occurred on June 10, 2007. Edna's father drove her to school. He dropped her off at school at 8:00 a.m. and drove away.
>
> Donna Lapp, the defendant, ran a red light and slammed into Mr. Smith's car. His car exploded, and Edna heard the explosion. Edna saw his car enveloped in flames. Edna also saw his severely burned body and the large gash on his forehead that was spurting blood.
>
> Edna now suffers from horrible, recurring nightmares, she is terrified of cars, and she has excruciating stomach pain. Donna Lapp negligently caused Edna's injuries.

The above example of a facts section is poorly written because it is not objective. The writer left out adverse facts, such as Edna's distance from the accident. In addition, the writer used value-laden words, such as "horrible" and "excruciating" to describe Edna's and her father's injuries.

The writer also made legal conclusions, instead of just stating facts. For example, the writer stated that the defendant negligently caused Edna's injuries. Moreover, the writer did not organize the facts clearly and logically.

§ 13.02. DISCUSSION

The discussion section is composed of legal arguments resolving the issues and sub-issues. Use the methods for writing legal arguments you learned in Chapter 5:

1. Use deductive reasoning.
2. Apply the law to the facts.
3. Make analogies.
4. Make policy and equity arguments.

Ideally, you want to use all of these types of arguments in the discussion section. Circumstances may limit the types of arguments available to you or may dictate that you emphasize one form of argument over another.

Divide the discussion into sections that correspond to the issues and sub-issues. In each section, discuss the law applicable to the issue or sub-issue, and apply it to the facts that are relevant to the issue or sub-issue. Remember that all the facts to which you refer in the discussion should be in the facts section of your memo.

Write the discussion clearly and logically. As we suggested in Chapter 7, give your reader a roadmap paragraph at the beginning of the discussion, including a statement of your ultimate conclusion. As noted previously, readers of legal prose are not looking for suspense, they are looking for explanations. Explain the organization of the discussion so the reader can follow it easily.

The discussion section must be objective. Include both favorable and unfavorable facts and legal authority. Discuss arguments in favor of your client first, and then potential counterarguments. If you can, distinguish cases that are unfavorable to your client's position.

Be objective, but think strategically. If any argument supports your client's position, discuss that argument. The senior attorney who assigned the memo wants you to find a way for your client to win. Do not, however, misrepresent the strength of your client's position. The reader relies on your research and analysis. If your client is going to lose, do not assert that the client will win. You do not want a senior attorney to take the wrong action for a client. It will come back to haunt you.

Remember to come to conclusions and make recommendations. Do not simply present the information and force the reader to reproduce your analysis. At the end of the discussion section, summarize all the conclusions you reached and recommend actions the reader can take. The conclusion at the end of the discussion should be brief but may offer more detail than the conclusion section of your memo.

Here is an example of how to write a discussion. The example is drawn from the case discussed in Chapter 11 and in the first section of this chapter.

Edna Smith has a valid cause of action for negligent infliction of emotional distress. In *Sinn v. Burd*, the court held that a bystander at an automobile accident has a valid cause of action for negligent infliction of emotional distress if the injury to the bystander is reasonably foreseeable to the defendant. 486 Pa. 146, 173, 404 A.2d 672, 686 (1979). The court formulated a three-part test to determine whether the bystander's injury was reasonably foreseeable:

1. whether the bystander was located near the scene of the accident;
2. whether the injury resulted from a direct emotional impact upon the bystander from sensory and contemporaneous observance of the accident, as contrasted with learning of the accident from others after its occurrence; and
3. whether the bystander and the victim were closely related.

Id. at 170-171, 404 A.2d at 685. The present case meets all three parts of the *Sinn v. Burd* test. Each part of the test is discussed separately below.

A. *Distance from the Scene of the Accident*

The issue in Edna's case is whether someone standing one block from the scene of the accident is located near the scene of the accident. The decided cases suggest that one block is close enough to meet the test.

In *Sinn*, the court held that a mother who witnessed an accident on the street from the front door of her house was located near the scene of the accident. *Id.* at 173,

404 A.2d at 686. Similarly, in *Anfuso v. Smith,* the court held that a mother who was inside her home when she heard an accident occur on the street was located near the scene of the accident. 15 Pa. D. & C.3d 389, 393 (Northampton Co. 1980). In *Bliss v. Allentown Public Library,* the court held that a mother who was twenty-five feet away from her child when she heard a metal sculpture fall on him was located near the scene of the accident. 497 F. Supp. 487, 489 (E.D. Pa. 1980).

In *Sinn, Anfuso,* and *Bliss,* the bystanders were close enough to the accident to see it happen or to see its aftermath. None of the cases required the bystander to be standing at the accident site in order to be located near the scene of the accident. In the present case, Edna was close enough to the scene of the accident that she could see its aftermath. Accordingly, Edna was located near the scene of the accident, and the first part of the test has been met.

B. Direct Emotional Impact

The issue here is whether someone who heard an accident rather than saw it had a sensory and contemporaneous observance of the accident. Edna's emotional distress was a direct result of hearing the accident as it occurred and, therefore, the relevant case law supports the conclusion that the second part of the *Sinn v. Burd* test has been met.

In *Bliss,* the court held that a mother who heard a metal sculpture fall on her child but did not see it fall had a sensory and contemporaneous observance of the event. *Id.* at 489. The court stated that it would not deny a suit simply because of the position of the plaintiff's eyes at the split second the accident occurred. *Id.* The court found that the entire incident produced the emotional distress the plaintiff suffered. *Id.* Similarly, the *Anfuso* court held that a mother who heard a car accident while inside her home and rushed out to see her daughter injured in the accident had a sensory and contemporaneous observance of the event. 15 Pa. D. & C.3d at 393.

The facts of the present case are similar to the facts of *Bliss* and *Anfuso.* Edna heard the accident and then turned and saw its aftermath. Her emotional distress resulted from a direct emotional impact on her from both hearing the accident and seeing its aftermath. Her observance of the accident was both sensory (hearing and sight) and contemporaneous (she heard it as it happened and then turned and saw its after-math). Therefore, the second part of the *Sinn* test has been met.

The present case is distinguishable from *Brooks v. Decker,* 512 Pa. 365, 516 A.2d 1380 (1986). There, the court held that a father did not have a valid cause of action for negligent infliction of emotional distress. *Id.* at 365, 516 A.2d at 1383. In *Brooks,* the father did not hear or see the car accident in which his son was injured. *Id.* at 367, 516 A.2d at 1381. Instead, he followed an ambulance, which passed him. *Id.* On arriving at the scene, the father saw his injured son lying on the ground. *Id.* The court found that he did not have a valid cause of action because he did not hear or see the accident as it occurred. *Id.* at 365, 516 A.2d at 1383. Moreover, the present case is distinguishable from *Mazzagatti v. Everingham* because there the court held that a mother who learned of an accident from a telephone call was not directly impacted by the accident and could not recover damages. 512 Pa. 266, 269, 516 A.2d 672, 674.

In the present case, however, Edna heard the accident occur. She did not learn that an accident had occurred by seeing an ambulance nor did she learn about the accident from another person. Therefore, the holdings in both *Brooks and Mazzagatti* are inapplicable to the present case.

C. Close Relationship

The final issue is whether a father-daughter relationship is a sufficiently close relationship to satisfy the third part of the test. Relevant decisions suggest that Edna and her father are closely enough related to meet the third part of the *Sinn v. Burd* test, although none of the cases involved a directly analogous relationship.

In *Sinn,* the court held that mother-child relationship was a sufficiently close relationship to satisfy the third part of the test. 486 Pa. at 173, 404 A.2d at 686. In *Anfuso,* the court held that a mother-child relationship and a sibling relationship were sufficiently close relationships to satisfy the third part of the test. 15 Pa. D. & C.3d at 391.

In *Sinn* and *Anfuso,* the courts held that the two types of blood relatives satisfied the third part of the test. Edna and her father are blood relatives. Parents, children, and siblings are immediate family members. However, since none of these courts suggest that immediate family members cannot satisfy the third part of the test, we should argue that a father-daughter relationship is sufficiently close.

The present case is consistent with *Blanyar v. Pagnotti Enters.,* 451 Pa. Super. 269 (1996). There the court recognized that only immediate family members can recover for negligent infliction of emotional distress.

In the present case, Edna is Mr. Smith's daughter. Therefore, the holding in *Blanyar* supports Edna's claim.

D. Conclusion

Edna Smith has a valid cause of action for negligent infliction of emotional distress. Edna was located near the scene of the accident, her injury was a result of a direct emotional impact from sensory and contemporaneous observance of her father's accident, and Edna and her father are closely related. Since all three parts of the *Sinn* test have been met, the firm should file suit on Edna's behalf.

In the above example, the writer divided the discussion into sub-issues that correspond to the three parts of the *Sinn* test. In each section, the writer discussed the law applicable to the specific part of the test and applied that law to the facts relevant to that part of the test. All of the facts referred to in the discussion came from the facts section example in the first part of this chapter.

At the beginning of the discussion, the writer provided a roadmap for the sections discussing the individual parts of the test. The writer gave conclusions at the beginning of each section and summarized those conclusions at the end of the discussions. The writer also recommended an action for the reader to take—to file suit.

Finally, the writer discussed unfavorable facts and cases. In addition, the writer distinguished an unfavorable case, *Brooks v. Decker.*

Now that you have seen an example of a well-constructed discussion section, the next segment of this chapter offers some tips on how to avoid mistakes that students and young lawyers commonly make when writing legal memoranda.

§ 13.03. MAKE YOUR REASONING READILY APPARENT

"Ambiguous" is a word that writing instructors often write on first-year law students' papers. The student will often respond by pointing out the intended meaning, perhaps not even seeing the alternate meaning that made the expression ambiguous to the reader.

Always put yourself in your reader's shoes. Assume your reader knows nothing about the subject, and strive for a self-contained document that treats your subject thoroughly. Your reader should have no trouble understanding your reasoning in applying the law to the case at hand.

1. Avoid the "Digest" Approach

A writer who uses the digest approach recites a series of mini-briefs of cases and fails to integrate the law and the facts.

In the following example of the "digest" approach, the writer "recites" the law but does not apply it.

> Article 2, § 8, of New York State's Bill of Rights (McKinney 2006) reiterates the "right of the people . . . against unreasonable searches and seizures" provided by the Fourth Amendment to the United States Constitution. "Searches conducted outside the judicial process, without prior approval by judge or magistrate, are *per se* unreasonable under the fourth amendment . . . subject only to a few specifically established and well-delineated exceptions." *Katz v. United States*, 389 U.S. 347 (1967).
>
> The application of the "plain view doctrine" is contingent upon a showing by the state that the officer's vantage point is a place in which it is lawful for that officer to be. *Ker v. California*, 374 U.S. 23 (1963).

The court sets forth the guidelines that govern the application of the "emergency" exception to the warrant requirement in *People v. Mitchell*, 39 N.Y.2d 173, 347 N.E.2d 607, *cert, denied*, 426 U.S. 953 (1976), as follows:

(1) The police must have reasonable grounds to believe that there is an emergency at hand and an immediate need for their assistance for the protection of life or property.

(2) The search must not be motivated primarily by intent to arrest and seize evidence.

(3) There must be some reasonable basis approximating probable cause to associate the emergency with the area or place to be searched.

Id. at 176, 347 N.E.2d 177–78.

In *People v. Gallmon*, 19 N.Y.2d 389, 280 N.Y.S.2d 356 (1967), the police officer's entry without obtaining a warrant was justified by his obligation to assist people in distress.

> Under the "fruit of the poisonous tree doctrine" the government cannot use information obtained during an illegal search. *Wong Sun v. United States*, 371 U.S. 471 (1963); *Silverthrone Lumber Co. v. United States*, 251 U.S. 385 (1920).

In this example, the writer has included several paragraphs about the law, but the reader still knows nothing about the case at hand. Each time a rule is articulated, the rule should be applied to the facts of the case being discussed, using the previously decided cases to explain the application.

2. Avoid the "Historical Development of the Law" Approach

The "historical development of the law" approach, as it implies, goes through the history of the law, often needlessly. Sometimes it is necessary to give some history of the development of a rule—but not often. This approach is often appropriate in a law review article but has limited usefulness in a legal memorandum or brief. The reader—whether a lawyer, a judge, or a client— usually will care little about where the law came from or what led to its development, but will want to see what the law is and how it applies to the current situation.

Here is an example of the "historical development of the law" approach:

At common law, an action for wrongful death did not exist. Nevertheless, the Ohio General Assembly recognized such an action in title 21, section 25.01, of the Ohio Rev. Code Ann. § 2125.01. *Werling v. Sancy*, 17 Ohio St. 3d 45, 46, 476 N.E.2d 1053, 1054 (1985).

Section 2125.01 provides as follows:

When the death of a person is caused by wrongful act, neglect, or default which would have entitled the party injured to maintain an action and recover damages if death had not ensued, the person who would have been liable if death had not ensued ... shall be liable to an action for damages, notwithstanding the death of the person injured. ...

Ohio Rev. Code Ann. § 2125.01.

Since § 2125.01 refers only to a "person," a key question is whether a viable, unborn child is a "person" within the meaning of § 2125.01. *Werling*, 17 Ohio St. 3d at 46, 476 N.E.2d at 1054.

The most recent case involving an action for wrongful death under § 2125.01 where the decedent is a stillborn fetus is *Werling v. Sancy*, 17 Ohio St. 3d 45, 476 N.E.2d 1053 (1985). In *Werling*, the Supreme Court of Ohio reaffirmed the position of the Court of Appeals for Madison County in *Stidam v. Ashmore*, 109 Ohio App. 431, 167 N.E.2d 106 (1959). The Supreme Court held in *Werling* that a viable fetus that is negligently injured in its mother's womb and subsequently stillborn may be the basis for a wrongful death action pursuant to § 2125.01. *Werling*, 17 Ohio St. 3d at 49, 476 N.E.2d at 1054.

Notice that you have read several paragraphs and still know nothing about the case the writer is discussing. You cannot even be sure of the specific issue being discussed. Unless it is actually relevant to your discussion to explain how the rule got to its present form, simply state the rule and begin your discussion at that point.

3. Avoid the Use of Too Many Quotations from Legal Authorities

Many court opinions contain numerous quotations from other cases, legal periodicals, and treatises. It is easier and faster to quote from authorities than to paraphrase them, so some writers tend to use many quotations.

Too many quotations distract the reader, and often the quotations themselves are not clear. A frequent flaw in legal writing is overuse of the "block quote," the indented, single-spaced quote. Many judges, attorneys, and students tend to skip over them. Avoid overuse of block quotes in particular, and avoid overuse of all quotations. Here is an example from a student memo:

> Mr. Walker has a valid cause of action for false imprisonment. In *Barletta v. Golden Nugget Hotel Casino*, 580 F. Supp. 614, 617 (D.N.J. 1984), the court found that "in order to support a claim for false arrest, the plaintiffs must allege two elements: First, that there was an arrest, and second, that the arrest was without proper legal authority, which has been interpreted to mean without legal justification." In New Jersey, false imprisonment and false arrest are merely separate names for the same tort. *Roth v. Golden Nugget Casino/Hotel*, 576 F. Supp. 262, 265 (D.N.J. 1983).

The court held in *Barletta v. Golden Nugget Hotel Casino*, 580 F. Supp. at 617-618, that:

> A taking into custody need not be done violently to constitute an arrest. . . . The inquiry goes to whether there was any unlawful restraint upon a person's freedom of movement. . . . Further, the assertion of legal authority to take a person into custody, even where such authority does not in fact exist, may be sufficient to create a reasonable apprehension that a person is under restraint.

Therefore, applying the law to the facts of the present case, we can conclude that an arrest was made.

The student should have used his own words instead of quoting the court. When you read the excerpt, you probably read the first quote hastily and wondered if you could avoid reading the block quote. Most people tend to skip over long quotes. The student also used quotations in place of analysis. He wanted to argue that Mr. Walker has a valid cause of action for false imprisonment. The student should have applied the rule of law to the facts in his case and compared his client's circumstances with those of the plaintiff in *Barletta*. Instead, he quoted generalities from the *Barletta* opinion.

4. Avoid the "Abstract Writing" Approach

The "abstract writing" approach reads like an essay. This form of writing is easy for students who have written essays in undergraduate school that earned "A's" in English or social sciences. Writers who use this form often discuss their viewpoints on what the law should be, but never get to what the law actually is. The following is an example of the "abstract writing" approach:

> The Court should uphold defendant's conviction for selling cocaine as a matter of public policy. This society is permeated by drugs, and courts should not allow drug dealers to go free.
>
> The President has recently declared a war on drugs. The use of drugs is so prevalent that recently many celebrities in the entertainment and sports worlds have either died or admitted drug abuse, setting a bad example for young people.
>
> Defendant's conviction should stand because she is a mother who is a bad example for her children. The evidence against her was overwhelming, and her guilt is indisputable. To let her go free to protect her constitutional rights would be an injustice not only to her drug customers but also to her family.
>
> That defendant's having to go to prison may split up her family should not be the court's major consideration. Her children will be better off in a drug-free environment. The defense argues that the police deprived defendant of her constitutional rights but ignores the fact that she is taking others' lives by selling dangerous drugs.

For all these reasons, defendant's conviction must stand.

The memorandum above could also be called the "soapbox" approach to legal writing. The student quite rightly addresses public policy issues, but fails to back up any ideas with constitutional provisions, statutes, or judicial rulings. There is no legal analysis.

5. Avoid the "Law Discussion Only" Approach

The next rule concerns the opposite of the "abstract" or "soapbox" approach— the "law discussion only" approach with no factual, policy, or equity considerations. This approach often gives a very accurate recitation of the law but fails to discuss policies and equities underlying the law or the case on which the writer is working. Here is an example:

> Ohio Rule of Evidence 501 allows Ohio courts to use their discretion in deciding what privileges they will allow. The rule states that "[t]he privilege of a witness, person, state or political subdivision thereof shall be governed by statute enacted by the General Assembly or by principles of common law as interpreted by the courts of this state in the light of reason and experience." Ohio R. Evid. 501.
>
> The Ohio courts have been consistent in their refusal to extend the privileges beyond those that are specifically listed in the statute. Section 2317.02 recognizes as privileged, communications between attorney and client, physician and patient, clergyman and parishioner, husband and wife, and professional counselor and client.
>
> In *Whipple v. Render*, C.A. No. 2480, 1989 Ohio Ct. App. LEXIS 3493, at *3 (Sept. 13, 1989), the court refused to extend the privilege of physician-patient to include dentists or dental surgeons.

The student tells us about an evidentiary rule that gives Ohio courts discretion in making certain decisions. The student tells us that the courts have not exercised that discretion liberally. We also learn about the holding in one case. The student, however, omits vital information. We need to know what policy considerations guide the court in deciding how to exercise its discretion. We also need to know why the court decided the *Whipple* case as it did. The "law discussion only" approach fails to give us the information we need to engage in legal analysis.

6. A Good Example

The following is an edited excerpt from a good discussion of the law, accompanied by appropriate discussion of policies and equities, but avoiding abstraction or "soapboxing":

Ohio Rule of Evidence 501 allows Ohio courts to use their discretion in deciding what privileges they will allow. The rule states that "[t]he privilege of a witness, person, state or political subdivision thereof shall be governed by statute enacted by the General Assembly or by principles of common law as interpreted by the courts of this state in the light of reason and experience." Ohio R. Evid. 501.

Because the statutory privileges of § 2317.02 controvert the general policy that disclosure of all information in the possession of witnesses in trials is necessary to insure the disclosure of the truth, the Ohio courts have been consistent in their refusal to extend the privileges beyond those which are specifically listed in the statute. Section 2317.02 recognizes as privileged, communications between attorney and client, physician and patient, clergyman and parishioner, husband and wife, and professional counselor and client.

In *Whipple v. Render*, C.A. No. 2480, 1989 Ohio Ct. App. LEXIS 3493, at *3 (Sept. 13, 1989), the court followed Ohio precedent and refused to extend the privilege of physician-patient to include dentists or dental surgeons. The court noted that the Ohio statute "is a derogation of the common law and must be strictly construed. Consequently, the aforementioned section affords protection only to those relationships which are specifically named therein." *Id.* That court thus aligned itself with the earlier case of *Belichick v. Belichick*, 37 Ohio App. 2d 95, 307 N.E.2d 270 (1973). That court stressed the importance of the disclosure of all information necessary to discover the truth. "The granting of privileges against disclosure constitutes an exception to the general rule, and the tendency of the courts is to construe such privileges strictly and to narrow their scope since they obstruct the discovery of the truth." *Id.* at 96-97, 307 N.E.2d at 271. Further, the court said, "R.C. 2317.02 is in derogation of the common law and must be strictly construed and consequently, the aforementioned section affords protection only to those relationships which are specifically mentioned therein." *Id.* at 97, 307 N.E.2d at 271.

Several other Ohio decisions have refused to extend the privileges of § 2317.02. *See Weis v. Weis*, 147 Ohio St. 416, 423, 72 N.E.2d 245, 252 (1947) (no physician-nurse privilege); *State v. Hallech*, 24 Ohio App. 2d 74, 81, 963 N.E.2d 916, 922 (1970) (no parole officer-parolee privilege); *Arnovitzs v. Wozar*, 9 Ohio App. 2d 16, 21, 222 N.E.2d 660, 665 (1964) (no attorney-witness privilege when witness was not client).

The Ohio courts' refusal to recognize privileges outside those authorized by statute is based on the policy that justice cannot be served if vital information is kept out of the record. The court so firmly believes this that it will refuse to recognize even those privileges authorized by statute where such recognition would protect criminal conduct. In *State v. Tu*, 17 Ohio App. 3d 159, 478 N.E.2d 830 (1984), a defendant who was being criminally prosecuted for vehicular homicide claimed the physician-patient privilege to prevent the introduction of a blood-alcohol test result into evidence at his trial. The court held that the privilege was not absolute and that "statutory privileges, unless they expressly provided otherwise, were simply not designed or intended to shield criminal conduct." *Id.* at 163, 478 N.E.2d at 833.

It follows that even if Ohio did recognize a parent-child privilege, it would never uphold the privilege in a case such as this one, where a defendant seeks to use the privilege to exclude vital evidence in a criminal prosecution for possession and sale of cocaine.

If you apply the lessons of this chapter, and the approach to legal analysis discussed in Chapter 5, to all legal memoranda you write, you should find that your writing will be well received by those who use it to guide their decisions in practice. You will write clear, concrete, and concise yet thorough documents that will earn you a reputation as a knowledgeable and thoughtful lawyer.

Exercise

Below is a poorly written example of part of the discussion of Edna Smith's case. Identify what is wrong with it.

In *Sinn,* the court held that a mother who witnessed an accident on the street from the front door of her house was located near the scene of the accident. *Id.* at 173, 404 A.2d at 686. Similarly, in *Anfuso v. Smith,* the court held that a mother who heard a car accident while inside her home and rushed out to see that her daughter had been injured in the accident was located near the scene of the accident. 15 Pa. D. & C.3d 389, 393 (Northampton Co. 1980). The *Anfuso* court further held that the mother had a sensory and contemporaneous observance of the event. *Id.* In *Bliss v. Allentown Public Library*, the court held that a mother who was twenty-five feet away from her son when she heard a metal sculpture fall on him was located near the scene of the accident. 497 F. Supp. 487, 489 (E.D. Pa. 1980). The *Bliss* court also held that the mother had a sensory and contemporaneous observance of the event. *Id.*

In *Brooks v. Decker,* the court held that a father did not have a valid cause of action for negligent infliction of emotional distress. 512 Pa. 365, 516 A.2d 1380, 1383 (1986). In *Brooks,* the father did not hear or see the car accident in which his son was injured. Instead he saw an ambulance race past him with its lights flashing and its sirens on. When he arrived at home, he saw his injured son lying on the ground. *Id.* The court found that the father did not have a valid cause of action because he did not hear or see the accident as it occurred. *Id.*

Edna was located near the scene of the accident, and the first part of the *Sinn* test has been met. Edna had a sensory and contemporaneous observance of the accident, and the second part of the *Sinn* test has been met. Therefore, Edna will win her case.

CHAPTER 14

Practice with Memos: Facts and Discussion

§ 14.01. INTRODUCTION

This chapter will give you the opportunity to practice developing a facts section and a discussion section of a memo. The legal issues to be developed here are similar to those covered in the previous chapter, but with a new set of facts and case law.

§ 14.02. DRAFTING THE FACTS SECTION

After meeting with the client, you dictated the following notes of the interview:

Lisa Ellington has come to see us because she was devastated by the recent death of her son Josh. A couple of weeks ago, her husband John Ellington, a ten-year veteran of the City of Chapman police department, shot and killed seven-year-old Josh and himself. He also wounded Lisa and their three-year-old daughter Katie. There was a long history of trouble in the nine-year marriage. John beat Lisa frequently, usually when he was drunk.

Lisa called the police whenever John got out of control, including at least seven or eight times over the last two or three years. All calls were responded to, and John was taken into custody twice. She doesn't know whether he was ever actually arrested, and he was never formally prosecuted because he always promised to change and get help with his drinking and she wanted to work things out, so she didn't press charges. Lisa was hospitalized once last year with broken ribs and other injuries and contusions. John took her to the hospital that time, and they both lied and said she had fallen down the stairs. John had seemed really upset that he had hurt her so badly, and she really thought that might be a turning point in the relationship. John had never before threatened Lisa or the children with a weapon.

On the night of the shootings, Lisa called 911, asking for immediate assistance because John was drunk and threatening her with a gun. John was yelling that she was no damn good and needed to be "taught a lesson." She doesn't know exactly what set him off, but he came home drunk and missed dinner. The children were crying, and she wanted to send them to their rooms, but John said no. After she called 911, John punched her in the face three or four times and threw her against a wall, right in front of the children.

Two officers responded to her 911 call. They knocked on the door, and John answered. He was holding his service revolver. The officers, Randy Miller and Jake Holmes, asked John to step outside. He complied, and they asked him what was going on. He started yelling again about how Lisa was no good and needed to be "taught a lesson." Randy and Jake took John's gun.

At this point, Lisa went to the door, bleeding from the nose and with a split lip, and told Randy and Jake that she had had enough, and she wanted John arrested. She said that she would follow through with the prosecution this time, and that she was going to take the children and go to her mother's. She also said she was finally going to divorce John. This seemed to enrage John even further, and he reached for his gun while screaming and cursing at her, calling her an "ungrateful *****" among other things. Randy and Jake took John away.

Lisa went back into the house to calm the children and clean up her face. She called her mother and told her they were coming. Lisa's mother was very relieved because she had been worried about the situation with John for some time. Lisa began to pack up some things for herself and the children. After about two hours, John returned home, came into the bedroom and found her packing, drew his gun, and fired at her, hitting her in the stomach. He then left the bedroom to find the children. Lisa heard the gunshots that killed her son and wounded her daughter, but did not actually see the shootings. John then took his own life.

Josh was shot in the head and died immediately. Katie was shot in the leg and will be physically okay, but she is showing signs of serious emotional trauma. She has nightmares every night and is always looking over her shoulder in fear. She jumps and screams at any sudden noise, like the phone ringing or a door slamming. She was always an outgoing child, but now Lisa can hardly get her to say three words. She hangs onto Lisa all the time. The doctors had to remove part of Lisa's spleen, but she should be okay physically as well. She has also been having nightmares and is having a lot of trouble coping. She feels as though she could have saved Josh if only she had left sooner, but it never occurred to her that the officers would keep John for only two hours. The last time they took him into custody, they kept him at the station overnight and then let him call her to see if she wanted him to come home.

Lisa believes that the officers did not take the situation as seriously as they should have, and that they gave John a break because he was a fellow officer. She told them about wanting to divorce John and taking the kids to her mother's because she wanted them to understand that she was really serious this time, and that she wanted them to treat him like they would any other criminal.

Lisa wants the police department and maybe the city to pay—it won't bring Josh back or give Katie back her smile, but she is really hurt and angry, and she is going to have a lot of bills to pay, including counseling for Katie and maybe herself. She can work as a secretary, but hasn't since Josh was born because John wanted her at home with the children. He always said he was man enough to provide for his family. Lisa doesn't know how much life insurance or pension John had, and she doesn't know whether the department will continue to pay for the health insurance she had before.

You can draft a facts section for your memo now, but it would probably be better to wait until you have read the applicable law because you won't know for sure which facts are relevant until you understand the law. When you do draft the facts section, be sure to include all facts that are legally relevant or otherwise necessary to tell a coherent story. Omit facts that do not meet those criteria. Remember to keep the tone of the facts section objective and to tell the story in a logical order.

Here is a synopsis of the governing case law:

Elden v. Sheldon, 46 Cal. 3d 267, 758 P.2d 582, 250 Cal. Rptr. 254 (1988)

1. In *Elden*, the court held that damages may be recovered for reasonably foreseeable emotional distress and physical injury resulting from plaintiff's witnessing of an accident in which a closely related person is injured or killed by the negligent act of the defendant. In determining whether defendant should reasonably foresee the injury to the plaintiff, the court took into account the following three factors:

1) whether plaintiff was located near the scene of the accident as contrasted with one who was a distance away from it;
2) whether the shock resulted from a direct emotional impact upon the plaintiff from the sensory and contemporaneous observance of the accident, as contrasted with learning of the accident from others after its occurrence; and
3) whether plaintiff and the victim were closely related, as contrasted with an absence of any relationship or the presence of only a distant relationship.

2. *Hoyem v. Manhattan Beach City School District*, 22 Cal. 3d 508, 585 P.2d 851, 150 Cal. Rptr. 1 (1978).

In *Hoyem*, the court held that a mother, who was not present at the scene of an accident where her ten-year-old son was struck by a motorcycle, could not recover for the emotional distress that she suffered upon observing such injuries in the hospital a few hours after the accident. The plaintiff urged the court to apply the *Dillon* rule that "courts should allow recovery to a mother who suffers emotional trauma and physical injury to her child for which the tortfeasor is liable in negligence." *Dillon v. Legg*, 68 Cal. 2d 728, 730, 441 P.2d 912, 914; 69 Cal. Rptr. 72, 74 (1968). The court declined to extend the *Dillon* rule, holding that "*Dillon* requires more than a mere physical presence: . . . the shock must also result from a 'direct emotional impact' on the plaintiff caused by a 'sensory and contemporaneous observance of the accident.'" *Justus v. Atchison*, 19 Cal. 3d 564, 584, 565 P.2d 122, 135; 139 Cal. Rptr. 97, 110 (1977). Therefore, the plaintiff mother's cause of action for NEID was properly dismissed.

3. *Molien v. Kaiser Foundation Hospitals*, 27 Cal. 3d 916, 616 P.2d 813, 167 Cal. Rptr. 831 (1980).

In *Molien*, a doctor misdiagnosed a patient as having syphilis and advised her to tell her husband so he could be tested and treated if necessary. Since the doctor's negligence was expressly directed at the husband as well as the wife, the husband was permitted to pursue a claim for negligent infliction of emotional distress. The risk of harm to the husband was reasonably foreseeable, therefore the defendant owed the plaintiff husband a duty to exercise due care in diagnosing the physical condition of his wife.

The *Molien* court also found that the plaintiff was not barred from recovery by the fact that he did not suffer a physical injury. The court held that "the underlying purpose of such an action [loss of consortium arising out of infliction of emotional distress] is to compensate for the loss of companionship, affection and sexual enjoyment of one's spouse, and it is clear that these can be lost as a result of psychological or emotional injury as well as from actual physical harm." *Agis v. Howard Johnson Co.*, 371 Mass. 140, 355 N.E.2d 315, 320 (1976).

4. *Thing v. La Chusa*, 48 Cal. 3d 644, 771 P.2d 814, 257 Cal. Rptr. 865 (1989).

In *Thing*, a mother who did not witness an accident in which a car struck and injured her child could not recover damages from the driver of the car for emotional distress she suffered when she arrived at the accident scene. The court held that in the absence of physical injury or impact to plaintiff himself, damages for emotional distress should be recoverable only if

(1) plaintiff is closely related to the injury victim,
(2) plaintiff is present at the scene of the injury-producing event at the time of the it occurs and is then aware that it is causing injury to the victim, and
(3) as a result, plaintiff suffers emotional distress beyond that which would be anticipated in a disinterested witness.

The court applied this three-part test to determine whether the mother's injury was foreseeable. The undisputed facts established that the plaintiff was not present at the scene of the accident in which her son was injured, did not observe defendant's conduct, and was not aware that her son was being injured. Therefore, the plaintiff mother could not establish a right to recover for the emotional distress that she suffered when she learned of the accident and its consequences.

5. *Ess v. Eskaton Properties, Inc.*, 97 Cal. App. 4th 120, 118 Cal. Rptr. 2d 240 (2002).

In *Ess*, the plaintiff, sister of a nursing facility patient, brought an action for negligent infliction of emotional distress against the nursing facility, alleging that she suffered severe emotional distress as a result of the injuries her patient sister received when sexually assaulted by an unknown intruder.

The court held that damages for negligent infliction of emotional distress (NIED) may be permitted in a "bystander" case where the plaintiff is closely related to the victim of a physical injury, is present at the scene of the injury-causing event and is then aware that it is causing injury, and suffers emotional distress beyond that which would be anticipated in a disinterested witness. In *Ess*, the plaintiff could not pursue a bystander cause of action because she was not present at the event that caused the injury to her sister.

The court also stated that recovery for NIED may be permitted if the plaintiff is a "direct victim." Direct victim cases involve the breach of a duty owed the plaintiff that was assumed by the defendant, imposed on the defendant as a matter of law, or arose out of a preexisting relationship between the two. In this case, the plaintiff alleged that she had a close familial relationship with her sister and had undertaken care for her since her sister's diagnosis with Alzheimer's disease. However, the court held that when the sister became a resident of the nursing facility, the defendants undertook to provide care to the sister. Therefore, the plaintiff incidentally benefited from defendants' duty of care to her sister, but this was not sufficient to support a direct victim cause of action for emotional distress.

6. *Powers v. Sissoev*, 39 Cal. App. 3d 865, 114 Cal. Rptr. 868 (1974).

In *Powers*, the plaintiff sought damages for emotional distress resulting from seeing her daughter thirty to sixty minutes after the daughter was struck by a truck. The court found that the mother could not recover because the circumstances were not materially different from those undergone by every parent whose child has been injured in a non-observed and antecedent accident.

7. *Ochoa v. Superior Court of Santa Clara*, 39 Cal. 3d 159, 703 P.2d 1, 216 Cal. Rptr. 661 (1985).

In *Ochoa*, the plaintiffs sought damages for emotional distress arising out of the death of their thirteen-year-old son. The parents were present when the medical needs of their son were allegedly ignored by personnel of the county juvenile hall. The court found that the parents could bring an action for emotional distress under the "percipient witness" theory pursuant to the court's holding in *Dillon v. Legg*, (1968) 68 Cal. 2d 728, 441 P.2d 912, 69 Cal. Rptr. 72. Mrs. Ochoa [the mother] was a foreseeable plaintiff, looking on "as a helpless bystander as the tragedy of her son's demise unfolded before her." *Ochoa*, at 173.

8. *Fife v. Astenius*, 232 Cal. App. 3d 1090, 284 Cal. Rptr. 16 (1991).

In *Fife*, the parents and brothers of an automobile accident victim sought damages for emotional distress. From their family home, the plaintiffs heard the automobile crash and saw debris fly. The court held that the plaintiffs could not recover because they did not know that the victim was involved in the accident at the time they heard the crash.

9. *Campanano v. California Medical Center*, 38 Cal. App. 4th 1322, 45 Cal. Rptr. 2d 606 (1995).

In *Campanano*, a patient's family brought a cause of action for NIED under the "bystander" theory pursuant to the court's holding in *Dillon v. Legg*. The family sought damages alleging that the hospital had improperly placed an intravenous line in the patient's arm, and that this negligence resulted in the swelling, blistering, and eventual amputation of that arm. The court held that "the only recoverable damages are those which arose from plaintiffs' observation of the injury-producing event, the infusion. Any distress which arose from observations of subsequent injuries . . . is simply not compensable." *Campanano*, at 1329.

10. *Moon v. Guardian Postacute Services*, Inc., 95 Cal. App. 4th 1005, 116 Cal. Rptr. 2d 218 (2002).

In *Moon,* the plaintiff sought damages for NIED after he observed abuse to his elderly mother-in-law in a skilled nursing facility. While at the nursing facility, the plaintiff observed that his mother-in-law had become "malnourished and dehydrated, had lost significant weight, had become immobile and bedridden, had contracted infection, and had become incontinent." The court held that the plaintiff was not "closely related" to his mother-in-law, such as was necessary for him to establish a claim to recover for negligent infliction of emotional distress under the "bystander" theory. *Id.* at 1008.

§ 14.03. EDITING THE FACTS AND DISCUSSION SECTIONS OF A MEMO

Assume that an associate drafted the following facts and discussion sections of a memo on the Ellington case. What feedback would you give the associate?

FACTS:

Mrs. Lisa Ellington (hereinafter "Lisa") is interested in filing a claim against the police department and possibly the City of Chapman for negligent infliction of emotional distress ("NIED"). Lisa desires to bring said claim as the result of a tragic incident which occurred at her home two weeks ago whereupon her husband John, a ten-year veteran of the police department, went gun-crazy and killed their seven-year-old son, Josh, and injured Lisa, as well as their three-year-old daughter Katie before he shot and killed himself. John was a wife-beater whose violent tendencies flared when he became intoxicated. There is a recorded history of domestic violence that occurred throughout John and Lisa's troubled nine-year marriage, resultant in numerous injuries, including Lisa's hospitalization one year ago for broken ribs. Lisa reportedly called the police when John was "uncontrollable," which occurred at least seven or eight times over the last two-three years. However, in typical victim fashion, Lisa never pressed charges against John, idealistically believing his promises that he would change. Prior to this event, John had reportedly never injured the children or threatened Lisa with a weapon.

On the night of the incident, Lisa telephoned 911 for emergency assistance and reported that John was drunk and had threatened her with a gun. The children were present and John refused to allow them to go to their rooms. The crying children were therefore present to witness Lisa being punched in the face several times and thrown against the wall by John. When the police arrived John answered the door holding his gun. The officers, Randy Miller and Jake Holmes, took John outside and took his gun away.

Lisa was visibly injured, with blood streaming down her face when she came to the door. She informed the police that she wanted John arrested and prosecuted. Lisa conveyed to the police that she was going to file for divorce and that she could no longer handle John's violent beatings. Lisa told the police that she was going to take the children and go to her mother's, and John was taken to the police station.

About two hours after the incident had ended, while Lisa was preparing to leave for her mother's house, John entered the bedroom and shot Lisa in the stomach; he then went to find the children. Lisa heard the gunshots that killed her son and wounded her daughter, but did not actually see the shootings. John then took his own life.

Lisa believes that the police were negligent in failing to hold John at the police station given their knowledge of the danger that John presented to Lisa and the children. Lisa believes that the police violated standard protocol by allowing John, a fellow cop, to leave only two hours after he was taken into custody, when in times past, he was not released until the following day contingent to Lisa's permission. While both Lisa and Katie are predicted to have a successful physical recovery, there are still many medical bills to pay and the emotional scars are likely to plague them forever. Lisa and young Katie suffer regular nightmares and are having difficulty coping, and Katie is easily frightened and unusually withdrawn as a result of the incident.

DISCUSSION:

Recovery under an NIED claim is an unquestionable challenge given its elemental requisites, but not an impossible one under our factual situation. Case history reveals some mixed results regarding recovery for plaintiffs who are mothers under a theory of NIED, and an often essential element is whether the plaintiff actually witnessed the trauma-inducing event, a fact which Lisa does not have in her favor, but Katie might. California's liberal courts seem to reserve a certain amount of sympathy for mother/child scenarios such as ours.

In *Elden v. Sheldon*, 46 Cal. 3d 267, 758 P.2d 582, 250 Cal. Rptr. 254 (1988), the plaintiff boyfriend sued a negligent driver who unlawfully drove his vehicle into the plaintiff's vehicle, which resulted in the injury and subsequent death of plaintiff's cohabitant girlfriend who was the automobile's driver. The plaintiff boyfriend claimed that as a result of their close relationship, and the fact that he witnessed the accident, he suffered foreseeable harm. Although the court recognized "[i]t is manifest . . . that a mother will suffer severe emotional trauma from the death or serious injury of her child in an accident whether or not she is present at the scene," not every relationship is close enough to warrant recovery. *Elden v. Sheldon*, (1988) 46 Cal. 3d at 274. While the relationship between plaintiff and victim is undoubtedly one of the primary factors for allowing recovery under negligent infliction of emotional distress (NIED), the additional elements of proximity and whether the plaintiff actually witnessed the event are becoming more of a concern for the courts.

For example, in *Hoyem v. Manhattan Beach City School District*, 22 Cal. 3d 508, 585 P.2d 851, 150 Cal. Rptr. 1 (1978), the California Supreme Court affirmed the trial court's dismissal of plaintiff mother's claims of emotional distress at having seen her son, injured in his hospital bed, hours after the event occurred. In this case, plaintiff's son was severely injured by a motorcycle while crossing the street. The trial court dismissed all causes of action, and on appeal, although the Supreme Court allowed the plaintiff to collect damages for medical expenses, recovery for emotional distress was not allowed because of the sheer fact that time and distance separated the plaintiff from the actual event and the defendant was therefore not proximately liable for plaintiff's emotional state as she was not a reasonably fore-seeable victim. In the instant case, our facts are distinctly more favorable than in *Hoyem*, considering that time and distance are not mitigating factors. The son was shot in the same house as Lisa, separated only by a thin wall. Lisa was present, without being actually in the room; she heard the fatal gunshot and was able to witness the horrific results of John's brutal act within moments of him committing it. A case similar to *Hoyem* is *Powers v. Sissoev*, 39 Cal. App. 3d 865, 114 Cal. Rptr. 868 (1974), where the court refused to allow the plaintiff mother to recover for emotional distress after she saw her child almost an hour after she was hit by a truck. The court held, "we do not think that this court should extend the rule to a case such as this where the shock, as claimed, resulted from seeing the daughter 30 to 60 minutes after the accident and thereafter under circumstances not materi-ally different from those undergone by every parent whose child has been injured in a non-observed and antecedent accident." Our facts can be distinguished from both cases on the basis of location. There was little to no time separating Lisa from the inevitable shock that she would suffer as a result of seeing her seven-year-old son dead. And her presence in the home, hearing the sequence of events unfold but unable to do anything about it, made the experience that much more visceral.

Another favorable case is *Molien v. Kaiser Foundation Hospitals*, 27 Cal. 2d 916, 616 P.2d 813, 167 Cal. Rptr. 831 (1980). In this case, a physician misdiagnosed a patient with syphilis and encouraged the patient to warn her husband so that he could be tested and treated if necessary. After the trial court dismissed the com-plaint pursuant to the defendant's demurrer, the California Supreme Court, with Justice Mosk writing, determined that the plaintiff husband had stated an appro-priate cause of action based on the doctor's misdiagnosis and the husband's resultant emotion distress and loss of consortium. Thus, even though the plaintiff was not present when the doctor informed his wife of her misdiagnosis, and therefore was not in the "zone of danger," he was still entitled to recover under NIED. "In order to limit the otherwise potentially infinite liability which would follow every negligent act, the law of torts holds defendant amenable only for injuries to others which to defendant at the time were reasonably foreseeable." *Thing v. La Chusa*, 48 Cal. 3d 644, 685, 771 P.2d 814, 842 257 Cal. Rptr. 865, 893 (1989) (citation omitted). And the foreseeable risk may entail not only actual physical impact, but emotional injury as well. (*Id.* at 666, 771 P.2d at 828, 257 Cal. Rptr. at 879). In our situation, it was reasonably foreseeable to the police that John was clearly a dangerous man who was likely to cause severe emotional and physical injury to Lisa and her children if he was to be released on that night. The police were aware of the danger that John posed to his family. Nevertheless, they neg-ligently released him despite his lengthy and brutal record of domestic violence coupled with Lisa's pleadings that he be arrested and prosecuted.

Thing v. La Chusa, 48 Cal. 3d 644, 771 P.2d 814, 257 Cal. Rptr. 865 (1989), is another leading case on NIED. This case also involves a mother plaintiff, who did not witness the accident wherein an automobile struck and injured her infant child. The Supreme Court held that damages for emotional distress, absent physical injury, are available only if (1) plaintiff is closely related to the victim, (2) plaintiff is present at the scene of the injury-producing event at the time it occurs and is aware that it is causing injury to the victim, and (3) as a result, the plaintiff suffers emotional distress beyond that which would be anticipated in a disinterested witness. Due to the mother's absence from the scene of the accident and the fact that she was unaware that it was occurring, she was unable to recover under NIED. Our plaintiff is mother and/or sister to the victim; both were present, in the home, at the time the injury producing event occurred and aware of what was happening; and lastly both suffer extreme emotional distress, including regular nightmares, difficult coping, and other depressive symptoms.

The final case for analysis of Lisa's position is *Ess v. Eskaton Properties, Inc.*, 97 Cal. App. 4th 120, 118 Cal. Rptr. 2d 240 (2002), wherein the plaintiff was the sister of a nursing facility patient who brought an action for NIED against the nursing facility after her sister was sexually assaulted by an unknown intruder while under the facility's care. The court acknowledged that bystanders are able to bring claims for NIED and referenced the three-factor test for recovery in *Thing v. La Chusa*. However, in this case, because the plaintiff was not a bystander when the incident occurred and was not aware of what was happening to her sister, her claim was not recognized. As has been established, Lisa was in the home with her children when John returned to the house; he had already shot Lisa and charged off to find the other children. Lisa was a bystander in this situation in every possible way; she was present and aware of what was happening in her home. While the defendant police department may offer the argument that its officers were informed, by Lisa, that she was going to be taking her children to her mother's house that evening, it is nonetheless extremely reckless and professionally negligent behavior for them to release a drunk wife-beater to undoubtedly seek out his family and finish the job only two hours after he was brought into custody. The police took a risk in allowing John to leave early that night, and it was reasonably foreseeable that a mere two hours after the incident, an understandably shaken and upset Lisa would still be at the house. She would have had to calm down two small children and herself, as well as pack for all three of them.

Pursuant to the three-factor test in *Thing v. La Chusa*, Lisa's claim for NIED will survive any demurrers filed by the defendant, and she will successfully recover damages for all medical bills resultant of the incident, and any additional claims for emotional damage. The police department made a grave mistake in allowing John to go early that night, and it was likely because he was a police officer too. John was reportedly visibly drunk, obviously dangerous, and threatening to continue to harm his family; the police department would not have allowed another person in this state to be released prematurely. The law favors Lisa, and NIED is definitely a viable theory for recovery based on an analysis of precedent, but also because of the particularly egregious conduct by the police.

§ 14.04. DRAFTING THE DISCUSSION

Now write your own discussion section (and facts section if you have not already done so). After you have analyzed all of the case law, predict the most likely outcome for your client's claim of NIED. Your discussion should begin with a statement of your conclusion and a roadmap paragraph that describes how the analysis is organized. Your analysis must be objective—acknowledge and address weaknesses in your claim as well as strengths. Where important questions are not directly addressed by the case law, you should explain them as well.

Writing the Client Opinion Letter

§ 15.01. INTRODUCTION

Writing and speaking to your client is perhaps the most important communicating you will do in your career as a lawyer. Attorneys sometimes become so involved in their cases that they forget the human element. Learn to communicate well with clients and you will have more work than you know what to do with. Clients like to be told what is happening in a case, why it is happening, and what is going to happen next.

One important way to keep the client informed is the opinion letter. An opinion letter advises a client how the law applies to a particular case and suggests action to be taken based on that law. The letter serves as a record of the progress of a case for the attorney and the client. This chapter gives you some simple guidelines to follow in preparing these important documents.

§ 15.02. WRITE IN AN APPROPRIATE STYLE

1. Focus on Your Audience

Remember to write for your reader. In the case of an opinion letter, your reader will usually be either an individual who does not have a great deal of legal knowledge or another lawyer, perhaps your client's general counsel, who is legally sophisticated. Such sophisticated clients often request "formal" opinion letters that involve analysis of, and citation to, relevant legal authority, much like the office memorandum. Each client is different. Your goal must be to write a letter that will help the individual client in a particular case. The better you know your client, the more likely it is that you will be able to achieve that goal.

2. Be Concrete

Your clients want to know what is likely to happen in their cases. A lengthy, abstract discussion of the law without applying it to the client's case will have very little meaning for the client. Explain the applicable rules to the client, but do it in the context of the case at issue.

In this chapter we use examples from student assignments. All of the examples in this chapter are taken from student opinion letters discussing a single case. The case involved a criminal attack on two guests at a hotel. The issue is whether the guests can sue the hotel for negligence. Under tort law, to find negligence in such a case, four elements are required:

1. The hotel must have a duty to protect its guests from criminal attacks.
2. It must unreasonably fail to perform that duty.
3. The failure must have caused the attack at least in part.
4. Damage must result.

Read this passage as if you were the clients to whom it is addressed. In this case, the clients are the hotel guests who were attacked.

> Although Florida law has no statutes for a tort action for the criminal acts of third parties committed on a hotel's premises and no security standards have been adopted by the hotel industry, we think that you can bring a successful negligence action against Palm Court Hotel. Our opinion is based on past cases tried in Florida that are similar to your case and that set precedent for the courts to follow. In these past cases both motels/hotels and landlords were held liable for assaults committed by third parties on their premises when plaintiffs could prove that the hotel/motel or landlord had acted negligently in protecting its guests. These rulings are supported by Florida statutes for landlords and innkeepers.

As the clients, what have you learned? Do you understand how previous cases will help the court decide your case? Do you understand the significance of the presence or absence of statutes or industry standards? These are the kinds of questions to which clients should be able to answer "yes" after reading a letter from you. The clients who read this letter would answer "no."

Compare the next two examples and decide which you would prefer to receive if you were the same clients.

First Example

A hotel has a duty to protect its guests from harm based on the nature of the business and the social policies involved. In general, a hotel's duty is to exercise reasonable care in protecting its guests. The test for "reasonableness" is whether a reasonable person knew or should have known that there was potential danger based on the circumstances (for example, area crime rate, occurrence of similar crimes on the premises, design of the hotel, etc.) and whether appropriate precautions were taken to prevent or deter such danger. This determination is made on a case-by-case basis.

Second Example

Generally, in cases like yours two things are required to find the hotel liable. First, the hotel must have had cause to believe that such an attack might occur. Second, a court must find that the hotel did not take reasonable steps to prevent such an attack.

The second example is much more concrete. The sentences are shorter and the language is simpler. Obviously, the analysis must be fleshed out and the law applied to the case, but at least you have a better understanding of the legal test. The concrete examples provided in parentheses in the first example would fit nicely in this paragraph. What else would you add?

3. Avoid Sounding Colloquial

Even when you are writing for lay clients and want to use language they can understand, maintain a formal tone. The rules for opinion letters are the same as for other legal documents. Avoid contractions, slang, and other colloquialisms. You do not want to sound stuffy or cold, but you do want to sound professional. Avoid sentences like these:

> I don't see any problem with this.
> We have several things going in our favor.
> I believe we can nail down a favorable settlement.
> FYI, the courthouse closes at 2:00 p.m. on Fridays.

4. Avoid Jargon and Stilted Language

You should avoid using unnecessary legal jargon and stilted construction. Again, remember your audience. If you are writing to a layperson, avoid legal terminology altogether if possible. But if you are writing to another attorney, he or she will expect you to use appropriate legal terminology. For example, you might include this passage in a letter to the general counsel for the Palm Court Hotel:

> Palm Court Hotel had a legal duty to exercise reasonable care for the safety of its guests. The hotel was obligated to use whatever security devices the average reasonable person would have used in the same circumstances. In view of the hotel design and location, and the criminal activity in the area, there should have been some control over access to the building.
>
> By failing to control or even monitor access to the guest building, Palm Court negligently breached its duty of reasonable care for the Smiths' safety.

Conversely, if you were writing to the Smiths, you would use simpler language, and explain legal concepts rather than using terms of art.

> Palm Court failed to provide chain locks on the guest room doors. While no hotel industry standard requires a chain lock, providing a lock in your case would have enabled Mr. Smith to keep the door locked when checking to see who was at the door.
>
> The extent of a hotel's liability depends in large part on the crime rate in the area surrounding the hotel and the occurrence of similar crimes on or near the premises. If Palm Court was not aware of the sharp increase in the crime rate in the area surrounding the hotel, it should have been. Palm Court was also aware of several similar crimes that had taken place at the Seaside Inn, a sister resort located directly across the street.

A hotel's response to foreseeable danger and its attempts to exercise reasonable care can be measured most easily by the security measures and personnel it provides. Palm Court provided only one guard to patrol the entire resort, including the main buildings, four outlying guest buildings, and the grounds. The hotel also kept the access doors to the guest buildings unlocked at all times. Our security expert will testify that such security measures are clearly inadequate to protect a facility as large as Palm Court.

5. Use Correct Spelling and Grammar

It is just as important to spell correctly when you write to a client as it is when you write to the courts or to other lawyers. Avoid the grammatical errors we discuss in this book. Failure to write proper English will destroy your credibility as a professional. A client quite rightly will wonder about the impression you will make on judges and other attorneys if it appears that you cannot write grammatically or spell accurately. A few extra minutes will help you avoid this problem.

§ 15.03. ANSWER THE QUESTION

Usually a client's specific question prompts you to write the letter. Make certain that your letter gives the client all of the information necessary to make an educated decision. Here are five guidelines that will help you provide this information effectively.

1. Include Important Facts Provided by the Client

Before you analyze the problem presented by your client, you should restate the important facts the client previously provided. The client knows what happened, but your job is to connect those events to the law and give your professional opinion on the probable outcome of the case. It is important to be certain that you and the client have the same understanding of the facts. Recording the known facts in a letter to the client may jog the client's memory about something else important that happened. If other, less helpful, facts surface later, you will be able to remind your client that your more optimistic assessment of the case was based on the facts that came from the client, as outlined in the letter. Your presentation of the facts in our case might look something like this:

I understand the facts of your case to be as follows: Palm Court is a Florida resort complex with 200 rooms and extensive grounds. It is illuminated mainly by pathway lights, and none of the five buildings have exterior lights. The access doors of the building in which you were staying were never locked. Although the steel door of your suite was spring-locked and had a doorknob with an anti-picking device, there was no safety chain on the door. The door's observation port did not permit you to see to the sides of the door. No trained security guard was on duty at the time of the attack, though there had recently been a dramatic increase in the crime rate in the area, including several thefts at Palm Court and several assaults on persons at the Seaside

Inn across the street. On the evening of the attack, you heard a knock on your door. You did not see anyone when you looked out the port, so you opened the door. The attack then took place.

2. Be Accurate

You should have legal authority to support any argument you make. Although you do not cite that authority in a letter to a lay client, you should be prepared to cite appropriate authority in a formal opinion letter. In either case, you must be confident that the relevant authority supports the conclusions you state. The client will make decisions about future actions based on your advice. Provide the best guidance you can.

In our sample case, one writer declared:

> One of the areas of law that pertains to your case involves the responsibility of Palm Court for the acts of your assailants. Palm Court is responsible for the crimes you suffered while you were its guests. A hotel is in the business not only of providing lodging but also of providing its guests with reasonable care for their safety.

The last sentence in the paragraph states the law fairly accurately, but the middle sentence creates a misleading impression. It is up to a court, not the lawyer, to decide whether the hotel is legally responsible for an attack on its guests.

3. Explain Your Answer

It is not enough to tell a client that you advise a certain course of action. Explain the reasons for your recommendation. The reasons may be legal or practical. In either case, make sure you explain the reasons clearly in the letter. In explaining the legal basis for an opinion, be sure you apply the law to your client's case. You learned to integrate your discussion of the law and the facts in Chapter 5. Apply the same rules here.

First Example

> We must prove that the hotel failed to exercise reasonable care. Though the hotel exercised some degree of care in the safety measures and procedures adopted, we believe this security was inadequate. We believe that there was a need for not one, but two, patrolling security guards whose shifts would start at 7:00 p.m., not 10:00 p.m. This proposed level of security would have been sufficient to deter the type of crimes which occurred. In addition, Palm Court was or should have been aware of the increasing crime rate in the area and the recent assaults in the vicinity that make this type of crime foreseeable. Palm Court will probably say that the security provided was adequate under the circumstances and, therefore, that it exercised the reasonable care required.

Second Example

> The security provisions of the hotel, both guards and physical security devices, were found to be inadequate. The number of guards was insufficient for a hotel of that size, and the hours patrolled were too few. The physical security devices were also

insufficient, since Mr. Smith had to open the door to see who was there when he heard the knock.

As far as the clients could tell from either of these examples, all the writers have presented are their personal opinions. In the first example, the writer even said "we believe" in two separate places. In the second example, the writer says the security measures "were found to be inadequate." By whom? In both cases, the writer should have given the client some legal basis for the conclusions reached.

The idea is not necessarily to cite cases or other authority, but to explain the legal standards by which a court will judge the actions of the parties. Here is a revision of the second example.

> A hotel has a legal obligation to take reasonable steps to ensure the safety of its guests. What is reasonable depends on the circumstances. In this case, the increase in crime in the area and the attacks at the Seaside Inn made the attack on you more likely and therefore legally foreseeable. Our security expert will testify that these facts made the security provisions of the hotel inadequate. The number of guards was insufficient for a hotel of that size, and the hours patrolled were too few. The physical security devices were also insufficient, since Mr. Smith had to open the door to see who was there when he heard the knock.

4. Do Not Promise What You Cannot Deliver

In addition to making sure that your conclusions are accurate, be certain that your advice is honest. One student wrote:

> In regard to your claim against Palm Court Hotel for the attack that occurred on May 31, 2003, I have concluded that if you decide to proceed, you will probably recover a large sum of money in damages because the hotel was negligent in failing to prevent the crime.

This is a dangerous approach. You may create expectations that you will not be able to fulfill. Even though the law may appear to be in your favor, there are many other factors that can affect the outcome of a legal proceeding. You do not have control over some of these factors, such as the judge or jury who ultimately decides the case, so you should not make promises you may not be able to keep.

Do not interpret this rule to mean that you should take a negative approach when you advise your client. As explained by one writer:

> Not only should advice be affirmative, but the giving of it, as of all things, should be cheerful. Even as with the physicians, while clients come to us for advice, it is usually more for comfort and assurance that they seek us and this is so whether the client be a poor widow or the president of a wealthy corporation. While we must not close our eyes to the bad or disadvantageous or dangerous aspects of the client's problem or situation, we should endeavor to find its most favorable aspect and, from that vantage point, advise him cheerfully and affirmatively what to do. One who has a problem which seems dark and hopeless is not helped by a lawyer who sheds only new darkness upon it. We should remember that the leaders of lost causes were never

men of dismal minds. No opinion letter should import fear into the client's mind, unless the writer of it at once eradicates that fear by strong affirmative advice.[1]

As with most legal tasks, you must strive to find the proper balance when you give honest advice to your client.

5. Address Your Client's Concerns

If you are aware of any special concerns of your client, address them in your letter. If your client is a cost-conscious businessperson, you might want to stress the cost-effectiveness of a particular course of action. If your client has never had any contact with the legal system and is somewhat afraid of it, be especially reassuring. Tell the client that you are available to answer questions and that you will be there every step of the way.

Clients like to feel that their lawyers think of them as human beings and not just as files or cases. It does not take much effort to add the little touch that lets a client know you have paid attention to what the client has told you. Listen carefully, be considerate, and communicate effectively.

§ 15.04. TELL THE CLIENT WHERE YOU ARE GOING

As you conclude the letter to your client, continue to think concretely. What is the next step? Who should take that step, and when will it happen? Use the final paragraph of your letter to give the client a clear idea of what happens next, so he or she feels more confident. It is not necessary to summarize what you have said previously in the letter. The document is not that long. Do not offer general predictions about what might or might not happen in the case. Avoid writing something like this:

> For all of these reasons our case against the hotel is strong. Because of previous attacks at the Seaside Inn and the size and expanse of Palm Court we should be able to prove the hotel should have realized the possibility of an attack on its patrons. Whether the judge or jury believes our security expert will be crucial to our case; however, established law does support our expert. The lack of TV monitoring equipment and security access doors also supports our case. Although I cannot assure a decision in our favor, I feel confident that the hotel will be found liable if we bring this action.

The writer could have concluded more effectively by offering to begin legal action upon instructions from the client. In some situations you might suggest a meeting with the client. Sometimes the next step is to wait for action from the court or the opposing party. If so, tell the client that you advise doing nothing and why. Tell the client what will happen next as precisely as possible. The client then will feel more comfortable with the progress of the case and with your representation.

---

1. Arthur Littleton, *Writing an Opinion Letter to a Client* (unpublished, 1959).

Exercise

Rewrite the following letter using the rules you have just studied. The letter discusses the same case you have read about throughout this chapter.

Dear Mr. and Mrs. Smith:

This letter pertains to the suit we are bringing against the Palm Court Hotel where you both were assaulted in May of 2003. We are asserting that the hotel was negligent of its required duties to the two of you as guests. To establish negligence we must first prove that the hotel was negligent of its required duties to the two of you as guests. To establish negligence we must first prove that the crime committed against you was foreseeable. Secondly, we must show that the hotel responded inadequately to that foreseeable crime. In establishing foreseeability of the crime, we will try to show that criminal activity within the community and within the immediate vicinity should have alerted the management that a similar crime may occur on its premises. After establishing that the crime was indeed foreseeable, we must then assert that the Palm Court Hotel took insufficient security measures to deter or prevent the occurrence of the crime. An analysis of the security precautions taken by the hotel and testimony from an expert witness will be instrumental in deciding whether the hotel instituted the necessary security system to deter or prevent the foreseeable crime.

We expect the outcome of the suit to be in your favor. There is ample evidence of similar crime within the immediate area of the Palm Court Hotel. We feel that the court will find that the hotel neglected its duties to secure the grounds in light of the foreseeability of the crime. We have evidence that the security staff was insufficient and that the premises were vulnerable to crime. With a judgment in your favor, we can request compensatory and punitive damages. Compensatory damages are damages to compensate you for some of the injuries you sustained and some of the grief you have suffered, however inadequate this may be in reality. Punitive damages are a form of punishment levied upon the hotel for negligence.

Sincerely,

CHAPTER 16

Practice with Client Letters

§ 16.01. INTRODUCTION

This chapter will give you the opportunity to practice drafting and editing a client letter, using the principles you learned in the previous chapter. Assume that you received a memo outlining the facts and law you need to know before drafting a letter to your client, Sandy Harmon. Sandy came to you looking for advice on what to do about a coworker who has been making her life difficult. The facts and legal analysis from the memo are reproduced below.

Memorandum

Facts

Sandy Harmon and Kris Martin both work for a software company, Playtime, Inc. Martin asked Mrs. Harmon out several times, and she refused each time. His behavior progressed into repeated telephone calls to her home and hanging up on her husband. He told Mrs. Harmon he would convince her husband there was something going on between her and Martin so that her husband would divorce her. Shortly after, she started receiving phone calls from strange men making "seriously lewd propositions." She found out from a coworker that Martin had put her phone number and later her address on his webpage. She asked Martin to stop, and he just laughed. More recently, guys have actually come to her house wanting to engage in sex. Her husband has had to chase them off their property. Some of the men even asked if the husband would join. At one point they had to call the police for assistance. Finally, Mrs. Harmon went into work one day and threatened Martin with a lawsuit, and he responded by laughing. She began to cry and yell, trying to convince him to stop. She then had to speak to her boss and explain her situation, and she took the rest of the day off. Mrs. Harmon has suffered emotionally, from lack of sleep and from not knowing what these strange men will do to her or when they will next show up at her doorstep. She is quite frightened and wants this to stop. She wants to know if she has a viable claim against Martin for stalking, either criminally or as a tort, or even both.

Discussion

In California, one can be liable for stalking either criminally or as a tort. Stalking as a crime is defined by California Penal Code § 646.9, which defines stalking as willfully, maliciously, and repeatedly following or harassing another person and making a credible threat with the intent to place the victim in reasonable fear for her safety, or the safety of her immediate family. *Id.* The three elements of the crime are (1) repeatedly following or harassing another person (2) making a credible threat (3) with the intent to place that person in reasonable fear of death or great bodily injury. *People v. Ewing,* 76 Cal. App. 4th 199 (1999).

Stalking as a tort is defined under California Civil Code § 1708.7. Although there are no cases dealing specifically with the tort of stalking, it would be appropriate to use the current cases dealing with the crime of stalking since the elements of the two are essentially the same. Under California Civil Code § 1708.7 the elements are:

(1) The defendant engaged in a pattern of conduct the intent of which was to follow, alarm, or harass the plaintiff. . . .

(2) As a result of that pattern of conduct, the plaintiff reasonably feared for his or her safety, or the safety of an immediate family member. . . .

(3) [That the defendant did] one of the following: (A) The defendant, as part of the pattern of conduct specified in paragraph (1), made a credible threat with the intention to place the plaintiff in reasonable fear for his or her safety, or the safety of an immediate family member and, on at least one occasion, the plaintiff clearly and definitively demanded that the defendant cease and abate his or her pattern of conduct and the defendant persisted in his or her pattern of conduct. (B) The defendant violated a restraining order. . . .

The main distinguishing factor is that the tort of stalking requires that the victim demand the defendant to stop his conduct.

Finally, in proving the stalking charges there are two ways the facts of the case can be interpreted. One approach would be that Martin is guilty of stalking based on his conduct of making repeated calls to Mrs. Harmon's home, hanging up on her husband, telling her that he will convince her husband there is something going on so that her husband will leave her, and publishing her phone number and address on his webpage. The second approach that can be taken is that of a co-conspirator. Although Martin did not actually make the lewd comments or appear at her doorstep soliciting sex, he knew that by placing her information on his webpage such actions would result. He actually intended those results, and as a result would be criminally liable for stalking as a co-conspirator.

The first way the facts of the case can be interpreted to determine whether Martin can be found guilty of stalking, either as a tort or criminally, is based solely on Martin's conduct. This approach is further developed throughout this memorandum and is most practically the stronger of the two. However, the second approach of viewing Martin as a co-conspirator has a viable standing in this case as well.

When Martin placed Sandy Harmon's phone number and address on his webpage he arguably met all three requirements of the crime and tort of stalking. He "harassed" Mrs. Harmon by taking her private information and making it available to millions of people. Second, the credible threat element is met through the conduct of the men who actually called her and appeared at her doorstep. They had the apparent ability to follow through on their credible threats and had to be chased away by her husband in order to stop them from committing the act. Finally, we would need to prove that both the strange men and Martin intended to place Mrs. Harmon in reasonable fear of death or great bodily injury. If we can demonstrate that Martin intended to inflict such injury, circumstantial evidence can also show that these men could have had the same intent, since they had to be chased away or the police had to be called. Martin knew that by invading Mrs. Harmon's privacy and publishing her private phone number and address she would be vulnerable to a variety of dangerous situations, which would not only put fear in a reasonable person, but actually caused Mrs. Harmon to fear for her safety.

The first element of stalking requires "repeatedly following or harassing another person, which causes that person to suffer substantial emotional distress." *Ewing*, 76 Cal. App. 4th at 199. In that case, the defendant initially was storing his belongings in the victim's garage, but became more intrusive and began to ask for food and money. *Id.* at 203. He then started to make explicit comments to the victim. Shortly after, the victim noticed that the defendant had set up residence in her garage without her permission. *Id.* He continued to stalk her by videotaping her home, calling her repeatedly, and vandalizing her yard and garage. He was finally arrested when he stole her television set and VCR. *Id.* at 204. The court began its discussion by defining the term "harass" as outlined in § 646.9(e) ". . . a knowing and willful conduct directed at a specific person that seriously alarms, annoys, torments, or terrorizes the person, and that serves no legitimate purpose." The court continued to elaborate that this course of conduct ". . . must be such as would cause a reasonable person to suffer substantial emotional distress, and must actually cause substantial emotional distress to the person." *Id.* at 206.

The court's holding in *Ewing* was that the victim did not demonstrate substantial emotional distress and therefore the defendant could not be found guilty of stalking. This holding should concern our victim, Mrs. Harmon, and we will need to get more detail from her about the nature and extent of her emotional distress. The court in the *Ewing* case went to great lengths to define every term in the statute. *Id.* at 207.

The rationale for the court's decision appeared to be based on its in-depth analysis and definition of each term in the statute, in order to demonstrate whether both the defendant and the victim met the requirements of stalking. The court went as far as analyzing what adverb precedes and qualifies the terms in the statute. The court defined "alarm" as "to strike with fear: fill with anxiety." *Id.* at 207. By placing Mrs. Harmon's private information on his webpage, Martin clearly has placed Mrs. Harmon in a position to be alarmed and anxious, not knowing who will show up at her doorstep. "Annoy" is defined as "to irritate with a nettling or exasperating effect." *Id.* Once again, Martin's conduct can easily be labeled as annoying and has had an exasperating effect on Mrs. Harmon, to the point where she had to take time off from work. The court continued to define other terms such as "torment," which is to "cause (someone) severe suffering of body or mind: inflict pain or anguish on," "terrorize," which is to "fill with terror or anxiety," and "terror," which is "a state of intense fright or apprehension." *Id.*

The court continued its analysis of these terms by pointing out that they are preceded and qualified with the adverb "seriously." So each term should be read with "seriously" preceding it. *Id.* at 208. The court then applies the reasonable person standard and rephrases the definition of "harass" as "a knowing and willful course of conduct directed at a specific person that [a reasonable person would consider as] seriously alarm[ing], [seriously] annoy[ing], [seriously] torment[ing], or [seriously] terror[ing] the person." *Id.*

Additionally, the court clarified that the reasonable person standard also applied to the victim when dealing with the course of conduct that would cause a reasonable person to suffer. *Id.* at 208. This would thus reduce the possibility that a victim's subjective reaction to a certain defendant would factor into play. *Id.* The court concluded that the "definition of 'harass' in section 646.9(e) establishes a standard of conduct which is ascertainable by persons of ordinary intelligence," so that a person could determine whether they are breaking the law by their conduct. *Id.* at 209. With that in mind, it is clear that we need to demonstrate that any ordinary person would suffer substantial emotional distress from Martin's acts of harassing phone calls and taking private information like a phone number and address and publishing them on the webpage for millions of people to access. In addition, we must demonstrate that this conduct did actually cause Mrs. Harmon to suffer substantial emotional distress.

The court in *Ewing* established guidelines to determine whether someone actually did suffer substantial emotional distress. "At the very least, we can safely assume that the phrase means something more than everyday mental distress or upset . . . the phrase . . . entails a serious invasion of the victim's mental tranquility." *Id.* at 210. The court continues its analysis of substantial emotional distress since it is not defined in the statute. By looking to the tort of intentional infliction of emotional distress as a guideline, the court concludes that substantial emotional distress means emotional distress of such substantial quantity or enduring quality that no reasonable man in a civilized society should be expected to endure. *Id.* The court wanted more than "sleepless nights" and "joining a support group." *Id.* at 211. The court concluded that ". . . there was insufficient evidence that Ewing's conduct, however offensive and annoying, actually caused Ferguson to suffer substantial emotional distress, within the meaning of §646.9." *Id.* at 212. Mrs. Harmon has mentioned that she is "furious," "frightened," and "short of sleep." There needs to be more than a mere inconvenience in her life. Therefore, more facts are needed to determine the extent of her emotional distress in order to prove that she suffered substantial emotional distress.

The second element of stalking is the making of a credible threat. Under §646.9(g), a credible threat is any verbal or written threat as well as a threat implied by a pattern of conduct. In *People v. Halgren,* the defendant stalked the plaintiff by repeatedly calling her at home and work, and saying such things like "[b]itch, you don't know who you are f * * * ing with. I am going to call you whenever the f * * * I want to, and I am going to do to you whatever the f * * * I want to." *People v. Halgren,* 52 Cal. App. 4th 1223, 1227 (1996). He also went to her place of work, watched her, called her, and made statements like "God, I've missed you. You look great in black today." *Halgren*, 52 Cal. App. 4th at 1224. The court in that case found the defendant guilty of stalking and stated, "[t]o meet the statutory definition the threat must be made with the specific intent to cause the victim to reasonably fear for her personal safety or the safety of immediate family." *Id.* at 1231. The issue in that case was whether his conduct constituted a credible threat. The court held that the facts of the case do indeed present a credible threat.

The court's rationale was that the mere making of a credible threat was not enough and that simply expressing one's feelings or emotions does not trigger the statute. The statute clearly specifies "(1) The credible threat was made with the intent and apparent ability to carry it out so as to cause the target to reasonably fear for personal safety or the safety of immediate family; and (2) the threat was made in combination with willful, malicious and repeated following or harassing of the target." *Id.* at 1231. This definition of credible threat gives the prosecution a broad range of activities without having to prove that the stalker actually intended to execute what he threatened he would do. Therefore, we will not have to prove that Martin actually intended for Mrs. Harmon to be hurt by the strange men or that he actually intended to convince her husband to leave her. All that is needed is that he intended to make the threat, to cause her reasonable fear, and that he did so by his willful and repeated phone calls and harassing.

The court in *People v. Falck* also followed this rationale. In this case, defendant met the plaintiff when she was nineteen years old, while she was working at a restaurant. *People v. Falck*, 52 Cal. App. 4th 287 (1997). The stalking behavior began when he started to repeatedly visit the victim at the restaurant. The stalking progressed to him sending her twelve black roses, and then letters being sent to the restaurant, professing his love for her and how he and the victim were meant to be together for eternity. *Falck*, 52 Cal. App. 4th at 291. He was finally arrested when he ignored the manager's request to not come to the restaurant. The defendant was given six months court probation and a court order to stay away from the defendant. *Id.* at 292.

Twelve years later the stalking commenced and by then the victim was married. *Id.* The defendant began studying astrology, and the movements of the planets convinced him that the time was right to try again. *Id.* After an exhaustive search the defendant was able to locate the victim and called her, identifying himself as George Frederick. *Id.* He said, "I found you. I can tell by your voice." *Id.* After her husband got involved the telephone calls stopped, but he started to write her letters professing his great anticipation of their impending wedding, sending pornographic pictures and astrological references. *Id.*

The defendant was finally arrested, and the search of his apartment found numerous photographs of the victim throughout his apartment. *Id.* The defendant argued that he did not have the specific intent to make a credible threat; he was just expressing his love for her and his need to marry her. The court outlined the two-prong test detailed in *Halgren* and concluded in its holding that "[b]y these requirements § 646.9 limited its application to only such threats as pose a danger to society and thus are unprotected by the First Amendment," and found the defendant guilty of stalking. *Falck* at 297.

The court explained that it is not imperative that a threat be made with the intent of actually carrying out the act that is threatened in order for it to be a credible threat. *Falck,* 52 Cal. App. 4th at 291. The court's rationale was that a "... true threat includes a threat which on its face and in the circumstances in which it is made is so unequivocally, unconditionally immediate and specific as to the person threatened, as to convey a gravity of purpose and imminent prospect of execution." *Id.* at 295.

The court in *Falck* continued to explain the premise of its decision by noting that § 646.9 has "... withstood constitutional challenge for its inclusion of the term repeatedly." *Id.* at 294. The court continued to highlight that the terms "harass," "credible threat," "willful," and "malicious" are all sufficiently defined and definite. *Id.* The defendant, however, challenged the word "safety" and claimed that the term is not defined by the statute and has no clear definition. *Id.* However, the court dismissed this reasoning and stated that the term has a commonly accepted usage and "... whether related to a defendant himself or to others, ... has a commonly understood meaning which gives adequate notice of the conduct proscribed." *Id* at 295.

Although Martin's conduct was not as extreme as the defendant in the *Falck* case, there is still sufficient evidence to show that a credible threat was made and that the requirements of the two-prong test were also met. It is true that no one act of Martin's would be sufficient to trigger the statute. However, when we look at his combined efforts and his intent to convince Mrs. Harmon's husband to leave her and to scare her by placing her private information on his webpage, she not only feared him, but actually had reason to fear him, especially since he reacted by laughing at her whenever she pleaded with him to stop his stalking.

As noted earlier, there is no significant difference between the tort and the crime of stalking. However, in the tort of stalking the third element requires that "... on at least one occasion, the plaintiff clearly and definitely, but unsuccessfully, demanded that the defendant stop his pattern of conduct." § 1708.7. This element differs slightly from the crime of stalking by adding the additional prong whereby the victim must clearly communicate her desire for him to stop the pattern of conduct. The court in the *Falck* case concluded that the defendant intended to cause fear in the victim when he insisted on making contact with her even though she clearly asked him to stop. Additionally, the defendant was warned by her husband, the police and the court to stop his behavior, yet he ignored all requests. *Id.* at 291. Similarly to our case, Mrs. Harmon has made it clear that she wants the harassment to stop, her husband has made it clear, and Martin still continued to harass her and cause her to fear for her life by not only ignoring her repeated requests to stop but also continuing to make her vulnerable to the strange men by not removing her phone number and address from his webpage.

The third element for both the crime and tort of stalking requires that the stalker have the intent to place that person in reasonable fear of death or great bodily injury. The prosecution must prove that the stalker intended to cause the victim to be afraid and that he had the ability to carry out his threat. There is no specific intent requirement that the stalker intend to execute the threat; the prosecution must only show the ability to execute the threat if he wanted or had the opportunity to do so. Because Martin placed her phone number and address on his webpage, Mrs. Harmon was swarmed with strange men soliciting sex from her. This would clearly put any woman and her family members in fear of bodily injury or death.

Martin may try to defend his actions and say that even if he had the intent to scare her into leaving her husband, he did not have the apparent ability to carry out the threats he made. Unfortunately for him, this line of reasoning will fail. In *People v. McClelland*, the defendant and victim married while the defendant was in state prison for attempting to murder his former wife by burning down her house. *People v. McClelland*, 49 Cal. Rptr. 2d 587 (1996). Soon after he was released, he became abusive with the victim and the victim's daughter. When the daughter went away to college he became obsessed with her and wrote love letters to her, but those letters then turned abusive. In one letter, the defendant stated that if he had seen someone " 'blow [Linda's] head off,' he would 'spit on [her] carcass.' " *McClelland*, 49 Cal. Rptr. 2d at 590. The victim got a restraining order, but the defendant still continued to stalk her by making repeated telephone calls, ramming into her front gate with his car, and even throwing explosive objects at her house. The defendant was finally arrested after he parked his car in front of her house. *Id.*

The defendant argued that there was not sufficient evidence that he made a credible threat with the intent to place the victim in reasonable fear; in other words, he did not have the apparent ability to carry out the threat. *Id.* at 593. The court responded and held that "[t]he circumstances leading to defendant's attempted murder conviction, his threatening display of matches to Erdman, his throwing of a bottle at the house, and his overall behavior during the period in question, constituted substantial evidence of his apparent ability to carry out the threat, a fire bomb at 6:00 o'clock." *Id.* The court's rationale was that since the defendant was convicted of attempted murder and other violent and harassing acts, he had shown he would have the apparent ability to execute his threat on this current victim. The court explained, ". . . a reasonable person, aware that the defendant had been convicted of attempted murder in burning his former wife's house, would reasonably fear for her safety. . . ." *Id.* at 154. It would be very helpful to Mrs. Harmon's case if we can determine if he had done this to any other women and, even more important, if she was aware that he is capable of this type of conduct. This is not a required element, that he stalked before or that she was aware that he was capable of violent acts against women, but it would certainly strengthen Mrs. Harmon's case if this information was known.

Our case is distinguishable from all the cases cited so far, in that the stalker in our case has not demonstrated the level of violent, neurotic, or obsessive behavior of the defendants who have been found guilty. However, the medium Martin has chosen makes his actions even more dangerous. He used his webpage, and by doing so, he has made Mrs. Harmon vulnerable to several stalkers, all at the same time. The victims in the other cases had only one deranged man after them; our plaintiff has had to deal with several men each night. What Martin has done has brought stalking to a new level by introducing a new level of fear in a victim, from several men at once. The potential for danger is far greater from several deranged men than it would be from one, who can possibly be traced because the victim knows who the stalker is. Mrs. Harmon does not have the advantage of knowing who her stalkers are or how dangerous they are.

The second approach we can take brings the analysis to another level and makes the stalking case even stronger. One can be found guilty of conspiracy to commit a crime when there is a meeting of the minds of two or more persons with the intent of performing a crime. The meeting of the minds element of conspiracy can be tacit, depending on the jurisdiction. We would need to further investigate exactly what Martin's webpage said and how he presented her private information. If her private information was portrayed in such a way that we could prove that whoever saw his webpage had an understanding that they were agreeing to some type of behavior that could be classified as stalking, then Martin would be guilty of conspiracy to stalk, as well as stalking. All co-conspirators are responsible for actions of their peers performed within the scope and in furtherance of the conspiracy. As stated earlier, more facts are needed, but we do not have to prove that Martin knew exactly what these men would do as long as their acts constituted "furtherance of the conspiracy," which in this case is stalking.

Mrs. Harmon has several avenues of retribution/justice available to her. If Martin is found guilty of the crime of stalking, the California Penal Code § 646.9 mandates ". . . imprisonment in a county jail for not more than one year or by a fine of not more than one thousand dollars ($1,000), or both that fine and imprisonment, or by imprisonment in state prison." § 646.9(a). If there is a restraining order, injunction, or any other court order, any person who violates § 646.9(a) will be "punished by imprisonment in the state prison for two, three, or four years." § 646.9(b). If a defendant is found guilty of stalking after having been convicted of a felony under § 273.5, 273.6, or 422, he ". . . shall be punished by imprisonment in a county jail for not more than one year, or by a fine of not more than one thousand dollars ($1,000), or by both that fine and imprisonment, or by imprisonment in the state prison for two, three, or five years." § 646.9(c)(1). Finally, Martin may also have ". . . to register as a sex offender pursuant to subparagraph (E) of paragraph (2) of subdivision (a) of section 290." § 646.9(d).

§ 16.02. EDITING A LETTER

Assume that an associate drafted the following letter to Mrs. Harmon based on the above analysis. What feedback would you give the associate on the draft letter?

Mrs. Sandy Harmon
32441 Mediterranean
Monarch Beach, CA 92677

RE: Stalking charges against Kris Martin

Dear Mrs. Harmon:

Thank you for contacting our offices and giving us the opportunity to represent you. The purpose of this letter is to explain your rights and remedies and tell you what we can do for you. Please remember that we are here for you and if you should need any assistance or have any questions, please do not hesitate to contact our offices.

Although we know you are aware of the facts of your case, we would like to reiterate them, just to ensure that we have the facts correct. Also, if there is anything missing or something you forgot to tell us, please be certain to notify our offices immediately. According to our last meeting you explained to us that you and Kris both work for a software company. Kris asked you out several times, but you refused each time. He then started making repeated telephone calls to your home and hanging up on your husband. He told you he would convince your husband there is something going on between the two of you so your husband would divorce you.

A couple of weeks ago, you started receiving phone calls from strange men making "seriously lewd propositions." You eventually found out from a co-worker that Kris had put your phone number on his webpage. So you confronted Kris and asked him to "knock it off," and he just laughed it off. He not only ignored your request, but Kris exacerbated the situation by placing your address on his webpage. You explained that within the past week men have actually appeared at your home wanting sexual favors from you. So, you went on his webpage and found out that he put your address on his webpage. Kris went so far as to say on his webpage that you would welcome all "comers" and that you would play hard to get, but that was part of the game, and that you really meant yes. It has become so bad that your husband has had to chase them off your property and at one point you had to even call the police for assistance.

Finally, while at work one day you once again asked Kris to stop and even threatened him with a lawsuit, and he again responded to your pleas to stop by laughing. You began to cry and yell, trying to convince him to stop. But when that failed, you were forced to speak to your boss about the situation and took the rest of the day off.

Mrs. Harmon, you have explained to us that you have suffered emotionally due to lack of sleep and not knowing what these strange men will do or when they will next show up. You have expressed how frightened you are and that you want this to stop. In our last meeting, you asked us if you had a viable claim against Kris for stalking, either criminally or as a tort, or even both. We believe you do; however we will need more facts from you to make our case stronger. The law does support your claim for stalking, but there are some weak points that we will discuss further with you. We will also discuss your remedies and the options you may pursue.

In California, one can be charged with stalking as a crime or as a tort. The requirements for the two are essentially the same, so you do have both options available to you. The basic definition that could cover both would be: willfully, maliciously, and repeatedly following or harassing another person and making a credible threat with the intent to place that victim in reasonable fear for her safety or the safety of her immediate family. The courts define "harass" as a knowing and willful course of conduct directed at a specific person that seriously alarms, annoys, torments, or terrorizes the person, and that serves no legitimate purpose. Additionally, "course of conduct" is defined as a pattern of conduct composed of a series of acts over a period of time, evidencing a continuity of purpose. Finally, the courts define "credible threat" as a verbal or written threat, including that per-formed through the use of an electronic communication device, or a threat implied by a pattern of conduct. The inclusion of the term "electronic communication" is important for your case because the term includes the use of computer to make a credible threat.

Kris willfully and it can be interpreted as maliciously called your house repeat-edly, hanging up on you and your husband. He also harassed you by taking your private phone number and home address and placed it on his webpage. Further-more, he made a credible threat that he will convince your husband that there is something going on between the two of you, with the intent to place you in fear. Also, by placing your private information on his webpage he has clearly placed you and your husband in reasonable fear of physical injury or death. We will argue that any reasonable person would be placed in fear if strange men showed up at her doorstep soliciting sex. However, please be aware Kris can defend his actions by saying that he did not intend to scare you or your husband and that he was just expressing his love for you. Fortunately, the law has made it clear that there is no longer free speech protection when you make a credible threat with the intent and apparent ability to carry it out and the credible threat was made in combination with willful, malicious, and repeated following or harassing of the target.

Although we went into great lengths regarding the facts of your case, we do need you to provide more specific information about the emotional stress you have suffered. This is one of the weakest areas in your case. The law is clear that you need more than sleepless nights and a few sessions of therapy. It needs to be more substantial than that. In our last meeting you explained to us that you have experienced sleepless nights and are frightened, but we need more specifics from you about how you have coped with this trauma in your life. Once we have all the details, we will be better prepared to move forward with your case.

We can also look at your case from a different perspective. Kris can still be charged with stalking, either as a tort or crime, or both; in addition, he can be charged with conspiracy to stalk. This is not the strongest perspective on your case, but it is a viable avenue. We can argue that by placing your information on his webpage Kris intended that these strange men come to your house or call you over the telephone and solicit sex from you. We can further argue that he knew this would place you in reasonable fear of physical injury or death and he intended for these men to place you in such fear for your life. Depending on what else he said or conveyed on his webpage, we can possibly prove that there was a tacit agreement between Kris and every guy who decided to telephone you or come to your doorstep harassing and soliciting sex from you.

Now we would recommend that our first step should be to send Kris a letter, asking him to stop his acts, remove your information off his webpage and to stay away from you and your husband. Although this decision is entirely up to you we think it is in your best interest that we make every attempt to convince him to stop his behavior, in order to avoid the court system. This will not only save you money, but also time and frustration. However, if he does not cooperate and insists on harassing you and continues his stalking behavior, or if you want us to altogether bypass writing a letter, we can press forward with a lawsuit against him. During this time we do ask that you document any new instances from here on out, just in case he does not cooperate and we do have to go to court. We need to have everything he has done to you well documented with dates and descriptions of the conduct. This will help make your case stronger and give us more ammunition if we have to go to court.

Finally, there are several remedies available to you. If Kris is found guilty of the crime of stalking, we can ask the court to issue a court order for him to stop his behavior and remove your private information off his webpage, in addition to facing imprisonment in county jail for no more than one year or a fine of no more than one thousand dollars ($1,000), or both. If you get a restraining order before we go to court and he continues to stalk you, then the court may punish him in state prison for no more than two, three, or four years. Also, if he has committed a felony prior to this and is found guilty of stalking, he can face county jail for up to one year, a fine of no more than one thousand dollars ($1,000) or both, or state prison of two, three, or five years. Additionally, he may have to register as a sex offender. Now, if Kris is liable for stalking as a tort, he may be liable to compensate you in damages, in addition to serving jail time.

Please advise whether you would prefer for our offices to first send him a letter, which we would provide to you for approval before we send it to him, or if you would rather we bypass that option and file suit immediately. Either way, please let us know of your decision within a week from the date of this letter. Please contact our offices if you have any further questions or information you need to provide to us. We will keep you apprised of any new findings or developments in your case.

Sincerely,

§ 16.03. DRAFTING A LETTER

Now write your own letter to Sandy Harmon. Remember to include a brief synopsis of the facts to confirm that you understood them correctly and to make clear that any legal analysis in the letter relies on those facts. You should outline the legal analysis without jargon or excess detail. You should give Sandy some options to consider, along with the advantages and disadvantages of those options. You should clarify what the next steps are, and what response you seek from the letter.

Advising the Client

§ 17.01. PURPOSE OF THE CONSULTATION

Once you have researched the client's problem and given the client some preliminary feedback in the form of a letter, you are ready to meet with the client again. This is the time to decide how to proceed with the client's matter. The process of decision making in a client-centered approach to counseling requires patience and thoroughness. Remember that the decision is not yours to make, but the client's (Model R. Prof. Conduct 1.2). Your purpose at this point in the process is to help the client arrive at a decision that will meet as many of the client's articulated goals as possible. Your purpose is not to tell the client what you would do or to substitute your judgment or priorities for those of the client. Your job is to provide the client with all relevant information so that he or she can make as informed a decision as possible. This includes discussing the most likely consequences of pursuing various options and the advantages and disadvantages of those options. Your plan for a follow-up meeting with the client should take all these considerations into account.

§ 17.02. THE SCENARIO

As we work through the planning process for a follow-up consultation, assume that you have already interviewed a client and gathered this information:

Susan Starkey is a member of a video dating service. On about December 20, she chose John Partlow from the video dating service. After speaking for hours on the telephone, the two agreed to meet at a dating service party on December 28. At the party, Partlow told Susan she was gorgeous, and she reported that she felt sparks, too. They exchanged e-mail addresses and sent more than a dozen messages back and forth.

After five days, Susan told Partlow to "get lost," feeling that he was trying to get too close too fast. He was already starting to talk about marriage and kids. On January 6, Partlow left a message on Susan's answering machine telling her he had secretly watched her leave work. She became worried and filed a police report on

January 7. Police told Partlow to have no more communication with Susan, computer or otherwise, but no official restraining order was issued.

On January 15, Partlow sent Susan another e-mail message. "I've been trying to court you, not stalk you. If you let me, I would be the best man, friend, lover you could ever have. I just want to show you how well we go together. You've turned my innocent and somewhat foolish love for you into something bad in your own mind."

When Susan received the message, she replied via e-mail. She sent Partlow a message stating that if he did not leave her alone, he would be sorry.

On January 24, Partlow sent Susan another e-mail, threatening to e-mail the story to all her computer friends, and mail it to her family and old boyfriends. He informed her that "this is the least of the many things I could do to annoy you." He said he knew she must be seeing someone else, and that he had figured out her password and was monitoring her e-mail messages to find out who the other guy was.

This last message frightened Susan, but she is afraid that police action might not deter Partlow, or that it might make things even worse. Since the incident, she canceled her membership with the video dating service. She is afraid to use her computer for any online services and gave a friend her password, asking that the friend delete any messages from Partlow before she logs on. She also changed the hard drive on her computer and completely rebuilt her system. She is having trouble sleeping and is considering contacting a counselor to help her deal with the situation.

Susan wants to know whether there is any way she can sue Partlow, to make him pay for all the disruption he has caused in her life. She would like compensation for her distress. She feels that Partlow has diminished the quality of her life with his threats. She told you that she wants her life back.

Susan also expressed interest in finding out if she has any claim against the dating service, since it certainly seems to her that it could screen its clients better. When she called the service to complain about Partlow, the person she talked to said, "Oh yeah, him. You know, this is the second or third complaint we've had about him. We may just have to cut him off." The person she talked to was the receptionist, Sandy Adams. Ms. Adams said she would relay Susan's complaint to Tony Benton, the head of the dating service, but she never heard anything from him. Susan made the original call three or four weeks before she came to see you. Assume that the last e-mail from Partlow arrived about two weeks before Susan came to see you.

§ 17.03. PLANNING THE CONSULTATION

As you plan the consultation, start with your understanding of the client's goals and priorities as they have been articulated to you thus far. Susan has told you that she wants compensation, both from Partlow and from the dating service, and that she wants her life back. Compare these goals and priorities with the results of your research as you have set them out in your memo and letter. Assume that your research and analysis have led you to the conclusion that you might be able to bring successful civil suits, against Partlow for intentional infliction of emotional

distress (IIED) and against the dating service for negligence in screening customers.[1] It is also possible to contact the police and pursue criminal charges.

Try to estimate the likelihood of various events with some degree of precision,
and think through the consequences, positive and negative, of making each
decision. Then, outline the topics you and the client need to discuss. Assume
that you believe the suit against Partlow has about an even chance of succeeding,
and that the odds of a successful suit against the dating service are slightly better.
One distinct disadvantage of either suing Partlow or trying to have criminal
charges brought is that Susan will likely have to face him in court at some
point. You should also evaluate the likelihood that Partlow will be able to pay a
substantial judgment. What other likely consequences can you think of? Advantages and disadvantages?

It is a good idea to find some way to keep track of all this complexity. You may
want to make a chart before you begin the consultation. The chart should list the
options you have considered in your planning process, and perhaps leave room
for other options that might be developed during the consultation. You should
identify any advantages and disadvantages that occur to you before the consultation, and leave space for others that might be identified by the client. You might
want to include the client's goals and concerns in the chart, so that you will have a
ready reference to check as the option development process proceeds. Here is one
way you might prepare such a chart:

Options	adv.	disav.	goals/concerns
civ. suit–IIED			
civ. suit–negligence			
crim. charges			

§ 17.04. BEGINNING THE CONSULTATION

You should begin this meeting, as with the initial interview, with a friendly
greeting and a little casual conversation. Again, you want the client to relax and
feel comfortable. You should also offer a brief preparatory explanation, so the
client knows what to expect of this meeting. Share your outline of the meeting
with the client, and ask if the client has any topics in mind that you have not
included. For example, your consultation with Susan might begin like this:

You: Hi, Susan. How are you today?
Susan: OK, I guess.
You: Are you feeling any better?
Susan: I'm hoping you can give me some good news today, and then maybe
           I will.

---

1. Depending on your jurisdiction, you might identify other possible causes of action as well.
For example, in California it is possible to bring a civil action for stalking.

You: I hope so too. Can I get you something to drink?

Susan: No thanks.

You: Did you get the letter I sent?

Susan: Yes.

You: Do you have any questions about the letter?

Susan: I don't think so; not right now anyway.

You: What I am hoping we can do today is discuss the options I mentioned in the letter, and any other options or concerns that may have occurred to you. I would like us to review the advantages and disadvantages of all the options, and then try to make a decision about how you wish to proceed. I prepared a little chart that we can use to keep track of our discussion. Do you have any questions, or is there anything you want to add before we get started?

§ 17.05. REAFFIRMING THE CLIENT'S GOALS AND PRIORITIES

Early in the consultation, you should check to make sure that your understanding of the client's goals and priorities is correct, and that they have not changed since you and the client last discussed the matter. If any material facts have changed, or if the client has reassessed the desirable outcomes, you want to know that before you get too deeply into the discussion you have already prepared based on your earlier understanding. Ask if the client has had a chance to review the letter you sent, and if she has any questions about the letter.

To determine Susan's priorities, you may want to ask some questions about choices she would make. For example, ask her whether it is more important that she never have to face Partlow again or that he be forced to compensate her. Can you think of other questions that might help you prioritize her goals?

§ 17.06. DEVELOPING OPTIONS

We have identified three preliminary courses of action:

1. A civil suit against Partlow for IIED
2. A civil suit against the dating service for negligence
3. Contacting the police in the hope of criminal charges being filed

1. Likely Consequences

In order to help Susan make a decision, you need to share with her your estimation of the likely outcome of these options. You should identify the most likely and least likely outcomes, and perhaps the "best case" and "worst case" scenarios. Clients would obviously like you to predict the likelihood of a particular outcome as precisely as possible, perhaps using percentages—e.g., "we have a 50/50 chance of prevailing in the intentional infliction of emotional distress suit, and a 70 percent chance of prevailing in the negligence suit against the dating service." Many lawyers are uncomfortable with the idea of attaching numbers to their estimates, fearing that there are simply too many variables to allow such precision. The law is fundamentally a human process, and trying to predict what parties, witnesses, judges, and juries are likely to do is often little more than an educated guessing game.

If you are uncomfortable with the idea of assigning numbers to your estimated chances of success, you must come up with some other way of communicating your perceptions to the client in a way that will be understood. Remember that the client will interpret whatever you say in a way that makes it meaningful for the client. Thus, if you say "we have a pretty good chance of succeeding on this claim," what is that likely to mean to the client? You may mean 50/50 or 60/40, but the client may hear 70/30 or 80/20. You may try to offer a range of numbers, or you may try to be very conservative and guess low. Remember, however, that the client is entitled to your honest assessment of the likelihood of success of the options you discuss.

If you have previous experience in the area, or if you have researched jury verdicts in similar cases, you can share that information with the client. You can discuss the variables that make perfect prediction impossible. If the client understands the complexity of the process, the client may also understand why you can't offer guarantees, or even odds, with any degree of certainty. We do not have the perfect solution to the dilemma; you will have to experiment to find a way of communicating the likelihood of success that you are comfortable with and that gives the client a reasonable opportunity to understand the situation.

2. Advantages and Disadvantages

You also need to discuss the advantages and disadvantages of each option, and of the various ways of approaching each option. For example, as you discuss the possibility of civil suits, you should always advise the client about the time and costs involved, and of the various alternative dispute resolution mechanisms available. You should discuss the advantages and disadvantages of filing a complaint before attempting to negotiate, and vice versa. You should explain the process of mediation, along with its advantages and disadvantages. Can you think of other consequences, advantages or disadvantages that should be discussed in this case?

You should also explore nonlegal considerations that create advantages and disadvantages, and ask the client to help you think these through. For example, in this case, Susan has obviously suffered a great deal of emotional distress, to the point where she has taken the extreme and possibly irrational action of rebuilding her computer. She needs to think about how it would feel to have this matter occupy another several months, if not years, of her life. Can you think of other questions you might want to ask Susan that would help you understand the implications of the nonlegal concerns that would affect the decision-making process in this case?

It should be clear by now that this option development process can get quite complicated. It gets even more so as you actually discuss the details of each option. You will find that the discussion of one option leads you into a discussion of another, as you compare and contrast likely consequences. You will move back and forth between the options and the client's goals to check whether proposed options are meeting the client's needs. You will shift back and forth between options, and you may discover that discussing consequences leads you to other options you had not considered.

§ 17.07. CHOOSING A COURSE OF ACTION

Once you have gone through this process of option development, it is time to make a decision. You and the client must sift through all the information you have produced as you discussed the options and choose a course of action. If your option development process has produced a clear choice in the form of a single option that has many more advantages and fewer disadvantages than other options, the choice will be easy. Unfortunately, this is frequently not the case. All of the options are likely to have advantages and disadvantages. You may find yourself with too many good choices, too many bad choices, or something in between. You should go back to the client's goals and priorities and try to make a choice that way. Is there one option that meets more goals, or does less damage to the client's goals, than other options? If not, ultimately the client will simply have to make a decision, and make the best of it. Here is one way part of your decision-making dialogue with Susan might go:

You: OK, Susan, we have discussed the advantages and disadvantages of our three options. What do you think?

Susan: I don't know. It all seems so complicated.

You: I can certainly understand that. Let's try going back to what brought you to see me in the first place. You wanted compensation, and you wanted your normal life back. Do I have that about right?

Susan: Yeah, that's about it.

You: Now, we have discussed the likelihood that you will have to face Partlow at some point if you sue him or if you contact the police about criminal charges. We have also discussed the possibility that Partlow may not be able to afford a lot of money and that it may be difficult to collect any judgment we do get. You also know how long a lawsuit might take to get resolved. Can you help me balance those concerns against what you were hoping to accomplish?

Susan: Well, that all makes suing Partlow seem like it might be more trouble than it's worth. And I don't know if I want him to go to jail. I just want him to leave me alone. What about suing the dating service?

You: I'm glad you asked that; I was going to mention that next. You would probably not have to deal with Partlow in that suit, but it could still take a lot of time to resolve. Like I said, I am hopeful that the dating service might be willing to negotiate a settlement, but you never know. Would you like me to contact them, and see how they respond?

Susan: Sure, let's see what they say. I would hope they would understand they made a mistake on this one.

You: So would I. Now, let's get back to the question of how we get Partlow to leave you alone.

If the client seems stymied, remind her that no decision is also a decision. In other words, discuss the advantages and disadvantages of doing nothing, and compare them to the other choices on the table. If the client asks you what you would do, there are two ways to present your choice. You can articulate the client's values as you understand them and tell her what choice you would make based on those values, or you can tell her what your values are and tell her what choice you would make based on those values. Either way, you should not tell her what you would do without articulating the values that guide you to that choice. For example, how risk averse are you, and how much are you guided by emotional as opposed to rational factors in making choices? You may also refuse to tell the client what you would do and insist that she make the choice.

What if you disagree with her choice? If you are satisfied that she has made an informed choice, and her decision does not pose any ethical or moral dilemmas for you, you should do whatever is necessary and appropriate to implement her decision. If you think she has made a mistake, perhaps because she does not understand some aspect of the likely consequences of her decision, you can try again to educate her by running through the advantages and disadvantages. Always remember, however, that the decision is hers and not yours, and that you owe the client an obligation of competent and diligent representation. There-fore, if you deeply disagree with what the client wants done, to the point that your representation is likely to be compromised, you should say so and offer the client the option of seeking other counsel. If the disagreement is extreme, you may seek to withdraw from the case.

§ 17.08. GETTING SETTLEMENT AUTHORITY

Once the decision is made, you should get explicit instructions from the client about the limits within which you must operate. For example, if you have decided to negotiate with the dating service on the negligence claim, you should discuss with Susan the elements of a settlement agreement that would satisfy her. How much money should you ask for, and what is she willing to settle for? If the dating service wants confidentiality of any settlement terms, does she have a problem with that? Can you think of other elements that might come up in these negotiations? If you do not have this conversation at this point, you may find yourself in a negotiation with no authority to settle. This may frustrate you, your client, and the other party. You will have to come back to her with simple questions that could easily have been answered at this stage if only you had thought to address them.

It should be obvious that we have touched only on the issues that go into helping the client to reach an informed decision. The process is much more com-plex, and the possibilities more numerous, than we can convey in a few pages. However, if you keep the basic principles in mind that we have discussed here, and come up with organizing strategies that help you and the client keep track of important factors, you should be able to help your clients reach informed decisions that offer as much satisfaction in the long run as is possible given the difficult circumstances that brought the clients to you in the first place.

Exercise

Make up a chart for your consultation with Susan Starkey that incorporates the issues we have already touched on, and any others that occurred to you as you were reading and answering the questions posed throughout this chapter. There is no particular format that is appropriate for such a chart; play with it until you come up with one that you think will work for you.

§ 17.09. CONSULTATION CHECKLIST

— Plan for the consultation by identifying options based on your understanding of the client's goals and priorities and the applicable law you have found. Think about likely consequences, advantages and disadvantages of those options.

— Prepare a chart outlining those options, consequences, advantages, and disadvantages. Leave room on the chart for contributions in all these areas that may come up during the consultation.

— Remember to greet your client warmly and have a bit of casual conversation if the client seems to need an opportunity to settle down and relax.

— Check with the client to see if anything has changed, if your understanding of the facts is correct, and if you understand the client's goals and priorities. Give the client a chance to react to your letter and to ask any questions.

— Go through the options you have developed, including likely consequences, advantages and disadvantages, and give the client ample opportunity to react and contribute. Give the client the best assessment of the likelihood of success that you can.

— Get a decision from the client and discuss how you will act on it. If you are going to negotiate, make sure you understand the limits of your settlement authority.

Negotiating

§ 18.01. INTRODUCTION

Negotiating skills are important in many aspects of life. We begin negotiating with our parents at a very young age. We negotiate with employers, with friends and colleagues. We negotiate major purchases such as cars and houses. Lawyers negotiate constantly—plea bargains, settlements, contracts, and many other types of transactions. Along with client counseling, negotiation is the most frequently performed and critical lawyering function. Nevertheless, most of us have never had any formal training or organized learning on the subject. We frequently do not even give much thought to the process. We don't plan our negotiating strategy or analyze how and why the process works the way it does. Nor do we reflect on our negotiations after the fact to figure out how we might have done better.

This chapter gives you an introduction to concepts that will allow you to plan for and learn from your negotiations in an organized way. We help you to begin to understand the inner workings of the negotiations process so that you can control both the process and results to a greater extent, and serve your clients better along the way.

As you study the material about negotiating, think about how the fact that negotiations are so common might influence your approach to research and writing. When you begin research for a memo, for example, think about the fact that the lawyer on the other side of the case is doing the same thing you are doing— looking for legal support for his or her client's position. Then imagine that after you have completed your research, you will be trying to negotiate a resolution to the problem. You will want to have thoroughly researched the law that supports both sides of the case, so you can respond to any arguments that might be put forth by opposing counsel. You will want your memo to reflect that research, so you can make cogent arguments in support of your client, and anticipate arguments from the other side. When you put your legal research and writing in the context of what lawyers actually do with the information, you will research and write more effectively.

§ 18.02. PURPOSES OF NEGOTIATION

The purpose of any negotiation is to reach an agreement. If that is not your purpose, you might as well save your energy and go to court. The essence of negotiation is compromise and problem solving. Whether you are trying to decide custody and visitation or how much money an injured victim is entitled to, you must assess the needs and interests of the parties and try to reach a resolution that meets as many of those needs as possible. Obviously some needs and interests will be in conflict, and there must be some balancing and decision making. The likelihood that you will be able to meet everyone's needs is very small, as is the likelihood that one party will walk away with all the marbles. Therefore, you must plan on giving as well as getting.

§ 18.03. THEORIES OF NEGOTIATION

There are many approaches to negotiating, but we will focus on two approaches here: the adversarial and problem-solving modes of negotiating.[1] Most lawyers, and probably most individuals, at least begin with an adversarial approach to negotiating—that is, the idea that someone must win while the other will lose. The problem-solving approach, which requires a great deal of trust, is less common, particularly among negotiators who have no history with each other. As you gain experience, you will develop a flexible approach to negotiating. You will adapt various methods of negotiating to suit your own personality and the many contextual variables that determine which negotiating approach is most appropriate in any particular situation.

1. Adversarial Models

We will briefly discuss three models for adversarial negotiating: game theory, economic, and social-psychological. We present the outlines of the theories so that you can gain a preliminary understanding of how theorists look at the negotiating process, and perhaps identify some frameworks that will help you in your negotiation planning. Understanding how and why the other party may be approaching the negotiation may help you plan your own strategy. Our belief is that models have some utility for conceptualizing the process, but that ultimately the process is sufficiently human and therefore unpredictable that you cannot rely too heavily on artificial constructions.

a. Game Theory
The game theory approach to negotiation views the negotiation as being composed of the usual components of a game: players and rules. If you know the rules, you can predict what the players will do. You can plot out the possible avenues of progress for the negotiation in advance because the players have limited options

---

1. For a more in-depth discussion of the theories touched on here, see Robert M. Bastress & Joseph D. Harbaugh, *Interviewing, Counseling, and Negotiating* (Little, Brown 1990).

based on the rules. The chief problem with this approach to negotiation is that it can only really work in a world of perfect information, where you know exactly what everyone else knows and how that information will affect the decisions of all the players. Fortunately or unfortunately, negotiation players do not all play by the same rules, they tend not to share all their information, and they don't behave predictably. Nevertheless, constructing a model for negotiating that uses some of the elements of game theory can be a useful organizing tool.

There are some "rules" of negotiation: for example, most negotiators don't start negotiating at the bottom line—they leave themselves some room to bargain. Also, it is frequently the case that concessions get smaller as bargainers approach their bottom lines. It is at least a convention of negotiating that it is poor form to revoke a concession once firmly made. You may learn or discover some other "rules" that offer some predictability for the process. Let us see how the first two "rules" might help you to predict the "moves" in a negotiation:

Assume that Party A, the plaintiff in a personal injury suit, demands $5 million to start. Because Party B, the defendant, knows that most negotiators set their opening demands to leave bargaining room, B knows that the next "move" is to make a counteroffer rather than simply offer to write a check. If subsequent concessions by A follow this pattern: $4 million, $3.5 million, $3.25 million, $3.125 million, then B can apply the "rule" of diminishing concessions to infer that A's bottom line is somewhere around $3 million. Of course, A can make strategic use of this assumption to suggest a false bottom line. Negotiation is nothing if not a complex strategy game!

You will rarely if ever negotiate in an environment of perfect information. Negotiations frequently take place before discovery is completed, perhaps even before it is begun. Even if discovery has been completed, the likelihood that you know everything there is to know is very small. People simply don't provide complete information in response to discovery requests—the requests may not seek the right information, the respondents may not remember everything, or there may be reasons, such as privilege, for not providing full information.

Finally, negotiators are human beings. They make decisions and choose courses of action for all sorts of reasons. Individuals have different priorities, different levels of risk aversion, and different personal styles. All of these can make it difficult to predict what a negotiator will do. This difficulty becomes compounded by the fact that a negotiator is representing a client, who also has idiosyncratic goals and preferences that may influence the negotiation.

b. Economic

The economic model of negotiation envisions a continuum along which the negotiation progresses. Each party begins at one end of the continuum, and the parties move together toward the middle until they reach their stopping point, or bottom line. If there is overlap between the stopping points, there is a "zone of settlement" within which the negotiation should settle:

(Assume that Party A starts negotiating at W and sets her bottom line at X)

W>>X
($500,000)   **($250,000)**

(Assume that Party B starts negotiating at Y and sets his bottom line at Z)

Z<<<<<<<<<<<<<<<<<<<<<<<<<<<<<<<<<<<<<<<<Y
($350,000)   **($100,000)**

Here the zone of settlement is between Z and X, or between $250,000 and $350,000.

(Party A) W>>>>>>>>>>ZooooaX<<<<<<<<<<<Y (Party B)

If the stopping points fall short of each other, there can be no settlement:

(Party A) W>>>>>>>>>>XooooooZ<<<<<<<<<<<Y (Party B)

This model of negotiation works reasonably well if the subject of the negotiation is an easily measured or relatively fungible item such as money, and the parties can take successive positions along the continuum. It does not work as well where the negotiation involves multiple items, at least some of which cannot be quantified or broken into pieces that can be given up. For example, if the negotiation involves custody of a child, there is no continuum to move along—one parent or the other will get custody, or they will share joint custody. There are no other options.

c. Social-Psychological Bargaining

We refer to this approach to bargaining somewhat cynically as the "head-game" theory of negotiation because it involves negotiation by manipulation of perceptions. "Head-game" bargainers don't bargain on the merits of the facts or law; they try to make you uncomfortable in one way or another or to affect your perceptions in a way that causes you to want to give in. They may try to make you feel intimidated ("I went to an Ivy League law school and have been practicing for twenty years"), or guilty ("How can you represent a client who did such reprehensible things?"), or physically uncomfortable or off-balance (turning up the heat or providing uncomfortable furniture), with the idea that you may give up just to get away.

There is virtually no limit to the aspects of negotiation process that can be manipulated by a bargainer determined to approach negotiation from this extremely adversarial position. The best defense against a "head-game" bargainer is to recognize the game and ignore it. If you insist on bargaining on the merits, you may be able to neutralize the tactics of your negotiating opponent.

2. Problem-Solving Negotiation

The problem-solving approach to negotiating requires a paradigm shift. The problem-solving negotiator does not think in terms of concessions, compromise, and positions, but rather analyzes needs and interests, and looks for solutions to the mutual problem facing the negotiators. The problem-solving negotiator looks for ways to make the pie bigger, rather than simply carving it up. A problem-solving negotiation involves more free-flowing information and brainstorming of possible solutions. The problem-solving negotiation is not constrained by the game board or the economic continuum, but moves outside the lines to address as many needs and interests as possible.

Since this mode of negotiating focuses on your client's needs and interests rather than bargaining positions, using it should enhance the probability of success. The challenge is to determine whether both the personalities and the subject matter involved in the negotiation lend themselves to this approach. If you determine that the subject matter is appropriate, which is particularly likely in a multiple item, nonmonetary negotiation, and that you are comfortable with your negotiating counterpart, you might ask about the needs and interests of the other party. Of course, you must be prepared to honestly share your client's goals as well. Then the negotiators can work together to devise options that take into account as many of the needs and interests on the table as possible.

§ 18.04. STYLES OF NEGOTIATION

The basic personal approaches to negotiation are competitive and cooperative.[2] This is not to say that these are polar opposites; most of us could place ourselves somewhere on a continuum from highly competitive to highly cooperative. Most of us also tend to believe that other people essentially behave the same way we do. Therefore, cooperative bargainers may be vulnerable to exploitation when faced with competitive opponents because the cooperative bargainer will tend to make concessions in an effort to induce reciprocal behavior. The cooperative bargainer tends to assume that sufficient cooperative behavior must induce reciprocity from an opponent, while the competitive opponent, believing that all people are essentially competitive, will take whatever is given and push for more. This individual does not believe that cooperative bargainers exist, and therefore assumes that the concessions made by the cooperative bargainer are not real concessions—no rational person would give things away unless they did not matter!

There are more effective cooperative negotiators than there are effective competitive negotiators, at least in part because more people tend to be cooperative. In addition, competitive negotiators can sometimes be so abrasive that they cause breakdowns in the process, and so they are less effective.

Cooperative negotiators can protect themselves by making contingent concessions. In other words, do not actually give anything away until you have gotten something in return. Make it clear that all proposals on the table are contingent on the final agreement being satisfactory. For example, in a collective bargaining negotiation over compensation, management's counsel might say, "My client might be willing to contribute more to the pension plan, but we would need your client to relax the demand for a large raise in salary. What is your client willing to give up?"

Negotiation models and personal styles can intersect in interesting ways. Cooperative bargainers can adopt adversarial strategies, and competitive

---

2. *See* Charles B. Craver, *Effective Legal Negotiation and Settlement* (6th ed., LexisNexis 2009). Nancy Schultz is grateful to Charlie Craver for many of the insights that guide her thinking and teaching about negotiations.

negotiators can be problem solvers. The cooperative negotiator using an adversarial model will offer concessions and compromise, while the competitive negotiator trying to function as a problem solver will focus only on his or her own client's needs and interests, and will push solutions that meet those needs and interests.

§ 18.05. PLANNING FOR NEGOTIATION

You should plan all aspects of the negotiation: the information exchange, your opening position, and subsequent concessions. You should establish an opening offer or demand, a target point at which you would like to end up, and a bottom line below which you will not or may not go. We will discuss each of these stages in turn.

1. Evaluating the Case

The first step in your planning process is to evaluate the case as objectively as possible. In order to do this effectively, you need to have a thorough understanding of the law and the facts, and how they intersect. The beauty of negotiation is that you are not limited by what a court is likely to do with your case, but assessing the likely result in court is a good starting point for evaluating acceptable settlements. Therefore, you need to research relevant law and, if possible, find jury verdicts in similar cases. The general rule of thumb for establishing an acceptable settlement point is the likely verdict multiplied by the likelihood of prevailing. For example, if you think you could get a jury award of $800,000, but you think you only have about a 70 percent chance of winning, you should settle for $560,000.

How do you figure out the likelihood of prevailing? In addition to the strength of your legal support, look at factors such as the novelty of the claim, the credibility of likely witnesses, the availability of admissible evidence, and the track record of other players in the game, including opposing counsel, judges, and juries. You should also evaluate opportunity costs associated with litigating or not litigating. This is obviously not a science, and it is impossible to calculate the value of the case with mathematical precision, especially given that different people have widely divergent value systems, but you must start somewhere.

2. Planning to Exchange Information

Inexperienced negotiators frequently underestimate the importance of information exchange to an effective negotiation. You will feel much more confident in your negotiated result if you have sufficient information about the underlying events, needs, and interests. You will be more successful at obtaining useful information if you plan for the process beforehand. It may help to think about information as belonging to one of three categories: information you want, information you don't want to divulge, and information you want your opponents to have.

You have control over the latter two categories, and it should be relatively simple to categorize the information in your possession. You should, however, think strategically about the dissemination of information. People generally give more weight to information they have to work to get, while ascribing lesser significance to information that is easily obtained. This means that you may be able to get your opponent to devalue damaging information by simply stating it up front. This may seem counterintuitive initially, but if you think about it, it should make sense. Before fighting information requests, you should be sure that information that seems dangerous at first blush is really all that damaging. Frequently there are perfectly logical explanations for facts that seem harmful, and sometimes you may even be able to turn an apparently damaging fact into a useful tool. You will find it easier to evaluate information objectively during your preparation than you will in the heat of the negotiation.

Plan your questioning of your opponent. Identify categories of information you want, and ask questions that are precisely designed to get that information.

3. Establishing an Opening, Target, and Bottom Line

Much strategizing is done on the subject of where to begin a negotiation. Some negotiators hesitate to begin negotiating at all for fear of appearing weak. There is little evidence that either party to a negotiation gains an advantage by starting or refusing to start the process. It is possible that the party that makes the first concession will do less well in the final result. Some experienced negotiators prefer to make the first offer or demand because doing so allows them to set the stage for the negotiation and begin to limit the playing field. Other negotiators prefer to draw an opening offer or demand to respond to, on the theory that they can set the midpoint of the opening positions (where many results tend to cluster) with their response. You should probably do whatever feels most comfortable to you or whatever is appropriate in the context of a particular negotiation. For example, plaintiffs in personal injury actions frequently make the first demand.

The trick in establishing an opening offer is to set the starting point at a place that is credible, but that also gives you some bargaining room. Starting too close to your bottom line in an effort to be fair or to make the negotiation more efficient may cause frustration all around. Most negotiators simply will not believe that your opening position is designed to be fair, and there will be quite a struggle to keep the final result in the range you had in mind. Conversely, an outrageous opening offer or demand may cause the other party to refuse to negotiate at all until you have come down to a reasonable point. Outrageous starting positions are difficult to defend and frequently require huge initial concessions just to get the bargaining started. Find a starting point that you can justify with a straight face and that leaves some room for bargaining, and even for the possibility that you may have miscalculated the value of the case. Remember that your opponent knows things you don't know, and this may affect the reasonable settlement point in ways you cannot anticipate.

Set a target point, a point at which you would like to settle and that you believe is reasonable based on the information you have. Head toward this target point during the negotiation and make a serious effort not to go below it unless you are persuaded that there can be no settlement in this range. Finally, set a bottom line before you go into the negotiation. This should be the point below which you absolutely do not intend to go, and you should hold firm at that point if you get there during the negotiation, unless you are satisfied that you have seriously misanalyzed the problem. Negotiators who do not preset bottom lines frequently find themselves "giving up the farm" during the negotiation. Once you start giving, and begin to feel a commitment to settlement, it can be difficult to refuse that final concession in the interest of finalizing a deal.[3]

You should also think about a concession pattern in advance. How do you plan to get from your opening to your target, and then ultimately to your bottom line if you have to go there? Obviously the actual concession pattern will to some extent be dictated by the events of the negotiation, but you will feel more confident if you have thought about where you want to go after the opponent rejects your opening offer or demand, as is virtually inevitable. If the opening offer or demand is accepted, you have almost certainly badly underestimated the value of the case!

4. Analyzing Needs and Interests

You should make an effort to identify the needs and interests of the parties as accurately as possible before the negotiation. You may want to classify the anticipated needs as essential, important, or desirable, and then try to figure out whether those needs are likely to be shared, independent, or conflicting.[4] The idea of shared needs may seem odd, but it is possible. For example, both parties may want to keep the agreement confidential, or both parties to a custody dispute may want the best for the children—they simply disagree about how to achieve it. Independent needs are those that can be met without creating an adverse impact on the other party. For example, if one party to a negotiation needs the terms of the settlement to be confidential, and the other party has no desire to talk about the deal, the need for confidentiality is an independent need.

This approach is particularly appropriate for a problem-solving negotiation, but it can be useful in virtually any situation. Thinking of a negotiation in terms of needs and interests rather than positions frequently makes the bargaining more flexible and the conversation less strained. It may also open up possibilities for resolution that would not have occurred to you otherwise.

If you can identify independent or shared needs, start the negotiation there. It is easier to get the process started if you can get an agreement on bargaining items that are not likely to create conflict. Beginning the negotiation with difficult or contentious items can lead to early breakdown. The most likely area of difficulty in the formulation we suggest is the area where essential needs of the parties are in conflict. If you arrive at this point in a negotiation, bring your creativity or prepare to go to trial!

---

3. Remember that all of this takes place in the context of your instructions from your client. You should know what your settlement authority is before you begin to negotiate, and you may not agree to anything outside of that authority. At best, you can offer to take a proposal to your client that does not satisfy the goals set by you and the client before the negotiation.

4. This formulation appears in a very useful chart in Bastress & Harbaugh, *supra* n. 1, at 483.

5. Planning for Personalities

Try to find out what you can about your negotiating partners or opponents. Negotiating style and personality can have a huge impact on the progress of a negotiation. Some people have so much trouble communicating that they simply cannot have lengthy face-to-face meetings. If you find yourself in a negotiating situation with someone who makes you so angry you cannot think straight, get out! You are likely to make mistakes if you are angry or in some other emotional state that clouds your thinking sufficiently that it becomes difficult to make rational decisions. Conversely, if you are negotiating with someone who is fair and reasonable, the process can be a pleasure. Remember that everyone's job is to represent their client, and try not to take it personally if you don't get everything you want.

§ 18.06. BEGINNING THE NEGOTIATION

If you have prepared adequately, the beginning of the negotiation should be easy. Try to establish a comfortable, constructive atmosphere for negotiating. If the negotiators don't know each other, a little small talk to allow everyone to relax may be helpful. It may be a good idea to set an agenda for the negotiation. For example, you may agree on an order of topics to be addressed; you may agree in advance that all options put on the table are contingent on an acceptable final settlement. The latter approach is a good way to avoid deadlock later on if the only item left to be discussed is a particularly difficult one, and you find yourself wishing that you had something else left to ask for or to give away. A lot of negotiators try to gain some sort of tactical advantage by playing "head games" in the early stages of a negotiation; this may be effective for some in the short run, but you will generally find that the process works better if everyone just gets down to business and concentrates on trying to deal with the joint problem to be solved that brought you to the table in the first place.

§ 18.07. INFORMATION EXCHANGE

As we mentioned earlier, this is obviously a critical phase of the negotiation. How can you reach the optimal resolution of a problem if you don't really understand what the problem is? Again, if you have prepared adequately, this phase of the negotiation should be productive. You want to find out as much as you can about the other side's needs, interests, and priorities. You want to obtain any facts that will help you understand the situation and that might be relevant if the case does go to trial. If you have filed a complaint, you may be able to get some of this information through discovery, but negotiations frequently take place before discovery is completed, and perhaps before it is even begun.

Open-ended questions, such as "What was your client doing right before the accident?", may get you more information, but they also allow more opportunities for evasion if a party is determined to evade the question. Listen very carefully to the answers you get. If the responder is hedging or seems to be choosing words very carefully, think about the precise words you used in your question and rephrase the question in a way that leaves less wiggle room or that is more precisely designed to get the information you seek. For example, if you are negotiating a settlement of the Smiths' claim against the Palm Court Hotel, and you want to establish the hotel's knowledge of criminal activity in the area, you might ask if hotel personnel were aware of any similar incidents in the area. This question allows the responder to define "similar incidents." If the negotiator chooses to interpret that phrase in a very limited way, he or she might decide that since there were no identical incidents, the answer is "no." You should ask instead whether the hotel is aware of any criminal activity within a specified radius of the hotel.

If you get questions you prefer not to answer, there are many blocking techniques available. You can answer with a question, you can "misunderstand" and answer a different question, you can hide your answer in a lot of irrelevant verbiage, you can refuse to answer, you can declare the question irrelevant or out of bounds, or you can answer part of the question. You should consider the likely effect of using too many blocking techniques on your own ability to obtain information. Why should the other party answer your questions if you refuse to answer theirs? You should also be aware of the likelihood that these techniques may be used against you and watch out for them. If you sense that information requests are being blocked, don't give up—rephrase your questions until you are satisfied that the information does not exist or will not be forthcoming. It is frequently disappointing or worse for negotiators to realize that critical information was available if only they had asked for it in the right way.

All in all, the negotiation will be much more productive if there is a constructive and thorough information exchange. If you want to obtain the best result for your client, you want to provide the information that supports the result you seek. The parties are much more likely to reach a mutually satisfactory resolution of the problem if there is genuine understanding of the issues on all sides. The exchange of information will frequently suggest possibilities for resolution that may not have occurred to anyone during preparation.

§ 18.08. TRADING

This is the point of the negotiation where the actual exchanges take place. The key here is to keep track of the concessions and to explain them in terms that are relevant and understandable. Do not make multiple unreciprocated concessions. Do not make concessions that are disproportionately large when compared to your opponent's concessions. Make sure that you explain the rationale for every concession and every refusal to make a concession. Concessions that are not justified in terms of the applicable law and facts are merely numbers or positions that come from nowhere and have little credibility or persuasive effect. There is nothing to distinguish one number from another if you cannot connect it to something concrete.

For example, if you are seeking damages for the Smiths, explain how you arrived at the number you request using factors such as lost wages and medical expenses; if you agree to accept a smaller number, explain the concession in terms if something that has happened during the negotiation—a fact of which you were unaware or a trade-off for something else that will benefit your clients. Negotiations will frequently get to a point where everyone is simply "horse-trading" to arrive at a resolution, and finally perhaps "splitting the difference" to finalize the deal. This should be the natural evolution of the negotiation—not the starting point.

§ 18.09. CLOSING THE NEGOTIATION

Once you believe you have achieved a negotiated resolution, take a few moments to find out if it is possible to adjust the agreement in some way that benefits both parties or that allows one party to benefit without damaging the other party. These few moments at the end of a negotiation can make a large difference in the parties' commitment to the agreement and willingness to carry it out. They can also go a long way toward preserving or rehabilitating the relationship between the negotiators. You will discover that the importance of reputation cannot be overemphasized in the legal community, and a reputation as a competent, fair negotiator will take you far.

You should also use this final stage of the negotiation to make sure that you have actually reached an agreement. Go back over the terms in detail and make sure that both parties have the same understanding of the agreement. Proper handling of this crucial step will save you much grief later on. Misunderstandings can cause serious problems and may end up unraveling the whole deal if it turns out that the parties had very different feelings about the meaning of a critical term. One good approach is to send a confirming letter to the other negotiator outlining your understanding of the agreement as you will take it to your client. If both sides are not "on the same wavelength," it should become clear very quickly, indicating a need for further negotiation or recognition of an impossible situation.

§ 18.10. NEGOTIATION ETHICS

There are very few written rules that govern negotiations. There will be no one there looking over your shoulder to see if you behave or not. One rule that does apply is that you may not make a false statement of material fact or law (Model R. Prof. Conduct 4.1(a)). This is obviously a simple statement of a complex range of possibilities. For example, when does an omission rise to the level of a misrepresentation? If you know that the opposing party is relying on a misconception about what the facts are, and you do nothing to correct it, are you misrepresenting the facts? Negotiators frequently try to skate this line very closely; you will have to make your own decisions about what kind of negotiator you want to be, and what kind of behavior will allow you to sleep at night. Do remember that your reputation will not only precede you, but will affect how and whether people interact with you.

It is a convention of negotiating that the client's value system is not considered a material fact. Thus you may "lie" about what your client is willing to accept and even about your bottom line. You do not have to respond honestly to direct questions about what your client wants, as you do to factual questions in other areas. You should know, however, that you may do damage to the negotiating process and to your reputation by lying about such things to the extreme. A certain amount of puffery is expected, but if people learn that you will look someone in the eye with a wounded expression and plead that you are being taken to the cleaners while you are in fact cleaning out your opponents, you will find future negotiations difficult.

Another type of behavior that causes damage to the process is lying about what kind of negotiator you are. Many competitive "sharks" can adopt the language of the cooperative problem solver while they are taking advantage of genuinely cooperative negotiators. If discovered, however, they may find later negotiations uncomfortable. Again, however trite it may sound, you must let your conscience be your guide in negotiations.

We have obviously only skimmed the surface of the complex set of interactions that is negotiation. However, we believe that we have given you sound advice that will serve you well as you develop your own negotiating style and ideas. You will learn a lot about the process through experience, and there are plenty of books on the market if you wish to do further reading.[5]

§ 18.11. NEGOTIATION CHECKLIST

— Prepare, prepare, prepare. Research the law. Know the facts. Plan your information gathering and exchange. Analyze needs and interests. Write down your opening, target, and bottom line, and think about likely and acceptable concession patterns. Find out whatever you can about your negotiating partners and opponents.
— Exchange information until you are satisfied that real bargaining can take place in an informed environment.
— Keep track of concessions. Justify all requests and concessions with thoughtful explanations of relevant facts and law.
— Close the negotiation by checking to see if you can adjust the agreement to benefit one or more parties without damaging others. Make sure all parties have the same understanding of the agreement.
— Think about what kind of negotiator you want to be and what kind of reputation you want to have in your negotiating community.

Exercise

Here is the general information for a negotiation exercise. Your instructor will distribute confidential information for each party and give you further guidance regarding how to conduct the negotiation.

---

5. For example, you might want to take a look at the classic *Getting to Yes* by Roger Fisher & William Ury (Houghton Mifflin 1981), or, for some very practical advice, *Negotiating Your Salary: How to Make $1000 a Minute* by Jack Chapman (Ten Speed Press 1996).

Landlord/Tenant Problem

General Information

Millie Graves is seventy-nine years old. For the past fifteen years, she has lived in a second floor apartment in Garden Grove. About a month ago, Millie was mugged outside the front door of her building. Her attacker had apparently followed her from the street, waiting until just before she entered the building, when she was in the shadow of the large bushes growing in the front yard. There is a light over the front door, but it was not on that evening. The attack took place sometime between 9:00 and 9:30 p.m. Millie was not seriously injured, but she suffered bruises and scrapes when her assailant knocked her to the ground after he grabbed her purse. She lost all her identification, credit cards, and approximately $80 in cash. There is normally a doorman stationed at the desk just inside the front door, but he was not at his desk at the time of the attack.

Millie has never been a problem tenant. She doesn't complain and she pays her rent on time. For the past three months, however, she has withheld $100 per month from her monthly rent of $500 in an effort to get the landlord, Sam Simolean, to make several repairs to her apartment. There is a leak in her shower, water damage to her kitchen ceiling from a leak in the apartment above hers, and two broken windows. Her apartment has not been painted in two years, and it shows. There are also quite a number of insects running around the building, particularly in the common areas. Millie has three cats, which was perfectly fine with her previous landlord, but Simolean has instituted a "No Pets" policy for new tenants. Based on Millie's failure to pay her full rent for the past three months, he recently served her with an eviction notice, giving her sixty days to vacate the premises. The lease requires thirty days' notice of termination for failure to pay rent. Millie still has fifteen months to go on a two-year lease.

Communicating Electronically

§ 19.01. E-MAIL ETIQUETTE

By now, most professionals are acquainted with e-mail, and certainly all law students and young lawyers are. They usually know the basic rules of e-mail etiquette. For example, they know to type in complete sentences and not to type in all capital letters or all lowercase letters. A quick search with a browser will bring up innumerable online lists of e-mail dos and don'ts, most of which will contain the same rules. What follows is a particularly comprehensive list from *Email Etiquette Guidelines for the Connecticut State Government*. Although some of the contents seem tailored to government employees, these guidelines offer sound advice for any professional.

I. Guidelines for Effective E-Mail Communication

A. Know Your Audience

1. Know your audience.

Communication and mail conventions may vary between groups. Remember that the recipient is a person whose culture, language, and humor may be different from your own. Acronyms, date formats, measurements, and idioms may not be universally understood. Also be mindful that different users have different levels of experience with technology applications like e-mail. Be patient with and supportive of new users.

2. Be aware of differences across e-mail systems.

Others may not have the same e-mail features or capabilities you have, in which case, avoid special control characters like bold, underline, and special fonts; even tabs can differ. With the exception of binary (program) files, keep your lines under 80 characters; if possible don't exceed 72 characters. Be sure that your e-mail software inserts carriage returns at the end of each line; if not, enter a hard return. Be extra careful with graphics. Whenever possible, find out in advance what e-mail features and software tools your recipients have.

B. Message Composition Guidelines

1. Identify yourself.

Identify your affiliation, title, background, and expertise in your e-mail message, especially if you are acting on behalf of an organization or professional association, or if you have relevant background or expertise in a matter. You can create this file ahead of time and add it to the end of your messages. (Some mail clients do this automatically.) In Internet parlance, this is known as a .sig or signature file. Your .sig file takes the place of your business card. If you include a signature keep it short.

2. Use subject entries.

Try to keep messages to a single subject. E-mail should have a subject heading which reflects the content of the message. The subject line of an e-mail message enables busy people to discern the subject of a message and when it must be read. The subject line is also important because it is used to index the message in mailboxes and file folders.

3. Avoid putting text in all capital letters.

Use appropriate punctuation and case as you would in a standard business letter. Most users suggest that you avoid putting all text in caps because it may seem ANGRY or HARSH. The recipient of your e-mail may feel that you are shouting at them.

4. Keep messages brief and to the point.

Make your messages concise, not cryptic. Shorter paragraphs have more impact and are more likely to be read by busy people. Most people can only grasp a limited number of ideas within a single paragraph, especially on a computer screen.

When replying to a message, include enough original material to be understood but no more. It is bad form to reply to a message by including the entire previous message unless it is relevant to an understanding of your response.

5. Format messages for easy reading.

White space enhances the look and clarity of an e-mail message, and a blank line only adds a byte to the message. Lengthy messages are almost always read in hard copy form and should be prepared accordingly (e.g., with cover sheets, headers, page numbers, and formatting). Be aware that complex formatting may be lost during translation through mail gateways and into mail systems that are not configured to support it.

6. Cite the appropriate references and context of a message.

Reference any related e-mail message or posting, and the event, topic, or issue that your message refers to, in order to avoid being taken out of context and misinterpreted. Back up your statements with references to documents or articles just as you would in written material.

If you are forwarding or re-posting a message you've received, do not change the wording. You may shorten the message and quote only relevant parts, but be sure you give proper attribution. If the message was sent to you and you are re-posting it to a group, you should obtain the sender's permission first.

7. Be aware of copyright restrictions.

Copyright laws are applicable to e-mail networks. Posting information on networks is publication. Be careful to cite references and avoid posting copyrighted material. For more information on copyright, see the U.S. Copyright Office website at: http://lcweb.loc.gov/copyright/.

8. Proofread your messages.

Spelling and grammar mistakes can be just as distracting in an e-mail message as they are in written communications. Proofread your messages, especially messages that are used to communicate or document agency business.

C. Communication Guidelines

1. Read the State of Connecticut Acceptable Use Policies.

The State of Connecticut has developed a comprehensive set of acceptable use policies for networking, telecommunications and electronic mail systems. Familiarize yourself with these policies. The "Electronic Mail Acceptable Use Policy for Connecticut State Government" can be accessed at http://www.state.ct.us/cmac/policies/emailcon.htm and the "Acceptable Use Policy Telecommunication Network (CTNET)" can be accessed at http://www.state.ct.us/cmac/policies/aup.htm.

2. E-mail messages are public records.

Don't be fooled by the illusion of privacy. E-mail messages are discoverable as evidence to support litigation. Don't commit anything to e-mail that you wouldn't want to become public knowledge.

There is always the chance that your message could end up in someone else's hands. Be aware that e-mail messages are often retained on system backup tapes and disks in central computing facilities after they are deleted from the mail system. In addition, unless you are using an encryption device (hardware or software), you should assume that electronic mail transmitted via the Internet is not secure.

3. Separate opinion from fact.

Use labels or explanatory notes to distinguish opinion from fact so that readers do not confuse personal opinion with agency policy or position. If necessary, include a brief disclaimer.

4. Be careful with your use of humor and sarcasm.

You can't control when and in what context a message will be read; it might be read at the wrong time or by the wrong party. The reader might not understand your intention.

What is humorous to you may be offensive to others. Use labels, explanatory notes, or emoticons to alert the recipient that a message is meant to be taken humorously. Facial expressions, voice inflection and other cues that help recipients to interpret a message are absent from e-mail.

5. Avoid sending e-mail in anger or as an emotional response.

It is best not to send these kinds of messages over e-mail. Such situations are better worked out in person or in another forum. If you are caught in an argument or disagreement, keep the discussion focused on issues rather than the personalities involved.

If you receive a message or posting that generates negative feelings, set it aside and reread it later. An immediate response is often a hasty response. On most systems, once you send a message you are committed to it, and cannot retract it. Re-read your e-mail for content and tone before you send it. Don't rule out the possibility that a misunderstanding or misinterpretation might occur. It is common with e-mail because of the lack of physical cues.

6. Respect the privacy rights of others.

Don't invade others' privacy. Don't read other people's e-mail. If you receive e-mail meant for someone else, use the same consideration you would with traditional mail. Inform the appropriate party, see that the mail is returned, and notify your network administrator.

D. Distribution Conventions

1. Don't label messages urgent when they don't need to be.

Most of us learned the lesson of "the boy who cried wolf" quite some time ago. In today's world, this lesson rings true for the misuse of priority mail notices. These notices will soon become meaningless with overuse.

2. Don't over-distribute e-mail.

Every message you send creates work for someone else who must read, consider, and deal with the message. It may be better to post some messages on an electronic bulletin board, website, or newsgroup to reduce the number of copies routed to individual users.

E. Sending Attachments with Your E-Mail Message

1. Sending attachments with your e-mail message

If you are sending plain text, do not use an attachment. Place the content in your e-mail message. Also consider including Uniform Resource Locators (URLs) or pointers to FTP-able (File Transfer Protocol) versions, or cutting the file into smaller chunks and sending each as a separate message. Most e-mail applications will allow you to attach almost any type of file to an e-mail message, including word processor documents, spreadsheets, sound files, and graphics. Attaching large documents, files, images or programs may make your message so large that it cannot be delivered or will consume excessive resources. A good rule is not to send a file larger than 50 Kilobytes or "KB." (This document, E-Mail Etiquette Guidelines for Connecticut State Government, is approximately 50 KB or 7 pages.) Never send large amounts of unsolicited information.

2. Specifying your attachments

Use proper naming conventions and file extensions to identify your documents. Within your e-mail messages, clearly specify that there is an attachment with its proper file name, application software version, content description and size of the attached file so the recipient can make an immediate judgement as to what will be required to view the file. It is important to keep in mind that your recipients may not have (1) the same suite of desktop application software that you have, or (2) if they do have the same application, they may not have the same version of the software as your attachment. If possible, one should always check with the recipient to verify the compatibility of the attachment that is being sent. If you are unable to verify the compatibility, send the file in a lower version (Excel 4.0 vs. Excel 97) or a more common format, i.e. text or HTML, to improve the chances that the file can be read by the greatest number of recipients.

3. Receiving attachments

After receiving an e-mail attachment, save the attachment to a local or network drive to avoid clogging your e-mail system's storage capacity with little used documents and files.

4. Protecting against viruses

At this time, reading e-mail messages does not pose a threat of catching a computer virus. Viruses can only be contained in attachments to your e-mail messages. One should be very careful about opening attachments to e-mail messages, particularly if they aren't from a known or trusted e-mail source. Do not allow your e-mail program to automatically download and/or execute an attached file. You can safely download a virus-infected attachment to your desktop, as long as you don't open the file. To protect your computer resources, detach the file and run an antivirus program that checks the attachment before you open it.

II. Guidelines for E-Mail Distribution Lists (LISTSERV®) and Newsgroups

1. Learn how the Listserv/Newsgroup operates and understand its culture

Save the subscription messages for any lists or newsgroups that you join. These will usually tell you how to post messages, how to unsubscribe, and the rules, guidelines and etiquette for the listserv. If there is an FAQ (Frequently Asked Questions) for the list, read it before posting or replying to your first message. Make an effort to understand the culture of the listserv or newsgroup that you are joining—know what is acceptable behavior and what is not.

2. Consider that a large audience will see your posts

Take care in what you write. Consider that a large audience will see your posts and this audience may include your colleagues and co-workers. Remember too that mailing lists and newsgroups are frequently archived, and that your words may be stored for a very long time in a place to which many people have access.

3. Identify yourself

Make things easy for the recipient(s). In order to ensure that people know who you are, be sure to include a line or two at the end of your message with contact information. This will guarantee that any peculiarities of mailers or newsreaders that strip header information will not delete the only reference in the message of how people may reach you. You can create this file ahead of time and add it to the end of your messages. (Some mailers do this automatically.) In Internet parlance, this is known as a .sig or signature file. Your .sig file takes the place of your business card.

4. Be brief and to the point

Messages and articles should be brief and to the point. Don't wander off-topic, don't ramble, and don't send mail or post messages solely to point out other people's errors in typing or spelling.

5. Distributing large files

Don't send large files to mailing lists when Uniform Resource Locators (URLs) or pointers to FTP-able (File Transfer Protocol) versions will do. If you want to send it as multiple files, be sure to follow the culture of the group. If you don't know what that is, ask.

6. Adding context with your reply

If you are sending a reply to a message or a posting be sure you summarize the original at the top of the message, or include just enough text of the original to give a context. This will make sure readers understand when they start to read your response. Giving context helps everyone. If you ask a question, be sure to post a summary. When doing so, truly summarize rather than send a cumulation of the messages you receive.

7. Be careful when you reply to messages or postings

Frequently, replies are sent back to the address that originated the post—which in many cases is the address of a list or group! You may accidentally send a personal response to a great many people, embarrassing all involved. It's best to type in the address instead of relying on REPLY.

8. Unnecessary replies to replies

Avoid sending messages or posting articles that are no more than replies to replies. Only post messages that are relevant.

9. Disagreement with one person

If you should find yourself in a disagreement with one person, make your responses to each other via mail rather than continue to send messages to the list or the group. If you are debating a point on which the group might have some interest, you may summarize for them later.

10. Do not use Auto-reply features

The auto-reply feature (and/or delivery receipt, non-delivery notice and vacation programs) of many mailers is useful for in-house communication, but quite annoying when sent to entire mailing lists. Do not use them. Consider unsubscribing when you cannot check your mail for an extended period.

11. Cross-posting

When sending a message to multiple mailing lists, especially if the lists are closely related, apologize for cross-posting.[1]

---

1. Parts of this Guide to E-Mail Etiquette incorporate conventions and similar guidelines compiled by: Gargano, "Guide to Electronic Communication and Network Etiquette" (1989); Goode and Johnson, "Putting Out the Flames: The Etiquette and Law of E-Mail," ONLINE (1991); Krol, "The Whole Internet User's Guide and Catalogue" (1989); and Robinson, "Delivering Electronic Mail" (1992); "Netiquette Guidelines," October 1995, http://www.ietf.org/rfc/rfc1855.txt, Sally Hambridge Intel Corporation. LISTSERV is a registered trademark licensed to L-Soft International, Inc.

§ 19.02. E-MAILING YOUR SUPERVISOR

In today's busy world, a junior attorney may find that he or she is writing fewer memos and letters and communicating more in e-mails. In these communications, the attorney must be especially careful to follow the rules of etiquette. In composing these documents, the attorney may have three particular questions. What tone should I adopt? How detailed should the document be? How should it appear visually?

1. Tone

The professional e-mail is a formal document directed to a boss or client and not to a close friend. Because of the nature of e-mails, the writer can be tempted to drop his or her guard. Even if you think you have developed a good friendship with your supervisor, you may forget that your e-mail may be forwarded to others who will find your tone inappropriate.

An emotional tone may become tempting if you are excited, disappointed, or angry over an assignment or turn of events. Wait at least a few minutes before hitting the "send" key so that you can think clearly about your tone and its possible consequences.

E-mails with an inappropriate tone can cause problems for the writer. You may know the story of the New Zealand accountant who had to fight her termination when she was fired for sending e-mails in all-caps with words in red and bold, which her employer argued "caused disharmony in the workplace." You may also have heard of the unfortunate e-mail that former Federal Emergency Management Agency director Michael Brown sent during the catastrophe that Hurricane Katrina caused in New Orleans. Brown received an e-mail stating that "thousands are gathering in the street with no food or water." His e-mail reply: "Thanks for the update. Anything specific I need to do or tweak?" When that reply became public, Brown seemed exceedingly heartless. In the same way, a thoughtless e-mail could cost you a client, a poor evaluation, a promotion, or a job.

2. Degree of Detail

An e-mail is not the venue for a complete memo of the sort that you might compose in hard copy. E-mail lends itself to briefer documents that can be read and digested in a short time. If your supervisor wants a full-scale memo, you should produce a hard copy or place it in an attachment that he or she can download and print.

As a general rule, an e-mail should be no longer than a page and should contain somewhat more detail than you would include in the conclusion or brief answer of a conventional brief. See Section 11.03.

3. Visual Appearance

In composing an e-mail document, you want to make it easy for the reader to read. Therefore, you must think about how to design your product. You will want a header that immediately tells the reader what the document pertains to. Because the reader may access the document on an iPhone, Blackberry, or similar device, you want to think about how it will appear on a small screen. Therefore, you will want to keep your paragraphs short, have blank space between them, and make the document no longer than is necessary.

Exercises

(1) When it comes to poorly composed e-mails, what is your pet peeve? What violation of etiquette or good format irks you the most? Please compose a short e-mail that exemplifies your pet peeve.

(2) In Section 11.03, you will find the examples of two good conclusions. Please redraft them as an e-mail memo that is no longer than one page. The other examples in Chapters 11 and 13 will give you enough additional information to permit you to complete this exercise.

CHAPTER 20

Drafting Pleadings

§ 20.01. INTRODUCTION

The parties in litigation use written pleadings to present their cases to the court. This chapter shows you how to write these pleadings. The pleadings determine the issues the court must decide. Pleadings also notify the parties of the allegations that each side intends to make at trial. The two most basic pleadings are the plaintiff's complaint and the defendant's answer. The litigants also may file other pretrial pleadings. For example, the defendant may file a counterclaim against the plaintiff, which may be included in the answer. Defendants may also file cross-claims against each other or third-party complaints to join additional defendants.

§ 20.02. THE PURPOSE AND LANGUAGE OF PLEADINGS

In drafting a pleading, remember that you are speaking to different audiences. When you are drafting a complaint, one audience is the defendant. Although the defendant probably knows the facts, he or she also needs to know what causes of action you are pursuing. The other audience is the court. The court needs to know both the facts and the causes of action.

To satisfy both audiences you need to tell the factual story and identify the causes of action. You will tell the story by arranging the facts in chronological order and presenting the sequence of events from your client's perspective. You do not editorialize or use unnecessary modifiers, but the reader of a well-drafted complaint should feel that a wrong has been committed and that something should be done about it. This feeling should be created even before the specific causes of action are presented.

There are different schools of thought about the level of detail that is appropriate for a pleading. There are also differences in expectations between state and federal courts. In your civil procedure class, you may learn about something called "notice pleading," which essentially means pleading only so much information as is absolutely necessary to put the defendant on notice of the nature of the claim. Additionally, some lawyers will tell you that, as a matter of strategy, they never want to tip their hands to opposing counsel by putting too much information into a pleading. You should follow the rules of your jurisdiction and the instructions of your supervisors. Nevertheless, it is our view that a good pleading tells a complete, coherent story in a persuasive way and gives the court solid perspective on your case.

The causes of action should be identified clearly and precisely. Be sure to allege all required elements. Use separate counts for each cause of action. To ensure clarity, you should follow the principles of writing set forth in this book: use plain English to the extent possible, write short plain sentences, and use concrete words.

In practice, pleadings often include substantial legalese. Court rules and decisions may require such archaic jargon as "complaint in Assumpsit" instead of "complaint in Contract" or "complaint in Trespass" instead of "complaint in Tort." Custom and practice have embedded in pleadings awkward sentences and confusing words. When local rules and precedents require you to use obscure language, you have no choice but to comply. Even when you are required to use some jargon, however, you still have considerable latitude to write short simple sentences in comprehensible English.

§ 20.03. FOLLOWING RULES

Pleadings must conform to the rules of procedure of the jurisdiction in which the action begins. Therefore, you must look at the rules in your jurisdiction before drafting a pleading. Our goal here is to give you a general understanding of how to draft a pleading.

In most jurisdictions, the party must make allegations in a pleading in consecutively numbered paragraphs so that the opposing party can answer each allegation using the same numbers. Each paragraph of the pleading must contain only a single allegation so that the opposing party can specifically deny or admit it.

You can find examples of how to draft pleadings in form books. Most jurisdictions have form books containing examples of pleadings. Law offices also develop forms over a period of time for use in many different situations.

§ 20.04. CAPTIONS

All pleadings begin with a caption that identifies the court, the number the court has assigned to the case, the parties, and the type of pleading. The caption may also include the month and year in which the action is filed. Here is an example of a caption for a complaint:

IN THE SUPERIOR COURT FOR THE
STATE OF CALIFORNIA

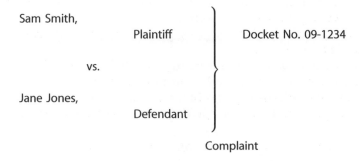

Sam Smith,

         Plaintiff   Docket No. 09-1234

    vs.

Jane Jones,

         Defendant

               Complaint

Exercise

Using the following information, draft a caption for a pleading.

Bob Dob has sued Joe Doe for assault and battery. You are drafting pleadings for this case in the District Court for Lincoln County. The court has assigned the case number as 98-502, and Bob filed the case in the April Term of 1998. Joe lives at 92 High Street, Hometown. Bob lives at 110 High Street, Hometown. Write a caption to use over a complaint, an answer, or any other pleading.

§ 20.05. THE COMPLAINT

Following the caption is the body of the pleading, which contains the material allegations and request for relief.

Suppose, for example, that your client, Marilyn Smith, wants you to file suit on her behalf so that she can recover damages for injuries she received from a dog bite. Before you draft the complaint, you might write out a summary of the facts provided by the client in paragraph, narrative form. The facts alleged in a complaint must show that the plaintiff has a cause of action. The complaint also must give the defendant notice of the plaintiff's claims and an opportunity to defend against them. To show that the plaintiff has a cause of action, the complaint must allege sufficient facts to demonstrate that the plaintiff has a right to relief under the applicable law. Therefore, you must research the law before you write the complaint to determine what facts to allege in it. Suppose that the law in your jurisdiction states that the victim of a dog bite can recover under either negligence or strict liability under the following circumstances:

An individual is liable in negligence to another party if

    (1) that individual owns or harbors a dog;

    (2) that individual knew that the dog had previously attacked at least one other person;

(3) that individual knew that the dog was likely to harm other persons unless properly confined or otherwise controlled;

(4) that individual fails to exercise reasonable care to confine or otherwise control the dog; and

(5) the dog attacks and injures the other party.

An individual is strictly liable in tort to another party if

(1) the individual knowingly owns or harbors a dog that is of a vicious nature that is accustomed to attacking and biting other persons;

(2) the individual had personal knowledge of the vicious nature of the dog and knew that the dog was accustomed to attacking and biting other persons; and

(3) the dog attacks and injures the other party.

The complaint that you would file on behalf of your client might look like this:

Complaint

1. Plaintiff, Marilyn Smith, is an individual and citizen of the Commonwealth of Pennsylvania, residing at 12 Main Street, Anywhere, Pennsylvania 19009.[1]

2. Defendant, Samantha Jones, is an individual and citizen of the Commonwealth of Pennsylvania, residing at 14 Main Street, Anywhere, Pennsylvania 19009.

3. On June 4, 2003, at about 8:00 a.m., the defendant was the owner of or harbored a dog.

4. On June 4, 2003, at about 8:00 a.m., Plaintiff was walking in a common driveway at her residence when the defendant's dog attacked and bit her without provocation.

5. The dog had attacked at least one other person before attacking the plaintiff.

COUNT I

STRICT LIABILITY IN TORT

6. Plaintiff incorporates by reference paragraphs 1 through 5 of this Complaint.

7. On June 4, 2003, at about 8:00 a.m., Defendant knowingly owned or harbored a dog that was of a vicious nature and that was accustomed to attacking and biting other persons.

8. Defendant had personal knowledge of the vicious nature of the dog and knew that the dog was used and accustomed to attacking and biting other persons.

9. The dog attacked and bit Plaintiff, causing her to suffer various physical and mental injuries, including but not limited to lacerations of her left hand and wrist, contusions of her left thumb, and a puncture wound in her left foot. The injuries led to scarring, infection, lameness, and present and future pain, suffering, and mental anguish.

---

1. Some jurisdictions, including the federal courts, require a jurisdictional allegation at the beginning of the complaint. Thus, you might begin the complaint with a sentence that says something like "This Court has jurisdiction over this matter under 28 U.S.C. § 1331."

WHEREFORE, Plaintiff demands that this court enter judgment in her favor and against Defendant in an amount in excess of $10,000, exclusive of interest and costs.

COUNT II

NEGLIGENCE

10. Plaintiff incorporates by reference paragraphs 1 through 5 of this Complaint.

11. Defendant knew that the dog had previously attacked at least one other person.

12. Defendant knew that the dog was likely to harm individuals unless properly confined or otherwise controlled.

13. Defendant failed to exercise reasonable care to confine or otherwise control the dog.

14. The dog attacked and bit Plaintiff, causing her to suffer various physical and mental injuries, including but not limited to lacerations of her left hand and wrist, contusions of her left thumb, and a puncture wound in her left foot. The injuries led to scarring, infection, lameness, and present and future pain, suffering, and mental anguish.

WHEREFORE, Plaintiff demands that this Court enter judgment in her favor and against Defendant in an amount in excess of $10,000, exclusive of interest and costs.

Attorney for Plaintiff

As you can see from this example, the introductory paragraphs of a complaint identify the names and addresses of the parties. Here the plaintiff is suing on two separate counts, or causes of action: strict liability in tort and negligence. The next paragraphs (3-5) set out any facts that are common to more than one count of the complaint. You incorporate those facts by reference in each count of the complaint. See, for example, paragraphs 6 and 10 of the sample complaint. This may appear unnecessarily repetitious, but it relates the information in the introductory paragraphs directly to each count and lets the court know that the basic information is the same with regard to each count.

The complaint shown above is written in plain English, following the principles of clear writing. You see no "hereins" or other stilted language. The writer used everyday language throughout the complaint and no legalese. The final paragraph does use "wherefore," which is the common way to end a complaint. Otherwise, however, there is no eccentric language.

Most sentences are in simple subject-verb-object structure, such as "The dog had attacked at least one other person," "Defendant had personal knowledge," and "The dog attacked and bit plaintiff." Just as you can present more than one cause of action in a complaint, you also can present alternative causes of action. Here, the two alternative causes of action are strict liability and negligence. Some jurisdictions require a demand for relief at the end of each count. Other jurisdictions require a demand for relief at the end of the complaint instead of at the end of each count. A demand for relief appears at the end of each count of the sample complaint.

The remaining paragraphs of the complaint present a concise summary of the facts that serve as a basis for the specific causes of action. Complaints do not set out case law or evidentiary matters. In the sample complaint, the writer did not discuss the elements of the strict liability or negligence causes of action. Instead, the writer set out the facts that establish the required elements of those causes of action. You must allege the required elements, but you do so with factual statements rather than legal arguments or conclusions.

§ 20.06. THE ANSWER

In an answer, the defendant admits or denies each factual allegation that the plaintiff makes in the complaint and raises any defenses to the causes of action presented in the complaint. The defendant answers each allegation by numbered paragraphs that correspond to numbered paragraphs in the complaint. The defendant's answer to the *Smith v. Jones* complaint set out in Section 20.05 might look like this:

ANSWER

1. Admitted.

2. Admitted.

3. Denied. Defendant denies that on June 4, 2003, at about 8:00 a.m., the defendant was the owner of or harbored a dog. The dog in question was owned by Frank Thomas, who had brought the dog with him while visiting Defendant.

4. After reasonable investigation Defendant is without knowledge or information sufficient to form a belief as to the truth of Plaintiff's allegation that Plaintiff was walking in a common driveway at her residence on June 4, 2003, at about 8:00 a.m., and therefore denies that allegation and demands strict proof. Defendant denies that the dog in question attacked and bit Plaintiff without provocation.

5. Denied. Defendant denies that the dog in question ever attacked anyone, including the plaintiff.

COUNT I

STRICT LIABILITY IN TORT

6. Defendant incorporates by reference her answers to paragraphs 1 through 5 of Plaintiff's Complaint.

7. Denied. Defendant denies that she owned or harbored a dog on June 4, 2003, at around 8:00 a.m. Defendant further denies that the dog in question was of a vicious nature or was accustomed to attacking and biting other persons.

8. Denied. Defendant denies that she knew that the dog in question was vicious. Defendant further denies that she knew that the dog in question was accustomed to attacking and biting other persons.

9. Denied. Defendant denies that the dog in question attacked and bit Plaintiff. Defendant further denies that Plaintiff suffered any illness or injury as a result of any action or inaction on Defendant's part.

WHEREFORE, Defendant demands judgment in her favor and against Plaintiff.

COUNT II

NEGLIGENCE

10. Defendant incorporates by reference her answers to paragraphs 1 through 5 of Plaintiff's Complaint.

11. Denied. Defendant denies that she knew that the dog had previously attacked at least one other person.

12. Denied. Defendant denies that she knew that the dog in question was likely to harm individuals unless properly confined or otherwise controlled.

13. Denied. Defendant denies that she failed to exercise reasonable care to confine or otherwise control the dog in question. Defendant did not have a duty to confine or otherwise control the dog in question. Defendant acted with all due care required of her under the circumstances.

14. Denied. Defendant denies that the dog in question attacked and bit Plaintiff. Defendant further denies that Plaintiff suffered any illness or injury as a result of any action or inaction on Defendant's part.

WHEREFORE, Defendant demands judgment in her favor and against Plaintiff.

AFFIRMATIVE DEFENSES

15. The Plaintiff's Complaint fails to state a cause of action, and this action should be dismissed.

16. The Plaintiff failed to join as defendants parties that are indispensable and necessary to a full adjudication of this action and, therefore, this action should be dismissed.

17. Upon information and belief, any injuries, losses or damages sustained by Plaintiff were caused by her own contributory negligence.

_____

Attorney for Defendant

Compare the paragraphs of the above answer with the paragraphs of the complaint in Section 20.05.

Unless you deny a factual allegation the plaintiff made in the complaint, the court will conclude that you have admitted it. Sometimes you do not have sufficient information to know if an allegation made in a complaint is true or not. In this case, the rules of procedure of many jurisdictions permit you to state that "after reasonable investigation [your client] is without knowledge or information sufficient to form a belief as to the truth of an allegation." In those jurisdictions, this statement has the same effect as a denial. See, for example, paragraph 4 of the sample answer.

After answering the plaintiff's allegations, set out any affirmative defenses that the defendant intends to raise at trial. Typical affirmative defenses in a tort case include assumption of risk, consent, contributory negligence, fraud, and the statute of limitations. Affirmative defenses operate to negate a claim even when all of plaintiff's allegations are true. The court may conclude that affirmative defenses are waived unless the defendant raises them. In some jurisdictions, the defendant can plead inconsistent defenses. Put the affirmative defenses in a separate section of the answer. See, for example, the "Affirmative Defenses" section of the sample answer. Some jurisdictions use a different title for affirmative defenses, such as "New Matter."

In some jurisdictions you also can raise counterclaims or motions to dismiss (sometimes called demurrers) in an answer. In a counterclaim, you allege that the defendant also has a claim against the plaintiff. Counterclaims are governed by the same rules that govern a plaintiff's complaint. In a motion to dismiss, you allege that the plaintiff has failed to make out a cause of action that can properly be decided by the court. In some jurisdictions, you will file a separate motion to dismiss the complaint, rather than demurring in the answer. We discuss motions to dismiss in Section 23.03.

§ 20.07. VERIFICATIONS

Attorneys must sign all pleadings. In addition, in many jurisdictions, the party signs a verification that is attached to the pleading. In it the party states that the allegations are true. Here is an example of a verification:

I, (name of party), hereby state that I am the (plaintiff/defendant) in this action and verify that the statements made in the foregoing (type of pleading) are true and correct to the best of my knowledge, information, and belief.

_____

Date

_____

Party

Practice with Pleadings

§ 21.01. INTRODUCTION

This chapter will give you an opportunity to practice the principles we explained in the previous chapter. You will be able to go through the process of preparing a complaint and answer based on a fictitious case. The complaint and answer will be filed in your state's trial court. You should determine the appropriate format for the caption and any local pleading rules before beginning this exercise.

§ 21.02. PLAINTIFF'S FACTS

Here are the facts for the plaintiff:

Sandy Harmon works as an executive assistant to Jack Burton, the CEO of a software company, Playtime, that makes games. The company's specialty is role-playing games. She thinks one of the guys in the company has gone completely around the bend. The guy, Kris Martin, the COO of the company, has asked her out several times, but she has refused since she is married (and, frankly, wouldn't be interested anyway). Kris does not like to take no for an answer. He has been calling Sandy at home, and hanging up when her husband answers the phone. He has told Sandy that he will convince her husband there is something going on between her and Kris so her husband will divorce her. He has also told her that he will complain about her to her boss if she doesn't "wise up." Sandy has told her husband what is going on, and he, too, would like to know how to make Kris stop. This has been going on for about three months.

About three or four weeks ago, Sandy started getting calls from other guys, who were making seriously lewd propositions. Sandy couldn't figure out why these guys all of a sudden started calling, until one of her coworkers, Mark, told her that Kris had put her phone number on his webpage, and said guys could call for a good time. Sandy told Kris to knock it off, and he just laughed.

Then, in the last week or so, guys started showing up at Sandy's door, saying they were there to give her what she wants. When she told them to go away, they said they knew she didn't really mean it. Sandy's husband had to chase most of the guys away, and once they had to call the cops. When a couple of guys found out her husband was there, they said they were happy to share. One wanted to know if he could bring another woman over, too. There have been about eight or nine guys each night.

On a hunch, Sandy went to Kris's webpage and discovered that indeed he had put her address on the webpage, and said that she would welcome any men who cared to "visit." He also said that Sandy would say no, but that was just part of the game, and that she really meant yes.

Sandy went to work a couple of days ago and told Kris she was going to get a lawyer to make him stop. He laughed at her again, telling her to "lighten up," and she got pretty upset. Sandy was crying, and started yelling, trying to make him listen. Finally she gave up and told her boss she was taking the rest of the day off. Kris is a good friend of Sandy's boss, Jack Burton; they started the company together. Because of this, Sandy has not told Jack about Kris's behavior.

Sandy is absolutely furious, not to mention short of sleep. She is also getting a little frightened since she doesn't know how crazy some of these guys might be.

§ 21.03. DRAFTING THE FACT ALLEGATIONS

Remember to check whether your state requires a jurisdictional allegation at the beginning of a complaint. You should allege that both the plaintiff and any defendants are citizens of your county and state. You can decide whether to sue anyone other than Mr. Martin, such as his employer, Playtime. Your factual allegations should be clear and to the point—include only relevant facts and keep each numbered paragraph to one idea. Don't forget to request appropriate relief!

§ 21.04. DRAFTING THE LEGAL CLAIM

Here is the applicable statute to support Sandy's claim. You might also want to include other claims, such as invasion of privacy, defamation, sexual harassment, and infliction of emotional distress. If so, you should look up the applicable law to be sure that you know the required elements. Each legal claim should be presented in a separate count.

§ 1708.7. Stalking; tort action; damages and equitable remedies

(a) A person is liable for the tort of stalking when the plaintiff proves all of the following elements of the tort:

(1) The defendant engaged in a pattern of conduct the intent of which was to follow, alarm, or harass the plaintiff. In order to establish this element, the plaintiff shall be required to support his or her allegations with independent corroborating evidence.

(2) As a result of that pattern of conduct, the plaintiff reasonably feared for his or her safety, or the safety of an immediate family member. For purposes of this paragraph, "immediate family" means a spouse, parent, child, any person related by consanguinity or affinity within the second degree, or any

person who regularly resides, or, within the six months preceding any portion of the pattern of conduct, regularly resided, in the plaintiff's household.

(3) One of the following:

(A) The defendant, as a part of the pattern of conduct specified in paragraph (1), made a credible threat with the intent to place the plaintiff in reasonable fear for his or her safety, or the safety of an immediate family member and, on at least one occasion, the plaintiff clearly and definitively demanded that the defendant cease and abate his or her pattern of conduct and the defendant persisted in his or her pattern of conduct.

(B) The defendant violated a restraining order, including, but not limited to, any order issued pursuant to Section 527.6 of the Code of Civil Procedure, prohibiting any act described in subdivision (a).

(b) For the purposes of this section:

(1) "Pattern of conduct" means conduct composed of a series of acts over a period of time, however short, evidencing a continuity of purpose. Constitutionally protected activity is not included within the meaning of "pattern of conduct."

(2) "Credible threat" means a verbal or written threat, including that communicated by means of an electronic communication device, or a threat implied by a pattern of conduct or a combination of verbal, written, or electronically communicated statements and conduct, made with the intent and apparent ability to carry out the threat so as to cause the person who is the target of the threat to reasonably fear for his or her safety or the safety of his or her immediate family.

(3) "Electronic communication device" includes, but is not limited to, telephones, cellular telephones, computers, video recorders, fax machines, or pagers. "Electronic communication" has the same meaning as the term defined in Subsection 12 of Section 2510 of Title 18 of the United States Code.

(4) "Harass" means a knowing and willful course of conduct directed at a specific person which seriously alarms, annoys, torments, or terrorizes the person, and which serves no legitimate purpose. The course of conduct must be such as would cause a reasonable person to suffer substantial emotional distress, and must actually cause substantial emotional distress to the person.

(c) A person who commits the tort of stalking upon another is liable to that person for damages, including, but not limited to, general damages, special damages, and punitive damages pursuant to Section 3294.

(d) In an action pursuant to this section, the court may grant equitable relief, including, but not limited to, an injunction.

(e) The rights and remedies provided in this section are cumulative and in addition to any other rights and remedies provided by law.

(f) This section shall not be construed to impair any constitutionally protected activity, including, but not limited to, speech, protest, and assembly.

§ 21.05. CRITIQUING A COMPLAINT

Here is a draft federal complaint on the same facts. Redraft any paragraphs that you think are problematic. Explain briefly the problems you see.

IN THE UNITED STATES DISTRICT COURT
FOR THE CENTRAL DISTRICT OF CALIFORNIA

SANDY Harmon,

PLAINTIFF

V.   No. 04-1234

KRIS Martin,
JACK Burton, and
PLAYTIME, INC.,

DEFENDANTS

COMPLAINT

1. This Court has jurisdiction under 28 U.S.C. § 1331.
2. Plaintiff Sandy Harmon is an individual residing in Orange County, CA.
3. Defendant Kris Martin ("Martin") is an individual residing in Orange County, CA.
4. Defendant Jack Burton is an individual residing in Orange County, CA.
5. Defendant Playtime, Inc. is a corporation organized under the laws of California.
6. Plaintiff is employed as an executive assistant at Playtime, Inc. She has always done good work and received numerous favorable performance evaluations.
7. Plaintiff's immediate supervisor is Jack Burton.
8. In July of 2003 Martin began making sexual advances toward Plaintiff.
9. Plaintiff refused all such advances, telling Martin that she was married and had no interest in extracurricular affairs.
10. Martin called Plaintiff's home and hung up when Plaintiff's husband answered the phone.
11. Martin threatened to convince Plaintiff's husband that "something was going on" between Martin and Plaintiff.
12. Martin threatened to complain about Plaintiff to Defendant Burton if she didn't "wise up."
13. In late September or early October 2003, Martin published Plaintiff's home telephone number on his webpage.
14. Martin made the outrageous and untrue suggestion on the webpage that men could call Plaintiff for "a good time."
15. Plaintiff received telephone calls from men making lewd propositions.
16. Plaintiff asked Martin to remove her telephone number from his webpage.
17. Martin demonstrated his heartlessness by laughing at Plaintiff's request.
18. In late October 2003, Martin published Plaintiff's home address on his webpage.
19. Martin's webpage, in a further demonstration of the outrageous lengths to which he would go, said that if Plaintiff said "no" to any visitors she really meant "yes."
20. Plaintiff has never had any desire to engage in sexual relations with men other than her husband.

21. Unwelcome male visitors, up to eight or nine per night, began appearing at Plaintiff's home.
22. Some visitors refused to leave voluntarily.
23. Plaintiff's husband had to chase many of the visitors away.
24. In at least one instance, the police had to be called to remove an unwelcome visitor.
25. On October 27, 2003, Plaintiff again requested that Martin remove her personal information from his webpage.
26. Martin responded by laughing and telling her to "lighten up," demonstrating a complete lack of concern for Plaintiff's physical and mental well-being.
27. Plaintiff was unable to continue working that day.
28. Defendants Martin and Burton are good friends and founded Defendant Playtime, Inc. together.
29. Plaintiff has suffered from sleeplessness.
30. Plaintiff was frightened and unsure what the unwelcome visitors might do.
31. Plaintiff no longer feels secure in her own home.
32. Plaintiff fears loss of employment.
33. Plaintiff suffers from extreme emotional distress.

COUNT I—INVASION OF PRIVACY (FALSE LIGHT)

34. Plaintiff incorporates Paragraphs 1-33 by reference.
35. Martin published outrageous, hurtful facts that falsely cast Plaintiff in a negative light.
36. Martin's portrayal of Plaintiff would be highly offensive to a reasonable person.

COUNT II—INVASION OF PRIVACY (PUBLICATION OF PRIVATE FACTS)

37. Plaintiff incorporates Paragraphs 1-33 by reference.
38. Martin published private information about Plaintiff in a manner that would be highly offensive to a reasonable person. There was no reason to put her address and phone number together with an invitation for men to come visit her for sex, other than to intimidate and harass Plaintiff.
39. There was no legitimate public interest in Plaintiff's private information.

COUNT III—CIVIL STALKING

40. Plaintiff incorporates Paragraphs 1-33 by reference.
41. Martin engaged in a pattern of conduct intended to harass or alarm Plaintiff, and maybe to cause her actual physical harm.
42. As a result of Martin's pattern of conduct, Plaintiff reasonably feared for the safety of herself and her husband. Anyone would have been scared of all these men coming to their house!
43. Martin made a credible threat with the intent to place Plaintiff in reasonable fear for her safety. What other reason could there be?!
44. Plaintiff clearly and definitively demanded that Martin cease his pattern of conduct.
45. Martin persisted in his conduct after Plaintiff's demands that he cease.

COUNT IV—SEXUAL HARASSMENT IN VIOLATION OF TITLE VII

46. Plaintiff incorporates Paragraphs 1-33 by reference.
47. Martin's conduct created a hostile working environment.
48. Plaintiff's job was threatened.

WHEREFORE, Plaintiff requests:

1. Injunctive relief, including a "stay away" order and the removal of her personal information from Martin's webpage.
2. Compensatory and punitive damages.
3. Such other relief as the Court deems appropriate.

ATTORNEY SIGNATURE

_____

VERIFICATION

I have read the foregoing Complaint, and the allegations are true and correct to the best of my knowledge, information, and belief.

_____

§ 21.06. DRAFTING THE ANSWER

Here are the facts Kris Martin has provided in response to the complaint:

Kris says he has just been having a little extracurricular fun. He did ask Sandy out several times, but she refused, saying she is married. Kris does not like to take no for an answer, and besides he's not sure what being married has to do with anything. He just wanted to have a little fun (i.e., sex). He did call Sandy at home, and hung up when her husband answered the phone. He told Sandy that if she didn't "go out" with him, he would convince her husband there was something going on between the two of them, so her husband would divorce her.

Kris did put Sandy's phone number on his webpage, and said guys could call her for a good time. He wasn't getting anywhere with her, and just wanted to get her attention. He thought he would look pretty good by comparison to some of the creeps who were likely to call. He also thought he could show off his understanding side if Sandy were to confide in him about the calls. However, when Sandy found out about the webpage, she got upset and told him to knock it off. Kris just laughed; this was getting more entertaining by the minute.

Kris later put Sandy's address on the webpage, and said that she would welcome all "visitors." Kris also said that Sandy would say no, but that was just part of the game, and that she really meant yes.

One day, Sandy came into work really upset (she was crying and yelling, making quite a scene), and told Kris that she was getting a lawyer to make him stop. Kris told her to "lighten up."

Kris can't figure out what he did wrong since he didn't actually *do* anything to her, and never meant for anything bad to happen to her. He just thinks she could stand to loosen up a little bit. He admitted that he might have threatened to complain about her to Jack, but didn't figure she would take that seriously since she knows how much Jack values her work.

Kris got a couple of e-mails from guys complaining that Sandy wasn't very cooperative when they went to visit.

Kris took Sandy's name and address off the webpage for now, but will probably come up with something else fun to do if this lawsuit goes away. He is convinced that Sandy would really appreciate his "talents" if she would only give him a chance.

Again, keep your fact allegations simple and to the point. Admit facts that you must admit, and indicate that you don't have adequate information only where that is true. Add any affirmative defenses that seem appropriate at the end of the answer.

§ 21.07. CRITIQUING AN ANSWER

Here is a draft answer to the foregoing federal complaint. Which, if any, paragraphs need to be changed, and why?

IN THE UNITED STATES DISTRICT COURT FOR THE CENTRAL
DISTRICT OF CALIFORNIA

SANDY Harmon,

                  PLAINTIFF

        V.   No. 04-1234

KRIS Martin,
JACK Burton, and
PLAYTIME, INC.,

                  DEFENDANTS

ANSWER OF DEFENDANT KRIS MARTIN

1. Admitted.
2. Admitted.
3. Admitted.
4. Admitted.
5. Admitted.
6. Admitted.
7. Admitted.
8. Denied.
9. Denied.
10. Admitted.
11. Admitted.
12. Admitted, but it wasn't serious.
13. Admitted.

14. Admitted.
15. Defendant is without knowledge or information sufficient to form a belief as to the truth of this allegation.
16. Admitted.
17. Denied.
18. Denied.
19. Denied.
20. Defendant is without knowledge or information sufficient to form a belief as to the truth of this allegation.
21. Defendant is without knowledge or information sufficient to form a belief as to the truth of this allegation.
22. Defendant is without knowledge or information sufficient to form a belief as to the truth of this allegation.
23. Defendant is without knowledge or information sufficient to form a belief as to the truth of this allegation.
24. Defendant is without knowledge or information sufficient to form a belief as to the truth of this allegation.
25. Admitted.
26. Admitted.
27. Defendant is without knowledge or information sufficient to form a belief as to the truth of this allegation.
28. Admitted.
29. Defendant is without knowledge or information sufficient to form a belief as to the truth of this allegation.
30. Defendant is without knowledge or information sufficient to form a belief as to the truth of this allegation.
31. Defendant is without knowledge or information sufficient to form a belief as to the truth of this allegation.
32. Denied.
33. Denied.

COUNT I—INVASION OF PRIVACY (FALSE LIGHT)

34. Defendant incorporates Paragraphs 1-33 by reference.
35. Denied.
36. Denied.

COUNT II—INVASION OF PRIVACY (PUBLICATION OF PRIVATE FACTS)

37. Defendant incorporates Paragraphs 1-33 by reference.
38. Denied.
39. Denied.

COUNT III—CIVIL STALKING

40. Defendant incorporates Paragraphs 1-33 by reference.
41. Denied.
42. Denied.
43. Denied.
44. Denied.
45. Denied.

COUNT IV—SEXUAL HARASSMENT IN VIOLATION OF TITLE VII

46. Defendant incorporates Paragraphs 1-33 by reference.

47. Denied.

48. Denied. She can't be serious!

WHEREFORE, Defendant requests that the Court enter judgment in his favor and against Plaintiff.

ATTORNEY SIGNATURE

_____

VERIFICATION

I have read the foregoing Answer, and the allegations are true and correct to the best of my knowledge, information, and belief.

_____

Writing Persuasively

§ 22.01. INTRODUCTION

In discussing appellate briefs, we move from expository writing to persuasive writing. When you represent a client and argue to a court, you must do more than state the facts, explain the law, and predict how a case will be resolved. You cannot merely present information to a court and rely on it to make a decision. You also must persuade the court to find in your client's favor.

Persuasion requires constructing a clear, concrete, and tightly written argument that presents your client's case in the best light. Learning to write persuasively is not a matter of mastering a grab bag of gimmicks or tricks. It also is not a matter of using exaggerated rhetoric. Lawyers and judges have seen all the tricks and flourishes too many times. If you rely on these devices, you will impress no one.

The chapters that you have read so far teach you how to write clearly and concretely, and how to construct a legal analysis. The following chapters teach you not only the mechanics of brief writing, but also how to write persuasively. You will learn that you must construct every part of the brief in a way that advances your client's position.

This chapter summarizes the methods of persuasion that the other chapters discuss. By presenting these methods in a single chapter, we offer you an overview and reinforce the thesis that persuasive methods are not simply a number of isolated techniques, but share a common theme. To reiterate, persuasive writing consists of constructing a well-written, well-reasoned analysis that puts your client's best foot forward.

Here is an list of this chapter's lessons:

1. Make your argument clear and credible.
2. Write a well-organized argument.
3. Adopt a persuasive writing style.
4. State your facts persuasively.
5. Use equity and policy arguments.
6. Use precedent persuasively.

§ 22.02. MAKE YOUR ARGUMENT CLEAR AND CREDIBLE

1. Make Your Argument as Simple as Possible

When you write a law school exam, you expect to get credit for identifying and discussing the critical issues. You also expect extra points for discussing issues that are barely arguable or exceptionally complicated, but that would be extremely artificial if raised in a real-world legal argument. When you include complicated, artificial arguments in a brief, you cannot expect the rewards that you gained in law school. These arguments will distract the reader from the arguments with real persuasive power. They also may detract from your credibility. Stick to the arguments that have the best chance of winning.

You also can expect to hurt your case if you make your critical arguments sound unnecessarily complicated. You are more likely to persuade the reader with arguments that seem logical and simple and sound like common sense. Stick to your main arguments and write them so that they are easy to understand.

A busy judge has many cases to consider and many briefs to read. He or she does not have the time or patience to digest peripheral arguments or even major arguments that are not stated clearly. Thus, unnecessary complexity hurts your client.

Here is a simple method for rooting out complexity. State your argument to a legal associate in a very few sentences. If he or she cannot follow your train of thought, revise your words and presentation and try again.

A major part of advocacy is to place your client's arguments in clear focus: What does your client want and why? Bringing the argument into focus requires striving for simplicity.

2. Write in a Persuasive But Credible Style

Some lawyers try to be persuasive by overstating their cases and by using emotionally charged verbs, adjectives, and adverbs. This tactic inevitably marks the practitioner as an amateur. Other lawyers state their cases without adding a persuasive edge of any kind. Their style also does the client a disservice. Strive for a style that is assertive, but reasoned and even a little understated.

Consider this excerpt from a brief:

> Next we have Wilmer's ludicrous explanation of the circumstances surrounding his secret taping of various people at the dental school. Instead of coming clean and admitting that he was gathering information for his malpractice case, Wilmer asks the court to swallow his tall tale about how he was merely furthering his education.

The writer has overwritten. Words like "ludicrous" and "swallow his tall tale" do not have the effect for which the writer is striving. Judges have seen too much of this hyperbole to find it persuasive.

Compare this version:

> Wilmer admits that he secretly taped various people at the dental school, but states that he was furthering his education.

Here, the writer has underwritten and does not advance the client's position. To be persuasive, strive for a style somewhere between these extremes. For example:

> Wilmer admits that he secretly taped various people at the dental school. However, he offers a curious explanation. He denies that he was gathering information for his malpractice case and instead claims that he was furthering his education.

Here is another acceptable revision:

> Wilmer admits that he secretly taped various people at the dental school. However, he denies that he was gathering information for his malpractice case and instead claims that he was taping for an educational purpose. He has not been terribly specific about how he would use the tapes to further his education.

These two revisions illustrate the proper tone. In the first revision, the writer draws attention to Wilmer's unbelievable explanation by terming it "curious." "Curious" adds flair, but not too much. In the second revision, the writer adds a final sentence to subtly highlight the improbability of the proffered explanation. In both, the writer juxtaposes Wilmer's explanation with what is apparently the real reason. As a result, the writer furthers the client's cause by painting the opposing litigant as untruthful and even pathetically comical.

§ 22.03. WRITE A WELL-ORGANIZED ARGUMENT

1. Structure Your Argument

An important key to persuasive writing is producing a document with a structure that is readily apparent. You want the reader to follow your argument as effortlessly as possible. Forgo stream-of-consciousness writing in favor of organization.

The key to organization is to write according to an outline and to put your conclusions first. Even if you are not the type of writer who is comfortable outlining first and then writing, you still can write first and then organize your results so that they fit an outline. That is, write the outline after you have finished and then, where necessary, reorganize according to the outline.

After you have written your first draft, make sure that you begin the discussion of each argument with a conclusion that applies the legal argument to the facts of your case. Briefly outline your argument in the first paragraph so that the court has a "roadmap" of where you are going. Review your paragraphs for topic sentences. In most paragraphs, you will want the topic sentence at the beginning.

2. Put Your Best Arguments First and Develop Them More Fully

When we read a document, we usually pay more attention at the beginning. After a while, our interest wanes. In addition, as readers, we expect the important arguments to come first and to be developed in proportion to their importance.

The lesson is clear. Place your most persuasive arguments first and allocate more space to them.

For example, suppose you are opposing the argument that a statute requires your client to give a neighbor an easement over her property. You have three arguments. First, the statute is unconstitutional. Second, in this case, the terms of the statute do not require granting an easement. Third, the neighbor did not follow the procedure the statute prescribes. Because courts are extremely reluctant to declare statutes unconstitutional, either your second or third argument probably gives you the best chance of winning. Decide which is your best argument and develop it fully. Then set out your second argument and give it less space. Finally, set out your argument on constitutionality and allocate it the least space.

As with all rules, there are exceptions. Sometimes you will decide to put your second-best argument first because it sets a good stage for your best argument. Then you will include your best argument. Nonetheless, in the overwhelming number of cases, you will do well to put your best argument first.

§ 22.04. ADOPT A PERSUASIVE WRITING STYLE

1. Be Concrete

When you argue for a client, you are not arguing for an abstract legal principle. You are seeking a holding that has practical consequences. In the same manner, judges are not interested in debating legal abstractions; they are interested in resolving specific disputes. The lesson: write about your case in concrete terms. In doing so you drive home the fact that your case is not an academic debate, but a conflict involving real people, particularly your client.

Consider this sentence:

The unforeseeability of the event absolved the defendants of liability.

This sentence is abstract. It could be about anyone. If you include facts about the relevant events, you make the issue concrete and compelling:

Because the defendant could not foresee that a twenty-year-old trespasser would dive head first from a lifeguard chair into a shallow pool, the defendant is not liable.

Here is another example:

A reasonable adult in plaintiff's position would recognize that the attempt to execute a head-first, straight dive into the lake without prior awareness of the depth of the waters might result in severe injury from the collision of one's head on the lake bottom.

Compare this revision:

A reasonable adult like the plaintiff would know that if he dived straight down and head-first into a shallow lake without knowing its depth, he could hit his head on the lake bottom and become paralyzed.

In the revision, the changes are subtle, but telling. They make the sentence far more concrete and persuasive.

2. When You Want to Emphasize a Word or Idea, Place It at the End of the Sentence

In a sentence, the beginning and the end are the best places to put information that you want to emphasize. Use the beginning of the sentence for information already familiar to the reader, usually the subject. Also use the beginning for information that the reader expects or can understand easily. Use the end for new information that you want to emphasize.

Suppose you are arguing about which law applies to your case, Missouri law or federal law. If you are arguing in favor of applying Missouri law, you might write this sentence:

Missouri law, not federal law, governs this case.

Although this sentence states your position, it does not make the best use of the end of the sentence. You will make your point more emphatically if you end with "Missouri law." Therefore, you should rewrite the sentence this way:

This case is governed not by federal law, but by Missouri law.

Although this revision forces you to use the passive voice, the loss of the active verb is far outweighed by the power of placing "Missouri law" at the end of the sentence.

The same principle applies to sentences with more than one clause. Consider this sentence:

The court barred the plaintiff's complaint as a matter of law because the plaintiff failed to notify the bank of the forgery within the time prescribed by the statute.

Suppose you want to emphasize that the court barred the complaint as a matter of law. You would rewrite the sentence this way:

Because the plaintiff failed to notify the bank of the forgery within the time prescribed by the statute, the court barred the plaintiff's complaint as a matter of law.

By placing the main clause at the end of the sentence, you stress the idea that you want to emphasize.

3. When Appropriate, Use the Same Subject for a Series of Sentences

By using the same subject for a series of sentences, you make it clear that you are telling the story of the subject. As a result, you give your sentences unity and direction.

Consider this paragraph from the brief of a convicted criminal defendant arguing ineffectiveness of counsel:

> The client and the defense counsel did not meet until one hour before the trial. As a result, there was never the personal exchange between the two parties so necessary to a strong defense. The defense counsel never had the opportunity to observe her client. Thus there was no opportunity to judge his mannerisms and overall appearance, the fact being that the defendant, being somewhat quiet and shy, would not make a strong witness at trial. When he testified at trial, he did not come across well to the jury. The tactical error of placing him on the stand could have been avoided if more time had been spent with the defendant and a personal interview had been conducted.

The argument becomes much more compelling when the defense counsel becomes the subject of every sentence and of virtually every clause:

> Until one hour before the trial, the defense counsel never met with the defendant and thus never had the personal exchange so necessary to a strong defense. Because she had never had the opportunity to observe her client, she could not judge his mannerisms and overall appearance. She therefore did not know that her client was somewhat quiet and shy and, at trial, would not come across well to the jury. By placing her client on the stand, the defense counsel made a tactical error that she could have avoided by taking the time to conduct a personal interview.

The rewrite makes it clear that the writer is discussing the failings of the defense counsel and detailing what she did and failed to do. As a result, the writer is presenting a persuasive argument for ineffectiveness of counsel.

§ 22.05. STATE YOUR FACTS PERSUASIVELY

At the beginning of your brief, you will have the opportunity to present the facts from your client's perspective. Judges expect your statement of the facts to be straightforward and accurate. They dislike rhetoric here and will form a negative opinion of your credibility if you attempt to mislead them by distorting or omitting critical facts. Therefore, you must present an objective narrative.

Nonetheless, you still must write the facts as an advocate. Here is how. Stress the facts that favor your case and deemphasize those that hurt it. Instead of stating your own opinions about the facts, report that someone else offered those opinions. In this way, you are stating a fact—what someone else stated—not your opinion.

This excerpt from a brief furnishes a good example. The plaintiff dived into a pool with only three feet of water and suffered severe injuries. The writer represents the defendant, the manufacturer of the pool.

> The plaintiff claimed that he perceived the water depth to be six feet and not its actual depth of three feet. At trial, several experts testified that this misperception was significant to their conclusion that the plaintiff caused the accident. As Dr. Luna, one of the experts, testified, if the plaintiff believed that the water was six feet deep, "his

mental and physiological processes involving visual perception and judgment of his surroundings were impaired by his ingestion of alcohol and hallucinogens.'

In this example, the writer makes the essential point without rhetoric or value-laden adjectives or adverbs. She does not call the plaintiff irresponsible or label him dissolute. She does not berate the opposing lawyer for pursuing a frivolous lawsuit. The writer simply reports the plaintiff's assertion and then reports the testimony of experts hired by the defendant.

The quotation from Dr. Luna is part of a sentence objectively reporting what happened at trial. Instead of quoting an expert, the writer might have stated the opinion as her own: "If the plaintiff believed that the water was six feet deep, his mental and physiological processes involving perception and judgment of his surroundings clearly were impaired by his ingestion of alcohol and hallucinogens." However, by placing the opinion in the mouth of another person, an expert, the writer makes it far more persuasive. (In the alternative, she might have attributed the opinion to Dr. Luna and then paraphrased his words in order to make the sentence better stylistically.) As you can see, it is possible to state facts in an objective manner and still write as an advocate.

§ 22.06. MAKE EQUITY AND POLICY ARGUMENTS

In most cases that go to trial, and certainly in most cases on appeal, both parties have sound legal arguments. Therefore, the advocate must argue more than the law. You also need to argue the equities and social policy. To argue the equities means to argue that your client is the most sympathetic litigant and should win as a matter of justice. To argue policy means to argue that the legal holding you seek has positive ramifications for society and your opponent's does not.

Here is an example. Suppose you represent a child whose mother was seriously injured in an accident. You are suing the party that caused the accident for loss of parental consortium. In other words, you are arguing that the child should recover for losing the companionship and affection of the parent.

To argue the equities, you would enumerate the ways in which the child has suffered. You would mention activities that the child and mother used to share. You might quote the child reflecting on her loss. You thus would paint a picture of a child deserving to recover.

To argue policy, you would assert that as a general principle, the court should recognize the right of a child to sue for loss of parental consortium and should be liberal in finding that the loss has occurred in specific cases. Your policy argument might read like this:

> The importance of a child's feelings and emotions merit more than lip service. The loss of a parent is a devastating injury at least as important as a spouse's loss of consortium, which this jurisdiction recognizes. For these sorts of injuries, tort law is the appropriate avenue of redress.

Thus, while an equitable argument focuses on the particulars of a case, a policy argument generalizes. In the illustration, the policy argument states that recognizing this cause of action is desirable, is logical because it is similar to another tort that the jurisdiction already permits, and is consistent with the development of tort law.

§ 22.07. USE PRECEDENT PERSUASIVELY

Judges prefer that their decisions be consistent with past decisions of their court. They also must be persuaded that their decisions are consistent with those of any higher court. Therefore, invoking favorable precedent is a powerful tool of persuasion.

The difficulty arises when the earlier case does not support your position or it is unclear whether the case supports it. You might argue that the earlier case was wrongly decided. However, such an argument is at cross purposes with the desire to claim consistency with existing case law. Therefore, an argument rejecting precedent should be an alternative argument of last resort. Your first argument should be that existing law supports your position or at least is consistent with it.

1. Argue that Adverse Precedent Is Consistent with Your Argument

To harmonize adverse precedent, argue that the contrary case is distinguishable from your case on its facts or that it does address the issue in your case. If possible, go one step further and argue that the policy underlying that opinion is the one you are advancing.

Return to your argument that the court should recognize a cause of action for a child's loss of parental consortium. Suppose that in another case, the same court rejected the argument. There, the court stated that because the parent will receive compensation from the defendant, that compensation probably will give ample recovery to both parent and child. Therefore, according to the court, permitting a separate recovery for the child would be unfairly duplicative.

If, in that case, the only plaintiff was the child, and in your case, the child's claim is joined with the parent's claim, you can distinguish the cases. Argue that the previous case's holding dealt only with cases in which the actions of parent and child were not joined at trial. Argue that if the same jury is deciding the claims together, the risk of a duplicative recovery is very small. Then argue that, in both cases, the underlying goal is just compensation. Here, you are advancing this goal in a situation that will not result in overcompensation. With this argument, you distinguish the adverse precedent and also argue that you are furthering the same goal that motivated that decision.

2. Interpret Precedent Narrowly or Broadly, as Appropriate

As you have learned in law school, a holding is open to more than one interpretation. When you are dealing with precedent, select the interpretation that furthers your case. Depending on the facts of your case, this endeavor may require you to interpret the holding narrowly or broadly.

Suppose you are arguing that an adult should be able to recover for the loss of consortium of a parent. Suppose your jurisdiction has an earlier case permitting a minor child to recover for loss of parental consortium. Opposing counsel would interpret the holding narrowly to permit the cause of action only when the plaintiff is a minor child. However, you would interpret the holding broadly to permit any child to recover.

The way you deal with precedent is illustrative of the way you make a persuasive legal argument. Interpret the law and facts in a way that is both credible and in your client's best interest.

CHAPTER 23

Writing Pretrial Motions

§ 23.01. PURPOSES OF MOTIONS

Pretrial motions are filed in an effort to persuade the court to make a decision in the early stages of a case. The decision requested may be to dismiss the case entirely, to decide it without trial, or to resolve a discovery dispute between the parties. Although there are other types of motions that may be filed, we will focus on these three as representative of common motions. Motions involve advocacy; you are trying to persuade the court to do something and so should follow all the advice about advocacy writing that is offered elsewhere in this book.

§ 23.02. FORM OF MOTIONS

There is no set format for writing motions. You should get sample motions from other lawyers in your office or look at motions that have previously been filed in the court for which you are writing. In most courts, the motion itself is a simple statement of the basis upon which relief is requested. The motion may be supported by a memorandum that sets forth the legal arguments in support of the motion and by other documents appropriate to the motion, such as affidavits. All memoranda, or briefs, in support of motions should include a statement of the relevant facts and an analysis of the relevant law.

§ 23.03. MOTIONS TO DISMISS

Under Rule 12(b)(6) of the Federal Rules of Civil Procedure, a defendant may move to dismiss a complaint on the grounds that it fails to state a claim upon which relief can be granted. Most, if not all, states permit a similar motion—sometimes called a demurrer—that allows a defendant to attempt to get a defective complaint dismissed. Under this standard, the defendant must demonstrate that even if the plaintiff can prove all the facts alleged in the complaint, there is no basis for legal relief. In ruling on such a motion, the court will interpret the facts in the light most favorable to the plaintiff. Motions to dismiss may also be granted when the plaintiff fails to allege some crucial element of the cause of action. In such a case, the court may dismiss the complaint with leave to amend, so the plaintiff can correct the defect.

In our case against the dating service on behalf of Susan Starkey (see Chapter 17), let us assume that you filed a complaint for negligence. Assume also that the dating service filed a motion to dismiss for failure to state a claim, alleging that it had no duty to protect persons in Susan's position, and therefore there is no basis for recovery. You should have researched the applicable law before filing the complaint, and you should have legal support for your argument in favor of such a duty. Your response to the motion should focus on establishing the duty to protect; you should not try to win your whole case on the motion because you will likely need discovery to establish the facts in support of your argument that the duty to protect was breached and that the breach was the proximate cause of Susan's damages—that is, the failure of the dating service to adequately screen its clients led to Susan's stalking and emotional distress. Proving this will require witness testimony and other evidence. The point here is that only purely legal arguments can be resolved in the context of the motion to dismiss. If the court needs to find facts in order to resolve the question presented, the case must go on. If the motion to dismiss raises factual issues, that may be reason enough to deny the motion.

Exercise

Write a paragraph or two explaining why a motion to dismiss should not be granted in the Starkey case. Focus on the facts you would like to prove and how they fit into your negligence claim, especially the issue of the dating service's duty to its customers.

Assume that you have found case law supporting the idea that the dating service may have a duty to protect customers, particularly if it makes any affirmative representations relating to safety or background checks or similar ideas. Assume that Susan brought you an ad from the dating service that includes the language "Looking for a safe, sane alternative to the bar scene?" Also, assume that Susan told you that she specifically asked about screening of prospective dates and was assured that the dating service took "all necessary precautions" to ensure that its clients were reputable.

Write your explanation as if it would go into your response to the motion to dismiss. In other words, your audience is the judge who will decide the motion. Remember that the judge will interpret the facts in the light most favorable to your client in deciding the motion. You do not need to cite cases; write as if you are summarizing your argument in the response to the motion.

§ 23.04. MOTIONS TO COMPEL DISCOVERY

Under Federal Rule of Civil Procedure 37(a)(3)(B), a party may move to compel discovery when the opposing party does not respond to a discovery request and the parties cannot work out the dispute themselves. For example:

- a deponent[1] fails to answer a question asked under Rule 30 or 31
- a corporation or other entity fails to make a designation under Rule 30(b)(6) or 31(a)
- a party fails to answer an interrogatory submitted under Rule 33
- a party, in response to a request for inspection submitted under Rule 34, fails to respond that inspection will be permitted as requested or fails to permit inspection as requested the discovering party may move for an order compelling an answer, or a designation, or an order compelling inspection in accordance with the request

The motion must include a certification that the movant has in good faith conferred or attempted to confer with the person or party failing to make the discovery in an effort to secure the information or material without court action. When taking a deposition on oral examination, the proponent of the question may complete or adjourn the examination before applying for an order.

Under Rule 37(a)(4) an evasive or incomplete answer may be treated as a failure to respond. Available sanctions under Rule 37(a)(5) include the expense of filing or opposing the motion, including attorneys' fees.

Assume that you served a request for production of documents on the dating service, and that the dating service refused to produce Partlow's file in response to your specific request, claiming confidentiality. Note that under Rule 37 you are required to confer with the dating service to attempt to obtain the material without court action. If you try to work the matter out but are unsuccessful, you may move to compel the production of the file. You would need to research the issue of confidentiality raised by the dating service and establish that under the law the service is not entitled to keep the file from you. You would make this argument in your memorandum in support of the motion.

Because the rule requires that you confer with the defendant, you should state in your motion that you have made the attempt to confer, and you should probably detail the attempts you made in your memorandum in support of the motion. It is always a good idea to put in writing all efforts you have made to comply with prerequisites to obtaining a hearing on the merits.

§ 23.05. MOTIONS FOR SUMMARY JUDGMENT

Rule 56 of the Federal Rules of Civil Procedure provides that either party may move for summary judgment. Rule 56(c) states that the motion will be granted "if the pleadings, the discovers and disclosure materials on file, and any affidavits show that there is no genuine issue as to any material fact and that the movant is entitled to judgment as a matter of law." This means that, as in the case of the motion to dismiss, if the question before the court is one of law, the case may be decided upon motion. The difference between a motion to dismiss and a motion for summary judgment is that the motion for summary judgment generally includes some supporting factual material such as responses to discovery or affidavits, while the motion to dismiss focuses solely on the complaint.

---

1. The term "deponent" refers to the person being questioned in a deposition.

Let us go back to Susan Starkey's case. If counsel for the dating service files a motion for summary judgment alleging that there was no breach of the duty to protect persons in Susan's position because the screening procedures were adequate, and attaches an affidavit from an employee of the service outlining those procedures, you would simply respond that the motion raises a genuine issue of material fact. Regardless of the existence of screening procedures employed by the dating service, you would want the opportunity to prove that those procedures either were inadequate or that they were not followed. The only way to prove these things is to cross-examine the employees of the dating service, and perhaps to hire an expert to testify that the service's procedures did not meet the standards of the industry.

The key to responding to any motion is to limit your argument to what you need to establish to overcome the motion. Many lawyers succumb to the temptation to argue the entire case at the motion stage, which only confuses the issue and may make it less likely that the motion will be decided in your favor. Thus, if in responding to the dating service's motion for summary judgment, you choose to argue the inadequacy of the screening procedures and the damages Susan suffered, you might actually suggest to the court that you think the case is ready for decision, when all you really want at this stage is the chance to prove your case in court. Understanding the standard in the applicable rule is critical. Read carefully and argue only what you need to in order to defeat the motion.

Note that the parties in some cases may actually agree upon the facts, in which case both parties may be content to submit the case for decision by summary judgment, and avoid the time and expense of a trial. This will probably be the exceptional case, but if there are no genuine issues of fact to be proved at trial, you may very well win the gratitude of the court by stipulating to the facts and submitting the case for a decision on the law.

Exercise

Write a few paragraphs explaining why Susan Starkey's case cannot be decided on summary judgment. Explain the genuine issues of material fact that must be addressed at trial. Again, assume that you are writing for the judge who will decide the motion, and do not cite cases. Focus on the basis for the motion and what you need to establish to persuade the judge to deny the motion.

§ 23.06. ETHICAL CONSIDERATIONS IN MOTION PRACTICE

As an officer of the court, you should never file a frivolous claim or make a frivolous argument. Your factual and legal support for your argument must be sufficient to justify taking up the time of the court and other parties to the matter. Rule 11 of the Federal Rules of Civil Procedure provides that pleadings and motions must be signed by the attorney of record. When you sign a pleading or motion, you represent that to the best of your "knowledge, information, and belief, formed after an inquiry reasonable under the circumstances,—

(1) it is not being presented for any improper purpose, such as to harass, cause unnecessary delay, or needless increase the cost of litigation;

(2) the claims, defenses, and other legal contentions are warranted by existing law or by a nonfrivolous argument for extending, modifying, or existing law or for establishing new law;

(3) the reversing factual contentions have evidentiary support or, if specifically so identified, will likely have evidentiary support after a reasonable opportunity for further investigation or discovery; and

(4) the denials of factual contentions are warranted on the evidence or, if specifically so identified, are reasonably based on belief or a lack of information."

Fed. R. Civ. P. 11(b). Violators of this rule are subject to monetary and other sanctions. If you believe that another attorney has submitted papers to the court in violation of this rule, you may move for sanctions.

§ 23.07. CHECKLIST FOR MOTIONS

— Before filing or responding to any motion, make sure that you understand the standard upon which the motion will be decided. Read the rule!
— Research the applicable law.
— Find sample motions of the type you will be filing for the court in which you will be filing the motion. You may want to make copies for your files.
— Prepare your memorandum in support of the motion to carefully articulate the factual and legal basis upon which the court may grant the relief you seek. Argue no more than necessary to obtain that relief, but make sure that you have met the standard set forth in the applicable rule. Do not try your case at the motion stage!
— When responding to a motion, carefully focus your argument on what you need to establish to overcome the motion. Do not argue your entire case and confuse the issue.

CHAPTER 24

Introduction to Writing Briefs

§ 24.01. WHAT IS A BRIEF?

A brief is a written argument that a lawyer submits to a court. Briefs may be written in support of motions (discussed in Chapter 23), to define issues for trial, or on appeal. Trial briefs do not generally follow any specific format and may not be submitted in every trial. In an appellate brief, the lawyer argues that the appellate court should reverse or affirm the lower court's decision, or asks for whatever other relief is appropriate. A court uses briefs to define the issues it will decide, to learn about the facts and the law, and to determine who should win.

Unlike a memorandum, which is an objective document, a brief is a persuasive document. Therefore you should write it in a way that will encourage the court to reach a decision favoring your client.

Although you should seek to convince the court that your client should win, do not overstate your case. Be sure to include a discussion of any adverse facts or cases. To win, you must not only argue that the law, policy, and equity support your client's argument, but also face up to damaging facts and contrary cases. You must downplay the significance of the facts and distinguish the cases. If you ignore adverse information, you will be embarrassed when your opponent brings it to the court's attention.

Write the brief persuasively, even the statement of facts. Argue that equity and policy, as well as the law, support your client's case. Chapter 22 describes how to make equity and policy arguments and gives an example of each. Because appellate briefs are the most complicated and involve the most precise rules, we focus on appellate briefs in the next few chapters. You should follow the rules articulated in this book for writing persuasively and for presenting the facts and analysis when writing any brief. You should try to get information from the court or from experienced lawyers who have written similar briefs if you seek guidance regarding the format or desired content of other types of briefs.

Before writing an appellate brief, read the record. The record usually consists of documents and exhibits filed in the lower court, transcripts of depositions, trial testimony and arguments before the lower court, docket entries, and the lower court's orders and opinions. The record defines the issues you may raise on appeal because you can argue only issues raised in the proceedings before the lower court.

The record also limits the facts on which you can rely in your brief because you can rely only on facts that are in the record. Chapter 26 describes the record in more detail.

§ 24.02. PROCEDURAL RULES FOR APPELLATE BRIEFS

Appellate courts promulgate their own rules of appellate procedure. You must follow these rules when you write an appellate brief. These rules regulate the appearance, length, and content of appellate briefs.

Many appellate courts have rules governing paper size, paper color, size of margins, size of type, line spacing, type of binding, numbering of pages, and the format of the title page. As a general rule, each part of an appellate brief must begin on a new page. For example, even if the table of contents takes up only half of a page, you cannot put the table of authorities on the same page. You must begin the table of authorities on the next page.

Many appellate courts also limit the length of appellate briefs. Judges do not have the time to read long briefs. The shorter your brief is, the more likely it is that the judge will read all of it. Even if the appellate court's rules allow you to write a fifty-page brief, write the shortest one possible that still permits you to make a compelling argument.

All appellate courts require appellants to file their briefs first because the appellant is appealing the lower court's order. The appellee then files a brief that responds to the appellant's brief. Most appellate courts allow the appellant to file a reply brief to the appellee's brief.[1]

Most appellate courts require that appellants include the following parts in their briefs:

(1) Title page
(2) Table of contents
(3) Table of authorities
(4) Statement of jurisdiction
(5) Questions presented
(6) Constitutional and statutory provisions
(7) Statement of facts
(8) Summary of argument
(9) Argument
(10) Conclusion
(11) Appendix (all or part of the record)

Although the appellee's brief has most of the same parts, most appellate courts do not require the appellee to include a statement of jurisdiction, questions presented, or a statement of facts. The appellee, however, is allowed to and should include its own version of the questions presented and a statement of facts.

---

1. If the parties have the right to appeal a lower court's decision, the party who initiates the appeal is called the appellant and the opposing party is called the appellee. When review of a lower court's decision is discretionary, the party seeking such review is called the petitioner and the opposing party is called the respondent.

§ 24.03. THE PARTS OF A BRIEF

This section briefly describes the parts of a brief that most appellate courts require. Chapters 26, 27, 28, and 29 describe the parts of the brief in greater detail.

1. The Title Page

The title page contains sufficient information to identify the case and who filed the brief. The title page usually sets out the names of the appellate and lower courts, the names of the parties, the numerical designation for the case, and the name of the attorney who is filing the brief.

2. Table of Contents

The table of contents tells the court the pages on which it will find each part of your brief. The table of contents provides a summary of your argument because it consists of the headings and subheadings of your argument in sentence form.

3. Table of Authorities

The table of authorities tells the court the pages on which it will find the cases, constitutional provisions, statutes, and secondary authorities you cite in your brief. The citation format in the table of authorities must be as accurate and complete as the citation format you use in the argument section of your brief.

4. Jurisdictional Statement

The jurisdictional statement tells the court what authority confers jurisdiction on the court to hear the appeal.

5. Questions Presented

This section frames the issues for the court. Frame the issues persuasively so that they suggest the answers you want the court to reach, but do not be argumentative.

6. Constitutional and Statutory Provisions

This section sets out the text of the constitutional and statutory provisions you cite in your brief. Do not set out the text of the jurisdictional authority you cite in the jurisdictional statement.

7. Statement of Facts

This section sets out a clear and concise statement of the facts relevant to the argument section of the brief. Write the facts in a light most favorable to your client, but do not omit adverse facts. Include references to the record but do not include arguments, conclusions of law, or citations in this section.

8. Summary of Argument

This section sets out a clear, concise, and persuasive summary of your argument. In this section, summarize your primary and most compelling arguments.

9. Argument

The argument section is the heart of the brief. In this section, analyze the pertinent legal authorities and apply them to the facts of the case. Divide the argument into as many subsections as there are issues and sub-issues. Unlike the discussion section of a memo, which is objective, the argument section of a brief is persuasive. Argue equity and policy as well as the law. You must discuss adverse facts and cases.

§ 24.04. THE HALLMARKS OF A WELL-WRITTEN BRIEF

The hallmarks of a well-written brief are the same as the hallmarks of a well-written memo, which are set out in Section 10.04:

- Clear writing style
- Good organization
- Thorough research
- Good judgment
- Writing for the reader
- Precision and clarity
- Creativity
- Correct citation format

There are certain strategic differences between memos and briefs. Your primary audience is the court, not the assigning attorney. Therefore, a brief is persuasive, not objective. The judges will not have read the case file or the applicable law before they read your brief. They usually will know less about the facts and the law than you do. For this reason, be very careful to discuss the facts and the law clearly and thoroughly.

Appellate Process and Standard of Review

§ 25.01. INTRODUCTION

Writing appellate briefs requires an understanding of the appellate process. The structure and ground rules of that process affect your ability to present an effective legal argument. In this chapter, we discuss in broad terms how cases come up on appeal, the record on appeal, and standards of review, that is, the tests an appellate court uses to evaluate the decision below. The discussion focuses primarily on the civil appellate process. If you are handling a criminal appeal, you should follow the applicable rules.

§ 25.02. HOW CASES COME UP ON APPEAL

Although each state court system and the federal system have their own rules on the proper procedure for taking an appeal, all systems share important similarities. Once a court or jury decides a case, the losing party may take an appeal to the appellate court. In a state with an intermediate appellate court, most appeals to that court are a matter of right. In most civil cases, the court of last resort, often called the state supreme court, has discretion in deciding whether to hear an appeal.

In general, the losing party can take an appeal from a final judgment, that is, a decision that disposes of the entire case. A final judgment might arise when a trial ends or when the court decides the case on a motion, for example, a motion for summary judgment. However, in certain instances, an appellant may take an appeal from an interlocutory order. An interlocutory order does not determine the final result of an action, but decides only some intervening matter, such as the grant or denial of an injunction. An appeal from an interlocutory order must follow procedural rules specifically applicable to interlocutory appeals.

§ 25.03. THE RECORD ON APPEAL

In reviewing the proceedings of the court below, the appellate court relies on the record. Rule 10(a) of the Federal Rules of Appellate Procedure sets out a typical definition of the record: "(1) the original papers and exhibits filed in the district court; (2) the transcript of the proceedings, if any; and (3) a certified copy of the docket entries prepared by the district clerk." Reliance on the record ensures that the appellate court will base its decision on only those matters presented to the district court, including both factual and legal questions.[1]

As a general rule, the court will not independently review the record for errors, but will rely on the parties to identify and brief any errors that should be reviewed. When you make your arguments on appeal, you must point to a specific reference in the record to justify each argument. In your brief, you must make constant references to the record so that the court can easily locate the parts of the record on which you are relying. If you fail to make sufficient precise references, you force the court to sift through the often voluminous stack of paper that comprises the record or you run the risk that the court will reject your argument as unsupported by the record. Such a failure will hardly endear you to the court or your client. For a further discussion of the record, see Section 26.01.

§ 25.04. THE STANDARD OF REVIEW

In deciding an appeal, a court cannot simply ignore the decision of the court below. The appellate court may decide only issues that the parties properly identified and objected to as erroneously decided at the trial level. This requirement allows the trial court to correct errors immediately, or at least gives the appellate court the benefit of the trial court's thinking on the issue. In addition, only issues or findings that are necessary to the trial court's decision may be appealed.

The test the appellate court must apply in passing on the lower court's decision is called the standard, or scope, of review. The standard of review varies depending on the jurisdiction and the type of case. You will explore the various types of review in detail in your civil procedure class. Our goal is to briefly introduce you to the most typical standards: clearly erroneous, abuse of discretion, and de novo review. These standards are part of a continuum, from extreme deference to the trial court on fact findings because of the trial court's firsthand exposure to evidence at trial, to little or no deference on purely legal questions.

1. Clearly Erroneous

The most deferential standard for review of a trial court's decision is the "clearly erroneous" standard.[2] The standard is set forth in Rule 52(a)(6) of the Federal Rules of Civil Procedure: "Findings of fact, whether based on oral or other evidence, shall not be set aside unless clearly erroneous, and the reviewing court must give due regard to the trial court's opportunity to judge the witnesses' credibility." The rationale for this standard is clear. Because findings of fact are based on in-court proceedings where the trial court can make judgments on the credibility

---

1. The appellate court may sometimes consider new legal theories or arguments on appeal, but only if those arguments can be resolved based on the facts found at trial.

2. Jury findings are accorded even more deference. The standard is the same as that employed in deciding motions for directed verdict or for judgment notwithstanding the verdict: whether a reasonable jury could have reached the verdict. Gene R. Shreve & Peter Raven-Hansen, *Understanding Civil Procedure*, 444-445 (2d ed. 1994).

and competence of witnesses after seeing them firsthand, these judgments are due substantial deference. Because the trial court has a greater familiarity with the case, the appellate court may not independently determine the weight or credibility of the evidence or assess the inferences drawn from the facts by the trial court.[3]

The Supreme Court described the standard this way: "A finding is 'clearly erroneous' when although there is evidence to support it, the reviewing court on the entire evidence is left with the definite and firm conviction that a mistake has been committed."[4] This standard obviously places quite a difficult burden on the appellant's attorney.

2. Abuse of Discretion

Slightly further along the deference continuum, and more difficult to define, is the abuse of discretion standard. This standard applies to matters that are within the discretion of the trial court because they are "largely ad hoc and situation-specific."[5] This standard is tolerant of mistakes that may be made by a trial court in the exercise of its acknowledged discretion. Trial courts have a great deal of discretion on issues relating to trial management, such as joinder, discovery, sanctions, and the grant or denial of a motion for a new trial.

The scope of the trial court's discretion in a particular instance will depend on and must be evaluated in the context of the source of its discretion. For example, Rule 35(a) of the Federal Rules of Civil Procedure gives the trial court discretion to order a mental or physical examination of a party "for good cause," when the mental or physical condition of the party is "in controversy." Such an order would normally be accorded great deference on appeal, but in *Schlagenhauf v. Holder*, 379 U.S. 104 (1964), the Supreme Court found abuse of discretion in a case where the trial court ordered that a defendant be examined in each of four medical specialties—internal medicine, ophthalmology, neurology, and psychiatry. There was nothing in the record to support any examination other than a visual examination, so the Court vacated the judgment of the district court and remanded for reconsideration and further proceedings.

The abuse of discretion standard "varies in intensity with the breadth of discretion. Accordingly, abuse of discretion really occupies a band in the middle of the spectrum of intensity of review, its precise locus in any particular case depending upon the nature of the discretionary order under review."[6] If abuse of discretion is the standard for the case you are appealing, you will need to research similar cases in order to understand and argue precisely how the standard should be applied in your case.

3. De Novo Review

The least deferential standard of review is applied to pure questions of law, or to mixed fact-law questions.[7] The appellate court is at no disadvantage in deciding

---

3. Jack H. Friedenthal, Mary Kay Kane & Arthur R. Miller, *Civil Procedure* 640 (4th ed., West 2005).
4. *United States v. U.S. Gypsum Co.*, 333 U.S. 364, 395 (1948).
5. Shreve & Raven-Hansen, *supra* n. 2, at 445.
6. *Id.* at 446.
7. Friedenthal et al., *supra* n. 3, at 639, 641.

these types of questions because it has the same access to relevant information that the trial court had. By making de novo decisions, the appellate court fulfills one of its primary functions: to provide guidance to the lower courts by ruling on questions of law.[8]

The de novo standard comes into play, for example, in reviewing pretrial motions. To illustrate, Rule 56(c) of the Federal Rules of Civil Procedure sets out the standard to apply when the federal district court grants a motion for summary judgment. According to the rule, summary judgment is proper when it appears that "there is no genuine issue as to any material fact and that the movant is entitled to judgment as a matter of law." The appellate court reads the record in the light most favorable to the party against whom the summary judgment was granted. Because the lower court heard no witnesses and weighed no evidence, the appellate court has no findings of fact to review. It therefore may decide the issue de novo. As you would expect, this standard is the one most favorable to the appellant.

4. The Importance to the Practitioner

As you can see, the appellate lawyer must know what standard of review the court should employ and should think strategically in presenting the appropriate standard to the court. If you represent the appellant, it is to your advantage to be able to characterize the issue on appeal as a question of law, or of mixed fact and law. If you succeed, the standard of review will be de novo. Conversely, if you represent the appellee, you want to characterize the issue as one of fact, or at least as one subject to the trial court's discretion. That way, the appellate court will be forced to give greater deference to the opinion of the trial court. Not surprisingly, complicated analysis and legal research may be required to distinguish the mixed fact-law question from the purely factual question.

Your understanding of the standard of review will also affect the way you argue and emphasize different aspects of the record. If you are representing the appellee and the court must find the decision below to be clearly erroneous in order to overturn it, you should stress the evidence that supports the trial court's decision and argue that the appellate court must defer to the judgment of the lower court. On the other hand, if you are representing the appellant and the court may hear the case de novo, you should point out that the decision below carries no weight and then make as few references to it as possible. Present the argument as if you are making it for the first time.

§ 25.05. AVAILABLE FORMS OF RELIEF

When the appellate court completes its review, it has the discretion to take certain specific actions. It may reverse or vacate the decision below, remand the matter to the lower court for further proceedings, or affirm. As an appellate attorney, you must tell the court precisely what action you want it to take. You may want the court to take different actions on different issues. If you fail to be precise about the relief you seek, the court can only guess at what your client wishes.

---

8. *Id.* at 639.

The Appellate Brief: The Introductory Parts

§ 26.01. USING THE RECORD

You must have authority for every fact you state in your brief. Your authority for facts and for the history of your case is the "record." Although some courts call the record the "appendix," in this book, we use the term "record." the record consists of docket entries, trial transcripts, deposition excerpts, and pleadings filed in the court below. You will make many references to the record in your statement of facts. You will also refer to the record every time you repeat a fact in the argument section of your brief and every time you refer to any event or filing of documents in the proceedings in lower courts.

An attorney prepares the record before writing the brief. In practice, attorneys for the opposing parties on appeal usually agree to the contents of the record. In the law school situation, the instructor gives students the record from which to write the brief. the record is the "reference book" for your brief. You must not rely on any fact that is not in the record.

Rules of court usually tell you what you must include in the record. For example, the rules may require all docket entries from the lower courts and all orders and opinions from the lower courts. You also should include in the record all relevant pleadings in your case and relevant excerpts from depositions and trial transcripts.

When you prepare the record, put all items in the order the court rules specify. If the court rules specify that you arrange items in groups, arrange the items within that group in order. Put other items, such as testimony, in the order that you think is logical. The record is bound into a volume or, in many cases, several volumes. The pages of the record are then numbered sequentially as "R-1," "R-2," "R-3," and so forth. (If the record is called "appendix," the pages are numbered "A-1," "A-2," and so forth.)

When you write your brief, make references to the pages containing the facts that you include. For example:

The defendant hit the plaintiff. (R. 35-37.) The plaintiff then skidded off the road. (R. 107-111.) The plaintiff's car was totally destroyed. (R. 103.)

If you have stated a fact that appears on several pages in the record, make references to all pages on which that information appears:

> The defendant hit the plaintiff. (R. 35-37, 86-89.) The plaintiff then skidded off the road. (R. 107-111, 332, 345-346.) The plaintiff's car was totally destroyed. (R. 103, 111, 462-465, 503.)

Do not include any fact in your brief that the record does not substantiate. Do not assume any facts that are not in the record. The court that reads your brief will rely only on facts in the record. It is also very important that all your record references be accurate because the court will refer to the pages of the record you cite.

Skim the sample briefs referenced in Appendix IV and notice that the writers have made record references throughout their briefs.

§ 26.02. THE TITLE PAGE

The title page of your brief gives the court necessary information. Look at the title pages of the sample briefs referenced in Appendix IV. The title page in your brief must conform to the rules of the court with which you file your brief.

There are many ways to type title pages of briefs. The one you choose should be pleasing to the eye and easy to scan for the necessary information it contains. Some courts require typeset briefs.

A typical title page contains the following eight elements:

1. the exact name of the appellate court with which you are filing your brief;
2. the term in which the court is to consider your appeal, including the month and the year;
3. the docket number for the case;
4. the names of the parties with the appropriate appellate designation ("appellant," "appellee," "petitioner," or "respondent");
5. the exact name of the court from whose order you appeal;
6. identification of the party: "Brief for Appellant," "Brief for Appellee," "Brief for Petitioner," or "Brief for Respondent";
7. the name and address of the attorney writing the brief; and
8. the name and address of the attorney representing the opposing party (optional).

If court rules tell you how to prepare a title page, follow those rules exactly.

§ 26.03. TABLE OF CONTENTS

The table of contents is a "roadmap" for the court and the opposing counsel. This section is the first summary of your argument. It also serves as a reference tool. You must be sure that the page references are accurate and that the headings of the arguments in the table of contents are exact duplicates of the headings in your brief. For a discussion of brief headings, see Chapter 29.

Read the tables of contents for the briefs in Appendix IV. Notice that the argument headings summarize the writer's arguments.

§ 26.04. TABLE OF AUTHORITIES

The table of authorities is a listing of all legal authorities you have used in your brief. The first and most important part of this table is the listing of cases.

In compiling the table of authorities, follow the rules of the court for which you are writing the brief. Some rules require that you list cases alphabetically and by court—all United States Supreme Court cases in alphabetical order, all United States Court of Appeals cases in alphabetical order, and so forth. Others require a single alphabetical listing of all cases from all courts.

Follow proper citation form, including the procedural history of cases. Again, accuracy is most important. The court and opposing counsel will rely on the accuracy of the page numbers in your table to find the location of the authorities in your brief. When you prepare your brief, checking these page references is the last thing you should do because they can change at any time.

When a writer uses an authority many times throughout a brief, the Latin word "*passim*" can replace page numbers in the table of authorities; it indicates that the authority is "everywhere." Be very careful about using this term, and do not use it in the table of authorities unless you actually use the authority "everywhere." For example, you may have cited a case on virtually every page. In this situation use "*passim*." However, if you use a reference only a few times, "*passim*" is inappropriate, and you should list all the pages on which that reference appears.

In the table of authorities a listing of statutes and constitutional authorities usually follows the listing of cases. Be thorough, list every statute and constitutional provision you have used in your brief, and follow the *Bluebook* for citation form.

After the listing of statutes and constitutional authorities, list all "secondary" sources you have cited in your brief. These include legal periodicals, treatises, restatements of the law, and other sources that are neither cases, statutes, nor constitutional provisions.

Again, list every authority you use, write accurate citations, and number the pages accurately. The court will use the page references to authorities while reading your briefs. A common question the court asks during oral argument of a case is "Where can I find that case in your brief?" Save yourself the embarrassment of referring the court to the wrong page. And remember: The court will get its first impression of the accuracy of your brief from the table of authorities section. If this section is inaccurate, the court may question the rest of your work. Attention to detail is very important.

§ 26.05. JURISDICTIONAL STATEMENT

Read the jurisdictional statements in the sample briefs in Appendix IV. You can follow those formats generally.

This section of your brief tells the court what authority permits the court to consider your case. Cite the authority, but do not quote it. It is not a statement of a statute governing the substance of your case, but a statement of a statute, a rule of court, or a constitutional provision authorizing the appellate court to hear the kind of case you are appealing. This statement tells the court that your case is in the right court.

A colleague may tell you to appeal a certain kind of case to a certain court. However, you cannot rely on word of mouth. Find the provision of law specifically stating that the court in which you are bringing your appeal is the right one to consider your case.

§ 26.06. QUESTIONS PRESENTED

The questions presented section is one of the most important sections of the brief. It frames the questions you want the court to answer and frames those questions in a way that encourages the court to decide them in your favor. The number of questions presented must correspond to the number of major headings in your brief.

Courts often give you specific rules about this section of the brief; however, most rules are the same:

- State the questions clearly and concisely.
- Avoid specific names, dates, and locations unless they help clarify the issues and are persuasive.
- Let the court know precisely what your case involves.

Writing the questions presented by your case is an art in itself. You can master this art only through practice. Writing the questions presented section is not a mechanical effort, but one to which you should devote a significant amount of time.

Here are examples of issues stated in different ways to illustrate what to say and what not to say in questions presented.

Bad: Whether Mr. Barnes proved his case of adverse possession.

Better: Does an adverse user satisfy the "continuous" and "exclusive" use elements needed to establish adverse possession to severed mineral rights by mining at times that are economically feasible and allowing neighbors to mine coal for personal use at other times throughout the statutory period?

Comment: In the first example the question is too broad and could refer to any adverse possession case. The second statement of the question includes the specifics of the case in question. Note that when you begin the question with "whether," you should end with a period, and, when you begin with a word like "does" or "can," you should end with a question mark. When you phrase the question presented as a question, phrase it so that the answer is "yes" and favors your client.

———

Bad: Did the trial court err in admitting the evidence the officers obtained through the search?

Better: Did the trial court err in admitting evidence voluntarily given to the police by the minor child, when the child obtained it as a result of his independent search of the property and without police direction?

Comment: The first example is too general and says nothing about the particular case. The second statement of the question states the important facts concisely and clearly.

In addition to writing the questions presented with particularity and sufficient information, write your issues persuasively in your client's behalf. Here is how counsel on each side of the case might write the first example above.

Plaintiff's phrasing of the question: Can a land user satisfy the "continuous" and "exclusive" use needed to establish adverse possession to severed mineral rights by mining at times that are economically feasible and consistent with local custom, and allowing neighbors to mine coal for personal use only at other times throughout the statutory period, particularly when he acted at all times and in all other ways as a true owner would have acted?

Defendant's phrasing of the same question: Whether sporadic mining of a property only at convenient times while allowing others to use the property at their will was insufficient evidence of the continuity and exclusivity required to deprive the record owner of his superior rights to the minerals on the land.

Comment: The first statement of the adverse possession question suggests that the plaintiff has acquired rights by meeting legal requirements, and the second statement of the same question suggests that plaintiff failed to fulfill the legal requirements and should not deprive the record owner of mineral rights. Some readers may find the phrasing of the questions too argumentative. For a less argumentative version of the plaintiff's question, omit the words "only" and "particularly." For a less argumentative version of the defendant's question, omit the word "only" and substitute "sufficient" for "insufficient."

———

Here is how counsel on each side of the case might write the second example above.

Prosecution's phrasing of the question: Whether the trial court was correct in admitting evidence when the child who provided the evidence voluntarily conducted a search of his home, with no direction from the police, and voluntarily offered that evidence to the police.

Defendant's phrasing of the question: Whether the trial court erred in admitting evidence provided by a child, who, at the direction of the police, searched his own home and provided the evidence after further prompting by the police.

Comment: The prosecution's phrasing of the question first suggests that the trial court was correct; it then places the child's activity on the child's shoulders and not on the police. It suggests that no police search occurred and that the search was an appropriate private search resulting in admissible evidence. The defendant's phrasing suggests that the trial court erred in admitting the evidence. It suggests that the child obtained the evidence only at the direction of the police in violation of the defendant's constitutional rights.

Some lawyers phrase the question presented by using more than one sentence. This technique permits them to avoid long, complex sentences that are difficult for the reader to comprehend. For instance, in the last set of examples, the defendant's lawyer might phrase the question this way:

> At the direction of the police, a child searched his own home and, after further prompting by the police, produced evidence. Did the trial court err in admitting this evidence?

§ 26.07. TEXT OF CONSTITUTIONAL, STATUTORY, AND REGULATORY PROVISIONS

This section of the brief contains the text of the constitutional, statutory, and regulatory provisions you use in your brief. See the examples of this section in the briefs in Appendix IV.

Do not include the text of any of these provisions if you do not rely on them in your argument. For example, do not include the statute or rule you use in your jurisdictional statement unless that authority is at issue in your case. If you make reference to a provision that is not at issue in your case, do not include its text.

Do not include full texts of provisions when only parts of those provisions are at issue. A statute, for example, may be very lengthy and may contain much language that has nothing to do with your case. Use only relevant portions as long as those portions make sense standing alone. Follow correct citation format.

Exercises

1. Using the information provided, prepare a title page for a brief. Type it the way it would appear in final form. Follow the format of the briefs in Appendix IV.

(1) The appellate court is the Supreme Court for the State of Ohio.
(2) The term of court is January 1998.
(3) The docket number for your case is No. 96-43360.
(4) The appellee is the State of Ohio.
(5) The appellant is Elyse Keaton.
(6) The case is on appeal from the Court of Appeals for the State of Ohio.
(7) The brief is for the appellee.
(8) You are the attorney for the appellee. Your address is 106 Main Street, Centerville, Ohio 90207. Your phone number is (302) 777-7777.
(9) Mary Smith is the attorney for the appellant, and her address is 100 Main Street, Centerville, Ohio 90207. Her phone number is (302) 555-5555.

2. Prepare a table of contents from the following information. Conform to the format in the sample briefs in Appendix IV. Omit page numbers.

(1) Conclusion
(2) Argument headings:
   I. The state did not violate the defendant's Fourth and Fourteenth Amendment rights, and the cocaine is admissible because the police found it as a result of a legal private search by defendant's child, without government involvement; and the child gave the evidence voluntarily to the police
       A. Officer Rambo did not direct Alex's search
           1. The interaction between Alex and Officer Rambo did not give rise to an agency relationship
           2. Alex conducted his search without Officer Rambo's knowledge, and he completed it before he notified Officer Rambo
       B. Alex was not acting as Officer Rambo's agent when he gave Officer Rambo the evidence
       C. Even if the search and seizure was subject to the Fourth Amendment, Alex's consent constitutes an exception to the warrant requirement
           1. Alex had authority to consent
           2. Alex voluntarily and knowingly consented to the search and seizure of the evidence
   II. Neither a husband-wife privilege nor a parent-child privilege provides a basis for defendant to exclude her child's testimony since neither would be available to defendant under Ohio law, the law of other courts and legislatures, or social policy
       A. Ohio law clearly prohibits defendant from invoking the husband-wife privilege
       B. The Ohio statute does not authorize a parent-child testimonial privilege, and the court should not recognize such a privilege where a child voluntarily testifies about a communication his mother made in his presence regarding her criminal activities
(3) Summary of the argument
(4) Table of authorities
(5) Statement of the case
(6) Constitutional and statutory provisions
(7) Statement of jurisdiction
(8) Questions presented

3. Prepare a table of authorities from the following information. Omit page numbers. Use correct citation form. Follow the format in the sample briefs in Appendix IV.

Ohio Rev. Code Ann. § 2317.02 (LexisNexis 2005)
Weis v. Weis, 147 Ohio State 416, 72 N.E.2d 245 (1947)
State v. Morris, 42 Ohio State 2d 307, 329 N.E.2d 85 (1978)
Three Juveniles v. Commonwealth, 455 N.E.2d 1203 (Mass. 1983)
Idaho Code 9-203(7) (1998)
United States v. Matlock, 415 U.S. 164 (1974)

Arnovitz v. Wozar, 9 Ohio App. 2d, 222 N.E.2d 660 (1964)

Belichick v. Belichick, 37 Ohio App. 2d 95, 307 N.E.2d 270 (1973)

Martin J. McMahon, Annotations, Presence of Child at Communication Between Husband and Wife as Destroying Confidentiality of Otherwise Privileged Communication Between Them, 39 American Law Reports Annotated 4th 481 (1985)

Fourth Amendment, United States Constitution

In re Terry, W., 130 California Reporter 913 (Ct. App. 1976)

Mapp v. Ohio, 367 U.S. 643 (1961)

Jeffrey Begens, Comment, Parent-Child Testimonial Privilege: An Absolute Right or an Absolute Privilege?, 11 University of Dayton Law Review 709, 1986

Oregon v. Scott, 729 P.2d 585 (Or. Ct. App. 1986)

Herbert v. Maryland, 269 A.2d 430 (Md. Ct. Spec. App. 1970)

Ohio Const, amend. IV. § 1

4. Rewrite the following facts into a question presented two ways: for the plaintiff/appellant and for the defendant/appellee.

Mr. Hale is a tenant, and Ms. Petrie is his landlady. Mr. Hale's apartment is in New Jersey. A few months ago a robber attacked Mr. Hale in the parking garage of his apartment complex and robbed him at gunpoint. The robber also beat Mr. Hale, causing him injuries and a broken arm.

Mr. Hale sued Ms. Petrie for negligence for her failure to provide adequate security in the parking garage. Although a guard was usually stationed in the garage, that guard was off-duty at the time of the criminal attack. Ms. Petrie contended in the trial court that, in New Jersey, she had no duty to protect her tenants from criminal attacks and was therefore not negligent. She also argued that, even if she had a duty, she provided sufficient security and that she had fulfilled any duty she had by taking reasonable steps to provide security. Her argument won in the court below. Mr. Hale now appeals that decision and argues that, once Ms. Petrie undertook to provide security, she also undertook to provide reasonable security but failed to do so.

5. Suppose you are working on a case concerning a confidential communication to a priest. Prepare the text of the relevant statutory provision from the following statute as if you were preparing this text for a section on constitutional and statutory provisions for a brief.

Section 2317.02 of the Ohio Revised Code Annotated (LexisNexis 2005), *Privileged Communications and Acts*, provides in relevant part:

The following persons shall not testify in certain respects:

(A) An attorney, concerning a communication made to him by his client;

(B) A physician concerning a communication made to him by his patient;

(C) A clergyman, rabbi, priest, or minister, concerning a confession made, or any information confidentially communicated, to him for a religious counseling purpose;

(D) Husband or wife, concerning any communication made by one to the other, or an act done by either in the presence of the other, during coverture, unless the communication was made, or act done, in the known presence of hearing of a third person competent to be a witness; ...

(G) A school guidance counselor ... professional counselor, counselor assistant, social worker, social work assistant or independent social worker concerning a confidential communication made to him by his client.

The Appellate Brief: Statement of Facts; Summary of Argument

§ 27.01. STATEMENT OF FACTS

The statement of facts, also called the statement of the case, should include all the facts that the court needs to know to decide the case. Turn to the statements of fact in the briefs in Appendix IV to get an idea of what the statements look like.

For the attorney, the statement has a purpose in addition to furnishing information. Use the statement to set the stage for your argument. Tell the truth, be complete, but put your best foot forward. This part of the brief offers still another opportunity for advocacy.

Organize the facts and state them clearly so that the court can readily understand them. You are writing a statement of facts; therefore, state the facts truthfully and write without editorializing. Nonetheless, write so that the court sees your client in the most favorable light possible. The following pages show you how to perform this feat.

Here are three rules for writing the statement of facts:

1. Tell what happened.
2. Tell the truth, but put your best foot forward.
3. Hold the court's attention.

To illustrate our discussion of these rules, we will examine excerpts from the statements of the petitioners and respondents in *New Jersey v. T.L.O.*, 469 U.S. 325 (1985). In this case, a high school vice-principal searched the purse of T.L.O., a student, and found marijuana. New Jersey began a delinquency proceeding against the student.

The issue was whether the Fourth Amendment's exclusionary rule should apply when a public school teacher or official illegally seizes evidence from a student. As you may know, the Constitution's Fourth Amendment forbids unreasonable searches and seizures by government officers. Under the exclusionary rule, evidence obtained during an unconstitutional search is inadmissible in court.

In *T.L.O.*, the trial court and the intermediate appellate court ruled that the evidence was admissible. The New Jersey Supreme Court, however, ruled that the exclusionary rule applied to the search and that the evidence therefore was inadmissible. Before the United States Supreme Court, New Jersey was the petitioner and T.L.O. was the respondent.

1. Tell What Happened

In the statement of facts, you are telling a story. Tell the story so that the reader can follow along with the least amount of effort.

An important part of the story is the case's procedural history: how the case started and what decisions the courts below have issued. A court will want this information readily available. Some attorneys set it out as a short, separate section of the brief. Others include it as an introductory subsection of the statement of facts, and still others weave pieces of it into the statement of facts as the pieces naturally arise in the course of the story. You should use the method that works best for you in a particular case. If the procedural history is brief and uncomplicated, you might state it in the opening sentences of the statement of facts. If it is complicated, you might set it out as a subsection of the statement or as a completely separate section labeled "Procedural History." If you choose the latter method, you also might discuss the lower court decisions near the end of the statement.

You will help the court to follow the story if you call the parties by their names and do not refer to them as "petitioner" and "respondent." Think of the times when you have read a court opinion and the court called the litigants "appellant" and "appellee." Remember how difficult it was to recall which label went with which litigant. In the *T.L.O.* case, call the juvenile "T.L.O." as opposed to "respondent." Call the petitioner either "New Jersey" or "the State."

Most of the time, you will want to tell the story chronologically. The historical approach is easy to follow. To illustrate, here are the opening paragraphs of the statements of facts in the *T.L.O.* briefs. The first excerpt comes from the brief of the petitioner, New Jersey:

> On the morning of March 7, 1980, a teacher of mathematics at Piscataway High School entered the girls' restroom and found the juvenile-respondent T.L.O. and a girl named Johnson holding what the teacher perceived to be lit cigarettes. (MT20-1 to 25).[1] Smoking was not permitted and the girls were thus committing an infraction of the school rules. The girls were taken to the principal's office where they met with Theodore Choplick, the assistant vice-principal. (MT21-1 to 3; MT21-24 to 22-11; MT31-18 to 20; MT33-20 to 34-10).

The second excerpt comes from T.L.O.'s brief:

> On March 7, 1980, a search was made by Mr. Choplick, vice principal of Piscataway High School, of a purse belonging to T.L.O., a student at the school. Ms. Chen, a

---

1. "MT" refers to the transcript of the motion to suppress heard before the Juvenile and Domestic Relations Court on September 26, 1980. "T" refers to the transcript of trial on March 23, 1981, the transcript of the juvenile's plea of guilty to other complaints on June 2, 1981, and the transcript of sentencing on January 8, 1982, all contained in one volume.

teacher, had made a routine check of the girls' restroom. She observed T.L.O. and another girl smoking tobacco cigarettes. (MT 20-7 to 25) Although smoking by students was permitted in designated areas, it was not allowed in the restrooms. (MT 33-20 to MT 34-6) Ms. Chen accompanied both girls to Mr. Choplick's office, where she advised him of the infraction. (MT 21-1 to MT 22-23)

In each paragraph, the attorneys told the story in chronological order in a way that is easy to follow. T.L.O.'s statement began with a sentence not in chronological order because the sentence offered a desirable way to begin the story. Which paragraph do you prefer? Note that both attorneys documented their facts by making reference to the record. You are expected to furnish this documentation as a convenience to the court.

In telling the story, keep the narrative moving. Stay on point and omit irrelevant information. You should include facts that help make your client's case sympathetic, even if they are not essential to your legal argument. Here is the second paragraph from New Jersey's statement of facts:

Mr. Choplick asked the two girls whether they were smoking. Miss Johnson acknowledged that she had been smoking, and Mr. Choplick imposed three-day attendance at a smoking clinic as punishment. (T49-24 to 50-7). T.L.O. denied smoking in the lavatory and further asserted that she did not smoke at all. (MT27-10 to 17). Mr. Choplick asked T.L.O. to come into a private office. (MT27-14 to 21; MT30-22 to 31-17).

T.L.O.'s brief does not contain a comparable paragraph. It offers a single sentence: "Upon being questioned, T.L.O. denied that she smoked." Do you understand why New Jersey's attorneys decided to include the additional information?

Here is another example. T.L.O.'s brief describes the juvenile court's disposition in the following words: "On January 8, 1982, a probationary term of one year was imposed." Here is how the New Jersey brief describes the disposition: "On January 8, 1982, T.L.O. was sentenced to probation for one year with the special condition that she observe a reasonable curfew, attend school regularly and successfully complete a counselling and drug therapy program." Arguably, the New Jersey brief includes more information than a court would need to make a decision about the applicability of the exclusionary rule. The additional information, however, helps place the state in a more favorable light. New Jersey's attorneys were correct in including it.

2. Tell the Truth, But Put Your Best Foot Forward

In writing your statement of facts, you must tell the truth and not otherwise mislead the court. If the court discovers that you have been less than truthful, you lose your credibility, severely damage your client's case, and hurt your reputation as a trustworthy attorney. Still, you should state your case in the most favorable way possible. Write in an objective, noneditorial style, but emphasize the facts that help your client's case. Here is an excerpt from the New Jersey brief:

Once inside this office, Mr. Choplick requested the juvenile's purse, and she gave it to him. (MT27-24 to 28-7). A package of Marlboro cigarettes was visible inside the purse.

(MT28-9 to 11). Mr. Choplick held up the Marlboros and said to the juvenile, "You lied to me."

This excerpt paints the picture by using facts, rather than adverbs, adjectives, or editorial statements. Instead of explicitly calling T.L.O. a liar—an editorial statement—New Jersey's attorneys furnish facts that permit the Court to reach this conclusion. The statement adds emphasis by quoting the vice-principal. Quoting another person's judgmental words is more effective than employing your own editorial words. In a statement of facts, employing your own editorial words is inappropriate.

As another illustration, consider how T.L.O.'s brief describes the items that Mr. Choplick found in the purse:

Looking further into the handbag, he found a metal pipe, and one plastic bag containing tobacco or some similar substance.[2] (MT29-10 to 16) He also found a wallet containing "a lot of singles and change," and inside a separate compartment of the purse, two letters and an index card.

Compare the description in New Jersey's brief: "There he found marijuana, drug paraphernalia, $40 in one-dollar bills and documentation of T.L.O.'s sale of marijuana to other students." Each statement tells the same story, uses objective words, offers accurate information, and yet favors the respective client.

Writing the statement of facts may require you to deal with information adverse to your client. You already have seen some examples of ways to confront the problem. For another example, compare the following accounts of T.L.O.'s encounter with the police. Here is the account in New Jersey's brief:

T.L.O.'s mother acceded to a police request to bring her daughter to police headquarters for questioning. (T18-12 to 18). Once at headquarters, T.L.O. was advised of her rights in her mother's presence and signed a *Miranda*[3] rights card so indicating. (T20-3 to 21). The officer then began to question T.L.O. in her mother's presence. (T23-4 to 6). T.L.O. admitted that the objects found in her purse belonged to her. She further admitted that she was selling marijuana in school, receiving $1 per "joint," or rolled marijuana cigarette. T.L.O. stated that she had sold between 18 and 20 joints at school that very morning, before the drug was confiscated by the assistant principal.

Compare the account in T.L.O.'s brief:

The local police transported T.L.O. and her mother to headquarters. Upon arrival, Officer O'Gurkins advised the juvenile of her *Miranda* rights. (T20-7 to T21-3). When Mrs. O. indicated that she wanted to have an attorney present during the questioning, she was permitted to telephone the office of her lawyer. (T34-10 to 24). He was not

---

2. At trial it was stipulated that the bag contained 5.40 grams of marijuana. (T12-17 to 25). [Would you have advised the writer to place this information in a footnote?—Ed.]

3. *Miranda v. Arizona,* 384 U.S. 436 (1966).

available, so the officer proceeded with the interrogation. According to Mrs. O., at no time did her daughter state that she had sold marijuana. (T35-15 to 22).

Officer O'Gurkins admitted that although it was standard practice in juvenile matters to reduce incriminating statements to writing, he did not follow this procedure with T.L.O. (T24-12 to 18). He nevertheless maintained that T.L.O. had confessed that she had been selling marijuana in school for a week. (T22-2 to 17). He conceded that T.L.O. explained to him that the $40.98, which was found in her purse, constituted the proceeds from her paper route, which she had collected the night before.

The New Jersey brief seems to deal with some adverse facts by omitting them. Controversy exists over whether T.L.O. admitted to selling marijuana. From a technical perspective, the controversy is not pertinent to the issue before the Supreme Court. Nonetheless, the possible innocence of T.L.O. on the selling charge may affect the Court's perception of the case. T.L.O.'s brief discusses the controversy. The Court might think less of New Jersey's brief for ignoring it. The New Jersey brief could have alluded to the matter without turning it into a major issue. It might have begun the critical sentence this way: "According to the officer, T.L.O. admitted that she was selling. . . ." It also might have included an additional sentence: "Her mother later denied that T.L.O. made this admission." The lesson is that you can own up to adverse facts without waving them about.

Another way to use facts to your advantage is to summarize or quote favorable opinions of the court below. These opinions are powerful support for your arguments. Use them. If a majority opinion goes against you, mention the opinion and then focus on the dissent. In either case, you have the opportunity to make your arguments while still writing objectively. You summarize the favorable words of a third party, a court. This summary is still one more presentation of your argument. In *T.L.O.*, for example, New Jersey's statement of facts summarizes the adverse holding of the state supreme court in a single sentence. T.L.O.'s statement, however, spends four paragraphs summarizing the majority opinion.

3. Hold the Court's Attention

Both New Jersey's and T.L.O.'s statements of fact hold the reader's interest. They tell the story in chronological sequence. They omit needless information. They use a concrete writing style. They refer to T.L.O.'s cigarettes as "Marlboros," as opposed to "tobacco cigarettes." New Jersey's statement quotes the vice-principal: "You lied to me." It also states that Mr. Choplick found "$40 in one-dollar bills" as opposed to "$40" or "some money." The attorneys writing these statements followed the rules of good writing style that you have learned. In these statements, the most important rules of style are using the active voice, keeping sentences and words simple and concrete, and avoiding the inflammatory rhetoric that marks the advocate as an amateur.

Exercise

Here is a paragraph from T.L.O.'s statement of facts. Rewrite it to improve it stylistically so that it more effectively holds the reader's attention.

An appeal was taken and decided on June 30, 1982. *In re T.L.O.*, 448 A.2d 493 (N.J. Super. Ct. App. Div. 1982). Two judges affirmed the denial of the motion to suppress the evidence secured by the search of the juvenile's purse, adopting the reasons set forth in the opinion of the trial court. However, they found that the record was inadequate to determine the sufficiency of the *Miranda* waiver which was allegedly made by the juvenile after her mother's unsuccessful attempt to summon counsel. *Id.* at 493. They therefore vacated the adjudication of delinquency and ordered a remand for further proceedings in light of the principles enunciated in *Edwards v. Arizona*, 451 U.S. 477 (1981) and *State v. Fussell*, 174 N.J. Super. 14 (App. Div. 1980). *Id.* One judge dissented, indicating that he would suppress the evidence found in T.L.O.'s purse because the search had been unreasonable. *Id.* at 495.

§ 27.02. SUMMARY OF ARGUMENT

In the summary of argument, you summarize your argument. According to United States Supreme Court Rule 34(h), the summary is a "succinct, but accurate and clear condensation of the argument made in the body of the brief. It should not be a mere repetition of the headings under which the argument is arranged." Please read the summaries of argument in the briefs referenced in Appendix IV. As you can see, the summary rarely is more than one or two pages.

This part of the brief is your chance to give the court a summary of your argument. It may be all some judges read before they hear your oral argument. Because of its importance, spend the time necessary to make it readable and persuasive. When a judge turns to your summary, he or she probably knows very little about your case. Therefore write the summary for an intelligent but uninformed audience.

The task is harder than you may think. After spending weeks or months grappling with a case, you may have difficulty in accurately reducing your analysis to a page or two. Stick to your main arguments and save the subtle points for the body of the brief.

Use the table of contents as an outline for the summary. Write a topical sentence stating a point of your argument at or near the beginning of each paragraph. Then flesh out the outline a bit. If you cite any cases at all, cite only those that are essential to making your summary understandable. For example, you might cite the major case that you are distinguishing or relying on.

CHAPTER 28

Practice in Writing the Statement of Facts and Summary of Argument

§ 28.01. EXERCISE I

Please read the following excerpt from the summary of argument in T.L.O.'s brief. Then write an outline of the summary. Note also how the writer fleshed out the argument. What suggestions do you have for improvement?

Assuming *arguendo* that the decision of the New Jersey Supreme Court does present a federal question for adjudication, petitioner's contention that the exclusionary rule need not be applied to the fruits of the illegal search at issue in this matter is clearly erroneous. The Fourth Amendment protects against unreasonable searches conducted by any governmental agency. Because public school personnel are employed by the state, act with state authority, and are responsible for carrying out state laws and regulations, their conduct constitutes governmental, rather than private, action. Thus the search of T.L.O. by the vice-principal comes within the ambit of the Fourth Amendment.

While petitioner is correct in asserting that this Court has not found the exclusionary rule to be constitutionally required in the case of every Fourth Amendment violation, those instances where it has not been applied have involved limited, peripheral uses of the evidence so obtained. This Court has not permitted the fruits of an illegal search to be introduced into evidence on the prosecution's case-in-chief in a criminal proceeding, as the State seeks to do in the present matter. In such circumstances, application of the rule is mandatory.

Even if petitioner is correct in maintaining that a balancing test—weighing the benefits of deterrence against the societal costs resulting from implementation of the rule— is constitutionally permissible to determine if the exclusionary rule should be applied in the present circumstances, it is clear that the expected benefits would outweigh the anticipated detriments. First, educators do have an interest in the successful prosecution of juvenile delinquency proceedings and would be deterred from conducting unreasonable searches by the knowledge that the resulting evidence would be excluded. Second, if evidence illegally secured by educators was not admissible at trial, the police would be deterred from instigating teachers to conduct illegal searches in order to provide otherwise obtainable evidence on "a silver platter." With regard to societal costs, statistical studies have shown that relatively few prosecutions are dismissed because of Fourth Amendment problems. School surveys do not support the conclusion that the crime rate in schools is rising or that an increase in searches by school personnel would be a significant factor in reducing the present rate.

Petitioner has demonstrated no alternatives to the exclusionary rule which would effectively deter violations of the Fourth Amendment rights of students. In addition, the exclusionary rule serves constitutionally recognized purposes other than deterrence: it protects the imperative of judicial integrity, and teaches respect for constitutional rights.

§ 28.02. EXERCISE II

At the end of this chapter, please find the statements of the case (statements of facts) submitted by the petitioner and respondent in *McIntyre v. Ohio Elections Commission*. Please compare them. How do they differ? Why did the attorneys write them the way they did? What suggestions would you make for improvement?

§ 28.03. EXERCISE III

At the end of this chapter, please find the summaries of argument submitted by the petitioner and respondent in *McIntyre v. Ohio Elections Commission*. Please compare them. How do they differ? Why did the attorneys write them the way they did? What suggestions would you make for improvement?

§ 28.04. EXERCISE IV

In *Rosenberger v. University of Virginia*, college students sought funding for "Wide Awake," a new student publication with an expressly religious viewpoint. They were denied funding because of a university funding guideline that categorically denies funding of religious organizations and religious activities. At issue is whether this prohibition violates the First Amendment.

At the Supreme Court, the petitioner students argue that the denial violates the guarantees of freedom of speech and freedom of the press. They also argue that funding their publication would not violate the Establishment Clause, which requires separation of church and state, as long as the university extends funding to a broad range of activities and publications without regard to their differing religious and nonreligious viewpoints.

The respondent university argues that the First Amendment permits it discretion in making funding decisions. It further argues that the funding guidelines are reasonable and neutral with respect to religious viewpoints and other viewpoints and are not designed to suppress expression.

At the end of this chapter please find the summaries of argument of the petitioner and respondent and compare them. How do they differ? What suggestions for improvement would you make?

McIntyre v. Ohio Elections Commission
514 U.S. 334 (1995)

EXCERPTS FROM THE BRIEF OF THE PETITIONER, MARGARET MCINTYRE

STATEMENT OF THE CASE

On March 19, 1990, Mrs. Margaret McIntyre was fined $100 by the Ohio Elections Commission for distributing leaflets opposing the passage of a local school tax levy. The Ohio Elections Commission imposed the fine because the leaflets did not contain her name and address as required by Ohio Revised Code §3599.09, which prohibits the distribution of all anonymous campaign literature. The Ohio Supreme Court upheld the fine on September 22, 1993.

The events in this case began on the evening of April 27, 1988, outside the Blendon Middle School in Westerville, Ohio. At that time, Mrs. McIntyre; her son, a student in the Westerville schools; and his girlfriend were distributing leaflets opposing the passage of a school tax levy that was to be voted on at a nonpartisan referendum scheduled for the following week. (J.A.30). Mrs. McIntyre was distributing the leaflets at the Blendon Middle School that evening because it was the site of a previously scheduled public meeting at which the Westerville superintendent of schools planned to address the merits of the tax levy. (J.A.28). During the meeting the superintendent specifically made reference to statements contained in the leaflets. (J.A.15).

Mrs. McIntyre stood outside the school near the doorway to the meeting room and handed leaflets to persons as they entered the building. (J.A.15). Her son and his girlfriend distributed additional leaflets in the school parking lot by placing them under automobile windshield wipers. (J.A.30). The leaflets stated:

VOTE NO

ISSUE 19 SCHOOL TAX LEVY

Last election Westerville Schools, asked us to vote yes for new buildings and expansions programs. We gave them what they asked. We knew there was crowded conditions and new growth in the district.

Now we find out there is a 4 million dollar deficit—WHY?

We are told the 3 middle schools must be split because of over-crowding, and yet we are told 3 schools are being closed—WHY?

A magnet school is not a full operating school, but a specials school.

Residents were asked to work on a 20 member commission to help formulate the new boundaries. For 4 weeks they worked long and hard and came up with a very workable plan. Their plan was totally disregarded—WHY?

WASTE of tax payers dollars must be stopped. Our children's education and welfare must come first. **WASTE CAN NO LONGER BE TOLERATED.**

PLEASE VOTE NO
ISSUE 19

THANK YOU, CONCERNED PARENTS AND TAX PAYERS

J. Michael Hayfield, Assistant Superintendent of Elementary Education for the Westerville schools, observed Mrs. McIntyre distributing the leaflets. He examined the leaflets and told her that she was not in compliance with Ohio election laws. (J.A.28).

On the next evening, April 28, 1988, a similar school meeting was held at the Walnut Springs Middle School. . . . Again, petitioner stood outside of the school and distributed leaflets opposing the school tax levy to persons entering the building to attend the meeting. Again, Mr. Hayfield observed her distributing leaflets and noted that they did not conform to Ohio election laws. (J.A.15).

Following Mrs. McIntyre's leafletting on April 27, 1988 and April 28, 1988, the school tax levy failed. It was again defeated in a second election. In November of 1988, on the third try, it finally passed. (Pet. App. A10). On April 6, 1989, five months after the passage of the twice-defeated levy, and approximately one year after her leafletting, Mrs. McIntyre received a letter from the Ohio Elections Commission informing her that a complaint had been filed against her. (J.A.10). The complaint, filed by Assistant Superintendent Hayfield, charged her with violating Ohio Revised Code § 3599.09 and two other statutes because the leaflets she had distributed at the Blendon and Walnut Springs Middle Schools, during the two evenings in April of the previous year, did not contain her name and address.[1]

Initially, the charges were dismissed for want of prosecution. (J.A.18). A short time later, they were reinstated at the request of Assistant Superintendent Hayfield. On March 19, 1990, a hearing was held before the Ohio Elections Commission on the charges against Mrs. McIntyre. At the conclusion of its March 19th hearing, the Ohio Elections Commission found that Mrs. McIntyre had distributed unsigned leaflets and fined her $100 for violating Ohio Revised Code § 3599.09; the other charges were dismissed.[2] (J.A.41).

On September 10, 1990, the Franklin County Court of Common Pleas reversed, holding that § 3599.09 was unconstitutional as applied. (Pet. App. A33). On April 7, 1992, the Ohio Court of Appeals reversed the Court of Common Pleas and reinstated the fine. (Pet. App. A16). That decision was affirmed by the Ohio Supreme Court on September 22, 1993, which concluded that: The requirement of R.C. 3599.09 that persons responsible for the production of campaign literature pertaining to the adoption or defeat of a ballot issue identify themselves as the source thereof is not violative

---

1. In addition to being charged with violating § 3599.09, prohibiting distribution of anonymous campaign materials, Mrs. McIntyre was charged with violations of Ohio Revised Code § 3571.10(D) (failure to file a designation of treasurer) and § 3517.13(E) (failure to file a PAC report).

2. Mrs. McIntyre was unrepresented throughout the administrative proceedings and the administrative record is, therefore, a sparse one. Prior to the March 19th hearing, Mrs. McIntyre wrote a letter to counsel for the Ohio Elections Commission acknowledging that some of the leaflets she had distributed were unsigned. (J.A.12). At the hearing, she both denied any intent to violate the law and objected to the law as "an infringement of her First Amendment rights." (J.A.36, 38-39). She also testified that she had talked to many other people who were concerned about the levy and felt she was representing their views as well as her own. (J.A.38). Assistant Superintendent Hayfield repeated the statement made in his prior affidavit, that he had seen Mrs. McIntyre distribute leaflets without her name and address.

The Commission's decision upholding the complaint was issued the same day. It was not accompanied by any written opinion and contained no factual findings other than the implicit finding that Mrs. McIntyre had distributed anonymous leaflets and thereby violated the law. Thus, the only issue raised or considered on appeal by the Ohio state courts was whether the ban on anonymous campaign literature set forth in § 3599.09 is constitutional.

of the right to free speech guaranteed by the First Amendment to the United States Constitution and Section 11, Article I of the Ohio Constitution.

(Pet. App. A1).[3]

Summary of Argument

Petitioner Margaret McIntyre has been fined under § 3599.09 of the Ohio Election Code for preparing and distributing leaflets urging a vote against a school tax levy because the leaflets did not contain her name and address. The Ohio Supreme Court held that § 3599.09 does not violate the First Amendment even though it indiscriminately bans the distribution of all anonymous political campaign literature. The Ohio Supreme Court erred in upholding the statute because its decision is inconsistent with *Talley v. California*, 362 U.S. 60 (1960), which holds that a flat ban on anonymous leafletting is unconstitutional because it deters the speech of those who fear retaliation and thereby restricts freedom of expression.

This Court's protection of anonymous speech in *Talley* rests on a firm historical foundation. The drafters of the Constitution were well aware of efforts by the government of England to punish political and religious dissenters for their anonymous publications. The drafters were also aware of the frequent use of anonymous political publications to criticize the English governance of the American colonies. The use of anonymous political publications as part of public discourse continues today. Consistent with this history and practice, the Court has repeatedly held that the First Amendment protects anonymous speech. *E.g., Thomas v. Collins*, 323 U.S. 516 (1945); *Bates v. Little Rock*, 361 U.S. 516 (1960); *Shelton v. Tucker*, 364 U.S. 479 (1960); *Lamont v. Postmaster General*, 381 U.S. 301 (1965).

The constitutionality of § 3599.09 is to be measured by the compelling state interest test because it is a regulation of the fundamental right to speech and press. Most recently, this Court applied the compelling state interest test in reviewing the regulation of election related speech in *Burson v. Freeman*, 504 U.S. 191, 112 S. Ct. 1846 (1992). The Ohio Supreme Court erred in concluding that the more relaxed standard of review applicable to ballot access and voting regulations was applicable to this case. This is because § 3599.09 is a regulation of political speech in public places intended to persuade voters and is not a ballot access or voting regulation. Applying a strict scrutiny standard, § 3599.09 is unconstitutional because Ohio has not demonstrated a compelling state interest and has not narrowly tailored its law. The failure of § 3599.09 to serve a compelling state interest is demonstrated by the fact that it covers all anonymous election related leaflets and pamphlets. It is not confined to intentionally false and fraudulent statements. In addition, it extends to communications about referendum issues that cannot be smeared or libeled. *Illinois v. White*, 506 N.E.2d 1284 (Ill. 1987). Section 3599.09 is not narrowly tailored because it extends to election related publications at any time in any place. As a consequence, it is a prophylactic rule requiring disclosure, even when no legitimate interest is actually served.

---

3. According to Rule 1(b) of the Ohio Supreme Court Rules for the Reporting of Opinions, this statement, which is the syllabus of the case, "states the controlling point or points of law decided. . . ."

Finally, § 3599.09 is unconstitutional as applied to the facts of this case. Petitioner is a street corner leafletter who has engaged in core political speech about a public issue. As a result, no law, including § 3599.09, can be applied to her speech without violating the First Amendment. *Lovell v. Griffin*, 303 U.S. 444 (1938).

Excerpts from the Brief of the Respondent, Ohio Elections Commission

Statement of the Case

In 1988, Petitioner Margaret McIntyre opposed passage of a property tax levy for the Westerville, Ohio school district. She prepared, or had prepared, flyers expressing this opposition.

Instead of placing her name and address on these flyers as required by Ohio Rev. Code 3599.09(A) (the "Disclosure Statute"), Petitioner identified those responsible for the flyers as "Concerned Parents and Tax Payers," Joint Appendix ("J.A.") 6-7, a fictitious organization. (J.A. 38-39). She distributed these flyers at two separate meetings that were scheduled as open forums for the public to discuss the tax levy. (J.A. 14-15).

On each occasion, an assistant school superintendent observed Petitioner distributing the flyers. *Id.* On the first occasion, he cautioned that her failure to include her name and address on them violated Ohio elections law. (J.A. 28). Petitioner, however, ignored his caution. At no time did anyone attempt to prevent her from circulating any literature, nor did anyone seek to prevent her from attending either meeting. Petitioner also was never threatened with any reprisals because of her opposition to the tax levy.

The assistant superintendent eventually filed a complaint with Respondent, the Ohio Elections Commission ("Commission"), alleging that Petitioner had violated the Disclosure Statute, among other provisions of Ohio elections law. (J.A. 3, 14-16). At a full hearing conducted by the Commission in a civil enforcement action, evidence was presented that some of Petitioner's flyers did contain the disclosure statement required by Ohio Rev. Code 3599.09(A), and Petitioner testified that she had intended to disclose this same information on all the flyers, though she had failed to do so. (J.A. 36-39). It was also revealed that no such organization as "Concerned Parents and Tax Payers" had ever existed. (J.A. 38-39). After considering all the evidence, the Commission found that Petitioner had violated the Disclosure Statute and fined her $100. (J.A. 42).

At the hearing and in the Commission's order, the viewpoint contained in the flyers, which expressed Petitioner's anti-levy message, was never considered with respect to any of the issues that were raised and determined. Instead, the sole focus was on whether the flyers included an attribution statement and whether any such statement was false or fraudulent as provided in Ohio Rev. Code 3599.09. (See J.A. 26-42.)

On appeal from this administrative order, an Ohio trial court ruled that Ohio Rev. Code 3599.09(A) was unconstitutional. (J.A. 45.) A state appeals court upheld the law and reversed. (J.A. 49).

Petitioner then took an appeal to the Supreme Court of Ohio, which analyzed her challenge to the Disclosure Statute under the established test for evaluating the constitutionality of election laws crafted in *Anderson v. Celebrezze*, 460 U.S. 780 (1983). *See McIntyre v. Ohio Elections Comm'n*, 67 Ohio St. 3d 391 (1993),

Appendix to Petition for Writ of Certiorari, A1-A15. That test requires a reviewing court to weigh any burden that the challenged legislation places on First Amendment rights against the legitimate interests of the State in regulating the subject matter involved. The Ohio Supreme Court conducted this balancing test and concluded that the Disclosure Statute places only a modest burden on First Amendment rights, which is outweighed by Ohio's proper interests in the deterrence of fraud, misleading advertising, and libel, and in requiring disclosure to the public of specific information that is pertinent to the electoral process. Consequently, the Ohio Supreme Court affirmed the appeals court's holding that the Disclosure Statute is constitutional. Petitioner then sought a writ of certiorari from this Court, which granted review on February 22, 1994.

Summary of Argument

1. The court below properly applied the test established in *Anderson v. Celebrezze*, 460 U.S. 780 (1983), to analyze the constitutionality of an elections measure such as the Disclosure Statute. Under that test, a reviewing court must weigh any burden the challenged legislation places on First Amendment rights against the legitimate interests of the State in regulating the subject matter involved. Here the Disclosure Statute imposes only a modest burden, if any, on First Amendment rights. This modest burden is substantially outweighed by the State's legitimate interests in the deterrence of fraud, misleading advertising, and libel, and in requiring the disclosure to the public of specific information that is pertinent to the electoral process.

2. *Talley v. California*, 362 U.S. 60 (1960), is inapplicable to this case. *Talley* specifically left for another day whether a measure such as the Disclosure Statute, which is designed to deter fraud, misleading advertising, and libel, is constitutional. In addition, *Talley* did not involve an election law requiring the Court to weigh two competing interests of equal constitutional magnitude—protecting the right to vote by preserving the integrity of the electoral process and assuring freedom of speech. The States are authorized to act to protect the integrity of the electoral process, even when First Amendment rights are implicated, as long as any such action does not discriminate against the viewpoint expressed in any political message.

3. Even if strict scrutiny were to be applied here, however, the Disclosure Statute would withstand such scrutiny because it advances the State's compelling interest in combatting fraud in the electoral process. The Disclosure Statute, moreover, is narrowly drawn to serve that compelling state interest. *Burson v. Freeman*, 504 U.S. 191, 112 S. Ct. 1846 (1992).

4. Disclosure statutes have long been upheld by this Court in many different fields, even where they impose some burden on First Amendment activities. In the field of elections law in particular, the Court's precedents confirm the constitutionality of disclosure statutes in elections both for candidates and for ballot issues. *See Buckley v. Valeo*, 424 U.S. 1 (1976); *First National Bank of Boston v. Bellotti*, 435 U.S. 765 (1978). The same result also holds for disclosure statutes that affect such First Amendment activities as lobbying, *United States v. Harriss*, 347 U.S. 612 (1954), and charitable solicitations, *Riley v. National Federation of the Blind of North Carolina, Inc.*, 487 U.S 781 (1988). Any countervailing interest in maintaining secrecy or anonymity is less powerful than Petitioner alleges, and must yield to the State's compelling interests in requiring the disclosure of a limited amount of pertinent information to

the public. In this case, for example, any burden allegedly imposed on Petitioner's First Amendment rights by the Disclosure Statute was either minimal or nonexistent, and the State has a compelling interest in requiring the limited disclosures specified in Ohio Rev. Code 3599.09(A).

Rosenberger v. University of Virginia
515 U.S. 819 (1995)

Excerpt from the Brief of the Petitioner, Ronald Rosenberger

Summary of Argument

This case involves the discriminatory exclusion of an otherwise qualified student publication from eligibility for student activity funding at the University of Virginia, solely on the basis of the content, indeed the viewpoint, of the publication.

The University of Virginia uses its Student Activity Fund to support a wide variety of student speech from different perspectives, including some 15 newspapers and magazines. Petitioners have started a sixteenth: Wide Awake, a student magazine that addresses national and campus issues of a political, personal, cultural, and educational nature from the point of view of its editors and members. They have satisfied all the necessary requirements for funding eligibility. The problem is their editorial point of view, which is rooted in their Christian religious faith. That (and that alone), according to the University, makes the magazine ineligible for funding. This raises the question: is the religious perspective of a student publication a lawful ground for excluding it from benefits otherwise available to organizations of its type?

We contend that the University's action violates the First and Fourteenth Amendments of the United States Constitution. Our argument is based on two important principles of constitutional law. First, discrimination on the basis of the content of speech, and especially its viewpoint, is presumptively unconstitutional and can be justified only on the basis of a compelling governmental purpose for the discrimination. *R.A.V. v. City of St. Paul*, 112 S. Ct. 2538, 2542-43, 2547-48, 2549-50 (1992). This principle applies to decisions involving benefits as well as regulation (*FCC v. League of Women Voters*, 468 U.S. 364 (1984); *Arkansas Writers' Project, Inc. v. Ragland*, 481 U.S. 221, 230 (1987)), and to religious as well as secular points of view (*Lamb's Chapel v. Center Moriches School Dist.*, 113 S. Ct. 2141 (1993); *Widmar v. Vincent*, 454 U.S. 263, 269-70 (1981)). Second, the nondiscriminatory funding of a broad range of publications and activities, without regard to their religious, anti-religious, or nonreligious point of view, does not violate the Establishment Clause. *Texas Monthly, Inc. v. Bullock*, 489 U.S. 1, 14-15 (1989); *Witters v. Washington Dep't of Services*, 474 U.S. 481 (1986).

Excerpt from the Brief of the Respondent, the Rectors and Visitors of the University of Virginia

Summary of Argument

Respondents' argument consists of three points:

First, in the expenditure of public funds, decisions based on the content of speech are familiar, necessary, and entirely legitimate. Routine academic decisions, such as the hiring and promotion of professors and the choice of courses for the curriculum, involve content-based evaluations of speech. To require that such decisions be made without regard to content would be to disable public universities from adopting or implementing educational policies. This the First Amendment does not require.

Second, the University of Virginia Student Activity Fee Funding Guidelines are reasonable. They exclude from funding religious, political, philanthropic, and social activities. They do not reflect, as petitioners allege, an ideologically driven attempt to suppress a particular point of view.

Third, the public forum doctrine confirms the constitutionality of the funding Guidelines. Under that doctrine, student activity fee funds constitute a non-public forum. In the non-public forum, content-based rules are allowed, "as long as the regulation on speech is reasonable and not an effort to suppress expression merely because public officials oppose the speaker's view." *Perry Educ. Ass'n v. Perry Local Educators' Ass'n*, 460 U.S. 37, 46 (1983). The University Guidelines fully meet that standard.

The Appellate Brief: Argument and Conclusion

§ 29.01. THE ARGUMENT

The argument is the heart of the brief. Its purpose is to persuade the court that your arguments rest on the applicable law and mandate a decision favorable to your client. While the other portions of the brief are important, you generally will win or lose your case on the substance of the argument. The argument section must be written persuasively and forcefully. It must be interesting enough to hold the attention of the court, and convincing enough to warrant a decision in your client's favor. This chapter instructs you how to structure and prepare the substance of an effective argument.

1. Structuring the Argument

a. Use Headings

A heading is a concise, persuasive statement of a conclusion that you want the court to accept with respect to a segment of your argument. Headings appear both in the table of contents and in the body of the argument at the beginning of different sections and subsections; they should be identical in both places. For examples of headings, turn to Appendix IV and examine the sample briefs. Here is an additional example:

> I. NALLY'S TAPE-RECORDED STATEMENTS ARE ADMISSIBLE IN EVIDENCE.
> A. Because Nally Contradicted His Taped Statements, the Taped Statements Are Admissible Under the Hearsay Exception for Prior Inconsistent Statements.
> B. Because Nally Testified About These Statements at the First Trial, They Are Admissible Under the Hearsay Exception for Judicial Admissions.

As you can see, the headings divide the argument into major sections, and subheadings further divide those sections. Together, the headings and subheadings create an outline of your argument. You can feel confident about your headings when you list them in the table of contents and they present a logical, compelling summary of your argument.

Headings, then, are an essential tool in writing an organized, logical, and therefore persuasive argument. They give the court guidance in understanding your arguments and their logic. If you write persuasive headings, they should help persuade the court to rule in your client's favor.

b. How to Write the Headings

The questions presented provide the foundation for the headings. To draft the headings, prepare a list of the specific conclusions the court must adopt to decide the case in your client's favor and identify the reasons that support those conclusions. These conclusions will become the arguments made in the headings and should serve as an excellent outline for drafting the brief. Make a separate list for each question presented. Then outline the necessary conclusions.

The order in which you present your conclusions or arguments is important. First, present your arguments in the same order as your questions presented so that the court will find it easy to follow you. Second, arrange your arguments for each question presented in a logical order, keeping related parts of the argument together. Third, begin with your strongest argument, unless doing so would strain the logic of the discussion. Your strongest argument is the one with which the court is the most likely to agree, based on your knowledge of its prior decisions and its members' predilections. It is not necessarily the one about which you feel the most strongly.

Once you have decided on the necessary conclusions and their order, you are ready to write the headings. Headings should be an integral part of the argument. They are more than section titles. A heading is a statement of the argument to follow. It should be a complete sentence and be affirmative, persuasive, and specific. It should not, however, be so partisan that it sounds unreasonable. Do not make arguments you cannot support.

Each question presented usually warrants only one major heading. If a question has several subparts, write one general major heading. Then use the subparts to write minor headings. Place a Roman numeral before each major heading and a capital letter before each minor heading. Capitalize the first word and the first letter of all words except articles, conjunctions, and prepositions, and underline each such minor heading. State the elements of the argument supporting a minor heading in subheadings preceded by numerals indicating their positions under the minor heading. Capitalize only the first word of subheadings and do not underline them. Always use a period after a heading, whether it is a major heading, a minor heading, or a subheading. However, when you list a heading in your table of contents, you need not place a period at the end. Single-space your headings. Do not use minor headings or subheadings unless you use two or more of them. The headings should look like this:

    I. FIRST MAJOR HEADING.
      A. First Minor Heading.
      B. Second Minor Heading.
        1. First subheading.
        2. Second subheading.
        3. Third subheading.
    II. SECOND MAJOR HEADING.

Each heading is the thesis sentence for the part of the argument it introduces. As such, a well-written heading identifies the legal issue or rule of law involved, indicates your position on the issue, and sets out the reasoning supporting that position by relating the rule to your specific factual situation. It thus includes both the law and the facts of your case. Parties are often identified by name in headings. When minor headings and subheadings are used, the major headings need include only your conclusion regarding the application of a rule of law to your particular facts, since the minor headings and subheadings will set out the reasons for that conclusion. The more specifically you state the question, the rule, your reasoning, and the facts, the more persuasive the headings will be. Framing a heading, however, remains a balancing process requiring good judgment and common sense. While the heading must contain sufficient information to effectively summarize the argument, it must also be easily comprehensible.

Here are a few examples of the types of headings that result when the writer does not adhere to the principles of effective heading drafting:

The elements of the foreseeability test.

Comment: Avoid general topical phrases that could be applicable to any number of cases.

———

Only blood relatives are permitted to recover for negligent infliction of emotional distress.

Comment: Avoid stating an abstract legal proposition by failing to show its relevance to your case. A better heading would be:

Because the appellant is not a blood relative of the injured person, she may not recover for negligent infliction of emotional distress.

———

Appellant fails to state a cause of action for negligent infliction of emotional distress since her claim does not fall within the parameters of the *Sinn v. Burd* foreseeability test.

Comment: Avoid using case and statutory citations as shorthand references to the applicable legal principle unless the reader would be familiar with them (e.g., *Miranda*). A better heading would be:

The appellant fails to state a cause of action for negligent infliction of emotional distress because she was not near the scene of the accident and was not closely related to the injured person.

c. Using Headings as an Advocate

Seek to advocate your position, to make your basic arguments, through the headings. When you write a heading, use persuasive sentence structure and language. How you phrase a heading will depend on which side you represent.

Consider the following headings as they appeared in the tables of contents of two student briefs.

As drafted by counsel for the appellant:

I. PAULA DIGIACOMO'S CLAIM FOR NEGLIGENT INFLICTION OF EMOTIONAL DISTRESS SATISFIES THE FORESEEABILITY TEST ADOPTED BY THIS COURT.

    A. Ms. DiGiacomo's Presence at the Scene Within Seconds After Farmer's Bat Struck Henry's Head Satisfies the Requirement of Physical Proximity.

    B. Ms. DiGiacomo, Hearing the Crowd's Screams After Seeing Farmer Lose His Bat, Sensed a Contemporaneous Threat of Danger to Henry.

    C. Ms. DiGiacomo's Long-Term Commitment to Henry Qualifies Her as Having a Close Relationship with Him Deserving of Legal Protection.

    D. Ms. DiGiacomo's Loss of Sleep, Need for Medication, and Frequent Visits to Her Psychiatrist Present Physical Manifestations of Emotional Distress.

As drafted by counsel for the appellee:

II. THE COURT BELOW CORRECTLY AFFIRMED THE SUMMARY JUDGMENT ORDER FOR THE APPELLEE BECAUSE APPELLANT DIGIACOMO CANNOT SATISFY THE REQUISITE FACTORS OF THE FORESEEABILITY TEST AND THEREFORE FAILS TO STATE A VALID CAUSE OF ACTION FOR NEGLIGENT INFLICTION OF EMOTIONAL DISTRESS.

    A. The Appellant's Relationship as an Unmarried Cohabitant with the Victim Does Not Satisfy the Requirement that the Appellant Be Closely Related to the Injured Party.

    B. The Emotional Distress Alleged by the Appellant Could Only Have Resulted from Her Observation of Her Cohabitant's Condition upon Arriving at the Scene of the Accident as the Appellant Neither Witnessed Nor Sensorially and Contemporaneously Observed the Accident as It Occurred.

    C. The Appellant Has Not Alleged or Suffered Any Bodily Harm or Severe Physical Manifestation of Emotional Distress as a Result of the Accident.

Note how each version uses identical facts but offers a different perspective on the same arguments, yet both are persuasive.

d. How Many Headings?

Headings should reflect your organization and simplify it by providing logical breaks in your argument. A well-written brief containing carefully drafted and logically placed headings will lead the reader easily from one point to the next. Too few headings will result in an argument that is difficult to follow and often poorly organized. Too many headings will interrupt the flow of the argument and may draw attention to insignificant or weak arguments. With these considerations in mind, use your judgment.

e. Final Considerations

When you have formulated your point headings, write them out in outline form as they will appear in the table of contents. Then ask yourself whether they conform to the principles discussed in this section. Are they complete? Does each point follow logically from the ones preceding it? Is the phrasing persuasive but reasonable? Is each heading readable? Only if you can answer each question affirmatively should you be satisfied with this crucial part of the argument section.

2. Preparing the Substance of the Argument

To be an effective advocate, you must be coherent and credible. The presentation of your argument may be as important as the substance of your argument. Your research must be complete, your organization clear, your argument logical, and your writing precise.

a. General Considerations

i. *Understanding the Appellate Process*

Remember that the judges are the ones who must be persuaded. In every appellate case, the judges seek to render a decision that is both fair and consistent with precedent. Write your brief with these dual concerns in mind. To achieve a favorable result, write a brief that is clear, interesting, complete, and reliable. Be honest about the law. Persuade with the strength of your arguments. Avoid excessive partisanship and statements without support. Never omit or distort the applicable law. If you do so, you will sacrifice your credibility, an essential element of a successful appeal.

ii. *Familiarity with the Record*

The record is your sole source of information about the case. To prepare an effective argument, you must have a clear and thorough understanding of the record. Read it carefully several times. Be certain that you understand the arguments and facts presented to the lower court, as well as the legal issues raised on appeal.

iii. *Research: Do It Right But Know When to Stop*

A carefully crafted and persuasive argument begins with thorough research. For an approach to doing research, review Chapter 3.

Here are some tips. Think through the legal question. Approach it from a number of perspectives. Be creative in using the indexes to the digests. Look under a variety of topical headings. You and the index's publisher may list a topic under very different headings. Keep track of what you have researched and how you arrived at each source. Do not rely on headnotes. Read a case critically before relying on it. Shepardize each case you intend to cite. Make certain your research is current—check the pocket parts.

How do you know when to stop? Stop researching when you begin to find the same cases again and again. You should know when you have reached the point of diminishing returns.

Students sometimes engage in excessive research for two reasons. First, they keep searching for the one case that will give them a definitive answer to the legal issue. However, if you fail to find such a case early on in your research, there probably is no such case. In law school assignments, most problems have no definitive answer and no dispositive case.

Second, students keep researching because they are avoiding the next step, organizing the material and starting to write. Avoiding this pitfall requires being honest with yourself and recognizing that doing excessive research will deprive you of the time you need to finish your brief before the deadline. Drafting an effective argument is not an easy task. Be certain that you leave yourself enough time to do it well and expect that it will take longer than you anticipate.

iv. Compliance with the Rules of Court

To be an effective advocate, you must be credible. One of the simplest ways to establish your credibility is to comply with the rules of court concerning briefs.[1] Failure to comply will not reflect well on you and may have a major adverse effect, such as dismissal of your client's case.

v. Simplicity in Substance and Style

Perhaps the single most important attribute of an effective argument is simplicity in substance and style. Limit the arguments presented to the court and make them as uncomplicated as possible. If your outline is too long and complicated, rethink it. Adhere to the plain English writing style discussed in Chapters 7 and 8. Most courts have a heavy volume of cases and therefore have limited time to spend on any particular case. You are more likely to capture and hold the court's attention with a brief that is straightforward in both substance and style.

b. Formulating the Arguments

Formulating the arguments you will make is a dynamic process involving analysis and evaluation of legal authority. You should consider not only the arguments suggested by your research, but also those that you develop based on your own insight into and understanding of a particular issue. Think carefully about the kinds of arguments that would be most effective for your client.

There are six distinct types of arguments you can make:

1. Arguments based on legal precedent
2. Arguments by analogy to similar situations
3. Arguments based on public policy
4. Arguments based on a "parade of horribles," i.e., the potential consequences of a precedent-setting decision against you
5. Arguments based on commonsense notions of justice and fair play
6. Arguments that stress certain sympathetic facts and rely on the emotional appeal of your case

Consider all six types of arguments when formulating your position. Use the ones that seem most persuasive in your particular case.

c. The Organization and Substance of the Arguments

When your appeal raises several independent issues, begin the argument section of your brief with the strongest issue. Similarly, where you have formulated several

---

1. All appellate courts have rules about brief format, content, and length. Your legal writing program most likely has rules that govern the briefs you write for it. Frequently these rules are online. For example, you can find the rules for briefs and other documents before the United States Supreme Court at www.supremecourtus.gov/ctrules.html.

arguments in support of your position on an issue, start with the most compelling argument, unless logic dictates otherwise. Your brief will be more persuasive if the strongest issues and arguments are presented first. The court's attention and time are limited. Beginning a brief with a strong argument will ensure that at least that argument will be read. Starting with a compelling argument will impress the court with the soundness of your legal position and enhance your credibility. In addition, the less persuasive issues and arguments are more compelling when they seem to support the stronger issues and arguments. Some advocates put the weakest arguments last, while others bury them in the middle.

An effective argument generally has five components. These components suggest an organization for discussion of each argument.

First, open the discussion of the argument with a fact-specific conclusion, even though you may, to a certain extent, be repeating what is contained in the heading. Do not begin with a broad statement of black letter law. If you do so, you risk losing the court's attention. Opening with an affirmative, specific statement is more persuasive and more likely to hold the court's interest.

Second, state the specific legal question raised by the argument under discussion and provide an answer, indicating how the applicable rule of law will apply to your facts. By doing so you are, in effect, giving the court a roadmap of your argument. With the aid of a roadmap, the court will know where the discussion is leading. Knowing where the discussion is leading is invaluable to understanding it and a prerequisite to being persuaded by it. If the court does not grasp your argument on the first reading, that argument is most likely lost as the court will not take the time to grapple with it. If the discussion requires more than one reading, the fault lies with the writer.

Third, give a full discussion of the authorities on which you rely. Unless you are citing a case only for a general legal proposition, be certain that you provide the reader with the relevant facts, the court's holding, and its rationale. Failure to sufficiently develop a case you cite will rob it of its persuasive value and frustrate the court. Remember that your role here is that of an advocate. Sometimes your discussion of a case will require a paragraph; other times it will require only a sentence or a parenthetical. Present relevant authority in the light most favorable to your position, but never mislead the court. Stress those portions of the opinion that are helpful to your argument, but do not take statements out of context.

Fourth, apply, explain, or relate that analysis to the facts of your client's case. Effective argument requires that you take your facts and work them into the authorities you have cited. Develop them in the context of the facts, the rationale, the policies, or the rules those authorities set out. In this section of the brief, you must argue—you must comment, compare, distinguish, find controlling, highlight, explain away. Demonstrate to the court why it should decide the case in favor of your client and how it can do so in a manner consistent with existing precedent. Remember to cite the record each time you refer to the facts of your case.

Fifth, when appropriate, restate your specific conclusion in regard to the argument under discussion.

This sample argument illustrates the suggested organization:

The appellant, Ms. DiGiacomo, cannot state a claim for negligent infliction of emotional distress because she fails to meet the first and second prongs of the foreseeability test in *Sinn v. Burd*, 486 Pa. 146, 173, 404 A.2d 672, 686 (1979). The first and second prongs require, respectively, that the plaintiff be near the scene of the accident and that the shock result from a direct emotional impact upon the plaintiff from the sensory and contemporaneous observance of the accident. Here, the appellant was neither near the scene of the accident nor was her shock the result of a sensory and contemporaneous observation of the accident.

When invoking the *Sinn* foreseeability test, this state's highest court considers both prongs simultaneously and then strictly construes both. *See Brooks v. Decker*, 512 Pa. 365, 516 A.2d 1380 (1986); *Mazzagati v. Everingham*, 512 Pa. 265, 516 A.2d 672 (1986). Consequently, the court has refused to recognize a cause of action when, as here, the plaintiff comes upon the accident scene immediately after the accident has occurred. As recently as October 1986, the Pennsylvania Supreme Court held against the plaintiff in two such cases. *Brooks*, 512 Pa. at 368, 516 A.2d at 1382; *Mazzagati*, 512 Pa. at 268, 516 A.2d at 679.

Two Pennsylvania cases particularly illustrate why Mrs. DiGiacomo was not a contemporary observer. In the first case, *Brooks*, a father, returned to his home in the afternoon and was passed by an ambulance. After the ambulance turned up the street to his house, it stopped at a crowd of people. As the father approached, he noticed his son's bicycle lying on the ground and discovered that his son had been in an accident with an automobile. The father accompanied his son to the hospital where the boy lay comatose for ten days and then died. 512 Pa. at 366, 516 A.2d at 1381. This Court dismissed the claim for negligent infliction of emotional distress because the parent did not witness the injury causing the accident. *Id.* at 367, 516 A.2d at 1382.

As in *Brooks*, Ms. DiGiacomo did not actually witness the defendant's negligent act. The act was completed when the bat struck its victim. Witnessing the bat leave the defendant's hands and hearing the crowd's uproar was analogous to Mr. Brooks seeing the ambulance turn down his street and then seeing his son's bicycle on the ground.

In the second case, *Bliss v. Allentown Public Library*, 497 F. Supp. 487 (E.D. Pa. 1980), a federal court applying Pennsylvania law permitted a mother to recover, even though she was not looking at her child at the exact moment a statue fell on him. The court held that the mother was a percipient witness because she observed her child immediately before the accident and heard the statue fall. She absorbed the full impact of the accident as if she had personally witnessed it. *Id.* at 489. There were no intermediary forces lessening her shock in witnessing her child's condition. *Id.*

The facts in that case differ from the facts here. In *Bliss*, the mother knew where her child was located and heard the accident happen. In contrast, Ms. DiGiacomo was unaware of her friend's location before the accident. She was unaware that he had been struck by a bat. She heard the crowd roar, but she did not know that it was because of an injury to her friend. As was true of the father in *Brooks*, Ms. DiGiacomo had no sensory and contemporaneous perception of the accident.

This Court's test is not unique to Pennsylvania. The facts of the instant case most closely resemble those of *Scherr v. Las Vegas Hilton*, 214 Cal. Rptr. 343 (Ct. App. 1985). In *Scherr*, the plaintiff watched live news coverage of a hotel fire and knew that her husband was in the hotel at the time of the fire. Because she did not witness her husband's injuries and did not know with certainty that he was being injured at that time, she could not recover for negligent infliction of emotional distress. *Id.* at 910-11,

214 Cal. Rptr. at 394-395. The court held that the "decisive question . . . is whether plaintiff, through whatever medium, received a sudden and severe shock by *actually* and *contemporaneously witnessing* not just the fire but the *infliction of injuries* upon her husband." *Id.* (emphasis in original).

By simply witnessing the throwing of the bat, Appellant DiGiacomo did not know with any certainty that her friend was in danger, let alone injured. The cry of the crowd provided no greater certainty. Therefore, like the wife in *Scherr*, the appellant was neither physically proximate to the scene of the accident nor was her shock the result of sensory and contemporaneous observation of the accident.

As these cases demonstrate, the appellant cannot state a claim for negligent infliction of emotional distress. She fails to meet well-established elements of the foreseeability test set forth by the Pennsylvania Supreme Court.

Review the sample briefs referenced in Appendix IV for additional illustrations of effective organization of the argument.

d. What to Avoid

Year after year, legal writing instructors see students make the same errors in organizing and presenting their arguments. In the world after law school, judges see the same errors. These errors are both well known and easy to avoid. You can find a discussion of them in Section 13.03. Take the time to review that discussion. To refresh your memory, you are on the way to writing a well-crafted brief if you

- avoid the "digest" approach,
- avoid the "historical development of the law" approach,
- avoid the use of too many quotations from legal authorities,
- avoid the "abstract writing" approach, and
- avoid the "law discussion only" approach.

e. Using Precedent

In writing the argument portion of the brief, you must select the authorities on which you will base your argument.

i. Hierarchy of Precedent

When choosing authorities, select those that have the greatest precedential value. Binding precedent is case law from the jurisdiction whose law is controlling, particularly from the highest court in that jurisdiction or sometimes from the court that is hearing your case. Therefore, these cases have the greatest relevance. Although decisions from lower courts are not binding, they still will be persuasive. Recent cases are generally more desirable than old cases. If you are in state court, federal court decisions interpreting the law of the controlling jurisdiction are not binding, but generally provide very persuasive authority.

You often will find that there is no binding authority directly on point, that the courts in your jurisdiction have not decided the issue, or that the case is one of first impression. In such a situation, you must rely on the decisions of other courts, decisions that are not controlling. Seek to persuade the court that those decisions are based on sound policy considerations and are compatible with your jurisdiction's existing body of law.

The law of some states will be more persuasive than that of other states. Generally those states that are geographically closer to your state will have case law that is similar to that of your jurisdiction. This case law will provide you with strong arguments urging the adoption of your client's position. Certain states tend to be in the forefront of developing areas of the law and may provide you with authority for your argument. You may also make an argument based on a trend in the developing law. Suggest to the court that the conclusion reached by a number of other jurisdictions is proper and warrants adoption.

ii. Handling Adverse Precedent

In researching your argument, you will encounter decisions adverse to your position. Both ethical and practical reasons dictate that you discuss adverse decisions in your argument. The ethical reason stems from your obligation as a lawyer. The A.B.A. Model Code of Professional Responsibility requires that "legal authority in the controlling jurisdiction directly adverse to the position of [your] client" be disclosed,[2] while the A.B.A. Model Rules of Professional Conduct state that "[a] lawyer shall not knowingly . . . fail to disclose to the tribunal legal authority in the controlling jurisdiction known to the lawyer to be directly adverse to the position of the client and not disclosed by opposing counsel. . . ."[3] The practical reason should be apparent. If you have found adverse authority, it is likely that your opponent has found it as well. It is far more desirable to address and minimize the adverse authority in the context of your argument than to allow your opponent to argue it from the opposite side. Your position will be far more credible if your argument is complete and includes adverse decisions. Seize any opportunity to explain why the authority should not be followed.

There are several ways to effectively harmonize adverse precedent. You might distinguish it on the facts of the case. You might argue that the policy goals stressed in the adverse case mandate a different result in your case. Suggest that a decision in favor of your opponent would set an unfortunate precedent with negative consequences. If the case is the most recent pronouncement of a well-established legal rule, you might want to argue that your case requires an exception to that rule. You might be forced to argue that the case is an aberration and was wrongly decided. Use this tactic only as a last resort. It is an admission that you cannot harmonize the precedent. This argument may be ineffective when there are other decisions espousing the same position.

When you are the appellant, consider as adverse authority the decision from which you are appealing. Seek to harmonize it by pointing out its errors or omissions. Counsel for appellee will stress the decision as favorable and argue that it is sound.

iii. Rebuttal of Opposing Arguments

Seek to defuse the impact of the opposing arguments by criticizing them in one or several of the ways outlined in this chapter. Do not make conclusory statements that characterize your opponent's position as wrong. A broad dismissal suggests

---

2. Model Code of Prof. Resp. EC 7-23 and DR 7-106 (ABA, 1980).
3. Model R. of Prof. Conduct 3.3 (ABA, 2009).

to the court that you cannot counter the position adequately and will adversely affect your credibility.

Resist the temptation to devote too much attention to your opponent's cases and arguments. The tone of your argument must remain affirmative and not convey a defensive posture. Use paragraph structure to your advantage. Never start an argument with a rebuttal of your opponent's position or the adverse cases. Do not devote a lot of time to your opponent's position or elaborate on the adverse cases. Doing either will focus undue attention on the opposing arguments and detract from the importance of your own arguments. Your argument should recognize that there is another position, address and dispose of it briefly, and move on.

iv. Parentheticals, String Cites, Signals, Quotations, and Footnotes

Use the authorities on which you rely to persuade the court that your client's position is correct. After you have fully discussed the cases that are critical to your argument, you may want to cite additional cases that have arrived at similar conclusions based on analogous facts. Those cases may not warrant full discussion, but you may want to include them to bolster your position. In this situation include a parenthetical after your citation of the case. Your parenthetical abstractions of the case should not be more than one sentence but should contain a brief summary of the relevant aspects of the case.

> See *Pearsall v. Emhart Indus.*, 499 F. Supp. 207 (E.D. Pa. 1984) (woman who arrived home to find firefighters attempting to control the blaze engulfing her house and who saw the unconscious bodies of her husband and children was a contemporaneous observer); *Corso v. Merrill*, 119 N.H. 647, 406 A.2d 300 (1979) (mother who heard and immediately witnessed a car accident involving her daughter contemporaneously observed the accident).

Signals such as *see, accord*, and *contra* can be used effectively in the argument. You might use a signal and a parenthetical to cite an adverse case, depending on how much discussion the case requires. Such a brief reference will demonstrate to the court that you have considered the case but will reduce its impact.

Avoid string citations, except perhaps where you are seeking to demonstrate the long-standing acceptance of a rule or an emerging trend in the law. String citations add nothing to your analysis. The court does not read them. Moreover, they are a distraction and break the flow of your argument. String cites suggest to the court that you think it is responsible for locating and reading the cited cases.

Exercise restraint when using quotations. Occasionally a judge will have phrased a certain point very effectively, and you will want to use a quotation. Most often your argument will be better if you paraphrase the opinion. Avoid long block quotes. Readers will often skip them entirely. If you must use them, use them very sparingly and delete all of the language that is not relevant by using ellipses indicated by three periods.

Use footnotes sparingly. Generally, if the thought is worthy of a footnote, you can fit it into your argument. Footnotes are undesirable because they interrupt the flow of the argument.

Use underlining or other methods of emphasis only very rarely. They are distracting. Rely on language and structure to emphasize a particular word or phrase.

f. Writing Persuasively

When drafting your argument, keep in mind the general principles of clear and effective legal writing. Take the time to review Chapter 22. In addition, take note of the following points.

i. Control Tone

Carefully control the tone of your brief because it affects the court's reaction to the substance of your arguments. Seek to establish an assertive tone. Make strong arguments, but do not overstate your position. Be scrupulously accurate. Do not use colloquialisms. Avoid informality and the use of abbreviations. Do not sound stuffy or pompous. Beware of humor, as an attempt at humor may annoy the judges. Sarcasm is always inappropriate, as is insulting or attacking the integrity of opposing counsel or the parties to the lawsuit. Do not adopt an arrogant tone—it will annoy and alienate a judge who may be favorably inclined to your opponent's arguments. Refer to the judges as "the court," opposing counsel as "counsel for appellant (or appellee)." Personalize your clients by referring to them by name, while referring to opposing counsel's client as "the appellant" or "the appellee." Never refer to the court as "you" or yourself as "I."

ii. The Final Touches

Rewrite, edit, and polish your argument. Make sure your language is clear, strong, and concise. Eliminate unnecessary words. Ask yourself whether your arguments are tightly reasoned. As you examine your brief, try to read it through the eyes of the judges who will decide the case. Will they find it easy to understand and persuasive?

Proofread your argument. Typographical errors may cause the court to question how careful you were in constructing the substance of the argument.

§ 29.02. THE CONCLUSION

The conclusion is a separate section of the brief and states precisely what action the party wants the appellate court to take. Here are two typical conclusions:

> For the above reasons, appellees respectfully submit that the judgment of the court below should be affirmed.

> For the reasons discussed above, we respectfully request that the judgment of the court below be reversed and the case remanded with instructions to dismiss the complaint against the appellant.

Because a wide variety of relief is available, you must specify the relief you seek. Do not assume the court will know what relief is sought. You will annoy the court by forcing it to guess, and you risk not having the desired relief ordered. The conclusion is not a summary of the arguments presented in the brief. Such a summary should be included at the end of the argument section. The conclusion should never consist of more than a short paragraph and may be only one sentence. Close the brief with "Respectfully submitted," and your signature as counsel.

For more illustrations, review the briefs referenced in Appendix IV.

§ 29.03. A CHECKLIST

In writing and revising a brief, some lawyers and law students find it helpful to use a checklist. A good checklist lists the important mechanical and stylistic rules that the writer should follow. You may find this checklist useful.

I. Title Page: Does the title page conform to the rules of the court?

II. Table of Contents
   A. When you read the headings, do they present a good summary of the argument?
   B. Are the headings exactly the same as they appear in the argument?
   C. Are the page numbers accurate? Is the brief within the page limitation that the court rules prescribe?

III. Table of Authorities
   A. Does the table include all the authorities you cite in the argument? Have you excluded the citations in the jurisdictional statement, unless jurisdiction is an issue in the argument?
   B. Have you listed the authorities in the order that the court rules require? If court rules do not prescribe an order, have you listed them in a conventional way: for example, cases alphabetically, then constitutional provisions and statutes, then other authorities?
   C. Are the page numbers accurate?
   D. Is your citation form accurate? When required, have you included a case's prior or subsequent history?

IV. Jurisdictional Statement: Have you cited the authority that gives jurisdiction to the court?

V. Questions Presented
   A. Does the number of questions presented correspond to the number of major headings in your brief?
   B. When you read each question, do you find it comprehensible?
   C. Is each question framed in a way that, while not argumentative, encourages the court to answer it affirmatively and in your favor?
   D. Does each question include sufficient specifics of your case without including too much detail?

VI. Constitutional, Statutory, and Regulatory Provisions
   A. Have you included the relevant text of all provisions at issue in the argument? Have you excluded the statute or rule in the jurisdictional statement unless it is at issue in your argument?
   B. Have you included only the pertinent parts of provisions, as opposed to the full texts?
   C. Are the citations in proper form?

VII. Statement of Facts
   A. Have you documented the facts with references to the record?
   B. Have you stated the facts truthfully?
   C. Have you avoided editorializing and using value-laden modifiers?
   D. Have you put your best foot forward and told the story from your client's perspective?

     E. If a court below or a dissenter supported your position, have you emphasized that fact?

     F. Have you organized the facts and stated them so that the court can readily understand the story you are telling?

     G. When appropriate, have you used a chronological sequence?

     H. Have you employed a concrete writing style?

VIII. Summary of Argument

     A. Is the summary succinct, but accurate?

     B. Does the table of contents serve as an outline of the summary?

     C. Have you avoided citing cases unless they are essential to making the summary accurate?

     D. Have you stuck to your main arguments and saved the subtle points for the argument?

     E. Will the summary be comprehensible and persuasive to an intelligent, but uninformed audience?

IX. Argument

     A. Are your headings effective?

       1. Have you structured the argument with sufficient headings and subheadings, but not too many?

       2. Do the headings correspond exactly to the headings in the table of contents?

       3. Is each heading a complete sentence?

       4. When appropriate, does each heading make specific reference to the facts in your case?

       5. Have you written the headings to be persuasive and advance your argument as opposed to just stating the law?

     B. Have you adhered to a plain English writing style?

     C. Have you chosen your arguments with care?

       1. Have you used your strongest arguments?

       2. Have you placed your strongest arguments first when it is logical to do so?

       3. Have you given your stronger arguments proportionately greater space?

       4. Have you made your arguments as uncomplicated as possible?

     D. Have you presented each argument clearly and persuasively?

       1. Have you begun the discussion of each argument with a fact-specific conclusion and an answer to the specific legal question that you are addressing so that the court knows where your argument is going? Have you briefly outlined your argument in the first paragraph so that the court has a roadmap?

       2. Have you given a sufficiently full discussion of the authorities on which you rely, including the facts of decided cases when appropriate?

       3. Have you applied, explained, or related your analysis to the facts of your case?

       4. At the end of your discussion, have you restated that your argument leads to the specific conclusion you advocate?

       5. Have you made your argument as persuasive as possible?

  E. Have you dealt with adverse arguments?

  F. Have you made the best use of authority?

       1. Have you used proper citation form?

       2. Have you relied primarily on authorities with the greatest precedential value?

       3. Have you dealt with adverse precedent?

       4. When cases have not needed extended discussion, have you briefly summarized them in parentheticals?

       5. Have you used proper citation signals?

       6. Have you avoided string citations?

       7. Have you exercised restraint in using quotations and footnotes?

  G. Have you written in an assertive tone that does not overstate your position?

X. Conclusion

  A. Have you specified the precise relief you seek?

  B. Have you closed the brief with "Respectfully submitted" and your signature as counsel?

CHAPTER 30

Basic Principles of Oral Communication

§ 30.01. INTRODUCTION

Oral presentations have several aspects that you should carefully think out or practice in advance of the presentation itself. This chapter asks you to think about the appellate argument the same way you would think about any other spoken presentation. We teach you some basic principles that will guide your preparation every time you are asked to speak, whether to a court, clients, other attorneys, or community groups. In Chapter 31, we will discuss in detail the steps that are unique to preparing for and presenting an appellate oral argument.

Knowing how to talk is not the same thing as knowing how to speak effectively; our goal is to help you do the latter. Inadequate preparation and poor presentation can so distract from a message, even a very important one, that the impact of the message can be virtually destroyed. Undoubtedly you have sat through your share of less-than-gripping speeches and presentations that have proved this rule. Make your goal to have your audiences hanging on your every word or, if not, at least processing *most* of the information you are trying to convey.

§ 30.02. CONSIDER THE AUDIENCE

If the purpose of speaking is the communication of ideas, audience evaluation is critical. How can you best communicate your thoughts to a particular audience if you have not considered who your audience is and what preconceptions they might bring to the topic and your position on that topic?

1. Do Your Homework

In the appellate context, you will seldom be faced with individuals on the bench who are unknown quantities. Your judges will likely have written opinions that you can read before you go into court. If they have written opinions on related issues, it would almost be negligence not to read them. Even if they have not written opinions in similar cases, you might gain some insight into the judges' styles of reasoning by reading unrelated opinions. You do not need to spend several days in this process, but it will be well worth your time to spend a few hours at it.

You should also try to find someone who has previously argued in front of these judges. Ask about the judges' styles of questioning, the types of arguments they seem to find persuasive, and the types of issues they like to focus on in reaching their decisions. Find out whether the judges concentrate on the facts of the cases in front of them or on policy implications for the future. When you have this kind of information, you can structure your argument accordingly.

If time and circumstances permit, consider going to court and listening to someone else argue in front of the same judges. Get a feel for the judges' reactions to various arguments and approaches, and think about what you might do to obtain the reaction you are seeking to your argument.

2. Adapt to Your Audience

Once you have developed a sense of what might persuade your audience, you need to think about how to accomplish that goal. The first thing you should consider is the image you want to present. If you have previously appeared before this court, you may already have established a certain ethos or credibility that will help you convey your message. If not, you need to determine how to suggest to the court a level of competence that will make the judges receptive to your arguments. Adequate preparation and a professional demeanor, which we will discuss in greater detail later, are good ways to accomplish this.

In order to persuade an audience, you must give them a reason and the means to identify with your position. You can do this most effectively if you establish common ground between you and the audience. Convince the audience that you are all on the same side, or at least that you have in some way attempted to adapt to your audience's perspective on the issues being discussed. If you have made some effort to ascertain your audience's attitude toward the topic before making your presentation, you will find this a lot easier to do.

If you sense, or have learned, that your audience's attitude toward the topic is different from yours, try to figure out the source of their attitude. If you understand where it comes from, your chances of changing it may improve if you can address the root cause. You should recognize, however, that extreme attitudes cannot usually be changed greatly or quickly, and that an attitude that has been expressed publicly (for example, in an opinion, article, or speech) will be more resistant to change than an attitude that has not been committed to in that manner.

There are strategies that can be employed to change audience attitudes. You can persuade the audience that circumstances have changed sufficiently that the original attitude is no longer appropriate. If there has been no change in circumstances, you may be able to persuade the audience that they were previously misinformed or that they had not been made aware of all the available facts. Or, you can point out that the situation you are discussing is sufficiently distinct from previous situations that it calls for a different result. If you are trying to "scare" your audience into changing their attitude, you should know that attitudes are generally changed more easily by moderate than by strong anxiety appeals.

§ 30.03. CONSIDER THE SETTING

The term "setting" in this context refers to both the physical surroundings in which the presentation will be made and the occasion, or reason, for convening the speaker and the audience. Spending a little time understanding the expectations created by these contextual factors will help you prepare a more effective presentation.

1. Study the Physical Surroundings in Advance

You should, if at all possible, take the time to visit the courtroom or other location in which you will be "performing." If you have a sense of the size of the space, its acoustical properties, and the location of any furniture or other objects that will be present when you speak, you can prepare in advance to deal with any problems that might be caused by any of these factors. For example, if the podium is too high or too low, find out whether it can be adjusted, as many of them can, by the simple push of a button. If you can manipulate the physical environment to make yourself more comfortable, do so. Greater comfort will mean greater confidence and, in all likelihood, a stronger presentation.

Another factor to consider is the time of day at which you will be speaking— are people likely to be tired because your turn comes at the end of a long day, or might they forget your message because it appeared in the middle of a long parade of other speakers? If you sense that these types of factors might create a problem for you, you can try to come up with ways of making your presentation stand out, such as an especially strong opening or closing statement. If you arrive early, you may even be able to make last-minute adjustments in your prepared material to account for the mood of the audience at that particular day and time.

If you need some sort of visual aid to make your presentation, you must plan for it in advance. Check to find out whether the courtroom has an easel, a projector, computers, or whatever else you might need. If not, find out whether the equipment you need can be brought in or whether you should supply it yourself.

2. Understand the Occasion

The reasons an audience convenes will largely determine the audience's expectations of what the speakers will say and of how they will conduct themselves. Make sure that your understanding of the occasion and the audience's understanding are the same. Ask questions about any traditions and conventions that must be followed to avoid surprising the audience in a way that will detract from your message.

In an appellate courtroom, for example, the expectation is that you will behave with proper formality and deference. If you go in expecting to dazzle the judges with the type of drama and emotional appeals that might be more appropriate for a jury, you are not likely to make a favorable impression or to be taken as seriously as you need to be.

§ 30.04. STRUCTURE FOR MAXIMUM EFFECT

Plan the structure of your presentation to reinforce your intended message. Remember that, from your audience's perspective, your meaning will come across sequentially and cumulatively. Thus, you want to be sure that the sequence of your ideas is logical and that the cumulative effect of your presentation is persuasive. Your ideas should progress in a manner that the audience can follow and be tied together appropriately, even explicitly where that will enhance understanding.

1. Structural Strategy

It is useful to have some basic understanding of human psychology and memory when deciding how to structure an argument for maximum persuasive effect. The concepts of "primacy" and "recency" refer to the likelihood that audiences will remember best the ideas they hear first and last, when their attention is most focused on the presenter. Bear this in mind when structuring your oral argument.

You should also consider whether to present your arguments in ascending order of impact, saving the best for last, or descending order, starting with your strongest point. Because both primacy and recency will work in most contexts, you should try to start *and* end on a strong note, and bury your weaker points in the middle, where they will be the least detrimental.

Virtually all appellate advocates will tell you to start with your strongest argument, for the simple reason that you may never get beyond your first argument if the judges have many questions. Because an appellate argument is not a "set piece," where you have total control over the presentation, but rather a dialogue between you and the court, you must plan your strategy accordingly.

2. Methods of Proof

There are two primary approaches to proving a proposition: the direct approach, from proposition to proof, and the indirect approach, which gradually builds up the building blocks of proof until the proposition being proved becomes the inevitable conclusion. The latter method is somewhat more difficult, but often more effective, particularly when dealing with a skeptical or hostile audience. The reason this method works better for such audiences is that they may decide not to listen to the proof after they hear a proposition stated with which they disagree. If they do not know what the proposition is until they have heard the proof, you may be able to keep their minds open longer.

Even so, most legal arguments will work from proposition to proof because that is the expected approach. Judges may get frustrated if they do not understand immediately where an argument is going and what an attorney is trying to prove. Because the judges have the right to interrupt at any point, the attorney trying to prove a point by indirection would probably have to be doing so in an especially fascinating manner to avoid an irritated, "Counsel, where is this going?"

Part of your proof should consist of anticipating and defusing adverse arguments. You do not need to deal with every possible argument that might be made against your position, but if you know that an opposing argument will be made, or that those who disagree with you do so for a particular reason, it is foolish not to address that point. Pretending something does not exist is not the best way to make it disappear, and it does nothing for your credibility or persuasiveness. Why should your audience believe your arguments if you ignore theirs?

Raising and then explaining away the negative arguments is known as the "straw man" approach to proof. It is called that because you are setting up the straw man arguments just to knock them down, demonstrating all the while how insubstantial they were in the first place. Just make sure that in the course of dealing with the "straw men," you do not inadvertently make them seem more substantial than your opposition would have been able to or that you do not create new arguments against your position that might not have come up at all.

3. Organizational Patterns

You must figure out which of the many ways to structure an argument makes the most sense for each project you undertake. The most important aspect of the choice, however, is that you make one. Structure does not take care of itself; you must make conscious decisions about what structure is most likely to enhance the message you are trying to convey. Here are several possibilities to consider.

a. Chronological

This approach to structure makes the most sense when you are relating a story and the exact sequence of events is important to the audience's understanding of the story. In the context of the appellate argument, a chronological organization will probably be useful in your presentation of the facts of the case you are arguing.

b. Cause to Effect

If you are trying to establish a causal relationship between two events, as you might be in a negligence case where proximate cause is an issue, you should be sure to structure the argument so that the causal link will be apparent to the audience. This will usually require you to begin with the statement of the cause and then to move on to the result, demonstrating the unbroken nature of the chain of events you are describing.

c. Problem to Solution

If you are arguing for a change in an existing rule, this structure will probably be useful. It is one of the most common approaches to persuasion. Begin by developing the need for change; discuss the harmful consequences of the current rule, being sure to connect those harms directly to the rule you seek to change. Once you have thoroughly proved that a change is necessary, move on to the solution you propose.

In order to make this structure really effective, you must establish a strong link between the benefits of your proposal and the harms you previously identified. In other words, now that you have made the case for change, you must convince your audience that your change is the right one and that it will solve all the problems previously identified. Many speakers simply present their proposal and assume the audience will immediately see that it is the perfect answer. This is very rarely persuasive—you run the risk that the audience will not find your solution as obvious as you do and will begin to think about other alternatives.

If you do a good job of convincing the audience that change is necessary, you will have created the perfect atmosphere for receptivity to your proposal. Do not waste that opportunity by failing to make explicit connections between your solution and the need for change; you may not get another chance!

d. Pro Versus Con

You may occasionally be in the position of offering an evaluation of which of two proposals is more likely to effect a desired result or of defending a proposal that you know has encountered strong opposition. If so, this might be the structure to choose. Where the positions on both sides are clearly defined, it will make sense to the audience that you choose to address those positions sequentially.

Your only remaining decision is whether to address the "pro" or the "con" first. This will depend on the context of the argument, and probably on which side you think is stronger—for example, if you think the audience is hostile to the proposition you support, you may want to deal with the "con" arguments first. If you can effectively negate those, the audience may be more receptive to hearing why you support the other side.

e. Topical

When you have several issues to address, you will generally take a topical approach to structure, presenting the various topics in any order that seems appropriate. It is here that issues of primacy and recency, and ascending versus descending order, arise. If there is a sequence that is naturally logical—for example, if one argument must be developed first to provide context for another, you should present the arguments in that order. Similarly, if you are making arguments in the alternative, or if one argument is conditional upon the acceptance of another, you should take that into consideration when structuring the overall presentation.

4. Introductions, Conclusions, and Transitions

These are important parts of the structure of any spoken presentation. We have included them last in this discussion because that is probably when you should think seriously about them. The conclusion obviously belongs at the end of the speech, but you should also construct your introduction *after* you have completed your substantive analysis. It is at that point that you will have the best idea of the tone you are attempting to create and of the central theme of your argument. Both of these should be reflected in the introduction.

The introduction and the conclusion should be short, pithy, and as powerful as you can make them, consistent with the subject of your argument. These are the first and last impressions you will leave with the audience, and you want them to be strong ones. Identify the one idea you would like the audience to take away from your presentation (assuming that that is all you can realistically expect them to take away) and then emphasize that idea in the introduction and conclusion. Ideally, the conclusion will echo the introduction in some interesting way so that the central idea is reinforced.

Consciously consider transitions after you have constructed the argument. The reason you move from one argument to another, or the relationships between arguments, will often seem obvious to you, and thus you may not state them directly as you develop the argument. After you have created the body of the argument, look at it as objectively as you can, and ask yourself whether the audience will see the flow of the argument as well as you do. Even if you think they will, consider adding brief transitions between major points. Remember that the audience has to process your message aurally; any help you can offer to make that message clearer will almost certainly be appreciated.

§ 30.05. WRITE FOR SOUND APPEAL

Remember, as you draft the language you intend to speak, that writing words to be spoken requires a different style from writing words that will be read in silence. You have additional tools at your disposal to enhance the impact your words will have on the audience. Try to hear the words as you write them and to picture how the delivery will go. What facial expressions will accompany your words? How will you use your hands to support your message? What will your volume and vocal inflection reveal about the importance of what you are saying? What tone will most enhance your message? Language shapes perceptions; use your knowledge of this fact to encourage or discourage particular responses.

1. Useful Tools

There are several ways you can maintain audience interest in your spoken message. Some of them are relatively simple but quite effective if used in appropriate contexts. Others may require more conscious effort on your part to use them effectively. Here are some of the ways you can keep an audience listening and wanting to hear more.

a. Humor

Humor can be a very good way to involve your audience in your message from the start. This is probably why so many speakers begin their presentations with a joke. Be sure that what you say really is funny and that it is appropriate to the audience. Also remember that subtle humor is often more effective than obvious humor; surprise is an important element of good humor.

b. Novelty

Novelty may also be a way to catch your audience's attention early on. If you have a different approach to an old topic or are discussing something with which the audience is not familiar, you can use the interest that most of us have in new things to your advantage. Choose an interesting way to present new information to your audience, and you may very keep their attention longer.

As with anything else, though, do not get carried away; novelty for its own sake will wear thin very quickly. Be sure that your approach is actually novel, present it in a way that is appropriate to the audience and the topic, and avoid "cuteness" that may succeed only in turning the audience off.

c. Conflict

You may be able to use the element of surprise in another way. If your topic lends itself to the creation of conflict, for example, between light and serious tones, a sudden shift can catch the audience off guard and make them sit up and take notice. Thus if you can begin with a humorous approach and then move unexpectedly into an aspect of the topic that is decidedly not funny, you may shock the audience into listening more carefully than they might otherwise. This is a manipulative approach to getting your message across, but if handled adroitly, it can be quite effective.

d. Suspense

This is a difficult technique to use effectively, particularly in a legal setting, but if done well it can really add to the impact of a message. You can use suspense in the introduction to your presentation by finding an interesting but somewhat ambiguous way of leading into your topic. In order not to lose or frustrate the audience, make certain that your mysterious introduction is genuinely fascinating and does not go on for too long.

You may find it more effective to at least signal your topic early on, but leave the audience wondering exactly what your approach or perspective is. It can be a very effective means of persuading a hostile or skeptical audience to begin by articulating the arguments for your opponents and suggesting that you understand them, and then suddenly revealing your true position on the issue. Once again, the element of surprise keeps the audience involved in the presentation.

Be very sure that you understand the expectations of your audience before you try this technique in a legal setting. In the appellate context, where presentations tend to assume nearly identical guise and where the judges can interrupt you if they get frustrated, too much suspense could be detrimental to the persuasiveness of your argument. With a jury, however, appropriate use of this technique could be quite powerful.

e. Emphasis

A spoken presentation gives you many opportunities to suggest appropriate emphasis. You can use your voice, hands, and face to guide the audience to the conclusion that what you are saying at any given moment is particularly important. Recognize too that the audience will generally expect that important information appears at the end of sentences rather than at the beginning. They expect the beginning of a sentence to contain contextual information that will help them orient themselves in the message and prepare for what follows. Here is a powerful example of the effect an understanding of this simple expectation can have on the impact of a message. Read this excerpt and think about how you would react to it as a listener.

> I have refrained directly from criticizing the President for three years. Because I believe that Americans must stand united in the face of the Soviet Union, our foremost adversary and before the world, I have been reticent. A fair time to pursue his goals and test his policies is also the President's right, I believe. The water's edge is

the limit to politics, in this sense. But this cannot mean that, if the President is wrong and the world situation has become critical, all criticism should be muted indefinitely.

A fair chance has been extended the President, and policies that make our relationship with the Soviet Union more dangerous than at any time in the past generation no longer deserve American support and support cannot be expected.

Reagan administrative diplomacy has had this grim result: We could face not the risk of nuclear war but its reality if we allow present developments in nuclear arms and United States–Soviet relations to continue.

This is an excerpt from a campaign speech by Walter Mondale. It seems very flat and leaves the reader wondering what exactly the speaker is trying to accomplish. If we simply restructure the sentences, leaving the meaning and vocabulary virtually intact, here is the result:[1]

For three years, I have refrained from directly criticizing the President of the United States. I have been reticent because I believe that Americans must stand united before the world, particularly in the face of our foremost adversary, the Soviet Union. I also believe a President should be given fair time to pursue his goals and test his policies. In this sense, politics should stop at the water's edge. But this cannot mean that all criticism should be muted indefinitely, no matter how wrong a President may be or how critical the world situation may become.

President Reagan has had his fair chance, and he can no longer expect Americans to support policies that make our relationship with the Soviet Union more dangerous than at any time in the past generation.

This is the grim result of Reagan administrative diplomacy: If present developments in nuclear arms and United States–Soviet relations are permitted to continue, we could face not the risk of nuclear war but its reality.

By simply restructuring the sentences to place emphasis on the appropriate information, we end up with something that actually sounds as though it might belong in a campaign speech.

f. Theme

One of the most important tools for effective speaking is the creation and emphasis of a central theme for any presentation. Find a way to tie your ideas together, to relate them to a single overarching principle, and be sure to clearly identify that theme for your audience and to refer to it wherever appropriate to emphasize its importance. Choose a tone for your presentation that reinforces this central theme (i.e., solemn, ironic, indignant, etc.) You should never assume that any audience will remember every subpoint of an argument, but if they walk away understanding the main goal you were trying to accomplish and why that goal is important, you will have achieved something to be proud of.

---

1. This example is taken from George Gopen, *Expectations: Teaching Writing from the Reader's Perspective* (A.B. Longman Publishers, Pearson Education Division, 2004, pages 145-148); he, in turn, got the example from Joseph M. Williams, and asked us to acknowledge that fact.

g. Language

Remembering always that your audience cannot go back for another look at something that was not immediately clear, keep your language concrete, precise, active, colorful, and simple. Most people will process information more efficiently if they can conjure up a visual representation of it. You can help your audience do this by using concrete analogies and examples to clarify points that might otherwise seem abstract. Here are some specific examples of stylistic devices that speakers have used to good effect in many contexts.

i. Rhetorical Questions

Asking questions to which you do not expect an answer can, if used sparingly, be a very effective means of keeping your audience involved in your presentation. Your goal is to frame the question in a way that suggests the desired answer but leaves enough room for thought that the audience will feel that they have arrived at the answer on their own, and thus feel a sense of commitment to it. You should be a little extra careful about using this technique with an appellate bench of course—you do not want the judges to feel that you are, usurping their role!

ii. Repetition

Strategic use of repetition, whether of sentence structure (e.g., antithesis), words, or sounds (e.g., alliteration), can be an effective signal of emphasis or simply a means of increasing the memorability of what you say. Part of the reason so many people remember and quote speeches by John F. Kennedy and Martin Luther King is because they used repetition so powerfully. You should be careful to avoid monotony, however, which will almost certainly result if you overuse this technique.

iii. Imagery

As mentioned above, giving your listeners the ability to "see" what you are saying will help them process and retain the message. There are several ways to do this, all involving comparisons, sometimes literal, sometimes of very dissimilar things.

The literal analogy is the most direct comparison; it identifies similarities between things or ideas that will help clarify a point. The more figurative similes and metaphors make comparisons between very different things in order to create a picture in the listener's mind that will suggest meaning quickly and powerfully. A simile is a comparison that actually uses the words "like" or "as," while a metaphor implies the comparison.

Martin Luther King's "I Have a Dream" speech is one of the strongest and most effective uses of metaphors you are likely to see; it creates an entire landscape in your mind through the simple use of words. Most of us cannot use metaphors nearly so well. They should be used sparingly and carefully; if you create a metaphor that is too startling or confusing, you run the risk of distracting your listeners as they struggle to deal with the visual image you have created.

Personification is another type of comparison that can be used effectively to create a lasting image in the mind of the listener. This is the giving of human traits to inanimate or intangible objects, as by suggesting that an institution is "ill" or that an idea "limps." Again, you should be careful not to create images that are so strange the audience will spend substantial time puzzling over them, or laughing where you did not intend humor.

2. Not So Useful Tools

As you can see, there are many ways you can enhance your message by making it more fun for the audience to listen to you. Similarly, there are some ways you can detract from the message and alienate the audience so that they stop listening or become less receptive to your message. For example, using slang, foreign phrases, vulgarity, euphemisms, or triteness might have this kind of effect, ranging from distraction to active annoyance.

Another tactic speakers sometimes resort to, particularly in the political arena, is name-calling. By this, we do not mean only the obvious mud-slinging type of name-calling, but also the more insidious, intellectually dishonest use of labels in place of analysis. When a speaker knows that a particular word will generate an emotional reaction, such as the word "quota" in a discussion of affirmative action, it may be tempting to simply use the word and thereby short-circuit a genuine examination of the topic under discussion. This technique may get results—it is always easier, both for the speaker and the listeners, to oversimplify an issue and thus discourage reason and evaluation—but it does so inappropriately.

Particularly in a courtroom setting, where your listeners are intelligent and at least somewhat informed, you should respect them enough to offer a straight-forward and thoughtful analysis of the topic you are discussing. Say what you mean and do not shy away from the difficult questions. If your audience is paying any attention at all, attempts to avoid the real issues are likely to be challenged and will cost you valuable credibility. There is simply no reason to take this kind of risk.

§ 30.06. APPLY THE FUNDAMENTALS OF GOOD PUBLIC SPEAKING

Delivery is the final element of any spoken presentation. When you have worked so hard to prepare your argument, it would be very unfortunate to diminish the impact of your efforts by not delivering the message effectively. Here are some suggestions about how to achieve maximum influence as a messenger.

1. Maintain Eye Contact

Maintaining eye contact with an audience is difficult for inexperienced or nervous speakers, but it is essential. In a courtroom, look the judges in the eye rather than at your notes or the ceiling. Eye contact lets the judges know you are interested in what they have to say. It also helps keep them interested in what you are saying.

2. Be Heard

Speak loudly and clearly enough that everyone in the room can hear you. Project but do not yell. Speaking at an appropriate volume suggests confidence in your position. If you speak so that everyone can hear you easily, you help ensure that your audience will understand your argument. You also increase the likelihood that your audience will find your argument persuasive.

3. Do Not Read

Reading will cause you to speak too fast and make you more difficult to understand. It suggests a lack of preparation and even a lack of interest in your argument. In addition, you will lose eye contact with the bench, and the judges' interest in your argument may decrease.

4. Use Emphasis

Sounding like you are interested in your arguments and believe them makes it more likely that your audience will find you persuasive. It is difficult to listen to someone who speaks in a monotone. We are not suggesting that you try to be flamboyant, but merely that you modulate your voice appropriately for the point you are making.

5. Use the Pause

Silence is often anathema to someone who is unused to speaking in public. As you develop experience and expertise in speaking to an audience, you will learn to use a well-timed pause to provide emphasis. A pause while you ponder a question or collect your thoughts can ensure that what follows the pause is more fluent and persuasive.

6. Use Appropriate Gestures

Not all people use their hands while speaking. If you are not comfortable using hand gestures, do not try them for the first time in the pressure-filled environment of a courtroom. If, however, it is natural for you to use your hands to add appropriate emphasis to your presentation, do so in your oral argument. Be careful not to use your hands excessively.

7. Watch Your Posture

The courtroom is a formal setting. Do not lean excessively on the podium. You may rest your hands on the podium, but not your elbows. Do not argue with your hands in your pockets or on your hips. Casual poses may suggest a lack of respect for the court and, at the very least, are likely to be distracting. Do not pace or rock back and forth. Stand in one place and maintain an upright, respectful posture.

CHAPTER 31

The Appellate Argument

§ 31.01. INTRODUCTION

This chapter teaches you specifically how to make an oral argument in appellate court. Although most attorneys do not find themselves in appellate court very often, the skills you learn in presenting an oral argument will be useful in other areas of practice. Attorneys also argue motions to the trial court and appear before various administrative agencies that may require argument.

Oral argument is the culmination of an attorney's efforts in an appeal. It complements the brief. You cannot expect, however, to present an argument every time you file a brief because the court has discretion about whether to grant oral argument. If you get a chance to argue, view it as a golden opportunity. You will have no other in-person, one-on-one contact with the judges who will decide whether you win or lose.

The oral argument provides you with an opportunity to interest the court in particular arguments presented in the brief and to convince the court that your client's position is correct. Generally, the argument is more provocative, more personal, and more lively than the brief. The oral argument affords an opportunity to answer the court's questions and address its concerns. Time is limited and therefore precious, which means that precision in presenting the argument is crucial.

Most lawyers will tell you there is very little chance you will win a case at oral argument that you otherwise would have lost. They will also tell you that you can lose a case based on your argument. On the other hand, some experts, including Justice Kennedy of the Supreme Court, will tell you that many cases are decided at oral argument.[1]

Many first-year law students view oral argument as an ordeal to be endured. Because the experience is new and the process unknown, the prospect of oral argument makes students nervous. Fortunately, despite their initial misgivings, most students find that the actual experience is worthwhile and even fun.

---

1. Justice Kennedy, in his address as part of the Enrichment Program at the George Washington University National Law Center, February 6, 1990.

§ 31.02. THE SETTING OF THE ORAL ARGUMENT

The appellate oral argument usually is conducted before a panel of three judges.[2] The court allots each side a specified amount of time in which to present its argument. The attorney addresses the bench from behind a podium. The appellant presents the first argument and may reserve time for rebuttal. The appellee argues after the appellant and does not present a rebuttal. If two teams are arguing in a first-year legal writing or moot court program, both appellants argue, followed by both appellees. The appellant delivers the rebuttal after the appellee has argued. The judges may interrupt at any time with questions.

As a matter of protocol, rise when the judges enter the room and remain standing until the judges have seated themselves. The court then calls the case and may ask whether counsel is prepared. After you indicate your readiness to proceed, step to the podium and begin your argument. Refer to any judge to whom you are speaking as "Your Honor." Refer to your opponent as "opposing counsel" or "counsel for appellant" (or appellee).

§ 31.03. PREPARING THE ORAL ARGUMENT

The key to a successful oral argument is preparation. If you are prepared, you will be confident and should be able to satisfactorily address any concerns raised by the judges. In preparing your argument, remember that time is limited, so you must state your arguments in general terms. Focus on controlling legal principles, policy, and equity rather than the details of case law, which should be presented in your written brief.

The judges' questions will probably force you to deviate from your prepared outline. You should be sufficiently prepared that you can shift back and forth from one part of your argument to another as necessary. The judges may not wish to follow your structure, and you should be prepared to accommodate them. Also, you must think through the consequences of your arguments and the relief you want the court to grant. Judges will want to know precisely what you want them to do and what effect your preferred result will have on future cases. Here are seven rules to help you achieve the required degree of preparation.

1. Know the Record

You must have all information about what happened in your case at your fingertips. This information includes not only the facts that gave rise to the cause of action, but also the entire procedural history of the case, including discovery. You may present a brief history of the case as part of your argument, but you must be able to answer the court's questions about any additional facts. The judges may doubt the accuracy of other aspects of your argument if you cannot tell them what happened previously in your own case.

---

2. This is true for intermediate appellate courts. The United States Supreme Court and other higher courts will have more judges hearing arguments—usually seven or nine. The party designations at the Supreme Court level are petitioner and respondent, or appellant and appellee.

2. Study the Authorities

Although you usually do not focus primarily on details of decided cases in presenting your argument, you must be able to answer questions about the major cases cited in your brief or in your opponent's brief and to use such cases in response to questions where appropriate. You must know the facts, holdings, and rationales of all such cases. The court will expect you to be able to apply them to the facts of your case.

3. Know the Arguments

You must be familiar with all arguments raised in your brief. For purposes of oral argument, however, select a maximum of three major arguments to present to the court. Use the organization of your brief as a guide. As explained in Chapter 30, try to begin with your strongest argument. This will help capture the judges' attention and set the tone for the rest of the argument. Also, the judges might ask so many questions that you never reach your second argument. You must, however, be prepared to answer questions about your weaker arguments because the judges may focus on those arguments. Also, remember that if your strongest argument does not logically come first, you may not be able to begin with it.

Be flexible about the order in which you present your arguments and be prepared to adapt your argument to what happens in the courtroom. For example, if you are the appellee, listen carefully to the questions the court asks the appellant. If the court focuses on a particular issue, you may want to begin by presenting your argument on that issue.

4. Outline Your Arguments

An outline is an essential part of preparing for an oral argument. Even if you do not use your outline during the argument, preparing one ahead of time will give your presentation clarity and structure. The outline should present the high points of your argument. When deciding how much detail to include in your outline, use the rule of thumb that you should have enough prepared material to occupy approximately half your allotted time. For a fifteen-minute argument, prepare an outline that should take you approximately eight minutes to present. Some people feel more prepared if they put virtually every word they intend to say on paper beforehand. Others prefer a sketchy outline that allows greater flexibility of word choice at the time of the argument. As a general rule, go to the podium with the fewest words on paper that will help you remember your key points. Regardless of which approach you choose, keep your arguments simple and straightforward, and use only minimal references to details such as case names in preparing your outline.

5. Prepare Argument Aids

After preparing your outline, think about the kind of notes and other aids you are likely to need while presenting your argument. You may choose to use the outline or you may find that some other form of prompting is more helpful to you. Many appellate advocates suggest putting your outline on the inside of a manila folder so that the entire argument is laid out in front of you. This approach makes referring to various parts of the argument in response to questions easier. If you are shuffling through loose papers to find needed information, you may distract the bench. Locating a particular part of your argument under pressure can be difficult.

When you go to the podium, take your brief, your outline, and notes or cards that summarize the relevant cases. The case notes should provide a short summary of the facts, holding, and rationale of each case about which you can reasonably expect questions during the argument.

Take your argument aids to the podium with you, but do not read from them. Use the argument aids only to remind you of the points you wish to raise with the court. Forcing yourself to speak without heavy reliance on notes will facilitate the all-important eye contact with the bench. One way to accomplish this is to follow the general rule stated above, and have only as many words in front of you as you really need to remember your key points. For example, use important words and phrases rather than full sentences.

6. Rehearse the Argument

Although some people may feel a bit foolish practicing an oral argument, it is an essential exercise. If you are not accustomed to public speaking, practice in front of a mirror. You will be able to see how effective your facial expressions and hand gestures are. You also may want to practice in front of other people—your friends, your family, or your partner if you are arguing as part of a team. The best way to gauge your effectiveness as a public speaker is to videotape your performance. Although videotaping is obviously not always a practical alternative, it definitely is an educational experience.

An important part of rehearsing the argument is anticipating questions the judges are likely to ask. Prepare for

- questions about the facts of your case;
- questions about the facts of cases cited in the briefs filed with the court;
- questions about arguments raised by your opponent;
- questions about arguments you intend to make but have not raised yet—that is, questions that require you to deviate from your prepared outline; and
- questions about the ramifications of your arguments and the rule or rules you are asking the court to adopt; understand and be able to articulate the policies behind the options available to the court and know your "bottom line"—what are the precise parameters of your arguments and the rule(s) you are advocating?

Although you cannot possibly predict every question the judges will ask during the argument, you will give a much more polished and persuasive presentation if you have anticipated and rehearsed answers to the majority of questions you receive.

7. Advise the Court and Your Opponent of New Information

Information or case law relevant to your case sometimes becomes available after you file your brief. You have an affirmative obligation to advise the court of any new case law that may be dispositive. If you decide that it is necessary to provide newly discovered case law to the court, do so before the argument and send a copy to your opponent at the same time. Not only is this practice a matter of courtesy, it also prevents the court from becoming distracted by reading a document you hand up during your argument.

§ 31.04. THE STRUCTURE OF THE ORAL ARGUMENT

1. Basic Argument Structure

The oral argument, whether presented by appellant or appellee, usually conforms to a basic framework that contains a number of elements:

a. The Introduction

The introduction usually begins with the phrase "[M]ay it please the court," briefly introduces counsel and the party represented by counsel, and reserves time for rebuttal if desired. For example, in the case of *Ace Trucking Co. v. Skinflint Insurance, Inc.*, counsel for appellant Ace Trucking Co. might begin:

> May it please the court, my name is Nancy Schultz, my co-counsel is Annemiek Young, and we represent Ace Trucking Co. We would like to reserve four minutes for rebuttal, with two minutes deducted from each of our arguments.

Then give a brief summary of what the case is about and indicate the relief requested. Your summary offers a good opportunity to explain briefly to the court why your client deserves to win and to set the tone for the rest of your argument. This is a good opportunity to create a "theme" for your argument. A theme is a one-sentence encapsulation of the core of your case that grabs the attention of the court. Themes are frequently used in trial court arguments, and some people will tell you they are more appropriate there, but they also have their place in appellate court. Any time you can help the judges understand the heart of your argument in an interesting and memorable way, you are advocating effectively. For example, in a Fourth Amendment case, you might introduce your case this way: "This case is about protecting our homes from unreasonable intrusion by law enforcement authorities."

b. The Roadmap and Key Facts of the Case

You should always provide the court with a roadmap of your argument. As noted elsewhere, you should be arguing two or three major points to the court, and you should tell the court up front what those points will be. This will allow the court to understand where your argument is going, and it may persuade the judges to wait to question you on particular parts of your argument until you get to them. It may not work that way, but at least you have announced to the court what you will be arguing.

The roadmap should be succinct and straightforward. For example, again assuming that you are arguing a Fourth Amendment case on behalf of the petitioner, whose mobile home was searched using a vision-enhancing device, you might offer this roadmap: "We ask this Court to reverse the decision of the court below for two reasons: (1) Petitioner had a reasonable expectation of privacy in his mobile home, and (2) the police required a warrant before using any kind of vision-enhancing technology."

Immediately following the roadmap, you should offer a very brief statement of key facts that will help the court understand what happened to your client. Ideally this statement will plant the idea that the court would like to find a way to rule for your client to right an injustice. Particularly in moot court competitions, some advocates will "waive a recitation of the facts," meaning they will not set the stage by talking about any facts, and sending the message that the facts do not matter. This is bad practice, as appellate advocates will tell you. Any time you appear in court, you are there on behalf of a client who has a story to tell. The fact that you are in appellate court, where legal issues predominate over factual ones, does not make the facts unimportant. The statement of the facts should be short, accurate, and persuasive. Frame it to present your point of view and the merits of your client's case. It must not be misleading, however, or you will lose credibility with the court. You should emphasize helpful facts, but you must appear fair.

c. The Argument

Providing the bench with a brief outline, or roadmap, of the arguments you intend to make indicates to the judges which arguments you believe are worthy of oral argument and advises them of the order in which you will be making those arguments. An outline enables you to at least mention all of the arguments you have selected, albeit broadly, and may encourage the court to defer its questions until the appropriate time. If you are arguing as appellee and will be presenting arguments in an order different from that used by your opponent, it may be wise to advise the court of that fact.

Present your arguments as you have outlined them. State conclusions first, then support them with facts and law. During your argument, refer to your client by name. This practice both humanizes your client and helps the court keep the parties straight. When referring to the opposing party, most advocates use an appropriate party designation such as "appellant" or "appellee." Expect that a substantial portion of your argument time will be devoted to answering questions from the bench.

d. The Conclusion

When your time has run out, finish your sentence and sit down. Before concluding, make sure you have answered any pending question to the questioner's satisfaction. If you finish your argument before your time has run out, do not keep talking just to fill the time. Present your conclusion and sit down. Conclude your oral argument by providing the court with a short, "punchy" statement of why your client deserves to win and is entitled to the requested relief. Depending upon how your argument has progressed and the time remaining, the conclusion may be a single sentence or it may be more detailed. You should prepare both. If, when time runs out, you have not had an opportunity to conclude, you must ask the court for permission to do so. If a question is pending, you should ask for permission to answer the question as well. The court may or may not grant such permission; for example, the United States Supreme Court will not give extra time.

2. Rebuttal

If, as appellant, you choose to reserve time for rebuttal, be prepared to use that time efficiently and effectively. If you are arguing as part of a team, usually one member of the team will present the entire rebuttal for the side and should be prepared to discuss any issues raised during the argument. In two to five minutes, you cannot rebut every argument made by your opponent. You also may not use this time to raise new issues. Select one or two major points made during the argument that you believe most require clarification or rehabilitation. Remember that your rebuttal is the last thing the judges will hear before they decide your case. Choose your arguments accordingly.

There are other effective ways to use rebuttal time. Listen carefully to your opponent's argument. Your opponent may make statements or mistakes that you can use to your advantage. If you do not have one or two major points that need reinforcing, you may want to use the time to give the court a brief and powerful summary of the reasons your client deserves to win. Some advocates choose to use the time to answer an important question they were unable to answer when the court asked it during the argument.

It may be worthwhile to prepare several possible rebuttals ahead of time. Canned rebuttals, however, are no substitute for listening to your opponent's argument. Tailor your rebuttal to the argument the court actually hears. It also is acceptable to waive your rebuttal if you are satisfied with the way the argument has progressed. The judges are likely to appreciate the time savings, and you send a distinct message of confidence when you waive rebuttal. If, however, you have reserved substantial time for rebuttal, perhaps five minutes or more, you may want to use the time to at least summarize your major arguments for the court. Also, some advocates will tell you that it is a mistake to give up the chance to have the last word. Always close your rebuttal with a request for the specific relief you seek from the court.

§ 31.05. QUESTIONS FROM THE JUDGES

Throughout your argument the judges are likely to interrupt with questions. Questions from the court are desirable because they signal the judges' interest and involvement in the matter. Questions from the bench reveal what the judges' concerns are and permit you to tailor your argument to respond. Oral argument is your only opportunity to directly address the concerns of individual judges. Do not be disturbed if the questions from the bench take you out of your prepared sequence. You use your allotted time most effectively by focusing on those matters about which the court is undecided. Do not consider every question as an attack on your position. Some questions are designed to support your view. If you are asked a helpful question, recognize it and use it to your advantage.

As noted previously, the types of questions the judges ask will vary. A judge might seek information about the facts or raise policy considerations. He or she could ask about the authorities upon which you or your opponent rely for support. You might be asked about the ramifications of a particular legal argument. If you have formulated answers to a variety of questions in advance, you should be able to use most questions to advance your argument.

To handle questions from the bench effectively, remember six basic rules:

1. Listen to the question very carefully. To respond to it, you must fully understand the judge's concerns. Never cut a judge off in the middle of a question.

2. Be sure you understand the question. If you did not understand the question, ask the court to repeat it. If you think you understand the question but are not certain, begin your answer by restating the question.

3. Think before you speak. If you need to think about the question before you can effectively answer it, do so. A brief pause will indicate to the court that you are considering the question and formulating a precise and thorough response.

4. Be responsive. Answer the question directly. If the question calls for a yes or no answer, the first words out of your mouth should be "Yes, Your Honor," or "No, Your Honor." Some first-time advocates have a tendency, particularly early in the argument, to give long, rambling answers that cover much more ground than the question requires. Such an answer may obscure the point you need to make and may bore or confuse your listeners. It also may suggest new questions to the judge.

Do not hedge when answering a question, or the judge may think that you are being evasive. If the question seeks information you do not have, say so. If you cannot answer a question for other reasons, it sometimes helps to fall back on a general statement of your fundamental argument on the issue. Do not overuse this device. Seek to explain and clarify your position to the judge's satisfaction. When you believe that you have answered the question and additional inquiries are not immediately forthcoming, move on. Do not wait for a signal from the bench giving you permission to proceed.

5. Be an advocate. Use your responses to the court's questions as a vehicle to present and advance your argument, even if you must depart from the order set out in your outline. If you are interrupted by a judge, be polite and answer the question immediately. Never ask the judge to wait until later in your argument for an answer. Once the court is satisfied with your answers and you have fully presented your arguments on a particular issue or point, make a smooth transition to the next issue or point. Try to get your argument back on track if it has been disrupted by questioning, but if you have fully discussed a point in response to questions, do not go back and present the argument again from your outline. You will waste valuable time and confuse the bench, and you may invite new questions that will force you back into issues you would rather not spend any more time on.

6. Prepare in advance for questions. At the risk of repeating ourselves, good preparation is the key to answering questions. A thorough understanding of your case will permit you to spot both your weak points and your opponents' strong ones. These areas will be the source of many questions from the bench.

Be prepared for a wide variety of personalities on the bench. Some benches take on personalities themselves, which may range from "cold" benches that ask very few questions to "hot" benches that rapidly fire questions at you. Sometimes the judges are not prepared and may not even have read your brief. Others may have read only parts of it. You may get very few questions or an unending stream of questions. You may get thoughtful, probing questions or questions that seem completely irrelevant. Your role in the argument is to address the particular concerns of the court, whatever they may be, and to answer all questions to the best of your ability.

§ 31.06. ORAL ARGUMENT CHECKLIST

— Identify and articulate the fundamental reason or reasons your client deserves to win; prepare a short explanatory statement for use during the argument.

— Select the two or three major points you intend to make during the argument and decide upon the order in which they will be presented.

— Think through the implications of your major arguments and identify the policy goals served by those arguments.

— Identify key facts and prepare a short statement of your client's perspective on those facts, if they are helpful to your case.

— Prepare your introduction, conclusion, roadmap, and outline.

— Anticipate questions and formulate answers to any questions you can be reasonably sure the judges will ask.

— Know the facts, holdings, and rationales of any important cases relied upon by you or your opponent(s).

— Prepare your argument aids, remembering to keep them as short as you can.

Memoranda

MEMORANDUM

TO: Jaded Old Partner
FROM: Eager New Associate
RE: John E. Walker,
         False Imprisonment Claim

ISSUE

Can a casino patron who is drunk and disruptive recover for false imprisonment under the law of New Jersey when security personnel detain him to "cool off" despite his repeated requests to leave?

CONCLUSION

A casino patron who is drunk and disruptive can recover for false imprisonment under the law of New Jersey when security personnel detain him to "cool off" despite his repeated requests to leave. The two requirements of false imprisonment are met because the patron was under a reasonable apprehension that the security personnel had the authority to detain him and because they did not, in fact, have such authority. There was no legal justification for the detention in this case because the patron was not cheating and had not committed a crime that the casino intended to report to the authorities.

FACTS

Our client, Mr. John E. Walker, recently visited the Empty Pockets Casino in Atlantic City, New Jersey. While there, he lost a great deal of money. Apparently believing that they had a "high roller" on their hands, casino officials instructed the waitresses on the casino floor to provide Mr. Walker with free drinks.

After accepting several free drinks and continuing to lose money, Mr. Walker became somewhat upset and began accusing the dealer and the casino of cheating and of stealing his money. He acknowledges that he was probably a bit loud and may have been annoying other patrons of the casino.

Mr. Walker was approached by two rather large men wearing suits who identified themselves as casino security guards and asked him to accompany them. Mr. Walker noticed that they were wearing identification badges that had the word "security" prominently displayed on them. Mr. Walker accompanied the men to a small room located near the casino floor, where they asked him to sit down and "cool off."

The guards remained with Mr. Walker for approximately two hours, denying his several requests to leave. At the end of this period, the guards told him he was free to go. Mr. Walker would like to know whether he can sue the Empty Pockets Casino for false imprisonment.

DISCUSSION

Mr. Walker has a cause of action for false imprisonment against the Empty Pockets Casino. Under New Jersey law, a cause of action for false imprisonment or false arrest is made out upon a showing that there was an arrest and that the arrest was without legal justification. *Barletta v. Golden Nugget Hotel Casino*, 580 F. Supp. 614, 617 (D.N.J. 1984). In New Jersey, false arrest and false imprisonment are merely different names for the same tort. *Roth v. Golden Nugget Casino/ Hotel, Inc.*, 576 F. Supp. 262, 265 (D.N.J. 1983).

Mr. Walker can establish that there was an arrest in his case. He must show that his liberty was constrained as a result of force, or the threat of force, by the defendant. *Id.* New Jersey courts have held that "the assertion of legal authority to take a person into custody, even where such authority does not in fact exist, may be sufficient to create a reasonable apprehension that a person is under restraint." *Bartolo v. Boardwalk Regency Hotel Casino*, 449 A.2d 1339, 1341 (N.J. Super. L. Div. 1982, 185 N.J. Super. 534, 537).

The court in *Barletta* found that an arrest had taken place where the plaintiff was escorted to the casino security office by two security officers after an altercation between the plaintiff and another casino patron. The fact that the plaintiff accompanied the security officers under her own power did not affect her claim where she testified that she did not feel free to refuse. The court in *Roth* found an arrest under virtually identical circumstances.

Mr. Walker's situation closely parallels the cited cases. He, too, was asked to accompany security officers from the casino floor, and, by his own account, did not feel that he was in a position to refuse. Here, as in *Barletta* and *Roth*, a court should find that there was a reasonable apprehension of force.

Mr. Walker should also be able to establish that the restraint was without legal justification. There are two possible justifications for the restraint that the casino might raise, but neither of them is likely to be accepted by a court.

First, the casino might argue that the security officers were entitled to detain Mr. Walker under a broad interpretation of the New Jersey statute that allows casinos to detain patrons upon suspicion of various offenses, all of which involve cheating. N.J. Stat. Ann. §5:12-121(b) (West 1977). Such a broad interpretation of the statute was rejected by the court in *Bartolo*. In that case the plaintiff was detained on suspicion of card counting, which the court held could not be equated with cheating. If card counting does not constitute cheating and therefore does not come within the ambit of § 5:12-121(b), being drunk and disorderly is certainly not a ground for detention under that section.

Alternatively, the casino might argue that it was entitled to detain Mr. Walker under the statutory provision that allows any person to detain another who commits a disorderly persons offense in the detainer's presence. N.J. Stat. Ann. § 2A:169-3 (West 1979). However, that statute has also been narrowly construed by the courts. In *Roth*, the court held that a disorderly persons offense must actually have occurred before an arrest without a warrant will be justified. There, the court denied defendant's motion for summary judgment because there was a genuine factual dispute as to whether plaintiff had committed the offense of criminal trespass.

It is not entirely clear whether Mr. Walker committed a disorderly persons offense, but the casino security personnel did not accuse him of committing one and took no steps to bring him before the proper authorities as is required by § 2A:169-3. Although the cases do not address the significance of the phrase "and take him before any magistrate," the previous narrow constructions of the statute would suggest that this phrase should also be read literally. Thus, the casino's failure to follow the procedure outlined by the statute should negate its claim of legal justification for the detention.

In Mr. Walker's case, the security guards simply told him that they wanted him to "cool off," and, when they were satisfied that he had done so, let him go. Such a detention is not authorized by the statutes or the decided cases. We should pursue a claim for false imprisonment on Mr. Walker's behalf.

MEMORANDUM

PRIVILEGED AND CONFIDENTIAL

TO: Paul Partner
FROM: Adam Associate
DATE: December 14, 2009
FILE NO.:   025499-0001
RE: Liability of individuals for discrimination under the DCHRA

I. QUESTION PRESENTED

Can individuals be liable for harassment and discrimination in violation of the District of Columbia Human Rights Act ("DCHRA")?

II. SHORT ANSWER

Yes. Both the plain language of the statute and case law allow individuals to be liable for violation of the statute. However, in each case to consider the issue, the court has found liability only with regard to individuals occupying a *managerial or supervisory* capacity. It is unclear whether the supervisor must have authority over the plaintiff in order to be subject to liability.

III. RELEVANT FACTUAL BACKGROUND

In February 2008, plaintiff Steven Smith ("Smith") amended his complaint to assert causes of action for discrimination under the DCHRA against individual employees of his former employer, Cafe Asia. Specifically, Smith alleged claims against May Stiltz, Karen Saweed, Joey Yimmer, Abu Baker, Elias Treer, and Shawn Yo in their individual capacities. Their specific job titles are as follows:

May Stiltz: day manager
Karen Saweed: operations manager
Joey Yimmer: night manager
Abu Baker: kitchen/chef supervisor
Elias Treer: Abu's supervisor
Shawn Yo: owner

IV. DISCUSSION

A. According to the Plain Language of the DCHRA, Any Individual Who Acts in Their Employer's Interest, or Who Aids and Abets Discrimination, Is Amenable to Suit.

Our analysis begins with the plain language of the DCHRA. Section 2-1402.11 provides that

(a) It shall be an unlawful discriminatory practice to do any of the following acts, wholly or partially for a discriminatory reason based upon the actual or perceived: race, color, religion, national origin, sex, age, marital status, personal appearance,

sexual orientation, gender identity or expression, family responsibilities, genetic information, disability, matriculation, or political affiliation of any individual:

(1) By an employer.—To fail or refuse to hire, or to discharge, any individual; or
otherwise to discriminate against any individual, with respect to his compensation,
terms, conditions, or privileges of employment, including promotion; or to limit,
segregate, or classify his employees in any way which would deprive or tend to
deprive any individual of employment opportunities, or otherwise adversely affect
his status as an employee[.]

D.C. Code §2-1402.11(a)(1). The DCHRA further makes it unlawful "for any
person to aid, abet, invite, compel, or coerce the doing of any of the acts forbidden"
by the Act. *Id.* §2-1402.62. The DCHRA defines "employer" as "any person
who, for compensation, employs an individual, . . . [or] any person acting in the
interest of such employer, directly or indirectly." *Id.* §2-1401.02. As the foregoing
citations make clear, the DCHRA is apparently not limited to constraining only the
employing entity, but extends as well to "any person acting in the interest of such
an employer," as well as "any person" who aids, abets, or otherwise assists
in violating the DCHRA.

This broad definition appears to allow suit against individuals, especially
when compared to Title VII's definition of employer. Title VII defines "employer"
as "a person engaged in an industry affecting commerce who has fifteen or more
employees . . . and *any agent of such a person.*" 42 U.S.C. §2000e(b). Generally,
courts to construe the italicized language have held that "the obvious purpose
of this agent provision was to incorporate respondeat superior liability into the
statute," *Gary v. Long,* 313 U.S. App. D.C. 403, 411 (1995) (citation omitted), and that
"individual employees cannot be held liable under Title VII." *Sheridan v. E.I.
DuPont de Nemours & Co.,* 100 F.3d 1061, 1077-1078 (3d Cir. 1996). The DCHRA
is not confined to cover only the acts of "agents," but by its terms applies to "*any
person*" acting in the interest of an employer or who otherwise aids and abets
prohibited conduct. Thus, based on its plain language, the DCHRA appears to
apply to any employee—even nonmanagerial employees—who are deemed to
have discriminated, or aided in discrimination, if the employee is also "acting
in the interest" of an employer.

B. Cases to Construe the DCHRA Have Allowed Suit to Proceed Against Partners, Supervisors, Managers, and Executive Officers in Their Individual Capacity.

The majority of cases to consider the question of an individual's amenability to
suit under the DCHRA have concluded that a case under that statute may properly
be brought against individuals. *See, e.g., Purcell v. Thomas,* 928 A.2d 699, 715 (D.C.
2007) ("[W]e hold that because Mr. Purcell was a high level official of [the corporate defendant] who exercised extensive supervisory, management and administrative authority over the corporation, he was individually liable to Ms. Thomas
under the DCHRA"); Wallace v. Skadden, Arps, Slate, Meagher & Flom, 715 A.2d
873, 888 (D.C. 1998) (holding that partners of law firm could be liable in individual
capacity under DCHRA); *but see Hunter v. Ark Restaurants Corp.,* 3 F. Supp. 2d 9,
15-18 (D.D.C. 1998) (holding that individual employees cannot be liable under

DCHRA);[1] Hodges v. Wash. Tennis Serv. Intl. 870 F. Supp. 386, 387 (D.D.C. 1994) (dismissing an individual defendant, who was "not a proper party because neither Title VII, 42 U.S.C. § 1981, nor the District of Columbia Human Rights law creates grounds for a cognizable claim against a co-worker").

1. The *Purcell* Decision Constitutes the Most Recent Interpretation of the DCHRA.

The *Purcell* case provides the most recent analysis of whether a DCHRA claim can be asserted against an individual. In that case, the court squarely considered whether Purcell, an individual and supervisor of the plaintiff, could be liable under the provisions of the DCHRA. *Purcell*, 928 A.2d at 702. In that case, the plaintiff alleged that Purcell made numerous sexual advances toward her, continually made inappropriate comments, and eventually terminated her for refusing to give in to his demands. *Id.* at 703-706. Purcell was the president, COO, controlling shareholder, and director of Fedora, the company for which the plaintiff worked. *Id.* at 715. Purcell was also the plaintiff's supervisor. *Id.* The court held that Purcell "was individually liable to Ms. Thomas under the DCHRA" because he was "acting, directly or indirectly, in the interest of Fedora and hence fell within DCHRA's definition of employer." *Id.*

In so holding, the court referred to its decision in *Wallace*, in which law partners were found to be "employers" under the DCHRA. *Id.* at 714 (citing *Wallace*, 715 A.2d at 888-889). Next, the court observed that the District Court for the District of Columbia "has found that supervisors are subject to individual liability." *Id.* at 715 (citing *Mitchell v. Natl. R.R. Passenger Corp.*, 407 F. Supp. 2d 213 (D.D.C. 2005); *MacIntosh v. Bldg. Owners & Managers Assn.*, 335 F. Supp. 2d 223 (D.D.C. 2005); and *Lance v. United Mine Workers of Am. 1974 Pension Trust*, 400 F. Supp. 2d 29 (D.D.C. 2005)). The court also noted that "[o]ther jurisdictions have imposed individual liability upon management and supervisory employees under state law in employment discrimination cases." *Id.* at 716 (citing cases).

2. The *Wallace* Decision Was the first Decision to Allow Individual Liability Under the DCHRA, and Is the Starting Point for Nearly All Subsequent Cases.

As with the *Purcell* decision, many cases to find individual liability under the DCHRA have cited to *Wallace* as important, if not dispositive, of their analysis. *See, e.g., Mitchell*, 407 F. Supp. 2d at 241 (discussing *Wallace*); *MacIntosh*, 335 F. Supp. 2d at 227-228 (discussing *Wallace*); *Lance*, 400 F. Supp. 2d at 31 (discussing *Wallace*). As such, a discussion of the *Wallace* decision is appropriate.

In *Wallace*, a former Skadden Arps attorney filed suit against the law firm and some of its individual partners for various causes of action, including defamation and violation of the DCHRA. *Wallace*, 715 A.2d at 875-876. After a series of procedural machinations that are not germane to the present discussion, the trial judge dismissed Wallace's DCHRA claim against the three Skadden Arps partners, holding that the individuals were "not amenable to suit in their

---

1. *Hunter* was decided before the final *Wallace* opinion was published.

individual capacities." *Id.* at 887. The plaintiff appealed, and the appellate court reversed.

In deciding that the individual partners could be liable under the DCHRA, the court focused on the language of the statute prohibiting "any person acting in the interest of such employer, directly or indirectly," from violating the provisions of the DCHRA. *Id.* at 888. The court attributed the "normal everyday meaning" to this language and concluded "that the partners fall within the ambit of the statute." *Id.* The court further noted that if the quoted language "does not extend to a partner in a law firm, it is difficult to conceive of any person to whom it would apply." *Id.*

The court then bolstered its conclusion by referencing the "aiding and abetting" language of the DCHRA. *Id.* ("Moreover, if Skadden, Arps unlawfully discriminated . . . then the partners who carried out the allegedly discriminatory acts aided and abetted the employer's discrimination. . . ."). The court further stated that the individual partners could be liable for violating the DCHRA under the "aiding and abetting" section "[e]ven if [the court] were to assume that the individual partners are not employers." *Id.*

The *Wallace* court then rejected the defendants' argument that the DCHRA is patterned on, and should be construed like, Title VII. *Id.* at 888-889. The *Wallace* court conceded that, in interpreting the DCHRA, courts have generally looked to, and in appropriate cases adopted, Title VII decisions. *Id.* at 889 n. 31. The court observed that the majority of relevant Title VII decisions "have held that individual employees cannot be held liable under Title VII." *Id.* at 888-889. However, the *Wallace* court declined to follow Title VII precedent because that legislation "does not contain the phrase 'any person acting in the interest of such employer,'" and because "there is no provision in Title VII proscribing 'aiding and abetting.'" *Id.* at 889. The court observed that although Title VII does define "employer" to include "any agent" of an employer, "'the obvious purpose of this agent provision was to incorporate *respondeat superior* liability into the statute.'" *Id.* at 889 n. 32 (citing cases). In contrast, the court reasoned, the plain language of the DCHRA includes "within the term 'employer' any person who acts on the employer's behalf." *Id.* As such, the DCHRA has a broader applicability than its federal counterpart.

3. All Cases to Allow Individual Liability Under the DCHRA Have Involved Managerial or Supervisory Employees.

Notably, in both the *Purcell* and *Wallace* decisions, the courts did not rely on the individual defendants' supervisory or managerial authority in deciding that the individuals were amenable to suit under the DCHRA. Indeed, as was discussed earlier, the plain language of the statute appears to allow *any individual*—regardless of status as a supervisor—to be liable under the DCHRA. Notwithstanding the plain language of the statute, however, there does not appear to be a case in which an individual, nonsupervisory employee was found to be liable under the DCHRA.

In the cases considering whether individuals can be sued under the DCHRA, the individual is almost always a high-level manager or company executive. For example:

- *Wallace*, 715 A.2d at 889: "[W]e therefore hold that the Skadden Arps *partners* were properly joined as defendants." (emphasis added)

- *Martini v. Fed. Natl. Mortgage Assn.*, 977 F. Supp. 464, 479 (D.D.C. 1997): "[T]he Court concludes that individual *supervisors* can be held liable for their acts of discrimination." (emphasis added)
- *Russ v. Van Scoyoc Assocs., Inc.*, 59 F. Supp. 2d 20, 24-26 (D.D.C. 1999): following *Martini*, and allowing suit under the DCHRA to be brought against Stuart Van Scoyoc, the *president of the corporation* that employed the plaintiff and plaintiff's supervisor.
- *MacIntosh*, 355 F. Supp. 2d at 227-28: relying on *Wallace* and finding that the *Executive Director* and *Vice President of Advocacy and Research* for plaintiff's employer could be sued in their individual capacities under the DCHRA.
- *Lance*, 400 F. Supp. 2d at 32: citing *MacIntosh* as stating that "a plaintiff [may] maintain suit against individual *supervisors* in a DCHRA action"; and finding *MacIntosh* consistent with *Russ*, "in which this court held that under the DCHRA a *supervisor* could be sued in his individual capacity." (emphasis added)
- *Mitchell*, 407 F. Supp. 2d at 241: reasoning that "[t]he text and purpose of the DCHRA, and *Wallace*, do not suggest that it would be appropriate to follow Title VII here and preclude a claim against individual *management* and *supervisory* employees involved in committing the allegedly discriminatory conduct"; holding that "Green [the former *director of the Workforce Development* unit in the HR Department] and Porter [the *Vice President of the HR Department*] . . . are proper defendants in plaintiff's DCHRA claim." (emphasis added)

Indeed, even the magistrate judge's decision in our case suggested that only management or supervisory employees could be defendants in Smith's DCHRA claim. *See Smith v. Cafe Asia*, 598 F. Supp. 2d 45, 48-49 (D.D.C. 2009). ("[T]he amended complaint alleges that the additional individual defendants were *managers* . . . the facts alleged regarding these *supervisory management employees* reflect that they acted in the interest of their employer . . . [whether] the individual employees fit that definition is not to be resolved at this stage.") (emphasis added).

Just as no case has ever held that a nonsupervisory employee is liable under the DCHRA, no case has stated that such employees are exempt from liability. Furthermore, no case has commented on whether an individual defendant must be the *plaintiff's* supervisor or whether *any* supervisor is a proper defendant under the DCHRA.

V. CONCLUSION

Although the plain language of the DCHRA allows for any individual to be liable for discrimination, all cases to construe the DCHRA in the context of individual's amenability to suit have involved a managerial employee. There is no authority addressing whether the individual sued under the DCHRA must be one of the plaintiff's supervisors.

For questions regarding the foregoing, please contact Adam Associate.

MEMORANDUM

TO: Jayne Taylor Kacer
FROM: Regan Dean
RE: Jeffrey Bing—Claim of Self-defense

Question Presented

Will Mr. Bing's act of shooting Mr. Geller be protected by the Illinois Self-defense Statute, which specifies that an individual is justified in the use of force that is intended or likely to cause death or great bodily harm if the individual (1) reasonably believes that he or she is in imminent danger of death or great bodily harm and (2) reasonably believes that such force is necessary to prevent imminent death or great bodily harm to himself (or herself) or another, or the commission of a forcible felony? 720 Ill. Comp. Stat. 5/7-1, 1961.

  (1) Did Bing reasonably believe that he was in imminent danger of great bodily harm or death if his assailant was armed with a deadly weapon, had already cut another, was undeterred by attempts to avoid a confrontation, and had a known history of violent and explosive behavior?
  (2) Did Bing have a reasonable belief that deadly force was necessary if he made numerous attempts to avoid the use of such force either by apologizing, retreating, or warning that he would retaliate if necessary prior to shooting?

Short Answer

Yes, our client has a strong claim that he acted in self-defense in accordance with the elements of the Self-defense Statute.

  (1) First, Bing had a reasonable belief that he was in imminent danger of death or great bodily harm because his assailant was armed with a deadly weapon. The assailant continued to advance on our client despite knowledge that Bing was armed, threats against Bing's life were made by his assailant, and his assailant was well known as a violent individual.
  (2) Second, our client had a reasonable belief that deadly force was necessary to prevent imminent danger of death or great bodily harm because all of the efforts he employed to avoid the use of such force proved futile, including defendant's attempts to apologize, retreat, and warn the assailant.

Statement of Facts

Our client, Jeffrey Bing, has been charged with the murder of his close friend of six years, John Geller. Bing claims he acted in self-defense. Bing and Geller had a friendship that was occasionally marred by violence. They attended college together (four years ago), where Geller ran cross-country. During college Bing sustained injuries (swollen knuckles, bloody noses, black eye) resulting from fights with Geller (6', 190 pounds), who was slightly larger than Bing (5'11", 175 pounds). However, more serious injuries were always averted when Bing, who is not particularly athletic, pleaded with Geller to stop. They have not had any fights since college, but one year ago Bing and another friend, Newton, had to pull Geller off his roommate after a violent fight wherein the roommate suffered a broken rib, black eye, and multiple bruises.

On the day of the incident, Bing and Geller were on a camping trip with their friend, Mr. Newton. They stopped five minutes from their lodge because Bing was winded. Newton then began joking with Bing about Jill Jacoby. Jacoby was Geller's former girlfriend with whom Bing had recently spent a weekend in New York. Bing previously concealed this information from Geller, and in fact had lied to Geller about the identity of his New York companion. Upon learning the truth, Geller became enraged. Newton later told the police that Geller "went beserk."

Mr. Geller pounced on Bing, threw him on the ground, and began beating Bing's face with his fists. Bing apologized for his actions, but Geller continued to beat Bing. Newton attempted to stop Geller by shouting at him to "calm down," but Geller replied: "Stay out of this. My fight is with Jeff." Newton attempted to physically separate the men and, in doing so, was cut on the arm by Geller, who brandished a hunting knife he retrieved from his knapsack. Newton then decided to run for assistance to the lodge nearby and stated that he had "never seen [Geller] like this before." While Newton left the scene for help, Geller, who continued to brandish his knife, and Bing, at this point unarmed, began circling each other. Geller attempted to charge at Bing, and when the men were separated by about twenty feet, Bing produced a gun from his knapsack that he had carried with him for safety while hiking. Bing attempted to keep Geller at bay by waving his gun around as the men continued to circle each other for about five minutes. During this time, Bing pleaded with Geller to "calm down," but Geller told Bing that he would "kill [Bing] for this." Bing warned that he would use his gun if necessary to which Geller replied, "Only one of us is getting out of here alive." At that moment, Geller charged at Bing, and when Geller was between five and ten feet away from Bing, Mr. Bing shot Geller, pulling the trigger once.

Discussion

Mr. Bing acted in self-defense under the Illinois statute for "use of force in defense of person" (hereinafter Self-defense Statute). Pursuant to the Self-defense Statute, Bing is "justified in the use of force which is intended or likely to cause death or great bodily harm only if he reasonably believes that such force is necessary to prevent imminent death or great bodily harm to himself or another, or the commission of a forcible felony." 720 Ill. Comp. Stat. 5/7-1. In order to successfully claim self-defense, two elements must be met, namely that Bing maintained a reasonable belief that he was in imminent danger of death or great bodily harm and also that Bing reasonably believed the degree of force used was necessary to prevent such harm to himself. If belief is merely subjective, Bing cannot claim self-defense. That Mr. Bing subjectively believed that he was in imminent danger of death or great bodily harm is presumed to be true given the facts and is not addressed in this memorandum. This memorandum will discuss whether Mr. Bing had a reasonable belief that he was in danger of death or great bodily harm and that Bing reasonably believed the degree of force used was necessary to prevent such harm.

Mr. Bing Had a Reasonable Belief that He Was in Imminent Danger of Death or Great Bodily Harm.

Mr. Bing had a reasonable belief that he was in imminent danger of either death or great bodily harm. In determining whether a reasonable belief exists, the courts evaluate various factors including whether the assailant had a weapon, whether the assailant was deterred by attempts made to de-escalate the situation, the known history of violence of one or both parties, the comparative physical size of the attacker and the defendant, the mental state of the assailant, and whether the defendant was cornered. Geller not only brandished a weapon, but used it to harm a third party. Geller was undeterred by the efforts made by Bing to curtail the situation. There is a known history of violence by Geller directed toward Bing and others. Geller was said to be acting in an irrational manner, and Geller was a bigger and more athletic man than Bing.

A person reasonably believes that s/he is in imminent danger of death or great bodily harm when s/he is outnumbered by drunken, armed assailants who are undeterred by attempts to avoid a confrontation. In *People v. S.M.*, 416 N.E.2d 1212 (Ill. App. 1st Dist. 1981), the defendant's belief that he was in imminent danger of death or great bodily harm was found to be reasonable because he was outnumbered four to one and cornered by his assailants; his attackers had been drinking and were all bigger than he; the assailants had weapons, which they threw at the defendant; and his attackers were not discouraged by the defendant's gun nor by his warning that he would use it. In *S.M.*, the defendant made an offensive comment to a group of four older, more athletic boys after he was nearly hit by their car. The defendant immediately apologized for his comment upon realizing that the boys were upset. However, the boys advanced on the defendant, who then fled. The assailants continued to chase the defendant, throwing asphalt and tin cans at him. The defendant yelled out for help, but was eventually cornered and unable to escape. The defendant had a gun because he was initially intending to hunt for raccoons, and he brandished it to scare off his attackers. However, the assailants were unfazed by the gun and continued to advance, which prompted the defendant to fire a warning shot and verbally warn the attackers that he would shoot if necessary. Upon realizing that the attackers remained undeterred in their pursuit, the defendant shot and killed two of the assailants and wounded two others. The jury found the defendant guilty of the commission of two counts of aggravated battery. The court of appeal reversed, holding that the defendant's fear of imminent great bodily harm or death was reasonable under the circumstances. 93 Ill. App. 3d 105.

A person has a reasonable belief that s/he is in imminent danger of death or great bodily harm when there is a known history of the assailant's propensity for violent behavior. In *People v. Shipp*, 367 N.E.2d 966 (Ill. App. 2d Dist. 1977), the defendant knew the assailant was capable of causing her great bodily harm or death with or without a weapon. The assailant was undeterred in his pursuit of the defendant and made threatening comments to the life of both the defendant and her male friend. The facts of *Shipp* describe a long history of violence between the assailant and the defendant. The defendant sustained numerous severe injuries resulting from beatings and gunshots fired at her by the assailant, whom she knew had killed his first wife. Eventually, the defendant obtained a restraining order against the assailant, which was meant to prevent the assailant from harassing, annoying, or talking to the defendant. However, this did not prevent the assailant from continuing to harm the defendant both verbally and physically. The assailant made numerous threats against the defendant's life, including holding a knife to her throat and telling her that he would cut her throat and go to the penitentiary. The assailant further warned her that he would kill her if he ever caught her with another man. On the night in question, after leaving a bar, the assailant went to the home of a man with whom the defendant was spending the evening. When the assailant entered the bedroom, the defendant became frightened and picked up a gun; she backed away from the assailant who continued to walk toward her with his hands in his pockets, not revealing whether he was armed. The assailant continued to approach her despite verbal warnings not to come any closer or the defendant would shoot, and then cornered the defendant saying that he was going to "take care" of both the defendant and her male companion who was hiding under the bed. When the assailant was six feet away from the defendant she shot and killed him. The jury acquitted the defendant of murder and unlawful use of weapons, but convicted her of voluntary manslaughter. The Appellate Court reversed, and the court believed the defendant's fear of imminent danger of great bodily harm to be reasonable. The court stated, "It is the defendant's perception of danger, and not the actual peril, which was dispositive."

Application of the factors recognized in the aforementioned cases to the Bing situation leaves little doubt that the court will find that Bing's fear that he was in imminent danger of death or great bodily harm was reasonable. Geller had a deadly weapon, which he was clearly not afraid to use, as evidenced when he cut Newton's arm. In *People v. S.M.*, the weapons used by the assailants, asphalt and tin cans, do not merit the same potential to cause death or great bodily harm as a knife. And in *People v. Shipp*, it was unclear if there even was a weapon, yet the court found the defendant's fear to be reasonable. Thus, the fear of a defendant whose attacker is armed with a deadly weapon that he has used on a third party will most likely be considered reasonable by the court.

Like the attackers in *S.M.* and *Shipp*, Geller was undeterred despite both Newton's and Bing's attempts to calm him down, the fact that Bing had a gun, and that Bing gave several warnings that he would shoot Geller if necessary. Based on prior altercations involving Geller and Bing, Bing's efforts to plead with Geller to calm down would have been sufficient, yet his employment of those efforts immediately prior to the shooting proved futile. In fact, Geller continued to make threats against Bing's life and charge at Bing while brandishing his weapon following Bing's warnings.

Like the defendant in *Shipp*, Bing had knowledge of Geller's propensity for violent behavior and knew firsthand that he was capable of inflicting harm upon another person when angry. The court in *People v. Shipp* believed such knowledge justifies the reasonableness of one's fear of great bodily harm.

Although Geller had not been drinking, as had the assailants in *S.M.* and *Shipp*, Geller was enraged and consumed by an unpredictable state of mind. The notion that Geller was acting out of character was reinforced by Newton's comment, "I've never seen him like this before." Additionally, while each court makes reference to the stature of the parties, it does not appear to be a primary factor in their determination of whether there was a reasonable belief of imminent danger of death or great bodily harm. There was only a slight disparity in the physical size of Bing and Geller; therefore this will not be a compelling argument for our case.

In determining whether the defendant had a reasonable belief that he was in imminent danger of death or great bodily harm, the court in *People v. Moore*, 357 N.E.2d 566 (Ill. App. 1st Dist. 1976), considered many of the same factors as the courts in *S.M.* and *Shipp*, namely whether the assailant had a weapon, whether the assailant was undeterred, the comparative physical size, and a history of violent behavior. Between the parties the defendant had previously engaged in a physical altercation with the decedent in which the defendant was the aggressor. On the night in question, the defendant said something that caused the decedent to get upset with him. The defendant then informed all present that he had a gun. He left the scene and went home to retrieve his gun. Upon returning, the decedent threatened to beat up the defendant. The onlookers held the decedent away from the defendant to avoid a fight. The defendant had an opportunity at this moment to leave and put the gun away, which he was encouraged to do by the onlookers. However, the defendant remained outside and stated that he would shoot the decedent if he came near him. The defendant eventually shot the decedent while he was fifty feet away. The court held that there was no reasonable belief that the defendant was in imminent danger of great bodily harm or death and upheld the jury's finding of voluntary manslaughter. The decedent was unarmed, there was substantial distance between the men at the time of the shooting, the defendant did not attempt to flee, and the defendant stated his intention to harm the decedent. The court acknowledged the disparity in stature of the parties, but said that despite the fact that the decedent was advantaged in physical size, this factor was irrelevant because only the defendant was armed.

The *Moore* case is distinguishable from the Bing situation as the defendant in *Moore* was the aggressor, while Bing acted in self-defense. Additionally, unlike *Moore*, Geller was between five and ten feet away and charging at Bing with a deadly weapon at the moment Bing pulled the trigger. In *Moore*, the threat to the defendant was less imminent because there was fifty feet between parties, the decedent was unarmed, and there was an opportunity for the defendant to avoid the situation altogether.

Mr. Bing Reasonably Believed Force Was Necessary to Prevent Imminent Death or Great Bodily Harm to Himself.

Bing reasonably believed that his use of force was necessary to prevent imminent death or great bodily harm to himself under the circumstances of his situation. The court determines whether the necessity to prevent imminent death or great bodily harm has been fulfilled by examining the efforts made by the defendant, such as apologizing, retreating, giving verbal warnings, brandishing, or firing a warning shot to avoid a physical confrontation. Bing made several such attempts. Bing apologized to Geller, he pleaded with Geller to calm down, and he attempted to keep distance between them. Additionally Bing brandished a weapon to scare Geller off and warned that he would shoot if necessary. Each attempt Bing made was ignored by Geller, who persisted in his advancement.

A person reasonably believes that deadly force is necessary to prevent imminent death or great bodily harm to himself or another when the defendant makes repeated efforts to avoid an altercation, such as apologizing, retreating, yelling for help, pleading with attackers to stop, brandishing a weapon, giving verbal warnings as well as firing a warning shot. In *S.M.*, the defendant was clearly desperate and did not want to resort to such action, but under the circumstances, felt that it was necessary. The defendant in *S.M.* employed each of the described efforts to avoid an altercation; additionally, he did not advance toward the attackers and he unsuccessfully sought help from the onlookers before he resorted to shooting his assailants. The court acknowledged each effort made by the defendant to resolve the situation and held that the defendant maintained a reasonable belief that the force employed was necessary.

To determine whether a person reasonably believes that deadly force is necessary to prevent imminent death or great bodily harm, the court in *People v. Shipp* examined the avoidance attempts made by the defendant. Upon the assailant's entrance, the defendant in *Shipp* brandished a weapon, presupposing a threat. The defendant then verbally warned her attacker, telling him that he was violating a restraining order. She pleaded for him to stay away and to the extent that it was possible, the defendant attempted to keep distance between her and the assailant by moving backwards, and it was not until she was cornered that she shot him. There were fewer efforts to avoid the use of a firearm by the defendant in this case than in *S.M.*, but the ruling was the same. The court ruled that the defendant was justified in her actions, stating that her fear was "highly reasonable under the circumstances" and that her actions were necessary.

Bing engaged in many of the same efforts employed by the defendants in the cited cases with no success. For example, like the defendants in *S.M.* and *Shipp*, Bing apologized to his assailant and pleaded with him to calm down. Similarly, Bing retreated to the best of his ability, brandished a gun, and gave verbal warning that he would shoot prior to doing so.

In determining whether a person reasonably believes that deadly force is necessary to prevent imminent death or great bodily harm to himself (or herself) or another, the court in *People v. Moore* examined avoidance techniques. The defendant in *Moore* had ample opportunity to avoid the situation and did not. There was no pleading, apologizing, warning, or retreat, and Moore was recognized as the aggressor in this situation. The court emphasized these facts: Moore could have avoided the altercation, he expressed intent to shoot the decedent, and he shot him from fifty feet away. Moore's use of force was not found to be reasonable under the circumstances because he demonstrated intent to cause harm instead of making efforts to avoid using force.

The court should recognize the significant variances in the two situations and find that, while no reasonable belief of the necessity to use deadly force existed for Moore, it did exist for Bing. Unlike the defendant in *Moore*, Bing made repeated attempts to avoid the use of force, while in *Moore*, the defendant demonstrated intent to rely on an unjustifiable amount of force. The disparity in the distance between the parties at the moment the force was used and Bing's attempts to reconcile the conflict without force will differentiate the cases and demonstrate that Bing should be acquitted of voluntary manslaughter because a reasonable belief to justify his use of force existed.

Conclusion

Bing can successfully claim self-defense. He reasonably believed that he was in imminent danger of death or great bodily harm because his assailant was armed with a deadly weapon, his assailant was undeterred despite knowledge that Bing was armed, he had a history of violent behavior, and he demonstrated an unpredictable state of mind. He also reasonably believed that deadly force was necessary to prevent imminent death or great bodily harm to himself because all of the efforts he employed to avoid the use of such force proved futile.

MEMORANDUM

TO: Jayne Taylor Kacer
FROM: Regan Dean
DATE: November 25, 2002
RE: Andrea Johnston—Defense to Claim of Negligence

Question(s) Presented

Is Andrea Johnston liable for negligence?

1. Was it foreseeable that her car would be stolen when she parked her highly visible Porsche sportscar on a public street with the keys in the sun visor and the doors unlocked in an area she was unfamiliar with as to its reputation and crime rate, while she entered a store with the intention of being away from her car for a few minutes?
2. Was it foreseeable that an unauthorized person would cause injury while driving Ms. Johnston's Porsche, which is not an inherently dangerous vehicle and requires no special knowledge to operate other than that required to drive an automobile?

Short Answer

No, Ms. Johnston will most likely not be found liable for negligence.

1. It was not foreseeable that her car would be stolen because Ms. Johnston was unaware of the crime rate in the neighborhood, she intended to leave her car unattended on a public street for only a few minutes, and the car is one that a reasonable person would not expect to be stolen because it is so readily identifiable.
2. It was not foreseeable that an unauthorized person would cause injury while driving Ms. Johnston's car because the car requires no special skill to operate, nor is it an inherently dangerous vehicle.

Statement of Facts

Our client, Andrea Johnston, is alleged to be negligent resulting in injuries sustained by the plaintiff, Bonnie Smythe, from a car accident in which an unauthorized person operating Ms. Johnston's car collided with plaintiff's parked car. Ms. Johnston is a well-known professional racecar driver who resides in Florida. The vehicle involved in the accident is Ms. Johnston's lipstick red Porsche, which she purchased two years ago. The Porsche has been modified to include wing-like appendages attached to the doors and a manual transmission engine traditionally found in racecars. The body of the car has been reinforced with roll bars added to better withstand an impact from a collision. Additionally, the car is able to accelerate to speeds over 185 mph. The car has had celebrity exposure and is widely recognized because Ms. Johnston has raced it in various celebrity pro-am races, and the car has also been featured on the David Letterman show in a skit involving Ms. Johnston.

On the day in question, Ms. Johnston was in Missouri to attend a race and stopped at a store, Party City, on her way to the race to pick up some refreshments.

Party City is located on Delmont Street, in the Central East End, which has undergone a recent transformation from a seedy, dilapidated area to a trendy neighborhood with many popular restaurants and shops. Despite its renovated appeal, the area is three blocks from the highest-crime community in St. Louis, an area called Crimtown. This area has received much publicity because of the propensity for nearby high-schoolers to steal cars. Ms. Johnston, being from Florida, was unaware of the former reputation of Delmont Street and that of its adjoining community, Crimtown. She intended to be inside Party City for only a couple of minutes to pick out a specific item. Ms. Johnston parked her car on a public street in front of the store, rolled up her windows, but placed her keys in the sun visor above the driver's seat and left the doors unlocked. While inside, Ms. Johnston checked on her car one time and it was empty. Ms. Johnston was slightly delayed while in the store, but left the car alone outside for no more than eight to ten minutes total.

When Ms. Johnston drove up to Party City, a woman standing at the bus stop across the street watched Ms. Johnston put her keys on the visor and enter the store. The thirty-five-year-old woman, Barbara Mandible, was late for a paid singing engagement and decided to take Ms. Johnston's car in order to arrive on time. Ms. Mandible drove the car over the 55 mph speed limit and was spotted by a police officer who followed her. Mandible then began to increase her speed to over 100 mph and spun out of control, colliding with the plaintiff's parked car occupied by the plaintiff. The plaintiff sustained numerous injuries when she was thrown from her Volkswagen, which was flattened by the Porsche. Upon recovery, the plaintiff will forever walk with a limp.

Discussion

Ms. Johnston will most likely not be found liable for negligence. A Missouri statute formerly addressed the issue of liability for car owners who left their vehicles unlocked, unattended with the keys readily available in Mo. Rev. Stat. § 304.150 (repealed by L.1996). The statute made it a misdemeanor for motor vehicle operators to leave the car keys in the ignition while unattended on a highway of any city with a population over 75,000, but stated that evidence of the statute and/or its violation was barred in a civil action. The statute was repealed in 1997 and will therefore not factor into the analysis contained in this memorandum. The fact that this statute was repealed, however, does seem favorable for our client, as it suggests that there is no longer any criminal liability for leaving a car unattended with the keys in the ignition. Prior case law in this area reveals that individuals who leave their vehicle unattended with the keys in the ignition are not found to be negligent when unauthorized third persons steal the car and operate it negligently. The determinative issues that will be discussed in this memorandum are the defendant's (1) foreseeability of theft and (2) foreseeability of injury resulting from unauthorized negligent operation.

Issue I. It Was Not Foreseeable that Ms. Johnston's Car Would be Stolen.

It was not foreseeable to Ms. Johnston that theft would result from leaving her keys in the sun visor while she left her car unattended for what she anticipated would be a few minutes in an area that appeared safe. In determining whether it was foreseeable that theft would result the courts evaluate various factors including the type of neighborhood, the defendant's knowledge of the neighborhood's reputation, the location in which the car was parked (i.e., a public road or a private street), the length of time the vehicle was left unattended, and the type of vehicle. Here, Johnston was new to the area and unfamiliar with the neighborhood's reputation. All Johnston could know about the area was from what she saw, and the neighborhood appeared safe. Further, she parked her car on a public street, which would seem to deter potential thieves knowing that there were many potential witnesses. Ms. Johnston left the car for only a few minutes while she entered a store nearby and did not intend for it to be unattended long. And lastly, Johnston's car is one that stands out; it is highly recognizable and would therefore seem to be a poor choice of prey for thieves as they would likely be readily caught.

It was not foreseeable that theft will result from parking a truck in an unlocked garage stall next to a business on private property with the key in the ignition despite knowledge by the defendant that the establishment had been burglarized multiple times and the truck stolen twice in the past. In *Kaelin v. Nuelle*, 537 S.W.2d 226 (Mo. App. St. Louis Dist. 1976), the defendant, who owned and operated a service station for forty-three years, customarily parked his truck in this manner in an unlocked garage. He had begun to experience thefts five years prior to the incident, but continued to park his vehicle in the same manner. On the night in question, the defendant parked his car, and it was stolen several hours later by a thief who proceeded to collide with another automobile driven by the plaintiff's husband, who was killed. The thief escaped the scene of the accident, and the plaintiff filed suit against the defendant for negligence in failing to foresee that his car was likely to be stolen because of the history of burglaries that had occurred on his property. The trial court entered a directed verdict for the defendant and the Missouri Court of Appeals affirmed, holding that the plaintiff "as a matter of law, failed to adduce sufficient evidence of negligence or proximate causation to make a submissible case even though there was some evidence that defendant's place of business had been burglarized and the truck stolen in the past." *Kaelin*, 537 S.W.2d at 231.

It was not foreseeable that theft would result from parking an unattended, unusually dangerous vehicle in a public place unlocked and ready to operate when owner had knowledge that for a period of over one month individuals had climbed onto and operated the vehicles without permission. In *Zuber v. Clarkson Construction Co.*, 315 S.W.2d 727 (Mo. 1958), the defendant parked tractor-trailers in a public area over nights and weekends while constructing a levee. The trailers were large "earth moving" machines that required special skill to operate, yet were left unlocked and ready to operate. The defendant company had knowledge that curious passersby would climb on the trailers and operate them, yet they continued to park their trailers in this fashion. On the day in question, the plaintiff's son and his cousin engaged in this behavior, and the plaintiff's son died as a result of his lack of knowledge in operating such a dangerous vehicle and subsequent inability to curtail its movement. The plaintiff brought suit against the defendant company for negligence in his son's death because the defendant left the vehicles unlocked in an accessible place, ready to operate with knowledge of prior attempts by unauthorized individuals to operate such vehicles. The trial court overruled the defendant's motion for a directed verdict, and the Supreme

Court reversed, holding that at the time of the decedent's death, he "was engaged in committing a criminal act, to wit: Driving, operating, using or tampering with a motor vehicle and trailer without the permission of the owner and, as a matter of law, no duty was owed by defendant to plaintiff's decedent to avoid negligently injuring him or causing his death." *Id.* at 732. Therefore, because the defendant owed no duty to the plaintiff's decedent, it cannot be found liable for negligence.

Theft was not foreseeable when an owner parks his Cadillac in an exposed and readily accessible parking garage with the keys in the ignition and the doors unlocked for an unstated period of time knowing there had been other vehicles stolen from the garage in the recent past. In *Dix v. Motor Market, Inc.*, 540 S.W.2d 927 (Mo. App. St. Louis Dist. 1976), the defendant parked his car in a parking garage with the keys in the ignition and the doors unlocked, behavior that was mandated by the garage owners whom the driver paid to park in that garage. The car was stolen by a thief who, while attempting to flee from the police, got into an automobile accident and killed the plaintiff's husband. Both the car owner and the garage owner were sued for negligence in failure to safeguard against theft of cars by leaving keys in the ignition and the car doors unlocked in an accessible garage where the garage owner knew and the car owner "should have known" about a history of stolen cars from the vicinity. The trial court granted the defendant's demurrer, and the Court of Appeals affirmed, stating "the defendant was under no duty to discover the presence of a thief in the vicinity where he parked his car." *Dix*, 540 S.W.2d at 930. The Court of Appeals further reasoned, "as a matter of law the duty of one who leaves keys in an unattended auto does not extend to a plaintiff injured in an accident with the thief driving the stolen auto." *Id.* at 931.

Prior case law reveals a potentially favorable outcome for our client. One fact that distinguishes our case from the other cases in a favorable manner is that Ms. Johnston did not leave her keys in the ignition of her vehicle; she attempted to conceal them by placing them in the sun visor above her seat. Although the car was unlocked and unattended with the keys inside, there was a seemingly greater effort to avoid car theft by removing them from the blatant view of potential thieves. In both *Kaelin* and *Dix*, there was no foreseeability of theft when the defendants left their keys in the ignition with the doors unlocked. While in *Zuber* there is no mention of keys, it is believed that vehicles of this type use starters not keys, which were connected and ready to operate at the time the vehicle was used. Considering there was no foreseeability of theft when keys are left in the ignition, our client's act of placing the keys in the sun visor should result in less foreseeability of theft.

In both *Kaelin* and *Dix*, cars were stolen from an area with a history of previous car thefts or burglaries, and the defendant in each case either knew this or had reason to know of it. In the *Zuber* case, the court found that the defendant was not guilty of negligence despite the fact that the defendant had knowledge that curious individuals had been tampering with the vehicles and operating them without permission and that the defendant had failed to attempt to abort this behavior. The area in our client's case had a history of car thefts by teenagers and has a notorious crime rate; however, our client was not privy to this information, as she is not from the area and had no reason to know the reputation of the neighborhood.

In both *Kaelin* and *Dix*, the vehicle was stolen from private property, while in *Zuber*, the vehicle rested on public property at the time of the theft. Yet in each case, the court found for the defendant. While location of the vehicle is a factor considered by the courts in determining whether there was foreseeability of theft, it does not appear to be outcome-determinative. Ms. Johnston parked her car on public property, which is an open and obvious location with both more accessibility and more witnesses. This factor does not appear to be especially critical particularly in light of the lack of foreseeability of theft decision rendered in *Zuber* where the vehicles were parked in a public location. This fact, coupled with the defendant's express knowledge that people were tampering with the vehicles, is decidedly a more serious situation than ours.

Ms. Johnston had no intention of being in the store for more than a few minutes. While she was delayed and therefore away from the car for slightly longer, she tried to keep an eye on the car while inside the store, and the car was actually unattended for only eight to ten minutes including the delay. In both *Kaelin* and *Zuber*, it is clear that the owner intended to leave the vehicles unattended for at least an entire night if not longer; in *Zuber*, the vehicles were unattended during entire weekends. While it is not made entirely clear what length of time the defendant in *Dix* intended for his car to be left unattended, it can be inferred from the fact that he paid for parking in a garage that it was meant to be unattended for a period of time exceeding a few minutes.

One last factor examined in determining the foreseeability of theft is the type of car driven by the defendant. Ms. Johnston drives a unique automobile that is highly recognizable not only because of its altered appearance, but also because of the media attention that Ms. Johnston has received, which has included her car. Although inviting curiosity, Ms. Johnston's car would seem to be an impractical choice for a thief because of the identity factor. The cars driven in both *Kaelin* and *Dix*, a pickup truck and Cadillac respectively, are more realistic prey because they are generic models and are found on the roads in abundance. The vehicle in *Zuber* may be more analogous to our client's car because of its unusual make and features, which would again seem to deter potential thieves based on the high level of attention one would receive simply by being seen in the vehicle. It is less foreseeable that thieves would target such easily recognizable vehicles.

Issue II: It Was Not Foreseeable that Injury Would Result When an Unauthorized Person Drove the Vehicle.

It was not foreseeable that an unauthorized driver would cause injury while driving the vehicle because Ms. Johnston's car is not an unusually dangerous car and requires no special skill to operate. Factors examined by the court to determine whether it was foreseeable to the defendant that injury could result include whether or not the vehicle was an inherently dangerous machine and whether it required special skill to operate. While Ms. Johnston's car has been equipped with an engine found in racing cars, which allows her vehicle to operate at over 185 mph, it is not inherently dangerous because of this feature. The car is able to function as a normal car, traveling at the speed limit. Additionally, the car does not require special skill to operate.

Pursuant to the decision rendered in *Zuber*, there is no foreseeability of injury when an unauthorized person operates an inherently dangerous "earth moving" vehicle, which rests on public property and requires familiarity with the technique of its operation. The vehicles in *Zuber* were large tractor-trailers known as "Euclids" (hereinafter "Eucs"), which intrigued the decedent and his cousin on the day in question to more closely examine and attempt to operate them. While the cousin of the decedent claimed to have driven one before, there is no evidence that either of the individuals who operated them on the day of the accident had ever operated a Euc before and therefore lacked the requisite skill; nor was there evidence that the users had permission from the defendant owner to operate any of the Eucs. Although the Eucs sat on public ground, the individuals' acts of climbing onto and operating them was found to be a trespass. In finding that the defendant was not liable for negligence because of lack of foreseeability of injury, the Missouri Supreme Court further stated that "no duty was owed by defendants to either (decedent or cousin) to protect them against their own criminal acts." *Zuber*, 315 S.W.2d at 735. The court reasons that the unauthorized acts of the plaintiff's son and his cousin do not demonstrate that the defendant was negligent with respect to the acts that caused the decedent's death.

There is foreseeability that injury will occur when an intoxicated, unauthorized driver operates an inherently dangerous commercial shuttle bus, which he has special skill to operate, belonging to the defendant company. In *Kuhn v. Budget Rent-a-Car*, 876 S.W.2d 668 (Mo. App. Western Dist. 1994), an employee for defendant allowed an intoxicated off-duty employee onto the company premises. The company manager learned that the individual was on the property in an inebriated state and did not request that he leave. The off-duty employee knew how to operate the shuttle bus and further, knew that the company left the keys in the vehicle's ignition; he drove the bus without permission off the company property and killed the plaintiff's decedent in a car accident. The trial court granted the defendant's motion for summary judgment, and the appellate court reversed and remanded, acknowledging that a genuine issue of triable fact does exist. The appellate court found that the trial court must determine whether the defendant company acted negligently in failing to prevent the intoxicated off-duty employee from entering the premises and operating a potentially dangerous vehicle that caused the death of the decedent. The court stated that by either failing to secure the vehicles or by allowing the off-duty employee on the premises, it was foreseeable that injury might occur.

Ms. Johnston's car does not qualify as an inherently dangerous vehicle when contrasted with the vehicles in these cases. While Johnston's car admittedly operates at high speeds, it is not a large vehicle capable of causing injury and damage to many people such as the vehicles described above. In both *Zuber* and *Kuhn*, the vehicles were both unusually large and used for purposes other than that of an automobile, namely carrying many passengers or digging up earth. While an argument may be made that if not for the racing engine in Ms. Johnston's car, the unauthorized driver would not have been able to slam into plaintiff's car at such a high speed, this argument should fail because at the time of the accident, the car was operating at just over 100 miles per hour, a speed that many cars are capable of reaching.

Similarly, Ms. Johnston's car does not require additional skill to operate other than that required to drive a car. The skill required to operate the vehicles in both *Zuber* and *Kuhn* was unique to each vehicle and therefore different than that required to drive a car. Therefore the court should not find that there is foreseeability of injury based on requisite skill to operate.

The varying outcomes in *Zuber* and *Kuhn* can perhaps be reconciled by acknowledging that while the vehicles were both inherently dangerous, the defendants in each case maintained a different responsibility because of where the accident occurred. The defendants in *Zuber* were entitled to park their vehicles on public property and therefore were not responsible for the intervening trespass. In *Kuhn*, the vehicles were parked on private property, and as such there was a higher duty to be responsible for the acts of individuals whom the defendants allowed onto their property. Thus, there was no duty attached to Ms. Johnston's behavior similar to the finding in *Zuber*. Ms. Johnston was entitled to park her car on a public road, and subsequent acts of injury to a third person based on a person's unauthorized use of the car would be the sole responsibility of the unauthorized person because of his or her criminal act in taking the car.

Conclusion

Based on precedential case law and, to a lesser extent, the state's reluctance to make it a criminal offense to leave one's keys in the ignition of an unlocked and unattended vehicle, Ms. Johnston will most likely not be found liable for negligence for the injuries sustained by the plaintiff. The negligence claim will fail because our client did not owe a duty to the plaintiff. Specifically, it was not foreseeable that Ms. Johnston's Porsche sports car would be stolen when she left her car unlocked with the keys in the sun visor while she entered a store for up to ten minutes in a seemingly safe neighborhood. Additionally the claim will fail because it was not foreseeable that once the car was stolen it would cause injury to a third person because it is not an inherently dangerous vehicle and does not require any kind of special skill to operate other than that required to drive a car.

Client Letters

The first two letters in this appendix are written for business clients. The first letter is written directly to a prospective client, offering advice on how to proceed in resolving a dispute. The second letter is written on behalf of a client to opposing counsel. Because that letter is written to another lawyer, you will notice that it includes case citations and in many ways reads like a memo or brief.

Thomas A. Vogele
tvogele@enterprisecounsel.com

April 27, 2009

**CONFIDENTIAL AND STRICTLY PRIVILEGED;
ATTORNEY-CLIENT COMMUNICATION**

Mr. Lance McCann   Mr. Kevin Norton
Chairman & CEO   President
Bright Art Skylights   Bright Art Skylights
18312 S. Ritchey Street   18312 S. Ritchey Street
Santa Ana, California 92705   Santa Ana, California 92705

Re: *Bright Art Skylights adv. Jackson Chemical, et al.*

Gentlemen:

It was a pleasure to meet both of you last Thursday and discuss your interest in retaining ECG to assist you in resolving a potential product/material warranty claim your firm has against Jackson Chemical Company ("Jackson") and Startek Corporation ("Startek").

As we discussed, and after speaking with Mr. Flannigan, here is an overview of how we view the dispute and how we recommend Bright Art proceed to resolve the dispute in the most effective and expeditious manner.

First, neither I nor Mr. Flannigan believes this problem necessarily must result in protracted and costly litigation. While large corporations such as Jackson and Startek often take a "hard-line" stance at the outset, based on your description of

Jackson's active involvement in specifying and supplying the defective material for your specialized requirements, Jackson's and/or Startek's liability seems clear. In the face of clear liability, even a large company can be persuaded that a fair and reasonable settlement is better than protracted litigation resulting in a potentially *"unreasonable"* damage award from a jury against an *"unreasonable"* defendant.

The key to persuading Jackson and Startek to accept your settlement demand is to have a complete and utter mastery of the facts and legal arguments on both sides of the dispute, to articulate a fair and defined statement of damages suffered as a result of their breach of warranty, and to present a highly professional, defined and commercially reasonable solution to the problem.

Faced with clear and potentially significant liability, and presented with a commercially reasonable solution, many companies will assess what is best for their own business interests and work out a settlement. This is particularly true when that company faces potentially greater risks in litigation, both to its sales and market value.

Jackson's and Startek's liability appears clear. By way of explanation, in a commercial transaction such as your purchase of specialty polymer/acrylic sheets, there are a number of warranties that can serve as the basis for recovering damages. Article II of the Uniform Commercial Code ("UCC") governs contracts involving goods with a value greater than $500.

UCC § 2-313 creates an express warranty any time a seller affirms a fact relating to the product's qualities or performance characteristics or where the seller provides a sample, performance specifications, or a description of the material such that a buyer, in this case Bright Art, relied on that specification or description. Nothing is required to create such an express warranty—it is created as a matter of law.

Similarly, UCC § 2-315 creates an implied warranty if the seller knows how a buyer will be using the product and knows that the buyer is relying on the seller's expertise to help select or specify the material. Since you indicated that Jackson worked closely with you to specify and select this material for your particular and specialized use, this implied warranty would apply and provide Bright Art with the basis for recovering damages caused by Jackson's breach of warranty. These warranties are in addition to any warranties extended by Jackson or Startek.

With that as a preface, here is how we would recommend Bright Art proceed and how we propose to assist your firm in solving this problem.

Phase I—Investigation and Testing

The first step in formulating a plan to resolve the dispute is to define the scope and exact cause of the problem. While you mentioned that Bright Art (and Tri-Star before it) has used this same material for twelve years, you did not mention any failures involving domes manufactured more than five years ago. I believe the Arizona failures were in skylights sold eighteen months ago while the Los Angeles failures were in three- to four-year-old products.

This prompts the question of whether Jackson and/or Startek have changed the composition of the material itself or the extruding process in a manner that compromised the material's formerly excellent physical properties. We need to determine, through testing, whether the problem exists in skylights shipped five to ten years ago. If not, it would seem to indicate a more recent iteration in the resin or extruding process might be the source of the induced stress and failures.

To accomplish this task, we would recommend that Bright Art retain a testing laboratory, preferably the acknowledged leader in this industry (to avoid having the results dismissed or refuted by Jackson's own testing). You mentioned a few names as possible choices in our meeting, and we would work with Bright Art to identify the premier facility for chemical, mechanical, and accelerated UV testing and to retain that firm immediately.

Concurrent with testing of Bright Art products in service for various lengths of time, we would recommend that you create a database of all installations by year of sale to enable Bright Art and ECG to quantify the scope of the problem, once testing determines if the defect afflicts all Jackson/Startek material or only that used in a circumscribed time frame. We would need to know the number and location of all skylights sold by year to then determine how best to remediate the problem with the least amount of adverse "marketing blowback."

Phase II—Remediation

To avoid allowing Jackson's and/or Startek's breach of warranty to damage Bright Art's standing in the industry and future sales, we believe a remediation plan needs to be developed and implemented as soon as the testing phase determines the scope and extent of the problem. This plan should include a short-term plan along the lines we discussed today, to minimize further UV degradation to the acrylic material. Since this is what Jackson has already recommended, it would be appropriate and commercially reasonable to follow the manufacturer's suggestions.

Next, Bright Art needs to determine whether it wishes to continue using the material in the future. If the current material is inappropriate for this application, you need to identify an alternate and make sure the alternate material will perform as intended. If testing determines the problem with the current material is limited to a quantifiable time frame, continued use will require Jackson and/or Startek to rectify their formulation or manufacturing problem and back their product with an extended warranty.

At the same time, Bright Art needs to develop a "fix" for existing installations along with an implementation cost analysis so that the "cost of cure" can be incorporated into your settlement demand. Until testing is done, it will be difficult to fully quantify the cost of remediation.

Phase III—Dispute Resolution

After we have a firm grasp on the scope and exact cause of the defect and failures, and have worked with Bright Art to develop and define a remedial action plan, ECG and Bright Art would meet with Jackson and Startek to present Bright Art's proposed solution. This "initial settlement meeting" should take place in a neutral location and involve decision makers from all parties to increase the likelihood of success.

ECG would draft and prepare Bright Art's presentation and assist and participate in presenting it to Jackson and Startek. The goal of this meeting would be to demonstrate to Jackson and Startek that they are liable for Bright Art's damages, that Bright Art's overriding goal is to solve the problem Jackson and Startek caused with the least amount of disruption to all parties, but that Bright Art is ready and willing to hold both companies responsible for their breach.

There is always the possibility that Jackson and Startek will respond to this proposal by turning it over to their attorneys; however, Bright Art will be far better prepared and equipped to deal with that potential by preparing for this meeting like it were a presentation to a jury. Compared to ECG, Jackson's and/or Startek's attorneys would be playing catch-up, and with ECG's help Bright Art could "control the high ground" throughout any litigation that ensued.

Other Considerations

Bright Art must bring a claim for breach of warranty/breach of contract within four years of any breach. Generally speaking, a breach occurs when a party has any reason to know or suspect that it has occurred. In your case, this could be the date you first learned of the failures in Arizona. However, there is also case law that holds a breach occurs, and your right to sue accrues, when the defective material is delivered, whether you knew of the defect or not. In either event, Bright Art may be limited to claims for material delivered in the four years prior to commencement of litigation.

ECG would need to review all of the correspondence between Bright Art and Jackson and/or Startek, all of the documentation you have regarding the initial decision to use Jackson's material, as well as the purchase and sale documentation for this material.

No company is fully prepared for a problem such as this, but with ECG's help Bright Art will be able to take a proactive stance and deal with the problem from a position of strength. We look forward to our next discussion and stand ready to assist you and your firm in whatever manner you feel is appropriate.

Enclosed is a proposed retainer agreement for your review and execution should you desire to retain ECG to represent Bright Art. Again, it was a pleasure to meet you, and I look forward to the opportunity to work with you to turn this problem into an opportunity.

Kindest regards,

ENTERPRISE COUNSEL GROUP
A Law Corporation

Thomas A. Vogele

Thomas A. Vogele
tvogele@enterprisecounsel.com

September 17, 2009

VIA U.S. MAIL

Ms. Heidi Hanson
Sanderson & Kimball, LLP
23226 Madero, Suite 175
Mission Viejo, CA 92691

Re: *Employment Claims of Trisha Strand v. ABCA Corporation*

Dear Ms. Hanson:

Please be advised that we represent ABCA Corporation in this matter. I received your August 30, 2007, letter to Gregory Weiss and have reviewed it with our client. ABCA does not acknowledge any liability in this matter, and we disagree with your conclusion that Ms. Strand's release is voidable.

The reasons for Ms. Strand's termination were communicated to her during a meeting she had with ABCA management on July 24, 2007. To claim she was terminated for any reason other than poor performance is to misstate the truth. While your analysis of the statutory requirements for a "knowing and voluntary" waiver under the Age Discrimination in Employment Act (ADEA) may be correct, that does not address the fact that any claim would be completely without merit.

Your sweeping conclusion that because the release may be voidable as to ADEA, it is voidable as to all claims is incorrect. Such a leap of logic is not supported by case law. In fact, the very case you cite for this proposition (*Oubre v. Entergy Operations, Inc.*, 522 U.S. 422, 428 (1998)) undercuts your assertion. Justice Kennedy wrote that, "[a]s a statutory matter, the release cannot bar her ADEA suit, *irrespective of the validity of the contract (release) as to other claims." Id.* at 428 (*emphasis added*). *Oubre* narrowly holds that a terminated employee covered by the ADEA is not required to return any consideration received pursuant to a release, and a release that does not comply with the statutory requirements is voidable as to an ADEA claim. It does *not* hold that a release voidable for want of ADEA-mandated language is voidable as to non-ADEA claims.

California sought to outlaw age-related discrimination through the Fair Employment and Housing Act, Government Code sections 12940(a) and 12941, and *Guz v. Bechtel National, Inc.*, 24 Cal. 4th 317 (2000), sets out the elements of a prima facie case. That said, your conclusory statement that Ms. Strand was discriminated against *because of* age is wholly unsupported by the facts. Ms. Strand was arguably a member of a protected class by virtue of her age at termination and she did suffer an adverse employment action; however, she was not performing competently in her position as you allege.

Your claim that "there are numerous circumstances suggesting a discriminatory motive, such as the fact that she was the only person over the age of forty at the management level of the company" is belied by the fact that the manager who replaced her in the position is older than your client. The *McDonnell Douglas* three-stage burden-shifting test discussed in *Guz* requires far more than a naked allegation of discrimination to satisfy element (4) of the test.

ABCA terminated Ms. Strand for cause, as required by her executive employment agreement. She was given the reasons for her termination, and it is entirely within the purview of ABCA to make that determination. To avoid privacy concerns, ABCA will not provide the specific reasons communicated to Ms. Strand without her express authorization; however, let me assure you that every reason for her termination was related to a lack of performance, not her age.

Your claim that "the impression Ms. Strand was given was that it was a cost-cutting measure" is perhaps a form of rationalization by Ms. Strand. In the July 24th meeting, ABCA management did not discuss anything that would reasonably lead to this false impression.

The sweeping conclusion that Ms. Strand would be entitled to the balance of her contract payments cannot be based on the holding of *Martin v. U-Haul Co. of Fresno*, 204 Cal. App. 3d 396 (5th Dist. 1988). I read *Martin* to mean that contract damages cannot exceed the notice period required in the contract. The court cited *Pecarovich v. Becker*, 113 Cal. App. 2d 309 (1st Dist. 1952), for the proposition that "contract damages are limited to the notice period." *Id.* at 318. The court went on to quote *Cline v. Smith*, 96 Cal. App. 697 (3rd Dist. 1929), and the seminal case of *Jewell v. Colonial Theater Co.*, 12 Cal. App. 681 (1st Dist. 1910), as being in concert with this rule.

Ms. Strand's employment agreement did not require advance notice of termination, and thus no damages could be awarded for ABCA exercising its contract right to terminate her employment for cause. In any event, the release, although possibly voidable as to any ADEA claim, is a valid and enforceable release of all other claims. A release is a contract, *Solis v. Kirkwood Resort Co.*, 94 Cal. App. 4th 354 (3d Dist. 2001); *Matthews v. Atchison, T. & S.F. Ry. Co.*, 54 Cal. App. 2d 549 (2d Dist. 1942); and release agreements are governed by the generally applicable principles of contracts. *Vahle v. Barwick*, 93 Cal. App. 4th 1323 (1st Dist. 2001).

There is no evidence to suggest that Ms. Strand lacked capacity at the time to execute the contract. Consideration was recited and paid. There is no allegation of fraud in the inducement or false representations by ABCA regarding the release. In fact, the release specifically mentions Ms. Strand's right to consult with an attorney before entering into the contract and afforded her a five-day right of rescission. Finally, the release was not executed under duress or coercion. As such, it is binding on Ms. Strand as to all contract and tort claims.

There is no basis to suggest that ABCA and its employees acted in a manner that would constitute any form of tortuous conduct. The inclusion of *Agarwal v. Johnson*, 25 Cal. 3d 932 (1979), and *Ewing v. Gill Industries, Inc.*, 3 Cal. App. 4th 601 (6th Dist. 1992), in your letter is quite inapposite. In *Agarwal*, the conduct of the plaintiff's supervisor was so beyond the bounds of human decency and civility that a contrary decision would shock the conscience. Likewise, the facts of *Ewing* are without any relation to the facts of this matter and should not serve as a guidepost for your client.

As with your discussion of contract and tort damages, the inclusion of compensatory and punitive damages presupposes actionable conduct by ABCA and is putting the proverbial cart before the horse. Ms. Strand's termination was based on her failure to competently fulfill her contractual duties. ABCA terminated her employment in strict conformance with the terms of her employment agreement and negotiated a settlement of all her claims, as evidenced by her execution of the settlement agreement.

We hope Ms. Strand will recognize that her termination, while understandably distressing for her, was a business decision made to resolve the problems her lack of performance caused. While the release she executed may be voidable as to any ADEA claim, please keep in mind that is merely a threshold matter. There is no merit to such a claim, and the right to sue is far different from having a meritorious claim.

The settlement agreement ABCA executed with Ms. Strand is fair and final. The company regrets that Ms. Strand feels otherwise, but is confident that the company handled the matter properly and with the respect Ms. Strand deserved as a member of the ABCA organization.

Sincerely yours,

ENTERPRISE COUNSEL GROUP
A Law Corporation

Thomas A. Vogele

ADAMS & ASSOCIATES, STUDENTS OF LAW

*12510 Inglenook Lane * Cerritos, CA 90703 * (888) 41 ADAMS * Fax (562) 809-2653*

Ms. Mary Louise Solomon
1240 South State College Blvd.
Anaheim, CA 92806

Re: Surrogate Contract between Mary Louise Solomon and James Kelk

Dear Ms. Solomon:

Thank you for choosing Adams & Associates to represent you. We are mindful of the importance of this matter, and we will do our best to justify the confidence you have placed in us. The purpose of this letter is to acquaint you with how we see your case, what you may expect to happen and, what you need to do to assist us as we move forward. We work for you, so if you have questions, or you think there are things we should know, please do not hesitate to contact our office. If we are not available when you call, please leave a message, and we will get back to you as soon as we can. We will be providing you with a monthly itemized statement of your account with us and any amounts we are subtracting from your retainer.

Before proceeding further, there are a couple of items that require your immediate attention. First, please sign the enclosed Substitution of Attorney letter, return it to us in the envelope provided, and keep the second copy for your files. We cannot act on your behalf if you have not released your prior attorney from any obligations to you. Second, it is imperative that you keep an accurate record of all of your expenses associated with the pregnancy. Please use the enclosed expense form to keep track of your mileage to and from the doctor, and any other expenses you incur as a result of your pregnancy, such as maternity clothes.

According to information you provided during our initial consultation, you entered into a contract with James Kelk, in which you agreed to be artificially inseminated, and to conceive and deliver a child. Mr. Kelk promised, among other things, to pay all medical and collateral expenses, and to give you $15,000 upon surrender of custody of the child to him. You have abided by all the terms and conditions of the contract up to this point and are in your twentieth week of pregnancy.

Recently, your husband contacted the Kelks and informed them that your father was an alcoholic and that your mother was addicted to pain killers, facts that you confirmed were true. Now the Kelks have decided that they do not want the baby and wish to terminate the contract, despite the fact that you have no history of drug or alcohol abuse, and that tests conducted on your fetus offer no evidence of any problems with the baby. In seeking legal counsel, your goal is to have the Kelks perform the contract, i.e., do what they promised to do, including taking custody of the baby after it is born. Based on what you have told us and on our preliminary research, and with the understanding that we cannot guarantee the outcome of your case, we believe we have a reasonably good chance to either force the Kelks to pay the monies promised under the contract, or to pay any expenses and losses you might incur involving the pregnancy. We do not believe that we would be successful in forcing the Kelks to take custody of the baby.

In contract law, breach of a contract is the same as breaking one's promise. The law offers various remedies to the injured party (the party who is willing to perform on her promise). The basic goal of the courts in contract disputes is to put the parties in the same positions they were in before they entered into the contract. Usually, this involves the court either ordering the breaching party to perform as agreed in the contract, or the awarding of monetary compensation to the injured party for any expenses incurred or losses sustained as a result of the contract not being fulfilled.

Ordinarily, the law requires that a breach of the contract must occur before a legal remedy may be sought. At this point, the Kelks have not legally breached the contract because they have performed the promises that are already due under the terms of the contract, i.e., paid expenses to the fertility clinic and the costs of the medical evaluations, etc. Normally, we would have to wait until the Kelks actually broke one of their contract promises before we could take any action. However, by verbally telling you that they did not want the baby, the Kelks may have committed an "anticipatory repudiation of the contract." This is like reneging on a promise before the time when you are required to carry out that promise. We would need to prove, either through the Kelks' own admission or through other acts on their part, that they do not plan to make good on their contract promises to you.

Assuming that we can prove that the Kelks committed an "anticipatory repudiation of the contract," there are three possible responses we would advise. First, we can urge the Kelks to perform on the contract—to cancel or undo their repudiation. Second, if they still insist they do not want custody of the baby, we can try to negotiate a settlement that would be agreeable to both you and the Kelks. Third, we can immediately file an action to try and force performance of the contract or recover any damages that may be appropriate.

We recommend first sending a letter to Mr. and Mrs. Kelk urging them to honor the contract. They may have been overreacting to the information provided by your husband and may have reconsidered their position. This is the preferred approach because it accomplishes your goal and avoids the more costly alternatives. We have enclosed a copy of the letter we will send as soon as you give us your approval. Please call us and let us know what you decide.

If the Kelks refuse to reconsider and remain steadfast in their position that they do not want the baby, then we can still attempt to negotiate with them for a mutually agreeable alternative to the enforcement of the entire contract. Of course you would have to approve any final agreement we negotiated. The advantage to you of solving this disagreement through negotiation is that the outcome may be the same as through litigating the matter, but it would be resolved more quickly and at considerably less cost to you.

Should the initial negotiations fail to generate an acceptable outcome, we recommend filing an action in Superior Court for anticipatory repudiation of the contract. Based on the information you provided us and our preliminary research, we believe that filing an action would be a prudent approach and that there is a reasonable chance of prevailing. With that said, we must caution that there are no guarantees that we would win the action.

Although we would file the action in Superior Court, if you so directed us, we recommend that we enter into nonbinding arbitration, rather than court litigation. There are three reasons for this strategy. First, we can arrange an arbitration hearing more quickly than we can obtain a hearing date in our crowded court system. This means that if we are successful at arbitration, we can receive a judgment that would cover your expenses including attorneys' fees, thereby minimizing any financial burden to you. Second, it is far less costly to you than a protracted court battle. Third, we may have a better opportunity for a ruling in our favor. There has never been a case in California quite like yours, and, in general, the law surrounding surrogate contracts is very unsettled. For a number of legal reasons too complex to discuss here, how the courts would treat our case is unpredictable. In addition, an outcome in our favor in court would almost certainly result in an appeal, which would increase the costs and the length of time to a final outcome. Because the arbitration proposed is nonbinding, neither side has to abide by the decision of the arbitrator. However, having heard the other side's arguments, we will have a better idea of our chances of winning at trial if we are forced to litigate.

Thus far we have focused only on the monetary issues of your agreement with the Kelks. We realize that you want the Kelks to also honor their commitment to take custody of the baby upon its birth. However, as we mentioned before, it is our opinion that the courts would be unwilling to force Mr. and Mrs. Kelk to take custody of the child. Should you wish to put the baby up for adoption, that will be a separate issue with which our family law specialist can help. Should you decide to keep the baby, it is very likely that Mr. Kelk, as the child's natural father, would be responsible for part of the child's financial support, until he or she attains the age of eighteen. Again, that is a separate action and would be handled by our family law specialist.

To recap, upon your approval, we will send a letter to Mr. and Mrs. Kelk asking them to reconsider their position and honor the contract. If that proves unsuccessful, we will negotiate to arrive at a mutually agreed upon settlement, and, failing that, we will file an action and seek to enter into arbitration. Should arbitration fail to produce the desired results, then we will go forward with a litigated action in Superior Court.

Please contact our office no later than Friday, February 14, 2010, to inform us of your decision regarding the letter to the Kelks. Also, please mail the Substitution of Attorney letter immediately. We will keep you informed of further developments in your case.

Sincerely,

Richard G. Adams
Sr. Student

encl: Substitution of Attorney Letter (2)
        Letter to Mr. & Mrs. Kelk
        Expense Sheet

ADAMS & ASSOCIATES, STUDENTS OF LAW

*12510 Inglenook Lane * Cerritos, CA 90703 * (888) 41 ADAMS * Fax (562) 809-2653*

Mr. Yves Bordeaux, Esq.
Law Offices of Yves Bordeaux
2323 Main St., Suite 200
Orange, CA 92666

Reference: Surrogacy Contract between James Kelk and Mary Louise Solomon

Dear Attorney Bordeaux:

Please be advised that effective immediately I have retained the legal services of Adams & Associates to pursue my claims related to the above referenced contract.

Accordingly, please forward my file to my law student, Richard G. Adams, as soon as possible. Your cooperation is appreciated.

Sincerely,

Mary Louise Solomon

Adams & Associates, Students of Law

*12510 Inglenook Lane * Cerritos, CA 90703 * (888) 41 ADAMS * Fax (562) 809-2653*

Mr. & Mrs. James Kelk
12345 Orange Avenue
Orange, CA 95555

Re: Surrogacy Contract between James Kelk and Mary Louise Solomon

Dear Mr. & Mrs. Kelk:

Please be advised that our firm has been retained by Ms. Mary Louise Solomon relative to the surrogacy contract entered into by Mr. James Kelk. Ms. Solomon has informed this firm that you no longer wish to take post-natal custody of the child that is the subject of the aforementioned contract, and of which Mr. Kelk is the legal father.

We believe Ms. Solomon would prevail in legal enforcement of the financial terms of her contract with Mr. Kelk. However Ms. Solomon does not wish to engage in protracted litigation to resolve this matter unless absolutely necessary. To avoid litigation, which could ultimately prove very costly to you, we respectfully request that you reconsider your position. Please indicate in writing via a letter to this office, your intention to honor all of the promises you made in the aforementioned contract.

If you have any questions, please contact me. If you have employed an attorney, then please have that person contact my office. Communicating directly with you is inappropriate if you are represented by counsel.

Sincerely,

Richard G. Adams
Student at Law

EXPENSES RELATED TO BABY

Date	Miles to Doctor	Miles from Doctor	Total Miles	Medical Expenses	Personal Expenses

RACHEL GOLDSTEIN
ATTORNEY AT LAW
426-1/2 BEGONIA AVENUE
CORONA DEL MAR, CALIFORNIA 92625
TELEPHONE: (714) 675-3242; FACSIMILE: (714) 675-3243

Mr. Dana Clark
Dana's Restaurant
101 S. Imperial Highway
Anaheim, CA 92807

Re: Ms. Julia Kidd's Right of Publicity Claims Against You

Dear Mr. Clark:

Thank you for meeting with me in my office yesterday. This letter is a follow-up to our meeting. It restates my understanding of the facts, addresses your concerns regarding whether famous chef and TV personality Julia Kidd can take legal action against you for airing a TV commercial that features an actress resembling her, and proposes a course of action for your review and consideration.

First of all, I want to be sure I have the facts of your case straight. Based on our discussion, I understand the facts to be as follows: you are the owner and chef of Dana's, a two-year-old restaurant in Anaheim, California. In January of this year you paid an ad agency to create a TV commercial (ad) that would promote your restaurant. The ad, which began airing in Los Angeles in March, appears on Channels 5, 13, and 50.

The ad you approved features an actress resembling famous cooking show chef and TV personality Julia Kidd. The actress stands in a kitchen and says, "You know me." The actress never says she is Julia Kidd in the ad, and there is no disclaimer on the ad. The ad agency titled the ad copy "Julia Kidding" for its own internal reference. You estimate the ad has increased business by 50 percent.

On October 1, you received a letter from Ms. Kidd's attorney warning you that Ms. Kidd will pursue legal action against you if you do not pull the ad by November 30th. The letter also demanded that you destroy all related ad material and give all your restaurant profits from the ad to Ms. Kidd.

Your primary concern is whether Ms. Kidd can bring any causes of action against you for continuing to run your ad. You want to continue running your ad because you have already paid for the ad and the ad time and the ad has increased your business. You are willing to put a disclaimer on the ad if it will protect you from liability. You have also expressed concern about whether you are required to give Ms. Kidd your profits resulting from the ad. Finally, you want to know what your options are at this time.

My research indicates that if you continue to run the ad, Ms. Kidd can pursue legal action against you under both state and federal laws. The California courts are especially protective of famous personalities' rights because there are so many celebrities living in the state. Therefore, the courts tend to look with disfavor upon individuals who even unintentionally use a celebrity look-alike without permission to promote their goods and/or services. In addition, a jury and not a judge will decide whether the facts support Ms. Kidd's claims against you. A jury is likely to be sympathetic to Ms. Kidd because she is trying to protect her name and reputation.

Ms. Kidd can bring two state claims against you. In order for you to prevail against the first claim, you must show the actress in the commercial does not bear an exact resemblance to Ms. Kidd, you did not knowingly intend to use Ms. Kidd's likeness, or there was no direct connection between the use of the actress resembling Ms. Kidd and the promotion of your restaurant. To prevail against the second state claim, you must show the actress does not bear a close resemblance to Ms. Kidd, you did not use the actress's physical resemblance to Ms. Kidd for commercial advantage, Ms. Kidd's consent was not required, and Ms. Kidd suffered no losses resulting from the airing of the TV ad.

With respect to the first state claim and the issue of resemblance, the court applies a strict "likeness" standard. California courts, in particular, tend to look for an exact likeness of the person being copied rather than a close resemblance. In other words, Ms. Kidd will have to prove the actress is an exact likeness of her to prevail on this issue. You may prevail by establishing that the actress merely resembles Ms. Kidd. On the other hand, Ms. Kidd may argue the resemblance is strong enough to meet the "likeness" standard. A jury will ultimately decide if the actress's resemblance to Ms. Kidd meets the "likeness" standard by viewing the ad.

Regarding whether you "knowingly" used Ms. Kidd's likeness, you could assert that the ad agency came up with the idea and you only knowingly intended to promote your restaurant. However, Ms. Kidd can argue you were aware of the actress's resemblance to Ms. Kidd when you approved the ad and that you knew the agency labeled the ad "Julia Kidding." Ms. Kidd can also say the warning letter has formally put you on notice regarding the unauthorized use of Ms. Kidd's likeness. Again, the jury will decide if the facts support the "knowing" requirement.

Regarding the existence of a "direct connection," you could argue that no direct connection exists between the use of an actress who happens to resemble Ms. Kidd and the promotion of a restaurant because the actress does not identify herself as being a chef. However, if Ms. Kidd establishes you used her "likeness," she can establish the "direct connection" between the use of an actress who is portraying a famous chef and the promotion of your restaurant. Once again, the jury will determine if the "direct connection" requirement has been met.

Ms. Kidd is even more likely to prevail against you on the second state claim because the resemblance standard is not as strict. Under this claim, the court only requires that Ms. Kidd show you used her "identity." This broader standard considers not just physical resemblance, but the ad's total impression on the viewer. Therefore, even though you could still argue the resemblance is not close, the combination of physical resemblance, a kitchen setting, and the line "You know me" is likely to be enough under this claim to show you used Ms. Kidd's identity. Ms. Kidd can show you used the actress's resemblance to Ms. Kidd for commercial advantage because the purpose of the ad was to promote your restaurant. Ms. Kidd can use the warning letter to show you did not have her consent. She can also show that she suffered lost profits because she was not paid for the ad. Finally, Ms. Kidd can show the ad damages her reputation and image because her identity has been used without her permission to endorse an unknown and, arguably, unproven restaurant that she has never visited and that is owned by a man she has never met.

Ms. Kidd can also bring a federal claim against you. To prevail against a federal claim, you must show that viewers of the ad are not likely to confuse the actress with Ms. Kidd. You may argue that viewers who know Ms. Kidd will know the actress is not Ms. Kidd. However, you have already said that people have asked you if the actress is Ms. Kidd and this evidence can be used against you. Ms. Kidd is a famous chef who has a cooking show on TV. She will try to argue that your ad features a Ms. Kidd "look-alike" who is standing in a kitchen and telling the audience "You know me" to indicate she is Ms. Kidd. She may also try to show that the absence of a disclaimer intentionally promotes confusion among viewers. Based on the facts of your case and the research I have done, it is my opinion that Ms. Kidd has a strong chance of prevailing against you on both state and federal claims if this case goes to trial.

You may consider joining the ad agency as an additional defendant if Ms. Kidd pursues legal action against you. You may then be able to recover some or all of your costs from the ad agency, assuming no agreement exists limiting your rights against the agency. I would need to see all documentation between you and the ad agency to determine if you have a potential claim against it.

You wanted to know if you could place a disclaimer on the ad to protect you from liability. As I already indicated to you over the phone on October 9th, Ms. Kidd's attorney rejected that idea. At that time, I also consulted another attorney who is an expert in the area of intellectual property. I relayed to you that he also advised immediately pulling the ad as requested to avoid having to pay punitive damages in addition to the regular damages you may have to pay if Ms. Kidd prevails against you in court. General damages can include compensating Ms. Kidd for using her identity. In addition, the court could make you disgorge all your profits from the ad to Ms. Kidd. The court could also make you pay punitive damages for acting in bad faith by disregarding the warning letter and continuing to run the ad, even with a disclaimer.

You also wanted to know if you are required to give Ms. Kidd all your profits resulting from the ad, as demanded in Ms. Steele's warning letter to you. You are not required to give your profits to Ms. Kidd. However, failure to make an alternative offer to Ms. Kidd may cause her to take legal action against you. I therefore suggest that you consider allowing me to negotiate a settlement on your behalf so that Ms. Kidd has no reason to pursue legal action against you.

The following settlement options may enable you to continue running the ad without risking liability. You may offer to pay Ms. Kidd a licensing fee in exchange for your being permitted to continue running the ad. Another option is to allow Ms. Kidd to modify the ad to her liking and agree to destroy the unmodified ad and all related material.

In the event Ms. Kidd is not receptive to either of these options, I suggest that you consider proposing a third settlement option. This option is not as appealing, but it will allow you to cut your losses. Such an option could include your agreeing to pull the ad, destroy all ad material, and pay Ms. Kidd a licensing fee that covers the entire six-month period the ad has run. This option could be proposed in the event Ms. Kidd insists on the demands made in the warning letter.

These settlement options are merely suggestions for your review and consideration. I am also happy to explore other options with you. Settlement negotiations will take approximately twenty hours and will be billed at the same hourly fee of $150.00 I quoted during our meeting. Upon your instruction, I will immediately arrange a settlement negotiation conference with Ms. Kidd's attorney.

Of course, another option you have is to continue running the ad. If you decide not to cooperate with Ms. Kidd and continue to run the ad even with a disclaimer, it is very likely that Ms. Kidd will pursue legal action against you. If you lose, you may be faced with not only paying Ms. Kidd all your profits, but also compensating her for using her identity and paying her punitive damages. You may even be forced to pay her attorneys' fees in addition to my fees. I advise you to carefully consider the possible costs and consequences of not cooperating with Ms. Kidd at this time.

If you decide to pull the ad by November 30th as requested, you could replace it with a new ad. Understandably, you may not wish to consider replacing the ad because of the expense involved. Therefore, more economical alternatives are also worth exploring at this time. You could obtain free TV, radio, newspaper, and magazine publicity by inviting restaurant reviewers, dee jays, and food critics to dine in your restaurant. You could also participate in food drive charities and local events, like "The Taste of Newport," to further publicize your restaurant. You could also submit articles to food magazines and even teach a cooking course.

If you have doubts about the strength of Ms. Kidd's claims, you may wish to consider having a random survey conducted on the TV ad to determined whether viewers are likely to identify the actress in the ad as Ms. Kidd. A random survey could give us some insight into how likely it is that a jury will identify the actress as Ms. Kidd. If you decide to enter into settlement negotiations, survey results that favor you could be used as leverage in negotiating a better settlement for you. Unfavorable results could also help you decide what to do if we cannot reach a settlement that is agreeable to you. The cost of a survey is approximately $150.00 and takes two days. Subject to your consent, I will arrange to have a random survey conducted immediately.

Mr. Clark, I recommend that you consider doing all that you can at this point to avoid what is likely to be an expensive and lengthy trial in a case that Ms. Kidd has a good chance of winning. A trial is also likely to result in negative publicity for Dana's. I understand that you want to do what you can to increase your restaurant business. I can also appreciate your not wanting to lose the cost of the ad and the ad time. However, it makes more sense to take appropriate action now while you still can to minimize your losses than to end up fighting what I believe will be an uphill battle that may ultimately cost you far more than the cost of the ad, the ad time, and lost business.

Ultimately, the decision rests with you. We can discuss the options further when I see you next week. In the meantime, please feel free to call me if you have any questions. I am here to help you in any way I can.

Sincerely,

Rachel Goldstein, Esq.

Pleadings

ATTORNEY OF RECORD
IDENTIFICATION NO.
Mr. Noel Lerner
11240 Stillwell Dr.
Riverside, CA 92505
1-909-689-9728
Attorney for Plaintiff

SUPERIOR COURT OF CALIFORNIA
COUNTY OF ORANGE

REVEREND TOMMY SMITH
1240 S. STATE COLLEGE BLVD.
ANAHEIM, CA
      Plaintiff

        v.

BOARD OF TRUSTEES
SALVATION BAPTIST CHURCH
1240 S. STATE COLLEGE BLVD.
ANAHEIM, CA
      Defendant

NO. XX-00000

NOVEMBER TERM, XXXX

COMPLAINT FOR PUBLIC
DISCLOSURE OF PRIVATE FACTS

Statement of Facts for All Causes of Action

Plaintiff argues:

1. Plaintiff is Reverend Tommy Smith, an adult individual who resides at 1240 S. State College Blvd., Anaheim, CA.

2. Defendant is the Board of Trustees of the Salvation Baptist Church, with offices located at 1240 S. State College Blvd., Anaheim, CA.

3. On or about 6/19/XX, Plaintiff entered into an employment contract with the Salvation Baptist Church, 1240 S. State College Blvd., Anaheim, CA.

4. Under the employment contract, Plaintiff's duties were to function as minister and run the day-to-day operations of the church.

5. On or about 4/17/XX, Defendant held a meeting of part of the congregation of the church. At this meeting, a vote of 101-7 was taken to terminate the employment of Plaintiff.

6. The Board told the congregation that Plaintiff was having extramarital affairs and was guilty of adultery.

7. Before this disclosure the information regarding Plaintiff's extramarital affairs was private, that is, not known to the public.

8. Fifty members of the congregation have sworn affidavits about the public statements made by the Board about Plaintiff. The members include statements that they did not know about Plaintiff's extramarital affairs before the Board's statements. The members also state that the outcome of the vote was influenced by the public statements made by the Board about Plaintiff to the congregation. These original sworn affidavits are attached to this Complaint and marked as Exhibits 1-50.

9. On or about July 10, XXXX, a second meeting was held. As a result of this meeting the congregation reinstated Plaintiff by a vote of 259-196.

10. Plaintiff has suffered damage to his reputation both personally and professionally.

11. Plaintiff has also suffered damage to his ability to be employed as a minister because of the highly personal and intimate nature of the disclosure of the extramarital affairs.

Cause of Action

Right of Privacy—Public Disclosure of Private Facts

12. Plaintiff incorporates by reference paragraphs 1 through 11 of this Complaint.

13. On or about 4/17/XX, Defendant made a public disclosure of a private fact about Plaintiff to members of the congregation. The private fact was the extramarital affairs of Plaintiff.

14. Prior to this date, the congregation had not known of this fact.

15. The Defendant disclosed the fact either with knowledge that it was highly offensive or with reckless disregard of whether it was highly offensive or not. The fact made known was an intrusion into Plaintiff's most intimate and private sexual affairs.

16. The public disclosure of this fact caused Plaintiff to sustain injury to his reputation, damage to his emotions, and harm to his employability as a minister.

Wherefore, Plaintiff demands that this Court enter judgment in his favor and against Defendant in an amount in excess of $10,000, exclusive of interest and costs.

Attorney for Plaintiff

Verification

I, Reverend Tommy Smith, state that I am the Plaintiff in this action and verify that the statements made in the foregoing Complaint are true and correct to the best of my knowledge, information, and belief.

_____
Date

_____
Reverend Tommy Smith

Certification of Mailing

I, Noel Lerner, certify that I personally placed a copy of this Complaint in the student mailbox of Kimchi Huynh, on November 22, XXXX.

I certify this under penalty of perjury.

_____
Date

_____
Noel Lerner

ATTORNEY OF RECORD:
IDENTIFICATION NO.

————————————————

ALAN and LINDA SHERMAN
123 BIRCH STREET
PHILADELPHIA, PA,
   Plaintiffs
    v.
KATHRYN JONES
UNIT 14
130 ELM STREET
PHILADELPHIA, PA,
   Defendant

ATTORNEY FOR PLAINTIFFS
COURT OF COMMON PLEAS,
PHILADELPHIA COUNTY,
PENNSYLVANIA CIVIL ACTION—
LAW DIVISION
APRIL TERM, XXXX NO. 0000

Complaint in Assumpsit

1. Plaintiffs are Alan and Linda Sherman, adult individuals who reside at 123 Birch Street, Philadelphia, PA.

2. Defendant is Kathryn Jones, an adult individual who resides at Unit 14, 130 Elm Street, Philadelphia, PA.

3. On or about December 3, XXXX, Plaintiffs entered into an agreement with Defendant Jones to purchase real estate ("the property") owned by her at Unit 14, 130 Elm Street, Philadelphia, PA. A true and correct copy of this agreement is attached to this Complaint and marked as Exhibit "A."

4. Under the agreement, Plaintiffs paid the sum of ten thousand dollars ($10,000) to Creampuff Real Estate, Inc. ("Creampuff"), as a down payment on the property for Creampuff to deposit in an interest-bearing escrow account.

5. At all pertinent times, Creampuff acted as Defendant Jones's agent, the Defendant having agreed that Creampuff was to receive a 6 percent commission for procuring Plaintiffs to buy the property.

6. Under paragraph 19 of the agreement, Plaintiffs' duty to proceed to settlement was expressly subject to their ability to obtain a mortgage commitment within sixty days at a cost of no more than 3 percent of the principal ("three points"). Failing to obtain such a commitment, at Plaintiffs' option, Plaintiffs were to receive all deposit monies and the agreement was to become null and void.

7. At Creampuff's insistence, Plaintiffs proceeded with due diligence to apply to Security Mortgage Service Co. for a mortgage that would meet the terms of the agreement.

8. As of February 1, XXXX, however, sixty days elapsed with no commitment. On February 17, XXXX, Plaintiffs received a written commitment, dated February 12, XXXX. A copy of the commitment is attached and marked as Exhibit "B."

9. The commitment offered Plaintiffs a mortgage which would cost them four points rather than the maximum of three points set forth in that paragraph 19 of the agreement.

10. The commitment further required Plaintiffs to meet special conditions that paragraph 19 of the agreement did not contemplate, namely (a) evidence of sale or lease of their present residence, and (b) proof of XXXX income of $110,997.

11. Upon receipt of the commitment, Plaintiffs asked the mortgage company to remove the special conditions, but Security refused to.

12. In view of the circumstances in paragraphs 9-11 above, Plaintiffs on February 25, XXXX, sent a letter to Defendant Jones notifying her that they could not meet the terms of the commitment and that they desired the return of their deposit with interest. A copy of the letter is attached and marked Exhibit "C."

13. Despite the request, by letter dated February 25, XXXX, Defendant Jones refused to return Plaintiffs' deposit, and despite many subsequent requests, persists in her refusal. She additionally has directed Creampuff not to release the funds.

14. Further, by letter dated March 3, XXXX, Creampuff notified Plaintiffs they would not return the deposit unless the parties agreed or the court so directed.

Count I

15. Paragraphs 1-14 above are incorporated as though set forth at length.

16. Defendant Jones is liable to Plaintiffs in the amount of ten thousand dollars ($10,000), together with interest from December 3, XXXX.

WHEREFORE, Plaintiffs demand judgment in their favor and against Defendant Jones in the amount of ten thousand dollars ($10,000), together with interest from December 3, XXXX, and costs of suit.

Count II

17. Paragraphs 1-14 above are incorporated as though set forth at length.

18. Defendant Jones's refusal to return Plaintiffs' money has at all times been willful, malicious, and utterly without foundation in law.

19. Defendant Jones is liable to Plaintiffs for punitive damages.

WHEREFORE, Plaintiffs demand punitive damages against Defendant Jones in an amount not in excess of twenty thousand dollars ($20,000).

Count III

20. Paragraphs 1-14 above are incorporated as though set forth at length.

21. On April 13, XXXX, Plaintiffs notified Defendant by hand-delivered letter that unless Defendant returned the deposit by April 15, they could not pay their income taxes on time and expected to be liable for penalties and interest.

22. Defendant is now liable to Plaintiffs for consequential damages since Plaintiffs could not pay taxes on time.

WHEREFORE, Plaintiffs demand judgment in their favor and against Defendant for consequential damages calculated from April 15, XXXX, until time of judgment.

Attorney for Plaintiff

ATTORNEY OF RECORD:
IDENTIFICATION NO.

_____

ALAN and LINDA SHERMAN,
Plaintiffs
v.
KATHRYN JONES,
Defendant

_____

ATTORNEY FOR DEFENDANT
COURT OF COMMON PLEAS,
PHILADELPHIA COUNTY,
PENNSYLVANIA CIVIL ACTION—
LAW DIVISION
APRIL TERM, XXXX No. 231

———

Answer, New Matter, and Counterclaim of Defendant Kathryn Jones to Plaintiffs' Complaint

———

Answer

Defendant Kathryn Jones, by her counsel, answers Plaintiffs' Complaint as follows:

1. Admitted.

2. Admitted.

3. Admitted.

4. Admitted.

5. Admitted in part and denied in part. Defendant admits that Creampuff was to receive a 6 percent commission for procuring a satisfactory purchaser (not necessarily Plaintiffs) for the property. Counsel advises Defendant that she need not respond to the remaining allegations in this paragraph because those allegations constitute conclusions of law which operation of law deems denied.

6. Counsel advised Defendant that she need not respond to the allegations in this paragraph because those allegations constitute conclusions of law which operation of law deems denied. Furthermore, the document speaks for itself. In any event, Defendant specifically denies that Plaintiffs' duty to proceed to settlement was subject to their ability to obtain a mortgage commitment "at a cost of no more than 3 percent of the principal ('three points')." On the contrary, paragraph 19 of the agreement provides that the commitment "shall not require the Buyer to pay more than 3 percent of the principal amount as 'points' or a 'commitment fee.'"

7. Defendant is without knowledge or information sufficient to form a belief as to the truth of the averments of paragraph 7 of the Complaint because the means of proof are within the exclusive control of adverse parties or hostile persons, and Defendant demands proof of them.

8. Admitted in part and denied in part. Defendant admits that Plaintiffs received a commitment dated February 12, XXXX, and that a copy of that commitment is attached to the Complaint and marked as Exhibit "B." As to the

remaining allegations of paragraph 8 of the Complaint, Defendant is without knowledge or information sufficient to form a belief as to the truth of these averments because the means of proof are within the exclusive control of adverse parties or hostile persons, and demands proof of them.

9. Defendant specifically denies that the commitment offered Plaintiffs a mortgage which would cost them four points rather than the maximum of three points set forth in paragraph 19 of the agreement. On the contrary, the commitment expressly provided that the Buyer pay 3 percent of the principal amount as "points" or as a "commitment fee."

10. Counsel advises Defendant that she need not respond to the allegations in this paragraph because those allegations constitute conclusions of law which operation of law deems denied. Furthermore, the document speaks for itself. In any event, the commitment does not require proof of XXXX income of $110,997. On the contrary, the commitment merely requires that Plaintiffs substantiate the income that Plaintiffs claim on their application for the commitment by providing a "XXXX IRS return substantially supportive of income claimed on application of $110,997 OR complete **AUDITED** profit and loss for XXXX on both businesses supporting same income figure." Also, Defendant specifically denies that any requirement as to "evidence of sale or lease of [Plaintiffs'] present residence" is a "special condition not at all contemplated" by the agreement. On the contrary, such an occurrence is a normal, expected, and understood condition in such circumstances.

11. After reasonable investigation, Defendant is without knowledge or information sufficient to form a belief as to the truth of the averments of paragraph 11 of the Complaint, and demands proof of them.

12. Admitted in part and denied in part. Defendant admits that Plaintiffs sent the letter described, and that the letter indicated that Plaintiffs could not or would not accept the commitment and desired the return of the deposit, with interest. Defendant also admits that a copy of the letter is attached to the Complaint as Exhibit "C." Defendant is without knowledge or information sufficient to form a belief as to the truth of the remaining averments of this paragraph because the means of proof are within the exclusive control of adverse parties or hostile persons, and Defendant demands proof of them.

13. Denied as stated. Defendant admits that her counsel, by letter dated February 26, XXXX, indicated that Plaintiffs would be held liable under the agreement between the parties, based on previous indications Defendant received that Plaintiffs had obtained an acceptable commitment and Defendant's detrimental reliance on those indications. Defendant further admits that her husband informed Creampuff that any release of the deposit would be in violation of the agreement between the parties.

14. Admitted.

Count I

15. Paragraphs 1 through 14 of this Answer are incorporated by reference.

16. Counsel advises Defendant that she need not respond to the allegations in this paragraph because those allegations constitute conclusions of law which operation of law deems denied. In any event, Defendant specifically denies

that Defendant is liable to Plaintiffs in the amount of $10,000, together with interest, from December 3, XXXX. On the contrary, Defendant is not liable to Plaintiffs.

Count II

17. Paragraphs 1 through 14 of this Answer are incorporated by reference.

18. Defendant specifically denies that her refusal to return Plaintiffs' money has at all times been willful, malicious, and utterly without foundation in law. On the contrary, Defendant has at all times acted properly and within her legal rights and has acted in conformance with a good faith belief as to her legal rights.

19. Counsel advises Defendant that she need not respond to the allegations in this paragraph because those allegations constitute conclusions of law which operation of law deems denied. In any event, Defendant specifically denies that she is liable to Plaintiffs for punitive damages. On the contrary, Defendant is not liable to Plaintiffs.

Count III

20. Paragraphs 1 through 14 of this answer are incorporated by reference.

21. Admitted in part and denied in part. Defendant admits that her counsel received the letter described indicating that Plaintiffs sought the return of the deposit by April 15, XXXX, in order to have the money to pay their income taxes. Defendant is without knowledge or information sufficient to form a belief as to the truth of the averment that Plaintiffs were unable to pay their income taxes on time and expected to be liable for penalties and interest because the means of proof are within the exclusive control of adverse parties or hostile persons, and Defendant demands proof of them.

22. Counsel advises Defendant that she need not respond to the allegations in this paragraph because those allegations constitute conclusions of law which operation of law deems denied. In any event, Defendant specifically denies that she is now liable to Plaintiffs for consequential damages since Plaintiffs were unable to pay their taxes on time. On the contrary, Defendant is not responsible for any alleged inability of Plaintiffs to pay their income taxes on time and is not liable to Plaintiffs.

New Matter

23. Creampuff, through its employee Sharon Sellit, acted for Plaintiffs as their agent.

24. Throughout the month of February, Plaintiffs or their representatives visited the property for the purpose of taking measurements and also performed other actions consistent with an intent to make settlement under the agreement.

25. On or about February 22, XXXX, Sharon Sellit indicated to Defendant that Plaintiff Linda Sherman had instructed that carpet tacking remaining on the floor after carpeting was removed pursuant to the agreement between the parties should be left there.

26. In reliance on the above, and in reliance on other indications from Plaintiffs and their agents that Plaintiffs had accepted or intended to accept the commitment, that the agreement was still in force, and that Plaintiffs intended to make settlement under the agreement, Defendant continued to act, at her own expense, pursuant to her agreement with Plaintiffs.

27. Based on the above, Plaintiffs are estopped from asserting: (1) that the commitment was not in conformity with the agreement; and (2) that the agreement became null and void.

28. Based on the above, Plaintiffs have waived the requirements and conditions of paragraph 19 of the agreement as a basis for failing to fulfill their obligations under that agreement.

WHEREFORE, Defendant Kathryn Jones requests an order dismissing Plaintiffs' Complaint.

Counterclaim

Count I

29. Paragraphs 1 through 28 above are incorporated by reference.

30. Plaintiffs have breached the agreement by failing to make settlement as the agreement requires.

31. As a result of Plaintiffs' breach, Defendant is entitled to the $10,000 deposit as liquidated damages under paragraph 10 of the agreement.

WHEREFORE, Defendant Kathryn Jones requests an order awarding her the sum of $10,000, plus interest and costs.

Count II

32. Paragraphs 1 through 31 above are incorporated by reference.

33. Based on the above, Plaintiffs have made misrepresentations of material facts for the purpose of inducing Defendant to act or to refrain from acting in reliance on those misrepresentations.

34. Alternatively, Plaintiffs' misrepresentations were negligent or fraudulent.

35. Defendant acted and refrained from acting in reliance on Plaintiffs' misrepresentations.

36. As a result, Defendant has sustained damages totaling $19,099.72.

WHEREFORE, Defendant Kathryn Jones requests an order awarding her $19,099.72, plus interest and costs.

Attorney for Defendant
Kathryn Jones

———

Affidavit

———

Commonwealth of Pennsylvania
County of Philadelphia

}

ss

KATHRYN JONES, being duly sworn according to law, deposes and says that she is Defendant in this action and that the facts set forth in the foregoing Answer, New Matter, and Counterclaim are true and correct to the best of her knowledge, information, and belief.

_____

Kathryn Jones

Sworn to and subscribed
before me this 27th day
of September, XXXX.

_____

Notary Public

My Commission Expires:

ATTORNEY OF RECORD
IDENTIFICATION NO. 0000

_____

ALAN and LINDA SHERMAN,
                    Plaintiffs,

                    v.

KATHRYN JONES,

                    Defendant

CREAMPUFF REAL ESTATE,
INC.,

                    Additional Defendant

ATTORNEY FOR DEFENDANT
COURT OF COMMON PLEAS
PHILADELPHIA COUNTY,
PENNSYLVANIA CIVIL ACTION—
LAW DIVISION
APRIL TERM, XXXX No. 231

Defendant's Complaint Against Additional Defendant

1. Plaintiffs have sued Defendant contending that Defendant wrongfully has refused to return $10,000 Plaintiffs deposited as a down payment toward the purchase of real estate located at Unit 14, 130 Elm Street, Philadelphia, PA. A copy of Plaintiffs' Complaint is attached as Exhibit "A."

2. Defendant has filed an Answer to Plaintiffs' Complaint in which Defendant (a) denies any liability to Plaintiffs and (b) asserts counterclaims against Plaintiffs. Copies of Defendant's Answer, New Matter, and Counterclaim are attached.

3. Additional Defendant, Creampuff Real Estate, Inc. ("Creampuff"), is a corporation organized and existing under the laws of Pennsylvania with an office at 456 Maple Street, Philadelphia, PA.

4. Creampuff is holding as escrow agent the $10,000 deposit that is the subject of Plaintiffs' Complaint under the Agreement of Sale between Plaintiffs and Defendant.

5. Creampuff, through its employee Joan Buyit, acted as Defendant's agent for purposes of the sales transaction.

6. Creampuff, through its employee Sharon Sellit, also acted as Plaintiffs' agent in this transaction.

7. Plaintiffs' obligation to make settlement under the Agreement of Sale was contingent on the receipt by Plaintiffs of a mortgage commitment that was to meet certain conditions specified in the Agreement of Sale.

8. Creampuff represented to Defendant that Plaintiffs had obtained a mortgage commitment that met the conditions specified in the Agreement of Sale.

9. Creampuff also represented to Defendant that Plaintiffs had accepted the mortgage commitment and intended to make settlement under the Agreement of Sale.

10. Prior to February 25, XXXX, and in reliance on Creampuff's representation, Defendant removed carpeting from the premises and took other action and incurred expenses in preparation for settlement under the Agreement of Sale.

11. Creampuff advised Plaintiff prior to February 25, XXXX, not to inform Defendant that Plaintiffs refused the mortgage commitment.

12. On February 25, XXXX, Joan Buyit indicated to Defendant for the first time that there was "a problem" with the Plaintiffs' commitment.

13. Plaintiffs refused to make settlement under the Agreement, allegedly because the mortgage commitment they received did not meet the conditions specified in the Agreement of Sale. Complaint, paragraphs 9-10.

14. Plaintiffs have also alleged that they never accepted the mortgage commitment. Complaint, paragraphs 11-12, and Exhibit "C" to Complaint.

Count I

15. Paragraphs 1-14 of this Complaint against Additional Defendant are incorporated by reference.

16. Based on the above, Creampuff is alone liable to Plaintiffs or, in the alternative, is liable over to Defendant in indemnity or contribution for any amounts which may be adjudged against Defendant.

WHEREFORE, Defendant Kathryn Jones demands judgment against additional Defendant Creampuff for any amounts that may be adjudged against Defendant and in favor of Plaintiffs.

Count II

17. Paragraphs 1-14 of this Complaint against Additional Defendant are incorporated by reference.

18. In the event the mortgage commitment did not meet the conditions set out in the Agreement of Sale, which Defendant specifically denies, then Creampuff misrepresented that fact to Defendant.

19. Creampuff additionally misrepresented Plaintiffs' intention to accept the mortgage commitment.

20. Creampuff further misrepresented Plaintiffs' intention to make settlement under the Agreement of Sale.

21. Creampuffs' actions violated the Real Estate Licensing Act, 63 Pa. Consol. Stat. § 455.604 (1976).

22. Based on the above, Creampuff has made misrepresentations of material facts for the purpose of inducing Defendant to act or to refrain from acting in reliance on those misrepresentations.

23. Alternatively, Creampuff's misrepresentations were negligent or fraudulent.

24. Defendant acted and refrained from acting in reliance on Creampuff's misrepresentations.

25. By reason of its misrepresentations to Defendant, Creampuff is liable directly to Defendant for any damages that Defendant does not recover from Plaintiffs under Defendant's Counterclaim against Plaintiffs.

26. As a result of Creampuff's misrepresentations, Defendant has sustained damages totaling $19,099.72, plus interest, costs, and Defendant's reasonable attorneys' fees.

Count III

27. Paragraphs 1-26 of this Complaint against Additional Defendant are incorporated by reference.

28. Based on the above, Creampuff has breached its duty as an agent of Defendant to act with standard care and with the skill that is standard in the locality for the kind of work which Creampuff was employed to perform.

WHEREFORE, Defendant Kathryn Jones demands judgment against Additional Defendant Creampuff for $19,099.72, plus interest, costs, and Defendant's reasonable attorneys' fees.

Count IV

29. Paragraphs 1-26 of this Complaint against Additional Defendant are incorporated by reference.

30. Based on the above, Creampuff has breached its duty to Defendant not to act on behalf of an adverse party in a transaction connected with its agency without Defendant's knowledge.

31. Alternatively, Creampuff has breached its duty to act with fairness to each of its principals and to disclose to each all facts which it knew or should have known would affect reasonably the judgment of each in permitting the dual agency.

WHEREFORE, Defendant Kathryn Jones demands judgment against Additional Defendant Creampuff for $19,099.72, plus interest, costs, and Defendant's reasonable attorneys' fees.

Attorney for Defendant
Kathryn Jones

THE STATE OF TEXAS COUNTY OF HARRIS   } KNOW ALL MEN BY THESE PRESENTS:

BEFORE ME, the undersigned authority, personally appeared KATHRYN S. JONES, known to me to be a credible person, and after being duly sworn, upon oath deposed and stated the following:

"That the allegations in the Complaint against the Additional Defendant are true and correct to the best of my knowledge, information, and belief."

Further deponent sayeth not.

_____

Kathryn S. Jones

SWORN TO AND SUBSCRIBED BEFORE ME by KATHRYN S. JONES on this _____ day of November, XXXX, to certify which witness my hand and seal of office.

_____

Notary Public in and for
The State of TEXAS

My Commission Expires:

_____

In the United States District Court for the Eastern District of Pennsylvania

QUALITY PRODUCTS
CORPORATION,
Plaintiff

v.

MIDDLEMAN STEEL COMPANY,
Defendant and Third-Party Plaintiff

v.

HEAVY METALS COMPANY, Third-
Party Defendant

Civil Action No. 75–4113

Plaintiff's Complaint Against Third-Party Defendant, Heavy Metals Company

---

1. Plaintiff, Quality Products Corporation ("Quality") is a Delaware corporation having its principal place of business in New York, New York.

2. Third-Party Defendant, Heavy Metals Company ("Heavy Metals"), is a Pennsylvania corporation having its principal office and place of business in Philadelphia, Pennsylvania.

3. Jurisdiction of this claim is based upon the diversity of citizenship of the Plaintiff and Third-Party Defendant, under Title 28, United States Code, Section 1332.

4. The amount in controversy in this claim exceeds $10,000 exclusive of interest and costs.

5. Plaintiff incorporates by reference, as if set forth separately and in full, the allegations in paragraphs 5-11 of its Complaint in this action, which Plaintiff filed with the Court on October 20, XXXX, and a copy of which was served upon Middleman Steel Company on or about December 18, XXXX.

Count I

6. In or about November and December, XXXX, Defendant, Middleman Steel Company ("Middleman"), made a contract with Heavy Metals to purchase certain quantities of steel, which Middleman afterward sold to Quality as abrasion-resistant steel. The terms of their contract required that the quantities of steel Middleman purchased from Heavy Metals were to be abrasion-resistant steel.

7. At the time of the contract for the sale of the quantities of steel to Middleman, Heavy Metals knew that Middleman was a steel warehouse, engaged in the business of reselling steel to others, and that the steel Heavy Metals sold would come to

rest in the hands of an ultimate consumer, who would be some person or company other than Middleman.

8. Quality was the ultimate consumer of the steel Heavy Metals sold to Middleman and is a third-party beneficiary of the contract between Middleman and Heavy Metals, and of all warranties, express and implied, on the part of Heavy Metals in that contract.

9. The steel that Heavy Metals sold to Middleman for resale to Quality under the contract was not abrasion-resistant steel, but was steel of different and inferior physical and chemical properties.

10. By failing to deliver to Middleman abrasion-resistant steel as Middleman had ordered, Heavy Metals breached the contract, and the express and implied warranties in that contract, causing loss and damage to Quality as alleged in its Complaint.

WHEREFORE, Plaintiff demands judgment in its favor against Third-Party Defendant Heavy Metals Company for all sums which Quality had to expend as a result of the Third-Party Defendant's breaches, plus interest and costs.

Count II

11. The allegations in paragraphs 1-10 are incorporated by reference.

12. Heavy Metals is engaged in the business of selling the steel it sold to Middleman and afterwards that Middleman sold to Quality.

13. Heavy Metals expected that the steel that it sold to Middleman could reach the user or consumer without substantial change in the condition in which it was sold, and the steel did reach Quality in that condition.

14. The steel Heavy Metals sold to Middleman was in a defective condition because it was not abrasion-resistant steel as Heavy Metals represented it to be, and was unreasonably dangerous to Plaintiff's property.

15. As a result of the defective condition of the steel, Plaintiff suffered damage to its property in that the machinery Plaintiff manufactured from the steel became inoperative and required the expenditure of large sums for repairs.

WHEREFORE, Plaintiff demands judgment in its favor against Third-Party Defendant Heavy Metals Company for all sums which Quality had to expend as a result of the Third-Party Defendant's sale of the steel, plus interest and costs.

Count III

16. The allegations in paragraphs 1-15 are incorporated by reference.

17. Heavy Metals failed to exercise reasonable care in supplying steel to Middleman under the contract in Count I by delivering steel that was labeled erroneously and described as abrasion-resistant steel when it was not abrasion-resistant steel.

18. As a result of Heavy Metals' negligence in delivering steel to Middleman knowing that Middleman was to resell the steel to another, Quality suffered damages by having to expend large sums of money to repair machinery components manufactured of the steel Heavy Metals delivered.

WHEREFORE, Plaintiff demands judgment in its favor against Third-Party Defendant Heavy Metals Company for all sums which it had to expend as a result of the Third-Party Defendant's negligence, plus interest and costs.

Count IV

19. The allegations in paragraphs 1-18 are incorporated by reference.

20. Heavy Metals knowingly and willfully supplied non-abrasion-resistant steel to Middleman, which had ordered the steel as abrasion-resistant, and misrepresented the character of the steel it shipped as abrasion-resistant, when it knew full well that the steel did not have the physical and chemical properties of abrasion-resistant steel.

WHEREFORE, Plaintiff demands judgment in its favor against Third-Party Defendant Heavy Metals Company for all sums that it had to expend as a result of the Third-Party Defendant's willful delivery of nonconforming steel, plus interest and costs, plus punitive damages.

_____

Attorney for Plaintiff

In the United States District Court for the Southern District of Florida

---

UNITED STATES OF AMERICA,
Plaintiff,
v.
THE GOOD CORPORATION,
Defendant

CIVIL NO. 78-6789

Answer

Defendant, the Good Corporation, answers the Complaint as follows:

First Defense

1. Defendant admits that Plaintiff seeks to bring this action under the statutory sections alleged but denies that it has violated any provision of the Federal Trade Commission Act or any rule issued by the Commission and denies that the Plaintiff is entitled to recover civil penalties or obtain any other relief.

2. Defendant denies the allegations in paragraph 2.

3. Defendant denies that venue in the Southern District of Florida is proper.

4. Defendant denies the allegations in paragraph 4 and further states that they constitute conclusions of law that require no answer.

5. Defendant denies the allegations in paragraph 5 and further states that it does not know what the term "purchase money loan" means as used in the Complaint and that these allegations constitute conclusions of law which require no answer.

6. Defendant admits the allegations in paragraph 6.

7. Defendant admits that the Federal Trade Commission purported to issue a Trade Regulation Rule concerning Preservation of Consumers' Claims and Defenses on November 18, XXXX, and that

Ninth Defense

73. The Rule concerning Preservation of Consumers' Claims and Defenses is vague, unspecific, confusing, and misleading, and is therefore void and unenforceable.

Tenth Defense

74. The Rule concerning Preservation of Consumers' Claims and Defenses is vague, unspecific, confusing, and misleading; and Defendant and all Credit Unions identified in the Complaint attempted in good faith, to comply with it.

Eleventh Defense

75. The Rule concerning Preservation of Consumers' Claims and Defenses attempts to regulate Defendant based upon acts of others who are not within the control of Defendant, in violation of the United States Constitution.

Twelfth Defense

76. Substantial evidence in the rule-making proceeding did not support the Rule concerning Preservation of Consumers' Claims and Defenses.

Thirteenth Defense

77. Defendant has not engaged in an "unfair or deceptive act or practice" within the meaning of Section 5 of the Federal Trade Commission Act.

Fourteenth Defense

78. Defendant did not accept the proceeds of purchase money loans with actual knowledge or knowledge fairly implied on the basis of objective circumstances that such acceptance was unfair or deceptive and prohibited by the Rule concerning Preservation of Consumers' Claims and Defenses.

Fifteenth Defense

79. At the time that Defendant made any alleged sale of a used car, Defendant had no knowledge, and no reason to know, that the Purchaser had executed a consumer credit contract that did not contain the notice in the Rule concerning Preservation of Consumers' Claims and Defenses.

Sixteenth Defense

80. No person has sustained any injury because of the matters alleged in the Complaint.

Seventeenth Defense

81. Defendant at all times exercised reasonable care and diligence to ensure that any consumer credit contract executed in connection with the purchase of a used car as alleged in the Complaint contained the notice in the Rule concerning Preservation of Consumers' Claims and Defenses.

Eighteenth Defense

82. Upon information and belief, Defendant alleges that this action is frivolous and without merit and that Plaintiff brought it under pressure from special interest groups that compete with Defendant in the sale of used cars.

WHEREFORE, Defendant, The Good Corporation, demands judgment in its favor and requests that the Court dismiss the Complaint and grant to Defendant the costs of this action and reasonable attorneys' fees, together with such other and further relief as may be just and proper.

Attorney for Defendant

By_____

Briefs and Oral Arguments

In this appendix, you will find a sample trial court brief that was filed in the California Superior Court. (The names of the parties have been changed.) As is true in some other courts, in the California Superior Court, the brief is called a "memorandum," not to be confused with an "interoffice memorandum."

As for finding good examples of appellate briefs and oral arguments, the Internet is a great source. Certainly, not all the samples that you find are good ones; not even all briefs and arguments presented to the United States Supreme Court are desirable models. However, with selective searches, you can locate any number of well-constructed examples.

The Office of the Solicitor General produces very good briefs. That office conducts all litigation on behalf of the United States in the Supreme Court and supervises the handling of litigation in the federal appellate courts. To access its briefs, go to its website, http://www.justice.gov/osg. Then click on "Briefs."

You may want to examine the Solicitor General's helpful brief in *Florida v. Powell* (2009 term), which deals with the Miranda warning. You would click on "Type of Filing by Term," and then click on "2009," the term in which the Court chose to hear the case. Then, under "Merits Stage," click on "Amicus Briefs." Although the brief is an amicus brief, it is drafted as if it were the main brief on the merits. Once you access the brief, you should click on "View PDF Version" to see the brief as it was actually formatted. In order to read the Solicitor General's main brief in *Johnson v. United States* (2009 term), which deals with the definition of "violent felony" under the Armed Career Criminal Act of 1984, you would follow the same procedure, except that you would click on "Briefs" instead of on "Amicus Briefs."

The Mayer Brown law firms offers an online collection of well-constructed briefs drafted by its attorneys at http://www.appellate.net/briefs/defaultNew.asp. To find the brief in *Day v. McDonough*, a case dealing with the statute of limitations in habeas corpus proceedings, you would survey the list until you found the name of the case. If a lawyer from the firm had presented the oral argument, you could click on "Oral Argument" and find both a transcript and a recording of the argument. In this instance, another lawyer gave the oral argument. Therefore, for a recording of the argument, you would access http://www.oyez.org, find "Recently Updated Cases," and click on "More." Locate opinions filed in 2006, click on the case, find "Media Items," and click on "Oral Argument."

Another source is the United States Supreme Court's website, http://www .supremecourtus.gov. It offers transcripts of oral arguments beginning with the Court's October 2000 term. It also provides a link to briefs in recent cases on the American Bar Association's website, "Preview of United States Supreme Court Cases," http://www.abanet.org/publiced/preview/briefs/home.html.

A note of caution: Different courts have differing rules for formatting briefs and making oral arguments, and different lawyers have differing ways of constructing briefs and making oral arguments within the prescribed formats. Thus any briefs that you consult may not conform exactly to the rules that your law school has for formatting briefs. The value in consulting other briefs and oral arguments lies not in finding a document to imitate, but in getting a general idea of what style and level of analysis you should seek to attain.

This is a pretrial motion brief. It follows California citation rules. Your jurisdiction may also have its own citation rules that you should follow when you file documents in court. The important thing is that you use one citation form consistently throughout the document.

RUTAN & TUCKER, LLP
Brandon Sylvia (State Bar No. 261027)
611 Anton Boulevard, Fourteenth Floor
Costa Mesa, California 92626-1931
Telephone: 714-641-5100
Facsimile: 714-546-9035

Attorneys for Defendant
ABC CORPORATION, INC.

SUPERIOR COURT OF THE STATE OF CALIFORNIA
FOR THE COUNTY OF SANTA CLARA

DAVID SALAZAR,
 	
                              Plaintiff,
 	
                    vs.
 	
ABC CORPORATION, INC., and
DOES 1 through 10, inclusive,[1]
 	
                              Defendants.
	Case No. 1-08-CV-126729
	
	ASSIGNED FOR ALL PURPOSES TO:
	THE HONORABLE JAMES KLEINBERG
	DEPARTMENT 1
	
	MEMORANDUM OF POINTS AND AUTHORITIES IN SUPPORT DEFENDANT ABC CORPORATION, INC.'S MOTION FOR SUMMARY ADJUDICATION OF PLAINTIFF'S THIRD AND FOURTH CAUSES OF ACTION
	
	[Notice of Motion and Motion; Separate Statement of Undisputed Material Facts; and Declarations filed concurrently herewith]
	
	Hearing on Motion for Summary Adjudication:
	
	Date: April 28, 2009
	Time: 9:00 a.m.
	Dept.: 1
	
	Date Action Filed: October 31, 2008
	Trial Date: Not Yet Set

---

1. In California, it is common for plaintiffs to leave open the possibility that additional defendants may be added when they are identified. This is typically done by naming the potential additional defendants "Does."

TABLE OF CONTENTS

TABLE OF AUTHORITIES

I. INTRODUCTION.

Prior to filing this action, Plaintiff David Salazar ("Salazar") sued his employer, alleging failure to pay overtime premium wages. Salazar eventually accepted Defendant's California Code of Civil Procedure Section 998 ("Section 998") offer and a final judgment was entered in his favor. Salazar has now filed this second wage and hour lawsuit against the same employer based on additional violations of the identical wage orders that were the subject of the first action. In his initial lawsuit Plaintiff sought and received a monetary judgment for wages, penalties, and attorneys' fees arising out of violations of Industrial Welfare Commission ("IWC") Wage Order No. 4-2001 ("IWC Wage Order No. 4") (8 Cal. Code Reg. § 11040.) In this lawsuit Plaintiff again seeks a monetary judgment for wages, penalties, and additional attorneys' fees arising out of violations of IWC Order Wage Order No. 4.

Plaintiff freely admits he was aware of the additional violations while litigating the first action, yet chose not to pursue them. By piecemealing a single lawsuit into at least two separate lawsuits, Plaintiff has succeeded in creating two opportunities to drag his ex-employer into court, and more importantly two opportunities to recover attorneys' fees for alleged wage and hour violations that absolutely could have and should have been addressed in the first wage and hour lawsuit. The two lawsuits focus on the identical plaintiff performing the identical job for the identical employer over the identical time period.

To permit Plaintiff to bring one lawsuit for overtime, another for meal breaks, theoretically another for rest breaks, and yet another for pay stub violations, violates the most basic concepts of res judicata. Since wage and hour claims typically take the form of class actions, permitting such claim splitting would transform one wage and hour lawsuit into four or five suits, encouraging multiple lawsuits, multiple claims for attorneys' fees, and create a feeding frenzy for wage and hour attorneys. For these reasons, as well as those detailed below, Defendant respectfully requests that this Court enter judgment for Defendant and against Plaintiff on Plaintiff's Third and Fourth Causes of Action for meal period premiums and penalties.

II. STATEMENT OF FACTS.

A. *Salazar I.*

On December 31, 2007, Salazar filed a complaint against ABC Worldwide, LLP ("Worldwide") in limited civil court ("*Salazar I*"). In *Salazar I* Plaintiff alleged that his employer, Worldwide, failed to pay overtime as required by the applicable IWC Wage Order, and that Worldwide had failed to provide itemized wage statements as required by Labor Code section 226(a). Salazar subsequently filed a First Amended Complaint to make minor technical corrections to his pleadings; the substance of his claims remained unchanged. (Ex. 1.)[2]

---

2. A true and correct copy of the First Amended Complaint in *Salazar I* is attached as Exhibit 1 to the Declaration, filed concurrently herewith. All further citations to exhibits refer to exhibits attached to the Declaration.

Discovery commenced, and pursuant to a Request for Production of Documents ("RFP"), Worldwide provided Salazar with his employee file, copies of Salazar's time cards, and other documents on April 21, 2008. (Decl. ¶3.) Because the photocopies of Salazar's time cards were difficult to read, on May 28, 2008, Worldwide subsequently provided Salazar with color copies of each time card. (*Id.;* Ex. 2.) On July 8, 2008, Salazar's attorney informed Worldwide that he had lost the time cards so Worldwide *again* provided Salazar with documents responsive to the RFP, including the color copies of Salazar's time cards, on July 14, 2008. (Decl. ¶3.)

On September 9, 2008, Plaintiff was terminated. At the time of his termination Plaintiff received his final paycheck as well as an additional check for $835.81, along with a document stating, "Although we do not believe any overtime wages are due and owing you, the attached payment for $835.81 is based on the following . . . :" (See Defendant's overtime computation provided to Plaintiff, attached hereto as Exhibit 3.) The letter detailed the times, dates, and amounts of overtime that Plaintiff was allegedly owed. (Ex. 3.)

On September 22, 2008, Defendant made a Section 998 Offer to Compromise of $7,500, "for all damages, actual or statutory, reasonable attorneys' fees and costs incurred" in *Salazar I.* (Ex. 4.) On October 8, 2008, Plaintiff accepted the $7,500 offer to compromise and on December 1, 2008, judgment was entered for Plaintiff and against Worldwide for $7,500. (Decl. ¶6; Ex. 5.) Pursuant to the terms of the judgment, Plaintiff's counsel received a check for $7,500. (See check for $7,500 made out to Polaris Law Group, attached here as Exhibit 6.)

B. *Salazar II.*

On October 31, 2008, Salazar filed this lawsuit arising out of his employment with Worldwide ("*Salazar II*") in unlimited civil court. Salazar named and served ABC Corporation, Inc.[3] as the defendant, and has alleged violation of the Fair Employment and Housing Act ("FEHA") based on discrimination, as well as claims for wages and penalties for failure to provide meal periods. Plaintiff concedes that he was well aware of these violations while litigating *Salazar I.* In response to a special interrogatory seeking the factual support for Plaintiff's meal period claim, Plaintiff responded under oath as follows:

> I determined these dates by reviewing the subject time cards provided to me by defendant in a previous lawsuit. The time cards confirm that I missed meal periods on the subject date because there is no clocking out for lunch on those days. (Exs. 7 and 8.)

Thus, Plaintiff concedes that despite having knowledge of these specific meal break claims, he opted not to pursue them. Instead, after prevailing in *Salazar I* on claims of wage and hour violations, and receiving payment of attorneys' fees as part of that award, Plaintiff immediately filed *Salazar II* alleging the additional wage and hour claims and seeking an additional attorneys' fees award out of the

---

3. ABC Corporation, Inc., is a majority-owned subsidiary of ABC Worldwide, LLP, the operating partnership of ABC Conglomerate, Inc. (Decl. ¶3.)

same conduct that occurred during the same time period while working for the same employer.

ABC filed an answer on November 17, 2008, consisting of a general denial of the claims alleged, and a number of affirmative defenses, including res judicata.

III. ARGUMENT.

A. In California, The Doctrine of Res Judicata Is Informed By the "Primary Right" Theory.

1. The Doctrine of Res Judicata Bars Subsequent Proceedings That Present Issues That Were or Should Have Been Raised in a Prior Action Between the Same Parties and in Which There Was a Final Judgment.

"Res judicata" describes the preclusive effect of a final judgment on the merits. Under the doctrine of res judicata, "if a plaintiff prevails in an action, the cause is merged into the judgment and may not be asserted in a subsequent lawsuit." *Mycogen Corp. v. Monsanto Co.* (2002) 28 Cal.4th 888, 896-97. The practical effect of the doctrine is that res judicata "bar[s] not only the reopening of the original controversy, but also subsequent litigation of *all issues* which were or *could have been raised in the original suit.*" *Gates v. Superior Court (Bonpane)* (1986) 178 Cal.App.3d 301, 311 (emphasis added).

A crucial aspect of res judicata is the *scope* of the preclusion. As the authorities quoted above imply, the doctrine does not only preclude those issues actually raised in a prior action. Instead, "[i]f the matter was within the scope of the action, related to the subject-matter and relevant to the issues, so that it *could* have been raised, the judgment is conclusive on it despite the fact that it was not in fact expressly pleaded or otherwise urged." *Sutphin v. Speik* (1940) 15 Cal.2d 195, 202 (underline added, italics in original). Thus, res judicata is properly invoked to bar a subsequent lawsuit "when that suit alleged a different theory of recovery for the same injury, or a different remedy for the same injury, or a somewhat greater factual elaboration of the same injury" already sued upon in a prior suit. *Grisham v. Phillip Morris U.S.A., Inc.* (2007) 40 Cal.4th 623, 642 (citations omitted); *see also Wick v. Wick Tool Co.* (1959) 176 Cal.App.2d 677, 687 ("The rule has the effect of coercing the plaintiff to present all of his grounds for recovery in the first proceeding, . . .").

The doctrine of res judicata promotes judicial economy by "preclud[ing] piecemeal litigation by splitting a single cause of action or relitigation of the same cause of action on a different legal theory or for different relief." *Id.* Judicious recognition of the doctrine "benefits both the parties and the courts because it seeks to curtail multiple litigation causing vexation and expense to the parties and wasted effort and expense in judicial administration." *Gates*, 178 Cal.App.3d at 311 (internal quotation and citation omitted).

In the present case Plaintiff concedes that that he was aware of these specific wage and hour issues while litigating *Salazar I*. (Ex. 8.) Given the above-quoted authorities, this fact alone compels a finding that these issues "could have been raised in the original suit." *Gates*, 178 Cal.App.3d at 311. As detailed below,

Plaintiff cannot bring a claim based on his employer's violation of IWC Wage Order No. 4 and simultaneously knowingly withhold a similar claim against the identical employer for additional violations of the same wage order.

A prior judgment bars a subsequent action if (1) the parties in the first and subsequent proceedings are the same, or are in privity; (2) there was a final judgment on the merits in the prior action; and (3) the issues decided in the prior adjudication are identical with those presented in the later action. *See Consumer Advocacy Group, Inc. v. Exxon-Mobil Corp.* (2008) 2008 Cal. App. LEXIS 2279, *15 (*Consumer Advocacy Group*) (citing *Citizens for Open Access to Sand and Tide, Inc. v. Seadrift Assoc.* (1998) 60 Cal.App.4th 1053, 1065, *review denied*, 1998 Cal. LEXIS 1960, *1 (*Citizens for Open Access*)). Additionally, even if these elements are met, res judicata will not be applied "if injustice would result or if the public interest requires that relitigation not be foreclosed." *Id.* at *16.

2. California Follows the "Primary Right Theory" in Determining Whether Issues Raised in an Earlier Proceeding Are "Identical" to Those Raised in a Later Case.

As noted above, a second suit is barred by an earlier action only if "the *issue or cause of action* in the two actions is *identical.*" *Citizens for Open Access*, 60 Cal.App.4th at 1067 (emphasis added). "To define a cause of action, California follows the primary right theory." *Id.* According to the primary right theory, "a cause of action is comprised of a primary right of the plaintiff, a corresponding primary duty of the defendant, and a wrongful act by the defendant constituting a breach of that duty." *Consumer Advocacy Group*, 2008 Cal. App. LEXIS 2279 at *16 (citing *Mycogen Corp.*, 28 Cal.4th at 904). The purpose of this doctrine is to ensure that "[a] party cannot by negligence or design withhold issues and litigate them in consecutive actions . . . on matters which were raised or could have been raised" in a prior action. *Sutphin*, 15 Cal.2d at 202.

The "most salient characteristic" of a primary right is that it is *indivisible.* *Mycogen Corp.*, 28 Cal.4th at 904. Thus, "[e]ven where there are multiple legal theories upon which recovery might be predicated, one injury gives rise to only one claim for relief." *Id.* (emphasis added). This is so even though the violation of one primary right "may entitle the injured party to many forms of relief," as the relief and the cause of action are "not determinative of the other." *Id.* As will be discussed below, Salazar's claims for overtime premiums (in the first case) and meal period premiums (in this case) are separate forms of relief arising from a single primary right.

B. Salazar's Third and Fourth Causes of Action Are Barred By Res Judicata.

Salazar's latest claims regarding meal period payments, and his attempts to recover penalties thereon, are barred by res judicata due to the earlier judgment between the parties. First, the parties to both cases are clearly in privity, as both are between Salazar and his employer. His transparent attempt to sue different entities does not hide the fact that he was employed by one employer during this time period. It is also indisputable that the first Salazar claim ended in a final judgment. Finally, as the following analysis will make clear, Salazar has attempted to impermissibly split his single right for unpaid wages into two separate lawsuits.

1.   The Identical Parties Are Involved in Both Salazar Cases.

Worldwide and ABC are clearly in privity with one another. As noted in an earlier footnote, the defendant in *this* case is a majority-owned subsidiary of ABC Worldwide, LLP. ("Worldwide"). (Decl. ¶3.) Worldwide, in turn, is the operating partnership of ABC Conglomerate, Inc., the defendant in *Salazar I*. As such, the interests of ABC and Worldwide are identical. Furthermore, that Salazar alleged wage claims against both entities—based on the same period of employment, same shifts worked, and the same *paychecks*—essentially admits that the two are in privity with one another.

2.   The Prior Case Ended in a Final Judgment on the Merits.

Salazar's first lawsuit ended in a final judgment. On December 1, 2008, judgment was entered pursuant to a Section 998 offer in Salazar's favor in the first case on all the claims alleged in Salazar's complaint—including the wage claims. (Ex. 5.) It is therefore undeniable that the first case resulted in a final judgment.

3.   Because the Wage Claims Asserted in *Salazar II* Involve the Same Primary Right as the Wage Claims Asserted in *Salazar I*, Salazar's Third and Fourth Causes of Action Are Barred By the Doctrine of Res Judicata.

Salazar's claim for unpaid overtime (in the first case) and for failure to provide meal periods (in this case) constitute two attempts to recover for injury alleged to the same primary right. The scope of a "primary right" will necessarily depend on how the "primary injury" is defined, and "[a]n injury is defined in part by reference to the set of facts, or transaction, from which the injury arose." *Federation of Hillside and Canyon Assoc. v. City of Los Angeles* (2004) 126 Cal.App.4th 1180, 1202-03. Courts have also analyzed the *source* of the primary right to determine whether separate claims may be alleged. *See, e.g., Branson v. Sun-Diamond Growers* (1994) 24 Cal.App.4th 327, 343 (holding that a *statutory* right to seek authorization for indemnity and *contractual* action for indemnity involve different primary rights).

Because the facts and transactions forming the basis of Salazar's present wage claims are identical to the facts upon which he already recovered, his wage claims in this case should be barred. First, both of Salazar's claims arise from an alleged breach by Worldwide of the statutory obligation to pay Salazar proper wages pursuant to IWC Wage Order No. 4. Furthermore, the facts underlying both claims are identical, and constitute attempts to recover wages allegedly owed to Salazar that accrued during the time he was employed by Defendant. As such, Salazar's meal break claims arise from the alleged violation of the primary right for which he already sued, and should therefore be barred.

a. Because Salazar's Claims Both Arise From the Same Factual Scenario, a Single Primary Right Is Involved.

Salazar's claims for overtime and meal period premium payments invoke a single primary right because the facts underlying each claim are identical. *See Tensor Group v. City of Glendale* (1993) 14 Cal.App.4th 154, 160 ("The cause of action . . . will therefore always be the *facts* from which the plaintiff's primary right and the defendant's corresponding primary duty have arisen.") (emphasis in original). Both claims allege, in different words, that Salazar's wages were not properly paid according to applicable statutes. Thus, although Salazar's claims differ superficially, they both seek recovery for the same primary injury: unpaid wages.

Additionally, the existence of all of the alleged wage and hour violations were apparent from Salazar's time cards and pay statements—documents that were *twice* provided to Salazar during *Salazar I.* (Decl. ¶3.) Plaintiff himself concedes he was aware of these wage and hour violations while litigating *Salazar I.* (Ex. 8.) Thus, Plaintiff made a conscious and knowing decision to not litigate a portion of wage and hour claims and to bring them in a separate action. Such a decision to intentionally transform one lawsuit into two violates the most basic precepts of California law. As stated earlier, "[a] party cannot by negligence or design withhold issues and litigate them in consecutive actions . . . on matters which were raised or could have been raised" in a prior action. *Sutphin*, 15 Cal.2d at 202. Salazar's meal period claims should have been brought in his first lawsuit, and because they were not, he cannot now assert them. *See Tensor Group*, 14 Cal.App.4th at 160 (explaining that res judicata bars a matter "within the scope of the [first] action, related to the subject matter and relevant to the issues, so that it *could* have been raised . . .").

b. Because Salazar's Right to Overtime and Meal Period Payments Both Arise From Statute, Both Claims Invoke a Single Primary Right.

Not only are the obligations to pay overtime and meal periods similar in *structure*, they share a common *source*. Both the first and second Salazar complaints refer to IWC Wage Order No. 4 as the wage order governing Salazar's employment with Worldwide. That wage order sets forth the various *statutory* obligations of an employer, including the obligation to pay overtime wages and to provide meal breaks or a premium payment for foregone breaks. *See* 8 Cal. Code Regs. §§ 11040(3)(A) (governing payment of overtime premium), 11040(11)(B) (providing for premium payment for missed meal breaks). These obligations exist independently from any employment contract an employee may have entered into. *Compare, e.g., Branson v. Sun-Diamond Growers* (1994) 24 Cal.App.4th 327, 343 (finding that *contractual* and *statutory* rights to indemnity involve *separate* primary rights). Thus, an employee's "primary right" to payment of either overtime or meal period premiums springs from a single source—the statutory obligation of the employer found in Wage Order No. 4.

c. Because Overtime and Meal Period Premium Payments Have an Identical Function and Purpose, They Serve to Protect a Single Primary Right.

That overtime and meal period payments arise from a single primary right is further manifested by the identical purposes of the statutes under which such claims are brought. According to a recent California Supreme Court decision, "[t]he IWC intended that, like overtime pay provisions, payment for missed meal and rest periods be enacted as a premium wage to compensate employees, while also acting as an incentive for employers to comply with labor standards." *See generally Murphy* v. *Kenneth Cole Prods.* (2007) 40 Cal.4th 1094, 1109-14 (concluding that meal period payments—like overtime premium payments—are "wages"). Thus, because the purpose of overtime and meal period premium payments is identical, both forms of recovery protect the same primary right.

d. Salazar's Fourth Cause of Action—For Penalties Due to Unpaid Meal Break Premium Payments—Is Similarly Precluded, as it Is Based on Alleged Violation of the Same Primary Right.

As already discussed, Salazar's claim for unpaid wages for foregone meal periods is precluded by res judicata. As such, Salazar's attempt to recover penalties *based on his meal period wages* must also fail. Like his meal period claim, this claim must have been brought—if at all—in the first case, where Salazar alleged that Worldwide breached its duty to pay proper wages. Thus, Salazar's Third and Fourth Cause of Action are barred by res judicata, and should be dismissed by this Court.

4. Application of Res Judicata to This Situation Serves the Interests of Justice, Fairness, and Judicial Economy.

Although a court may decline to apply res judicata when application of the doctrine would result in injustice, such is not the case here. Instead, the interests of justice, fairness, and judicial economy all dictate that res judicata be applied to the wage claims asserted in Salazar's second lawsuit.

Allowing Salazar to bring separate lawsuits for overtime premiums and meal break premiums would open the door for the endless splitting of wage and hour claims. Within the specific realm of wage-and-hour law, a plaintiff's attorney interested in generating fees could bring separate lawsuits for minimum wage payments, overtime payments, meal break payments, rest break payments, and pay stub inaccuracies, as well as penalties for nonpayment of each form of wages. One court appearance then becomes five court appearances, one deposition of one plaintiff becomes five depositions of the same plaintiff, and one trial becomes five trials. This explosion of litigation is further incentivized because wage and hour attorneys will be permitted to collect fees for all five court appearances, all five depositions, and all five trials. To allow *separate lawsuits* for each claim would have the same effect as *encouraging* plaintiffs' counsel to bring five suits instead of one because their counsel could recover five times the attorneys' fees.

Given the frequency of wage and hour *class actions* and sheer tonnage of concomitant documents and billing, permitting such claim splitting in this area of the law will exponentially increase these inefficiencies. Permitting plaintiffs' counsel to transform one action, let alone one class action, into five separate actions, undercuts the most basic concepts of fairness and judicial economy. The entire purpose of the doctrine of res judicata is to promote judicial economy by precluding piecemeal litigation, and limiting the wasted effort and expense of multiple lawsuits. *Gates*, 178 Cal.App.3d at 311.

This unfortunate outcome is compounded by the knowledge that all the facts, evidence, and proof necessary to proceed on all five actions is typically available in the initial wage and hour action where the time records, job descriptions, and relevant information is produced and analyzed. In the case at bar, Plaintiff admittedly had all of this information while litigating *Salazar I.* As of May 28, 2008, he knew the date, time and duration of every meal break he had ever taken. (Ex. 2.) He took this information and did nothing, opting instead only to pursue a relatively small overtime claim. Now he seeks to be rewarded by garnering a second attorneys' fees award for refusing to combine these actions. As stated above, a party cannot negligently or intentionally withhold claims and then litigate them in successive actions. *Sutphin*, 15 Cal.2d at 202. This Court should prudently refuse to allow Salazar to split his wage claim into separate lawsuits, and should find that the wage claims asserted in Salazar's second case are barred by res judicata.

IV. CONCLUSION.

For the foregoing reasons, ABC respectfully requests that this Court find that Salazar's Third and Fourth Causes of Action are barred by res judicata, and that the Court enter judgment in favor of Defendant and against Plaintiff on the Third and Fourth Causes of Action in Plaintiff's First Amended Complaint.

Dated: December 14, 2009   RUTAN & TUCKER, LLP
                                          BRANDON SYLVIA

                                    By: _____
                                          Brandon Sylvia
                                          Attorneys for Defendant
                                          ABC CORPORATION, INC.

Grammar and Punctuation

Some people enjoy the great fortune of having learned the rules of grammar and punctuation in eighth grade, high school, or college. Others have learned a few rules here or there or by osmosis. If you fall into the latter group, it is time to make sure that you know at least the basics. If you are very deficient, you need to consult one of the many books on writing composition and grammar. If you do not already have one of these grammar books from college or high school, you should get one. You also should consult with a writing specialist at either your law school or college.

This appendix is not designed to be a comprehensive remedial handbook. Instead, it reviews the rules of grammar and punctuation most likely to create difficulties for the law student. Part A explains six rules of grammar and offers exercises to help you test your learning. Part B reviews the main rules for using commas, semicolons, colons, and dashes. It also discusses quotations.

Part A: Grammar

Part A discusses six rules:

1. Make sure each modifier unambiguously refers to the word that you want it to modify.
2. Make sure each pronoun clearly refers to the word for which it is a substitute.
3. If you are referring to a singular noun, use a singular pronoun. If you are referring to a plural noun, use a plural pronoun.
4. Make the subject agree with the verb.
5. Use "its" to denote the possessive and "it's" to abbreviate "it is."
6. Use "which" to introduce a nonrestrictive clause. Use "that" to introduce a restrictive clause.

Rule 1. Make sure each modifier unambiguously refers to the word that you want it to modify.

A modifier is a word, phrase, or clause that describes, alters, or clarifies another word in the sentence. For example:

The statute gives manufacturers a second incentive to comply with the regulations.

"Second" tells us more about "incentive." It modifies "incentive." "To comply" also is a modifier. It tells us more about "incentive." The incentive is designed to encourage manufacturers to comply with the regulations.

Watch out for misplaced modifiers. A sentence has a misplaced modifier when the reader might think that the modifier applies to a word different than the one the writer intended. The problem arises when the modifier is in the wrong location. Here is an example:

The court discussed the need for a written contract in a brief paragraph.

"In a brief paragraph" might modify "discussed" and tell us how much space the court's opinion devotes to this topic. Alternatively, it might modify "written contract" and tell us how long the written contract should be. Because of the location of the modifying phrase, the reader may not know which message you intended to communicate. Presumably the phrase modifies "discussed." If so, the sentence has a misplaced modifier. You can clear up the ambiguity by relocating the phrase. Here are some acceptable alternatives:

In a brief paragraph, the court discussed the need for a written contract.
The court discussed, in a brief paragraph, the need for a written contract.
The court, in a brief paragraph, discussed the need for a written contract.

Sometimes, a poorly written sentence contains the modifier, but not the word to which the modifier applies. Here is an example:

Faced with a statutory deadline, it is important to proceed quickly.

Who is faced with a statutory deadline? The sentence fails to tell us. The initial phrase is a dangling modifier because the sentence does not contain the word it modifies. The problem is easy to fix:

Faced with a statutory deadline, counsel must proceed quickly.

The next example illustrates a related problem:

Faced with a statutory deadline, quick action by counsel becomes necessary.

As written, the initial phrase seems to modify "quick action." However, the phrase must modify the actor, "counsel." To solve the problem, place the modifier next to the word it modifies:

Faced with a statutory deadline, counsel must act quickly.

Exercise

Please rewrite so that the modifiers unambiguously refer to the words you want to modify.

1. To prevail before an appellate court, a sound record must be developed before the trial court.
2. Once considered a major part of the civil procedure course, only modest attention is paid to the forms of action in today's law school curriculum.
3. The commission encouraged the companies immediately to go into production.
4. They only praised the decision, but not the rationale.
5. After examining the complaint, it is necessary to consider possible pretrial motions.

Rule 2. Make sure each pronoun clearly refers to the word for which it is a substitute.

The professor questioned the student about the issue that he was exploring.

Does "he" refer to the professor or the student? Was the professor exploring the issue or was the student exploring it? The sentence does not tell us in an unambiguous fashion.

Here are three ways to rewrite the sentence, assuming "he" refers to the professor:

1. The professor questioned the student about the issue that the professor was exploring.
2. In exploring the issue, the professor questioned the student about it.
3. The professor explored the issue and questioned the student about it.

Be particularly careful when you use "this," "that," or "those." Make sure the pronoun clearly refers to an antecedent. For example:

The court encountered criticism for making a de novo review of the evidence. This is not the function of an appellate court.

To what does "this" refer? We can solve the problem with a simple revision:

The court encountered criticism for making a de novo review of the evidence. Making such a review is not the function of an appellate court.

Exercise

Please revise these sentences so that the pronouns clearly refer to the words for which they are a substitute.

1. A friend of the decedent testified that she had been harassed at work in the weeks before the assault.
2. The plaintiff granted a single interview to a reporter. This would be inconsistent with the court's definition of media access.
3. The evidence was quite scanty. That made the prosecutor nervous.
4. Although taking exams dominates the month of December, it rarely is as taxing as students expect it to be.

5. The distinction between public and private figures is that they have media access to refute any defamation.

Rule 3. If you are referring to a singular noun, use a singular pronoun. If you are referring to a plural noun, use a plural pronoun.

Study this sentence:

If the corporation files for bankruptcy, they must notify their creditors.

"Corporation" is singular. The proper pronouns are "it" and "its." "They" and "their" are incorrect.

If the corporation files for bankruptcy, it must notify its creditors.

Here is another example:

Although the insurance company's representatives accepted the premiums, they now refuse to honor the policy.

The subject of the second clause is the insurance company, not the insurance company's representatives. Therefore, the correct pronoun is "it."

Although the insurance company's representatives accepted the premiums, it now refuses to honor the policy.

Exercise

Please revise these sentences so that single pronouns refer to single nouns and plural pronouns refer to plural nouns.

1. The Third Circuit was correct in determining that the statements were capable of defamatory meaning. Their decision should be upheld.
2. This practice creates a monopoly-like situation for the third party in which they are free to do whatever they wish.
3. The appellant's punitive damage claim should be dismissed because their fraud claim has been dismissed.
4. Every person in the neighborhood was asked to sign their name to the zoning petition.

Rule 4. Make the subject agree with the verb.

If the subject of the sentence or clause is singular, the verb must be singular. If the subject is plural, the verb must be plural. Although we know this rule, we sometimes break it by being careless.

In each of these examples, the subject and verb do not agree:

1. A variety of rhetorical devices appear in the appellate brief.
2. A lay dictionary, as well as a legal dictionary, are essential to an office library.

3. Either of the appellant's rationales require the court to accept a highly innovative argument. ("Either" means "either rationale.")

Exercise

Please revise these sentences so that subjects and verbs agree.

1. Everyone in the office say they met the deadline.
2. None of the memoranda recommend pursuing the matter.
3. The newspaper coverage in the surrounding counties were extensive.
4. Neither of the cotenants wish to partition the acreage.
5. The best part of the brief are the last five pages.

Rule 5. Use "its" to denote the possessive and "it's" to abbreviate "it is."

"It's" is the contraction of "it is." "Its" is the possessive of "it." Just as the possessive pronouns "her" and "his" have no apostrophe, the possessive pronoun "its" has no apostrophe.

Although the argument appears innovative, its roots extend well into the last century.

"Its roots" means the roots of the argument. The pronoun refers to the argument. Because "its" is a substitute for "the argument's," it is in the possessive and has no apostrophe.

Because legal writing is formal, contractions should be used only rarely. Therefore, rarely, if ever, will you use "it's." If you tend to confuse "it's" and "its," remember that in legal writing, the correct word almost always is "its."

Here are two correct examples.

1. Although both parties claimed the privilege of using the easement, neither was willing to pay for its maintenance.
2. According to the first witness, the defendant shouted, "It's time for a couple more beers."

Rule 6. Use "which" to introduce a nonrestrictive clause. Use "that" to introduce a restrictive clause.

Here is a simple way to decide when to use "which" and when to use "that." If you can or should place a comma before the clause, use "which." Otherwise use "that."

The memo that I wrote under considerable time pressure is surprisingly good.

Suppose I wrote only one memo. The clause gives the reader additional information: I wrote it under time pressure. The information in the clause is not essential to identify the memo that is discussed in the sentence. We call this clause a nonrestrictive clause because it adds information but is not essential to identifying the word or clause that it modifies. In a sense, it is parenthetical. We should place a comma before the clause and begin the clause with "which."

However, suppose I wrote several memos and wrote one of them under time pressure. In this case, the clause does more than give the reader additional information; it identifies the memo that I am discussing. We call this clause restrictive clause because it is essential to identifying the word or clause that it modifies. We do not place a comma before the clause, and we begin it with "that."

Exercise

Please rewrite the sentences that use "which" and "that" improperly.

1. Every business that qualifies can seek a tax exemption.
2. The building, which overlooked the river, attracted many tenants. (Assume several other buildings also overlooked the river.)
3. The building which overlooked the river attracted many tenants. (Assume that only this building overlooked the river.)
4. The comma that precedes the clause is unnecessary. (Assume that the sentence contains two commas.)

Part B: Punctuation

Part B explains how to use the comma, colon, semicolon, and dash correctly. It also discusses how to punctuate quotations.

1. The Comma

The rules concerning commas are in flux. The conventional rules require commas in specified situations. In many of these situations, however, the trend is to omit the comma when it does not help the reader to understand the sentence.

Here are six rules for using commas:

1. When using a conjunction to separate the independent clauses in a compound sentence, place a comma before the conjunction.
2. Use a comma after an introductory phrase or clause.
3. Use commas to set off words, phrases, and clauses in a sentence.
4. Use commas to separate words, phrases, and clauses in a series.
5. Use a comma between two adjectives that modify a verb.
6. Use commas in dates.

Rule 1. When using a conjunction to separate the independent clauses in a compound sentence, place a comma before the conjunction.

An independent clause is a clause that could stand alone as a sentence. A compound sentence has two or more independent clauses joined by a semicolon, colon, or a conjunction, such as "or," "but," or "and." Place a comma before the conjunction. Here are two correct examples:

> An independent clause must have a subject and a verb, but a phrase need not have them.

> An independent clause must have a subject and verb, and it must be able to stand alone as a sentence.

When the subject of both clauses is only in the first clause, place a comma before the conjunction, unless the conjunction is "and." Here are two correct examples:

An independent clause must have a subject and verb and must be able to stand alone as a sentence.

An independent clause must have a subject and verb, but need not include a preposition.

Pitfall: Do not separate two independent clauses with a comma. This construction is called a comma splice. Here is a bad example:

An independent clause can stand on its own as a sentence, a dependent clause cannot.

If you wish to place two independent clauses in the same sentence, separate them with a semicolon or with a comma and a conjunction. We can correct the bad example this way:

An independent clause can stand on its own as a sentence, but a dependent clause cannot.

Pitfall: Do not confuse a conjunction with a transitional word that functions like an adverb. Such transitional words include "however," "therefore," "thus," and "moreover." Do not treat these words as conjunctions. Consider this bad example:

The word "and" is a conjunction, however, the word "however" is not.

This sentence is a compound sentence consisting of two independent clauses. Because "however" is not a conjunction, no conjunction separates them. In the absence of a conjunction, you must separate them with a semicolon:

The word "and" is a conjunction; however, the word "however" is not.

Rule 2. Use a comma after an introductory phrase or clause.

The rule is self-explanatory. Here are two good examples:

1. After an introductory phrase, use a comma.
2. In the absence of a conjunction separating independent clauses, you may decide to use a semicolon.

Rule 3. Use commas to set off words, phrases, and clauses in a sentence.

Use commas when the word, phrase, or clause is really parenthetical or otherwise interrupts the sentence. Here are three good examples:

1. A comma, one type of punctuation mark, is overused more than other punctuation marks.
2. A comma, however, has many uses.
3. A grammarian would agree that, as a general rule, a writer should use commas to set off a parenthetical.

Instead of using a comma, you also can use parentheses or dashes. See the discussion of dashes later on in this appendix.

Rule 4. Use commas to separate words, phrases, and clauses in a series.

Here is an example:

Punctuation marks include the comma, the period, the colon, the apostrophe, the question mark, and the semicolon.

Sometimes writers find the last comma unnecessary—here, the comma after "question mark"—and omit it. However, sometimes the last comma is necessary to avoid ambiguity:

The curriculum includes courses in property, contracts, trusts and estates, and legal writing.

Here, the last comma makes it clear that trusts and estates is a separate course from legal writing.

Rule 5. Use a comma between two adjectives that modify a noun.

Here is an example:

An obtrusive, well-placed comma helps the reader out. If the clause does not seem necessary, you may omit it: A comma helps the reader to understand a long, complex sentence.

Rule 6. Use commas in dates.

Place a comma between the day of the month and the year:

September 22, 1945.

Under the traditional rule, you should use a comma between the month and the year when you are not specifying the day:

March, 1952.

However, most writers omit the comma.

2. The Colon

A colon indicates that the words before the colon lead the reader to expect what comes after the colon. For example:

There are three ways to punctuate the end of a sentence: a period, a question mark, and an exclamation point.

The words before the colon lead us to expect the writer to tell us what three punctuation marks can end a sentence. The words after the colon fulfill the expectation. Sometimes a comma will serve the same purpose:

In legal writing, there is one punctuation mark that we almost never use, the exclamation point.

Here we could have used a colon instead of the second comma. Because a colon is more dramatic and legal writing tends to prefer understatement, most legal writers use a comma instead of a colon when they can.

You also can use a colon to introduce a quotation:

The judge frequently quoted Justice Holmes: "The life of the law has not been logic; it has been experience."

2. The Semicolon

Use the semicolon in three situations:

a. When you want to combine two sentences into one sentence, separate them with a semicolon. The semicolon indicates that the two sentences—now independent clauses—have a close connection, but not close enough to use a conjunction. For example:

A semicolon can separate two independent clauses in a sentence; its use indicates a close connection between the clauses.

b. When the second independent clause in a sentence begins with a transition acting as an adverb—such as "however," "therefore," or "moreover," separate the clauses with a semicolon. For example:

You can join independent clauses with a conjunction; however, sometimes a semicolon seems more appropriate.

c. Use a semicolon to separate items in a series when there are commas within some of the items. For example:

Use a semicolon to show the close connection between independent clauses; to precede a transitional adverb such as "however," "therefore," or "thus"; and to separate items in a series when there are commas within some of the items.

3. The Dash

Use dashes to set off words that interrupt the continuity of a sentence. For example:

Use dashes—make one by typing two hyphens next to one another—to set off words that interrupt the continuity of a sentence.

Use dashes when the interruption is a major one. Otherwise, use commas or parentheses, whichever seems appropriate. Usually parentheses draw the least attention to the interruption. For example:

A dash (not a parenthesis) signals a major interruption in a sentence.

4. Quotations

The Bluebook, Rule 54 and the ALWD Citation Manual, Rules 47-49, prescribe the rules for punctuating quotations. Here is a summary of important rules:

a. Do not enclose block quotes with quotation marks.

b. When you omit words from the middle of a quoted sentence, insert three periods separated by spaces and put a space before the first period and after the last one (. . .). For example:

James Madison recognized a limitation on the danger of factions: "The influence of factious leaders may kindle a flame within their . . . states, but will be unable to spread a . . . conflagration through the other states."

c. When you are using the quotation as a full sentence and are omitting words at the beginning of the quoted sentence, do not use the three periods. If the first word you are quoting is not capitalized, capitalize the first letter and put it in brackets. For example:

James Madison recognized a limitation on the danger of factions: "[F]actious leaders may kindle a flame within their particular states, but will be unable to spread a . . . conflagration throughout the other states."

d. When you are using the quotation as a full sentence and are omitting words at the end of the quoted sentence, use four periods. Separate the periods with spaces and put a space before the first period. The last period is the period that ends the sentence. For example:

James Madison recognized that factions could disrupt the political process in an individual state: "The influence of factious leaders may kindle a flame within their particular states. . . ."

e. When you are quoting two consecutive sentences and omitting words at the end of the first sentence and at the beginning of the second sentence, use four periods. Separate the periods with spaces and put a space before the first period and after the fourth period. If the first word of the second sentence, as quoted, is not capitalized, capitalize the first letter and put it in brackets. For example:

For James Madison, the cure for factions lay in the great size of the republic: "In the extended republic of the United States . . . a coalition of the majority of the whole society could seldom take place on any other principles than those of justice and the general good. . . . [T]he larger the society . . . the more duly capable it will be of self-government."

f. Place a period or comma inside the quotation marks. Place a semicolon or colon outside the quotation marks. Place a question mark inside the quotation marks if it is part of the quoted material. Place a question mark outside the quotation marks if it is not part of the quoted material.